SURPRISE

Volume 2

Illegitimacy, Inheritance Rights, a

Formation of Imperial B

SURPRISE HEIRS

Volume 2

Illegitimacy, Inheritance Rights, and
Public Power in the Formation of
Imperial Brazil, 1822-1889

LINDA LEWIN

STANFORD UNIVERSITY PRESS

STANFORD, CALIFORNIA

2003

Stanford University Press
Stanford, California
© 2003 by the Board of Trustees of the
Leland Stanford Junior University
Printed in the United States of America

Library of Congress Cataloging-in-Publication Data

Lewin, Linda.
  Surprise heirs, vol. 2 : illegitimacy, inheritance rights, and public
power in the formation of imperial Brazil, 1822–1889 / Linda Lewin.
     p. cm.
  Includes bibliographical references and index.
  ISBN 0-8047-4606-0 (cloth : alk. paper) —
  1. Illegitimacy—Brazil—History—19th century. 2. Brazil—
Social conditions—19th century. I. Title.

KHD520 .L49   2003
346.8105'2—dc21   2002010019

This book is printed on acid-free, archival-quality paper.

Original printing 2003

Last figure below indicates year of this printing:
12 11 10 09 08 07 06 05 04 03

Designed and typeset at Stanford University Press in 10/13 Minion

In Memory of

DOROTHY D. VELLENGA

and

JOYCE F. RIEGELHAUPT

Acknowledgments

In writing this book, I incurred many debts over the course of two decades. Several people stand out for the tutoring and encouragement they offered me in the project's early stage. I am especially grateful to Mary Ann Glendon, of Harvard University Law School, and to Boston College Law School, for jointly sponsoring me as a visiting scholar in residence. Mary Ann, as a specialist in comparative family law, introduced me to the features of a civil law tradition. Without her guidance and personal interest in my project, I could not have unraveled the knotty complexities of a legal tradition deriving from eighteenth-century Portugal. Two very special friends, in whose memory I dedicate this book, seconded my original determination to integrate an old interest in the history of the family in Brazil with a new focus on that country's inheritance system. Joyce Riegelhaupt of Sarah Lawrence College, as an anthropologist, encouraged me to write on a Luso-Brazilian system of inheritance at a crucial juncture. She also recruited me as a participant in the Social Science Research Council's two-year seminar on Latin American kinship, an experience that sharpened my awareness of how far matters of inheritance can reach. Dee Dee Vellenga of Muskingum College shared her insights as a sociologist who "read" an inheritance system from the ground up, using oral data from women who were cocoa farmers as the key for unlocking individual strategies of heirship. While regaling me with anecdotes about how those women used Ghana's local court system to reclaim the cocoa trees that were their family patrimony, she reminded me that my own forays into oral history in Paraíba had led me from eliciting kinship patterns to the Philippine Code.

To Ann Twinam of the University of Cincinnati, as one historian of Latin America to another, I am extremely indebted. She not only read the drafts of both volumes of this study, and offered me the most valuable set of comments and criticisms one could hope to receive for undertaking revisions, but she also proved an enthusiastic and encouraging collaborator. Through countless discussions on the subjects of crown legitimization and the Iberian context of legal bastardy, she helped me more than anyone else to delineate and clarify the central arguments in this study. Mariza Corrêa of the University of Campinas, a historical anthropologist, invited me to present some of the arguments of this book to her graduate seminar, where she inspired my use of the "*herdeiro de surpresa*" for the title for this book. The late Jorge Pacheco Chaves Filho, of Rio de Janeiro, willingly gave me a missing piece of his Prado family history that proved a fruitful clue and an unforgettable moment. Finally, Norris Pope, Editorial Director of Stanford University Press, deserves singular recognition, and my deep appreciation, as a collaborator who believed in the value of this book, even when it could no longer be contained in a single volume. His encouragement, suggestions, and willingness to entertain two books on the subject of illegitimacy and inheritance law in Brazil were an inspiration.

A long list of librarians or archivists, many of whom I am unable to thank personally here, made this book possible. In particular, I would like to express heartfelt appreciation to Rachel Barreto Edensword, formerly of the Oliveira Lima Library, Catholic University of America, Washington, D.C.; Martha Maria Siqueira Cavalcanti, formerly of the Library of the Faculdade de Direito do Recife, in Pernambuco; Pedro Tórtima of the Instituto Histórico e Geográfico Brasileiro, Rio de Janeiro; Iêda Wiarda of the Hispanic Section of the Library of Congress, Washington D.C.; and Eliane Pereira, of the Biblioteca Nacional, and José Gabriel Pinto, of the Arquivo Nacional, Rio de Janeiro. Each of them uncovered documentation indispensable for plotting the course of the legislation central to this book. Finally, Ida Lewcowicz facilitated my access to the library of former justice minister, Alfredo Buzaid, on deposit at the Universidade Estadual de São Paulo, Franca. During a rewarding residence as a visiting professor, I located the last missing texts outstanding in the research for this book in Buzaid's impressive collection. My students in Franca, both in history and in law, enriched my appreciation of family history in imperial Brazil. In addition, the following graduate students tracked down precious primary and secondary materials: Louise Avila and Mariano Plotkin of the University of California, Berkeley, and Mary Ann Mahoney of Yale University. Paloma Fernández Pérez generously shared her own research and clarified Spanish inheritance law for me. Matthew Gerber, also of UCB, provided guidance on French law.

Special thanks are due to those who gave me detailed written comments on chapter drafts: Muriel Nazzari, Brian Juan O'Neill, Ted Riedinger, Patricia Seed, Sandra Lauderdale Graham, Mary Karasch, Dauril Alden, Keith Rosenn, Charles Hale, Marty Jay, Donna Guy, Jeff Needell, Bert Barickman, Paloma Fernández Pérez, and Hendrik Kraay. Keith Rosenn set me straight on Roman law and clarified my understanding of "legal nationalism," while calling that term to my attention. Marty Jay brought Continental liberalism into a more finely tuned focus vis-à-vis a Brazilian variant. Any errors I have made in failing to heed their invaluable written comments and conversational pointers are strictly my own responsibility. Donald Ramos, of Cleveland State University, provided me with an important missing text of eighteenth-century law. Hendrik Kraay generously provided me with excerpts from compendia of military laws and regulations. Osvaldo Agripino, of the Complexo de Ensino Superior de Santa Catarina and Stanford University's Brazil Working Group, provided excerpts from Brazil's 1941 Criminal Procedural Code and complementary statutory law. Tom Cohen, Director of the Oliveira Lima Library, supplied data for final corrections.

The financial support I received for this two-volume project was generous, extensive, and indispensable. A Tinker Post-Doctoral Fellowship, in tandem with a research travel grant from the Social Science Research Council and the American Council of Learned Societies, initially enabled me to spend an academic year as a research fellow in residence at Boston College Law School and the University of São Paulo. The latter venue facilitated access to a treasure trove of legal materials for imperial Brazil, housed in the Library of the Faculdade de Direito de São Paulo, one that supplemented the offerings detailed in the preceding volume for the FDSP's sister institution in Recife. A Humanities Research Fellowship from the University of California, Berkeley, and a research travel award from the American Philosophical Society later offered me opportunity for a sabbatical semester of leave for follow-up research, as a visiting research scholar at the Fundação Casa de Rui Barbosa, Rio de Janeiro. Rui's enormous archive and marvelous private library were placed at my disposal.

Another Humanities Research Fellowship from UCB contributed generously to a year of sabbatical leave for write-up in the mid-1990s and enabled me to expand considerably the project's focus. Assistance from my department's Shepard Fund facilitated retrieval of parliamentary debates from the Oliveira Lima Library and the Library of Congress, making possible this volume's legislative focus on a liberal agenda broadly addressing family and inheritance law. The Shepard Fund further contributed to publication of this volume. I especially wish to thank my friends and colleagues in the History Department, University of California, Berkeley, for believing in the merits of this book and for showing me infinite patience in waiting for its publication.

At all of these institutions, I benefited from faculty, research staff, and graduate students, who as friends and colleagues shared their enthusiasm for a project that for me has been as much an amazing intellectual journey as the authorship of a book. It was a journey that made many disparate pieces of Brazil's history fit meaningfully together for the first time. I hope this book proves worthy of their support and curiosity.

Contents

————◆◆————

Preface

This book began as a simple inquiry into rules of heirship that in Brazil were exceptionally generous to individuals born outside legal wedlock. Given a historical focus on the nineteenth century, those rules derived from a Luso-Brazilian inheritance system originating in three centuries of Portuguese colonialism. Natural offspring best exemplified the generosity of inheritance rights. Whenever recognized by a parent, their legal status approximated legitimate birth. On the other hand, rules of heirship excluded from succession rights a variegated category of illegitimate offspring who were collectively identified as spurious. Their legal position offered a sharp contrast to natural offspring because law denied them rights in heirship, sometimes prohibiting even a parent's modest bequest. Unlike their counterparts of illicit birth, natural offspring, those who were of spurious birth were taken by law to be true bastards. Yet, historically, bastardy proved remarkably mutable. Law provided remedy, offering another reason why a Luso-Brazilian legal tradition deserves to be evaluated as exceptionally generous. Only in twentieth-century Brazil did bastardy become legally irreversible.

For a North American reader, Brazil's legal tradition will contrast sharply with an Anglo-American one. Above all, rules of heirship have historically treated illegitimate individuals differently, thereby revealing the key features that differentiated succession rights in each legal tradition. Volume 1 of this study brought the major differences between Anglo-American and Luso-Brazilian legal traditions into explicit focus, underscoring how the meaning of bastardy historically imposed a pivotal distinction between what were two, distinctive sub-systems of European inheritance. Not only were rules of heirship divergent, but the fundamental concepts encoding the key features of Luso-Brazilian succession law differed from those deriving from Anglo-American succession law. As a result, paternal recognition, solemn vs. simple legitimization, a legal identity as a foundling, or the benefits of legitimization by subsequent marriage, proved to be culturally loaded notions that possessed special meaning for how, in given contexts, rules of heirship were to be applied in eighteenth- and nineteenth-century Brazil.

The detailed consideration paid in the preceding volume to those rules of heirship also made clear how their inherent concepts specifically applied after 1754, when they systematically came under revision by the Portuguese state. A Luso-Brazilian system of inheritance, as those chapters made clear, not only demonstrated dual ladders of *ab intestato* and testamentary succession prescribing how the bulk of any estate devolved to the appropriate heirs, but it also distinctly isolated those ladders from a secondary form of diverging devolution: bequests disposed by means of a will. From an Anglo-American legal perspective, consequently, the dual nature of succession in imperial Brazil—a circumstance derivative of the crown's solemn legitimization proceedings—complicates an understanding of how the inheritance system operated.

Beginning in the 1750s, Portugal's legal tradition underwent important reformulation by crown jurists, suggesting a final area of difference vis-à-vis Anglo-American legal tradition. Contrary to what many have assumed, Brazil's inheritance system at independence no longer closely approximated the one spelled out in Portugal's national law code of 1603, the *Ordenações Filipinas*. That is, the juridical foundation in Roman and canon law inherent in that "Philippine Code" had been significantly altered. The movement known in Portugal as legal nationalism—*direito pátrio*—recast the Luso-Brazilian inheritance system in accordance with new principles appropriate to the apogee of royal absolutism. Hence, what by 1750 had become an excessive reliance on canon law, and a parallel recrudescence of the "written reason" of Roman law, was systematically restricted or discarded. Legal nationalism represented the instrument for reformulating positive law in Portugal, specifically to privilege the statutory law of the king, national custom, and the practical rulings of the crown judges who both applied and made law in the royal courts. The impact of that politico-juridical movement has been analyzed in the preceding volume. Nevertheless, its prime mover, the marquis of Pombal (Sebastião José de Carvalho e Mello), who was the first minister of D. José I (1750–1777), continued to cast a long shadow in Brazil after independence.

Thanks to Pombaline reform, and the outstanding jurists who reinterpreted both the Philippine Code and other national positive law in eighteenth-century Portugal, legal nationalism represented the new orthodoxy in a juridical heritage that Brazil received from Portugal at independence. Readers of this book will discover, therefore, that Brazil's first generation of legislators behaved as the heirs of Pombaline regalism and legal nationalism. As a result, they invoked the interpretations of the two jurists most closely associated with Portugal's reformulated legal tradition: Paschoal José de Mello Freire dos Reys (1738–1798) and Manoel de Almeida e Souza de Lobão (1745–1817). The legal commentaries authored by the latter, in addition to the one subsequently produced by their standard bearer, Manoel Borges Carneiro (1774–1833), the brilliant martyr of Portuguese liberalism, defined the principal authoritative texts that Brazil's imperial legislators studied or consulted through the 1840s.

Inheritance and family law defined the central areas of private law where the impact of legal nationalism had been felt during Pombal's ministry (1750–1777). For Brazil's first generation of national legislators, independence in 1822 offered timely and compelling opportunity to modify the legal tradition they inherited from Portugal. Although they sought immediately to bring that tradition into conformity with the political demands dictated by the fact of a constitution, their efforts to rework private law also proceeded apace. As a result, far from being primordially fixed, rights in succession for Brazilians born outside wedlock historically have fluctuated dramatically since the independence era of the 1820s. This book, consequently, examines and interprets how Brazilian legislators, during the first three decades of independence, proposed to rewrite those inheritance rights vis-à-vis illegitimate individuals, and, in so doing, revised or discarded portions of the enduring national code of law received from Portugal.

Initially, the pivot of inquiry for this book rested on Law No. 463 of September 2, 1847, due to the great divide it defined in the history of inheritance rights enjoyed by one category of illegitimate individuals: natural offspring. The Law of September 2 amounted to the most important piece of nineteenth-century legislation affecting illegitimate individuals until promulgation of Brazil's 1916 Civil Code. As it turned out, Law No. 463 of 1847 possessed an exceptionally protracted history, for its genesis lay in the decade of liberal political experimentation known as the Regency (1831–1840). Further research revealed the significant extent to which, from the late 1820s through the 1840s, liberal legislators had sought to change either the position of illegitimate individuals in inheritance law or the legal rules that prevented many parents from marrying. In fact, the features of a Luso-Brazilian inheritance system came under scrutiny immediately, due to the ideological values early legislators held. They were also determined to make national law reflective of Brazilian social organization and cultural values.

Consequently, this book tells the previously unknown story of those reform efforts, beginning with the occasion when marriage was first placed on the agenda of national legislative debate, in 1827. At the same time, the approach adopted herein integrates attention to legal reform with a focus on common patterns of family organization during the era of independence

(1822–1830), the Regency (1831–1840), and the first decade of the Second Empire (1840–1889). That focus extends to some of the key legislators who sponsored reform bills, for their biographies illustrated the peculiar features of family organization inherent in their legislative discourse devoted to illegitimacy, marriage, and inheritance. New rules of heirship in early imperial Brazil were authored largely by men of property on behalf of propertied groups. Precisely because those at the top of society might choose to live outside legal marriage, and ignore or dispense with either the vows of matrimony or those of clerical celibacy, early imperial society offers a special context for investigating a rich multiplicity of family arrangements. Furthermore, legislators occasionally articulated their awareness of Brazil's rapidly growing proportion of natural offspring, that is, those whose parents were legally marriageable, but had declined to marry. An imperial deputy representing the province of Minas Gerais, for instance, offered data he collected in the 1840s to estimate that natural offspring amounted to one-third of Brazil's total population.[1] No one hazarded an estimate of the proportion who were spurious.

The propensity for Brazilians from all walks of life to live in consensual unions, whether they pertained to ubiquitous arrangements of adulterous and clerical concubinage, or, alternately, what liberal legislators by the 1840s termed "natural" marriage, not to mention less stable unions of cohabitation, explained the attention the national legislature paid to the legal position of natural and spurious children in the inheritance system. The diversity of conjugal unions, and the legal variegation among the non-legitimate offspring who resulted from those unions, defined the important sub-text of legislative debates that addressed illegitimacy, marriage, and inheritance rules between the 1820s and the 1840s.

Hence this book offers a selected view of that family sub-text of parliamentary debate and integrates the major features of family organization that made the subject of illegitimate birth significant for Brazil's first generation of imperial legislators. In this respect, it builds on the foundation laid in volume 1, tying late colonial patterns of family formation to discrete legal rights in heirship that depended on individual "*qualidade*," or quality of birth. That is, rights in patrimony varied, according to whether individuals were either natural, spurious (incestuous, adulterine, sacrilegious), legitimized, or foundlings. Initially sympathetic to mitigating the "stain of bastardy," liberal reformers made enlightened proposals on a broad range of family matters. In so doing, they subjected the private sphere of the family, including "skeletons in the closet" theretofore unremarked in parliamentary debate, to the scrutiny of public power. In this regard, their anxiety over the appearance of the "surprise heir," whom they conventionally identified as "a stranger" or an "outsider," but preferred to construe as an "imposter," prefigured the climactic adoption of Law No. 463 of 1847.

As they tinkered with rules of heirship and argued over legal marriage or the uncertainties of paternal recognition, legislators demonstrated a belief that public power in Brazil ought to be exercised over the most intimate private relations. That assumption, of course, was not new. In the colonial period, public power frequently had been exercised in order to sanction the religious morality of an established church, either through adoption of specific laws or the administration of crown justice, including punishment of sin executed by the secular arm. However, with each decade of the eighteenth century, ecclesiastical power less successfully asserted legal jurisdiction over private, intimate behavior. Portuguese absolutism restricted drastically the reach of religious tribunals and proved increasingly reluctant to enforce their determinations or to apply canon law in royal courts.

What stood out as different by the independence era of the 1820s was the fact of a triumphant Portuguese regalism, one that had largely succeeded in separating "sin" from "crime" in the private law of the family. The chief instrument of Portuguese regalism from the 1750s onward was national positive law, wielded by the crown jurist. Volume 1 has examined the impact of the 1769 Law of Right Reason (*Lei da Boa Razão*), in relegating canon law to a marginal position prior to Brazilian independence. Yet Brazil's early liberal legislators still tried to expand the mandate of "*boa razão*." By sponsoring bills to reform the private law of the family or the inheritance system, they fulfilled an agenda reaching to the 1760s. By the end of the 1830s, they had also transformed the national legislature, the General Assembly, into a stage for expressing their private views on sexual morality, views that never before had they committed to a public forum. As a result, a great deal of legislative discourse reflected keen awareness of what imperial legislators themselves believed should define quintessential, *Brazilian* family values. The formal record of their parliamentary debate therefore stands as a permanent and rich repository of those values.

As an interpretation of the family in past time, this book uses the process of making law as the principal focus for drawing conclusions about how public power confronted illegitimacy and inheritance rights during Brazil's crucial passage from colony to independent nation. In assessing the usefulness of legal change for the historian of the family, I have attempted to connect law to customary values and family patterns, especially those reflecting unwritten community standards explaining the widespread toleration of multiple forms of family organization characteristic of imperial Brazil. When, as minister of justice in the late 1860s, José de Alencar averred that a civil code was as much a work of customs and traditions as it was a work of juridical science and talent, his pronouncement merely affirmed a central tenet of legal nationalism. Of course, his statement also revealed his alternate persona as Brazil's most acclaimed novelist in the era of Romanticism. Possibly because he was himself a *sacrílego*, fathered by a priest, Alencar expressed an intuitive understanding of how unwritten standards of community toleration were embedded in laws that either reached deeply into family life or imposed differential patrimonial outcomes depending on individual quality of birth.

On the other hand, family and illegitimacy received significant attention from liberal legislators during the first three decades after independence in good part because those lawmakers questioned the rules regulating how property devolved intergenerationally. Those rules assigned rights to non-legitimate individuals in a national system of inheritance that permitted them to receive shares of the patrimony that belonged to the legitimate family. Initially, political and social change suggested to many that the rules had become out-of-date and deserved liberalization. Procedures of paternal recognition, inherent in the rules of heirship, captured legislators' central attention because they mediated the devolution of patrimony. Eventually, the extent to which non-legitimate individuals enjoyed legal rights to patrimony belonging to the legitimate family fell under negative public scrutiny, causing those rights to be restricted. As a result, the legal position of non-legitimate individuals in the inheritance system framed a public issue that catapulted a congeries of family behaviors and arrangements into the open arena of Brazil's national legislature.

The principal primary sources for this study are twenty-three years of the published record of Brazilian parliamentary debate known as the *Anais do Parlamento do Imperio Brasileiro*. Spanning 1826 to 1848, they are not quite aptly termed "minutes." Yet they are the only official record of public discourse for Brazilian legislators set down in discrete volume sets for both the Senate and Chamber of Deputies.[2] The Philippine Code of 1603, as well as several legal codes adopted by Brazilian legislators in the 1830s, together with colonial and national statutory law and the legal commentaries elucidating them, round out the primary sources supplying the key evidence for this book. Although this volume focuses on the process by which legislators attempted to modify or revoke sections of the *Ordenações Filipinas* after Brazilian independence, readers should keep in mind that Portugal's national code of 1603 was not replaced by a Brazilian Civil Code until 1916.[3]

Part I, by examining Brazilian liberalism, seeks to locate the impetus for reforming family and inheritance law in the programmatic assault that early nineteenth-century liberals carried out on the vestiges of the Portuguese *an-*

cien régime. More to the point, discussion of liberalism focuses on the attack that early liberals leveled against a society of estates. Chapters 1 and 2, consequently, develop from the preceding volume's analysis of Pombaline reform of the inheritance system, one that simultaneously undermined the economic position of church and nobility. By extending that analysis to the independence decade of the 1820s, these initial chapters set aside the conventional bifurcation of Brazilian history at 1822. In other words, the legal nationalism that undergirded the aggressive regalism associated with the Portuguese absolutist state after 1750 accounted for many of the reformist positions taken by liberal legislators during the 1820s and early 1830s. Even granting that Brazil's historical liberalism failed to generate enduring ideological divisions, when political parties emerged around 1840, it remains the case that legal nationalism and regalism survived the age of absolutism and the French Revolution to flourish throughout Brazil's era of independence and Regency. They especially left an imprint on matters of church and state.

An agenda of dismantling the state apparatus belonging to the former colonial regime implied the creation of new Brazilian political institutions that carried important consequences for illegitimacy and inheritance rights in imperial Brazil. Chapter 2 therefore analyzes the extinction of royal tribunals closely associated with the colonial order, especially the Desembargo do Paço, whose tribunal issued certificates of crown legitimization with concurrent rights in succession. The impact of the national judiciary that replaced the Desembargo do Paço in 1828, together with new procedures and legal assumptions about solemn legitimization that resulted, defines one of the dual themes of this chapter. Judicial legitimization, in supplanting crown legitimization during the independence decade, is evaluated as both an innovative liberalization and a problematic development that quickly drew renewed attention from reformist legislators. By situating nineteenth-century liberalism within the broad context of a reaction to Portuguese absolutism, both Chapters 1 and 2 tie the liberal credo of "equality before the law" to the eighteenth-century Pombaline attack on a society of estates. Chapter 2's other dual theme, consequently, is elaborated against the backdrop of the liberal credo of "equality before the law." By paying equal attention to color and race, the chapter reformulates the relationship between legitimate birth, gender, and nobility by descent previously developed in Volume 1. Alternatively, Pombaline civil nobility figures importantly in the chapter as a special juridical feature precisely perpetuating the "distinctions" that liberal reformers presumably opposed. Thus juridical equality, rather than political equality, defined the essence of the liberal attack on legal "distinctions."

Part II approaches the subject of illegitimacy and inheritance by examin-

ing the agenda on marriage that many liberal lawmakers endorsed, one preliminary to their sponsorship of bills directly reformulating the rights of illegitimate individuals. It isolates the efforts of reformers who challenged the
canons imposed by the Council of Trent on marriage and ordination. Chapter 3 takes as its subject the important 1827 debate that defined a strict definition of legal marriage throughout the imperial period, one reversed only with
the advent of a republic in 1889. The chapter explores why the legal definition
affirmed in 1827 was congruent with the sacrament of holy matrimony, that is,
narrowly framed by the canons laid down in the 1550s at the Council of Trent.
The fact that Brazil's first legislators found it necessary to reaffirm Tridentine
marriage may come as a surprise to many readers. However, the chapter's
other purpose, to clarify the ambiguous position that "*mancebia*" enjoyed in
late colonial and early imperial law, offers the explanation, given that *mancebia* continued to be an outcome tied directly to the position of Tridentine
marriage in national positive law. Consequently, Chapter 3 traces the fate of
"marriage according to the *Ordenações*" in the independence era, enlarging
on the impact that legal nationalism made on juridical interpretations of matrimony discussed in Volume 1. The multiple incarnations of "marriage according to the *Ordenações*," as de facto and assumed marriage, not to mention their generic manifestation—as "*mancebia*"—that really might not be
synonymous with the latter, highlight what has been a historiographically
confused discussion in the literature on Brazil's family history. *Mancebia*,
historically much more than a sexual union of cohabitation, continued to
remain pivotal for the high rate of out-of-wedlock births in imperial Brazil.
Even more than in the late colonial era, during the Empire it was directly tied
to the high rate of natural offspring in the general population as well as to a
sizable population of *sacrílegos*.

Chapter 4 pursues the liberal reaction to the canons adopted at the Council of Trent by examining the famous 1827 proposal of Dep. Diogo Antonio
Feijó, calling on the imperial government to permit priests to marry. Debate
over the forgotten bill sponsored by Sen. Nicolao Pereira de Campos Vergueiro, introducing civil marriage on behalf of all Brazilians regardless of religion, also figures centrally in this reassessment of "forced celibacy." The
latter implied that priests should have the right to marry, but it further implied their children should be relieved of the legal stigma of birth that labeled
them "*sacrílegos*," sacrilegious offspring. Feijó's famous campaign to permit
priests to marry, which ended only in 1835, is revisited in light of late colonial
patterns of clerical *mancebia*, or concubinage, and the latter's even more
widespread social acceptance after independence, in demonstration of the

impressive sentiment in favor of eliminating the "defect" of sacrilegious birth. On the other hand, Vergueiro's bill on civil marriage benefited the children of Catholic parents prohibited by Tridentine rules from marrying in the church, including priests, although the children of Protestants, as well as those of mixed, Protestant-Catholic parents, defined the major beneficiaries. Both proposals, in drawing the ire of the head of the Catholic Church in Brazil, became inextricably linked.

Part II concludes with Chapter 5, which leaves legislative debate aside in order to look at the plethora of family arrangements at the elite level of Brazilian society, the social basis of the situations legislators tried to address in their bills and resolutions. By taking the imperial court as a principal focus for exploring adulterine illegitimacy, the chapter illustrates both the patrimonial considerations that mattered importantly among groups possessing substantial property and the special stigma that law and society attached to one variant of spurious birth. Primary attention is paid to Emperor D. Pedro I's "polygamous" family, in contrast to the historiographical gaze conventionally cast toward his adulterous liaison with a noblewoman from São Paulo. Pedro's personal example also offers a means for isolating the restrictions that law placed on parents of noble birth whenever they wanted to legitimize their non-legitimate children, usually for purposes of heirship. His idiosyncrasies as a profligate husband who fathered a brood of adulterine children are reassessed, therefore, in light of his determination to remove the "stain" of bastardy visited on some of those children. Pedro's successes and failures are interpreted in the overlapping context of efforts by legislators during the final year of his reign to initiate legal reform, either liberalization of the procedures of paternal recognition or a parent's institution of both natural and spurious offspring as heirs in testamentary succession.

Part III, spanning the next three chapters, examines in detail the resolutions, bills, and laws that liberal legislators proposed as an impressive agenda to reform the position of illegitimate individuals in Brazilian inheritance law. Chapter 6 focuses on the turbulent Regency era, a decade that opened with the abdication of D. Pedro I in 1831. Its subject is the earliest effort to undo "damnable" birth, told in terms of two bills, a story concluded in Chapter 7. Both chapters exploit the parliamentary debate that provided valuable insight into courtroom conflict exacerbated by the 1828 Judiciary Act. Growing litigation on the part of necessary and collateral heirs, on the one hand, and, on the other, by natural and spurious children who claimed to be paternally recognized or legitimized, arose from the recently liberalized opportunity to plead inheritance claims in local courts. Legislators' opinions on accepted court practices, abuses, or the misapplication of law pertaining to legitimization procedures, provides an important dimension to judicial reform missing in conventional political narratives of the 1830s.

Chapters 6 and 7 thus assess the radical phase of liberal reform that sought to mitigate or undo "damnable" birth, one coinciding with the related effort to extinguish the private, or family, entail known as the *morgado*. An institution that directly privileged legitimate birth as well as noble descent, the *morgado* and its abolition in 1835 are connected to wider efforts by liberals to privilege all necessary heirs—including recognized natural offspring—with "equality before the law." Extinction of the ecclesiastical entail known as the *capela* proved more difficult and less comprehensive, but in 1837 its suppression accomplished the liberal goal of denying the church family patrimony that rightly belonged to *ab intestato* heirs. Tied to the broader political fortunes of historical liberalism, the radical trajectory of reforming marriage, liberalizing the rights of those born outside legal wedlock, and abolishing entail, peaked by 1835. Yet the reform impetus foundered for the same reasons that liberalism dissolved as a mobilizing ideology. Additionally, reform of marriage and the legal position of illegitimate individuals foundered on the Achilles' heel of an established church.

Chapter 8, which concludes Part III, in tandem with Chapter 9, surveys the evolution of the bill that became Law No. 463 of 1847. Together, these chapters follow the bill from its origin in 1836, as a measure exhibiting both radical and reactionary features, through a slow progression that kept in step with the country's return to a centralized monarchy by 1840. Finally, its fate after the emergence of the party system associated with the Second Empire is dissected in Chapter 9. The pivotal focus of both chapters, however, explores the logical tension between legislators who assumed that "good law" should reflect the customary practices and values of the Brazilian people and those who proposed new law as an instrument for changing behavior. At issue was not only the now common specter of the "surprise heir" but also a different model of family organization appropriate to new forms of wealth and property. Thus 1847 amounted to a watershed in the history of the patrimonial rights enjoyed by natural offspring, given that bastardy was legally redefined as more inclusive and less mutable. It also marked a turning point in how legislators viewed the adoption of new inheritance law, for a majority voted in favor of legal innovation inspired by French law as the instrumentality for domestic social change. Passage of Law No. 463 of 1847 also prefigured the direction the 1916 Civil Code adopted, by denying historic rights to both natural and spurious individuals. Finally, an epilogue discusses the position of the latter in the 1916 Civil Code, bringing their rights into a relevant, twentieth-century focus.

In conclusion, this book raises the nineteenth-century issue of whether law should validate existing family arrangements, legitimating what custom has long determined, or whether law should and can be used instrumentally to impose change, by privileging legal marriage and legitimate birth. Although Minister of Justice José de Alencar was a voice crying in the wilderness when he came down firmly on the side of validating custom in 1869, a century later his view had gained impressive support. Today, this book's focus on the role family law should play in Brazilian society remains as much an issue for Brazil's lawmakers as it does for social historians. The pendulum of social change continues to swing. As the twenty-first century opened, and Brazil promulgated a new Civil Code, in 2002, it was clear that family and inheritance law had moved away from the rules programmatically imposed by the 1916 Civil Code. Legislators again were inclined to validate social arrangements that reflected customary practices, simultaneously contradicting the role the authors of the 1916 Civil Code intended for law to play in upholding legal marriage. How bastardy was redefined initially in republican Brazil no longer commanded legitimacy.

Today, the "surprise heir" still enjoys prominence in Brazil's social landscape—as an individual newly equipped with rights following from both the 1988 Constitution and the 2002 Civil Code. Furthermore, the arrival of DNA in the 1990s has reinforced those rights in ways that have been dramatic, if not always accepted by the parties openly challenged. One has only to turn on the television to find the beguiling figure of the surprise heir writ large in Brazilian popular consciousness. Woven into the plots of Brazil's entertaining *telenovelas*, from the 1970s onward, he or she continues to raise alarm among legitimate heirs, threatening the devolution of family patrimony and sometimes raising even the possibility of incest committed in ignorance of the true ties of blood kinship. Like Machado de Assis and other nineteenth-century novelists who drew on the mysterious surprise heir as a stock character in imperial fiction, contemporary Brazilian scriptwriters continue to find their characters and plots in the stuff of real life.

A Note on Legal Language and Brazilian Orthography and Names

Language, especially the language of law in the eighteenth and nineteenth centuries, plays a central role in this study. The terms used in this book frequently differ from legal terminology currently in use in Brazil. Deviation often reflects more than merely a linguistic shift, however. Today, the legal concepts have often changed from what they were two hundred years ago. Consequently, English cannot always supply precise equivalents. If they exist in Anglo-American law, equivalent terms may imply different outcomes. Consequently, I have sometimes used archaic English to render language derived from a Luso-Brazilian legal tradition, as in the practice of "calling" the legitimate heirs to succeed. Otherwise, Brazilian readers will discover constructs that are central to discussion, such as "*qualidade*," an individual's quality of birth, no longer matter in their inheritance system. In matters of inheritance, Jack Goody has reminded us, "It is not easy to be precise unless we are technical."[1] Although I have translated Portuguese legal terms into English wherever they do correspond to Anglo-American legal concepts, there is a strong case to be made for retaining Portuguese where English "synonyms" either do not exist or imply different constructs, meanings, or outcomes. Rather than trying to harmonize linguistically what are really notions fundamentally alien to Anglo-American usage today, I have deliberately left a small number of those terms dissonant by retaining Portuguese terms. To do otherwise would be to blunt, to distort and misrepresent, or to confuse analysis of change over the century this book addresses.

Readers may initially be puzzled as to why I have not spoken consistently throughout the book of "illegitimacy" and "illegitimate" offspring, and, instead, alternated the latter with terms like "non-legitimate" or "out-of-wedlock." One reason is to avoid reliance on the dichotomy familiar from Anglo-American law that rigidly opposes "legitimate" to "illegitimate." Luso-Brazilian legal tradition demonstrated a spectrum of intermediate positions rather than a bifurcation of legal birth status. Another is to favor deliberate usage of "natural" and "spurious" offspring, as opposed to merging both as "illegitimate offspring." Sometimes even much finer discrimination is warranted, for alternate terms were operative in Brazil and Portugal until the twentieth century: *incestuosos, adulterinos,* and *sacrílegos,* as well as *quaesitos* and *expostos.* Basically, however, I have retained the language Brazilians used to designate those born out of wedlock for the period under study, because I wanted to convey how individuals from all walks of life labeled and thought about people who lacked legitimate birth. Although, historically, Anglo-American legal tradition has not discriminated finely among those who were illegitimate, it is also the case today that even Brazilians are much less likely to apply the finely tuned discrimination that was second nature to their grandparents or great-grandparents.

"Illegitimate" is a term taken from the civil law. Normally, Brazilian vernacular speech during the Empire and colonial period preferred the fine discrimination supplied by canon law. Although "illegitimacy" and "illegitimate" were not alien to the vocabulary of either jurists or ordinary people throughout the period this book spans, the language of canon law supplied the analytical constructs of an individual's "quality of birth." Those constructs, received in national positive law, underlay the social categories people regularly used in vernacular speech. Therefore, a crown jurist in Pombal's Lisbon and an illiterate farmer in Brazil's era of independence spoke the same language when they identified an individual as a "natural" child rather than an "illegitimate" child. In other words, religion, as much as inheritance law, inculcated the vocabulary of heirship used in this book and accounted for why the language of canon law penetrated popular speech. Rather than applying constructs of illegitimacy contemporary with the twenty-first century, I have tried to suggest those appropriate to the context spanning 1821 to 1889. The result is greater nuance and cultural shading, not to mention legal precision.

In one case, I have opted to retain a Latin term as the equivalent for Portuguese usage when a perfectly acceptable English equivalent exists: *ab intestato.* The reason that I have not adopted "intestate" as a translation is that it would only distract North American and British readers from appreciating the fundamental difference between their system of succession and the Luso-Brazilian system analyzed in this book. My initial effort to isolate the essence of what nineteenth-century legal commentators usually wrote as "*abintestado*" led me to discard "intestate," the better to focus on what a Luso-Brazilian context implied. The term conjures up a fundamental difference in an Anglo-American legal tradition—nearly the opposite meaning in a Luso-

Brazilian legal tradition. "*Ab intestato*" is synonymous with "legitimate" or "natural" succession and it presumes the natural order of events in Luso-Brazilian succession. That order is one where a will is unnecessary, because the rules of forced heirship determine the division of an estate and offer reassurance that the identity of the heirs is already known. In Anglo-American legal tradition, on the other hand, "intestate" implies a lapse—the failure to write a will. "Intestate" therefore can imply a family catastrophe, or at least a dissonant order of events that threatens to overturn normative expectations about heirship.

Finally, "intestate" implies the state's intervention is needed to identify and verify the authenticity of the heirs in an Anglo-American legal tradition. Those heirs, like wills, must be proved in a court of law. In the Luso-Brazilian legal tradition relevant to this volume, as opposed to the colonial period, the state ceased to play a marginal role vis-à-vis the identity of the heirs in legitimate or natural succession, by virtue of the greater attention it paid to taxing those heirs. However, *ab intestato* succession still took place without the state's intervention, a circumstance largely explaining why, with one exception, no tax was levied on *ab intestato* heirs by Brazil's imperial government until the second half of the nineteenth century.

Ab intestado succession in Luso-Brazilian law was also carefully distinguished from testamentary succession, the latter being the exception rather than the rule—and again, the opposite of Anglo-American practice. Hence, by relying on the device of "*ab intestato*" throughout the text, I am encouraging North American and British readers to stop thinking in terms of the assumptions, concepts, and rules of Anglo-American succession. I am asking them to don the mentality of an eighteenth-century civil law tradition, one where the heirs were already known and the lack of a will frequently defined the best scenario.

Brazilian orthography has varied considerably since the eighteenth century. The text of this book has modernized the spelling of archaic legal terms as well as the titles of legal codes, but left them unaltered in the notes and bibliographies. I have, however, spelled the names of individuals mentioned in the text of this book according to the usage in vogue when they were alive, meaning that names have usually been left consistent with the orthography specific to the sources cited in the notes. Given the latest orthographic reform that removes many diacritical marks from Portuguese, early nineteenth-century spelling more closely approximates early twenty-first-century spelling. Because historically there were no firm rules governing how people in Portugal and Brazil projected their names, not only the spelling of names but also the ways that individuals idiosyncratically manipulated their discrete name sets varied considerably. To a much lesser extent, this phenomenon continues to be true in Brazil down to the present. This is to say that Portuguese often prefers first names, even nicknames, wherever they are sufficiently uncommon or unique to obviate use of a concatenation of family names. Consequently, sometimes I have applied a lone rule of thumb that is still used in Brazil today. Individuals with uncommon or unique first names are often identified on a first-name basis. Thus Aureliano de Souza e Oliveira Coutinho is frequently identified as "Aureliano," just as in the 1980s the Brazilian press referred to Prime Minister Margaret Thatcher as "Margaret." Alternatively, his name is shortened to "Souza Oliveira," the parliamentary redactor's usage. In homage to Candido Mendes de Almeida, imperial Brazil's great jurist, he is identified obliquely in this book by the name Brazilians still use to refer to him, given his fame and the uniqueness of his first, Brazilian edition of the *Philippine Code*: "Candido Mendes."

Like the politicians mentioned in this text, the jurists discussed herein are identified initially in terms of their full names and then only mentioned by the short forms they routinely used to refer to each other in their own citations in legal commentaries. Thus Manoel de Almeida e Souza de Lobão was universally identified simply as "Lobão," and Lafayette Rodrigues Pereira became "Lafayette." The list of Legal Primary Sources Cited facilitates the referencing of their full names for readers. A decided preference for unique first names also implied that individuals who possessed extremely common given names frequently opted to project only one or more of their family names. They either omitted their given names altogether or they reduced them to initials. Finally, I have discriminated by given names several legislators in the same delegation who shared the same family name, due to being close relatives.

Politicians in this study are identified by their noble titles only where relevant in the period under study. I have declined, except in a few instances, to employ the convention of identifying anyone as a future bearer of a title. The title of the chief executive of a province throughout the imperial period was "president." I have retained the honorific "*dom*," which the Portuguese and Brazilians employed in lieu of the title, "King," abbreviated as in "D. Pedro I." Otherwise, I have followed standard usage and applied "*dom*" to several prelates of the Brazilian church. As the preceding volume of this study clarified, the honorific "*dom*" still applied widely at independence, to all individuals who either were noble by descent or were ennobled by the monarch. Women were analogously identified as "*dona*." Those whose nobility was merely civil, conferred by the law and therefore "secondary," did not enjoy the right to be addressed as "*dom*." With independence, use of "*dom*" rapidly eroded. By the close of the Regency, in 1840, the honorific was confined largely to the royal family and prelates of the church.

The monetary unit of the Empire was the *mil-réis*, written 1$000. The *conto* equaled one thousand *mil-réis* and was written 1:000$000, conventionally abbreviated as 1:000$.

The laws that comprise the primary sources for this volume are identified in terms of a myriad of designations originating in the usage of the Portuguese crown. Throughout Brazil's colonial history, statutory law, the most important source cited herein, was attributed to the sovereign and identified as "legislation," notwithstanding the absence of a legislature. Statutes were issued in the form of an *alvará* synonymous with "law" in English. After Brazilian independence, either "law" (*lei*) or "decree" (*decreto*), and even "decree-law" (*decreto-lei*), supplanted "*alvará*." However, the latter term continued to refer to crown law adopted prior to 1822. The indiscriminate use of both "law" and "decree," sometimes for the same statute, may confuse readers. It also confounded jurists, who understood "law" and "decree" were virtually synonymous. The persistence of this dualism seems to have originated in the monarch's historic loss of his role as "the Legislator" in the 1820s. In Portugal, lamented legal historian João Gomes B. Câmara, "the inexplicable distinction between 'law' and 'decree' was not resolved until 1936," when "law" triumphed. He offered a fine point doubtlessly accounting for the persistence of a dual nomenclature. A decree emanated from the legislature, but only the monarch's sanction, or signature, made it a "law."[2] In Brazil's case, the abolition of the monarchy in 1889 brought this duality to a close.

The other main source of law cited in this volume is, of course, the *Ordenações Filipinas* of 1603, the final of four compilations of Portuguese positive law that were promulgated as national codes of law between 1446 and 1603. Generically, these codes were referred to as "the *Ordenações do Reino*"—or simply the "*Ordenações*"—implying also the particular code currently in effect. During Brazil's Second Empire (1840–1889), usage moved away from the emphasis on what was, after all, a code derived from "the Kingdom of Portugal," to favor the politically less loaded alternate term, "*Código Filipino*," or Philippine Code. References to the *Ordenações Filipinas* of 1603 herein refer to Candido Mendes de Almeida's monumental 14th edition, published in 1870, the first to offer commentary in terms of *Brazilian* law: *Codigo Philippino ou Ordenações do Reino do Portugal* . . . . Otherwise, law in both colonial and early imperial Brazil consistently drew on administrative orders and clarifications, such as *avisos*, that were issued by the king's ministers or, in imperial Brazil, by the cabinet ministers associated with parliamentary government. Procedural law, such as that pertaining to high crown courts like the Tribunal of the Mesa do Desembargo do Paço, usually was defined in discrete "*regimentos*" or sets of regulations having the force of law. By the same token, the decisions of high crown courts, termed "*estilos*," frequently were cited as law throughout colonial and imperial centuries, given that the 1828 Judiciary Act perpetuated them in force throughout the Brazilian Empire. A list of abbreviations for these administrative and judicial forms of law has been prepared for readers.

The published sources used to write this book have been divided into two parts, one that pertains exclusively to legal primary sources, consisting of commentaries, treatises, and notarial manuals, or codes and collections of laws, gathered together as Legal Primary Sources Cited. Remaining sources, including legal histories, appear in Other Sources Cited. The lengthy nature of legal titles means that several have been abbreviated. Legal citations in the notes employ the standard abbreviations appearing in works contemporary to the nineteenth century. Therefore, I have also cited a legal commentary's discrete divisions: book, volume, part, chapter, title, section, and item number. Page numbers appear in parentheses, given that editions vary and the footnotes are often lengthy.

SURPRISE HEIRS

Volume 2

———◆———

Illegitimacy, Inheritance Rights, and Public Power in the

Formation of Imperial Brazil, 1822–1889

A civil code is not solely a work of science and talent. It is, above all, a work of customs, of traditions—in a word, of a people's civilization.

Minister of Justice José de Alencar, 1869

PART I

Liberal Beginnings

CHAPTER 1

The Context of Inheritance Reform

Liberalism in the Era of Independence

————— ◆ —————

Frei Joaquim do Amor Divino Caneca, martyr of liberty, being
condemned to death, was shot on the thirteenth of January, 1825,
because no executioner was willing to hang him . . . .
   The Chamber of Deputies for 1826 was, as it had to be, timid.
The dissolution of the Constituent Legislative Assembly and the
violence of power were the cause of this. But in 1827 and 1828 the
Legislative Assembly took heart, demonstrating a distinct independence.

   Mello Moraes the Elder, *Chronica geral do Brazil,* 1886[1]

Brazilian independence, hailed as the Cry of Ipiranga (*Grito de Ipiranga*) and
proclaimed in September 1822, found formal confirmation only on October
12. On that day, the birthday of Brazil's monarch, the municipal council of
Rio de Janeiro formally acclaimed D. Pedro emperor in the manner of Portugal's unwritten constitution. What historian Roderick J. Barman has aptly
characterized as "stumbling into independence" initiated a decade during
which Brazilians first managed to cut their ties with the Portuguese monarchy and then to expel their young sovereign.[2] A Portuguese by birth, Pedro
would leave the shores of his adopted land in 1831, protesting that in his heart
he would always be Brazilian. The crucial decade that opened in January
1822, on the banks of an inconsequential stream on the road to São Paulo,
witnessed Brazilians repudiating Portuguese colonial rule, receiving a constitution "written" by their twenty-six-year-old emperor, and then attempting to define the national polity as a constitutional monarchy.

   Over the course of the independence decade, the task of the national political elite would be to repudiate many of the institutions of Portuguese absolutism, while enacting legislation that gave full effect to the country's
monarchically imposed 1824 Constitution. Conflict in the political system
would logically polarize over the answer to one question: What should the
nature of constitutional monarchy be? Reluctantly joined in political sym-
biosis with a European power, by virtue of a dynastic arrangement that con-

nected Brazil's monarch to the throne of Portugal, the former colony began
the task of defining itself as politically distinct from the metropole. In less
than a decade, Brazil would reject its founding emperor because he failed to
reassure a suspicious legislature that he was indeed a constitutional monarch
and one committed to occupying an exclusively Brazilian throne. The first
decade of independence thus ended with a very different question mark:
Would Brazil continue to be a monarchy?

The rhythms of elite politics during the 1820s, when the national legislature struggled to implement a constitution that deprived the sovereign of his
absolute power to make law, resounded among actors who were usually
privileged men, notwithstanding that many in the lower house possessed
middle-class identities. Moreover, the national political elite comprised an
extremely small group: around 150 legislators, together with several dozen
individuals who belonged to the emperor's inner coterie of cabinet ministers,
imperial councilors, and courtiers. "The Corte," as the city of Rio de Janeiro
was designated until 1889, hosted legislators only between late April and October, when the General Assembly, a bicameral parliament, convened. The
dispersal of legislators to the provinces for six months each year, given the
absence of provincial legislatures until 1835, reinforced the role of the Corte
in the nation and that of the palace in the imperial capital. Ordinary Brazilians, however, proved far from passive spectators to political events in the
1820s. They would observe the break with Portugal according to a different
tempo than what applied to legislators. The populace, in fact, came alive politically in the wake of independence. With the exodus of D. João VI in 1821,
the crowd began to play an important role in national politics, from Pedro's
acclamation in October 1822 to the mass demonstrations that culminated in
"the night of the bottle throwing" in March 1831 and signaled his abdication.

The role of white political agitators notwithstanding, the crowd in the national capital was overwhelmingly comprised of people of color, slave and
free, a circumstance recently causing historians to reassess the implications
of "independence" for those who took to the streets on behalf of "the defense
of the Empire" or the "national cause."[3] Slavery, a legal condition that still
defined nearly half of Brazil's population at independence, also left its mark
on many individuals who had passed over to freedom. Given that the servile
institution defined the economic foundation of the new monarchy, it would
not be openly defied until the 1880s. "Gradual abolition"—manumission on
an individual basis—nevertheless would continue to accelerate in each decade after independence.[4] As the "letter of liberty," the manumission certificate worked its inexorable effect throughout society. *Pari passu*, a tiny but
significant stratum of the free population of color acquired greater social

mobility by virtue of individual talent and the unique opportunities presented by independence.

Paradoxically, even as the free population of color grew exponentially, greater and greater numbers of Africans would continue to set foot on Brazilian shores. Their importation bore witness to the fear that British opposition would end the slave trade, as well as to coffee's expanding demand for labor in the hinterland, west of the national capital. If the price for British recognition of independence was the Anglo-Brazilian Treaty of 1826, ostensibly ending the Atlantic traffic in 1830, then that treaty was better comprehended in the popular cliché it occasioned, "*para o inglês ver*," mere window dressing to impress the British.[5] As coffee and sugar planters reacted to boom conditions in the world market, and British diplomacy threatened to curtail the supply of coerced labor, the quest for profit fastened slavery's yoke more securely on the nation. Despite enlightened predictions that slavery in Brazil was doomed, or outright calls for abolition, Brazil's legislators remained firmly committed to the servile institution. If, individually, a select few lawmakers intelligently recognized the wisdom of ending the institution of slavery, or at least the traffic in human flesh, the domination of the government by pro-slavery forces persuaded them that any initiatives in that direction would be absolutely futile.[6]

The country's largest cities—Rio de Janeiro, Salvador, and Recife—testified to a changing national identity whose demographic refraction portended a larger cultural role in the Empire for forced immigrants who were African rather than European. The same refraction contained another, more immediate consequence. The growing free population of color, which in the cities represented an impressive reservoir of talent, presaged a new cultural equilibrium that attested to the challenge of social mobility. Overall, the nation's population steadily inclined toward a cultural visage that was creole rather than European. The physical presence and cultural imperatives imposed by thousands of Portuguese émigrés, who had arrived in 1808 with the Lisbon court, drastically receded after a mass exodus in 1831. "Creolization," a cultural process that affirmed a New World identity for Brazilians, would depend inevitably on cultural collaboration between those of European and African descent, as the passage of time attenuated affinities with the former metropole.

Never again would Brazilians be more antagonistically aligned against the Portuguese than by the end of the first decade of independence. Out of the confrontation a nascent sense of Brazilian national identity forced the Portuguese to choose between allegiance to the land of their birth and the land of their adoption. The disharmony of interest between peninsular Portuguese and former colonials, evident by 1831, would unite Brazilians of all colors in a common historical destiny. However, the cultural identity of the political elite, which inscribed a number of Portuguese expatriates, continued to be strongly European, in direct contradiction of the popular equilibrium moving toward creolization.

A national system of political parties did not clearly emerge in imperial Brazil until the mid-1840s. Prior to the creation of provincial legislatures in 1835, "faction" exclusively captured the essence of Brazil's partisan organization. Pedro I's preemptory closing of the national legislature in November 1823 served as the catalyst to align support for his brand of New World monarchy. Otherwise, it defined a growing opposition based on adherence to liberalism. He paved the way for the extremely factionalized conflict that consumed national politics, as the Second Legislature (1830–1833) opened. In this respect, the genesis of the nation's first constitution proved pivotal. Once the emperor and his councilors had revised an 1823 pending committee draft setting out a constitution for the nation—a document originally redacted by legislators who admired much in European, especially Portuguese, liberalism—Pedro then substantially revised and promulgated it as his own, "more liberal" Constitution of 1824.[7] However, the monarch imperiously declined to reopen the General Assembly for another two and a half years.

Predictably, the re-opening of the national legislature, on May 6, 1826, acted as a fillip to the growth of factional alignments, for now politicians held misgivings about the suitability of the young emperor. The appropriateness, if not the legitimacy, of the constitution Pedro now claimed as his own charter, remained open to question. Although the factional alignments that jelled by early 1830 forced Pedro's abdication the following year, the division posed by a liberal opposition had been clearly discernible at the close of the First Legislature (1826–1829). The genesis of conflict lay both in the constitutional issues thrashed out in legislative debates and the highly charged personalism of imperial court politics.

CONSTITUTIONAL MONARCHY AND
LIBERAL REFORM

The Monarch Disposes: Constitutionalism

Brazil's General Assembly consisted of an upper house of fifty senators and a Chamber of Deputies whose membership encompassed 102 provincial representatives. In the Chamber, where members were indirectly elected and did not enjoy life tenure in office, a core of legislative leaders immediately sponsored measures designed to implement constitutional arrangements that would extinguish the vestiges of the Portuguese *ancien régime*. By the opening of the 1828 session, the lower house, under firm liberal leadership, embarked on a program of implementing the 1824 Constitution. The central controversy between D. Pedro I and the bicameral General Assembly, especially the Chamber of Deputies, crystallized around the issue of who would rule: legislature or emperor? Tension during the 1820s turned on interpretation of the 1824 Constitution, notwithstanding the personal pride the emperor took in referring to himself as a constitutional monarch.

Brazil's new charter remained silent regarding the distribution of political authority in several important respects. Furthermore, in 1826, its most important innovations, such as a national judiciary, still awaited enabling legislation. For most legislators, sovereignty lay in the General Assembly simply because the Constitution vested the authority to make law in that body. For Pedro, who viewed himself as the bestower of the Constitution—even its author—abandonment of the sovereign's historic role as "the Legislator" for the Portuguese nation proved a difficult task. Despite demonstrating a more mature grasp of his political role by the late twenties, the monarch's willingness to confirm the constitutional redistribution of the power to make law, in favor of the legislature, remained ambivalent.

Prior to independence, D. João VI had personally vested sovereignty over Brazil in his eldest son, by virtue of what was regarded as Portugal's "historic," or unwritten, constitution. Such an assumption ran contrary to the new ideological emphasis on popular sovereignty that gained instant currency in the Lisbon Cortes of 1820–1821, and then was quickly diffused among a widening circle of Brazilian converts to constitutionalism. Not surprisingly, Pedro's Constitution of 1824 remained silent on the fundamental notion of popular sovereignty. The emperor understood his sovereign power as deriving explicitly from his father's formal devolution, at D. João's departure for Lisbon in 1821, when he bestowed on his son all the powers of Portuguese kingship in Brazil. Pedro confirmed those assumptions at his coronation, on December 1, 1822.

An investiture choreographed by the monarch himself, as Roderick J. Barman has correctly noted, the coronation "affected the character of the monarchy and the complexion of the new nation."[8] Although inspired by Napoleon's coronation, Pedro followed a ritual used for the Holy Roman Emperors when he knelt before Rio de Janeiro's bishop to have the nearly three-kilogram weight of a 22-carat, diamond-encrusted crown placed on his momentarily submissive head. The ceremony contrasted starkly with Pedro's official acclamation six weeks earlier at the Campo de Santana. Historically, Portugal's kings constituted themselves monarchs by the "acclamation" (*aclamação*) of their people, for the municipal councils customarily sent resolutions concurring that the heir should ascend the throne. Only then was the sovereign publicly "acclaimed" by the populace and an oath administered without any clergy present. D. João, for instance, took an oath with stark simplicity, placing the hat that he wore instead of a crown on the table beside him.[9] On the occasion of Pedro's acclamation at the Campo de Santana, Jozé Clemente Pereira, on behalf of the Corte's municipal government, had extolled "holy liberalism" from the balcony before which the multitude acclaimed their emperor in a pouring rain. As president of Rio de Janeiro's municipal council, Clemente Pereira—a Portuguese immigrant who was a passionate devotee of liberalism—had "begged the perpetual defender [of the nation] to bow to the will of the people and consent to be their constitutional emperor."[10]

By arraying his councilors and palace functionaries, almost all of whom were Portuguese, in the official uniform of the Portuguese court for his coronation, Pedro reaffirmed his identity as the heir of the Bragança royal house; by having himself anointed with holy oil by the royal chaplain, who was also bishop of Rio de Janeiro, he conveyed not only his identity as head of the church but also the divine sanction bestowed on his candidacy; and by selecting Latin as the language for the ceremony—deliberately excluding the vernacular customarily used by Portugal's kings in the oath, one now administered by the minister of justice—he sacralized the proceedings.[11]

Brazil's first emperor devised a coronation spectacle that would impose on his subjects both the "splendor of the house" of Bragança and the special position of the Brazilian monarchy vis-à-vis the throne of Portugal. Following the *Te Deum Laudemus* and holy communion in the imperial chapel, the emperor addressed the crowd assembled before the balcony of the City Palace. Looking across the capital's main plaza, he uttered an oath to the populace that later would be recalled as much for its *sotto voce* reservation as for its commitment to the ideological imperative of liberalism: "I swear to defend the constitution that is going to be made, *if it turns out to be worthy of Brazil and of me.*"[12] Thus did Pedro embark on the odyssey of his reign, one characterized by the contradiction between his reluctance to abandon basic tenets of an absolutist monarchy and the naiveté of his personal conviction that he was a liberal monarch.

Practically speaking, Pedro relied on two revisions in the 1824 Constitution that he himself imposed, both of which enabled him to challenge the national legislature's power to make law and affirmed his counterclaim to sovereignty: a Council of State and the moderating power. Neither idea originated with him; each was traceable to the ideas of Benjamin Constant de Rebeque. Previously, however, a Council of State had also functioned under the Portuguese monarchy as part of the executive branch. The creation of a new Council of State dated to the day following Pedro's closing of the national legislature in 1823, the act prompting him to establish such a body. The Council's first task, and its original *raison d'être*, had been to sponsor the modified draft that became the Constitution of 1824—and then to propose it for ratification to municipal councils throughout Brazil. This meant that neither the Constituent Assembly nor the reopened national legislature ever ratified Brazil's imperial Constitution, affording reason later for historians to term it a "charter" rather than a "constitution."[13] Ostensibly an advisory body, the Council of State would enjoy constitutional authority as part of a "fourth branch" of government introduced by Brazil's revised national charter. The Council consisted of a body of personal advisors appointed by Pedro, whom he preferred to draw from the ranks of senior colonial officials, overwhelmingly men of Portuguese birth. By 1826, Pedro had appointed almost all of them to the Senate, meaning that they held offices in two branches of government concurrently.

Equally significant, by 1826, Pedro had either ennobled or raised in the peerage virtually every one of his councilors, together with all the members of his cabinet. The occasions of his twenty-seventh and twenty-eight birthdays—October 12, 1825, and 1826—witnessed these ennoblements *en masse*, but they also portentiously bracketed the reopening of the national legislature in April 1826. The Constitution of 1824 conferred on the emperor authority to appoint and dismiss cabinet ministers, without providing that the latter were to be drawn from the legislature (Article 101, Paragraph 66). As a result, the cabinet universally reflected the emperor's personal choices rather than the preferences of the national legislature. A genuine parliamentary system could not take root. Not only did D. Pedro I fail to consult with legislators in many of his cabinet appointments, but he also did not feel bound to confine those appointments to members of the General Assembly.

Pedro's real challenge to the sovereignty of the national legislature, however, drew on the famous "moderating power" (*poder moderador*), sometimes referred to as the emperor's "regulating power" (Articles 98 through 101). Defended theoretically as a "balancing" or "neutral" power to counteract a legislature that might become unaccountable to the people, or unable to govern by virtue of deadlock, the moderating power conferred on the monarch certain prerogatives that potentially could impede or override the General Assembly's otherwise nearly exclusive authority to make law. Benjamin Constant had therefore construed his invention "the royal power."[14] Rather than "a fourth branch of government," as it has often been construed, the moderating power practically buttressed the executive, compensating the throne for the loss of all legislative functions.

For instance, under Article 98 of the Constitution, the moderating power conferred on the emperor the right to postpone or dissolve the General Assembly without consulting Parliament. Constitutionally, he could do so only where "the salvation of the state demanded it of him" and he was then required "to convoke immediately another to substitute" for the dissolved legislature. Pedro instead used his moderating power to dissolve the legislature, according to an *ex post facto* interpretation, and then ruled by decree from November 1823 until May 1826. The emperor derived his authority to appoint senators (Article 101, Paragraph 1) from the moderating power, selecting them from "triple lists" of candidates indirectly elected for this purpose (Article 43). The Constitution expressly directed that the emperor would nominate one-third of those on the triple list to the Senate; however, Pedro often named senators from among those who gained the least number of votes. He also disregarded the notion of provincial representation by declining to respect the geographical affiliations of senatorial electors and their candidates.

The moderating power also meant that legislators would be barred in public debate from criticizing the emperor directly, in terms of his policies. This point, sometimes overlooked in assessing Pedro's presumed commitment to liberalism, followed Article 99 of the Constitution, which stipulated—à la Constant—that "the person of the emperor is inviolable and sacred." By construing the emperor in absolutist terms, the Constitution gave him a unique, countervailing power vis-à-vis the legislature: "He is not subject to any responsibility." Thus the emperor, whose "imperial sanction"— his signature—was required for a bill to become a law, was not constitutionally required to offer reasons for vetoing legislation laid before him by the bicameral legislature.

As much by adopting the "brake" of the moderating power on the national legislature, as by its abuse, the emperor exercised an arbitrary veto on representative government. He could therefore influence the fate of bills simply by letting it be known he opposed their adoption. Similarly, the increasingly resented Council of State, under Pedro's direction, called into question his claim that he was indeed a liberal monarch. By frequently ignoring the spirit of the Constitution when he selected senators and ministers, who largely reflected his personal inclinations, Pedro alienated legislators and ignored the historical realities of a nascent Brazilian nationalism.

The General Assembly Disposes: Legislator of the Nation

Reform of succession and family law during the first two legislatures (1826–1833) has to be appreciated within the broader context of efforts by legislators who called themselves liberal to assert the constitutional powers of the General Assembly. Although bills taking aim at inheritance rules and the legal position of illegitimate individuals in Brazilian law did not represent their first priority, they nevertheless deserve consideration as part of broader efforts to strip the monarchy and the absolutist state of many of its former, legally defined, prerogatives. The latter historically had depended on the monarch's role as "the Legislator" for the nation, but the liberal attack also associated them broadly with a society of estates. Thus reform of inheritance law and the legal position of illegitimate individuals logically fell within a liberal agenda that implemented the 1824 Constitution. Furthermore, the focus on reforms addressing the rules of heirship and the legal fate of those born outside holy wedlock—or the role of sacramental marriage in national positive law—cannot be fully appreciated unless the nature of Brazilian liberalism is understood within the context of the 1820s and 1830s.

Liberals in particular emphasized that the emperor's power to legislate was no longer legitimate under the Constitution of 1824. They were correct that the monarch could not be deemed sole legislator for the nation; however, the emperor, much to their annoyance, played an indispensable role in all legislation. The Constitution jointly designated legislature and emperor "the representatives of the Brazilian nation" (Article 11), deeming him its "first representative," the "supreme chief of the nation" (Article 98). Yet it nevertheless relegated the emperor's former role as exclusive "Legislator" to a secondary and subordinate plane: "The Legislative Power is delegated to the General Assembly with the sanction [signature] of the emperor" (Article 13). The emperor, in fact, became fundamental for the implementation of any legislation. What José Murilo de Carvalho has correctly interpreted as the "ambiguity" of imperial institutions rendered the emperor a strong competitor with the Parliament for the representation of the nation in the making of law. If it was the case that the constitutional representation the emperor enjoyed was Burkean—attending to the general interest of the realm by better reflecting the public interest than Parliament—then the absolutist character of the Constitution also imposed practical limitations on Parliament.[15] Simply by refusing to sign a bill into law, he could exercise a *de facto* veto over legislation passed by the General Assembly. Consequently, he played an important role in making law, even if he could no longer initiate or independently promulgate legislation. His veto was one that could not be overridden. This circumstance limited support for bills wherever it was understood the emperor would not endorse them. On the other hand, by 1828 liberal legislators sought to force the imperial sanction by pushing the emperor to concede—in the face of public opinion—that overwhelming support for a bill in the legislature demanded his endorsement.

Reformers of inheritance law, usually as part of a liberal opposition, frequently implied that the emperor's power to legislate for the nation was no longer legitimate under the Constitution. They had in mind a more subtle dimension of the shifting balance of power between executive and legislature: the sovereign's ancient prerogative to dispense law in force, an attribution dating to medieval times. Until late 1828, when a national judiciary was established, Pedro possessed the sovereign power to suspend law. As the preceding volume has explained, the Tribunal of the Desembargo do Paço defined the institutional mechanism for bestowing such royal privilege. The latter, known as the "*mercê*," therefore remained fundamental for bestowing crown legitimization with concurrent succession rights or for confirming establishment of an entail. Now that "the Legislator" was the General Assembly, liberals argued, the executive power to dispense law should end. Full implementation of the Constitution, they correctly reasoned, would extinguish the monarch's power to dispense the law, making this unresolved aspect of sovereign power a source of tension within the legislature.

Pedro's two-year postponement of the legislature's first, four-year session, from 1825–1828 to 1826–1829, further explained why representatives in both houses paid immediate attention to constitutional implementation. Limiting the emperor's authority, by protecting the civil liberties of legislators, loomed uppermost. Initially, avoidance of a second, disastrous confrontation with Pedro, for fear it might expand his prerogatives, became a priority. The General Assembly's confidence in its exclusive power to make law also rested on an implicit power to deny legal effect to Portuguese law, although wherever the law of the former metropole was patently unconstitutional, action by the national legislature was not constitutionally required. Brazil adopted Portuguese legislation enacted only on or before April 25, 1821, meaning that the liberal laws introduced subsequently by the Lisbon Cortes did not apply in the former colony. This circumstance accounted for why Portugal's national law reflected a great deal more influence exerted by the French Revolution than did Brazilian law. The 1824 Constitution also offered considerable latitude to municipal councils either for denying effect to Portuguese law or for implementing new law within their localities. Article 178 provided: "All which is not constitutional can be changed, without reference to [constitutional] formalities, by the ordinary legislatures [municipal councils]."[16]

Interestingly, the important principle that Portuguese law was to be received in Brazil did not follow from the Constitution of 1824. Instead, the devolution of authority that D. João VI had conferred on his older son in 1821, as his chosen representative in Brazil, automatically conveyed the reception of Portuguese law. As a result, the task of the national legislature was to abrogate or clarify, by means of either new legislation or interpretive resolutions, important and fundamental laws received from Portugal. The Constitution anticipated that Brazilians would not depend in the long run on the law of the former metropole, for it called for adoption of both civil and criminal codes, "founded on the bases of justice and equity" (Article 179, Paragraph 18). Until the latter became realities, the *Ordenações Filipinas* of 1603, whose Book 5 constituted a criminal code, remained in force. Together with other statutory law promulgated in either Portugal or the colony after 1808, known as "*leis extravagantes*," the Philippine Code enjoyed full effect as received law in Brazil. Reception notwithstanding, Brazil's legislators believed that they possessed an implicit mandate to repeal or alter much of their outdated Portuguese national code—in the name of legal nationalism.

LIBERALISM IN A BRAZILIAN CONTEXT

First Liberals

Legislators who first advocated changes in succession and family law considered themselves liberals. The term "liberal," of course, had been initially diffused in Brazilian politics by events in the metropole, beginning in early 1820, when, spontaneously, a Cortes was called in Porto. In November, a Provisional Junta then formally convened Portugal's defunct Estates General as a constituent assembly—the Cortes Gerais Extraordinarias e Constituintes that met in Lisbon. However, both "liberal" and "liberalism" had appeared earlier in Europe's political lexicon, when the authors of Spain's 1812 Constitution met at the Cortes of Cádiz, in 1810–1812. Consequently, Brazilian intellectuals, politicos, and publicists initially were exposed to the ideas of liberalism as part of an Iberian reaction to the French Revolution, especially the Napoleonic invasion. The attack on corporate privilege, so inherent in Spanish liberalism, nonetheless defined a theme that from Pombal's era (1750–1777) onward had drawn support from enlightened sectors of Portugal's nobility and the emerging middle classes on both sides of the Atlantic empire.[17] By means of the Masonic lodges, which in Spain opposed the Bourbon restoration of Ferdinand VII in 1814, liberalism took clandestine root in Brazil and acquired a distinctly non-European revolutionary connotation. More firmly implanted in Pernambuco than in Rio de Janeiro, "revo-

lutionary liberalism" offered fertile ground for a secessionist, republican revolt from the metropole in 1817. The Portuguese crown quashed rebellion in
that northeastern province in a matter of months.[18]

In the royal capital of Rio de Janeiro, neither king nor court politicians
reacted to political change in post-Napoleonic Europe by concluding that
positive changes in Portugal's historical constitution should follow from
events in Spain. Rio de Janeiro was far removed from Cádiz, and the impact
of the Spanish Revolution of 1810 and the Constitution of 1812 did "not appear to have created a big commotion [at the Portuguese Court]." Nor did
the specter of republican revolt in Pernambuco, five years later, provide political incentive for the Portuguese crown to adjust itself to "the new practices and customs of the century."[19] Yet another liberal revolt in Spain, in
1820, proved the catalyst for a constitutionalist revolt in Lisbon.

In Rio de Janeiro, events in Spain, on February 26, 1820, obliged D. João
VI to promulgate a decree committing himself to respect a Portuguese constitution then about to be elaborated at the Lisbon Cortes. In the interim, the
resurrected Spanish Liberal Constitution of 1812 would be in force in both
Portugal and Brazil. When news of a liberal uprising in Lisbon reached Rio
de Janeiro, in 1821, the political situation in Brazil changed dramatically. A
steady stream of pamphlets began circulating, dedicated to the anticipated
constituinte, or constitutional convention, to be held in Lisbon. In tandem
with the press, Brazilian pamphleteers diffused the meanings of both constitutionalism and liberalism among the Corte's literate population, including
the pivotal ideas of Benjamin Constant de Rebecque. Drawing directly on
that Swiss-French survivor of Napoleonic revolutionary excess, an 1821 pam-
phleteer pointed out that a constitution was not "an act of hostility against
the monarch." It was "an act of union, determining the relations between
monarch and people." In the provinces, however, "constitution" elicited
confusion and suspicion.[20]

Initially, in an Iberian context, "liberal" connoted "constitutionalist." In
the Brazilian context of 1820, however, the word registered "constitutional
monarchist." Of the seventy-odd delegates Brazil sent to the Lisbon Cortes in
1821, most of those who balked at signing the draft of the 1822 Portuguese
Constitution were destined to become leaders in Brazil's first Parliament.
Their objections to the constitutional provisions pertaining to Brazil gained
them the respect of Manoel Borges Carneiro. That royal jurisconsult-turned-
liberal-leader in the Cortes fervently lent credence to Brazilian reservations
over the draft constitution. So much so that "the darling of the Lisbon
populace," along with a group of his fellow liberals, was accused by moderates of "subtly plotting Brazilian independence."[21] Although the charge that

Portuguese liberals favored Brazilian independence was exaggerated, the partisan baptism under fire that restive Brazilian delegates experienced in Lisbon lent new currency to the political label of "liberal" once they returned home. For the first time, Brazilians came into direct contact with European liberalism in a truly national context. Delegates who refused to sign the draft of Portugal's 1822 Constitution, Nicolao Pereira de Campos Vergueiro, Antonio Diogo Feijó, Antonio Carlos Ribeiro de Andrada, Jozé Ricardo da Costa Aguiar de Andrada, Cypriano Jozé Barata, Jozé Lino Coutinho, and Antonio Manoel da Silva Bueno, defected from the Cortes and fled to Falmouth, England—excepting Vergueiro. Instead, he found secret refuge in his native country.[22] The experience sealed their espousal of liberalism for life. Especially Vergueiro, Feijó, Costa Aguiar, and Lino Coutinho consistently sponsored reforms of inheritance law vis-à-vis illegitimate individuals, the abolition of entail, and the adoption of a form of civil marriage.

On returning to Brazil, delegates to the Lisbon Cortes found that independence was a fact. While they had been debating in Lisbon, their prince declared independence and transformed himself into a New World monarch. In May 1823, Pedro called a Constituent Assembly where many of the Lisbon delegates took their seats to write a constitution for Brazil. They found that liberalism was understood imperfectly, sometimes in polar opposition to absolutism, as synonymous with the "popular will." The absence of freedom of the press and institutions of higher education in Brazil created an ideological climate where few understood European political thought in sophisticated terms. By 1823, however, the collective experience of drafting Brazil's first constitution accelerated the process of "catching up" with European ideological currents. Liberal ideology was enthusiastically diffused among the new nation's political elite as well as the urban populace, thanks to Pedro's "despotic act" of closing the Constitutional Convention in November 1823. In 1822, the coincidence of Portugal's adoption of a written constitution with Brazilian independence flavored liberalism in the former colony with a strong anti-colonial accent. The Lisbon Cortes had underscored for Brazilians that parliamentary sovereignty repudiated Portuguese absolutism. In a New World context, European liberalism resonated with the same intensity that nationalism had reverberated in the wake of Napoleon's armies.[23]

The European Roots of Brazilian Liberalism

The denouement of the 1823 Constitutional Convention brought into stark relief the contrast between the constitutional situations of Brazil and Portugal. Brazil's 1824 Constitution stopped short of endorsing certain liberal tenets that had been incorporated in Portugal's 1822 Constitution. The latter, however short-lived, continued to function as an ideological bellwether for more radical Brazilian liberals throughout the 1820s. Despite the contradictions in D. Pedro's espousal of liberalism, the comparatively conservative constitution that he imposed on his adopted nation in 1824 demonstrated faithfulness to an Iberian liberal heritage. In contrast to the Portuguese Cortes, Pedro favored maintaining existing social divisions, meaning he leaned closer to the corporate basis associated with the *ancien régime* than many of his liberal critics. He also resisted any concession to popular sovereignty, believing sufficient the notion that he himself embodied the nation. Less venturesome than the Constitution that Portuguese liberals imposed on Pedro's father in Lisbon, Brazil's 1824 charter nevertheless shared with the latter a number of basic characteristics making it worthy of the label "liberal."

As Charles Hale has pointed out with reference to Mexico's 1824 liberal Constitution, the attraction of Benjamin Constant's writings, especially his "theoretical impulse" from post-restoration France, proved formative for Latin American liberals intent on implementing constitutionalism in the independence era.[24] Constant's accessibility for Spanish- and Portuguese-speaking intellectuals, most of whom read French, was accelerated once the 1820 Cortes of Cádiz resuscitated Spain's 1812 Constitution. Publication of his works in Spanish immediately ensued.[25] A post-1814 political milieu, consequently, remained uppermost in their formulations. The historical features of liberalism in Spain and Portugal nevertheless looked to the pre-1789 eras of reform under Bourbon and Pombaline monarchies that suggested long-term continuities. Constant's appeal to both Brazilian and Spanish American constitutionalists therefore deserves to be appreciated against Iberian crown attacks on ecclesiastical and noble privilege, the guild system, and entail in the latter half of the eighteenth century. Brazil's 1824 Constitution is best assessed against the key features of what amounted to an Iberian liberalism. Attention to the affinities between the ideas of Benjamin Constant and the political outlook of many Brazilian liberals can clarify considerable misunderstanding in the scholarly literature concerning the nature of early liberalism in Brazil.

First, rather than stressing the value of democratic rule—popular representation in terms of individual voting rights in the manner of Anglo-American liberalism—Brazil's Constitution of 1824 favored Iberian liberalism's louder accent on guarantees of personal liberties. The latter represented a check on the sovereign's absolute power. Indispensable for protecting the citizenry against a tyrannical monarch, those liberties were to counterbalance the enormous power that had accrued to the Portuguese crown since 1750. In this respect, consequently, the claim that the 1824 Constitution was a liberal document rang genuinely true. Although Brazil's Parliament subsequently implemented and broadened certain constitutional guarantees, such as the Law of the Free Press, the national charter reflected Constant's great concern for "the defense of individual liberty against the invasions of arbitrary authority."[26] It is in this regard that D. Pedro I legitimately could claim to be a liberal—and to have appropriated Constant as his idol. Having reluctantly accommodated himself to the political reality of a written constitution, Pedro enthusiastically embraced a commitment to individual liberties, one thoroughly congenial to his unbridled personal passions.

Second, the 1824 Constitution reflected a European post-restoration need for checks and balances whose purpose was to prevent the excesses of either enlightened despotism or the "Rousseauan" popular will.[27] Brazil's Constitution, consequently, reflected a strong consensus on the political necessity to repudiate egalitarian ideology, given how the latter was associated with the notion of the general will popularized by the Declaration of the Rights of Man and Citizen. For many of the same reasons that Charles Hale has argued Benjamin Constant's ideas appealed to the authors of Mexico's 1824 Constitution, Brazilian legislators favored the ideas of that "classic Continental constitutionalist."[28] Thus, in Constant's view, Hale argues, the historical position of the Spanish nobility, relative to the power of the monarch, did not represent a counterposing institutional safeguard against despotism. Iberian polities lacked what had slowly evolved in England as a counterweight to monarchical excess, a strong Parliament with an upper house jealously protective of its prerogatives.[29]

In Portugal's case, the nobility had been brought to heel prior to Pombal, whose legislation stood as a requiem for a second estate that lacked the political strength of even France's pre-1789 nobility. The nobility could not challenge the throne. The Portuguese Cortes, which had not met since the 1690s, was defunct. Consequently, nobility was incapable of functioning as an obstacle to the excess of monarchical absolutism, just as the church no longer posed a corporate check to absolute power. Furthermore, popular attachment to monarchy in Spain and Portugal continued very strong after 1814, reinforcing and perpetuating regimes of corporate privilege that remained intact when liberal revolts occurred in 1820–1821. As Hale has noted, "The dilemma of trying to forge a constitutionalist system where historic precedents were weaker than in France" produced a special Iberian context.[30] That dilemma was one shared broadly throughout Ibero-America, above all in Brazil.

Constant's concern for checks and balances, of course, harkened to

Montesquieu's scheme for balancing powers and the emphasis he placed on written constitutions for insuring civil liberties. In this respect, Montesquieu's notion of "intermediate bodies"—corporate groups enjoying legal status, such as the nobility, parlements, towns, and guilds—still mattered as important guarantees where individual liberty was threatened. Although he favored a hereditary assembly on the English model, Constant repudiated the old French nobility as "a corporation without a base and without a fixed place in the social body." Privileged corporations, consequently, could not for Constant fulfill the role of intermediate bodies, given that they lacked basic functions.[31] The assumption that corporate privilege had lost its utility for a nineteenth-century political system founded on a written constitution was one that genuine liberals in Brazil shared not only with Constant but also with their peers in Portugal. However, many self-styled liberals remained ambivalent, stopping short of calling for an end to all corporate privilege.

Ambivalence over liberalism could be readily detected in the partisan labels of the 1820s. Nor did any term clearly opposable to "liberal" register in Brazilian political parlance, largely because the emperor appropriated that label for himself. Republican revolutionaries in 1824 attributed the label "legalist" (*legalista*) to the imperial forces that quelled their northern revolt. In Portugal, the opposable camps were known on the one hand as "absolutists," or "royalists," and on the other as "liberals," or "constitutionalists."[32] Mello Moraes' identification of three Brazilian groups, or factions, all opposable to each other in 1822, is therefore instructive. "Pure royalists" (*realistas puros*) amounted to conservatives, those who had to accept constitutionalism as fait accompli, but preferred a stronger monarchy as well as a privileged "aristocracy." This group inscribed largely senators, as opposed to imperial deputies, together with the majority of the emperor's councilors and courtiers—the latter being largely Portuguese. Mello Moraes divided the liberal opposition roughly into two, sometimes antagonistic, currents: "liberal royalists" (*realistas liberais*), by which he meant the majority of liberal constitutionalists—those genuinely committed to a constitutional monarchy and loyal to the throne, but of divergent views—and "republicans" who comprised a "left wing" of liberalism. Thus "liberal" in Brazilian parlance deviated from a European connotation of anti-revolutionary and anti-republican.

By the end of the 1820s, liberal royalists were known as "Moderates" (*Moderados*) and the republican current as "Extremists" (*Exaltados*).[33] Applying Mello Moraes' categorizations, the preponderance of "pure royalists" increased in the Senate—those construed herein as either "ultra monarchists" or "conservatives." Perhaps a minority of senators initially were "liberal royalists." By 1827, the Chamber of Deputies became the pivot of liberal reform, making the liberal royalists known as Moderados—augmented by a republican fringe—predominant in the lower house.

A third, related, area that captured the nature of Brazilian liberalism, as well as the difference between the chambers of Parliament, turned on the denial of popular sovereignty, by means of relying on an alternative notion of representation. Because the 1824 Constitution vested the power to legislate in the bicameral General Assembly, that branch was carefully defined: indirect elections for imperial deputies who served four-year terms, but sovereign-appointed senators who served for life. By the same token, the notion of popular sovereignty conjured up susceptibility to the tyranny of democracy. Therefore, Brazil's Constitution spoke only of "representation" and harmonized the latter with monarchy by the device of identifying both emperor and legislature as the "representatives of the nation," a compromise fostering conflict between those branches. In contrast, Portugal's 1822 Constitution deprived the executive power of representation in a new, unicameral, national legislature, and withdrew from the monarch the power to dissolve the Cortes.[34] The institutional novelties of the moderating power and the Council of State, both traceable to Constant, reflected the distrust of popular sovereignty that proved integral to Brazilian liberalism. Those key innovations demonstrated the appeal that Constant's formulations in a post-restoration context exercised over Brazilian liberals for not altogether dissimilar reasons.[35] Consequently, the Council of State and the moderating power amounted to Pedro's constitutional legacy, institutions designed to militate against the power of the general will. They defined the pivot of a strong executive that by the early 1830s would prove repugnant to many early liberals.

Promulgation of the Constitution of 1824 precipitated a republican revolt in the northeastern provinces, where secessionists rallied under the banner of "the Confederation of Equador." Royal authority swiftly dispatched the martyred leader, a Carmelite known as Frei Caneca (Joaquim do Amor Divino Caneca). His execution stood as a gruesome object lesson for the nation that made his brand of "liberalism" intolerable. Frei Caneca's revolt responded directly to Pedro's "despotic" dissolution of the Constituent Assembly and his preempting of its right to articulate the people's sovereignty through a constitution. Caneca rejected the moderating power outright, as "a new Machiavellian invention and the master key for oppression of the Brazilian nation, the strongest garrote of the people's liberty." He denounced Pedro's rewritten 1824 Constitution for imposing life tenure on senators, a titled nobility, and, above all, "a monstrous inequality between the two chambers . . . giving to the emperor, who already has the Senate on his side, the power to change . . . the deputies he understands to oppose his personal interests . . . ." Defrocked in 1825 by his church, Caneca was shot by an imperial firing squad.[36] The martyred friar's call to establish a republic never gained meaningful support among any but a small minority of legislators whose liberalism therefore amounted to an ideological aberration.

Secessionist movements arising in the northern provinces in 1817 and 1824 clearly demonstrated a special context for what in Brazil was deemed a radical variant of "liberalism," but amounted to republicanism. The latter, tinged with treasonable secession, not only stood apart from mainstream liberalism in the south of Brazil, but afforded a context for people of color, including slaves, to play a key role in revolt. The great preponderance of Brazilian liberals, consequently, regarded what passed colloquially as a liberalism aligned in revolt, especially when it depended on the participation of people of color, to be a menacing demonstration of the general will. Liberalism fundamentally rejected the notion that political representation should rest on popular sovereignty, proffering instead the assumption it lay in the national legislature, if not primarily in the person of the emperor. Disfranchisement logically followed from opposition to popular sovereignty, for Brazilian liberals apprehended that republicanism could transform Brazil into a Spanish American situation, one where Bolívar's grand design of political unity rapidly fragmented throughout the 1820s. Most liberals, in addition to preferring monarchy as support for a slave regime, viewed republicanism as a threat to a unity of national culture that rested on a shared historical past. Republicanism, consequently, portended a proliferation of "the Brazils" into discrete political territories. Even in 1831, contemplating a vacant throne, the vast majority of liberals remained "liberal royalists" who would not espouse republicanism.

Liberalism in Brazil, like its European counterpart, sought to forestall popular sovereignty because the latter threatened liberty as well as order. If post-restoration France had provided the theoretical impulse for Constant, then most Brazilian legislators of the 1820s drew analogously on the impact the French Revolution had exerted on St. Domingue. They took the fate of Haiti's white population, between 1791 and 1794, as a cautionary tale for their own slave society. The so-called Revolt of the Tailors, a conspiracy that erupted in Salvador in 1798, had offered white Brazilians a domestic gloss on the watchwords of the French Revolution.[37] Led by a freed slave and captained by free mulattoes, Salvador's foiled insurrection took inspiration from the *sans culottes* of Paris. The parallel that white Brazilians saw between their slave society and the Haitian experience reinforced the espousal of liberalism, because the latter rejected the French Revolution's ideological assertion of political equality and popular sovereignty. Threat of "Haitianization"—a generalized slave uprising implying reversion to an "African" society—was explicitly voiced during the 1823 Constituinte and amounted to a rare instance of airing issues of race relations in a public forum. Although fear of becoming another Haiti also inspired several delegates, including the "patriarch of independence," Jozé Bonifacio de Andrada e Silva, to advocate gradual abolition, their voices amounted to a whisper.[38]

A strong throne allayed fears that the abolition of slavery would become a fact, forestalling "anarchy"—the tyranny of the mob. Taking a cue from Constant and the Spanish Liberal Constitution of 1812, Brazil's liberal legislators looked to indirect elections and property and income requirements for both voters and electors as the necessary safeguards against popular tyranny. They constitutionally denied active citizenship to freedmen, based on the assumption that their civil condition was legally reversible. Thus slavery compromised individual political representation by denying the right of suffrage to all men who were emancipated slaves. Again, Spain's Liberal Constitution of 1812 provided the precedent, for it denied suffrage to mulattoes, a group presumed, often wrongly, to be born of slave mothers.[39] Contemporary research continues to make clear that color, not merely the status of freedman—*liberto*—defined an important question mark for citizenship in the new nation of Brazil. A growing animosity between peninsular Portuguese and white Brazilians during the 1820s injected race as an issue that "jeopardized" emerging national identity, due to the tendency of Peninsulars to condemn race mixture. Although constitutional ambiguity ostensibly derived from the conditional nature of manumission, because law admitted reversal, the belief that "under no circumstances should men of color be allowed to become 'active citizens'" imposed a formidable qualifier on the exercise of citizenship.[40] Basically, Brazilian liberals viewed the population of free color as potentially dangerous—the catalyst for slave revolt.

Liberals and the Attack on Corporate Privilege

How individual legislators identified themselves as "liberal" can be better understood by appreciating another connotation of that term in an Iberian context, namely the attack on a society of estates. That Brazil's Constitution of 1824 diverged significantly on issues of corporate privilege from liberal constitutions adopted in Portugal, or reinvoked in Spain during the early 1820s, provides a useful point of comparison. Brazil's national charter, considerably influenced by Portugal's Constitution of 1822, thus drew directly on the Spanish Constitution of 1812, briefly restored in 1820.[41] Although Spain's Constitution was the first to be promulgated in Brazil, it was withdrawn by D. Pedro after twenty-four hours. Inspired by Benjamin Constant de Rebeque, liberal drafters of the Spanish and Portuguese constitutions struck at corporate privilege, but the full list of their anti-corporate provisions was not written into Brazil's 1824 Constitution. The emperor's preemptive authorship largely explained those omissions.[42]

For instance, Spanish liberals extended substantially the Bourbon monarchy's incipient disentailment of church property that had begun in the 1790s. In 1811 the Liberal Cortes initiated dissolution of family entails; in 1820, another Liberal Cortes abolished all entails in Spain and Spanish America: the family entail known as *mayorazgo*, corresponding to the *morgado* in Portugal, as well as the ecclesiastical entail known as *capellanía*, the counterpart of the *capela* in Portugal. Although initially the Audiencia of Mexico City concurred with the Spanish order to abolish all entails, a newly independent Mexico left ecclesiastical entails intact, abolishing only the *mayorazgo* in 1823. Meanwhile, in direct defiance of liberals in Spain, a restored Bourbon throne under Ferdinand VII quickly resuscitated the *mayorazgo*, in May 1823. Only in 1836 did a liberal revanche definitively end the *mayorazgo* in Spain— the same year that Portugal also effectively abolished the *morgado*.[43]

Portugal's liberals, who, like those in Spain, advocated abolition of all entails, similarly were thwarted by absolutist revanche. Led in 1823 by the count of Amarante on behalf of D. Miguel, a royalist faction successfully championed the legal prerogatives of church and nobility. Liberal constitutionalism proved no match for D. Miguel and his Spanish Bourbon mother. The 1822 Constitution was shelved and, for over a decade, the liberal cause was routed. In contrast to Portuguese and Spanish constitutionalism, Brazil's 1824 national charter left both types of entail intact and implicitly sustained the emperor's right to establish them. Controversial in an age of liberalism, entail stood out in Brazil as the sine qua non of noble privilege during D. Pedro's reign, defining an important difference between his views on legal privilege and those of liberal reformers in the Chamber of Deputies.

When Brazilian liberals spoke of "equality before the law," they had in mind the destruction of what they deemed legal "distinctions." Their emphasis on juridical equality emanated from their opposition to Bragança absolutism, rather than being inspired by either French or American Revolutionary notions of political equality. Like Portuguese liberalism, therefore, the Brazilian variant condemned the legal "distinctions" identified with corporate privilege. The idea that individuals should be juridically discriminated as "clergy, nobility, and the people" was now repugnant to many Brazilian legislators. The 1824 Constitution's stipulation that "the law will be equal for everyone, whether it protects or whether it punishes" (Article 179, Paragraph 13), prefaced the Charter's abolition of legal "corporations, their judges and staffs" (Paragraph 25). They were repugnant features of a society of estates that tolerated discrete codes of legal rules resting on corporate membership.

Liberal opposition to noble privilege also explained why Brazil's 1824 Constitution stopped short of establishing a hereditary nobility. In this respect, the emperor proved much less liberal than a majority of imperial legislators. When Parliament reopened, in 1826, a core of liberal legislators sought to dilute, counteract, or nullify the emperor's constitutional legitimation of a titled nobility. However, the restoration of Bragança absolutism in Portugal redefined the Cortes as bicameral in 1826, again privileging the upper house as the representative of the first two estates—church and nobility. That change stood in marked contrast to the situation in 1821–1822, when the Portuguese Cortes was convened as a unicameral body without representation for "clergy, nobility, and the people."[44] The change did not go unnoticed among liberals in Brazil, where a Senate based on life-tenure reflected an increasingly ennobled membership and seemed to fulfill a similar function. Liberals in the Chamber of Deputies, who largely identified with the third estate, found the emperor's progressive expansion of a titled nobility disturbing. Of course, senatorial life tenure was a constitutional device tied to checks and balances, but it redounded to the power of the throne. For instance, amending the Constitution required the Senate's concurrence, as well as the emperor's consent. Long-term continuity in the upper house, consequently, made constitutional revisions nearly impossible and underscored the uniqueness of the Chamber of Deputies as a renewable body largely restricted to either the third estate or to individuals whose nobility was minimal.

Following a common nineteenth-century formula, the titled nobility nonetheless had to be ideologically justified for a liberal era. The eighteenth-century notion that nobility was a reward for "service" to the nation rhetorically predominated. Although the Constitution ignored nobility by descent, the concept survived juridically, accentuated by the greater stress placed on civil nobility. The "splendor of the great houses"—noble lineages that testified to the perpetuation of heritable titles of nobility—was politically suppressed by the 1824 Constitution, notwithstanding entail's renewed vitality. Nevertheless, blood lines were replaced with the operative concept of "merit." The Constitution also spoke of "capacity and virtue," rather than aristocratic values, when it enumerated the qualifications of senators (Article 45, Paragraphs 3 and 14). The emphasis on merit, capacity, and virtue in-

sured that the third estate, whom D. João VI had favored prominently in elevating Brazilians to the peerage after 1808, presaged expectations of social
mobility in the new imperial era.

A constitutional arrangement of a different nature sharpened divisions
between the Senate and the Chamber of Deputies: an established church.
The latter ignored a fundamental formulation of Benjamin Constant, who
had insisted on the separation of church and state. "Hard-core" liberal legislators, who included a number of priests, proved themselves secularizers.
They favored a public education system devoid of ecclesiastical content or
control. More to the point, they found that Brazil's constitutionally established religion proved inimical to their efforts to reform both family and inheritance law. As liberals who attempted to rewrite law pertaining to illegitimacy and marriage, they had to confront how canon law penetrated private
law on marriage and therefore the quality of birth. Usually, the votes they
needed to overturn canonical provisions were not forthcoming.

Finally, the fact that Brazil's 1824 Constitution deliberately declined to
mention slavery, an institution abolished in Portugal prior to the French
Revolution, spoke more to fundamental consensus than irreconcilable differences in the Constituent Convention. However much liberals decried the
inequality of legal "distinctions," few of them connected chattel slavery to
the juridical foundation of a society of estates, one where birth ascribed an
individual's legal and social "quality"—*qualidade*. In conventionally referring to slavery as "captivity," both juridical and vernacular language eluded
any direct reference to either the servile condition or the legal imprint of a
society of estates. The fact that reformist legislators failed to see slavery as a
contradiction of their attack on legal distinctions, and viewed it as a legal
"condition" determined by birth, defined an important limitation to their
political assault. However, the acceptance of slavery was not inconsistent
with the essence of liberalism. Far from being hypocritical or "ersatz," Brazilian liberalism remained faithful to Iberian and European roots. In the
context of what was a neo-colonial polity, chattel slavery did not stand out as
ideological "falsehood."[45]

Although some have seen the liberal affiliation worn by reformist legislators in the 1820s as only window dressing, and construed the label "liberal" as
"clothes merely to be worn on occasion, perhaps unfashionable, but uncomfortably tight," it was not the case that Brazilian liberalism amounted to
"a system of displacement."[46] Nor did it represent a "debased" form of a
European importation to an "outpost of slavery," for being equated with
"favor" or "arbitrariness."[47] The assumption underlying such an attempt at
historiographical revision rests on the erroneous premise that European lib-

eralism demanded political equality, when, in fact, it was an ideology antagonistic to leveling. As a result, European liberalism excluded the working class from suffrage, supported slavery in the colonies, and denied outright the vote to women. It firmly rested on property and income qualifications for granting suffrage and endorsed a titled nobility justified by "merit."[48]

The yardstick taken for measuring "equality" in revisionist discussions of Brazilian liberalism often has assumed that the Declaration of the Rights of Man and Citizen represented the standard of equality appropriate to European liberalism. That yardstick European liberalism firmly rejected. On the other hand, the liberal constitutionalism of Benjamin Constant rarely enters into revisionist attacks on Brazil's first liberals.[49] The yardstick of 1789 is presumed as appropriate, largely because Brazil's 1824 Constitution did incorporate certain phrases verbatim or notions found in the Declaration. But, as Emília Viotti da Costa noted, what the 1824 Constitution omitted from the Declaration holds greater ideological significance than what it appropriated. Thus Brazil's national charter declined to incorporate the Declaration's assertion that "the nation is the source of all sovereignty; no individual or body of men can be entitled to any authority which does not expressly derive from it." Nor did it echo the belief that "the law is an expression of the will of the community."[50]

The point worth stressing is that the revolutionary Declaration of the Rights of Man and Citizen hardly fit the post-1814 restorationist context so fertile for constructing European liberalism. By the time liberals took power, the watchwords of the French Revolution had been relegated to the past. The truth of the matter is largely what Emília Viotti has asserted, that Brazilian liberalism reflected a historical moment tied to independence—"a revolutionary moment" during the 1820s wherein liberalism exercised appeal in the struggle against the metropole for independence. Attainment of that goal in 1825 explained the short duration of Brazil's "age of heroic liberalism." By the 1830s, argues Viotti da Costa, liberals were "pro-Parliament" rather than "democratic," although they favored federalism—decentralization—and the nationalization of trade.[51] Nevertheless, in the struggle to determine the balance of power between legislature and emperor that consumed Brazilian politics in the 1820s, liberalism mattered.

Consequently, evaluations critical of liberalism in nineteenth-century Brazil, as "hypocritical" vis-à-vis its European counterpart, usually ignore an Iberian liberal tradition and posit a "European" construct falsely committed to "liberty, equality, and fraternity." The same assessments have pointed to England and the United States, and uncritically taken parliamentary rhetoric in Brazil at face value. They have failed to distinguish enthusiastic, public pronouncements by Brazilian legislators during the 1820s and 1830s, especially endorsements of a successful war of independence in the United States—a "revolution" in parliamentary parlance—and the obliteration of the society of estates in France, from the Iberian bedrock of Continental liberalism. They have usually ignored how Portuguese and Spanish regalism implied a crown attack on many features of the society of estates that articulated a "liberal" tradition prior to the French Revolution. In Portugal, for instance, the French occupation of 1807–1811 accelerated change along lines that essentially resonated Pombaline reforms, extinguishing institutions like the Inquisition and the guilds.[52] Freedom of religion, also introduced under French rule, earlier had been presaged in Pombaline policy.

Opposition to legislative footdragging on issues pertaining to corporate privilege in Brazil defined an important element of ideological coherence between Brazil's early liberals and their Iberian counterparts. Furthermore, the assault on corporate privilege underlay a liberal interest in reforming family and inheritance law. As "liberal royalists," Brazilian legislators dedicated themselves to fulfilling many Pombaline reforms whose completion coincided with a post-1812 Iberian liberal agenda attacking legal "privilege." The commitment to uprooting a society of estates was not "cultural mimicry," but proceeded as much from a national political tradition as from post-1812 events. Far from being an "ideological comedy" ensuing from "misplaced ideas," the attack by Brazilian liberals on legal distinctions was grounded in both regalism and legal nationalism, the cultural baggage ignored by the critics of Brazil's early liberalism.[53]

REGALISM AND LIBERAL REFORM

Regalism As Pombaline Political Tradition

The attack on corporate privilege that stamped Brazilian liberals as distinct from their "purely royalist" counterparts in the General Assembly extended to the church. Although their conservative colleagues subscribed to established regalist tenets, liberals proved to be the legitimate heirs of Pombaline regalism. In this respect, they pushed regalism to new limits in their efforts to reform private law by challenging canon law. From the beginning, liberals created considerable controversy in the national legislature over the appropriate role the church would play in the new polity of Brazil. A very small number were better appreciated as radical regalists, the partisans of a Gallican, or independent, national church. Most liberals, however, thought more modestly, preferring to maintain the Catholic church as an institution firmly subordinated to the Brazilian crown. They upheld conventional regalist policies of the Portuguese crown that dated to the late colonial era, when D. João VI himself behaved as a firm regalist.

Soon after arriving in Brazil, D. João became embroiled in a dispute with the papal nuncio, Lorenzo Cardinal Caleppi, archbishop of Nizibi. That conflict demonstrated immediately the crown's defense of its historic *regalias*. Above all, the incident illustrated a political consensus on regalism that circumscribed all partisan shadings, including the bishop of Rio de Janeiro, for ranks closed against Nizibi. Initially, the nuncio had unwisely confronted D. João over his right to exercise the placet, the right of the monarch to approve or exclude communications (bulls, encyclicals, and Decretals) expedited by the Roman Curia or the Pope and intended for the instruction of all Catholics in Portugal and Brazil. The prerogative dated to the thirteenth century, when Portugal's monarchs had claimed they possessed the power to approve (*exquatur*) delivery of papal documents to their Portuguese subjects. Those monarchs had also asserted the power of their royal courts to hear appeals from ecclesiastical courts (*recursua ad principem*).[54]

The placet figured implicitly in Nizibi's highly unpopular denunciation of D. Jozé Caetano da Silva Coutinho, who, as bishop of Rio de Janeiro, served as the regent's imperial chaplain and personal confessor. A cultured man who leaned in the direction of religious toleration, D. Jozé Caetano clashed with the nuncio when he refused to follow the nuncio's public suggestion he modify a basic catechism used in Brazil. The catechism, it was argued, had been authorized in 1707 by the famous diocesan council called by Bahia's archbishop, D. Sebastião da Vide. In 1809, Nizibi accused D. Caetano of being "a Jansenist on Carioca soil," because of his refusals to withdraw or revise what was a modified Montepellier catechism. The latter reflected congruities with Lorenzo de Valla's Lyon catechism, one condemned by the Curia in 1780. It had continued to circulate in Portugal with crown permission. The trigger for the nuncio's objection, however, pertained to a popularly circulating "pamphlet" catechism, derived from the Montpellier catechism. Entitled a "Catechism of Christian Doctrine in Accordance with the National Church," the pamphlet had been designed for propagating the faith among both Indians and the illiterate poor. Its author was none other than Jozé da Silva Lisboa, future viscount of Cayru, and the title's reference to "the national church" pertained to the 1707 *Constituições Primeiras* of Salvador's diocese.

The nuncio, consequently, insulted a greatly respected figure of the Brazilian church, together with the politically influential layman who had advised D. João in 1808 to open Brazil's ports to free commerce. Both had taken degrees at Coimbra University. When D. Jozé Caetano responded authoritatively that the catechism served Brazil's needs very well, and received backing from the prince regent, then Nizibi could do nothing.[55] That the bishop prevailed, despite the nuncio's public questioning of his orthodoxy, testified not only to the independence of crown and religious hierarchy vis-à-vis Rome, but also to the unanimity of their defense of the nation's *regalias*.

The international political context presented new elements in church-state relations during the independence era. The formation of the Holy Alliance in Europe, the Vatican's reinstatement of the Society of Jesus in 1814, and growing ultramontanism in Rome made Brazilian liberals apprehensive, reinforcing their defense of national sovereignty. The fact that Nizibi and his successors spoke as fervent ultramontanists complicated enormously Brazil's relationship with the Vatican, but, by the mid-1820s, that relationship became more problematic due to the fact of a national legislature. Pope Leo XII proved antagonistic toward independence throughout Latin America, first in Spanish America, and then in Brazil. Rome demonstrated considerable ill will toward the fact of decolonization, to the point where the pope identified himself with resurgent absolutism in both Spain and Portugal, even siding with the Portuguese government when it delayed diplomatic recognition for Brazilian independence.

The papal nuncios dispatched to Rio de Janeiro after Nizibi, beginning in 1817, did little to cement good relations between the Vatican and Brazil, for they meddled in Brazil's internal political affairs. By advocating religious intolerance, whether during negotiations for the 1810 Anglo-Brazilian Commercial Treaty, or even as the 1824 Constitution was being drafted, they managed to antagonize a broad spectrum of politicians, priests, and prelates. By 1823, Bishop D. Jozé Caetano da Silva Coutinho had evolved considerably on matters of religious toleration from his position in 1810, when he had argued that the English, being "proud and obstinate," should be permitted to open houses of worship. He had reasoned then that if they were granted this right in the commercial treaty with Brazil, their unmarked chapel "will be built and nobody will ever go near it." Even so, according to the Anglican clergyman Robert Walsh, D. Jozé Caetano came under fire from the papal nuncio, for advocating a limited religious toleration. Caleppi proposed turning the clock back, by reestablishing the Inquisition "for the purpose of watching over the interests of the Catholic religion and restraining the progress of that heresy [Anglicanism] among Brazilians." In the Constitutional Convention, allied with Jozé Joaquim Carneiro de Campos, future marquis of Caravellas, D. Jozé Caetano nevertheless became instrumental in the inclusion of a guarantee of religious freedom to Article 5 of the Constitution.

The nuncios who followed Caleppi in the 1820s alienated national politicians who regarded themselves as good Catholics. The fact that a majority of Brazilian legislators routinely espoused the Jansenist tenets inherent in Pombaline regalism did not, in their eyes, make them any less devout Catholics.[56]

Unlike newly independent Mexico, where the royal patronage of the church led to a bitter dispute that witnessed the Vatican prevail, the Brazilian monarchy managed to retain the impressive instrument of Bragança regalism known as the royal patronage of the church, the *Padroado Régio*. The legal argument relying on a personal devolution of royal authority, transmitted by D. João VI to D. Pedro I, defined the trump card that accounted for why Brazil would retain the *regalias* of the Portuguese crown. The latter amounted to a complex of privileges conceded or confirmed by the Vatican to the national monarchy in matters of church administration and discipline. At Brazilian independence, their cornerstone remained the original *Padroado Régio* of the late fifteenth and early sixteenth centuries. However, those privileges, known as the *regalias*, stood as a cumulative bundle of concessions or confirmations by the popes to the Portuguese monarchs that either bestowed new prerogatives or acknowledged previously unconfirmed patronage over the national church. Most important was the sovereign's right to nominate prelates for the church in Portugal and then to present them to the pope for confirmation. The Vatican did not, however, concede that Portugal's monarchs enjoyed the inverse right—*not* to present bishops for confirmation by Rome.[57]

Since papal confirmation normally was perfunctory, the *Padroado Régio* placed control of the secular clergy firmly in the hands of the Brazilian crown. Collection of the tithe by the imperial government, on behalf of the church, followed from this arrangement. Seventeenth- and eighteenth-century concordats between the Portuguese monarchy and the papacy redounded to the benefit of a rapidly expanding national monarchy. Pombal stood as the eighteenth-century champion of Portuguese regalism at the end of the decade that opened in 1759, when he broke relations with Rome. Earlier, in the course of ambassadorial service at the court of Maria Theresa, in the 1740s, he came into direct contact with Jansenism. The context was the Austrian crown's dispute with the papacy, an ideological exposure that later served Pombal well. By continuing to legitimate a Jansenist position in domestic politics, Pombal insured that over the long run the papacy's ultramontane ambitions would be thwarted in Portugal.[58]

Pombal's break with Rome (1760–1769), occasioned by his persecution and expulsion of the Jesuits in 1759, fundamentally sought to counteract the centralization agenda of the Roman Curia, and a concomitant expansion of papal prerogatives over the national church. Despite a decade of schism, Pombal's position was not the most extreme, for some European monarchs advocated the supremacy of the state in religious matters. Theoretical positions articulated by Scot Buchanan, Francis Bacon, Thomas Hobbes, Jean Bodin, and Hugo von Grotius were all more radically inclined toward a national church. In contrast, Pombal willingly granted the superiority of the church in spiritual matters and sought merely "to position the church within the mold of the national state."[59] D. João VI and D. Pedro I subscribed to the basic outlines of Pombal's policy, taking it as a legacy to be jealously defended. In turning to the Oratorians—the Order of St. Philip Neri—as allies against both Jesuits and pope, Pombal had enlisted crucial support from the guardians of Jansenism in Portugal. It was they who sponsored wider use of the Montpellier Catechism.[60] Henceforth, the Oratorian adherence to Jansenism and Febronianism stamped Portuguese regalism with a uniquely national character, making it more radical than in Bourbon Spain.

The remarkable relationship Pombal cemented between the Portuguese crown and the Vatican, following restoration of relations between the papacy and Portugal in 1769, was one in which the Vatican even recognized Pombal's services to the church. It distinguished Portuguese regalism as a stunning triumph throughout Europe and Pombal as its genius. As a result, the awesome patronage exercised by the Portuguese absolutist state over the national church rested even more firmly on theoretical arguments privileging the primacy of ecclesiastical councils. Those arguments survived in Brazil during the 1820s and continued to color the regalist stance of liberal legislators in the 1830s, when they regarded Rome with greater suspicion and hostility. Pombal merely carried farther than most European monarchs a movement found throughout the Catholic monarchies of western Europe, one that appropriated Jansenist principles for a reinvigoration of the authority of church councils.[61]

The notion that conciliar decisions might take precedence over those of the Pope implied that the Portuguese had accepted for centuries the premise that councils played a special role in issuing binding determinations on ecclesiastical dogma. Historically, what jurists labeled the "Lusitanian church" had been characterized by organization and discipline effected through the collective deliberations and determinations of the bishops in "the Portuguese realms." Pombal's successful rapprochement with the Vatican, in 1769, following a decade of severed relations, thus underscored the national hierarchy's independence in deciding administrative questions. The tradition of episcopal independence, coupled with Pombal's earlier failure to include Brazilian seminaries in his design for curricular reform of education, accounted for why, during the colonial period, Brazil's dioceses operated as disparate administrative units lacking common rules. Only in the 1820s were the 1702 *Constituições Primeiras* of the diocese of Bahia officially imposed on all of Brazil's bishoprics. Moreover, the agent was the national legislature. During the independence decade, therefore, the historical accent on conciliar authority, reinforced by royalist ideology in the 1760s, remained a central tenet for Brazilian politicians of all factional persuasions.

When Pombal tightened the subordination of the secular clergy, the ecclesiastical orders, and the Inquisition to the Portuguese crown, he also enlarged the power of bishops in Portugal and Brazil. Thanks to the papal nuncio, Inocêncio Cardinal Conti—"putty in Pombal's hands"—the Holy See conceded new, formal authority to bishops to dispense canonical prohibitions on marriage. The Pope granted Conti's 1770 petition that, on the basis "of existing [Portuguese] practice in Portugal"—*a praxe portuguêsa*—the matrimonial dispensations formerly reserved to the Pope henceforth would be conferred directly on Portugal's bishops. In other words, Rome officially conceded what Portugal's bishops had already arrogated to themselves. The new arrangement further stipulated that consultations and communications directly with the Holy See pertaining to the rulings rendered in Portugal's ecclesiastical tribunals would cease. Henceforth, the Portuguese crown was to be the sole source of appeal.[62]

The most important concession extracted by Pombal from Rome pertained to papal confirmation of the famous placet, the crown's right to approve papal communications destined for Portugal. Although the Portuguese monarch's claim to the placet predated by centuries Pombal's negotiations, what mattered was the way that he prevailed on Rome to legitimate the placet. By resorting to the good offices of the papal nuncio in Lisbon, who did not read Portuguese, Pombal secured papal confirmation not only of the placet but of other *regalias* claimed by the crown. Furthermore, a year after Pombal fell from power, in 1778, D. Maria I signed a concordat with the Holy See that reconfirmed the *Padroado Régio* on behalf of the Portuguese monarchs in perpetuity. A fundamental instrument of Pombal's regalist state, the placet denied the papacy independent jurisdiction to communicate with Catholics in the Portuguese realms. The crown had to concur. Thus D. João, as regent, brought a reinvigorated royal patronage, including the jealously guarded placet, to Rio de Janeiro in 1808, as part of the regalist edifice of a "Lusitanian church" that belonged within the framework of the Apostolic Roman Catholic Church. First as regent and then as king, he assiduously maintained the gains that had accrued during the reigns of his mother, Maria I, and grandfather, D. José I. For instance, he reaffirmed with penalties the monarch's prerogative dating to the reign of D. José, that no one could be excommunicated without the king's consent. Similarly, D. João's decree of August 3, 1813, echoed peninsular practice, that Brazilian bishops were prohibited from ordaining priests without first obtaining crown permission. D. Pedro I perpetuated the procedure. Each individual priest's ordination required a crown license.[63]

Liberal legislators who sought to reform inheritance and family law took for granted a Pombaline tradition of regalism when they proposed bills addressing either legitimization or marriage and questioned the authority of Pope and Curia, even in matters that Rome defined as dogma. In attempting to remove or mitigate distinctions of birth, they challenged canonical determinations, because their political system assumed a high degree of crown independence on matters of church organization and discipline. On regalist issues, the gap between D. João VI and D. Pedro I—or between Pedro and his liberal critics—proved very narrow.

Regalism's Constitutional Imprimatur

The placet, as the eighteenth-century jewel in the crown of Portuguese regalism, found direct incorporation in Brazil's 1824 Constitution. Article 102, Paragraph 14, stipulated the emperor's powers included "conceding or denying the placet to all conciliar decrees and apostolic letters [bulls and encyclicals], and whatever other ecclesiastical constitutions not in conflict with the Constitution." Of course, a cardinal change followed from Brazil's new identity as a constitutional monarchy. After 1825, the monarch no longer exclusively exercised the placet as royal prerogative. The 1824 Constitution provided that the national legislature had to give prior approval to any placet conceded by the emperor. Ecclesiastical committees in each chamber of the legislature—whose members were nearly all clerics—now crafted policy on the placet. Approved bicamerally, determinations on the placet were then sent to the emperor for his sanction. By the same token, the emperor unilaterally lacked authority to present episcopal nominees for Brazil's eight dioceses or the archbishopric of Bahia to Rome. Thus the Constitution created a potentially public forum on any prelate's nomination or the dissemination of any papal document sent to Brazil by the Vatican. Ecclesiastical committees in each chamber, through reports they submitted to their legislative branch, basically set the terms for negotiation with Rome that normally contested or defended essentially ultramontane policies.

Regalism, consequently, enjoyed broad consensus among Brazil's legislators. Whether "royalist" or liberal, they had often imbibed that tenet of absolutism at its source, Coimbra University. By 1800 it permeated the classroom. No one better summed up the triumph of Pombal's regalist legacy than Carlota Joaquina, wife of D. João VI. Four years after the couple returned to Lisbon, she wrote to Pope Leo XII, in order to complain about the textbooks adopted at Coimbra University. Correctly, she alluded to their Jansenist content when she described them as "full of errors and therefore justifiably on the Apostolic See's Index of Prohibited Books." The Spanish mother of Brazil's new emperor deplored the intellectual leavening that had ensued, for "everyone, from bishops to parish priests," from "secretaries of state to lower crown officials, directly or indirectly, has drunk the poison of this University." Calling for another reform of Coimbra University as "most necessary," she concluded, "We shall end up as quasi-heretics."[64]

Most of the clerics who served in the national legislature prior to 1840 fervently defended the *regalias* of the Brazilian crown. They comprised an important proportion of legislators. In each of the first three legislatures (1826–1837), between 21 and 23 imperial deputies were men of the cloth—nearly one-fifth of the lower house. In the Senate, 13 of the total 16 ecclesiastics named to that body by 1889 had already taken their seats by 1837.[65] To the extent that they could be said to define a consistent ideological orientation, the partisan allegiance of clerics was largely liberal, but rarely radically republican. Their liberalism frequently was traceable to the seminary or mentorships with radical clerics in an older generation for whom regalism provided an intellectual matrix. Otherwise, a select group of priests imbibed regalism in Portugal. Of the 74 Brazilian clerics who received Coimbra degrees between 1746 and 1827, 60 belonged to the secular clergy.[66] The prelates of the Brazilian church, an archbishop, seven bishops and several abbots, administered an ecclesiastical court system as men universally educated at Coimbra University. Systematically indoctrinated with regalism, they shared an ideological homogeneity that extended to the clerical rank-and-file. Because bishops derived considerable authority and influence from a tradition of Lusitanian regalism that historically endowed them with near autonomy in their dioceses, they tended to close ranks with lay politicians on regalist issues.

A final constitutional feature in the relationship between the Brazilian state and established religion best captures the direct impact of European liberalism on Brazil: religious toleration. Nevertheless, in the eyes of foreigners who were not Roman Catholic, the constitutional toleration of religion remained heavily qualified. Only Roman Catholic places of worship could publicly proclaim their purpose. All other religious sects were constitutionally confined to holding services in unmarked buildings.[67] Primarily Anglicans benefited, given their pre-independence presence as an expatriate colony in Rio de Janeiro. Soon, however, a widening spectrum of Protestant sects, especially Calvinists and Lutherans, initially foreign residents, as well as Brazilian and Portuguese Jews, benefited from the genuine political innovation of religious toleration. The fact that the established church was nonetheless "Apostolic Roman Catholic" imposed considerable limits, even contradictions. Legal marriage did not exist in national positive law, except for Roman Catholics. Furthermore, only the latter could hold high political office and vote as electors. The liberal principle of equality before the law therefore was compromised as long as the Catholic Church was constitutionally established.

LIBERAL VERITIES

Since Pombal's era, the society of estates had been subject to progressive, legal redefinition. Consequently, "equality before the law" did not resonate in a Luso-Brazilian context as a novel, post-1789 concept. Rather, the impact of the French Revolution simply modernized that notion for the liberal era of the 1820s, conferring a political legitimacy consonant with the new century. Introduced into Brazilian political parlance via constitutionalism and the ferment of liberal revolutions in Cádiz and Lisbon, the notion of juridical equality repudiated corporate privilege. Thus Brazil's liberal legislators understood "equality" in terms of a late eighteenth-century historical context that associated legal "distinctions" derived from a society of estates with the absolutism of the *ancien régime*. They did not ordinarily connect the notion of "equality before the law" with the radical egalitarianism and popular sovereignty of the French or American Revolutions, but viewed it as a logical outgrowth of their own political tradition.[68]

What was new in 1824 was the stress on a written constitution. In Brazil's case, the emperor's revisions of the national charter circumvented debate over popular sovereignty as the basis for the national legislature's authority to make law. The General Assembly constitutionally enjoyed the power to make law, but the constitutional assumption that it shared that power with the emperor, who equally represented the nation, further denied assumptions of popular sovereignty. The novelty of constitutionalism, of course, meant more than replacing an absolutist sovereign, whose legitimacy rested on divine right, with a constitutionally legitimized sovereign. Political representation in a liberal era no longer depended on the discrete identities of estate inherent in Portugal's former Cortes Gerais. Although Brazil's 1824 Constitution introduced a bicameral legislature organized without regard to estate, the upper house resembled a body projecting certain "aristocratic" attributes. Not only did senators sit for life, but the majority of them possessed—or acquired from the emperor—noble titles held in life tenure. At least until the mid-1830s, one archbishop and three bishops also sat in the national legislature, further compromising representation along non-corporate lines.

Rather than viewing the titled nobility established by D. Pedro I as an obstacle to absolutist excess, many liberals viewed that group as a buttress to the throne, finding reason for apprehension. Although the titled nobility ceased to be a legally defined corporate group, as an institution that perpetuated corporate privilege along hereditary lines, it was far from clear that senatorial titleholders acted independently of either quasi-corporate interest or that of the imperial court. Appearances were deceptive, given that, since 1808, members of the third estate had been the most prominent sector recruited to Brazil's nobility. An informality of behavior belied the political influence and economic weal that titled nobles commanded in either the Senate or the palace.

The Rev. Robert Walsh alluded to the innocuous impression that Brazil's noble titleholders conveyed in observations he made about a dinner party for the emperor's inner circle. The guests included the entire cabinet. Held in 1827, at the home of the Austrian Plenipotentiary, Baron Mareschal, the gathering "had not the least appearance or pretension of a similar class in Europe," Walsh was surprised to discover. "The greater number had been engaged in business," he learned, "being men of opulence when the separation of the countries took place." The ministers and legislators he met were "men of the plainest manners, laughing and good-humored, and accessible, like common-councilmen at a London feast." Those "common-councilmen" nonetheless advertised their prestige and the power of their political positions. "Their dress, however, was rich and expensive; and some of them wore large golden keys, attached like small swords to their sides, intimating that they performed the office of chamberlain to his Majesty . . . ."[69]

Walsh's evening with many of the men who belonged to the emperor's nobiliary coterie demonstrated the latter's special identity—unpolished manners and low social origins notwithstanding. However inept, individual behavior captured the way an erstwhile middle-class cohort of entrepreneurial talent functioned as an extension of the imperial court. In the context of the Senate, the same men enjoyed a quasi-corporate identity. Their titles amounted to "distinctions" in a society where all were equal before the law. Furthermore, the 1824 Constitution did not preclude the possibility that a hereditary nobility might still emerge. By the end of the 1820s, consequently, many liberals viewed the titled nobility as a direct projection of the emperor's political arm. They took inspiration from the aforementioned constitutional stipulation that "the law will be equal for everyone, whether it protects or punishes, and it will offer compensation in proportion to the merits of each individual" (Article 179, Paragraph 13). This provision suggested at least that equality could be conceived according to a sliding scale reflecting merit, largely economic achievement, rather than bloodlines ascribed by birth.

Until 1828, however, the emperor exercised the sovereign prerogative of dispensing the law, via determinations made by either the conjoined Mesas do Desembargo do Paço and Consciência e Ordens or the Casa da Suplicação. The Mesa da Consciência e Ordens oversaw legally constituted corporations pertaining to the religious and military orders, while the Mesa do Desembargo do Paço removed legal "defects" of birth that enabled individuals, among other privileges, to become members of those entities. D. Pedro I, consequently, still retained important attributes of the sovereign's role as "the Legislator," where distinctions of birth defined Brazilians as noble or commoner, clergy or laity, and legitimate or illegitimate. When the national legislature reopened in 1826, not surprisingly, liberals contested his power to mediate those distinctions of estate and birth. They discovered in their opposition to Pedro's vestigial role as the legislator a much broader agenda in the reform of private law, one that spelled out the constitutional implications of "equality before the law" by applying that principle to the rules of marriage and heirship.

CHAPTER 2

Dismantling the Colonial Regime

Estate, Birth, and Color

—————◆◆————

> When I drew up this bill, I had in mind putting an end to the De-
> sembargo do Paço, for the reason that it was not needed. It was
> created here, only because there had been a Desembargo do Paço
> in Lisbon.
>
> Dep. Bernardo Pereira de Vasconcellos, July 24, 1827[1]

> What should come to an end is the effective jurisdiction of the tri-
> bunal for dispensing laws, whose function belongs to the legislative
> body.
>
> Dep. Jozé Clemente Pereira, July 24, 1827[2]

The central importance of a legally embedded society of estates for reform of
matrimonial and inheritance law emerged as soon as Brazil's national legislature convened. A plethora of arrangements touching on both public and
private positive law attracted attention from liberal reformers, due to their
determination that corporate privilege for church and nobility should cease.
Yet legislators construed distinctions of estate very narrowly. During the
1820s, for instance, they still thought in terms of social divisions they identified as "orders"—divisions that roughly corresponded to legal estates rather
than to those of social class. They also closed ranks on the issue of color—
what they usually construed as African ancestry. By maintaining silence, liberal reformers not only declined to confront the most blatant reminder of a
society of estates—slavery—but they also endorsed the increasingly extra-
legal barrier of African ancestry that explained why church, nobility, military,
and even Parliament itself would be upheld as lily-white institutions.

This chapter examines several ways that a society of estates still mattered
juridically after independence and how it shaped key social divisions in early
imperial Brazil. It is an effort to clarify both the juridical and the judicial
context for reformist bills addressing illegitimate birth and inheritance rights
discussed in the chapters that follow. Major attention is paid to the criterion
of legitimate birth, in tandem with the related notion of racial purity, extending a focus the preceding volume introduced. Each continued to be cen-

tral considerations in a post-independence context that witnessed the attenuated survival of many features of the old colonial order. The changing significance of legitimate birth and color is examined against the erosion of—
and legislators' efforts to dismantle—a society grounded in legally defined
orders and corporations. Attention is paid to a tacit assumption running
through much of the historical literature, that after independence the formal
criterion of "purity of blood" ceased to operate. Although legally discarded,
purity of blood continued to matter as a correlate of legitimate birth. Historians have not undertaken systematic research to establish the persistence of
what formerly had been the key attribute of membership in the colony's
multiple elites of European descent: legitimate birth. By suggesting how
rarely articulated "rules" of legitimate birth and European descent implicitly
operated, even as liberals attacked corporate privilege, or left it alone, much
of what follows stands as a preliminary effort to trace the elusive connections
between legitimate birth and race in the formation of imperial society.

The reopening of Brazil's national legislature, in May 1826, inaugurated an
era of liberal reform against the backdrop of constitutional implementation.
Although historians have long understood that "legitimate birth" and "legitimate marriage" defined key distinctions in imperial society, specific insight into how individual *qualidade* resting on legitimate birth operated after
independence, especially as a marker for racial ancestry, remains limited. The
implications of documents scrupulously identifying individuals as a "legitimate child" have often been left implicit, even when scholarly commentary
has suggested that the attention paid to legitimate birth has bordered on the
obsessive. This chapter, consequently, broadly articulates connections between legitimate birth and race in the context of the 1820s deserving closer
scrutiny, as liberals sought to remove the institutional vestiges of a society of
estates.

The reopening of Brazil's national legislature, in May 1826, inaugurated an
era of liberal reform against the backdrop of constitutional implementation.
Between 1826 and 1831, legislators would strive to restrict the sovereign's prerogatives, especially those he still enjoyed by default as a result of having
closed the General Assembly. Although a number of innovative bills anticipating reform of family and inheritance law were introduced, the most far-
reaching change derived from the 1828 Judiciary Act. The latter, by implementing a constitutional mandate, extinguished important crown tribunals
which theretofore had executed the sovereign's power as either judge or legislator. From the standpoint of family and inheritance law, consequently, the
major change introduced by the Judiciary Act lay in transferring to an imperial judiciary what formerly had been the monarch's exclusive power to dispense the law. No longer the result of the sovereign's "justice and grace," solemn legitimization became redefined as judicial writ.

Before the General Assembly could address the nature of a national judiciary, however, it had to dismantle the institutional apparatus of the Portuguese colonial regime. What proceeded initially amounted to an attack on the legal vestiges of the society of estates, meaning the privileges or immunities enjoyed by the established church as well as those potentially applying to the new nobility created by the emperor. Absolutism defined a second, parallel target, given the Constitution's restrictions on the sovereign's powers. In approaching these tasks, liberal legislators sponsored bills that took succession and family law indirectly into account. In paying direct attention to three broad areas of reform that responded to constitutional provisions, however, they anticipated bills that subsequently addressed the inheritance system and individual *qualidade* of birth, whether illicit or spurious.

The first set of constitutional arrangements claiming the attention of reformers pertained to the fact of a constitutionally established church. The Constitution, which proclaimed itself "in the Name of the Holy Trinity," prescribed that "the Apostolic Catholic Religion will continue to be the religion of the Empire" (Article 5), and designated the emperor as "protector" of the church (Article 103). Yet the exclusivity of religious commitment implied by an established church did not necessarily conform to the liberal values of many legislators who supported reforms in family or inheritance law, given their objections to the rigidity of canonical rules pertaining to marriage, legitimate birth, and clerical celibacy. In contrast to the other two sets of constitutional arrangements scrutinized by liberals, an established church left intact prominent vestiges of a society of estates. Canon law, as we have seen, directly affected how rules of the inheritance system were defined in positive law. Ecclesiastical courts pronounced on the validity of marriage or granted legal separations known as divorce. The important dimension of liberal reform that sought either to alter or to restrict the Tridentine canons on marriage has been reserved for the following chapter, given how the sacrament of matrimony fundamentally determined who would be legitimate in positive law.

The second set of constitutional arrangments drawing reformers' attention responded to the emperor's exclusive constitutional authority to bestow noble titles and, implicitly, the "feudal" privileges flowing from the latter, especially eligibility for entail. Jealous of their constitutional responsibilities and prerogatives, liberal legislators would strike at nobility and privilege in ways that, incrementally, would alter the inheritance system in fundamental respects by the mid-1830s. Initially, however, they were unconcerned with the underlying importance of legitimate birth as intrinsic to the rule of nobility by descent—the minimal, or natural, nobility of birth. The liberal attack responded instead to D. Pedro's preference for a hereditary nobility after the Portuguese model. Indeed, his coronation ceremony demonstrated to assembled legislators how much the emperor favored a titled nobility linked to the former metropole. Pedro's investiture prominently displayed the Portuguese noble orders, underscoring that he was the Grand Master in Brazil of the three great orders of Portuguese chivalry—of Christ, São Bento, and Aviz. In that capacity, the emperor would subsequently confer on select Brazilian subjects what amounted to membership in Portugal's most prestigious orders of chivalry, corporations that underscored the link with Lisbon as the source of his regal authority for issuing titles in Brazil.[3]

Pedro's establishment of the entail of Torre, bestowed on Bahia's Garcia d'Ávila family during his coronation, left no doubt where he stood on the delicate issue of a hereditary nobility. The emperor referred explicitly to his role as the creator of a Brazilian nobility in a decree issued on the same day, that proclaimed his establishment of a new "honor," or noble order, for Brazil, one emulating those associated with Portugal: the Imperial Order of the Cruzeiro. As Roderick J. Barman has emphasized, this act not only established a titled nobility in Brazil but it also affirmed Pedro's authority to create one.[4]

The opposition voiced by many delegates to the 1823 Constituent Assembly, either to a nobility or to heritable titles, manifest during the early stages of drafting a national charter, persuaded Pedro to restrain his ambition. The revised document that became the 1824 Constitution left the key point of the heritability of titles moot. Among the emperor's prerogatives was included "the bestowal of titles, honors, military orders and distinctions," in compensation for "service rendered to the state" (Article 102, Paragraph 11). Whether future titles might be heritable was therefore left to the emperor's discretion. The same article that conferred the power to grant noble titles also provided that "the pecuniary compensations" for such awards would depend on the approval of the General Assembly, "if they were not already specified and enumerated by law." Given considerable opposition to a hereditary nobility, and the knowledge that legislative control over the purse strings could restrict the noble entitlements he might bestow, Pedro reluctantly granted titles only for the life of the holder.

Perpetuation of noble rank juridically mattered a great deal to liberal reformers on a plane apart from the political connection they implied to the Portuguese monarchy. On the one hand, expansion of a titled, higher nobility evoked the corporate manifestations of a society of estates; it also drew a line between favored peninsular Portuguese and native-born Brazilians. Liberal legislators, especially in the lower house, were drawn largely from a minimal nobility of birth, but frequently they possessed civil nobility whenever their origins lay in the third estate. They therefore viewed the institutionalization of a titled nobility ambivalently, or with outright hostility, for it threatened the social mobility of their personal networks in the context of a court where Brazilians usually yielded rank to peninsular Portuguese.

On the other hand, in tandem with the privileges of secular and ecclesiastical entail, a titled nobility raised the issue of an important feature of the inheritance system, one directly depending on legitimate birth: entail. At odds with the liberal principle of equality before the law, entail quite literally represented an exception to the rules of equality inherent in Brazil's partitive system of forced heirship. It carried direct consequences in private law for the transmission of family patrimony. Liberal reformers therefore found in entail's association with a life-tenure nobility an important patrimonial issue that contradicted the system of *ab intestato* succession.

Initially, liberal reformers ignored the issue of nobility wherever it did not pertain to titles. Natural nobility, or nobility by descent, as we have seen in the preceding volume, amounted to a birthright of minimal noble rank. It was so widely diffused that the vast majority of imperial legislators enjoyed it, a circumstance accounting for why it did not figure in the attack leveled at a society of estates during the 1820s. This chapter considers a key attribute intrinsic to nobility by descent—the *qualidade* of legitimate birth—especially in terms of what the latter implied for the barrier implicit in racial ancestry. Otherwise, natural nobility, like its counterpart of civil nobility, figured directly in the rules of heirship. The recognized natural offspring of parents who were minimally noble, like those of titleholders, were excluded from *ab intestato* succession. Because liberal legislators did not raise this feature inherent to a society of estates until the late 1830s, it has been left for consideration in the final chapters.

The final set of constitutional arrangements receiving lawmakers' attention restricted the emperor's power in terms of prerogatives that the 1824 charter rendered anachronistic. They pertained largely to the sovereign's authority to dispense law and, therefore, to the attributes of absolutism that legislators viewed as contradictory to a constitutional separation of powers. Otherwise, the sovereign's prerogatives implied the exercise of arbitrary power. Those attributes would be curbed by extinguishing royal institutions through which, historically, the monarch had acted as the nation's lawmaker. Thus the extinction of two central institutions of royal power, implied in the 1824 charter, formed an important first step in a constitutionally mandated effort to restrict the emperor's prerogative to dispense law. Those institutions were, on the one hand, the Casa da Suplicação and, on the other, the conjoined Tribunals of the Mesa do Desembargo do Paço and Mesa da Consciência e Ordens. Abolition of the latter tribunals directly bore on the inheritance system and drastically transformed how certificates of legitimization would be issued in imperial Brazil.

The anticipated demise of these high crown tribunals followed directly from the fact that the Constitution mandated a third branch of government, a new judiciary whose apex would consist of a national Supreme Court of Justice (Articles 163 and 164). By introducing a national judiciary, legislators created what would become both the stage and the pivot for future efforts to reform private law pertaining to illegitimacy and inheritance. Consequently, this chapter pays final attention not only to abolition of the Desembargo do Paço but also to the procedural changes pertaining to legitimization that followed from the 1828 Judiciary Act. Due to the impact that new procedures made on individual behavior, both within and without the courtroom, liberals would sponsor bills in the 1830s and 1840s that specifically focused on the legal position of illegitimate individuals. Thus the starting point for appreciating their agenda on inheritance reform necessarily begins with the replacement of the Tribunal of the Desembargo do Paço by a national judiciary.

ATTACKING THE SOCIETY OF ESTATES

Beginning in 1826, liberal deputies and senators sponsored legislation directed at eliminating the legal vestiges of a society of estates whose organizational features shaped family and inheritance law. Better understood as political mavericks than as ideologically "pure" liberals, a core of determined reformers attempted to purge private law of many distinctions of estate, including canonically derived notions that no longer were in harmony with a liberal accent on "equality before the law." The impetus for their reforming zeal lay in the system of status they confronted, grounded in the bestowal of noble titles, "decorations," and honorific orders that implied prerogatives conferred by law ranging from carefully prescribed forms of address to legal immunities. By invoking a demand for equality before the law, and insisting on the benefits of individual "liberty," Brazil's early liberals attacked what they saw as their colonial heritage, one broadly framed by absolutism and mercantilism.

Viewed from the prism of nationalism, the vestiges of ecclesiastical and noble privilege embodying the Portuguese *ancien régime* underscored for liberals how Brazil's fragile identity amounted to little more than that of an imperfectly emancipated colony. Furthermore, the nature of national independence remained inconclusive under a monarch who might yet be enthroned as Portugal's king. More to the point, fear of absolutist revanche merely heightened the tendency to view the vestiges of corporate privilege as anomalies in a constitutional age. Liberals turned to the 1824 Constitution, believing that its effective implementation promised to jettison a colonial identity. Corporate privilege, viewed as impeding social mobility, merited attack because the Constitution called for legislation to dismantle absolutist institutions that upheld a much eroded legal order of estates. This circumstance gave greater significance to the constitutional refrain that echoed in the Chamber of Deputies: "The law will be equal for everyone, whether it protects or whether it punishes, and it will offer compensation in proportion to the merits of each individual" (Article 179, Paragraph 12).

Equality was expected to replace privilege in two constitutionally explicit respects. Each guaranteed that as emerging middle classes shed the juridical chrysalis of the third estate, they would enjoy full opportunity for social mobility and legal equality. First, "Each citizen can be admitted to public civic service, political or military, without any other distinction than those of his talents and virtues" (Article 179, Paragraph 14). And, second, "All privileges not essential and intimately connected to office by public utility will be abolished" (Article 179, Paragraph 16). Furthermore, the Constitution abolished the important corporate entity of the guild, as well as guild judges, scribes, and masters (Article 179, Paragraph 25), underscoring again that juridical barriers of rank would no longer deny crown employment or appointment to office.

Ecclesiastical Privilege

In the context of the first session of Brazil's national legislature, from 1826 to 1829, liberalism meant an end to the corporate privileges of the church. In this regard, lawmakers sought to fulfill the legacy of legal reform initiated under Pombal, one that had progressed under D. João VI and then been espoused by Portugal's liberals at the Cortes Gerais. Writing in the early 1840s, Portuguese jurist Coelho da Rocha offered a retrospective appraisal of the loss of corporate power the church suffered in Portugal from Pombal's era onward. He singled out none other than royal jurisconsult Paschoal José de Mello Freire (1738–1798), whose determination to secularize law amounted to what Coelho da Rocha identified as the fundamental cause for the demise of the political influence the church. He concluded that a quiet revolution in law had achieved its desired effect, thanks finally to a restoration of Portugal's 1822 liberal constitution.[5] Indeed, by 1808, the Portuguese church had been deprived of a great many of the legal prerogatives that historically explained its political power. Application of the 1769 Law of Right Reason (*Lei da Boa Razão*), Section 12, eventually extinguished most of the legally defined privileges of the church—especially the so-called *foro eclesiástico* whose centerpiece was a separate system of ecclesiastical courts. "*Boa razão*" whittled down the jurisdiction of the latter by progressively removing from the purview of such courts what were juridically construed as "*mixti fori,*" mixed cases involving the intersection of civil and religious law. Otherwise, regalism bore down on the clergy by obliging all ecclesiastics to pay the same taxes as other subjects of the crown.[6]

By Brazilian independence, the church's tribunals largely reviewed matters that were either spiritual or internal to church discipline.[7] The important exception pertained to ecclesiastical tribunals that ruled on matters of marriage. In this respect, Portugal's 1822 Constitution acted as a beacon for Brazil's first generation of liberal politicians, although the enduring impact of the liberal movement in the former metropole reached ascendance only after 1836. By specifically singling out the corporate privileges of the clergy, the constitution adopted in Lisbon provided inspiration for a number of bills introduced in Brazil's first legislative session. Although the formidable *privilegium fori*, the right of all clerics to be tried before an ecclesiastical judge, irrespective of whether the case involved civil or criminal law, no longer offered monolithic protection, some of its benefits lingered in the 1820s. The emphatic affirmation of Portugal's liberal constitution, that "the *privilegium fori* must not be tolerated" (Article 9), resonated across the Atlantic in 1827, perhaps even more powerfully because the "usurpation" of D. Miguel and his pro-clerical counterrevolutionary regime had placed liberal reform in jeopardy.[8]

Brazil's liberal legislators raised the issue of ecclesiastical privilege immediately, in 1826, as preparations began on a series of bills to implement the 1824 Constitution. Many of the latter would eventually be incorporated in either the 1828 Judiciary Act, the 1830 Criminal Code, or the 1832 Code of Criminal Procedure. Consistent with Portuguese regalism, Brazil's new constitution had specifically proscribed the clergy's right to special tribunals. However, it added the ambiguous qualifier, "except in conformity with the laws" (Article 179, Paragraph 17), that left open the door for perpetuating those that remained. This proviso pertained to law received from Portugal, meaning that the proscription on "privileged courts" and "special commissions in civil or criminal cases" was far from absolute. Among the special courts, several that were ecclesiastical had survived the eighteenth-century assault on the first estate and therefore continued to issue determinations on cases that were *mixti fori*. Thus liberal legislators looked to further restriction of received law from Portugal, arguing that the detested *"foro eclesiástico"* deserved to be consigned to Brazil's colonial past.

Debate over the ecclesiastical *foro* resulted in only a compromise between the more radical bill offered by São Paulo's Dep. Nicolao Pereira de Vergueiro and the version his opponents in the lower house succeeded in adopting. The opposition was led by two prelates—D. Romualdo Antonio de Seixas, soon to be confirmed as Brazil's metropolitan and archbishop of Bahia, and D. Marcos Antonio de Souza, bishop-elect of Maranhão. Although D. Marcos defended the autonomy of the ecclesiastical courts, maintaining they were a public good, D. Romualdo sagely declined to do so. As a moderate regalist, he had been educated at Coimbra in the decade after Pombal's fall, explaining why he was disposed to defend "the liberties of the Brazilian church," even to invoke Mello Freire in the bargain. Like so many of his fellow ecclesiastics in 1826, D. Romualdo was tainted with Jansenism. In affirming to the Chamber of Deputies that "times of confusion have now passed," he offered a noteworthy observation: "No one any longer believes in the infallibility of the Pope. Everyone today knows that he is not superior to a General Council and that it is only the latter that has the privilege of inerrancy or infallibility."[9] Not surprisingly, therefore, D. Romualdo upheld the crown's patronage over the church and the Constitution's denial of the ecclesiastical *foro*.

On the other hand, D. Romualdo declined to endorse Vergueiro's efforts to apply the Law of Right Reason to cases deemed *"mixti fori"*—a small group of disputes or appeals still determined by ecclesiastical courts that presented issues appropriate to a civil jurisdiction. He jealously defended the church's eroding legal jurisdiction where it pertained to many aspects of marriage and sexual morality, even though positive law had suggested since Pombal's era that the *"mixti fori"* were more appropriately heard in royal courts. Unlike Bourbon Spain, where the crown had removed trials for crimes like bigamy from ecclesiastical jurisdiction, Portugal had left jurisdiction in the hands of the Inquisition.[10] With the formal extinction of the Inquisition by the crown, in 1821, the church—and D. Romualdo—were determined to retain jurisdiction for episcopal tribunals over many issues pertaining to marriage, including adultery and bigamy.

Vergueiro's argument focused on the full spectrum of *mixti fori* cases, those involving not only the "sins" of public adultery, concubinage, bigamy, and procuring, but also perjury, sacrilege, and incest, where, in the absence of a criminal code, ecclesiastical courts in the 1820s retained jurisdiction by default. Asserting the famous formula of the Law of Right Reason, he proposed that "sins" be converted to "crimes," thereby removing them from the jurisdiction of the church.[11] His bill also called for an innovative end to the ecclesiastical monopoly of what positive law construed as "civil" registries of birth, marriage, and death records: parish registers. Over the next twenty years, Vergueiro would fight for the establishment of an authentic civil registry a number of times, always to no avail. Finally, he proposed stripping the church of its fiduciary responsibilities over wills, chapels, confraternities, and lay brotherhoods.[12]

Vergueiro's liberalism defined him in his very first year in the national legislature as a strong proponent of secularization. He emerged as the central figure among a group of liberal deputies who continued to sponsor bills attacking corporate privilege, the most prominent of whom were Jozé Lino Coutinho, Jozé Ignacio Borges, Jozé da Cruz Ferreira, Raymundo Jozé da Cunha Mattos, Jozé Clemente Pereira, Manoel Odorico Mendes, and Diogo Antônio Feijó. In the end, Vergueiro had to bow to the compromise amendment proposed by his more moderate liberal colleague and the head of the Minas Gerais delegation, Bernardo Pereira de Vasconcellos, already a leader in the lower house. The bill addressing the abolition of ecclesiastical tribunals that carried the Chamber of Deputies was a much watered-down version of the original, for Vergueiro's bill initially had offered a numbered list of sixteen special tribunals making determinations for the church, military, customs houses, and orphans. However, liberals who endorsed Vasconcellos' compromise deliberately invoked the "Golden Law" of 1769 and appealed vaguely to "right reason" for confining determinations of ecclesiastical courts to merely spiritual issues.

The bill's final version ambiguously called for ecclesiastical judges to limit themselves to ecclesiastical cases.[13] As a result, important determinations on the validity of a marriage would remain a spiritual matter and lie within the exclusive jurisdiction of the church. Throughout the imperial period, consequently, only ecclesiastical courts could annul a marriage or authorize a legal separation known as a divorce (*divórcio*). In this regard, ecclesiastical judges rendered important rulings that determined whether certain offspring would be legitimate or illegitimate in legal proceedings tried in the imperial courts. Subsequently, passage of a compromise version of the bill in the Senate meant that only the contractual, civil effects of valid marriages would fall within the purview of the imperial judiciary.

Coelho da Rocha identified a final, important reason for the church's declining political influence that carried both political and sociological import for Brazil's independence era. Thanks to legal change, he argued, the appeal of a priestly vocation no longer exerted strong attraction. The loss in political prestige the church had suffered since the reign of D. José I was irreversible.[14] By independence, the latter helped to explain why clerical vocations had ceased to be avenues of upward career mobility for men in wealthy families. More to the point, the impact of curricular reform had finally been felt at Coimbra University. The age of the canonist, like the church's monopoly of higher education, came to an end during the reign of the prince-regent, D. João VI. No longer could it be said that "the university is the church; to raise the number of canonists is to serve her and to increase her. The state serves itself from the latter."[15] By 1808, a doctorate in canon law no longer opened the widest possible opportunities for those aspiring to elite careers, especially the position of crown magistrate.[16] The era of the law school graduate had arrived. As Brazil's new law faculties demonstrated from the 1840s onward, the Mandarin class synonymous with the administrative arm of the Second Empire would be drawn almost exclusively from graduates who took degrees in civil law.

By the 1820s, consequently, the Brazilian clergy faced a crisis, a fact not lost on liberal reformers seeking to strip the church of corporate privilege. The reasons were multiple and the consequences far reaching. The Rev. Robert Walsh, the astute Anglican priest who observed every aspect of Brazilian life during his 1828–1829 residence in the Corte, identified what was a key shift in clerical recruitment. The imperial government continued to draw on a colonial *modus operandi* dating to the mid-eighteenth century, when the Vatican first permitted the Portuguese crown to collect the tithe. In return, the crown paid the clergy a regular stipend. However, contrary to the flush times of the late eighteenth century, noted Walsh, "Now the order of things is reversed." By the 1820s, declining clerical incomes forced country priests to depend fundamentally on the fees they collected for administering the sacraments. The clergy's former "considerable comfort, and even opulence" no longer attracted candidates for the priesthood, for clerical stipends had been outstripped by rising costs, despite the population growth that meant tithe revenues collected by the government now "amounted to an enormous sum."[17]

Walsh attributed the disinclination of men from wealthier families to follow a clerical career to the "comparative trifle" that an annual clerical stipend represented by 1827—a mere 200 *mil-réis*. He implied the priesthood no longer represented a viable vocation at society's higher levels. "None but persons in the lowest ranks" of life dedicated their children to clerical vocations, while men of "brilliant abilities always prefer some more attractive or profitable avocation."[18] Raymundo Jozé da Cunha Mattos, another liberal deputy, made the same point in 1828, but much more forcefully. He noted that "few wealthy men want to be priests," singling out as the key change the "grandeur of representation" that belonged to the clergy in "another time." He pronounced an ecclesiastical career "eclipsed," explaining that "intellectual styles have changed. Now the career aspirations of young men focused on "the high positions of civic office." Pointing a finger at the Portuguese court, Cunha Mattos charged that entities associated with government, such as "royal tribunals and crown secretariats," had "diverted the wealthy from being ecclesiastics."[19]

Bereft of talented personnel and denied significant support from the Vatican, the institutional church in Brazil could not respond vigorously to the liberal attack on its corporate privileges. Change in the church's institutional position accounted for how clergymen defined themselves in the era of independence, not only as active politicians but also in their private lives. The crisis over recruitment explained, to a certain extent, why, after 1822, clerics increasingly chose to live publicly in concubinage—in *"mancebia."* Priests had to make their own arrangements for economic support; a family economy offered an important part of the solution. Moreover, the inability of the institutional church to discourage or prohibit those consensual arrangements of cohabitation encouraged wider social toleration and acceptance. The singularity of the *sacrílego*—the offspring of a priest—in Brazil's imperial history usually has been of remark only in terms of a small number of specific, often famous, individuals. Scholarly inquiry has been seriously impeded by the etiquette of concealment and subterfuge that has characterized primary sources, wherever priests were to be shielded posthumously from scandalous exposure. Yet the *sacrílego* signified only one of several important dimensions in family formation in imperial Brazil that took place outside marriage and accounted for high rates of non-legitimate birth. The greater prominence of the children of priests throughout the imperial era, especially in politics, deserves assessment within the wider changes that occurred between the institutional church and the new political order.

The Church and "Defects of Birth"

Through the monopoly it enjoyed over birth, marriage, and death registries, the church in imperial Brazil would exercise considerable corporate power within secular society. This circumstance followed from how the clergy mediated legitimate birth in individual contexts. Custodianship over recordkeeping also provided clerics with opportunity to attribute color, or non-European ancestry, to illegitimacy, given the constructs and the subjectivity associated with conducting genealogical investigations. Alternatively, corporations of the church and lay organizations closely affiliated with the latter defended the membership criterion of European ancestry, tying the latter to legitimate birth. In a society where all citizens were equal before the law, the church therefore played a crucial, if indirect, role both in assigning individual *qualidade* and mediating identity.

One of the most important responsibilities deriving from the church's recordkeeping monopoly pertained to the obligatory genealogical investigations required for marriage and ordination. Parish priests were charged with conducting them by the Council of Trent in order to declare couples in the "free state to marry"—that is, to verify no impediment of close consanguinity or affinity existed between the partners. Legitimate birth also remained a precondition for ordination, as did "purity of blood"; however, indigenous ancestry no longer defined an impediment to be dispensed. Although the church imposed no barrier to interracial marriage or to marriage where a partner was illegitimate, it did require mandatory genealogical investigation that routinely revealed ancestry devoid of either purity of blood or legitimate birth—the twin attributes of respectable *qualidade*. Otherwise, an individual who wished to clear himself of the charge that he or she was not legitimate, or did not possess European ancestry, had to resort to the parish priest for genealogical confirmation from parish registers.

Historically, genealogical investigations established the crucial criterion of "purity of blood," answering whether or not individuals possessed exclusively European (Old Christian) descent, and implying ancestors who were not Jewish or Muslim converts (New Christians). Although those investigations routinely established whether a candidate was of legitimate birth, that finding acquired greater significance as the nineteenth century progressed and the value placed on nobility by descent eroded. Until the 1770s, ecclesiastical investigations of "purity of blood" and legitimacy exerted crucial influence on individual career choices, including university entrance, commission as a military officer, and appointment to the higher judiciary.[20] As it has been noted, Pombaline policy widened recruitment to royal service by relaxing, repealing, or ignoring the requirements of purity of blood and legitimate birth. Yet independence did not mean all the barriers were dismantled.

In Brazil, of course, purity of blood mattered most fundamentally where an individual possessed some degree of African ancestry. Beginning in 1555, when Pope Nicholas V granted the Portuguese the right to perpetually enslave Africans who "refused" Christianity, reliance on the doctrine of the "just war" facilitated the fiction that the color of one's ancestors was proof that they had rejected Christianity. In other words, the European notion that Christians should not enslave each other remained a rule of racial descent and failed to evolve into a broader concept of fraternal love inscribing all believers. Following the specious reasoning that "African" connoted "Muslim" ancestry, and then by equating such ancestry with "color," individuals of mixed African-European ancestry, such as *mulatos* or *pardos*, were legally deemed to possess a "defect" of color. The latter amounted to a variation on the older term, "defect of birth," a notion which passed into Portuguese law directly from the Latin usage of canon law—*Defectu natalium*. A "defect" of birth, however, pertained to more than illegitimacy, for it also inscribed physical impairments, such as epilepsy and paralysis, or forms of emotional illness. In the nineteenth century, colloquial reference to the notorious "defect of color" was common, offering a variation on the defect of birth, largely due to the greater social mobility free people of color enjoyed. More to the point, African ancestry *per se* was often taken to derive from a different "defect": illegitimate birth.

The conflation of African ancestry with illegitimate birth probably dated to the church's very early prohibition against marriage for slaves. However, it was the church that first overturned this feature of Roman law and set an example for Portuguese positive law to emulate.[21] As marriage rates rose among Brazilians of free color, or, for that matter, even among selected slave populations, such an absurd logic should have been harder to sustain. Nevertheless, it persisted in the face of rapidly changing social realities. Albeit crudely, non-legitimate birth thus operated as a basis for racial discrimination that essentially preserved imperial society's key social divide: color.

Scholarly research on imperial Brazil has not systematically established precisely how legal or extra-legal barriers resting on individual *qualidade*— either color or birth—came to be dismantled following independence. The Constitution presumably disregarded discrimination on the basis of those determinants, leaving intact only those of gender, religion, and, implicitly, servile condition. Although liberal legislators almost never directly challenged barriers founded on color or African ancestry, they nevertheless did so indirectly, as part of a challenge to the corporate privilege of the church. By attacking the church as the keeper of the "civil" registry, for instance, they were undermining its agency over genealogical investigations whose conclusions routinely were entered in imperial court proceedings treating family matters or inheritance claims. In the 1830s, as we shall see, some legislators tried to go much farther, rewriting the canonical formulas by which individuals were legally defined as natural or spurious. They, too, sought to deprive the church of its exclusive powers to regulate marriage as well as to determine legal definitions of illegitimacy.

In contrast to the state, which did not explicitly discriminate on grounds of color or race—except for upholding slavery and the constitutional denial of full citizenship to freedmen—the church did not abandon a policy of discriminating against those of either illegitimate birth or African ancestry. Non-legitimate birth, like African ancestry, closed the door to an ecclesiastical career, because it defined the ground for denying ordination. Although the church liberally dispensed defects of birth and color, it always did so on a case-by-case basis. Henry Koster, the English merchant who resided in Recife between 1811 and 1820, was so persuaded by the token representation of men of color in the clergy that he concluded "negroes are excluded from the priesthood" and "the law forbids the ordination of mulattos." Misreading what was the prescription of canon law as one sanctioned by positive law, Koster revealed how certain individuals got around such "trifling" regulations. "A mulatto enters into holy orders or is appointed a magistrate," he explained, "his papers stating him to be a white man, but his appearance plainly denoting the contrary." Given the absoluteness of the canons on ordination, Koster also isolated the preferred criterion in ecclesiastical dispensations for defects of color—putative whiteness. "What mulattoes may obtain through evasion of the law," he concluded, "the unequivocal color of the negro entirely precludes him from aspiring to."[22] Thus passing for white merely rested on appropriate documentation "proving" that one was white.

Following independence, appearances still could be deceiving. In 1827, the Rev. Walsh expressed admiration for the marked presence of men of color in the priesthood, after his keen eye registered amazement for a spectacle that he witnessed in Rio de Janeiro: Three priests—one white, one black, and one mulatto—celebrating mass in unison before the high altar of a downtown church.[23] Walsh offered an insightful hypothesis for this demonstration of interracial harmony, isolating an important clue in what he saw as a pragmatic relaxation of racial barriers. Noting that even the seminaries did not offer good intellectual preparation for the priesthood, he concluded that candidates for ordination who were white and of legitimate birth now presented deficiencies of liberal education. Hence "the admission of Negroes to holy orders, who officiate in churches indiscriminately with whites" that he witnessed. Walsh attributed racial toleration to expediency on the church's part, failing to mention that ordination still depended on a case-by-case dispensation of the "defect" of color.[24] He believed that the failure of white candidates to measure up to academic or moral standards demanded by bishops, as much as the reluctance of whites to take up the cassock, had opened the door to ecclesiastical vocations for men of color, insuring that the church would recruit talent. Dispensations of a "defect" of color or illegitimacy, especially for the secular or diocesan clergy, according to Walsh, reflected a recruitment emphasis on talent that overrode preference for white skin.

Not all bishops in the post-independence era were as willing to dispense defects of color as Rio de Janeiro's D. Jozé Caetano da Silva Coutinho. Marcus de Carvalho has documented a contrasting policy that rested on outright racial discrimination, laid down by the bishop of Olinda (Pernambuco) during the early 1830s. D. João da Purificação Marques Perdigão, by birth a Portuguese and by vocation an Augustinian educated in Porto, refused outright to permit the ordination in his diocese of friars who were not white. He appeared to perpetuate a practice dating to Koster's residence in Recife, although twenty years earlier the bishop of Olinda had been a native-born Brazilian. Making explicit a connection tying African ancestry to illegitimacy, Olinda's bishop justified a lily-white policy on the ground that "racial purity" provided the only guarantee for insuring that ordination candidates had been born in Catholic marriages.[25] Thus ostensible concern over legitimate birth proved the stalking horse for color. By adopting a blatantly racial criterion, the bishop ignored the fact that, increasingly, family formation in Olinda-Recife's large population of free color depended on the bonds of legitimate marriage.

Examination of a list of all the candidates ordained in the secular clergy in the province of Paraíba do Norte, which, until 1894, belonged to the same diocese of Olinda, similarly confirmed a very striking absence of men of color.[26] Those dispensed for the defect of illegitimacy numbered only three; those defined as non-white also totaled three. As late as 1903, one seminarian's dispensation for non-legitimate birth was linked to his slave ancestry, even though he was singular among all candidates for his *qualidade* as a legal *exposto*—someone whose parents' names were unknown.[27] Alternatively, Brazilians attributed this pattern of institutional race discrimination, especially on the part of the regular orders, to peninsular Portuguese. Dep. Manoel Odorico Mendes, in a rare acknowledgment from the floor of Parliament, explicitly cited the fact of racial discrimination in an 1827 debate over whether to prohibit certain monasteries from accepting novitiates. He charged that, as a rule, "the friars of Conceição do not admit any Brazilians to their corporation, because they hold that anyone born in this country does not have what they call 'clean and pure blood.'"[28]

By continuing to apply rules that defined color and birth as "defects" for recruitment to the priesthood, the church perpetuated the colonial value system predicated on purity of blood and legitimate birth. The fact that such defects might also be dispensed merely underscored the importance of keeping a lily-white rule in place after independence. Consequences spilled over into secular life. The importance of legitimate birth for racial purity would continue to matter in informal behavior throughout the imperial era, in no small part due to the widely perceived importance that ecclesiastical institutions placed on it. In any case, individual exceptions could always be made to exclusionary rules, as the example of Pe. Jesuino do Monte Carmelo illustrated. The founder of the famous "Congregation of the Padres of Patrocínio," established between 1806 and 1810, in the city of Itu (São Paulo Province), Monte Carmelo was another talented man of color who became a priest. As a popular *pardo* intellectual in Itu, he was refused admission to the prestigious Third Order of Our Lady of Carmo on the ground that his ancestry was not exclusively European or Christian.[29]

Eventually, Pe. Jesuino do Monte Carmelo gained admission to the Third Order of Carmo, for he was admired and well-liked by its members in Itu. They petitioned the Holy See, requesting a dispensation for Monte Carmelo's "defect of color" and cited the ground of "the postulant's virtues." In this case, racial discrimination led directly to Rome, where an exception was made and his defect of color removed. The head of the corporation in Itu, Capitão-Mór Vicente, was so pleased with the Roman Curia's decision that he added a Brazilian flourish. It was one congruent with Henry Koster's observations in Recife: The *capitão-mór* ordered Monte Carmelo's color changed in Itu's crown census rolls and moved his name into the column reserved for whites.[30]

The social dimension laid bare by Monte Carmelo's rejected application to the Third Order of Carmo pertained to a membership criterion that catered to the "cream" of late colonial society. Pombaline law had addressed racial discrimination in the lay brotherhoods known as *cofradias* or *irmandades*, which fell under the control of the secular clergy and, therefore, of the Portuguese crown.[31] However, Brazil's third orders did not meet the test of a lay brotherhood; they fell outside the jurisdiction of crown law. Legally, they were lay affiliates of the regular orders of the clergy that blended elite membership with a chain of command reaching to Rome. Third orders came under the jurisdiction of a provincial or a general of an ecclesiastical order— and, ultimately, of the pope. "To be admitted to one of the Third Orders signified that one belonged to the social elite and to have incontestably Catholic and white ancestry."[32]

The third orders survived the independence era with their lily-white membership criterion intact, enrolling an impressive number of imperial politicians. Although not all third orders barred non-whites, the prestigious Third Order of São Francisco, which counted Sen. Diogo Antonio Feijó among its members, certainly did. They rivaled in social prestige the secular military orders of Christ, Aviz, and the Cross. As elite organizations in secular society, the third orders projected a corporate identity affiliated with the church and perpetuated the value of European descent implying legitimate birth.[33]

Minimal Nobility and a Society of Rank

Nobility's legal character as a privileged corporation at the upper levels of society ostensibly withered in the face of a liberal constitution. Yet the post-1822 society of "orders" continued to be mediated by nobility in respects that forestalled or qualified the emergence of class divisions. The corporate facets of a higher nobility rested uniquely on the emperor's bestowal of life tenure titles and honors, complemented by the important distinction of "*grandeza*" that further enhanced a titleholder's prestige. The constitutional stipulation that titles be conferred on the basis of "service rendered to the state," subsequently dictated that titleholders would receive their patents of nobility as reward and recognition for their "productive economic activities."[34] In her study of dress during the reign of D. João VI, Maria Beatriz Nizza da Silva has analyzed how the clothes individuals wore on ceremonial occasions fit a prescribed etiquette, including distinctive attire that advertised membership in either of the first two estates.[35] Besides meticulously prescribed sartorial differences, there was special dress occasioned by the awarding of honorific "*graças*," or privileges, during the ceremonial fêtes when the sovereign bestowed the latter as honors. Ceremonial garb projected the key resource of individual prestige, explaining why many at the imperial court aspired to being seen on the frequent state occasions where personal resplendence could be publicly displayed.

Difficult to grasp today, the privileges of attending state functions "in court dress," and the right to be addressed according to one of an imaginative number of honorific formulas, mattered a great deal in the 1820s. Entitlement to honorific address, according to precisely gradated formulas, was hotly debated on the floor of Parliament during deliberations over the 1828 Judiciary Act, suggesting the important extent to which society remained grounded in prestige—rank—rather than social class. When the Rev. Robert Walsh was presented at court, on the occasion of a *beija-mão*, or ceremonial hand-kissing, for the emperor's birthday in 1828, he commented on how "very rich" dress identified gradations among those assembled. Walsh distinguished the key groups from "the respective costumes of their orders," as either nobility, military officers, public functionaries, or distinguished ecclesiastics."[36]

Controversy over the privilege of wearing court dress nonetheless hinted at emerging class identities. In the 1820s, "class" was a word that had entered contemporary speech, but not yet acquired a modern connotation. As Rev. Walsh suggested, at society's upper levels, people still thought in terms of "orders," the rough equivalents of estates. Yet an important corollary had developed. By the 1820s military officers tended to be discriminated from nobility, as an order apart. They constituted a nobility of the sword composed of a corps of commissioned officers. A comment of Frei Caneca, leader of Pernambuco's 1824 secessionist rebellion, offered insight: "The *fidalgos* of Brazil do not form a body; they are isolated individuals and do not constitute a class."[37] He correctly implied that, discounting the means by which they had acquired noble rank, nobles were extremely variegated in terms of prestige, privilege, and income. Furthermore, at the lowest rank, *fidalgos* overlapped with the third estate, placing those who were noble by descent above not only non-nobles in the third estate but also above the so-called "second order" nobles who possessed merely civil nobility.

As we have seen from the preceding volume, minimal nobility was defined by "natural descent," usually presumptively through common knowledge. Legitimate birth was inherent in a three-generation rule of nobility by descent, the presumption being that the holder, as well as his or her parents and grandparents, had been born of legitimate marriage. No liberal politician ever attacked the value or utility of what amounted to minimal nobility—whether by descent or by acquisition, the latter implying the civil nobility conferred by law. In imperial Brazil, civil nobility rapidly became a common option within the third estate, once faculties in law and medicine were founded in the late 1820s. Albeit inferior to nobility by descent, civil nobility greatly mattered because it separated the bearer from the third estate. Two Prussian visitors to the court of D. João VI confirmed the substantial social divide separating the third estate from those possessing any degree of nobility. At a palace fête, men who were commoners had to wear monotonously identical attire, being allowed only toy-like sabers:

He who does not have the right to a uniform puts on a black suit, white vest, and black trousers and shoes; he carries a curved, golden saber a foot in length and a "*chapeau á claque*" on his arm. Thus, without any differences, do all present themselves who are not *fidalgos*, that is teachers, artists, businessmen, and artisans, etc., who do not have the right to a sword.[38]

The fact of noble privilege, of course, contradicted the constitutional provision that "every citizen shall be admitted to public offices—civil, political, or military—without regard to differences, except those pertaining to talent and virtue" (Article 179, Paragraph 14). Nevertheless, possession of a title attested to a "social category with exclusive civil and political rights," as well as entitlement to "exemptions."[39] The attributes of nobility largely rested on entitlements to prestige, no small reward in a society still grounded in "orders." Those attributes found their best validation and long-term perpetuation in the imperial officer corps, precisely where men of talent in the third estate looked for careers promising upward social mobility.

Legitimate Birth, Color, and the Imperial Officer Corps

Just as racial discrimination remained conspicuous where individual career paths led to the church, so also it played a significant, though not exclusive, role in gaining entry to the army's commissioned officer corps. Race, more appropriately color, in such a context operated as a variable subordinate to legitimate birth, posing an anomaly in a liberal era. Liberal legislators, who normally did not debate issues of race, understood that race tacitly mediated service as a military officer. In 1829, for instance, the liberal deputy Cunha Mattos, also an army brigadier who was expert in military law, sponsored a salary bill to bring the pay for officers in the colonial militias to parity with those in the regular army. The former were to be eliminated, making the issue one of their absorption into the regular army. Because the militias survived independence as racially segregated entities, Cunha Mattos' proposal tacitly attempted to end pay discrimination on the ground of African descent. No legislator, however, directly acknowledged this motive. Amended by Bernardo de Vasconcellos, Cunha Mattos' bill restricted "equal pay" to the white officers in command of what were still black militias. The refusal to raise the subject of the differential pay for black officers demonstrated how reluctant liberals were "to deal with race questions." As Hendrik Kraay has pointed out, "Indeed, by refusing to discuss them, they were implicitly defining the Brazilian officer corps as an exclusively white institution, one in which there was no room for black men."[40]

Racial discrimination in the officer corps implicitly continued to rest to an important degree on the three-generation rule of nobility by descent. From the preceding volume's exploration of nobility, it will be recalled that the 1757 Law of the Cadets, which remained in force until the republican era, required officer candidates accepted as cadets to be not only the sons of commissioned officers but also to possess natural nobility. Consequently, they, like their parents and grandparents, had to be of legitimate birth. Although the officer corps of the army did not rely exclusively on cadets for commissioning officers, and men who were neither noble nor legitimate were promoted from the ranks, thereby automatically acquiring nobility, the corps did rely on those twin criteria for recruiting officers when they came from the cadet graduates of the Royal Military Academy in Realengo. Shortly before the Lisbon court was established in Rio de Janeiro, Brazilian fathers who enjoyed merely civil nobility brought pressure on the crown to place their sons in the military academy, because theirs was the wrong kind of nobility. It was "second-class" due to being conferred by the law rather than by descent or directly from the monarch. As "nobles who are not *fidalgos*," those fathers were crown officials and high judges, businessmen, wholesalers, and industrialists, not to mention graduates of law and medical faculties. Ennobled by the law, they were commonly "called 'good men' or 'men of good' [*homens bons*] in very old speech"—precisely because they could not be addressed as "*dom*."[41]

Protest against the exclusive rule of natural nobility as a criterion for cadet candidacy proved effective once the context became an incipient liberal revolution in Portugal. By the decree of February 4, 1820, D. João VI created exclusively for his Brazilian subjects the categories of "second-class," or "second," cadet and officer for the army and navy. This law addressed the sons of fathers who possessed merely civil nobility. The innovation deserves appreciation as a reaffirmation of what was previously discussed as the Pombaline expansion of nobility "by the law." The decree of 1820 specifically applied to the sons of men who possessed three types of nobility not deemed "natural": nobility automatically conferred by virtue of admission to either a military or secular order; or nobility due to "some civil consideration," that is, civil nobility acquired through the exercise of a profession or certain occupations; or nobility enjoyed by virtue of the "[civil] employment or corporate membership [*cabidos*]," again implying civil nobility. Additionally, civil nobility took into account the sons of men of wealth, such as the owners of sugar mills who, throughout the colonial period, presumptively possessed minimal nobility, or otherwise enjoyed wide, arbitrary inclusion. Thus civil nobility might inscribe the sons of "persons who, by virtue of their property or who, in other respects, deserve consideration."[42] Henceforth, the legitimate sons of all of such civilly noble individuals would be eligible either for candidacy as "second" cadets or as "private soldiers" in the army, navy, and militias. The sons of second-class nobles would thus take their place alongside "first" officers or cadets who enjoyed natural nobility. In tandem with the 1757 Law of the Cadets, the law of February 4, 1820, continued to regulate recruitment to the Royal Military Academy until the republican era.[43]

The cupola of Brazil's officer corps, consequently, continued to rely on legitimate birth or, alternatively, on the remedy of solemn legitimization, as the sine qua non of noble status. If elite officers and cadets were distinguished as "first," by virtue of natural nobility, then their corporate identity as members of the second estate, by perpetuating the three-generation rule for defining "natural nobility," retained long-term affinity with a society of estates rather than one of social classes. Although civil nobility assumed greater significance by the 1840s, imperial law upheld another Pombaline notion that reinforced the old order: ipso facto, an officer's patent signed by the emperor conferred nobility.[44] This reason alone accounted for why military officers who had fathered natural sons in illicit relationships, and wished them to be cadets, possessed special incentive to have their offspring solemnly legitimized, either by the crown, or, after 1828, by an imperial judge. Otherwise, simple legitimization failed to make their sons eligible as first cadet candidates or officers. In 1848, imperial legislators went so far as to reiterate the 1818 loophole sanctioning solemn legitimization—by then, accomplished through judicial writ—for equipping a natural offspring for cadet candidacy. That is, they rejected as insufficient the simple legitimization fathers frequently committed to a will or executed as a notarized declaration of paternal recognition.[45]

Although a moratorium on issuing noble titles held fast throughout the nine years of the Regency, minimal nobility continued to be tacitly endorsed. There was, however, one exception. For three decades, a small group of liberals consistently protested the criterion of minimal *fidalguia*, nobility by descent, incorporated in the 1757 Law of the Cadets. From the late 1820s into the 1850s, Cunha Mattos and Luiz Jozé de Oliveira consistently condemned the criterion of *fidalguia* by descent. The bills they sponsored to abolish this prerequisite for admission to the Military Academy at Realengo proved to no avail.[46] In his compendium of laws regulating the military, Cunha Mattos later observed that, although Article 179, Paragraph 16, of the 1824 Constitution abolished all privilege not essential to discharging public office, it was "in so many ways vague as to raise many questions."[47] He had in mind the controversy that arose in the 1840s over the intertwined criteria of natural nobility and legitimate birth, because significant numbers of the sons of National Guard officers were reaching the age when cadet candidacy for the officer corps of the army beckoned.

The 1831 legislation establishing the National Guard had been interpreted to mean that officers in the Guard were considered "equal in nobility to those in the army of the line."[48] In fact, Guard officers, who were chosen in local elections, did not have to be either noble or of legitimate birth. Resistance to admitting their sons to the Realengo Military Academy, consequently, turned on the fact that the Guard stood as a quintessential liberal institution. By rejecting the recruitment criterion imposed by the Law of the Cadets, the Guard, a liberal creation, broke with the society of estates. That its officers might lack minimal *fidalguia* or even be born outside legal marriage proved to be only part of why Guard officers were regarded as inferior in status by career officers in the regular army. The issue of the questionable nobility that certain Guard officers enjoyed was not resolved between 1850 and 1854. Additional legislation and related ministerial rulings eventually determined that only the legitimate or solemnly legitimized sons of officers in the National Guard could indeed be eligible for entry to the Realengo Military Academy. Yet controversy continued, even beyond the affirmative ruling of 1854 that concurred with the 1850 law: "Therefore, it seems that all of the officers of the National Guard are in general reputed to be noble, and their sons have the right to be recognized cadets, in conformity with their ranks."[49]

Natural offspring fathered by National Guard officers, like their counterparts in the army and navy whose fathers were noble by descent, did not qualify for admission to the military academy under the 1850 law. The resolution of May 12, 1818, still held. That is, the requirement of solemn legitimization endured, even after 1847, when the distinctions in inheritance law between the natural offspring of nobles and commoners were removed by law. The minister of war, seconded by the Council of State, upheld the 1818 resolution requiring solemn legitimization for the natural offspring of fathers noble by descent.[50] The Pombaline rule of nobility by descent, *fidalguia*, implying legitimate birth, was not set aside. In 1862, this principle of descent again was reaffirmed in imperial law.[51] As late as the 1880s, when solemn legitimization had become a legal anachronism, applicants for cadet candidacy were rejected on the ground that they merely possessed a father's notarized affidavit of paternal recognition. The criterion of legitimate birth dating to the 1857 Law of Cadets, together with the 1818 corollary requiring legitimization of natural or spurious offspring to be solemn, endured into the first decade of the republic, until the presidential administration of Prudente de Moraes (1894–1898), when it was abolished.[52]

Those who enjoyed minimal nobility, whether by descent or civilly conferred, possessed certain immunities in law. For instance, military personnel, especially officers, enjoyed the protection of their own code, when they were not subject to civil jurisdiction. Even when a civil magistrate held jurisdiction, he was restricted from arresting military personnel unless the commanding officer was first notified. Except where apprehended *in flagrante delicto*, military officers were to be handled "with consideration" by civil authorities and favored with house arrest in their home towns.[53] However, the law school graduate, wherever he practiced law, survived as the key exemplar of civil nobility in imperial Brazil. "The privileges of a *doutor*" validated the concept of "nobility conferred by law" in practice.[54] For instance, *pátrio poder* was waived for the *bacharel* who had not reached legal majority, whenever he sought to marry without parental consent. Along with medical school graduates, the *bacharel* could not be imprisoned with common criminals.

Even in twenty-first-century Brazil, the right of "special prison"—immunity from confinement in a "common jail cell"—survives as the enduring legacy of the eighteenth-century society of estates. This immunity originated in the legal privilege historically enjoyed by members of the first and second estate, validated by each promulgation of the *Ordenações do Reino*. Then in the eighteenth century it was widely extended to those "ennobled by law." Today, immunity from confinement in a common jail cell in Brazil is a legal right enjoyed by millions of citizens. It was comprehensively reaffirmed by the 1941 Code of Criminal Procedure, and, subsequently, by statutes, applied on behalf of the legal heirs of the first and second estates: all clergy, officers in either the armed forces or a plethora of police forces, as well as those in the merchant marine and "the corps of firemen." More to the point, a long list of quasi-corporate groups who today trace legal descent from the Pombaline possessors of civil nobility still enjoy the right to special prison: cabinet ministers, elected representatives to Congress and the state legislative assemblies, state governors, magistrates and local judges, ex-members of juries, holders of college degrees and many other post-secondary degrees, primary and secondary teachers, commercial pilots, and labor union leaders.[55]

Entail, Hallmark of the Society of Estates

Although the establishment of an entail stood as the privilege par excellence of an individual who enjoyed any degree of nobility, the right to succeed to an entail was predicated on legitimate birth. Alternatively, the institution of an entail could be on behalf of someone born outside wedlock, provided the individual had been legitimized, either by the crown or the parents' subsequent marriage. A bill to abolish entail, submitted in 1827 by Dep. Manoel Odorico Mendes, stood as an important liberal repudiation of the society of estates. The measure would need more than eight years to become law and, in 1829, the controversy it generated produced nineteenth-century Brazil's most prolonged debate on inheritance law. Introduced on July 17, 1827, the original bill called for the extinction of all entails, both the secular, or family, form known as the *morgado* and the more common form that was ecclesiastical, known as the *capela*, or chantry. Taking into account that historically entail comprised a mélange of secular and ecclesiastical forms, the bill additionally proposed extinction of a generically denominated body of arrangements identified simply as "any entails whatsoever" (*quaisquer vínculos*).[56] All secular entails were to be extinguished with the death of their current owners, while those controlled by corporate entities, meaning the church, would immediately cease to exist. An important exception was made for entails administered by charities, hospitals, and orphanages operated by the church. After being struck from the bill, this exception was then restored by amendment.

From the time of the bill's introduction, on July 17, it enjoyed very strong support in the lower house. Where the church mattered, ecclesiastical entail testified to considerable economic wealth. Several regular orders, like the Benedictines and the Carmelites, owned impressive amounts of urban real estate, probably acquired before the Pombaline prohibition on instituting ecclesiastical entails for real property. Nowhere was this truer than where the Corte's downtown streets surrounded the original houses of Parliament.[57] Walsh's estimate placed the proportion of the capital's inhabited houses (15,623) owned by the regular clergy at five percent, with the Benedictines owning around 700 houses. The arrival of the Portuguese court in 1808, however, exposed the urban real estate owned by the regular orders to selective appropriation by the crown. Again, in 1827, when lawmakers needed a large, central building to house the new law school authorized for São Paulo, they requisitioned the Franciscan Convent in the city's oldest neighborhood—the Largo do São Francisco.[58]

Given the crowded legislative agenda for 1827, the second discussion of the bill to abolish entail took place early in the 1828 legislative year. On June 3, Dep. Manoel Jozé de Souza França, a liberal lawyer, presented it for brief discussion.[59] Dep. José da Cruz Ferreira summarized the objections of liberals to entail, echoing arguments voiced in Europe since the enlightenment. His rhetorical exaggeration perhaps was better suited to a twentieth-century call for agrarian reform; however, Cruz Ferreira's words resonated with the Pombaline demand that real property should freely circulate. Besides the "evils" that entail had worked historically in both Portugal and Spain, he pointed to the "immense" tracts of land that in Brazil were administered as family entails. Those families, he charged, lacked the power or resources to cultivate them. Nor would they permit others to do so. Primogeniture, on which the majority of secular entails rested, drained the country of the services that otherwise their administrators, also known as *morgados*, might offer to a national economy. Cruz Ferreira dismissed the favorite argument of entail's defenders, that the nobles who administered family *morgados* "served the brilliance and the splendor of the throne." Rather than by means of stewardship over land that was fiduciary, he proposed that the "brilliance and splendor of the throne" be better served by "clemency, justice, and many other virtues of the highest type."[60]

Souza França and Cruz Ferreira resisted the procedural suggestion that the bill be sent to committee for a written opinion on its juridical implications—and an official redaction—leaving deputies free to amend or reword it from the floor and speed the measure toward a final vote. When the bill returned for a final discussion, only on June 9, 1828, debate proved lengthy. The newly consecrated bishop of Maranhão, D. Marcos Antonio de Souza, led the opposition. Although he claimed to favor abolition of the *morgado*, D. Marcos adamantly opposed extinction of ecclesiastical entails. The *capela*, together with "all other types of entail (*vínculos*)" the bill attempted to outlaw, provided the charitable income needed by church institutions, he insisted.[61] When he insinuated that no law on entail was necessary, because Pombal's famous and comprehensive law of August 3, 1769, was sufficient, then his logic was caustically rebuffed. The bishop made the mistake of referring, correctly, to entail as emanating from the monarch's power to legislate, an attribute of sovereign power that liberals were determined to abolish. Cruz Ferreira objected, noting that the monarch's authorization of entail reflected a "royal prerogative," but that the 1824 Constitution vested the power to make law in the national legislature.

Both were saying the same thing, although ideologically, the bishop and his liberal opponents struck distinctly different emphases. The monarch's prerogative to suspend law historically had been interpreted as intrinsic to his role as "the Legislator." For liberals, the distinction between the monarch's "grace," on the one hand, and his persona as "the Legislator" on the other, went straight to the heart of the matter. By definition, any establishment of an entail implied suspending inheritance law in force, given that the *Ordenações Filipinas* mandated a partitive rule of "equal shares for all" by virtue of *ab intestato* succession. Therefore, establishment of a family entail under a sole administrator, usually according to the rule of male primogeniture, defined an exception that deprived necessary heirs of their patrimonial rights. Pombaline reform, in fact, had tightened the monarch's sanction of entail. The law of September 9, 1769 (§17), required that the establishment of all new entails be approved by the Tribunal of the Desembargo do Paço as preliminary to confirmation by the sovereign's "justice and grace."

Again, the 1824 Constitution introduced ambiguity. Brazil's charter remained completely silent on the matter of entail, giving the emperor only the right to confer "titles of nobility, honors, membership in military orders, and distinctions in compensation for services to the state" (Article 102, Paragraph 11). In fact, D. Pedro himself, prior to promulgation of the Constitution, perpetuated the prerogative of crown privilege that sanctioned the establishment of entail, starting with his creation of the *morgado* of Torre on behalf of Bahia's Garcia d'Ávila family. That prerogative had been juridically interpreted in an age of absolutism as intrinsic to the sovereign's role as "the Legislator." Under a monarchy that was now constitutional, liberal legislators argued that the sovereign should no longer enjoy the power to dispense law. By insisting that the power to suspend the law was vested in the General Assembly, as "the Legislator," they also anticipated abolition of the Tribunal of the Mesa do Desembargo do Paço, the royal organ authorizing the establishment of an entail.

For liberals, abolition of entail would accomplish a dual goal that fulfilled a constitutional mandate: extinction of an important corporate privilege pertaining to both church and nobility as well as an attribute of the emperor's role as legislator. Debate went to the heart of controversy: Who made law, the monarch or the legislature? Legislators argued over whether the bill ought to be amended to define the national legislature as the sole body authorized to institute entail, but, as Dep. Lino Coutinho pointed out, such an approach was no safeguard. It logically contradicted the bill's *raison d'être*—the extinction of all entails—because the door would remain open for a future legislature to reestablish entail.[62] In the end, controversy erupted over a more fundamental issue, when the liberals, Clemente Pereira and Bernardo de Vasconcellos, backed by Francisco de Paula de Almeida e Albuquerque, Luiz Paulo de Araujo Bastos, and Francisco de Paula Souza e Mello, disagreed on how to extinguish entail: Where should the patrimony from extinguished entails go? To the public treasury? Or to the forced heirs of the last administrator? They also disagreed substantially over whether to exempt charities from abolition of ecclesiastical entail.[63] These issues would arise anew in what became a much more protracted Senate debate on the same bill in 1829.

The Chamber of Deputies resumed debate on July 2 and 7, after the bill had been returned from the Committee on Civil Justice for revised redaction. Adoption by the lower house came on July 7, with the final redaction approved July 10, 1828.[64] On July 12, the bill was forwarded to the Senate, but the vote was deferred until 1829.[65] The Senate proved the greatest obstacle to abolishing entail, proof of the importance of the *morgado* as a perquisite of nobility within a body dominated by titleholders. Although entail acquired a political significance for liberals that may have outweighed the institution's actual impact on economic organization, historians have underestimated its significance in the latter respect, including the role entail played for generating income for ecclesiastical corporations, clerical stipends, and charitable ends. The eagerness of the Chamber of Deputies to extirpate entail from the body politic drew directly on a liberal aversion to corporate privilege traceable to a legal tradition of Pombaline reform. In the Senate, on the other hand, Pombaline reform frequently supplied the reason that supporters and opponents of the bill disagreed over whether any action should be taken.

Odorico Mendes would propose the identical bill two more times, following several narrow defeats in the upper house, before the Senate finally adopted his bill in 1835.

REFORMING CROWN JUSTICE: THE 1828 JUDICIARY ACT

Once the national legislature reopened, judicial reform figured highest on the list of bills for adoption. As pivotal legislation, the 1828 Judiciary Act addressed the real work of modifying the institutional framework of the Portuguese *ancien régime*. It followed logically from the Constitution, which mandated a judicial branch and redistributed powers vested in the sovereign to either the legislature or the judiciary. The Judiciary Act also prepared the way for codification. Indeed, the two most important legislative accomplishments of Brazil's fledgling legislature during the initial decade of independence pertained to codification: the 1830 Criminal Code and the 1832 Code of Criminal Procedure. As Thomas H. Holloway has shown, both of these enduring codes represented conscious efforts to break with the colonial past, rewriting law and judicial procedures along lines that reflected notions consonant with a post–French Revolutionary Europe. Each, nevertheless, perpetuated the authoritarian tendency of the old regime to wed the power of the police to that of the judiciary. As a result, the judiciary never amounted to an independent branch of government. A series of complementary bills, such as the one adopting a jury system in 1827, belied the succinctness of the 1828 Judiciary Act; however, collectively, they found comprehensive articulation in the Procedural and Criminal Codes.[66]

Constitutional implementation proceeded *pari passu* with liberalism's rapid trajectory, defining an incoming tide that by 1828 witnessed the Chamber of Deputies firmly in the hands of liberal legislators. Judicial reform was the product of a two-year effort in both houses of the General Assembly. Bernardo Pereira de Vasconcellos, by 1828 the principal liberal leader in the Chamber, emerged as the author-redactor of the complex bill that established the new judicial system and the 1830 Criminal Code. He played a leading role in the abolition of the key crown tribunals associated with Portuguese absolutism, fully exploiting their rhetorical significance on behalf of liberals eager to indict the corporate privileges of clergy and nobility—and to strike a blow against absolutist principles of governance. Historians have paid little attention to what Brazil's legislature destroyed in order to establish a national judiciary in 1828. Yet, for an understanding of why inheritance law received significant legislative attention, starting with entail in 1827, the extinction of royal tribunals of appeal defined the first step in procedural reform.

Abolishing the Casa da Suplicação

Following the 1824 Constitution, legislators abolished the key institutions of high crown justice, extinguishing the monarch's role as supreme judge and legislator. As a result, the sovereign's prerogative to suspend prevailing law, in response to appeals to his "mercy and grace"—what for a liberal era were his "justice and mercy"—became negligible. The first tribunal to fall casualty to judicial reform in 1828 was the most all encompassing: the Casa da Suplicação. Dating to 1425–1429, and originally known as the Relação, or High Court, of Lisbon, the Casa had served as a model for all other courts. It possessed civil and criminal divisions that heard appeals from the colonies as well as in the metropole. By virtue of the *alvará* of May 10, 1808, D. João had recreated the Casa da Suplicação in Brazil. He appointed as its head the incumbent Regidor of the Casa da Suplicação in Lisbon, the same individual he had appointed in 1786 and who accompanied him into exile.[67] Continuity between the metropolitan and the colonial incarnations of this high crown court of appeal endured until 1828. Historically, the Casa heard appeals cases referred by the *Relações*, or courts of first appeal, including those that in the colonies sat in Bahia and Rio de Janeiro. The regional *Relações* received appeals cases directly from the local crown judges known as *ouvidores*, who, as judges of the first instance resided in their judicial districts, or *comarcas*.[68] The Casa da Suplicação clarified, as well as ruled on, decisions issued by the *Relações*. Beginning in 1808, the Casa created for Rio de Janeiro heard cases from the *Relações* in Pará and Maranhão, as well as from the Azores and Madeira. In 1821, another *Relação* was established in Pernambuco.

Extinction of the Casa da Suplicação, on September 18, 1828, was mandated by the simultaneous establishment of a Supreme Court of Justice (Supremo Tribunal de Justiça). In reality, however, the Casa survived until 1831. Due to Emperor D. Pedro's reliance on it as an instrument of patronage for his palace clique, the Casa operated on an interim basis for nearly three years beyond its legal "extinction."[69] Occupying the pinnacle of a new imperial judiciary, the Supreme Court hailed the arrival of a government purportedly reorganized on the basis of a separation of powers. In fact, the Judiciary Act retained the old Pombaline reliance on a fusion of executive (police) and judicial powers, in addition to a three-tiered organizational structure modeled closely on the Casa da Suplicação. Notwithstanding obligatory retirement of the Casa's high crown judges, a high degree of continuity in both personnel and jurisdiction accompanied the constitutional transition. For instance, judges of the new Supreme Court were drawn from the senior ranks of high judges presiding on the regional *Relações*. In keeping with the former prestige of the Casa da Suplicação, the sixteen justices of the Supreme Court bore their predecessors' prestigious title of "councilor" (*conselheiro*) and enjoyed the perquisite of being addressed as "Excellency." Like the former Casa da Suplicação, the Supreme Court heard appeals from the provincial *Relações*. Disputes in inheritance law continued to figure in their determinations, including cases turning on the succession rights of illegitimate and legitimized individuals. In reality, the most important changes mandated by the Judiciary Act pertained to the base, not to the pinnacle, of the new system of justice.

Abolishing the Mesa da Consciência e Ordens

Recreated on Brazilian soil by the *alvará* of April 22, 1808, the Mesa da Consciência e Ordens was established jointly with the Mesa do Desembargo do Paço in what amounted to the supreme expression of royal power. It exercised ecclesiastical jurisdiction on behalf of the temporal arm of the state, for its main function since establishment in 1532 was administration of the *Padroado Régio*, the royal patronage of the church. Until 1808, the Mesa da Consciência had discharged those responsibilities vis-à-vis Brazil in tandem with the Conselho Ultramarinho, the crown's principal organ of colonial rule. The Mesa's personnel was composed of theologians and jurists recruited from among the secular clergy or the knights of the military orders. Prestigious representatives of the first and second estates thus advised the monarch on all matters involving the royal patronage of the church. The Mesa da Consciência e Ordens organized new parishes or reorganized existing ones. It supervised the catechization of the native population, maintained seminaries, administered the examinations by which priests received parishes, and enjoyed responsibility for collecting the tithe and paying stipends to the clergy. The Mesa also resolved "obligations of conscience" for the three military orders of Santiago, Christ, and São Bento de Aviz. In resolving cases of conscience it disposed over disputes involving the lay brotherhoods known as *irmandades*, for they comprised important corporations falling under its jurisdiction. Finally, the Mesa da Consciência heard judicial disputes over the royal patronage and settled conflicts among ecclesiastics—or between the latter and their parishioners.[70]

Liberal legislators interpreted the Mesa da Consciência e Ordens as the crown organ of corporate privilege par excellence. Antipathy toward both the military orders, and the church accounted for such sentiment. Liberals who regarded the emperor with suspicion or hostility saw his role as Grand Master of the Order of Christ in Brazil as the embodiment of the old order.[71] Extinction of the Mesa da Consciência e Ordens in 1828 therefore produced a political effect analogous to the abolition of the Casa da Suplicação, implying the end of the colonial regime and the imposition of constitutional limitations on the emperor's power. Liberal legislators refused to uphold the sovereign's prerogative to regulate the corporate power of the church and sought to make the crown's *regalias* the mandate of the new legislature.

The 1828 Judiciary Act redistributed the centralized functions of the former Mesa da Consciência e Ordens between the legislature and the judiciary. Ecclesiastical committees in both houses of the Brazilian Parliament henceforth directly exercised sovereignty over the royal patronage, approving ordinations and nominating candidates for papal confirmation as bishops and archbishops. Contrary to what certain liberals liked to assert, however, the emperor, in his capacity as protector of the church, retained a shared sovereignty vis-à-vis the *Padroado*, by virtue of the imperial sanction required to make bills and resolutions bear the force of law. Accordingly, judges of the first instance acquired responsibility under the Judiciary Act for annulling disputed elections in the lay brotherhoods, while the provincial High Courts now ruled on jurisdictional disputes between prelates or other ecclesiastical authorities. Finally, the Imperial Treasury and administrative agencies of the Interior Ministry jointly oversaw collection of the tithe and payment of clerical stipends.

Abolishing the Desembargo do Paço

Unlike the abolition of the two high crown courts discussed above, whose jurisdictions extended to matters of inheritance law only indirectly, the Tribunal of the Mesa do Desembargo do Paço exercised a direct jurisdiction in matters of heirship. Indeed, the power it wielded when functioning as a tribunal was fundamental to the operation of the inheritance system. All exceptions to the law of *ab intestato* succession had to be referred to its high judges. Thus it controlled the process of crown legitimization, what amounted to a judicial oversight over the rights of necessary or collateral heirs. For the same reason, it passed on all petitions for instituting entails, whether secular or ecclesiastical. On very rare occasions, it sanctioned what amounted to adoptions, drawing on Roman law to approve an arrangement known as "*adrogação*." More than any other crown tribunal, "the Paço" conveyed the sovereign's power to make law. The monarch's prerogative to suspend law meant that it could overrule decisions appealed from the Casa da

Suplicação. Prior to 1822, in tandem with the Overseas Council, the Mesa do Desembargo do Paço had been a key organ of Portugal's colonial administration, although many of its responsibilities were routinely discharged through the Relação of Bahia. In the eighteenth century, the Desembargo do Paço had also enjoyed a shared responsibility for censorship. All of these attributes explained why it received major attention from lawmakers—and a great deal of antipathy from liberals. The fact that the Paço embodied the old order, absolutism and colonialism, accounted for the punitive language that Bernardo Vasconcellos originally wrote into the Judiciary Act, which declared the Mesa do Desembargo do Paço extinct—"as if it had never existed."[72]

The personnel of the Desembargo do Paço further explained the hostility many liberal legislators bore toward it. From 1590 onward, the presidents of the Mesa do Desembargo do Paço had always been drawn from a higher nobility, usually from candidates of royal blood. After 1821, the high judges, who technically served on an interim basis, were nearly all beneficiaries of the emperor's personal favor. Most had been elevated in the peerage by Pedro I. Their future, either in permanent retirement, reappointed to the appeals courts, or even named to the Supreme Court, defined a sore point for legislators. In any event, they would be obliged to forfeit their prestige and coveted emoluments of office.[73] Parliamentary debates alleged a number of the Desembargo do Paço's colonial judges had been guilty of malfeasance, provoking legislators to caustic frankness. In contrast to the Chamber of Deputies, where most deputies lacked titles of nobility, the crown judges of the Mesa do Desembargo do Paço conducted themselves as a nobility of the robe, graced by royally conferred titles. Although high office had conferred on them the privilege of *fidalgo* of the royal palace, as well as the honors of a royal councilor, almost always, the Paço's judges possessed *fidalguia* of birth, if not an inherited title. Titles awarded by D. Pedro usually enhanced a nobility already enjoyed.

The Mesa do Desembargo do Paço stood out as a glaring contradiction in the new political order. Legislators in the lower house who did not condemn it as a safe refuge for "aristocracy" concluded that it had become so corrupt as to be of little service to the new nation. Condemnation proceeded from allegations that the high judges had arrogated what was intrinsically a royal prerogative of absolute power. Furthermore, the tribunal served a noble clientele often identified as Portuguese rather than Brazilian. Even nomenclature, incorporating "Paço"—the palace—resonated a political connection to the imperial court. Debate over extinguishing this organ of high crown justice pivoted on the terms on which the incumbent high judges, known as *desembargadores*, would retire. Principal controversy over the bill to extinguish the crown tribunals occurred in the Senate, because the perquisites of a titled nobility mattered a great deal more to senators than to members of the lower house. Less inclined to strip the *desembargadores* of their honors and emoluments, the upper house delayed extinguishing the crown tribunal precisely on that ground. Sen. Luiz José de Oliveira, who did not have a noble title, tactfully expressed the quandary many of his colleagues shared: "The retired *desembargador* of the Paço has, up to now, enjoyed the honors and privileges of a magistrate of the Paço. But now that this judicial category is being ended, what are those judges who do not move to the new tribunal going to do? End up having nothing?"[74]

Debate over the magisterial destiny of the Paço's crown judges carried little significance for the outcome of the vote—extinction was a foregone conclusion, thanks to the Constitution. Instead, senatorial arguments revealed how fervent the sentiment on behalf of privilege and prestige remained in the upper house, where a society of rank received strong reinforcement. The more conservative stance of that body contrasted markedly with the Chamber. Eventually, a solution to the forced retirement of the high judges of the Desembargo do Paço emerged: They would be assigned the rank of a retired high judge of the Supreme Court of Justice. The marquis of Caravellas, one of a handful of liberals in the Senate, brokered the 1827 compromise that then moved the bill forward and established the new judiciary:

I ask you: Who are you going to find retired on the Desembargo, when some [*desembargadores*] will argue, "I should not have to remain retired on a tribunal that no longer exists"? . . . It does not matter that the Tribunal [of the Paço] will not exist. The honors and privileges that belong to it will continue to exist. All of the magistrates of the Paço, simply put, are old men, and they have grown old in the service of the nation. Therefore, it is not much to compensate them for years of service by giving them retirement on the Supreme Court.[75]

Caravellas shrewdly used the debate to make reference to the nature of nobility in Brazil's constitutional order. It was no longer hereditary: "After all, [the retiring high judges] are not even being favored, as formerly would have been done, if not by law, at least by custom, by having had conferred [on them] the titles of Commenda, Senhorio, or an Alcaldoria-Mór—*as well as [on] their sons* . . . ."[76] He sought to mollify Senate colleagues who were strongly dedicated to the perquisites of noble rank. By virtue of their office, the Paço's high judges were accorded the treatment befitting honorary gentlemen of the royal household and "ministers of the king." Their annual salaries amounted to four *contos*, three or four times that of a bishop. As a result, the 1828 Judiciary Act made special provision for the *desembargadores* who no longer would sit on the Tribunals of the conjoined Mesa do Desembargo do Paço and the Mesa da Consciência e Ordens. Law would consider them "retired from the Supreme Court of Justice," confirming "the treatment, honors, and perquisites conceded to its members, preserving the emoluments [*ordenados*] that they had won in tribunals where they no longer served."[77]

Just as the Casa da Suplicação survived legal extinction under the Judiciary Act, so, too, the Desembargo do Paço endured beyond September 22, 1828, the official date of its extinction. Out of deference to D. Pedro's appointees, who were often his closest advisors, like the count of São João da Palma (Francisco de Assis Mascarenhas), the emperor simply declined to comply with the law. The Paço was perpetuated on an interim basis until March 23, 1831, a few weeks before Pedro abdicated.[78] However, the juridical legacy of the Tribunal of the Desembargo do Paço proved more enduring. The Judiciary Act adopted the Paço's *Regimento*, giving full statutory effect to its procedures and rules, as well as to the body of its rulings (Article 2, Paragraph 1). Hence, an important strand of the Pombaline legal tradition determined how judicial proceedings were conducted, as well as the rules of evidence, until Empire gave way to Republic in 1889. For instance, the stipulation that *ab intestato* heirs within the fourth civil degree had to be consulted, before a solemnly legitimized offspring could be awarded concurrent rights in succession, remained the procedural rule after 1828.

RECASTING "PER RESCRIPTUM PRINCIPIS"

Legitimization "Por Escrito"

When the conjoined Mesas do Desembargo do Paço and Consciência e Ordens were abolished by the Law of September 22, 1828 (Art. 1, §1), the same law rudimentarily established a national judiciary. Consequently, the far-reaching judicial functions of both boards were redistributed within the new judicial structure. Two major innovations further shaped an imperial judicial system, both inspired by the 1824 Constitution: a locally elected judge known as a justice of the peace, or a parish judge, and a jury system. The former was instituted in 1827, but the latter arrived only with the adoption of the 1832 Code of Criminal Procedure.[79] The Procedural Code, rather than the 1828 Judiciary Act, destroyed the legal structure inherited from Portugal, embodying the unfulfilled goals of liberal legislators ascendant in the aftermath of the emperor's abdication. In many respects, it stood as the liberals' answer to Pedro's 1824 Constitution. The Judiciary Act, on the other hand, established only the skeleton of new legal structure, conserving intact much of the old judicial system. The Procedural Code therefore elaborated the former and redefined the powers and jurisdiction of specific judges, including the parish judge.

Judicial authority reached upward from judges of the first instance—either a justice of the peace, an orphans judge, or, beginning in 1832, an appointive municipal judge. In the latters' absence, a higher magistrate discharged the functions of a judge of the first instance. The colonial High Court known as the Relação essentially acquired a provincial venue in 1828, ceasing to exercise a regional jurisdiction. The Relação heard cases that either originated in its jurisdiction or, more frequently, were forwarded on appeal. Given that only the Relação could authorize a six-month extension for filing estate inventories, it played an important role in disputes over family patrimony.[80] The judges of the Relação continued to be known as *desembargadores* and, as in the colonial regime, their tribunal occupied the second tier of a tripartite structure. Now, however, a Supreme Court of Justice capped a national judicial structure, replacing the former dual hegemony of the Desembargo do Paço and the Casa da Suplicação, not to mention the "justice and mercy" of the monarch.

Beginning in 1832, a municipal judge, corresponding roughly to the former circuit judge known as a *juíz de fora*, was appointed by the provincial president for a three-year term. He was selected from three candidates presented from a list submitted by the local, or *município*, council. Finally, the *juíz de direito*, or imperial (district) judge, who roughly corresponded to the colonial *ouvidor*, also appeared in 1832, as a creation of the Procedural Code. As the superior magistrate to whom the municipal judge answered, the imperial judge combined the responsibilities of a circuit judge and a police chief, for he presided over jury trials in his district seat and applied the 1830 Criminal Code to those who were convicted. Normally not involved in matters of family or inheritance law, except in disputes, the imperial judge mattered first as the linkage between his district and the imperial government that appointed him. Second, like his predecessor, the *ouvidor*, and his subordinate, the municipal judge, he was "*letrado*," a credentialed law school graduate and therefore a career judge.[81]

The Judiciary Act produced immediate consequences for family and inheritance law, given that crown legitimization, adoption arrangements, and contracts establishing entail no longer could be authorized by the Tribunal of the Mesa do Desembargo do Paço. Starting in 1828, judges of the first instance, who ordinarily were locally elected justices of the peace, inherited what since 1560 had been the prerogative of the Tribunal of the Mesa do Desembargo do Paço: the power to issue legitimization certificates (Article 2,

§1). "*Perfilhação solemne*" continued to be the legal operative term for describing what until 1828 had been the crown's "solemn legitimization." However, instead of being conferred "*per Rescriptum Principis,*" now solemn legitimization would be deemed "*por rescrito*"—determined by the judicial writ issued by a local judge.

On matters of inheritance, the justice of the peace worked in tandem with the orphans judge. The latter played a direct role in ruling on rights in heirship, wherever the parties were either under legal age, married women, surviving spouses, or widows who rapidly remarried (Article 2, §§1,4).[82] The orphans judge could override *pátrio poder* and enable a minor to marry, when a parent refused to give consent (Article 2, §4). He exercised the important authority to grant emancipation certificates on behalf of the *filho-famílias,* the unmarried adult offspring who continued to live under a parent's roof (Article 2, §4). When an individual attained the legal age of majority—25 years in 1828—but still resided under the parental roof, he did not become legally emancipated; *pátrio poder* could not be terminated without the parent's permission and necessitated the order of a judge.[83] The orphan's judge was authorized to override *pátrio poder*, thereby emancipating the child when permission was withheld. Finally, the orphans judge functioned as a surrogate judge, exercising jurisdiction where individuals died without heirs—or the heirs were absent—in addition to supervising transfers of heritable property to orphans and minors under guardianship (Article 2, §5).

The impact of the Judiciary Act accounts for why the judge of the first instance, especially the justice of the peace known as the parish judge, became the key figure in grass-roots imperial politics. He originally possessed primary jurisdiction in civil matters, with his criminal authority confined largely to gathering evidence. The 1832 Procedural Code reversed this relationship, expanding his police powers in investigating crimes and charging him with making arrests. By 1833, the parish judge possessed jurisdiction in civil cases amounting to 50 *mil-réis*, underscoring his role as a "small claims" judge whose job was to conciliate local disputes.[84] Locally elected to a three-year term after 1832, and serving voluntarily without pay, the parish judge became a power in his own right, largely independent of the imperial government. He mattered for inheritance law, because he presided over the filing of estate inventories and *partilhas*, and many of his rulings in private law reached directly into family factional disputes, enhancing his local influence.

Bride abduction, known as *rapto*, provided one of the best illustrations of how the parish judge's political influence rested on his judicial authority to uphold family and inheritance law. "Abductions" often were staged elopements that ended up with one or both partners petitioning a local judge as minors for the opportunity to marry. If friendly to the groom's family, the judge might be asked to override *pátrio poder*, authorizing a marriage that was not paternally sanctioned by the bride's family. Where allied with the woman's father, the judge might apprehend the would-be bridegroom, and, using his post-1832 police powers, charge him with the crimes of *rapto* and deflowering a virgin. In other words, the parish judge would be expected to take sides in family disputes in his community, including those that erupted into violent feuding, given his police powers. Alternatively, legitimate heirs might petition the justice of the peace to set aside the recognition of paternity that a deceased father had declared on behalf of a natural offspring whom they denounced as a bogus heir. However, it was the imperial judge who would acquire ultimate jurisdiction in such disputes, due to the crime of fraud. For the same reasons, the orphans judge, as an alternative judge of the first instance, occupied a pivotal position in local inheritance conflicts after 1828. He supervised guardianships for minors and other legally incapacitated individuals, but he, too, oversaw the dispositions in inventories, *partilhas*, and wills pertaining to their patrimony. Orphaned minors and the heirs of individuals who died in distant places comprised his most common responsibilities (Article 2, §5). For the first time, the legal machinery relevant to the inheritance rights of all Brazilians, including every type of illegitimate individual, operated within a local venue under the jurisdiction of two resident magistrates.

Unforeseen Consequences: "Scandal in the Courtroom"

Beginning in 1828, legal change transformed the social context for petitioning for legitimization or resolving claims of heirship where illegitimate individuals either asserted rights or forced heirs contested the latter. Now the parents—or the children themselves—could turn directly to a parish judge in order to settle issues touching on the claims of both natural and legitimized children. This changed circumstance would enormously expand the caseloads of judges of the first instance by the 1830s. Specifically, legitimate and collateral heirs who contested the inheritance claims of their natural or legitimized relatives would take their grievances to the local justice of the peace. Formerly, they had been instructed by the Tribunal of the Mesa do Desembargo do Paço to defend their rights in the *ouvidor*'s court, normally a more distant and impersonal venue, or in proceedings presided over by an itinerant circuit judge (*juíz de fora*). After 1808, Brazil's Desembargo do Paço had explicitly distanced itself from disputes between either legitimate or collateral heirs, in cases where illegitimate offspring sought to displace them as forced heirs. Beginning in 1828, however, access to the machinery of justice became "democratized." Where before only the relatively wealthy could afford to petition the *ouvidor* and the Tribunal of the Mesa do Desembargo do Paço for legitimization certificates, now many individuals, even of modest means, could petition a local judge for what formerly was beyond their grasp. This was liberalization at its finest. In 1842, when a newly formed Conservative Party revised the 1828 Judiciary Act, the power to issue legitimization certificates and confirm adoptions remained in a local venue, being assigned to the municipal judge.[85]

The magnitude of change that ensued in a new socio-political context of local appeals to judges transformed the meaning of solemn legitimization. As a result of the Judiciary Act, the local courthouse became a forum for disseminating the most intimate of family secrets, given that it defined the venue for acquiring or contesting judicial legitimization certificates conferring concurrent rights in succession. Transgressions of family honor now would be exposed in testimony uttered in local courts: the identity of a concubine, the violation of a priest's concealed paternity, the revelation of a respectable husband's adulterine child or a wife's concealment of her child's adulterine paternity, and the more scandalous details of incest. The "polygamous" nature of family formation would now be subject to detailed scrutiny in the arena of a courtroom that was local, converting truths left elegantly tacit into real and permanent damage. The blunt veracity of courtroom testimony—or its mendacious slander—would now elicit ridicule, vituperation, shame, and revenge. The result was a compounding of the worst kind of "public and notorious scandal" that, as we have seen, Pombaline law had adroitly suppressed. The consequences were irreversible. Wealthy and influential Brazilians no longer could expect to have illegitimate children legally equipped as their heirs with a minimum of gossip or scandal. Additionally, where rights in forced heirship were contested before a resident judge, the local venue multiplied the possibilities for exposing family secrets that sharpened conflict to the point of explosive violence.

By comparison, the centralized proceedings of the Tribunal of the Desembargo do Paço had shielded petitioners from public scrutiny in their own communities, while the expense discouraged all but a few would-be plaintiffs. Frequently, both forced heirs and legitimized offspring testified before a crown *ouvidor* largely free of personal embarrassment or notoriety in their hometowns. Arguments could be presented in writing and witnesses deposed in writing. Declarations of paternity or maternity made in private, sealed by a public notary, could be presented to the *ouvidor*, minimizing embarrassment to the parties. Above all, geographical distance had protected family secrets or facilitated local denial, given that the Tribunal of the Mesa do Desembargo do Paço had been located first in Lisbon and then in Rio de Janeiro. True, legitimization proceedings still had to be initiated locally, but with a crown *ouvidor* who dispatched a petition to Lisbon or the Corte. Unlike the ubiquitous justices of the peace, the *ouvidores* were less numerous and confined to cities and larger towns.

The case of Josefa Maria Francisca de Paula, mentioned in the preceding volume, illustrated the relative privacy that crown legitimization afforded until 1828. She petitioned the Desembargo do Paço in 1816 to legitimize her adulterine son, Nicolao, asking to have the name of her deceased husband removed from Nicolao's birth registry—as his putative father. She wanted to substitute the name of her adulterine son's biological father, the man she subsequently took as a second husband. D. Josefa could proceed with relatively little attention, thanks to the semi-private nature of the legal procedures. Initially, she and her legitimate daughter by her first husband executed a private affidavit with a local notary in Recife, one declaring Nicolao maternally adulterine and divulging the name of his biological father. That document went forward as evidence for her petition and the *ouvidor* in Recife forwarded it to the high judges of the Tribunal of the Desembargo do Paço in Rio de Janeiro, who granted her petition.[86]

Had Josefa Maria initiated her petition after 1828, then she and her legitimate daughter would have been obliged to testify in open court before a justice of the peace in their place of residence, under circumstances that would have placed her at center stage before relatives, neighbors, and strangers. Courthouses customarily were positioned on a town's principal public square. They attracted spectators seeking to pass time, to keep abreast of events in the community, and to exchange valuable gossip. Their shuttered windows—lacking glass—afforded street accessibility for legal proceedings and, even when closed, permitted testimony to carry outside. Finally, the local judge's interrogation would have revealed how Josefa Maria had misrepresented her maternity of Nicolao to her first husband, and whether or not he been complicit in the deception of his fraudulent paternity.

Consequently, Brazil's liberal era witnessed the local courtroom become a public stage for dramatic revelations about private family life. The justice of the peace, a key player in local politics and ordinarily himself a politician, rendered judicial decisions subject to considerations of local patronage. He contrasted with the *ouvidor*, who had represented a professional judiciary credentialed at Coimbra and been an outsider in the judicial district. Although not as ideally professional as the legal rules assumed, the *ouvidor* was prohibited by law from negotiating business in his own district. Nor could he marry a woman living there, except with permission from the sovereign.[87] Periodic rotation to a new judicial district further maintained his professional "neutrality."

The juridical ineptitude characteristic of the justice of the peace during the liberal era also should not pass unremarked, although, as Flory correctly pointed out, the criticism often reflected anti-liberal opposition to the newly instituted local judgeship.[88] Even as he was casting his vote in favor of the 1828 Judiciary Act, the marquis of Caravellas decried the absence of professional credentials among those who would staff the lowest rung of Brazil's fledging judiciary. Referring to the self-taught lawyers who would fill the post of justice of the peace, Caravellas pronounced, "These so-called '*rábulas*' lack the education of a law school graduate. Their knowledge is only chicanery."[89] Justices of the peace did indeed comprise a rather motley crew in the 1830s. Typically, they lacked both the experience and academic credentials that the *ouvidor* possessed as a matter of course. As a result, matters of succession law could be misinterpreted or left moot, accounting for many of the gaps that historians have detected between legal rules and dispositions in documents. Parliamentary debates in the 1830s and 1840s exposed the ignorance of this "front-line" judiciary in matters of inheritance law. More to the point, transgressions of law fueled the 1831 reform that dictated a new procedure for instituting certain illegitimate offspring as heirs.

The circumstance of widespread ignorance of law among local judges, coupled with the "pull" of local power under a liberal aegis, may have been what prompted Candido Mendes de Almeida to condemn the transfer to the judiciary of the sovereign's historical power to suspend the law and grant legitimization certificates. The "grace" of the Prince intrinsically rested with the executive power, he insisted, and the national legislature had, in the words of Teixeira de Freitas, been "improvident" in reassigning it to the national judiciary. Candido Mendes published this conclusion, however, from the hindsight of four decades, when the juridical pitfalls of "democratizing" crown legitimization had become obvious, indeed, when solemn legitimization had itself become a juridical relic.[90]

FROM REFORMING JUSTICE TO REFORMING PRIVATE LAW

Those who voted for the Judiciary Act in 1828 could not have foreseen the extent to which the transfer of legitimization proceedings from the executive to the judicial branch would bring troubling complications. Many legislators viewed the shift of power from sovereign to local judge as merely the first of several steps in liberalizing the legal position of individuals born out-of-wedlock. They would try to carry reform further, having in mind rewriting the rules of heirship—including the canonical definitions of illegitimacy—as a means for resolving the legal inequality enjoyed by those born outside holy matrimony. Rather than stopping at reform of the judiciary, liberal law-makers widened the parliamentary dialogue. By moving from reforming the judiciary to reforming the rules of marriage, they directly addressed Brazil's historically low rate of marriage and the rising incidence of illegitimate births that resulted. Yet, in seeking to impose what they understood as a modern notion of "equality before the law"—rejecting the legal privilege embedded in a society of estates—those liberals failed to challenge successfully the legitimacy of a juridical order that still rested on an established church whose canonical determinations reached to the very heart of family law.

PART II

Confronting the Canons of Trent

CHAPTER 3

Mancebia Bows to Legal Matrimony

Legislating Marriage à la Trent

———◆◆◆———

> There is nothing more public or known to everyone than a mar-
> riage. The news of a wedding travels even faster than news of a
> death . . . . There is not anyone who does not know it, even if only
> two or three people showed up for the banns.
>
> Dep. Raymundo Jozé da Cunha Mattos, June 27, 1827[1]

Throughout the nineteenth century, foreign travelers commented on the
domestic arrangements of Brazilians that departed from either legal marriage
or monogamy. In the late 1830s, the English traveler George Gardner referred
directly to the widespread existence of consensual unions that Brazilians
identified as "living in *mancebia.*" Depending on a couple's circumstances,
the latter ranged from customary to de facto to serial marriage, and inscribed
polygeny and either clerical or extra-marital concubinage. From his vantage
point of Crato, in the remote interior of the northeastern Province of Ceará,
Gardner pronounced that city's inhabitants comparatively "low" in morality,
observing during a five-month residence that gambling and knife fights defined the most important activities for individuals of all social classes. What
he described of family life in Crato may have represented an extreme situation, for he asserted that "scarcely any of the better class live with their
wives."[2] However, at least in Brazil's back-country districts, his observations
about intimate domestic arrangements that departed from legal matrimony
do not seem to have differed from those reported for Rio de Janeiro, Minas
Gerais, or Bahia.[3] Even in the large coastal cities, such arrangements thrived.
In the bustling port of São Luis de Maranhão, Dunshee de Abranches recalled that in his native city "among commercial people especially, almost all
the innkeepers and clerks possessed a second house." Although legitimate
families disparaged the offspring of the latter, as "counterfeit families," it was
not unusual, he noted, for the sons of those households to be the classmates
of their legitimate half-brothers.[4]

Gardner confirmed that at the elite level of Crato society both national and local politicians elaborated polygamously extended families. The husbands he described often relied on a separate "*casa chica*," a second home for maintaining a consensual partner in adulterine *mancebia*. He offered examples of men from "the better class" whose wives had been "turned out of the house to live separately," and replaced "by younger women who are willing to supply their place without being bound by the ties of matrimony." He cited the case of Crato's imperial judge—the prestigious *juíz de direito* who was a law school graduate—as well as "the local orphans' judge and most of the larger shopkeepers."[5]

Members of the secular clergy routinely enjoyed long-term domestic arrangements in *mancebia*, Gardner further elaborated. Crato's parish priest, then between seventy and eighty years old, had fathered six children. One of the padre's godsons, who had followed him in the priesthood, was appointed Ceará's provincial president in 1840. During Gardner's residence, this individual was serving as a senator-for-life, representing the neighboring province of Pernambuco. When Gardner observed him visiting his godfather's home in Crato, he was accompanied by "his mistress, who was his own cousin," and no less than eight of their ten children. The senator-priest, whom Gardner declined to name, was none other than the famous liberal politician, Jozé Martiniano de Alencar—father of the novelist José de Alencar. He also had five children from an earlier relationship of *mancebia* with another woman, who had died in childbirth.[6] Gardner mentioned no fewer than three other priests in Crato who similarly lived openly in clerical *mancebia* with their consensual partners and children, including one who cohabited with another man's wife.

BRAZILIAN VARIATIONS, IBERIAN PATTERNS

Consensual Cohabitation: Mancebia

The Englishman's graphic vignettes, like those of other foreign travelers, illuminated patterns of family life commonplace within imperial Brazil. They underscored that members of the political elite who lived in *de facto* bigamy, adultery, or clerical *mancebia* enjoyed widespread acceptance in the community, apart from any disrespect that critics implied their personal behavior reflected on the sacrament of holy matrimony. In the colloquial speech of the 1820s and 1830s, "*mancebia*" continued to cover a wide range of consensual relationships pertaining to cohabitation and sexual union that in the late colonial era had ranged from valid marriage to casual sexual encounters. The word retained great elasticity of application simply because consensual unions, like illegitimate births, were becoming more numerous after independence. Moreover, popular speech tended to be faithful to some eighteenth-century applications that imperial jurists had recently discarded. For good reason, "*mancebia*" continued to be widely preferred to "concubinage" in nineteenth-century colloquial speech.

Deriving from Roman law, "concubinage" did not really "catch on" in popular idiom, being reserved as a term of opprobrium or disparaging insult—usually uttered in terms of female agency. Clerics tellingly spoke of "*mancebia*" in the 1820s, for they employed a usage standardized by Brazil's late eighteenth-century equivalent of an ecclesiastical constitution, the *Constituições primeiras do arcebispado da Bahia*. Contrary to what some historians have asserted, "*mancebia*" remained a usage firmly embedded in ecclesiastical law, despite linguistic coexistence with "concubinage." Thus, rather than "clerical concubinage," priests and lay persons alike preferred to speak of "clerical *mancebia*." "*Mancebia*" originated in a Portuguese vernacular dating to the seventeenth century, while "*concubinato*" (concubinage) connoted an alien and erudite term appropriate to Roman law.

Bereft of the many customary variations that *mancebia* implied, "concubinage" tended to be associated in the public mind with punitive juridical norms. Hence, it gained greater currency in Brazilian speech after 1830, when a criminal code was adopted, one that, incidentally, declined to mention "*mancebia*." Notwithstanding the architectonic reliance of the *Ordenações Filipinas* on Roman law, Portugal's 1603 code perpetuated the use of "*mancebia*" because the range of meaning it conveyed in an early seventeenth-century context could not be reduced to "concubinage." "*Mancebia*" captured attitudes toward cohabitation, as much as a range of living arrangements, that survived into Brazil's early republic. For that matter, the English of this chapter favors "*mancebia*" over "concubinage" given that the Anglo-American usage would trample on subtleties of Luso-Brazilian meaning.

Anecdotal evidence on *mancebia* drawn from nineteenth-century travel accounts testified to the presence of what were merely Brazilian variations on Latin American patterns of family organization. Compared with Spanish America, however, the ubiquitousness in Brazil of both the *casa chica* and clerical *mancebia* was striking. *Mancebia* relationships testified to the relatively weaker position of Brazil's established church as an enforcer of both monogamy and clerical celibacy than in colonial Spanish America. Episcopal authority was weakly institutionalized in colonial Brazil; parish priests were accustomed to a large measure of autonomy. Even the sacraments might be administered in deviation from Tridentine norms, due to the failure of bishops to impose reforms that established both their own authority and administrative uniformity.[7] A shortage of parish priests outside the colony's major cities left an impressive proportion of Brazil's population unchurched, for dioceses were vast. For instance, until independence, the Diocese of Olinda stretched from coastal Pernambuco's episcopal seat to beyond the western bank of the São Francisco River, a distance of over a thousand kilometers.

An incompletely inculcated official morality, prescribed by the Council of Trent, reinforced the relative powerlessness of the higher clergy in Brazil to discipline their flocks in matters of sexual behavior. The orthodox respect the institutional church demanded for both the sacrament of marriage and the vow of celibacy might be dramatically communicated during a sporadic episcopal visit, only to be neglected thereafter. Although Minas Gerais appears to have led the colony in the number of episcopal visits, no less than 53 between 1721 and 1802, that gold-mining captaincy's experience appears to have been singular, corresponding to its unrivaled reputation as the province with the largest number of priests living in *mancebia*.[8] Great deficiencies of religious education extended to clergymen, whose individual ignorance over matters of theology and doctrine reinforced a widespread toleration of domestic arrangements that deviated markedly from the orthodox canons. Finally, beliefs that drew as much on Luso-Brazilian popular values as on folk Catholicism, or Afro-Brazilian religions, accounted for the impressive disparity in attitudes about sexual morality held by the official church, on the one hand, and its millions of communicants on the other.

The oft-cited eclecticism and wide ambiguity of religious belief evidenced in Brazil's popular Catholicism explained only to a point the disparity of moral values distinguishing prelate from parishioner. As Donald Ramos has argued, what amounted to a "popular voice"—*a voz popular*—both shaped and expressed values defining popular opinion at the community level. A popular voice articulated community standards that inscribed a sexual morality often divergent from the official canons.[9] The imprint of a popular voice long had been evident in law, as the force of custom. What the church defined as the sin of "*mancebia*"—concubinage—public opinion often refused to condemn, and tolerated, even approved. After all, the *Constituições Primeiras* minimally construed "*mancebia*" as "an illicit conversation between a man and woman lasting a considerable time."[10] The official church not only was obliged to tolerate the values embedded in a *voz popular* but it also took them into account when it enforced, or failed to enforce, doctrine and discipline sanctioned by the Council of Trent.

For that matter, the Brazilian church's early eighteenth-century constitution directly incorporated community standards associated with a popular voice. The most important standard it proclaimed pertained to notions about the public nature of sinful behavior. That is, the creation of considerable public scandal, widely diffused in the community, mattered more than the sinful behavior responsible for scandal. The public forum mattered enormously for the discretionary enforcement prescribed by the *Constituições Primeiras*. Usually, scandal implied the loss of public reputation (*fama*) for offender and/or victim. In prescribing which kinds of individual behavior would receive ecclesiastical censure and punishment, or those deliberately ignored, Brazil's only episcopal synod took into account a majoritarian public opinion projected by a popular voice.[11]

Clerical *mancebia* in the eighteenth century did not normally imply cohabitation, although a priest might be encountered living openly in the company of a daughter. Limited evidence suggests that by the final decades of colonial rule a significant minority of lay couples lived "behind closed doors"—cohabiting in popular parlance. But priests found it much harder to cohabit.[12] By the independence era, religious authority had become more relaxed. The imperfect episcopal vigilance that in colonial times usually kept the sexual behavior of clerics discreet, if not virtually concealed, no longer restricted them largely to brief and erratic encounters.[13] By the 1820s, the shift from clandestine to open clerical concubinage was patently manifest, defining an upward trend that would attain its zenith by the advent of a republic in 1889.

Clerical Mancebia

Historians have not adequately explained the factors accounting for the well-pronounced phenomenon of open clerical *mancebia* that emerged during Brazil's early imperial decades. It must have received initial encouragement from the Pombaline suppression of the Inquisition, long before either the Napoleonic occupation abolished the Holy Office or the Lisbon Cortes definitively extinguished it in 1821.[14] Gradually, both prisons and judges of the Inquisition ceased to be available for what had always been sporadic visits to root out immoral behavior in a given city or town. When the Portuguese Court arrived in Brazil, in 1808, the Inquisition's days were numbered. Formerly, prosecution of concubinage had, to a certain extent, relied on the terror of the Holy Office for persuading Christians of good conscience to "denounce" sin in their communities; however, the visit of a bishop or his provisor served the same purpose.[15] It is difficult to judge the coercive power of such inquiries, even their frequency, for mostly scattered reports have survived. Denunciations of sin, however, were not always readily forthcoming.[16] The disappearance of the coercive power of the Inquisition, on the other hand, made it harder to persuade parishioners to testify against their own priests.

After the arrival of the Portuguese Court, regalism better explained why priests and lay persons alike escaped or defied the tough censure of public exposure imposed by a visiting episcopal inquiry on sinful conduct. Although clerics charged with concubinage fell under the exclusive jurisdiction of an episcopal court, the colonial church had relied on the cooperation and support of secular authorities for prosecuting the laity. As in Bourbon Spanish America, the impact of Pombaline regalism secularized political authority to the point where the crown no longer reinforced or carried out the determinations of ecclesiastical tribunals.[17] Those who sinned in matters of heterosexual morality, especially priests, were not likely to be disciplined by the crown, unless their sins extended to committing a serious crime or generating widely diffused scandal. Besides, as Ronaldo Vainfas has noted, the "great concern" paid to clerical concubinage by the Council of Trent did not receive similar emphasis in Bahia's *Constituições Primeiras*. Even so, members of the clergy who were discovered and charged with concubinage could count on being tried by a diocesan tribunal in closed proceedings; punishment for first and second offenses was comparatively light.[18]

In the eyes of the church, investigation conducted in private, or non-prosecution, was juridically justifiable for priests. The reason was not only the higher moral standing of a priest over a lay person but also the prudence counseled by a "popular voice" endorsing avoidance of public scandal. Evidence suggests that penalties meted out to clerics fell short of what either the Council of Trent or the *Constituições Primeiras* prescribed. In contrast to clerics, their lay paramours—often slaves or freed slaves—were judged in the community and required to confess and repent publicly. The punishment of concubines, administered by the temporal arm, almost always was harsher than what a clerical partner received, not to mention the concubines of laymen.[19] Notwithstanding the misogyny that colored ecclesiastically prescribed punishments, the lack of good reputation—*fama*—on the part of many prosecuted concubines, intrinsic in women of color, predisposed them to be judged by a different yardstick. Their priestly consorts, by definition, possessed *fama*, explaining why a priest's public reputation as an upstanding individual deserved to be shielded in private judicial proceedings conducted by a bishop. By the same token, a respectable married woman "who maintained her good reputation," while sexually involved with a priest, was equally entitled to judgment by the bishop behind closed doors.[20]

Fundamentally, Iberian roots explained the toleration shown to clerical concubinage in Brazil, although by the 1820s the tacit recognition that many men were obliged by their parents to pursue clerical careers, against personal inclinations, created additional sympathy. The intrinsic strength of family ties, especially their utility for forging the partisan networks that sustained priests who pursued political careers, also deserves important credit for why this salient feature of Brazilian family organization persisted so openly in both Empire and First Republic. By the independence era, Brazilian clerics who transgressed their vows had less to fear from either episcopal or crown punishment than in colonial times. Parish priests counted on even greater community support for *mancebia* relationships when they demonstrated willingness to discharge paternal responsibility.

Lay Mancebia

The same historical factors that eroded episcopal authority, an under-staffed and poorly educated clergy, dioceses of immense territory, and as-cendant regalism, explained the impressive toleration granted to the other feature of family organization that amazed George Gardner: the polygenous nature of lay domestic arrangements. Whether they pertained to the mainte-nance of a separate "*casa chica*" by husbands belonging to the "respectable classes," or to open cohabitation by legally separated individuals, the grow-ing trend of extra-marital *mancebia* was explained by the same factors that encouraged clerical concubinage to flourish. Of course, *mancebia* grew even more rapidly as an illicit relationship, that is, between unmarried partners for whom no dire impediments applied—what in positive law was deemed "un-qualified concubinage." As Francisco Londoño has argued, the church failed to formulate a "pastoral policy on marriage" that would have viewed the sac-rament of matrimony as "an instrument for affirming ecclesiastical power throughout the population." By declining to facilitate access to the sacra-ment of matrimony, through simplified procedures and lower fees, the church insured that *mancebia* would thrive.[21]

Juridically, the central point about both lay and clerical *mancebia* was the high degree of toleration that law paid to them. Ecclesiastical law supported those arrangements in most cases, including when they were defined as the "qualified" concubinage of adultery.[22] Where the partners were not clerics, the *Constituições Primeiras* defined a restricted yardstick of prosecution that echoed a popular voice. They singled out only "*mancebia* with infamy, scan-dal, and persistence of the sin" as worthy of ecclesiastical investigation. De-nunciations of concubinage against married individuals, in other words, should be investigated only where public scandal resulted in loss of personal reputation (*fama*) and, additionally, the partners persisted in the liaison.[23] Eighteenth-century inquisitors, however, did not always follow the injunc-tions of the *Constituições Primeiras*. Concubinage between master and slave defined a case in point, for the *Constituições Primeiras* obliquely acknowl-

edged that the slaveowner's dominion extended to sexual relations with female slaves. Evidence for prosecution on this important point, however, is
contradictory, because slave women were harshly treated as concubines in
many visiting inquisitions.[24]

Late eighteenth-century episcopal inquisitions into *mancebia* were obliged
to stress the public scandal that accompanied the relationships of concubinage they prosecuted for a different reason. The *alvará* of September 26,
1769, as the preceding volume elaborated, significantly reinterpreted the
standard for prosecuting *mancebia*. That law, following the Law of Right Reason by one month, implied that the church should exercise caution in prosecuting *mancebia*. In fact, by pronouncing concubinage both a crime in positive law and a sin against moral law, late colonial episcopal investigations
overstepped the boundaries imposed by the 1769 *alvará*. Therefore, when
they prosecuted *mancebia* relationships that were merely illicit, or unions of
unqualified concubinage, ecclesiastical authorities exceeded their mandate in
positive law.

As we have already seen, Pombaline legal tradition went much further
than the church when it explicitly validated most concubinage arrangements
by protecting them from criminal prosecution. The *alvará* of 1769 imposed
no criminal penalties on unqualified concubinage, between unmarried lay
persons who, as potentially marriageable, transgressed no dire impediments.
Borges Carneiro reiterated that conclusion for readers in the mid-1820s:
"Among us, though considered contrary to Christian purity and good customs, none of the three codes [the *Ordenações Afonsinas, Manuelinas*, and
Filipinas] imposes punishment on simple [unqualified] concubinage."[25] The
1769 law surpassed the protection the Philippine Code offered to illicit relationships, because the law's main purpose was to spare respectable families
public scandal. Legal accusation and criminal investigation, as its text
pointed out, brought daughters and wives into the courtroom as "innocent
parties." Consequently, even when *mancebia* was qualified as adultery, the
same law narrowly circumscribed criminal prosecution, confining it to cases
where the offender's spouse brought such a specific complaint. Of course,
zealous crown officials, as well as bishops, did not always respect the law's
limitations, but even their excessive zeal accounted for the stress they placed
on accusations of public scandal.[26]

The adoption of a criminal code for the Empire, in 1830, complemented
and perpetuated the Pombaline juridical protection of *mancebia* that was
adulterous. The cardinal principle of the Law of Right Reason, that positive
"law would punish crime, not sin," could be said to have been definitively
applied to adultery only when the Criminal Code of 1830 was promulgated.

The latter suppressed or severely modified a great many of the punitive provisions contained in Book 5 of the *Constituições Primeiras*, including the ecclesiastical crime of concubinage. Moreover, adoption of a criminal code freed adultery from all penalties formerly prescribed by ecclesiastical law.[27] Ostensibly liberal, the Criminal Code of 1830 fundamentally perpetuated distinctions of gender hallowed by the *Ordenações Filipinas*, classifying crimes according to categories that respected decidedly unmodern and illiberal distinctions, such as rank, honor, and public reputation. In reality, the Code conveyed a great deal of the post-1750 crown legislation that already had modified the *Ordenações Filipinas* during the era of Pombal, wherever family law raised implications for criminal law.[28] As Jurandir Malerba has observed, the Empire's Criminal Code, which preceded those of the newly independent Spanish American republics, remained "anchored in the preceding foundation of agro-export latifundia and slave labor." Notwithstanding that it "pushed aside the Gothic rust of the *Ordenações Filipinas*," by opening a new era where criminal penalties rejected torture and sadistic cruelty, at least for Brazilians who were not slaves, the Code's *raison d'être* remained frankly patriarchal and hierarchical.[29]

Although the Criminal Code of 1830 dropped explicit reference to the motive of avoiding notorious and public scandal, it nevertheless paid silent homage to that principle by making criminal prosecution for adultery highly unlikely. The Code validated behavior long sanctioned by custom, as if to confirm that Brazil's political elite would continue to endorse the consensual unions that underlay the high proportion of illegitimate births. In fact, the new code enhanced the Pombaline shibboleth of family decorum, based on an older respect for "good customs," by placing adultery under the intriguing and seemingly illogical category of "private crimes" listed in Part 3. "Private crimes" made perfect sense, not in terms of liberalism or even the preceding Philippine Code, where they historically had been embedded, but by virtue of the community standards manifest in a popular voice attuned to the public morality of the church. Private crimes were rooted in the important distinction between private and public sins. The former were deemed sinful regardless of whether they were known by others, while the latter were "those acts which are important only if and when they are known."[30] In the context of the Criminal Code of 1830, this distinction implied that private crimes were susceptible to volitional concealment. That is, they became crimes only when they ceased to be private and became publicly revealed.

Consequently, Part 3 of the 1830 Criminal Code paid attention to adultery under a chapter encompassing "crimes against civil and domestic security." The chapter narrowly circumscribed offenses committed against the institution of legal matrimony, such as polygamy or a wife's fraudulent representation of her husband's paternity of an offspring. Interestingly, adultery was not subsumed in the preceding chapter addressing crimes against personal honor—those of rape, abduction, and slander. Rather, the Criminal Code intoned, adultery was a crime against society whose foundation, the "good family," "reposed in the unity of marriage."[31] Under Article 250, a wife's adultery failed to be juridically defined, testifying to the legal privileging of husbands, who exercised the courtroom option of exposing as public a wife's private crime of infidelity. Rules of evidence meant that a wife's adultery would be patent in court, even when proof was merely presumptive. On the other hand, the Criminal Code stipulated that a married man could commit adultery only in one narrowly circumscribed respect: When he maintained a concubine in his own or a separate residence, that is, following the principle of "*teúda e manteúda*" derived from the *Ordenações*. Thus Article 251, by narrowly circumscribing a husband's adultery, simultaneously crystallized a definition of concubinage that would endure into the late twentieth century.[32]

That the Criminal Code of 1830 generously continued to protect private sexual behavior that extended to a range of public relationships encompassing *mancebia*, whether adulterous or not, validated public toleration of consensual unions as much as it sanctioned a husband's juridical entitlement to a double standard for adultery. Article 252 of the Code directly discouraged criminal indictments for adultery by reiterating another Pombaline rule: Only the offended spouse could authorize a criminal investigation, by bringing the charge of adultery. The Code further militated against prosecution of adultery by providing that, "if at any time" the accusing spouse "had consented to adultery"—implying merely discreet silence—then the right to accuse was automatically forfeit. Finally, a husband had to accuse both his wife and "the adulterer," complicating and frequently compromising his personal situation to the point where no charge would be brought.

REAFFIRMING TRIDENTINE MARRIAGE

Holy Matrimony and Liberal Reform

Liberal reformers who sought to modify the inheritance system inevitably addressed the rules of marriage. They therefore embarked on a strategy that led to direct confrontation with the established church over both the legal definition of marriage and the canonical procedures for declaring individuals in the "free state to marry." The latter signified that a couple was equipped under canon law to be married by a Catholic priest. Entries in nineteenth-century marriage registers affirmed those procedures had been satisfied whenever they routinely described couples as married "in the form of the Holy Council of Trent." As we have seen, procedures adopted at Trent became part of received law in Portugal during the 1550s and 1560s. Reform of matrimonial law, or merely authority to oversee its application, offered liberal lawmakers opportunity to assert their constitutional power. In proposing legislation addressing marriage, they were nonetheless prompted by regalist motives. Liberals appreciated that an established church made the Brazilian government vulnerable to ultramontane intervention. Among even moderate liberals, xenophobia became normative, given the humiliating settlement they were obliged to strike with Portugal in 1825, over the terms of independence. However, the fear of "foreign intervention" in Brazilian affairs, articulated in the 1827 legislative session, found its nemesis in Rome rather than in Lisbon.

First, antipathy toward Rome accounted for why liberal legislators zealously asserted their constitutional mandate to administer the secular clergy. Many resented the Vatican's proposal to create, in 1827, bishoprics for Goiás and Mato Grosso. Those dioceses, they charged, implied the pope exercised authority over the government and compromised national sovereignty. "Is Brazil a fief of the Roman Curia? Or the Order of Christ?" asked a member of the lower house.[33] Consequently, the legislature delayed approval of the bishoprics for twelve years. Liberals vociferously proclaimed their authority to discharge the responsibilities of the *Padroado Régio*, the royal patronage over the church that formerly had been the exclusive prerogative of the crown. Extremists argued the Constitution gave the national legislature exclusive responsibility for nominating bishops and bestowing the imperial *placet*, making the emperor's role merely confirmatory.

Second, more narrowly, a core of liberal legislators who were secularizers believed that canon law should not determine the rules of marriage in the new nation. They viewed as anachronistic the assumption that only the church should determine who might marry, as well as the legal validity of a marriage, an annulment, or a legal separation known as a "divorce." The state held a severely limited juridical responsibility for marriage, pertaining only to its civil, or contractual, effects, such as the disposition of marital property following death or legal separation, the transfer of property as dowry or gifts *intervivos*, and the administration of an orphaned legal minor's property. Conflicts pertaining to *poder marital*, a husband's legal authority over his wife, and to *pátrio poder*, the parental authority ordinarily vested in the paterfamilias, similarly fell under the jurisdiction of the imperial courts.

The fact that a Pombaline tradition of regalism had affirmed the church's authority over purely spiritual matters placed Brazil's reformist legislators in an uncomfortable, if not untenable, position wherever they sought to introduce change vis-à-vis matrimonial law.[34] Marriage defined a sacrament as well as a contract, accounting for why the institutional power of the church was committed to defending the definition of holy matrimony elaborated by the Council of Trent. As a spiritual matter, marriage nevertheless commanded the protection of the state, given that the Constitution committed the imperial government to protect the church. Yet the church had pronounced the Tridentine canons defining rules of marriage as accepted doctrine, making them, practically speaking, immutable. In an era when notions of papal supremacy were promoted by Rome, and conciliar authority relegated to a secondary plane, the canons on marriage stood as politically unassailable. Any changes proposed to accommodate them to Brazilian national positive law would be deemed non-negotiable by the church. Short of disestablishment, or, alternatively, of establishing a Gallican church that rejected outright the spiritual authority of pope and Curia, little room was left for Brazilian liberals to recast the rules of marriage in positive national law.

Canonical Procedures as Positive Law

On June 26, 1827, Brazilian legislators formally addressed marriage for the first time, in terms of a resolution that had been introduced on the floor of the Chamber of Deputies on June 18.[35] The resolution succinctly decreed that "the disposition of the Council of Trent, Session 24, Chapter 1, of *De Reformatione Matrimonii*, and the Constitution of the Archbishopric of Bahia, Book 1, Title 68, Section 291, would be observed in all of the bishoprics and parishes of the Empire."[36] Drawing the remainder of its text from the above-cited Section 291 of the *Constituições primeiras do Arcebispado da Bahia*, adopted in 1707, the resolution prescribed that "parish priests would proceed to receive before the altar [*na face da igreja*] in marriage" couples from the same bishopric, if either one of them belonged to the parish, "after the canonical banns had been read and no impediment was [discovered], the permission of the bishops or their delegates being unnecessary."[37] As a resolution, this proposal represented a clarification of existing law rather than new law. It was authored by the Chamber's Ecclesiastical Committee, whose chair, Jozé Clemente Pereira, was a lawyer, a moderate liberal leader, and soon to be the acknowledged leader in the Chamber. The rest of the committee consisted of four priests: D. Marcos Antonio de Souza, bishop-elect of Maranhão—who signed the proposal with reservations—Antonio da Rocha Franco, Diogo Antonio Feijó, and Miguel Jozé Reinaut.[38]

Strictly speaking, a resolution affirming the validity in Brazilian positive law of one of the Tridentine articles on marriage was unnecessary. The Constitution of 1824 specified that what had been promulgated as Portuguese positive law automatically became Brazilian law by devolution, except where specifically repudiated. Thus the Tridentine canons on marriage, promulgated by the Portuguese crown in 1564 and 1565, became part of Brazilian law at independence. In establishing the Apostolic Catholic Church, by declaring it "protected," Brazil's Constitution further implied that legal marriage would derive solely from the Roman Catholic sacrament of holy matrimony. Additionally, Book Four of the *Ordenações Filipinas*, which imposed rules of marriage adopted at Trent, was also received law in Brazil. Finally, the episcopal synod convened in Bahia in 1707 confirmed in its *Constituições Primeiras* that the content of *De Reformatione Matrimonii* was received in ecclesiastical law as a conciliar determination of that archbishopric. Toward the end of the eighteenth century, a majority of Brazil's dioceses had adopted the *Constituições Primeiras*, signifying that the Articles of Trent had been explicitly received by the Brazilian church as ecclesiastical law. In fact, the fundamental task of the *Constituições Primeiras*, which served as a primer for parish priests by the 1820s, had been to disseminate the Tridentine canons in terms of uniform ecclesiastical practices through the colony. One might well ask, consequently, why Brazilian legislators should want to reaffirm those canons in 1827.

Taking Control: The Padroado Régio

The answer lay in the opportunity that Tridentine marriage afforded legislators for demonstrating to the secular clergy that they, rather than either bishops or the emperor, were in charge of the institutional church. Liberal legislators, including a significant number of priests, together with an impressive number of their ultra-monarchist colleagues, found fault with Brazil's bishops. They charged that those prelates had failed to follow the uniform procedures in Chapter 1 of *De Reformatione Matrimonii*. The latter spelled out the steps for declaring an engaged couple in the free state to marry. The phrasing of the resolution contained its *raison d'être*, for it drew directly on the text of the *Constituições Primeiras* in order to restore to parish priests what certain bishops had arrogated unto themselves.

The Ecclesiastical Committee of the Chamber of Deputies sought, therefore, to impose as uniform law throughout Brazil the Tridentine procedures adopted by the archdiocese of Bahia that had gradually been accepted in other dioceses over the course of the eighteenth century. Its report charged that "in many parts of Brazil," couples "were obliged to obtain the authorization of ecclesiastical councils or so-called matrimonial judges, one and the

same, without which they could not marry." Because of "this manifest in-
fraction of ecclesiastical laws," it noted, "the legal equipping [of couples] has
no other ostensible end but the enlargement of the fees for those who demand them." In fact, unlike *De Reformatione Matrimonii*, the *Constituições
Primeiras* stipulated that neither the bishop's permission nor that of his provisor was required for the parish priest to marry a couple whenever there was
an absence of impediments. In singling out "the protection owed religion by
the temporal power," the report cited protection "from abuses introduced
into [religious] discipline." Legislative oversight of the church therefore was
necessary in order to insure that the "discipline" imposed by the canons on
marriage would be "one and the same throughout the Empire."[39]

Reaffirmation of the key provisions in Tridentine marriage may have
sounded a strange note in 1827; however, the motive behind the resolution
proved more ambitious than merely promoting procedural uniformity
throughout Brazil's dioceses. As the first foray made by national lawmakers
into the dense thicket of Tridentine rules on marriage—what they discussed
in parliamentary parlance as "*De Reformatione Matrimonii*"—the 1827 legislative deliberations on canonical procedures reflected the genuine goal of
making marriage accessible to larger numbers of Brazilians. Greater insight
into the debate's significance can be gained by appreciating that 1827 marked
the first time that Brazil's national legislature exercised its constitutional
authority over the *Padroado Régio*. Tridentine marriage therefore provided
an ideal issue for asserting the ascendance of the temporal over the spiritual
power. Although legislators justified the resolution by arguing they wanted
to remove obstacles to marriage for the Empire's citizenry, in reality, they
found in canonical procedures a powerful weapon for criticizing Brazil's
higher clergy. In sum, considerations of regalism overshadowed the genuine
effort to promote legitimate marriage.

Militant liberals used the issues surrounding their endorsement of Tridentine marriage as part of a decimating anti-clerical attack. Otherwise, more
moderate liberals, and even ultra-monarchists, found legitimate fault with
Brazil's bishops, who, it was charged, had usurped authority vested in parish
priests by the *Constituições Primeiras*. Because the bishops enjoyed considerable independence within their respective dioceses, couples seeking to marry,
even when impediments were absent, sometimes found themselves forced to
undergo an onerous and expensive set of investigative steps before they
could be declared in the free state to marry. In certain dioceses—those of Rio
de Janeiro, São Paulo, and Mariana (Minas Gerais) were specifically cited—
the parish priest could not on his own authority marry couples even after the
banns had been read and no impediments discovered. Instead, bishops in-

volved themselves routinely in all determinations pertaining to the free state to marry simply for financial gain. Neither *De Reformatione Matrimonii* nor the *Constituições Primeiras* sanctioned the procedural authority they exercised. In some dioceses, bishops appointed subordinate clerics to conduct investigations to determine if a couple was in the free state to marry, depriving the parish priest altogether of this responsibility.[40]

The Anti-Clerical Promotion of Marriage

Debate extended to issues beyond that of censuring bishops for appropriating the parish priest's authority to declare couples in the free state to marry. By turning to the fees bishops levied for dispensing impediments, a function they canonically enjoyed, liberals in the lower house widened their attack. Under *Magnam profecto Curam*, the bull issued by Pope Pius VI, on January 26, 1790, the papacy had conceded to Brazil's bishops "full power to dispense gratuitously in all degrees of kinship," except in the first lineal and collateral consanguineous degrees. That is, only marriages between grandparent or parent and child, or between siblings, could not be dispensed. Similarly, the first lineal degrees between affines, or in-laws, were excluded. The Vatican's decision to delegate authority directly to the bishops, as the preceding volume explained, could be traced to Pombal's diplomatic triumphs. However, the Curia was also prompted by a huge backlog of petitions from Brazilians seeking to marry within prohibitions of either consanguinity or affinity.[41] Petitions forwarded to Rome entailed years of delay, a circumstance that disposed many couples to opt to live in *mancebia*, within consensual unions that often defined a permanent alternative to legal marriage.

Despite the bull's explicit language—"*gratis dispensare*"—bishops quickly converted their newly acquired authority to dispense the impediments to marriage into a lucrative source of diocesan income. What Rome had intended as a grant of power for the aggressive promotion of sacramental marriage in Brazil—wider episcopal authority to dispense prohibitions of consanguinity and affinity—most bishops quickly transformed into onerous requirements. They obliged couples to pay substantial clerical fees and to expend additional resources in travel to the diocesan seat for a dispensation. In fact, this criticism was hardly new. As Dep. Nicolao Vergueiro pointed out, it dated to the 1790s, when Portugal's Overseas Council had responded to a complaint by São Paulo's municipal council in 1795. As a result, São Paulo's bishop had been ordered to observe the procedures of the Council of Trent, a directive he nevertheless managed to evade.[42]

Although liberal deputies proved the most strident critics of the church's failure to facilitate marriage, the resolution commanded "bipartisan" support. Its backers ranged from ultra-monarchists, like the marquises of Inhambupe (Antonio Luis Pereira da Cunha) and Queluz (João Severiano Maciel da Costa), to the liberal priest Diogo Antonio Feijó, who, as a moderate, espoused genuinely radical social ideas. What many legislators viewed as an episcopal abuse of power dating to the colonial era led some of them to confront those of their colleagues who were prelates. Turning to the bishop-elect of Maranhão, Lino Coutinho expressed indignation: "Why all this vigilance?" Were not the banns intended precisely to discover if some impediment existed between the couple contracting marriage? Parodying the Tridentine formula read by the priest to the congregation, he asked, if "the citizen" was not obliged by the banns, "under penalty of excommunication," to denounce a prohibition on marriage. Souza França and others questioned the utility of the local priest's genealogical investigation and the banns themselves, arguing it was preferable to let some individuals marry, even if they committed bigamy. Those situations could be sorted out afterward, he concluded.[43]

Several deputies concurred on the uselessness of the procedural steps required to declare couples in the free state to marry. Dep. Antonio da Rocha Franco, a member of the Ecclesiastical Committee who identified himself as former vicar of the mining center of Vila Rica, testified that his own genealogical investigations had been habitually reduced to merely eliciting oral testimony from a couple, prior to reading the banns aloud. Where prospective bridegrooms were not native to Brazil, and bigamy posed a possibility, he insisted, witnesses swearing to bachelorhood were never lacking. Dep. Lucio Soares Teixeira de Gouvêa doubted bigamy was a problem in Brazil. He attributed its rarity not to episcopal investigations, but the criminal penalty imposed by positive law. Seconding him on the uselessness of canonical investigations, Dep. Candido de Deus e Silva read Section 11 of the 1769 Law of Right Reason, in support of the precept that all laws that are useless are also noxious and therefore ought to be abolished.[44]

The partisan satisfaction that liberals derived from denouncing the Empire's bishops for usurping a power that De Reformatione Matrimonii clearly delegated to the parish priest amounted to only one dimension of debate. Alternatively, legislators contributed valuable insight into how ordinary Brazilians got married—and why many of them did not.[45] Unlike most foreign travelers, Brazilian lawmakers were intimately acquainted with how the established church declared individuals in the free state to marry. Debate elicited anecdotal examples revealing how canonical procedures, by serving to generate clerical income, deprived many ordinary Brazilians—and some not so ordinary—of the opportunity to marry. Even the very conservative bishop-elect of Maranhão, who signed the resolution with reservations, voiced the opinion that "the poor should not pay anything; only the rich ought to be subject to the expense of procedures equipping them [to marry]."[46]

Outrage over clerical fees subsumed the issue of forfeited parochial power as the debate's central focus. Teixeira de Gouvêa's estimate went uncontradicted, that in many places the fees levied by bishops for dispensing impediments amounted to more than 300 *mil-réis*, exclusive of the considerable expense of traveling to the bishop's palace, a distance that might be 60 leagues—as much as 360 miles.[47] The cost of clerical fees triggered an angry exchange over how the government meted out the stipends paid to parish priests. After independence, the tithe no longer provided substantial revenue for the church. It was still paid directly to the central treasury and the government then paid all clerical stipends for the secular clergy; however, the latter was more modestly remunerated than in colonial times.

Mon. José de Souza Azevedo Pizarro e Araujo, one of the few defenders of the clergy in the debate over *De Reformatione Matrimonii*, revealed the complexity of this issue when he protested "the extortion of the bishops" by the government. In his view, clerical fees deserved to be addressed because they were rooted in the modesty of a bishop's annual government stipend, which amounted to merely one *conto*. By comparison, it can be noted that the bill to establish a national judiciary, also before the lower house, provided annual salaries for justices of the future supreme court amounting to four *contos*. Mon. Pizarro specifically objected to the "stinginess" of a bishop's stipend, claiming the bishop was obliged by his office to spend 120 *mil-réis* of the one *conto* on official expenses and another 80 *mil-réis* for alms, in effect netting a mere 800 *mil-réis* for personal subsistence. He also hinted at the higher clergy's nobility of birth, exclusive of any title-holding status, when he complained that the stipend did not take into account a bishop's many expenses, including those for "maintaining the splendor of his family's dignity" and "the necessities of his flock."[48]

Deputies did not confine their remonstrances to the most expensive layer of fees, those pertaining to episcopal dispensations, but singled out the parish priest for analogous criticism. They echoed a common refrain in Spanish America during the post-independence era. Clerical fees—the notorious *arancel*—defined a common bone of contention between priest and parishioner, one that worked its way into liberal attacks on the corporate status of the church throughout Latin America.[49] Reference to the specific amounts paid in fees for matrimonial procedures, offered in debate, appeared to understate the situation. Evidence from four São Paulo parishes in the middle of the eighteenth century revealed that fees might vary from 700 to 1500 *mil-réis*, reaching nearly two *contos* in extraordinary situations. In calling attention to what was taken as a "customary" fee for the sacrament of matrimony, Dep. Teixeira de Gouvêa laid bare the reason that marriage remained largely confined to propertied groups: "The origin of this custom lies in the necessity to provide a decent living for the parish priest." He objected, consequently, "to the price weighing heavily on the people," primarily in country districts, "where frequently can be found couples contracting marriage who never in their lives would jointly possess the quantity [of money] demanded for a marriage."[50]

Souza França protested the fees more bluntly, noting that many among the poor lacked "what it takes to buy a shirt." When they want to marry, he objected, "they have to search for money to borrow in order to pay for an investigation, an odious provision." The fees paid for the basic investigation, moreover, merely "vest in the parish priest a power he already possesses—to receive the contracting parties in marriage before the church."[51]

Although no legislator connected the priest's power over matrimony to his position in local politics, the French botanist, Auguste de Saint-Hilaire, came to precisely this conclusion during his travels through Minas Gerais in 1822. Delayed in arranging a burial, due to the need to pay the relevant clerical fees and obtain signatures from a priest and his superior, Saint-Hilaire described in detail why the parish priest, then known as "the priest of the *vara*," a judicial district, was adept at translating sacramental authority into secular authority. He singled out precisely permission to marry as the cornerstone of the quasi-judicial authority the parish priest wielded, even construing the latter as "the matrimonial judge." Noting that "no marriage can be contracted without his authorization," Saint-Hilaire termed the proceedings that pronounced an engaged couple in the free state to marry "a bizarre action requiring payment of from 10 to 12 *mil-réis*." If only "the shadow of an impediment exists, then the expense rises to 30, 40, 50 *mil-réis*," he continued. Yet another 1$200 would be needed for the banns, a small fortune.[52]

Like other informed observers, Saint-Hilaire connected the system of clerical fees to the widespread incidence of *mancebia*:

Thus, in a country where there is so much repugnance toward legitimate unions, and where it should be so essential for the State and public morality to encourage them, the indigent are, so to speak, impelled, for lack of resources, to live in an irregular manner. I heard a priest lament bitterly that the respectable and generous bishop of Rio de Janeiro, during his distressing pastoral visits, had to marry, or give the order to marry, persons who could not pay the customary costs.[53]

Law Triumphs over Custom: Mancebia Yields to Marriage

A broad ideological spectrum of legislators defined an important consensus over the need to restore the authority of the parish priest in matrimonial determinations. Much as they would adopt a decentralized judiciary the following year, liberal legislators sought to assert the local authority of the parish priest vis-à-vis central episcopal authority. The resolution on *De Reformatione* faced little vocal opposition, except from the ultra-conservative bishop-elect of Maranhão, who steadfastly upheld the power of each bishop to make rules in his own diocese. After adoption in the lower house, on June 30, the resolution on *De Reformatione Matrimonii* was forwarded to the Senate on July 2, where it passed on August 18. Adopted by a joint session of the legislature, on October 11, the emperor's sanction was bestowed on November 13, 1827. Senate deliberation over the resolution proved minimal, although the viscount of Congonhas do Campo's (Lucas Antonio Monteiro de Barros) impassioned speech urging adoption demonstrated a conservative counterpoint to the liberal rhetoric in the Chamber. Pronouncing the measure "for the general utility and well being of the people," he dissected, diocese by diocese, the compliance or non-compliance of Brazil's seven bishops to the rules laid down in Session 24, Chapter 1, of Trent. The obstacles that "certain bishops" created to marriage in the church, he charged, produced concubinage and illegitimate children, which thanks to a lack of general education, produced social ills.

The resolution's final version was amended in the Senate prior to adoption, at the suggestion of the marquis of Inhambupe. He recommended a provision that, wherever couples lacked impediments, there should be no fee charged for the canonical procedures equipping them in the free state to marry. His amendment set the precedent for Brazil's 1890 Civil Marriage Act and all subsequent legislation, that stipulated the cost of marriage should always be gratis.[54]

By implying the authority of the Council of Trent was being flouted, and the *Constituições Primeiras* had not been implemented, legislators seized the opportunity to promote and firmly define legal marriage. In doing so, explicitly and implicitly, they condemned *mancebia*, bearing witness to the important historical shift that had taken place in the term's definition by independence. When Dep. Souza França decried the "illicit relationships that ordinarily are scorned"—due to lack of marriage—and insisted that "marriages have to multiply for the greater satisfaction" in which families live, he was confirming how, in the eyes of most legislators and jurists, *mancebia* amounted to no more than concubinage. Lino Coutinho struck a comple-

mentary note when he lamented, "Amongst us, marriages are few," and ex-
horted his colleagues to "do everything in their power to remove the obstacles that are barriers to marriage." A bachelor, he was the father of an eight-
year-old natural daughter. Rather than ranting about *mancebia*, Lino
Coutinho singled out "celibacy"—the stock cliché that anti-clericals opposed
to sacramental marriage. He invoked the canard that young men were forced
into the priesthood or holy orders as a result of an oppressive system of canonical impediments that frequently foreclosed the option of marriage.[55]

Other imperial deputies similarly underscored the growing importance of
marriage, defined exclusively as the sacrament of holy matrimony, to the
detriment of two, closely associated variants validated by the Philippine
Code as marriage in positive law. Each had continued to be juridically recognized in eighteenth-century Portugal, as "marriage according to the *Ordenações*," notwithstanding the Council of Trent. Contrary to their earlier legal
effect, either as customary or de facto marriage, these variants no longer possessed validity, although technically they remained "on the books" until 1830.
The *Ordenações Filipinas* most explicitly validated non-sacramental marriage
in Book 5, devoted to criminal law. Title 26 explicitly referred, for instance,
to adultery committed with a married woman who had not been married in
the church, when it punished "those who sleep with a woman married de
facto [*de feito*], and not de jure [*de direito*], or a woman who enjoys the
reputation of being married [*em fama de casada*]. . . ." The reason Book 5,
Title 26, separated *de facto* from *de jure* marriage was not to criminalize the
former, but to underscore that committing adultery was the same crime,
whether the woman's marriage was de facto or sacramental.

Similarly, Title 26 ruled de facto marriage invalid wherever it was contracted in the knowledge of the dire impediment of close kinship between
the couple, either by blood or ritual. It pronounced the concealment criminal, because either the man, or both partners, knowingly resorted to de facto
marriage from the motive of evading a canonical prohibition (Paragraph 1).[56]
As we have seen, concealment also caused couples to resort to the ruse of
clandestine marriage, condemned in national law in the seventeenth century.
Although Pombaline legal reform rendered criminal penalties for adultery
largely inoperable, and the crown ceased to enforce ecclesiastical crimes like
adultery, the fact that Book 5 specifically recognized de facto marriage had
continued to matter for Portuguese jurists into the early nineteenth century.

Notwithstanding wide acceptance that *mancebia* enjoyed in "a popular
voice," Brazilian legislators irrevocably rendered both variants of "marriage
according to the *Ordenações*" a dead letter in 1830.[57] The Criminal Code they
adopted in that year, replacing Book 5 of the Philippine Code, derogated all

forms of marriage, except that celebrated according to the canons of the Council of Trent. The old fiction of clandestine marriage was again prohibited by the new criminal code (Art. 248), a circumstance that lends credence to the assumption that those clandestine unions survived beyond the 1820s.[58] The church continued to acknowledge the existence of clandestine marriage in the determinations of its ecclesiastical courts, by handing down annulments granted on the ground that couples were not married according to the sacrament, but merely in their own eyes. Those ecclesiastical rulings ipso facto made clandestine marriage a crime under the 1830 Criminal Code.[59] Just as it had done in the colonial period, the church carefully distinguished clandestine marriage from concubinage, out of concern to condemn the former for dispensing altogether with the canonical requirments imposed by Trent.

The pejorative attitude imperial deputies showed toward *mancebia* testified to how "marriage according to *Ordenações*" had entered juridical eclipse. As the marquis of Caravellas would pronounce in the Senate two years later, "A woman who is not received by the church in marriage, according to our laws, is not married."[60] However, the problem for legislators, judges, and churchmen was that social behavior would continue to validate non-sacramental forms of marriage. Complicating this situation, not all legislators concurred in 1827 that *mancebia* should be synonymous with concubinage. A minority defended it as worthier than concubinage, if inferior to Tridentine marriage, explaining why the term continued to be reserved in popular speech for consensual unions akin to "marriage according to the *Ordenações*." Although in 1827 they did not explicitly defend *mancebia*, by the late 1830s liberal legislators explicitly did so when they spoke of it as "natural marriage." Thus the familiar dichotomy of meaning that *mancebia* projected, as either de facto marriage or concubinage, survived into the era of the Mature Empire.

Even among jurists, consensus was not unanimous during the 1820s that Tridentine marriage alone constituted the only valid marriage. None other than Portugal's eminent royal jurisconsult, Borges Carneiro, pronounced ambiguously on how positive law treated marriage according to the *Ordenações*. Some Brazilian legislators probably drew inspiration from his views, because they were published between 1826 and 1828. Although Borges Carneiro asserted that "marriage ought to be celebrated according to the form of the Council of Trent," he obliquely acknowledged that sometimes it was not. In listing the evidence for proving a valid marriage, he explicitly cited the age-old formula for "marriage according to the *Ordenações*," derived from Book 4, Title 46, Section 2: "when the couple have lived together in the public reputation of being married, for a time sufficient to assume marriage [exists]."[61] Social practice—custom—died hard. Borges Carneiro, though disagreeing with Mello Freire on important points, including his definition of valid marriage, nevertheless revered his predecessor for the emphasis he place on Portuguese custom as a source for national positive law.

Jurisconsult Manoel de Almeida e Souza de Lobão deserves the major credit for repudiating, once and for all, in a Brazilian context, the juridical recognition paid to alternate forms of marriage rooted in custom. Although he was not the first jurisconsult to condemn marriage according to the *Ordenações*, Lobão administered the *coup de grace* to the assumption that in certain situations *mancebia* amounted to what jurists called "assumed marriage." He alone possessed the juridical stature sufficient to contradict Mello Freire, given his predecessor's enormous popularity among liberal politicians of the First Empire. In Lobão's view, the reception in Portuguese law of the canons defined by the Council of Trent, prior to promulgation of the *Ordenações Filipinas*, rendered all forms of marriage except sacramental matrimony legal anachronisms.[62]

Customary marriage, the first type of "marriage according to the *Ordenações*" that Lobão condemned in the *Notas à Mello*, was once the most popular throughout Portugal, given that it presumed the church played a tacit, albeit non-sacramental, role.[63] It was described in Book 4, Title 46, Section 1, of the *Ordenações Filipinas* as produced by the exchange of "words of present promise" by the conjugal couple at the church door (*à porta da igreja*). The exchange might also be uttered inside the church. Otherwise, with permission from a prelate, those vows could be exchanged in another place, usually a private home. However, even with a blessing by the priest, customary marriage, whose form varied enormously from region to region in Portugal, failed to conform to the procedures established by the Fourth Lateran Council in 1215. It omitted the reading of the banns and, subsequently, other procedural requirements demanded by the Council of Trent. Carnal relations had to follow for a valid marriage to exist.[64]

The second variant of marriage according to the *Ordenações* was described in Section 2 of Title 46. It amounted to what jurists called "assumed," meaning de facto, marriage, and it was founded on a couple's public cohabitation, in either their own, a parent's, or another's house. In the words of the two most famous clichés pertaining to customary conjugal relations in the *Ordenações Filipinas*, the woman was taken to be the exclusive partner of the man who lived with and supported her—"*teúda e manteúda*"—and the couple was "in common knowledge and public reputation—*de fama pública*—taken to be husband and wife." As with "notorious scandal," reputation that was public made a crucial difference, converting what otherwise would be regarded as *mancebia* into valid marriage. The language of the *Ordenações* explained why Lobão carefully distinguished de facto marriage from concubinage, given how that royal code applied the cliché of "*teúda e manteúda*" to both. The same language distinguished concubinage as either adulterous ("qualified") or merely illicit ("unqualified"). Although Lobão explained that cohabitation was "for such time that, according to law, is sufficient for the marriage between them to be assumed, even if the words of the present cannot be verified," this definition no longer could be upheld in positive law.[65]

Ronaldo Vainfas has pointed out that the law of the church carefully distinguished both customary and clandestine marriage from concubinage, because the variants of customary marriage represented the "two rivals" to a "sacramental model of marriage." This important distinction in ecclesiastical law presumably underlay one that, he emphasized, also existed in positive law, accounting for why in the sixteenth and seventeenth centuries, customary and de facto marriage were carefully kept separate from concubinage. Furthermore, as he noted, the *Ordenações Filipinas* preferred to speak not of "concubinage"—"*concubinato*"—but of "*barreguice*," a term derived from "*barregão*," a young bachelor, and "*barregã*," the corresponding female term. The *barregã* is mentioned repeatedly in the *Ordenações Filipinas* as a woman "*teúda e manteúda*"—living exclusively with and supported by either a clerical or a lay partner, within what Vainfas denotes as "concubinage." By the eighteenth century, however, "*barreguice*" was termed "*mancebia*" in popular speech and statutory law. Indeed, "*barregã* and "*barregão*" were replaced by "*manceba*" and the more rarely used "*mancebo*." Similarly, in imperial Brazil, "*manceba*" would give way to "*amásia*," and "*mancebia*" to "*amasia*."[66]

Vainfas isolated the key distinction the *Ordenações* made between what he defined as "concubinage"—*barreguice*—and either customary or de facto marriage, explaining that the difference turned, once again, on the central importance of public reputation: "*fama*." Thus, where *barreguice* was taken in the community to be an assumed marriage, then all it needed as evidence for legal effect was confirmation by the popular voice that the couple enjoyed a public reputation taking them to be married: "*em voz e fama de casado*." By the same token, where a man wanted to establish he lived as a "married *barregueiro*," it was sufficient for him to prove he enjoyed the public reputation of being married.[67] Rather than a synonym for concubinage, as Vainfas tends to assume, "*barreguice*," like *mancebia*, connoted consensual cohabitation that ambiguously could be construed in positive law as either non-sacramental marriage or concubinage. Its juridical meaning depended strictly on the context of "a popular voice."

What fundamentally mattered about both non-sacramental variants of valid marriage recognized by the *Ordenações Filipinas* was that they conferred on couples a legal identity as *meeiros*. That is, law assumed the partners lived according to a *"carta de ametade"*—a community property regulation. Juridically, therefore, they possessed the same rights as couples married in the sacrament. By the early nineteenth century, considerations of matrimonial property played a pivotal role in the marginalization and suppression of "marriage according to the *Ordenações*." As much at issue as the lack of the sacrament, the lack of documentary proof for marriages contracted according to the *Ordenações Filipinas* disposed jurists to assess those unions as devoid of civil effects. "Today," Lobão noted in the first decade of the nineteenth century, "for the purpose of transmitting a heritable estate, no other proof of marriage can be accepted except that which a parish priest certifies was validly contracted with the solemnities of the Council [of Trent]."[68]

Conversely, lack of heritable rights in property served to confirm the new nature of all *mancebia* relationships. They were legally reducible to concubinage: "Because, not thus proven to be contracted, [a marriage] cannot be said to be valid; and, being null, it cannot produce effects. It remains, according to the terms of a concubinage relationship, insufficient for transmitting an estate." Neither form of non-marriage required written documentation, suggesting a key reason why jurists and legislators, not to mention bishops, found Session 24, Chapter 1, of the Council of Trent so appealing: It introduced the requirement that priests keep books for recording the names of the couple and the witnesses, as well as the place and date of marriage, and all information pertinent to the free state to marry.[69]

Lobão proved especially persuasive for Brazilian liberals because he repudiated Mello Freire's enthusiastic endorsement of all forms of customary and de facto marriage. The latter expounded his views in *De jure personarum*, Book 2 of the *Institutiones juris civilis lusitani*, as the preceding volume has analyzed. Going beyond what was sanctioned by Books 4 and 5 of the *Ordenações Filipinas*, Mello Freire attempted to reinvigorate pre-Tridentine definitions of marriage for a Joanine era. Furthermore, he did so in the late 1780s, when most jurists had begun to question the legal validity accorded "marriage according to the *Ordenações*." As we have seen, basically, he argued that a juridical view of marriage should take into account "custom"— what social behavior in his own time readily reflected as widespread practice, two centuries after Trent. He argued that not only was Tridentine marriage largely reserved for "the nobility," the propertied classes, but also that the "common people" did "not want their marriages proclaimed from the place of the high altar, but in their homes."[70]

Although Lobão wrote Book 2 of the *Notas à Mello* in 1805, it did not see publication until 1824. Meanwhile, another of Mello Freire's contemporaries, jurisconsult Joaquim Jozé Caetano Pereira e Souza, had published his authoritatively received *Classes de crimes* in 1802, only four years after Mello Freire's death. Pereira e Souza interpreted Book 5 of the *Ordenações* against the backdrop of Pombaline revision of criminal law. Obliged to comment on whether concubinage amounted to criminal behavior, he used the opportunity to point out that marriage according to the *Ordenações* constituted an anachronism. He condemned as outright "concubinage" the cohabitation in *mancebia* by couples taken to be husband and wife in public reputation, "without having fulfilled the legal solemnities that give to this union the quality of legitimate marriage."[71]

LIBERAL DILEMMA

Beyond the ostensible facilitation of marriage, adoption of the 1827 resolution reaffirming Session 24, Chapter 1, of *De Reformatione Matrimonii* placed definitive juridical distance between *mancebia* and legal marriage. It carried profound consequences for illegitimacy in imperial Brazil, because the resolution foreclosed alternatives to valid marriage that would have conferred the *qualidade* of legitimate birth on tens of thousands of individuals whose parents lived in "marriage according to the *Ordenações*." By underscoring the obligation of the church to follow the rules of Tridentine marriage, legislators took a public stand, emphasizing the sacramental form of marriage was one and the same with legal marriage. They thus placed all forms of *mancebia* outside any juridical recognition as valid marriage. Three years later, Brazil's new criminal code prescribed a punishment of two months to one year in prison for any priest who married a couple "contrary to the laws of the Empire." By stipulating that couples had to be "equipped in conformity with the law," Article 247 of the 1830 Criminal Code implied that they had to be declared in the free state to marry by a Catholic priest or bishop. Imperial law would continue to uphold the new exclusivity of legal marriage founded on Trent until the 1860s. Consequently, wherever liberals sought to reform family law, their 1827 affirmation of Tridentine marriage would prove a double-edged sword. They had boxed themselves in, leaving no alternative form of marriage juridically viable.

When Dep. Nicolao Vergueiro told the ultra-conservative bishop-elect of Maranhão, "To fight this resolution is to fight the Council [of Trent]," he may well have enjoyed the irony of watching so many of his anti-clerical colleagues band together in defense of canon law.[72] Yet, by closing the door tightly on an older definition of marriage rooted in the customary arrangement implied by "*teúda e manteúda*," liberals deprived themselves of ground to maneuver when they addressed Brazil's soaring illegitimacy rate. How could they expect success in sponsoring bills to introduce civil marriage, thereby alleviating illegitimacy, or to abolish the vow of clerical celibacy, eliminating a canonical impediment to marriage, if they reaffirmed Tridentine marriage? By the same token, how could they pass bills relaxing canonical rules on heirship for those born out-of-wedlock, after recommitting positive law exclusively to marriage in the Catholic Church? In 1829, Vergueiro, now a senator, would try to provide an answer to this conundrum, by sponsoring a bill to introduce civil marriage. First, however, Diogo Antonio Feijó, his liberal colleague in the Chamber of Deputies, would make that task more difficult by proposing that priests be permitted to contract valid marriage.

CHAPTER 4

The Liberal Challenge to the Canons of Trent

Clerical Celibacy and Civil Marriage

———◆◆◆———

The temporal power cannot take away from the citizen the right to marry; it can only regulate this right. To decree, therefore, that a priest can never contract marriage is an absurdity, a despotic act, and an injustice, because it is in opposition to human nature.

Dep. Antonio Diogo Feijó, *A Demonstration of the
Necessity To Abolish Clerical Celibacy* (1828)[1]

I, having said that the Discipline of Celibacy already belongs to the integrity of the National Religion, that it was guaranteed by the Fundamental Law, and that it is a Discipline approximating Dogma whose opposite sentiment was condemned by Trent . . . No Catholic bishop in any time or country has the authority to dispense or abrogate the General Law of Celibacy.

D. Romualdo Antonio de Seixas, Metropolitan of Brazil,
"Reflections on the Ecclesiastical Committee's Report
on Clerical Celibacy" (1834)[2]

By the late 1820s, clerical *mancebia* proved commonplace throughout Brazil. Crown legitimization offered important evidence for its toleration. The Lisbon Mesa do Desembargo do Paço had routinely legitimized the offspring of priests, even after 1800, in stark contrast to policy in Bourbon Spanish America. Toward the end of the reign of Charles III (1759–1788), Spanish crown legitimization of *sacrílegos*, which had never been impressive, ceased altogether.[3] On the other hand, between 1808 and 1828, no fewer than forty-five *sacrílegos* were legitimized before the reconstituted Desembargo do Paço in Rio de Janeiro.[4] The most significant finding revealed by petitions for that crown privilege was "the marked monogamy of the clerics, who had managed to have seven, eight, even eleven, children with the same concubine." Depositions testified to the paternal solicitude of priests. Relatives and neighbors recounted the efforts of individual clerics to support and educate the children they acknowledged as their own.[5] Where a priest lived with his children and their mother, clerical *mancebia* was tantamount to de facto marriage.

Although the Anglican clergyman Robert Walsh refused "to acquit" Brazilian ecclesiastics of the "serious charge" that they "too frequently" violated their vows of celibacy, he confirmed the monogamous nature of their relationships during the late 1820s:

Their attachments, however, are constant, and want only legal sanction to render them even laudable; for they consider their connection as binding, as if it had taken place. Many of them are excellent *fazendeiros*, or farmers, and leave behind a family in the midst of the wilderness, to extend the improvements they have commenced; and this is deemed in the countryside so important a benefit, that the thing is not regarded with the same degree of scandal as it ought, or as it is in other places.[6]

Clerical concubinage reached into Parliament, just as it did into municipal politics. A number of priest-legislators were known to maintain concubines; a more select group were recognized by colleagues as devoted family men. The most widely known example was the aforementioned Pe. Jozé Martiniano de Alencar, the liberal senator who so shocked the English traveler, George Gardner. Pe. Jozé Bento Leite Ferreira de Mello, a member of the Ecclesiastical Committee of the Chamber of Deputies during the 1826–1829 session, was another prominent example. He "had in his company a daughter who did the honors of the [lady of] the house."[7] Twenty years later, papal nuncios would still complain to Rome about Brazilian priest-legislators who had fathered children.[8]

Otherwise, several prominent liberal leaders of the 1820s and 1830s were the sons of priests. Feijó's identity as a *sacrílego* is the most prominent example, for his quality of birth was used to insult and discredit him. In all likelihood, Antonio Maria de Moura, himself a priest, was a *sacrílego*. He held a seat in the lower house from 1830 to 1837, serving as vice-president and president, before moving to São Paulo's provincial assembly and accepting the directorship of the São Paulo Faculty of Law. The Rev. Daniel Kidder, an American missionary who arrived in Brazil shortly after George Gardner, expressed amazement at the frankness with which Brazilian legislators publicly discussed Moura's *qualidade* as an *exposto* on the floor of the Chamber of Deputies.[9] One of the four reasons given by the Roman Curia for refusing to confirm Moura as bishop of Rio de Janeiro pertained to the dispensation of his "defect of birth" for ordination by São Paulo's bishop.[10] Francisco de Salles Torres Homem, viscount of Inhomirim in the Second Empire, also deserves mention as a legislator who was a *sacrílego*, although he did not become an imperial deputy until 1844. Politically, he, too, distinguished himself—as a senator, councilor of state, and provincial president.[11]

By 1827, the Brazilian clergy was facing a crisis more demographic than political, for recruitment had declined precipitously. The Rev. Walsh alluded to the diocese of Rio de Janeiro when he noted, "Many of the clergy are old and are every day leaving vacancies by deaths."[12] To the economic disincentives discussed earlier, the vow of celibacy deserves to be added. Walsh not only confirmed that popular sentiment ran in favor of permitting priests to marry, but he also referred to the key argument leveled against clerical celibacy that circulated in 1827–1828: "The Brazilians are all anxious to have the rule of celibacy, which they say is a mere matter of regulation, and not of doctrine, immediately repealed, and the discipline of their church adapted to the state of the country."[13]

FEIJÓ'S CAMPAIGN TO ABOLISH
"FORCED CELIBACY"

The Argument

The fact that celibacy was widely regarded as a matter of "regulation" or "discipline," rather than of "doctrine" embedded in the sacred canons, meaning a matter of faith, confirmed how profoundly the argument developed by Diogo Antonio Feijó had penetrated popular consciousness by Walsh's arrival in 1828. The issue of "the law of forced celibacy," as opponents dubbed the vow of clerical celibacy, first gained significant attention in the Chamber of Deputies on October 10, 1827. Tridentine marriage having been safely reaffirmed two days before, Feijó took the opportunity to introduce a bill calling on the pope to end the vow of clerical celibacy.[14] The project responded to a previously introduced bill, authored by the deputy for Bahia, Antonio Ferreira França. He had called for abolition of all monastic orders in Brazil and the obligatory marriage of priests.[15] Feijó, however, had to submit his bill "independently," because, even as a member of the Ecclesiastical Committee, he could not obtain its sponsorship for the measure. The ultra-conservative member, D. Marcos Antonio de Souza, bishop-elect of Maranhão, vetoed endorsement of the bill. Nor was Feijó permitted to publish and circulate the bill prior to taking the floor, a violation of standard protocol.[16]

Feijó's education explained his views on clerical celibacy only to a point. As a priest ordained in the secular clergy in 1808, his intellectual gifts were impressive, especially because he was largely self-taught. The only time he left Brazil was as a delegate to the Lisbon Cortes in 1821. Too poor to pursue full-time secondary study at the seminary, he imbibed Coimbra's regalist tradition through several teachers.[17] He perfected his Jansenist views in the decade following ordination, when he belonged to a congregation of clerics who studied theology and political philosophy in the rural center of Itu, São Paulo.[18] As a member of this intellectual circle of the "Patrocínio de Itu," he acquired the ideological foundation that prepared him for the 1821 Lisbon Cortes and his subsequent career as an imperial legislator. In his case, clerical *mancebia* contained a personal dimension. Registered at baptism as an *exposto*, he almost certainly had been fathered by a priest. Belated discovery of his father's identity confirmed his own identity as a disparaged *sacrílego*. This revelation accompanied his passage into the priesthood, for he had to appear before the tribunal dispensing his defect of birth prior to ordination.[19] Systematic research will no doubt confirm what the historical literature has suggested, and Feijó's enemies employed to slander him in broadsides and the press: He had also fathered children in a long-standing relationship of *mancebia*.[20]

Feijó's bill rested on a dubious argument, the state's implicit obligation, as protector of the church, to enforce disciplinary sanctions against priests whom ecclesiastical authority found guilty of violating vows of celibacy. In light of the imperial government's disinclination to impose punishments prescribed by ecclesiastical tribunals, his position remained highly tenuous. Nevertheless, it was extremely effective. By focusing on relieving the temporal power of any obligation to enforce the vow of celibacy, Feijó's argument distracted attention from the Tridentine canons on both ordination and marriage. They not only prohibited a priest from marrying but also prohibited any lay person from marrying a religious who had taken vows of celibacy. The prohibition was a dire impediment to matrimony. Feijó's repudiation of forced celibacy turned on the crucial argument that the vow of celibacy pertained only to priestly discipline—that it was not prescribed by church doctrine, or dogma.

Even though he was obliged to concede that the legislature could not abolish the vow of celibacy, because that right belonged exclusively to the spiritual arm, Feijó construed the royal patronage over the church, the *Padroado Régio*, to confer such a right on the legislature. Having in mind that secular priests were employees of the state, he informed his fellow deputy, D. Romualdo Antonio de Seixas, who was archbishop-elect of Bahia, and therefore future metropolitan of the national church, that "abolition of the rule of celibacy falls to the private competence of the temporal power and therefore to this house." When D. Romualdo objected to the 1827 legislative session coming to a close on "the truly exotic and ridiculous act of marriage for priests," Feijó countered: "Concubinage for the clergy is exotic and ridiculous." He received applause as Cunha Mattos seconded him from the floor: "It is much better for priests to be married than to live in *mancebia!*" Feijó nevertheless made a lasting and formidable enemy of Brazil's future metropolitan.[21]

The Strategy

Feijó failed to bring his bill to a vote on a first discussion in 1827, and the legislative year soon ended. Public reaction to his cause proved immediate and largely favorable. Two effects followed. First, he reintroduced the bill during the following year, on July 9, 1828. The Chamber of Deputies published it, together with his revised report, developed now as a lengthy historical treatise on clerical celibacy. Second, he took his case to the press. Or, rather, the polemic he provoked caused the press to confront, and to promote, his campaign. Feijó entitled his treatise on the evolution of clerical celibacy over two millennia of church history *A Demonstration of the Necessity To Abolish Clerical Celibacy by the General Assembly—and Its True and Legitimate Competence in the Matter*. The argument also contained the verbatim text of his bill. Not surprisingly, the *Demonstration* became the most discussed text of 1828. Although Feijó did not acknowledge a debt to Mello Freire, his repudiation of the vow of celibacy drew indirectly on that jurist for regalist inspiration, given how Feijó appropriated arguments contained in an 1822 published treatise against clerical celibacy written by a Coimbra University professor.[22] The historical arguments he employed proved important for Feijó's efforts during the 1830s to use Brazilian positive law for overriding the Tridentine canons on ordination and marriage. Feijó argued that, prior to the popes and the sacrament of marriage, it was the temporal power— originally constituted in the Roman emperors who preceded Constantine— that first established any impediments to marriage. From this historical circumstance, he concluded it was proper for the state to determine valid impediments and to modify or revoke them. Furthermore, the church's authority vis-à-vis impediments amounted to a privilege conceded by the essential power of state, sufficient reason for the temporal arm to redefine impediments.[23]

Insisting that neither "divine law nor even apostolic institution prescribed priestly celibacy," Feijó offered his bill on the moral ground that "I deem it my obligation, as a man, a Christian, and a deputy."[24] His proposal offered a daring, if doomed, strategy for persuading the pope to abolish the rule of celibacy, given that it amounted to an ultimatum. The bill called on the gov-

ernment "to obtain from His Holiness the revocation of the spiritual penalties imposed on clergy who marry, making him understand the practical necessity of so doing, given that the legislature could not derogate the rule of
celibacy." By urging the government to call "upon the pope to place the laws
of the Church in harmony with those of the Empire," the measure initially
proposed "the delineation of a sufficient time period in which the Brazilian
representative to the Holy See would definitively obtain from the Vatican
agreement" to revoke the penalties.[25] His bill envisioned the Vatican's refusal
and prescribed retaliatory steps. Basically, the legislature would "suspend the
placet for all of the disciplinary ecclesiastical laws found in opposition to the
government's existing decrees."[26] Much as medieval popes used the threat of
interdict, Feijó proposed that Brazil's imperial placet serve as the government's weapon for coercing the Holy See. By suspending or withholding the
placet, wherever a resolution or a law conflicted with a disciplinary rule of
the church, Brazil's national legislature could bring pressure to bear on the
pope to concede that the vow of celibacy pertained exclusively to discipline.[27]

Radical support for ending forced celibacy in 1827 and 1828 came from the
same group of liberal deputies who earlier had called for the abolition of entail, as well as those who in 1829 would support civil marriage. The key group
of stalwarts inscribed Lino Coutinho, Vergueiro, Cunha Mattos, Vasconcellos, and Clemente Pereira, joined by Pe. Jozé Custodio Dias. A formidable
opposition, seconded by the bishop-elect of Maranhão, but led by D. Romualdo de Seixas, newly confirmed in 1828 as Brazil's metropolitan and Bahia's
archbishop. In the same year, D. Romualdo became president of the Chamber of Deputies. Although he could not prevent Feijó from expounding the
case for abolishing the vow of celibacy, his presence in the legislature contributed to the bill's defeat. Despite the repeated applause that Feijó's arguments elicited from the floor of the Chamber of Deputies, passage of his bill
proved impossible. D. Romualdo, who as president of the Chamber was prevented by house rules from taking a major role in debate, was not averse to
using the press. The views he expressed in print over the same issue, again in
1834, left little to conjecture. Feijó's endorsement of marriage for priests encouraged his enemies to brand him a schismatic as early as 1827.[28] The fundamental principle, as D. Romualdo later argued to the minister of justice,
was that the civil power could not revoke the law of celibacy, for the reason
that it lacked "competence in matters of ecclesiastical discipline."[29]

D. Romualdo's determined opposition to any suspension of the rule of
celibacy continued even beyond 1829, when he no longer occupied a seat in
the Chamber of Deputies. In marshaling every possible argument in support

of the "law of celibacy," Romualdo argued against those who, like the bishop of São Paulo, believed more virtuous men would be persuaded to enter the priesthood if they might marry. Marriage, the archbishop haughtily responded, would only enhance the greater penury of the parish priest, already hard-pressed to live on an annual stipend of 200 *réis*. Marriage for priests, D. Romualdo insisted, would "multiply the proletarians and so many disgraced families," given that "the Brazilian clergy is reputed to be the bottom class of society."[30]

Thanks to an extensive press campaign that began in 1827 and continued through 1834, Bahia's archbishop employed incisive canonical logic, genuine indignation, and dismissive ridicule in order to rebut the highly popular and truly modern proposal that priests in Brazil should be free to marry. Romualdo de Seixas would remain Brazil's metropolitan until his death in 1860. The circumstance that he became the longest-tenured primate of the Brazilian church enabled him to oppose clerical celibacy effectively, and to tie his opposition to related attempts by liberals to introduce civil marriage or to replace canonical impediments with those that were civil.

Dogma Trumps Natural Law

Feijó's project threatened the unity of the national institution that united Brazilians even more strongly than the monarchy. Brazil's established church could not have permitted priests to marry and remain within the Apostolic Roman Catholic Communion. The vast majority of legislators, including liberals, were simply not willing to take the fatal step that would have isolated the Brazilian church from Rome. Portuguese regalism had always been based on aggressively defending the interests of the crown, while acknowledging the superiority of the church in purely spiritual matters. Despite the strong case to be made that the rule of celibacy was merely a matter of discipline—one again argued in the twenty-first century—legislators balked. Reluctance to be abandoned by Rome, however, was shrewdly tempered by a pragmatic note. Legislators understood that Brazil's bishops tacitly tolerated clerical *mancebia* within their dioceses. By turning a blind eye, bishops could avoid confrontation as long as the Vatican did not compel compliance. Their complicity—often their genuine support for clerical *mancebia*—accounted for why Thomas Ewbank concluded in 1845 that the Brazilian government "will be compelled eventually to carry out the intentions of the late regent Feijó—suppress every convent and adopt the system of the Greek Church in requiring priests, other than bishops, to marry."[31] Consequently, for the remainder of the imperial period, social practice continued to validate the family arrangements of priests who lived in *mancebia*, even when they openly acknowledged their offspring. Until Pope Leo XIII (1878–1903) brought the full weight of the Vatican to bear on the Brazilian hierarchy, and enlisted episcopal cooperation for the enforcement of the vow of celibacy, clerical *mancebia* thrived openly and unchallenged in imperial Brazil.

By bringing clerical *mancebia* into the public arena of the national legislature, Feijó and liberal reformers paid significant attention to an important variant in Brazilian family formation, one deemed "illegitimate" by both positive and ecclesiastical law. His courageous attempt to legalize marriage on behalf of Brazil's Catholic clergy addressed the intimately connected issue of illegitimacy. Feijó's argument demonstrated that the rule of forced celibacy was unfair, because it deprived clerics of a natural right to live as sexual beings. But he also attracted support for the assertion that "the immorality of the clergy originated in the impediment" of celibacy itself. That is, the vow of celibacy being "imprudent" and "useless," it "led to disobedience." "Given the lack of respect paid to it, it introduced immorality." Feijó's *Demonstrasão* also pointed a finger at another consequence of priestly "immorality," one that he had personally overcome in his own adolescence: "The exclusion from ordination of the sons of priests."[32] By proposing that priests be free to marry, therefore, his bill promised to remove the "defect of birth" that stigmatized all *sacrílegos*. His campaign against forced celibacy, which received strong support from the bishop of São Paulo, brought into clear focus the marked dissonance between popular moral standards and an official ideology resting on canon law. By enlisting "a popular voice" in support of his campaign, Feijó brilliantly refocused the issue of forced celibacy, making it inimical to Christian morality and the root cause of paternal irresponsibility.

Feijó's bill to abolish the rule of celibacy demonstrated how liberal legislators could radically apply notions of natural right and contract to the reform of private, family law. Although his proposal provoked a rapid and heavy-handed political reaction from D. Romualdo, even the archbishop was obliged to concede, obliquely, that celibacy was a disciplinary matter, for he qualified the latter when he construed it as "of a type approximating dogma." Contradiction of the rule of celibacy, Brazil's new metropolitan pontificated, was "proscribed and anathematized by the formal definition of the padres of Trent."[33] The vow of celibacy therefore amounted to a taboo, officially untouchable. The fact that for nearly a decade D. Romualdo commanded a public campaign to repudiate Feijó's bill also hardened that prelate's opposition to civil marriage. The two proposals were inextricably linked by being joined in the canonical prohibitions on marriage enshrined in the dogma of Trent.

SECULARIZING HOLY MATRIMONY:
CIVIL MARRIAGE

Protestant Colonization, Impetus for Change

The absence of any form of legal marriage in Brazil, other than that acquired through the Roman Catholic rite of holy matrimony, caused difficulty once D. João decreed the opening of the ports to foreign trade in 1808. Thereafter, a steady stream of resident foreigners, especially in the Corte, Salvador, and Recife, rapidly expanded. Beginning in 1817, the first immigrants, a group of German-speaking colonists, some of whom were Protestants, arrived under crown sponsorship. European couples already married in a non-Catholic rite experienced no legal difficulties after arrival in Brazil. Their children were deemed legitimate because marriages legally contracted abroad enjoyed validity in positive law. By the late 1820s, however, a new situation arose, thanks to a first generation of Protestant citizens born on Brazilian soil. By then, the children of European immigrants, together with newly arriving Europeans, constituted a small, but significant, population. Yet, Brazilian law denied Protestants opportunity to marry with civil effects, notwithstanding that the imperial government actively promoted immigration from Europe irrespective of religious creed. Until the 1860s, the only road to legal matrimony for Protestants was conversion to the Roman Catholic and Apostolic faith. Their rising numbers, given the inability to contract marriage, offered another reason why illegitimate births soared during the Empire.

European men who were not Roman Catholic increasingly sought to marry Brazilian women who were Catholic, due to the demographic preponderance of males among early immigrants. Consequently, as either resident aliens or naturalized and native-born citizens, a burgeoning male population that was Protestant could not contract legal marriage with Brazilian Catholic women. Initially, immigrant Protestant women rarely sought to marry Brazilian Catholics, but, as time passed, their daughters faced the same problem as their sons. The severest limitation, of course, occurred where both bride and groom were Protestant. Not only was a Protestant marriage null for all civil effects, but it might also be impossible to perform, due to the small numbers of Protestant clergymen available. In the eyes of the law, marriage contracted in a Protestant rite conveyed only social effects. Consequently, marital property was left unprotected, especially in situations of spouse abandonment, or when a Protestant divorce led to remarriage. The fact that certain European countries recognized divorce and remarriage imparted a legal murkiness to the inheritance position of the illegitimate children of

Brazilian Protestants, for legitimate half-siblings, parental relatives, and even a competing, legitimate wife might press patrimonial claims from distant Europe.

Given that Protestant unions juridically amounted to no more than *mancebia*—legal concubinage—the impact of the inheritance system could be devastating to a surviving spouse or minor children in a Protestant marriage. Under the rules of forced heirship, the children of Protestant parents at the very best were natural offspring; at the very worst, they were adulterine or incestuous and therefore excluded from any rights in *ab intestato* succession. The real difficulty turned on the nature of *mancebia*. It was purely consensual and therefore dissoluble at will. Spousal abandonment, the subsequent marriage of one parent in the Catholic church, or merely a parent's death—all threatened the children's juridical position vis-à-vis heirship. A consensual wife, even when not abandoned, might face widowhood impoverished, if her partner had not provided for her by the testamentary assignment of his *terça*. "Widows" might find it impossible to recover property they brought to a consensual union or subsequently acquired while living in one, given that law did not regard them as *meeiras*.

In 1829, Sen. Nicolao Vergueiro, himself a Portuguese immigrant, introduced a bill to establish civil marriage in Brazil. A talented lawyer turned planter-entrepreneur, Vergueiro acquired important political and economic connections soon after his arrival in São Paulo, around 1802. Thanks to his identity as one of only three lawyers practicing in the provincial capital, he rose rapidly in municipal and provincial politics. Gradually, after marriage to a Brazilian woman of good family, he amassed an impressive amount of land to the west of that city by the 1820s. In the 1840s and 1850s, his own "Paulista West" would become Brazil's new dynamic frontier, with coffee the leading sector by the late 1850s.[34] More than any other imperial legislator, Vergueiro consistently promoted European immigration, leaving his name permanently associated with a notorious experiment in "free labor" that he sponsored to attract Swiss immigrants to his own and neighboring coffee plantations.

By 1829, consequently, Vergueiro was approaching the pinnacle of what would be a remarkably long and successful political career. Promoted from the Chamber of Deputies to the Senate in 1828, for the Province of Minas Gerais, he proved a brilliant debater. Atypically for someone born and brought up in Portugal, Vergueiro was respected for his fidelity to the cause of independence, standing almost alone as an exception in a political milieu where anti-Portuguese sentiment continued to build in explosive proportions. He thus commanded the political stature and possessed the intellectual adroitness to take on the Senate's more intimidating, senior members. In 1829, consequently, he used his expanding prestige to rally limited, but significant, support in the Senate for a bill proposing what no other nation in Latin America had yet contemplated: the establishment of civil marriage as a legally valid alternative to marriage in the Catholic Church—and for all citizens, Catholics as well as Protestants.

Vergueiro's effort, initiated in the upper house, proved an impossible gamble, given the preponderance of the monarchy's Old Guard of "royalists," whom Pedro had appointed for their loyalty to the palace. Vergueiro, however, owed nothing in his career to the former Portuguese crown. Nor, for that matter, did he owe any debt to D. Pedro I, as some historians have claimed. The emperor had denied Vergueiro a deserved seat in the Senate in 1826; however, by 1828, Vergueiro was so popular that pressure from São Paulo's delegation forced Pedro to place him in the Senate. Despite the lack of a vacancy for his home province, Vergueiro took a seat in the Senate, representing Minas Gerais.[35]

Vergueiro's bill on civil marriage, proposed on July 4, 1829, a year after he entered the Senate, also called for the creation of registries of marriages, births, and deaths. It failed to distinguish between either Protestants or Catholics or between citizens and non-citizens, for all Brazilians would be able to contract civil marriage.[36] Undeniably, the availability of civil marriage would serve Vergueiro's personal interests as a businessman and promoter of European immigration to Brazil's sparsely populated hinterland. Although he intended to improve Brazil's image in Europe, by encouraging northern European, and therefore Protestant, immigration, he also acted from a liberal's espousal of equality before the law and a commitment to religious toleration. His strongly secular sympathies on the matter of marriage followed from firm regalist convictions, doubtlessly acquired while studying law at Coimbra University during the late 1790s. His bill on civil marriage reflected consistency with the positions he took on other bills, such as the abolition of entail. In the Senate, his most important ally was the aging marquis of Caravellas. The senior liberal in that body, and one of the principal authors of the guarantees of religious freedom written into the 1824 Constitution, Caravellas effectively co-sponsored Vergueiro's bill on civil marriage.

Debate over Vergueiro's proposal to introduce civil marriage, like the one in 1827 on *De Reformatione Matrimonii*, offers historians of the family several fascinating glimpses of how Catholic Brazilians addressed a new situation accommodating Protestants: the so-called mixed marriages unofficially celebrated between spouses who were Catholic and Protestant. Alternatively, Senate debate brought the circumstances of Protestant Brazilians bereft of their own clergy into a public focus for the first time. Finally, the debate exposed the actions of enlightened Catholic priests who believed in making ecumenical concessions while attempting to keep faith with the canons laid down at Trent.

Liberal Argumentation

Vergueiro introduced his bill by offering vignettes portraying the plight of "mixed couples" denied the sacrament of marriage in the Catholic church by their bishops. He intended to call into question the official position of Archbishop D. Romualdo de Seixas, for the anecdotes underscored the significance of a popular voice favoring a community standard that sharply deviated from the orthodox position defended by Brazil's metropolitan.[37] Initially, Vergueiro observed that "there have been many marriages between Catholics and Protestants," alluding to the priestly subterfuge that rendered those unions null in the eyes of positive law. "Necessity has obliged [mixed couples] to celebrate their marriages in the presence of a parish priest who does not preside over the sacrament, which, in this case, is not there, because he presides over a purely civil contract."[38] He was referring to the willingness of sympathetic priests to "marry" mixed couples, omitting both the banns and the final blessing that made the ritual a sacrament.

Vergueiro's defense of civil marriage rested firmly on the argument that marriage was a contract not only in the eyes of the church but also in the eyes of positive law. In fact, liberals were able to argue that the contractual identity of marriage, originating in natural as well as civil law, predated its sacramental identity. However, Vergueiro took the risky step of arguing that, even without celebration of the sacrament of matrimony, the priest was empowered to solemnize a marriage contract, rendering it valid in civil law. Of course, he knew this was a big leap and exceedingly dubious at that, given that only a Tridentine solemnization of matrimony was axiomatic for marriage to take place. Basically, Vergueiro tried to narrow the difference between the purely civil marriage he was proposing and the civil contractual implications of sacramental marriage that extended to positive law. D. Romualdo, together with several other prelates, would seize on just this point to argue the opposite—avowing there was no marriage, and therefore no contract, unless the sacrament of holy matrimony was celebrated.[39]

Alternatively, Vergueiro employed a persuasive, anecdotal strategy about mixed marriages, including those where Catholic priests had officiated. His motive was to produce indignation or shame, in an effort to move good Catholic consciences in the Senate. He stooped to a mocking, bigoted stance that otherwise, as an enlightened Catholic, he never employed in his public oratory, when he sought to disparage the hypocrisy in such pseudo-marriages:

But is there not a certain religious scandal in seeing a heretic come before the altar where the divine mysteries are celebrated, those he repudiates ... the images he disparages, before the cleric of the faith he does not recognize? And for what? In order to celebrate an act for which he denies any religious significance.[40]

Vergueiro recounted an even more appalling scene, one conjuring up the absurdity of the Protestant conundrum: The absence of both church and clergyman. "I witnessed a wedding in São Paulo in which the bride's mother was the minister," Vergueiro confided. "She asked the parties if they wanted to marry. They replied 'yes,' and she joined their hands, saying, 'You are married.'"[41] Although this description offered the absolute nadir in possible scenarios, due to female agency, it shockingly dramatized how Protestants were deprived of any ritual affirmation of matrimony.

The marquis of Caravellas, ever the champion of religious toleration, introduced a different argument in favor of civil marriage, one sounding an old and very Catholic note. Deprived of the sacrament of marriage, Protestants and, he implied, Catholics not in the free state to marry were left to live in permanent *mancebia*. Otherwise, as Caravellas himself had done when he entered Coimbra University, in the late 1780s, they resorted to a religious career that imposed the vow of celibacy.[42] Like many liberals, he rhetorically posed "celibacy" as the only alternative to a consensual union, whenever the church denied an individual the free state to marry. Civil marriage was necessary, he reasoned, "because we should take cautionary note of such *mancebia*; not everyone wants to embrace celibacy."

Caravellas shrewdly brought up a point he knew male legislators found appalling, that families constituted on a foundation of *mancebia* posed a threat to the male partner's prerogative of *pátrio marital* as well as to the children's right to paternal support. Correctly, he referred to law in force where legal marriage was absent: "The law does not concede that right the husband has over the wife, [nor] those that the children ought to possess." Men did not exercise *poder marital* over a *manceba*, who, in the eyes of the law, was a concubine. Nor did they hold *pátrio poder* over the children they fathered with her. Correctly, he was implying that jurists had interpreted the child support fathers provided to natural or spurious children could fall short of what the law expected them to provide their legitimate offspring.[43] Otherwise, *poder marital* could be exercised only over a wife recognized by positive law. A surviving partner in a relationship of *mancebia* lacked any claim to one-half of the matrimonial community, because law did not recognize his or her existence.

Finally, such situations led to patrimonial conflicts that deprived children of their inheritances. Where one partner was non-Brazilian, European consuls defended the rights of their nationals, who, as children born in what were *mancebia* arrangements, claimed a parent's property that had been jointly pooled with that of a Brazilian partner. The same situations produced claimants who were the surviving partners in those *mancebia* arrangements. Diplomatic friction eventually led to clauses inserted in international treaties that were designed to protect Europeans from the rules of forced heirship in Brazil. The latter favored either legitimate heirs or a legal spouse, at the expense of either the children of European nationals born in *mancebia* or their foreign parent.[44]

Fundamentally, however, Caravellas raised the issue of equality before the law, concurring with Vergueiro on the constitutional principle civil marriage would validate: "If we admit to our political association men who are not of the Catholic communion, we ought to make new legislation in this respect, out of necessity. The remedy ought to be by a law that legitimizes matrimony, even though the parties are not Catholics."[45] In the view of Vergueiro and liberal supporters of his bill, treating marriage as a civil contract provided that remedy. They looked to the Constitution, which, as Caravellas observed, "admits that foreigners may be naturalized, whatever their religion," and inferred the right of all Brazilians to contract marriage with the same civil effects. Because positive law on matrimony derived from canon law, he argued, it was "impaired." What was needed was to adapt old law to a Constitution that bestowed citizenship on non-Catholics, in a country where now Protestants also lived.[46] Reverting to the 1769 Law of Right Reason, Vergueiro cited the necessity of "filling the large lacuna that had opened in our legislation" due to a Constitution that did not restrict citizenship to Roman Catholics. Noting that "marriage is a contract in natural law," he injected the social menace posed by *mancebia*. For all who could not marry in the church, celibacy would be their fate. It was necessary, he warned, not to confuse marriage with "unions determined by purely animal mechanisms."[47]

Vergueiro carried the argument that "marriage was a civil contract . . . founded on the consent of the parties," to the familiar ground of regalism, asserting that the Constitution permitted the temporal power to regulate the purely civil, or contractual, results following from the sacrament of marriage. Correctly, he pointed to "the most orthodox canonists," who recognized that the temporal aspect of marriage was contractual, but insisted that the priest's task was to administer the sacrament once that contractual character had been established. Existing law, it followed, should provide the same civil effects for non-Catholics as for Catholics. Clinching his point, Vergueiro insisted that national positive law, nevertheless was being violated in one important contractual respect, due to the emphasis Tridentine marriage placed on "free will." Wherever someone married below the age of majority, which was twenty-five in 1829, canonical free consent was insufficient, he maintained. The church said that individuals could marry at twelve and fourteen, but from the perspective of positive national law they were not legally equipped to marry, due to being minors, parental consent notwithstanding. Mischievously, he proposed that what was a simple impediment in the eyes of the Council of Trent—lack of parental consent for minors—be defined in Brazilian positive law as a diriment impediment, one that nullified such a marriage.[48]

The Defeat of Civil Marriage

Opponents of civil marriage declined to respond to the liberal argument that all citizens should enjoy the right to contract legitimate marriage and possess the civil effects thereby produced. Their aversion to civil marriage originated in a commitment to canonical orthodoxy defined by the Council of Trent. As the viscount of Cayru reminded the proponents of civil marriage, they had boxed themselves in when they adopted the resolution on *De Reformatione Matrimonii* in 1827: "Already in this Senate, in conformity with the resolution passed by the Chamber of Deputies, we agreed that the requirements for marriage would be made in the form determined by the Council of Trent." Therefore, the "exotic innovation" of civil marriage "should be rejected *in limine*." In sticking to an exclusively Tridentine definition of legal marriage, opponents of civil marriage preferred to turn the liberal argument on its head: To be opposed to civil marriage was to defend the population *against mancebia*. Arguing that civil marriage would open the door widely to consensual unions, they had in mind Brazil's Roman Catholic population. Sen. João Evangelista de Faria Lobato offered the opinion that "the ignorant common people," not recalling the difference between the sacrament of marriage and a contract, "would be induced to believe that in civil marriage could be found the dispensation of the sacrament."[49]

Civil marriage proved less the issue than mixed marriages that opened the door to conversion to the Protestant faith. Religious chauvinism surfaced in debate. For instance, to those who deplored the perpetual *mancebia* to which Protestants were condemned, Sen. João Evangelista answered, "In my view, to be Protestant is worse than to be *amancebado*"—living in *mancebia*. The viscount of Cayru feared civil marriage because it "prepares the way to Protestantism, or to gentilism," relaxing discipline among Roman Catholics. He stated the opposition's case in the strongest terms and connected anxiety over sectarian purity to that famous nineteenth-century predator, "the libertine":

As to the specious argument that civil marriage will prevent concubinage and offer the security of legitimacy for offspring, I tell you that the worst concubinage is that which takes place with public authorization. . . . The foreigners and libertines would easily be able to seduce Brazilian women, promising them marriage and winding up the affair before a justice of the peace.[50]

In reality, civil marriage posed a threat to the paterfamilias' control of his daughters—and sons. By introducing the justice of the peace as a rival agent to the parish priest, it undermined the patriarchal support that locally dominant families expected from the latter. The government's judge also threatened the church's control of vital records. In order to perform civil marriages, an imperial magistrate would need to be privy to the contents of confidential parish registers. He would also generate a separate archive on civil marriages over which the priest would have no control.

On the one hand, fear of Protestantism reflected anxiety over divorce and conversion—apostasy. In Cayru's words, civil marriage "prepares the way to gentilism." Manoel Caetano de Almeida e Albuquerque, another liberal senator, sought to allay such fears by mentioning the paucity of Protestant clergymen in Brazil and emphasized the absence of offensiveness shown to the Catholic religion by Brazilian Protestants. These were reasons civil marriage should be adopted, he suggested. Failure to do so would merely "serve to make apostates."[51] Given how the bill's utility outweighed its shortcomings, he proposed amending it to restrict civil marriage to non-Catholic foreigners. Vergueiro stood fast. By flatly declining to amend the bill, he demonstrated a general preference that it serve Catholics whom the church would not declare in the free state to marry.

What really mattered as the underlying defense of exclusively Roman Catholic marriage was the homogeneous nature of community in Brazil. Immigration, originating from European countries outside Portugal, now was perceived as a regular feature of social life. Freedom of religion applied to Brazilian-born citizens rather than merely to small enclaves of resident foreign merchants and diplomats. Protestantism, consequently, challenged the colonial notion of community based exclusively on a shared identity as Roman Catholic. To be Brazilian one no longer had to be part of an established church, a circumstance that raised the anxiety that community values would be corrupted. Equally important, a Protestant identity rendered a select population of Brazilian citizens immune from the authority of the church, removing them outright from the jurisdiction of ecclesiastical tribunals and exempting Protestant clergymen from regulation by the legislature as a national clergy.

Ultra-Catholic opponents of civil marriage refused to endorse the bill on a final ground. They anticipated, incorrectly, that the Brazilian government would negotiate a concordat with the Vatican. Cayru proposed, consequently, that once "dissidents from the Catholic faith" had increased, then the imperial government could protest their situation to the Holy See—by resorting to a concordat. Those who favored a concordat, however, feared that any government action taken on behalf of Protestants in 1829 would jeopardize negotiations with the Vatican.[52] This position, of course, antagonized liberals, prompting Vergueiro to reformulate the suggestion: If Protestants were to be construed as "ex-communicants, that is, outside our community, how is it that this matter has to be taken to the Vatican?" Answering his own question, he retorted, "The pope will say, 'What do I have to do with marriages of Protestants?'" In fact, liberal domination of the Chamber of Deputies had already cast the fate of a concordat—the imperial government would never sign one.

Although opposition to civil marriage relied on a conservative argument, grounded in an established church and a homogeneity of religious community supportive of the throne, political arguments alone did not account for why civil marriage failed to be adopted in 1829. The active opposition of the institutional church played a principal role in defeating the bill, and continued to do so after 1829. The person of Brazil's metropolitan and Bahia's archbishop, D. Romualdo Antonio de Seixas, proved a most powerful opponent. Although he did not return to the Chamber of Deputies for the second session (1830–1833), D. Romualdo again sat in the lower house for the third session (1834–1837). The seventeenth bishop of Bahia also returned to the fifth session (1842–1845) of the national legislature, at age 81. He used the press and the pulpit continuously to denounce civil marriage from the late 1820s until the end of his life. During the Regency crisis over the twin demons of civil and clerical marriage, in 1832–1834, he publicly defended the church's exclusive right to pronounce on both dogma and discipline. He expressed misgivings that, at a popular level, any secularization of marriage would be understood in terms of theological distinctions pertaining to the sacrament and the contract of matrimony. Interestingly, he also acknowledged that only one Brazilian had been guilty of apostasy and become a Protestant.[53]

Yet fear of Protestantism defined a key motive in defeating subsequent bills on civil marriage. In the 1840s, for instance, the Rhineland German immigrant community in Petrópolis came under attack. Gaetano Bedini, the papal nuncio, prevailed on the Brazilian government to end the practice of "heterodox" marriages between Catholics and Lutherans in Petrópolis, which were being celebrated there in a Lutheran church. For want of a Catholic priest—due to episcopal prohibition—Catholics and Protestants were marrying in ceremonies conducted by a Lutheran minister. Bedini pressured the foreign minister to issue a decree prohibiting "mixed" marriages from being celebrated by a Protestant pastor and to order that the procedural rules of the Council of Trent be observed.[54] The foreign minister was none other than the baron of Cayru (Bento da Silva Lisboa), the son of the first viscount of Cayru who in 1829 had strongly opposed civil marriage. The imperial government thus capitulated on constitutional guarantees of freedom of religion in the Second Empire.

That Vergueiro's bill did not pass the Senate is unsurprising. What stands out is the truly pioneering nature of his effort. After the passage of almost two centuries, it is easy to overlook his bill's radical content. Although his proposal did not call for compulsory civil marriage, it anticipated the establishment of a civil registry that would have ended the church's exclusive monopoly on marriage. Throughout Spanish America, for many decades after 1829, civil marriage encountered militant opposition, sometimes from armed camps willing to make war. When the Argentine Province of Santa Fé adopted civil marriage, in 1867, the sponsoring governor reversed himself and the bill was rescinded. Yet he was forcibly deposed.[55] Mandatory civil marriage, regardless of religious affiliation, did not appear in Spanish America until Chile adopted such a law in 1884. Uruguay followed suit in 1885 and Argentina in 1888–1889.[56] Brazil would wait until 1890.

The historiography on Brazilian liberalism, as well as the scholarly literature on the family in imperial Brazil, has ignored the efforts of Brazil's historical liberals to enact civil marriage between 1829 and 1847. The assumption has been that the famous but doomed bill written by Councilor Jozé Thomaz Nabuco de Araujo, as minister of justice, represented the first attempt to introduce civil marriage. In fact, Nabuco's 1855 bill represented the fourth time civil marriage was defeated in the national legislature. And it departed from preceding attempts in one significant respect: It was not intended "for the mass of the population that is Catholic."[57] The bill narrowly applied to mixed marriages or to those of Protestant couples. Despite this concession, Nabuco's bill was defeated in 1858. Heavy opposition from the church, including the octogenarian D. Romualdo, whose denunciation of the bill was published a year before his death at age ninety-eight, helped to explain why the legislature declined to endorse civil marriage. Just as significant, a Conservative Catholic bloc in parliament still supported religious homogeneity as a guarantee of political stability.[58]

"THE LEGITIMATE FAMILY": MARRIAGE, NOT "MANCEBIA"

Having been identified by legislators as a social problem in the late 1820s, *mancebia* did not disappear from future public discourse. Although increasingly it received official condemnation from legislators as "concubinage," only very gradually did that pejorative view become accommodated by a more tolerant popular consciousness. Notwithstanding the 1827 reaffirmation of *De Reformatione Matrimonii*, ordinary Brazilians found it no easier to marry in the church after 1827 than before. Foreign travelers in Brazil continued to be astonished by the difficulty they faced when attempting to marry in the church. As late as the 1870s, Thomaz Lino D'Assumpção, a Portuguese resident in the diocese of Rio de Janeiro, criticized the expense and difficulty of the procedures for declaring couples in the free state to marry.[59] Although after 1829 many couples in imperial Brazil would claim to be living in the public reputation of man and wife, even describing themselves as married "according to the *Ordenações*," the line between social behavior and a juridical validation of marriage was now firmly drawn. Rights in matrimonial property juridically demanded legal marriage.

From a different perspective, the defeat of civil marriage in 1829 portended the direct attention paid by legislators to illegitimacy in the 1830s and 1840s. The absence of a legal alternative to holy matrimony encouraged them to consider the situation of illegitimate Brazilians in positive law. They appreciated that an impasse over reform of marriage contained a demographic corollary. The proportion of illegitimate individuals would continue to expand, because larger numbers of Brazilians would simply be unable to marry. Finally, individuals born out-of-wedlock would enjoy greater prominence in social life and make their presence more frequently felt within legislators' personal networks, including their own families. Only by modifying positive law to take the rights of those individuals directly into account could their social position—and that of their parents—be redressed. Failure to reform marriage by making it accessible to all Brazilians, including Catholics prohibited by canonical impediments, led to an agenda of change that after 1830 focused on illegitimacy and the inheritance rights of those born outside wedlock. Liberals would return to natural law and contract theory as the common grounds for challenging the canons on marriage. The arrival of the Regency provided the propitious political opening for them to address the legal condition of those whom law still stigmatized with the defect of birth.

CHAPTER 5

Illegitimacy and the National Elite
in the Independence Era

I declare that there was a daughter born to a noblewoman enjoying purity of blood, whom I ordered to be called D. Izabel Maria
de Alcantara Brasileira and to be raised in the home of a Gentleman of my Imperial Household, João de Castro Canto e Mello.
D. Pedro I, Declaration of Paternity, May 24, 1826[1]

In trying to explain why, between 1830 and 1836, a number of proposals were
introduced in Brazil's national legislature designed to broaden succession
rights on behalf of illegitimate individuals, the political context offers only a
partial answer. Political determinants deserve to be connected to deeply
rooted social patterns, especially evident among the political elite that inscribed Brazil's legislators and ministerial cupola. Standards of behavior at
the very highest social levels contributed to a widespread toleration of illegitimacy. On the other hand, they enforced social norms that imposed limits
where offspring were spurious rather than natural.

The patriarchal prerogative of founding a polygamous family, or, alternatively, of establishing an exclusively illegitimate one, was as closely associated
with the upper ranks of Brazilian society as it was with the common people.
A careful reading of elite biographies offers innumerable instances of prominent individuals who lived in stable unions and constituted families devoid
of the sacrament of marriage. Otherwise, the same couples married only after
producing progeny within consensual unions of *mancebia*. The historiography of the family in nineteenth-century Brazil has begun to make clear that a
significant proportion of couples at the pinnacle of society, like their counterparts among the common people, simply dispensed with the legal formal-
ity of marriage. Among those with substantial property, marriage was not
necessary for guaranteeing succession rights for natural children born in relationships of *mancebia*. As we have seen, parents relied on the rules of heirship for recognized natural offspring to safeguard their children's patrimony.

ELITE CONTEXTS OF ILLEGITIMACY:
"INEQUALITY" AND MANCEBIA

The late colonial emphasis on equality of social status between marriage partners carried over into imperial times. Individuals of substantial property, consequently, might decline to marry a partner with whom they had established a stable relationship because the woman, or the man, was not deemed a social "equal." Frequently, color proved the factor defining "inequality"; however, social origins and family pedigrees entered into such calculations. On the other hand, protestations of "inequality" could mask idiosyncratic objections to a marriage, as the brother of the future marquis of Barbacena (Felisberto Caldeira Brant Pontes) discovered. Ildefonso de Oliveira Caldeira Brant lived in *mancebia* with "the richest heiress in Brazil, who had as many suitors as Miss Tilney Long." He worked as the steward of this heiress, known universally as "Maria Bangu" (Anna de Moraes e Castro), whose name derived from her large property of Bangu that bordered on the imperial estates at Santa Cruz, in the Province of Rio de Janeiro. Although "she formed an attachment" to him, and they "lived unmarried 'til her death," the "Senhora of Bangu" found her steward's social credentials inferior. Nevertheless, she left him all of her property. "A great favorite of the emperor," the former steward was ennobled as viscount of Gericinó in 1826.[2]

Ordinarily, however, as an alternative to marriage, *mancebia* preserved a man's higher social status, not a woman's. Anecdotal evidence suggests that it was far from uncommon in many families to find at least one son who had declined legitimate marriage in favor of living in a stable consensual union. When the reason did not lie in an undispensed canonical impediment, then usually the woman's color explained the element of inequality. On the eve of independence, Maria Graham referred directly to the formidable barrier to matrimony that color presented. She noted that color was the reason that Portuguese colonists were "extremely anxious to avoid intermarriage with born Brazilians."[3] Early in the century, when Councilor Jozé de Oliveira Pinto Coelho Mosquera, who was a high judge of the Tribunal of the Mesa do Desembargo do Paço, fathered a natural child known as the *parda*, Joanna Mosqueira, his noble *qualidade* precluded obtaining royal permission to marry a woman of color.[4]

Johann Moritz Rugendas, the gifted artist who resided in Recife during the second decade of the nineteenth century, aptly described an important variation on *mancebia* that adapted the liaisons of privileged white males with women of color to patriarchal authority. What Rugendas observed more properly illustrated a type of serial marriage, one common in the 1820s:

So when parental objections impede a man from marrying a *mulata* to whom he is attracted, he takes her home. She remains there for years, at the head of arrangements, receiving the most respectable ladies and paying them visits. Sometimes the marriage is performed only after years, and when there are many children . . . If "imperious reasons" [parental dictates] oblige the man to take another woman for a wife, he gives a dowry to the *mulata* and she thus easily finds a husband of her color and position, because she is considered a widow and not a woman of bad habits.[5]

This arrangement eased tensions between parents and sons due to the "inequality" of sexual partners not fated to marry within a patriarchally ordered matrimonial system. As Maria Graham noted, in Recife, a city of 70,000, where only one-third of the residents were white, marriages were settled "without the parties having ever heard each other's voices. The general mode is for parents to settle their children's nuptials, without consulting anything but pecuniary convenience."[6]

Rugendas, on the other hand, ignored an important limitation presented by the serial marriage he described: the status in heirship enjoyed by the natural offspring born in such *mancebia* relationships. The natural children of the *mulata* abandoned for a white wife nonetheless enjoyed the right to be their father's *ab intestato* heirs. The children of such unions might seek a judicial determination of paternity if their fathers later evaded paternal recognition. The "amicable" circumstances Rugendas detailed for terminating those arrangements, the offer of a dowry to the mother—and a stepfather of color for her children—forestalled claims by the natural children to their father's *legítima*. Yet such compensation proved increasingly less likely to discourage the appearance of a "surprise heir," once the 1828 Judiciary Act became operable during the Regency.

Arrangements in which the sons of "good families" cohabited with women of color and brought up their mulatto children caused more scandal during the Second Empire than in the 1820s and 1830s, when they were more likely to be tolerated as commonplace. The tone of disapproval, even scandalized condemnation, with which many family anecdotes on interracial unions were set down in print after 1880 reflected, of course, the new importance placed on legal marriage.[7] As the foundation of the bourgeois family, legal marriage meant that unions of *mancebia* were also condemned for removing eligible white bachelors from family marriage pools. When Eleuterio da Silva Prado's (1836–1905) family would not permit him to marry the woman of his choice, he was past forty. He cast aside social position, for he was a half-brother of the baron of Iguape (Antonio da Silva Prado), then the wealthiest man in Brazil. In protest, Eleuterio reverted to living openly with two black cooks. The older Prados snubbed him as "*o negreiro*"—the slave trader—for what they took as his deliberate affront to the family. Subsequently, Eleuterio recognized and educated his mulatto children, giving them his Prado name. One, Armando Prado, became valedictorian of his 1903 class at the São Paulo Law Faculty. He went on to become a state and a federal deputy, as well as a newspaper publisher and director of the state archives. Yet the "family-sponsored genealogy," authored by Armando's cousin Martinho ("Martinico") Prado Junior, followed the convention common in elite families; it omitted reference either to Eleuterio's consensual unions or to his mulatto natural children.[8]

In contrast to *mancebia* unions that resulted in natural offspring, those that generated adulterine children proved problematic at the highest social levels. Spurious offspring might be acknowledged and accepted within the bosom of the legitimate family, but convention demanded that fathers keep silent in public and leave their adulterine paternity tacit. When Jozé Bonifácio de Andrada returned to Brazil in 1819, in the company of his wife and teenage daughter, his conjugal family included an infant adulterine daughter, on whom his wife had bestowed her name. A decade later, when Jozé Bonifácio, now a widower, was presented to Empress Amelia by D. Pedro, the aging "patriarch of Brazilian independence" introduced the empress to his adulterine little girl, explaining that Narcisa was his "adopted daughter."[9] No doubt, Narcisa's adopted status represented more than a subterfuge for propriety's sake—which it was—given that Jozé Bonifácio could not expect to bestow solemn legitimization on her when he already had legitimate children. Informal adoption, coupled with a widower's simple paternal recognition, permitted him to exercise *pátrio poder*, to give Narcisa his family name, and, above all, to pave her entry into the highest social circles of the Corte by "repairing" her bastard birth.

Reform of succession law therefore deserves consideration in terms of how legislators personally were affected, even inscribed, in arrangements of *mancebia* characteristic of Brazil's independence era. Those relationships provided the foundation for either the elite "polygamous" families that often received attention from visiting foreigners or the consensual unions tantamount to marriage that many Brazilians elaborated as alternatives to marriage in the church.

ILLEGITIMACY WRIT LARGE AT

THE IMPERIAL COURT

New Royal City and "Old Vices of Europe"

Arrival of the Portuguese royal court in Rio de Janeiro in 1808 imparted a special tone to illegitimacy at the elite level. Prostitution became more widespread, as well as inevitably more accepted, after the arrival of Regent D. João and his massive entourage. A city which in 1799 numbered slightly over 43,000 had grown to around 60,000 by the time the Lisbon court arrived; by the eve of independence it contained around 112,695 inhabitants. An influx of somewhere between 10,000 to 15,000 Portuguese, who accompanied the royal family as forced immigrants in early 1808, not only imposed a net population gain of about twenty-five percent but it also introduced a large, cosmopolitan contingent of residents. Twelve years after the arrival of the court, Maria Graham remarked on the special features both the city and its residents projected to visitors. Not only did she find Rio de Janeiro "more like a European city than either Bahia [Salvador] or Pernambuco [Recife]," but she also singled out its women as distinctive: "The Portuguese and Brazilian ladies are decidedly superior in appearance to those of Bahia; they look of higher caste; perhaps the residence of the court for so many years has polished them. I cannot say the men partake of the advantage . . . ."[10]

Graham did not comment on the extent to which the Portuguese courtiers of D. João VI patronized the world's oldest profession; however, the nature of "prostitution" in what was the world's biggest slavocracy hardly fit a European pattern. As a burgeoning south Atlantic port, Rio de Janeiro became home to a growing number of resident Portuguese, English, and French, whose commercial activities reflected the opening of the colony's ports to foreign trade in the same year that the royal family established its court. Foreign sailors, and, if Walsh is to be believed, especially those who were English, Irish, and North American, now defined a familiar population of itinerants whose offshore behavior would sometimes end in brawling and head-on collisions with the city's police forces. They also offered new incentive for promoting what the city's police chief described as "scandalous customs."[11]

Although prostitution was not, strictly speaking, illegal, the police regulated and punished the behavior of both prostitutes and their rowdiest customers. By the 1840s, "the most repulsive and scandalous houses of prostitution" were being shut down and their customers and operators either jailed or deported.[12] In 1823, the city acquired its first and infamous curfew, the "*toque do Aragão*," named for the police chief who ordered the bells of the São Francisco Church to be tolled to signal the curfew's start. What functioned as "an antique euphemism for promoting prostitution"—the curfew—signaled to "well-known persons of integrity" that police patrols would not discourage them if they were encountered in the streets.[13] The wealthy and influential, however, possessed little need to resort to either streetwalkers or houses of prostitution. In the 1820s, the latter largely catered to the poor or foreign sailors. A visiting Frenchman, Jacques Arago, who lived in Rio de Janeiro between 1817 and 1819, commented that prostitutes could be found "in every quarter and in every street." Moreover, he speculated, they were "perhaps as numerous as in Paris."[14]

In the words of the Spanish consul general to the Imperial Court, the capital of the Kingdom of Portugal, Brazil, and the Algarves was "the royal city where the vices of Europe are to be found everywhere."[15] The substantial income of succeeding waves of crown officials and courtiers, together with their imported tastes, offered further reason for the newcomers to indulge the pleasures of the flesh. Nor were the morals of Rio de Janeiro's elite women beyond reproach. Maria Graham, a guest at a ball hosted by a high official of the imperial court, soon after her return to the Corte, in 1822, was lectured by an Englishman on the morality of the female guests she had been admiring in the dance. Seeing her skepticism, Graham's informant offered his "wager" that at least ten of these well-bred women, married or unmarried, had arrived with notes "to slip into the hand of her gallant." He tied his point, however, to the New World circumstance of slavery. That "women, even the unmarried, are less pure here than in Europe," was due, in his view, to "the servants being slaves." Graham's countryman maintained that slaves resorted to sexuality as retaliation for their captive status and treatment, for, "as enemies of their masters, [they were] ready and willing to deceive them, by assisting in the corruption of their families."[16]

Throughout the nineteenth century, the opinion offered by Graham's English acquaintance was one Brazilians themselves commonly asserted. That the slaves were responsible for corrupting the behavior and morality of their masters was a notion turned on its head, exchanging symptom for causality. In reality, slavery in Portugal's New World colony, especially the royal capital, offered a favorable context for encouraging "the corruption of Portuguese and blacks."[17] Not all European visitors spared the slaveholders. The French naturalist Auguste Saint-Hilaire, who preceded Empress Leopoldina in 1816, unsparingly condemned elite morals in the imperial capital. Offered from a vantage point that brought him into contact with scores of prominent politicians, intellectuals, and crown officials, during a residence of six years, his judgment singled out D. João VI's court as the crucial factor for promoting immorality. Although he believed "conditions are going to change with time," a "relaxation of morals" had become part of custom. "Forgetfulness of morality has become universal," he deplored, pointing to the "example offered by the Court of Portugal during its residence in Rio de Janeiro. The venality it introduced in everything," he noted, "redounds to the general corruption."[18]

The magnetism exercised by the tropical city on a heavily male, European immigrant population is difficult to gauge with exactitude. D. João's stubborn postponement of his politically indispensable return to Lisbon—for five years—suggested the wholehearted conversion to a Brazilian ambience that many Portuguese expatriates experienced. The Rev. Robert Walsh, alone among foreign visitors, was impressed by "the decency and decorum" of Rio de Janeiro. He found it "striking" in comparison to "the awful display of licentiousness which besets [visitors] in the streets and public places of Paris and London." Clearly, he left much unsaid.[19] The otherwise astute Walsh is to be forgiven for his ingenuousness in concluding that "no women of bad character are ever seen in the streets, either by day or night," adding, "so as to be known as such."[20] Naively, he failed to appreciate the identity of "women of the night" when he encountered them.

Jacques Arago clarified the situation. Streetwalkers did not solicit openly. Instead, they wore "a distinctive mantilla trimmed in black velvet" that distinguished them from other women.[21] Walsh's comment seemed to reflect that where prostitution in the imperial capital was publicly identified, then it was confined compactly to bordellos in the Bohemian district. The latter emerged in the eighteenth century and was set apart from the city's downtown streets. Restricted by proximity to a mangrove swamp, from which it took its historical name of "Mangue," the Corte's red-light district was an unhealthy place to visit.[22] Fifteen years following the 1829 establishment of the Medical-Literary Society of Rio de Janeiro—inspired by the Paris Academy of Medicine—Brazilian medical students began to publish the first dissertations on prostitution and syphilis in the Corte.[23]

Among the capital's exotic attractions, the Lisbon émigrés found women of African descent especially appealing. The slave status of the majority of them in 1808 lent their carnal appeal a coerced accessibility for European patrons that most were powerless to deny. Luiz de Freycinet, a French observer of the royal court, identified "libertinism" as the dominant vice, characterizing Brazil as "the country where it is not unusual to see all manner of excesses regnant."[24] During the two decades witnessing the residence of the

Lisbon court, the city's slave population reached its apogee as a proportion of the total population. Although the absolute number of slaves would continue to rise throughout the first half of the nineteenth century, especially after 1830, their proportion of the capital's residents reached a maximum between 1799 and 1821, rising from 34.55 to 48.88 percent of all inhabitants. By 1821 over 55,000 slaves lived in Rio de Janeiro. Many worked as "*escravos de ganho*," hired out by their owners to perform tasks taking them into the streets. Free to move about in pursuit of their work, usually they were expected to arrange their own lodgings. Mary Karasch established that both slaves and free individuals of color took over the occupation of street vending from immigrant Portuguese during the first decades of the nineteenth century. Those who were women, a minority, sometimes pursued prostitution on either a part-time or a full-time basis.

Travelers from Schlichthorst to Adéle Toussaint Samson "reported that black women who were street sellers or household slaves during the day often earned extra money on their own at night."[25] In working at the city's fountains and markets, slave women turned to prostitution as a secondary pursuit, seeking either to acquire cash resources or augment their meager earnings. Both those who were rented and those who worked directly for their owners were expected to turn over daily minimum earnings. Therefore, slave women would turn to prostitution "voluntarily," merely to earn the minimum sums of money they were obliged to surrender.[26] Alternatively, part of what they were permitted to keep would be set aside in anticipation of securing the coveted *carta de alforria* that bestowed manumission.

Prostitutes of all hues and nationalities multiplied once "free trade" became a permanent feature of post-independence life; poor white Brazilian and European women worked side-by-side with their darker-skinned sisters in selling themselves to an equally variegated clientele. Throughout the country's cities, the oldest profession flourished. Saint-Hilaire, whose travels took him to the city of São Paulo, offered reasons for the large numbers of prostitutes he encountered in what was still a sleepy, provincial backwater. "The rich women informed me that they undertake light work inside their houses—they embroider, make flowers, while in grand number the poor women remain in idleness during the day. And when night arrives, they scatter themselves throughout the city, dedicating themselves to the commerce of their charms, as their only means of existence."[27] The city of São Paulo had yet to mushroom on the coffee trade, for in 1820 it was still the hub of a sugar production zone in the surrounding countryside. Consequently, Saint-Hilaire was shocked to find a cosmopolitan population of prostitutes plying their trade: "In no part of the world that I have traversed did I see such a large number of prostitutes. They were of every color; the sidewalks were covered, so to speak, with women of that low station."[28]

More reprehensible was the proprietary prerogative inherent in chattel slavery. Rangel connected it to upper-class consumption of erotic pleasure: Rio de Janeiro's Valongo slave market embarcadero "satisfied at the same time lubricity and industry, providing the flesh for love and the labor for the hoe," sustaining both "agriculture and the harems."[29] Karasch identified one of Harro-Harring's drawings, completed in 1840, as depicting a middle-aged madam purchasing young slave women at Valongo for the purpose of placing them in prostitution.[30] The circumstance that so much of slavery was domestic obviated to a considerable degree the need for bordellos, especially for the wealthy. An 1821 advertisement confirmed that some slaveowners used Rio de Janeiro's newspapers to solicit business for the slave women they rented as prostitutes. More commonly, "young *mulata* slave women whom their owners advertised in the newspapers for household work in a single gentlemen's home might also have to serve as mistresses."[31] The distinction between slave and free, however, could be confounded, as newspapers revealed. Advertisements like the one asking "to rent a mulatto woman, freed," disregarded the fundamental divide between slave and free, suggesting they belonged on the same continuum.[32]

In rural Brazil, planters ordinarily cohabited with their slaves, isolated from the rest of society. José de Alencar delicately intimated the situation in his novel *Senhora*, when he described a Minas planter's "household routine," noting that it demonstrated "some ingrained habits that tend to become established on some farms, especially when the owners are unmarried."[33] Dunshee de Abranches proved much franker, conveying in his memoirs the vast gulf separating back-country Brazil from the refined world of the Corte: "I was entertained by a rich farmer who even then, without the least constraint, called my attention to a group of small dwellings in the vicinity of the family house, each one occupied by a concubine, his ex-slave, and respective heirs."[34] That slaveowners exploited a multiplicity of women whom they also owned as "real property"—and fathered children who started life as family chattel—is beyond dispute. Nor was it unusual for slaveowners to retain their own offspring as part of their servile labor force. Warren Dean found that the coloration of the slave population in rural Rio Claro, São Paulo, which in each decade after 1820 reflected a rising proportion of mulattoes, offered strong confirmation that the offspring of white fathers with slave women remained in bondage. Among slave children, "as many mulattoes as blacks existed, even though there were three and one-half times more black than mulatto female slaves!" By the 1860s, nearly all of the increase in the county's free mulatto population was attributed to self-reproduction.[35]

Wealthy slaveowners enjoyed the opportunity to exercise a libertine prerogative. Dean collected oral history on a situation that had existed on Fazenda Angêlica, in Rio Claro, where it was said that "sadistic orgies presided over by the baron [of Grão Mogul] in his cellar" took place. Guálter Martins, the baron, summoned the "honorable members of the town's elite" as invited guests to those occasions of cruelty and debauchery.[36] Alternatively, planters' multiple unions with their slaves could complicate enormously their relatives' situation vis-à-vis *ab intestato* succession. Two of the sons of the marquis of Baependy (Manoel Jacyntho Nogueira da Gama), for example, were reputed to have kept a harem of *mulata* slaves, fathered by "well-known local gentry and aristocrats," leading to the facetious aside that this "gang" or "bevy" of young women was "ennobled." The younger son, the count of Baependy (Brás Carneiro Nogueira da Gama), fathered two children by the slaves, although he recognized neither, given that he had eight legitimate children.[37] His older brother, the baron of Juparanã (also Manoel Jacintho Nogueira da Gama) offered the contrast of lifelong bachelorhood, coupled with substantial property, extending to more than 400 slaves. Between 1852 and 1872, Juparanã fathered no less than sixteen natural children with mothers who were either slaves or *libertas*. When he died, his will left one-half of his estate to his two brothers and the remaining half to his sixteen children, whom he recognized posthumously with the proviso they were prohibited from using his family names.[38]

In urban contexts like Rio de Janeiro, the slave offspring of slave owners—or their close relatives—often fared better when the fathers were counted as members of the social and political elites. Their mothers usually belonged to what amounted to an urban elite of slaves who were "richly dressed ladies-in-waiting or personal maids of the wealthy, known as *mucamas*." The father-child relationship proved more complex, given that the mother's identity as a favored slave could determine not only the child's passage into freedom as a *liberto* but also considerable social mobility and good occupational or professional prospects.[39] "A *mucama* was often the half-sister, child, or concubine of her owner." Where the master was unmarried, she might be his housekeeper or supervise the other slaves, doubling as mistress or common-law wife.[40] Her value to the household could determine that the children she had with her owner would remain within or near the premises, at least until they reached the marketable age of around eight years.

The fate of many of these children, when their city-dwelling owners were well-off, tended toward manumission, either as the decision of their white fathers or as the result of purchase. Certainly, the city offered greater possibility for self-purchase. Caring relatives might also contribute to a slave child's freedom. Maria Graham underscored both the visibility and viability of Rio de Janeiro's free mulatto population, precisely because of the predominant role it played in most forms of skilled labor. "The orchestra at the opera house is composed of at least one-third mulattoes," she discovered on a visit in 1821. "They are the best artificers [artisans] and artists ... All decorative painting, carving, and inlaying is done by them; in short, they excel in all ingenious mechanical arts."[41] She singled out "creole negroes," by which she meant the native-born, free population of color, as the key achievers in late colonial society. Graham viewed them favorably, compared to both Portuguese and white Brazilians. In Recife, where free mulattoes "have amassed great fortunes in many instances," Graham emphasized they were "more active, more industrious, and more lively than the other classes." That there were "few rich negroes" to be found in Salvador she tied to how skin color predisposed those who were lighter skinned mulattoes to benefit disproportionately from their ties to slaveowners.[42]

Growth of the slave population from 1830 onward mattered fundamentally for the rising proportion of free color in the total population. "Gradual manumission" was an even greater fact of life by the independence decade than it had been in the final decades of the eighteenth century. Although the free population of color presented a much more likely source of recruitment for prostitutes, the demographic transition it captured mattered more for the growing number of stable unions that produced family units. Whether those unions were founded on interracial concubinage or legal marriage between partners who were usually of color, they increasingly involved free individuals. It was from the ranks of the free population of color that white men, often those of good prospects, increasingly selected mistresses. Otherwise, whites lower in status, like Portuguese immigrants, found the partners with whom they lived in *mancebia*, and occasionally married in the church.

In 1830, an illegitimate child was typically of color and freeborn—or likely to be soon manumitted. Where formerly the illegitimate child's slave status might have been deliberately left intact by his father, demographic change now presented white fathers with a new situation. Their children who were illegitimate increasingly tended to be freeborn or destined for manumission. The substantial number who were natural offspring, consequently, were potentially heirs in *ab intestato* succession. Alternatively, even children who were spurious tended more and more to be freeborn. In other words, less and less did the fathers of illegitimate children have it within their power to determine whether or not their children would be their legal heirs in succession. Even where the child remained a slave, the father had to take into account the greater possibility that his offspring might gain freedom through purchase or testamentary manumission.

Bragança Dynastic Legacy and Princely Example

The establishment of the Portuguese royal court in Rio de Janeiro fostered an ambience in which illegitimacy was tolerated for reasons that went beyond merely a general climate of relaxed sexual morality, if not outright licentiousness. The royal family itself offered demonstration of why, at the very pinnacle of the social pyramid, adultery was an accepted behavior and adulterine children were sometimes socially tolerated. Between 1808 and 1821, the anomaly of family life enacted by the royal couple—D. João Carlos de Bragança and D. Carlota Joaquina de Bourbon, daughter of the Prince of Asturias and, since 1788, Charles IV of Spain—found genealogical validation in the person of their second, surviving son: the prince of Beira, D. Pedro de Alcantara Bragança e Bourbon (1798–1834). The heir apparent's well-documented adventures as a womanizer deserve to be connected to his parents' rather bizarre union, especially his mother's sexual escapades and political intrigues. D. João and D. Carlota Joaquina resided in isolated, separate households for most of their nearly forty years of matrimony.[42]

Even before they embarked for Brazil, a singularly unhappy marriage had led the future monarchs, who were also uncle and niece, to live apart. Yet, despite a rocky union, they had nine children, beginning with Maria Tereza, princess of Beira, who was born in 1793. When their oldest son, Antonio, born two years later, lived only four years, then his younger brother Pedro became the heir apparent. Separate residences in Portugal also accounted for the queen's access to men whom gossips identified as the fathers of several of her children. Her lovers ranged from candidates chosen from the common people to Marshal Junot himself. The marquis of Marialva, the king's master of the horse, was reputed to have fathered her youngest son and favorite, D. Miguel.[43] Although it was commonly believed that D. João had not fathered the queen's three youngest daughters, Pedro, duke of Beira, was spared any intimation of spurious birth.

Pedro, who was nine when he arrived in Brazil, grew to adulthood in his father's São Cristovão Palace at Quinta da Boa Vista, in the company of his younger brother Miguel and his oldest sister, Maria Teresa, her father's private secretary. In 1810, she had married her first cousin, D. Pedro Carlos de Bourbon, Spanish Infante and the son of Ferdinand VII, king of Spain, her mother's brother. Consequently, Pedro paid visits to his mother and four younger sisters at Carlota Joaquina's seaside residence in Botafogo, three miles' distant, on the other side of the city. Mello Moraes, trenchant chronicler of Bragança court life, castigated D. João for having been so careless in the education of his heir and forfeiting responsibility to Carlota Joaquina. "Without doubt," he added, "he would have been one of the best sovereigns in the world, if he had had an education appropriate to his high rank." Instead, the Prince of Beira "sat a horse very well and made a handsome impression . . . taking pride in driving a four or a six-horse carriage team." Between the ages of ten and eighteen, Pedro spent his time in "pranks, gallantries, and roguish pastimes," in the company "of stable boys and minions," which caused his speech to be "coarse and his pronunciation bad."[44] In adolescence, the heir exhibited sexual behavior exaggerative of the general climate in the imperial court, his "gallantries" playing out in a context where "prostitution occurred without reproach and adultery was common," accounting for "the declarations of 'de pais incógnitos' that followed the names of newborns" in baptismal registries, "with little edification."[45]

Pedro's amatory inclinations, beginning when he was no more than fourteen, contributed to a climate at court highly tolerant of his wanton womanizing and, eventually, his illegitimate progeny. Escragnolle Doria aptly summed up Pedro's amatory style: "He did not know how to love only once. He partook of love by the mouthfuls."[46] His insistence on acknowledging or recognizing a number of his adulterine children by various mothers in the 1820s set a new standard for progeny of royal blood. Pedro's genuine concern for the children he fathered outside marriage, including the steps he took to rectify their stigmatized *qualidade*, defined a royal subtext that called into question the law's "damnable and punishable" treatment of spurious offspring.

Initially, both the prince's parents and the imperial court accepted his libidinous propensities for bedding the daughters of high crown officials or any other women who took his fancy. Good fathers barred the young prince's entry to their homes, while loyal palace officials and employees occasionally accepted as wives the daughters of colleagues offered in marriage with a dowry bestowed by Pedro.[47] His amatory conquests extended to the wife of the commander of the capital's Portuguese army garrison, Gen. Jorge de Avilez, a husband who later complicated Pedro's orchestration of the break with Portugal.[48] Chasing after the sedan chairs of highborn women or importuning their lowborn sisters in the streets did not always bring success. Singular rebuff came from a beautiful *mulata* whom Pedro so fancied that he grabbed her for a kiss on a Santos street. When she slapped him in the face and ran home, he wanted her even more. In this instance, his actions belied the abolitionism that some historians have ascribed to his liberalism. Pursuing royal advantage to the doorstep of the house where the young woman took refuge, and discovering she was a slave, he attempted to buy her. When the woman's owners refused to part with her, Pedro had to admit defeat.[49]

When the prince fell truly in love for the first time, with Noémi Thiery, a young French theatrical dancer, he threatened the marriage that his parents had carefully arranged in Europe. His adolescent impulses had to be checked. In May 1816, D. João had elevated Brazil to political equality with Portugal and the Algarves, following the death of Maria I in 1815. Pedro was officially recognized as the heir to the throne of the new United Kingdom of Portugal, Brazil, and the Algarves, during an investiture as prince royal and duke of Bragança on January 9, 1817.[50] His marriage the same year, at age eighteen, insured dynastic succession within a family soon to be divided into parallel royal lines dedicated to Rio de Janeiro and Lisbon. Pedro's bride was Archduchess Leopoldina, the daughter of Francis of Austria. She was already en route to Brazil when the bridegroom was informed his marriage by proxy had taken place in Vienna on May 13, 1817.

Leopoldina's imminent arrival in Rio de Janeiro, on November 5, provided the catalyst for bringing Pedro's affair with Noémi Thiery to an abrupt conclusion. By then, "Moemi," as she was known, was living in a house that Pedro had ordered built for her on the grounds of the São Cristovão Palace. She was also expecting their child in three or four months. When Pedro would not give up the woman he insisted on calling "my wife," a crisis of state played out in the confines of the palace.[51] Moemi proved resolutely devoted to Pedro, but, eventually, Carlota Joaquina persuaded her son's mistress to forsake him. She convinced her of the overriding importance of princely destiny—and the real possibility that Pedro would be disinherited in favor of Miguel if he did not set her aside. Moemi, whom Maria Graham described, as "very well brought up," extracted one condition, that the queen not send her into exile abroad. She was permitted to remove herself to another region of Brazil, due to the imminence of her child's birth.[52]

While D. João's ministers and councilors had personally implored the Frenchwoman to sacrifice herself for affairs of state, the entire court awaited the birth of the prince's love child—at the same moment they anticipated Leopoldina's arrival. Three months after being dispatched with a generous dowry on a packet to the northern port city of Recife, Moemi gave birth to a stillborn baby. Yet the affair had initiated a new standard of openness at court, for Pedro frankly acknowledged his paternity of the dead infant and publicly mourned its death, setting the precedent for the adulterine children he fathered in the 1820s. Moemi's care had been entrusted to the provincial governor-general and his wife. Following the public memorial for Pedro's dead child, no less than a public funeral was carried out with great pomp in Recife's streets. Organized by Gov.-Gen. Luiz do Rêgo Barreto, the solemnities amounted to an affair of state. Moemi herself slipped into the void of history.[53]

Pedro's well-documented remorse over Moemi's self-sacrificing departure in an advanced state of pregnancy, and his grief over their child's stillbirth, explained much about his subsequent concern as a monarch for the illegitimate children he would father with his notorious paramour, Domitila de Castro Canto e Mello. The grotesque anecdote that he kept the corpse of the stillborn infant Moemi delivered in Recife, in his royal apartment, after Gov. Gen. Luiz Rêgo brought it to him, underscored both a genuine paternal concern and the painful loss of the first woman he openly called "wife."[54] Although Pedro proved a devoted father to his legitimate children, beginning in 1819, with the birth of Maria da Gloria, he also concerned himself on behalf of a number of his illegitimate offspring. Several whose mothers had been only a passing fancy nonetheless enjoyed his protection.[55] More important for the political climate in which legislators would attempt to reform the position of adulterine children, Pedro acted to rectify the situation that defined his children as the "fruit of a crime."

PEDRO'S POLYGAMOUS FAMILY

"Teúda e Mantéuda" in São Cristovão

Conventionally and correctly, historians have concluded that Pedro's scandalous relationship with his famous mistress, Domitila de Castro Canto e Mello (1797–1867), indirectly contributed to his abdication, on the ground that his outraged ministers and councilors, not to mention many members of Parliament, came to resent his well-born and wealthy paramour as an influential "Madame de Maintenon." Certainly after Leopoldina's death, in December 1826, they regarded Domitila more dangerously, as a possible successor to the empress. On the other hand, this judgment conventionally ignores the position Domitila enjoyed by virtue of her motherhood of no less than five of Pedro's children between 1823 and 1830. The shadow that she cast over the expectations of politicians extended to the specter of what is best described as Pedro's polygamous family. It was a family he deliberately established at court and gave access to the royal apartments in the São Cristovão Palace. Nor have conventional treatments of Pedro's "affair" with Domitila explored the implications of the family they formed between 1823 and 1829 for changing social attitudes about *mancebia*, illegitimacy, and paternal recognition.

The emperor's elevation of Domitila to the position of first lady-in-waiting to the Empress Leopoldina, in April 1825, deserves reappraisal in light of the growing family he had fathered with his paramour. As the act that drew the ire of many in the political elite, Domitila's elevation in rank was a first step in Pedro's intended integration of his illegitimate and legitimate families within the walls of the Palace of São Cristovão. It carried a high price, due to breaking with conventional court decorum and offering direct, public insult to the empress. Domitila's rank of first lady-in-waiting did not merely confer prestige on a beloved mistress formerly excluded by protocol from the company of the empress. Nor did it merely gain her a place near Pedro at court—or even vindicate her, after the group insult she suffered when Leopoldina's ladies-in-waiting "cut her dead" during Holy Week services in 1825. All of these motives were genuine, but another has gone unremarked: Pedro wanted his adulterine daughter—and a second adulterine child anticipated in December of that year—to be part of his family life in the palace. He wanted them to join his legitimate children in play, to witness their father receiving his ministers, and for the court to partake of his paternal affection and pride. Above all, he wanted his adulterine children to be raised in a context where they would not be subjected to the social slights associated with the "stain" of damnable and punishable birth.

Yet Empress Leopoldina's unanticipated death at age twenty-nine, in December 1826, caused Pedro's ministers, as well as the capital's populace, to reappraise his motives. The negative verdict they returned, one difficult to reverse, cast Pedro's illegitimate family in a more unfavorable light and spelled its eventual eclipse. Once the emperor became a widower, the fear that Domitila might become his wife, and Brazil's next empress, grew irrationally. It led to speculation that the emperor might have her estranged husband murdered. It was one thing to acquire the reputation of a libertine emperor and then to be appreciated as the devoted lover of a mesmerizing and dangerous courtesan—a woman who bore Pedro illegitimate offspring *"em série."* It was quite a different proposition for the emperor of Brazil to impose a polygamous imperial family on the court. "Polygamous household" gets closer to the young monarch's goal, for, although Pedro did not ask Domitila to reside in the palace until after Leopoldina had died—and she wisely declined—by 1825 the concubine possessed the freedom to call on the empress. As first lady-in-waiting to Leopoldina, Domitila enjoyed entrée to Leopoldina's private apartments, a privilege belonging only to her confessor and the palace chamberlain, in addition to her husband. Domitila, who resided directly across the street from the São Cristovão Palace, in a home constructed for her on Pedro's orders, could visit the palace at will.[56]

Pedro began his formal liaison with Domitila in November 1822. In the manner of many men at court, he established a prized and beloved mistress according to the formula of the *Ordenações Filipinas*, domiciling and maintaining her—"*teúda e manteúda*"—as a concubine. In fact, Domitila was very wealthy in her own right, a legally separated woman of twenty-five and the mother of three legitimate children. When summoned to the Corte by Pedro, initially, she took up living quarters in the Rocio, the capital's downtown district. This arrangement afforded the emperor ready access to her household from the nearby City Palace, explaining why Empress Leopoldina became the last to learn of her husband's new passion. Five children followed from Pedro's liaison with Domitila de Castro, starting in 1823. The first three arrived in sequence with Pedro's legitimate offspring. The emperor's penchant for bestowing the names of his sisters on his adulterine daughters, as well as giving his own name to both legitimate and adulterine sons, reinforced the image of a dual imperial family.

What Pedro imposed directly on Empress Leopoldina, from April 1825 until her death at the end of 1826—that his Austrian wife accept his illegitimate children in her household, so that they would be brought up in the company of their legitimate offspring—was not as shocking as it seemed. By Brazilian standards, law permitted fathers to impose their adulterine children on their wives, and defined as a wifely obligation that they raise them in the legitimate household. Wives did not gain the right to refuse to bring up a husband's illegitimate child until the republic. Consequently, Pedro's behavior in this respect amounted to a transgression of court decorum and husbandly good sense rather than any violation of a wife's rights. As a foreigner, Leopoldina was unaccustomed to the expectations of a Brazilian husband. Although she wisely did not challenge Pedro on the matter of his Paulista paramour, and reluctantly tolerated his adulterine children, his insistence on integrating both sets of children within her household eventually became unbearable for her.

On October 12, 1825, Domitila de Castro was ennobled as viscountess of Castro, while two of her brothers and her father were elevated to gentlemen of the court. That she received a title and later was elevated in the peerage acquired special significance in view of the children she bore the emperor. The noble title and distinctions *en famille* amounted to rewards for having given birth to Pedro's daughter, on May 24, 1824. Domitila was also seven months' pregnant with Pedro's son when she became a viscountess. The

French representative to the Bragança court reported that earlier, in 1823, Domitila had given birth to a son of Pedro, who survived only hours. The daughter, however, had arrived two days after an ecclesiastical tribunal ruled that Domitila was legally separated—"divorced"—from her estranged husband.[57] Nevertheless, the child was maternally, as well as paternally, adulterine. Marriage was dissoluble only by death. When the "baby girl Izabel" was baptized, on May 31, 1824, the priest noted her *qualidade* in the baptismal register of Engenho Velho's parish church as "*de pais incógnitos*," of unknown parents. Both parents, however, apparently witnessed the christening of the legal *exposta*.[58] The child's father named her "Izabel Maria," after his younger sister. The parish register also reported that the infant had been "abandoned" at the house of Col. João de Castro Canto e Mello and Escolastica Bonifacia de Toledo, her godparents who were also Domitila's parents.

Five days after Empress Leopoldina gave birth to Brazil's future emperor, Pedro Alcantara Gonçaga, on December 2, 1825, Domitila de Castro gave birth to a third child fathered by D. Pedro, a baby boy. His father named him Pedro Alcantara Brasileiro, perhaps due to his belief that only one of his two sons would live, a reasonable assumption. More probably, he concluded that each baby was his mother's second son, for whom he—as a second son—had deliberately reserved his own name. Accidents of fate historically meant that no first-born son of the house of Bragança had lived long enough to inherit the throne of Portugal. D. Pedro, like his father and grandmother, became the heir due to the death of an older brother.[59] Pedro's adulterine son was baptized "in danger of his life," on December 27, the priest from Engenho Velho being called in haste to administer the sacrament in the imperial chapel. The marquis of Mareschal, witness to the christening, was impressed with the emperor's reserve at what Pedro determined would be a public event. The British representative to the imperial court also underscored the public nature of the christening ceremony.[60]

According to the representative of the United States to the imperial court, Pedro Alcantara Brasileiro's baptism occurred just as the emperor was preparing to bestow the title of duke on the infant. However, the frail newborn did not live long enough to attain a title. The fact that the child was a legal *exposto*, a foundling, would have complicated his ennoblement enormously, for, like his adulterine sister a year earlier, little Pedro Alcantara was baptized of "unknown parents." However, unlike Izabel Maria's registration, the word "*exposto*" was not recorded next to his name in the parish register. The curious omission of such a notation may have been due to the circumstance that the baptism took place as an emergency measure, removed from the church in Engenho Velho. There may have been no time to arrange a false set of adoptive parents with a separate residence, due to the baby's critical illness. Although Domitila's sister and her husband stood as godparents, no information was recorded on the baby's parentage.[61] Presumably, the emperor, whose plans for recognizing and ennobling his children with Domitila already were in evidence, found it repugnant to register the couple's only son as a legal foundling. Pedro apparently prevailed on the parish priest to leave the infant's parentage moot, for the parish registers of the Engenho Velho church catered to such delicate situations. Confined to the care of wet nurses on February 2, 1826, when Domitila accompanied Pedro and Leopoldina on a state visit to the northern provinces, the sickly Pedro Alcantara Brasileiro lived less than three months. He died on March 13, before his parents returned to the capital on April 1.

The death of Pedro's adulterine baby, which coincided with Domitila's notorious presence in the imperial entourage to the north, widely publicized the existence of Pedro I's polygamous family beyond the confines of São Cristovão, making it common knowledge in the Corte. Prior to the funeral, the presence of the empress' first lady-in-waiting aboard the *Pedro I*, the royal yacht, advertised to the emperor's subjects the intimate co-existence of his legitimate and illegitimate families. After three and one-half years, Pedro's relationship with his paramour became not only overtly public but also integrated within his legitimate family. On board the *Pedro I*, Domitila de Castro was seated to the emperor's right at dinner, with his eldest daughter, Maria da Gloria, on his left, leaving everyone else, including the empress and Domitila's brother and brother-in-law, to sit wherever they would. When the entourage reached Salvador, Pedro took the first floor of the Governor's Palace and installed Domitila on the floor above. The empress, however, stayed in the adjacent Palace of Justice and the six-year-old Maria da Gloria occupied rooms in a connecting bridge between the two buildings.[62]

Meanwhile, on March 17, the tiny body of the adulterine infant Pedro Alcantara Brasileiro had been embalmed and placed in the church in Engenho Velho. Fearful of the decision they must make, the emperor's ministers met in confusion, but finally determined they should proceed with the funeral. Their anxiety derived from the apprehension that a public funeral would divulge the news of the infant's death throughout the city. The viscount of Paranaguá (Francisco Vilella Barbosa) sent invitations to those at court; the marquis of São João da Palma (Francisco de Assis Mascarenhas) did the same for legislators. They were thus obliged to reveal to startled onlookers assembled outside the church that the funeral was being held for "a son of their sovereign." The presence of imperial carriages in the streets, conveying high-born occupants to Engenho Velho, as well as "a flock of children in festive mood," who by custom accompanied "the little *espúrio*" from the palace to the church, alerted all of Rio de Janeiro to the death of the emperor's love child.[63] "Gaiety," an emotion in evidence at the funerals of small children in the 1820s, followed from the belief that they went to be with the angels in heaven. For this reason, even at the close of the nineteenth century, it was "not the custom of the country that the parents follow the body" of their child in the funeral. "Along the procession to the cemetery, ladies would throw roses to the little angel," whose casket often looked more like an "elegant embroidered trunk enveloping the body in artificial flowers."[64]

Displayed on a catafalque within the church of São Francisco Xavier de Engenho Velho, the handles of the tiny coffin containing Pedro Alcantara Brasileiro were grasped by the marquis of Santo Amaro (Jozé Egydio Alvares de Almeida), soon to be president of the Senate. Accompanying him as pallbearers were three courtiers close to the emperor: the viscount of Aracaty (João Carlos Augusto d'Oeyenhausen), the viscount of Taubaté (Luiz de Saldanha da Gama), and the above-mentioned viscount of Paranaguá.[65] The prestige of these noble pallbearers merely underscored the significance of the occasion throughout the city, for a populace that two months earlier deliriously celebrated the christening of the dead child's half-brother and namesake, the emperor's male heir. In fact, rumors abounded that the infant who died in the palace was Pedro's legitimate son and that the babies had been switched. The political necessity of distinguishing the dead Pedro from the living Pedro who was his legitimate half-brother had dictated "the little *espúrio*'s" public funeral as much as any appreciation of his father's sentiments. It also confirmed for the capital's populace that the emperor's progeny had indeed been growing in multiples of two.

Per Rescriptum Principis: Sovereign vs. Bishop

The deaths of two infant sons fathered with Domitila, in 1823 and 1825, may well have prompted D. Pedro to try to persuade the bishop of Rio de Janeiro to cooperate in obtaining crown legitimization for the couple's surviving offspring, Izabel Maria. Over the weeks following Pedro Alcantara's funeral, the emperor attempted to arrange "a solemn proceeding for recognizing [paternal] filiation."[66] "Solemn" signified nothing less than a coveted certificate of crown legitimization issued by the Tribunal of the Mesa do Desembargo do Paço. Historically, Portugal's monarchs had sometimes resorted to papal legitimization in order to succeed. D. Dinis I, for instance, was the adulterine son of D. Afonso II (1248–1279) and his paramour, D. Beatriz of Castile, herself a natural offspring. Beatriz' father was none other than the lawgiver king of Castile and León, Alfonso X, El Sabio. Papal legitimization in 1263 enabled Dinis to be crowned king of Portugal in 1279.[67] However, by the fourteenth century, the Portuguese king's illegitimate children were exempted from rules applying to the offspring of other nobles, because their right to enjoy their father's nobility was deemed automatic with paternal recognition—simple legitimization.

Eventually, legitimization was not required for succession to the throne, probably due to the precedent set by the founder of the House of Aviz, Mestre João d'Aviz. The natural son of the king, D. Pedro, and his Spanish paramour, Inêz de Castro, João d'Aviz dispensed altogether with legitimization after persuading the Avignon pope to release him from his vows of celibacy so that he could marry Philippa of Lancaster. He then laid before João das Regras his mother's claim that she and his father had contracted a clandestine marriage. Placing confidence in his royal jurisconsult's celebrated knowledge of Roman law, he ascended the throne as D. João I (1383–1433).[68]

By the eighteenth century, consequently, even an heir to the throne whose legitimacy was questionable needed only the simple paternal recognition of the king—or his legitimate brother. Otherwise, crown legitimization, as Lobão confirmed, was not the usual course of action for the "bastards of the king." They did not depend on *per Rescriptum Principis*.[69] Considerable precedents existed among the eighteenth-century Bragança monarchs for acknowledging their adulterine offspring, tacitly or publicly, including those who were doubly adulterine or maternally *sacrílegos*. D. João V (1717–1750), for instance, had several long liaisons with women who had taken the veil, giving rise to Voltaire's quip: "When he wanted a mistress, he took a nun." Moreover, the great-great grandfather of D. Pedro I publicly acknowledged one of his sons by Mother Paula Teresa da Silva, a future inquisitor-general. D. João V also acknowledged D. Antonio, a son whose mother was French, and D. Gaspar, born to a lady-in-waiting at court. The latter became bishop of Braga.[70]

D. José I, who succeeded his father D. João V, in 1750, proved more circumspect. The marquis of Távora (Bernardo Jozé de Lorena) was an instructive example. Bernardo Jozé de Lorena was widely reputed to be the king's illegitimate son, given D. José's affair with the wife of the preceding marquis of Távora, Lorena's putative father and the individual later executed for high treason in the concocted plot to murder D. José. Unacknowledged publicly by the king, the adulterine Bernardo de Lorena was raised in the Monastery of Chellas and then posted to the colonies. Entrusted with the captain-generalcy of São Paulo and Minas Gerais, he established a sixteen-year relationship of *mancebia* with Marianna Angelica Fortes de Bustamonte Sá

Leme, a Brazilian woman of gentle birth. The couple had at least five natural children, before Lorena left in 1806 to become viceroy of India. All were baptized *expostos* to conceal their parents' names, although the relationship was common knowledge. Marianna did not become Bernardo de Lorena's wife due to her social inequality, for she lacked high nobility. The queen's permission, needed for a high crown official to marry, would not have been forthcoming, although Bernardo was presumably Maria I's half-brother. In compensation, the municipal council of the city of São Paulo accorded Marianna "recognition of her filiation of *fidalguia* of Andalusian roots." Her *qualidade* of minimal nobility, by descent, could thereby be raised, entitling her to be addressed in a form reserved for nobility—appropriate to the un-married governor-general's consort.

In 1818, when the oldest child of Lorena and Marianna, Francisco de Assis Lorena, was legitimized by Rio de Janeiro's Tribunal of the Desembargo do Paço, he was twenty-eight years old. His father's identity still had to be con-cealed, even though his mother was dead, presumably due to the late mar-quis' identity as a royal bastard. The petition, filed in 1818 by Francisco's fa-ther-in-law and former guardian, therefore disguised his father, Bernardo Jozé de Lorena, as his uncle; it made no mention of his parents' names. A year later, Francisco received paternal recognition, posthumously, when Bernardo Jozé de Lorena's 1819 will declared paternity of him and his three sisters.[71]

Historically, the so-called bastard of the king did not need crown legitimi-zation. Merely his or her father's recognition was sufficient, an act permitting the king's bastard then to be addressed as "*dom.*" That D. Pedro I could not be content with his open acknowledgment of his fatherhood of an adulterine daughter—kingly behavior tolerated in the eighteenth century—spoke to his determination to see his spurious children accepted as equal in rank with his legitimate offspring. He wanted to bestow recognition more formally, as sol-emn legitimization, due to his intention to equip his adulterine children with titles and make it appropriate for them to be addressed as "your highness." Theoretically, "the mercy and grace of the Prince" conferred by the Tribunal of the Desembargo do Paço extended to the sovereign's own offspring; how-ever, Pedro's situation was highly unusual, even unique. The fact that he al-ready had five living legitimate offspring—and expected more—did not make Izabel Maria a good candidate for solemn legitimization. In addition, as the previous example of Francisco Lorena illustrated, crown legitimization ordinarily was effected without naming the "offending" parents, especially when they were living, prominent, and highborn. Moreover, custom dictated that solemn legitimization was posthumously bestowed on adulterine individuals. Pedro, in declining to be circumspect about his paternity of Izabel Maria, publicly testified to Domitila's maternity as well. Furthermore, their liaison was one of "qualified" concubinage, deemed in law to be "notorious and scandalous," as well as ongoing. Finally, the father of Empress Leopoldina was the Austrian emperor. His approval or disinterest could not be assumed, given that solemn legitimization would directly affect his grandchildren's social position and threaten their position as *ab intestato* heirs.

Pedro declined to delay his daughter's legitimization until she reached adulthood, because he intended for Izabel Maria to be received by Empress Leopoldina and his ministers and courtiers on a parity with the child's legitimate half-siblings. Therefore, he had to make her a duchess in order for her to be addressed as "your highness." These motives nevertheless were subordinate to the emperor's goal of rectifying the stain of her adulterine quality of birth. By legally equipping her for ennoblement and a title, he expected that she would cease to be regarded a royal bastard. In acting publicly on a sentiment that many fathers of adulterine children shared, consequently, the emperor dramatized the deep resentment felt by socially prominent fathers when their innocent offspring paid the price of the "crime" of adulterine or sacrilegious birth.

D. José Caetano da Silva Coutinho, bishop of Rio de Janeiro and imperial chaplain, would not be moved to support solemn legitimization for Izabel Maria, even when the emperor used his considerable resources of persuasion.[72] That Pedro believed he needed the support of the man who was his personal confessor for a legal procedure that did not depend on canon law spoke to the complexity of his personal situation. D. Jozé Caetano, who commanded considerable moral authority and popular respect, was a skilled politician as well as a prelate of the national church. He had been named royal chaplain in 1808 by D. João VI, whom he followed into exile.[73] Pedro needed his approval, or at least D. Jozé Caetano's tacit consent, in order to amend and revise the baptismal register of the Engenho Velho church so that it would establish his simple *perfilhação*, or act of paternal recognition. The latter served as the basis for initiating crown legitimization proceedings. Hence, he could not afford to have the bishop of Rio de Janeiro oppose his petition to the Desembargo do Paço. On the other hand, the emperor's close confidant and friend, the marquis of São João da Palma, was president of the Tribunal of the Mesa do Desembargo do Paço. Pedro doubtlessly expected Palma to cooperate fully in granting a legitimization certificate for Izabel Maria.

In 1823, the bishop of Rio de Janeiro had sat as a deputy to the Constituent Assembly. Therefore, he continued to be a member of the lower house in the first session of Parliament, dismissed by the emperor and then convened in April 1826. Although Pedro first approached D. Jozé Caetano on the matter of legitimizing Izabel Maria in April or May of that year, in February, he had named the bishop to a life tenure seat in the Senate. Indeed, it is difficult to resist the conclusion that D. Jozé Caetano's senatorial appointment reflected the emperor's attempt to enlist his support for legitimizing Izabel Maria. From 1827 through 1831, in his official capacity as "president-bishop-royal chaplain," Silva Coutinho presided over the Senate. Of liberal opinions, he was "exceedingly temperate"—a man who "fasts all year on one meal a day."[74] By the time Pedro sought his support for Izabel Maria's legitimization, however, D. Jozé Caetano had acquired a reputation for butting heads with Pedro's coterie of advisers and courtiers, over the morality prevailing at court. Earlier, D. Jozé Caetano had been thwarted in several attempts to reform the comportment and sexual conduct of individual clerics. In 1821, he had even enlisted D. Pedro's support in admonishing priests "to dress decently" in order to earn the respect of the common people.[75] By 1828, partly as a result of chilled relations with the emperor, Rev. Walsh reported, "the court party has been for some years in open hostility with him."[76]

Pedro failed to enlist the bishop's support on behalf of his adulterine daughter's legitimization. The overriding obstacle was the simple fact that, as imperial chaplain, D. Jozé Caetano also served as personal confessor to Empress Leopoldina.[77] In the end, the emperor had to settle for much less than he wanted. The bishop balked at breaking the convention that demanded adulterous fathers keep silent and he refused to uphold Izabel Maria's legitimization *per Rescriptum Principis*. Instead, "that solid son of the church relaxed his inflexibility before the vehemence of the imperial will only in order to permit a succinct rectification be entered in the original parish registry's entry." That is, the bishop offered the emperor one, not inconsequential, concession that amounted to simple legitimization in law: the sovereign was permitted to correct the baptismal entry of 1824, altering Izabel Maria's *qualidade* from an *exposta* to a child fathered by the emperor. However, she would continue to be matrilineally spurious—of unknown mother—in the baptismal register.[78]

D. Pedro, of course, could not be content with merely an altered parish register. Denied solemn legitimization, he transformed his simple legitimization, no more than a declaration of his paternity, into a formal state occasion. On May 20, 1826, a few days before his daughter's second birthday, a delegation consisting of the emperor's councilors of state and ministers met in Pedro's presence to witness his handwritten affidavit recognizing Izabel Maria as his daughter. The emperor postdated his signature to May 24, the date of Izabel Maria's second birthday.[79] In keeping with custom, he did not reveal the name of the child's mother, because she was a gentlewoman and remained another man's legal wife. Pedro recognized his daughter according to a suitably discreet formula that subtly implied his paternity through the act of bestowing his dynastic names on the recognized child: "I declare that there was a daughter born to a noblewoman enjoying purity of blood, whom I ordered to be called D. Izabel Maria de Alcantara Brasileira and to be raised in the home of a Gentleman of my Imperial Household, João de Castro Canto e Mello [Domitila's father]."[80]

By virtue of an accompanying "note," witnessed by three of Pedro's ministers or advisors, dated May 28, the sovereign's declaration of paternal recognition was then presented to the same parish priest in Engenho Velho who had baptized "Izabel the innocent" in 1824. It attested to the paternity of the child described in the baptismal record of May 31, 1824, and instructed the priest to correct the baptismal register to read "Izabel Maria de Alcantara, daughter of his majesty, the emperor."[81] The words of this instruction specifically directed that "the stain of unknown paternity was to be removed and modified." "Modification" stopped short, however, of accomplishing what solemn legitimization would have done. Izabel was still excluded from *ab intestato* succession, or receiving a paternal bequest, given that Pedro had legitimate children. Later, her father ignored the law and generously disposed from his *terça* on her behalf. Even without solemn legitimization, her father's simple legitimization went far in repairing Izabel Maria's "stain of birth." On the other hand, the baptismal register continued to read "unknown mother," an unalterable circumstance.

In a complete departure from custom, the emperor ordered that his formal declaration of paternal recognition be published in Rio de Janeiro's *Diario Fluminense*, on October 12, 1826. He timed the announcement to coincide with the palace release of the list of individuals ennobled or raised in the peerage on his twenty-eighth birthday. The reason that Pedro published his declaration of paternity on this date lay in the second of two documents he had drawn up on May 24. He revealed the second document on July 7, when he had it transcribed onto a somber parchment, embellished by a silken ribbon and georgette that carried his personal seal and signature. By means of the lavish parchment, he raised his adulterine daughter to the noble rank of duchess of Goyaz, "wishing to do her the honor and the favor" of conceding not only a title but the equally important privilege of being addressed as "highness." The official list of ennoblement also raised Izabel's mother to marquise, justifying her elevation in the peerage as imperial reward for her maternity of "my loved and beloved daughter, the duchess of

Goyaz. . . ." Thus Pedro recognized Domitila's motherhood by "wishing to do her honor and favor in addressing such distinct services, which have so greatly claimed my heart," and pronounced that "Demetilia de Castro Canto e Mello is now called marquise of Santos from here on."[82]

A different well-born mother of another adulterine offspring of Pedro also received her reward on October 12, 1826, albeit indirectly. Pedro made the husband of Domitila de Castro's sister, Boaventura Delphim Pereira, baron of Sorocaba. In reality, the emperor honored his wife, Maria Benedicta de Castro, for she acquired her husband's title, as baroness of Sorocaba. Maria Benedicta had also borne Pedro a son in 1823. Her husband accepted the adulterine Rodrigo Delfim Pereira in his household and gave him his family names, sparing the child the stain of bastardy by the time-honored subterfuge of putative paternity.[83] The emperor fondly remembered the nine-year-old Rodrigo by his full name in his last will and testament executed in 1832, bequeathing one-sixth of his *terça* to Maria Benedicta de Castro's son.[84]

Pedro's ennoblement of Izabel Maria Alcantara Brasileira accomplished her integration within his legitimate family in the São Cristovão Palace, for her rank of duchess was equal to that of the royal couple's eldest legitimate daughter, Maria da Gloria. The latter, at age seven, was the apple of her father's eye. Enchanted by her beauty, he had promised at her birth that she would become wife to his only brother, Miguel.[85] Maria Graham, on first seeing Maria da Gloria at age four, stressed not her beauty, but her intelligence.[86] Perhaps for that reason, several months after ennobling his adulterine daughter, Pedro was obliged to use his full force of persuasion to make his oldest legitimate daughter accept Izabel Maria's company in the palace household. Aware of the antipathy her mother had felt toward the marquise of Santos, Maria da Gloria, like her sister Paula, resented her presence.[87] The emperor made similar demands of acceptance on his ministers and councilors, as well as the national legislators who were permitted to resume their seats in the General Legislative Assembly that reopened on May 1, 1826. They were expected to pay the little duchess of Goyaz the same public homage routinely offered to his legitimate children, according to the court's stylized etiquette.

Publication of Izabel Maria's rank as the duchess of Goyaz was followed by a gala dinner on the same day, hosted by Domitila at her home in Mataporcos. The festive occasion affirmed a social parity attained between the illegitimate and legitimate divisions in Pedro's polygamous family. Izabel Maria's proud parents celebrated their daughter's noble rank by urging courtiers, palace functionaries, ministers, councilors, and legislators to congratulate the little Goyaz personally in what was a royal ceremony of "*beija-*

mão." That is, the emperor's supporters were expected to bestow individual kisses on the duchess' tiny hand as acts of personal loyalty to her father. The marquise's dinner party offered the emperor opportunity for assessing personal loyalty, given that the news of Izabel Maria's elevation to the peerage "had fallen like a bombshell."[88] Four months earlier, on June 6, Pedro had presented Izabel Maria to Empress Leopoldina, in order to prepare his wife to accept the future duchess into their legitimate household at the São Cristovão Palace.[89] Having "normalized" his adulterine daughter's situation at court in October, Pedro demonstrated his disfavor toward ministers and politicians who declined to dote on Goyaz. The emperor "lived with her in his lap, asking everyone who approached if he or she had kissed the child's hand." When Manoel Caetano de Almeida e Albuquerque, a liberal deputy who became vice-president of the lower house, refused the child this homage, "the emperor rudely regarded him." He also ignored the motive that brought the duke of Lafões to the palace in 1826 "because of the way he behaved in the presence of the bastard."[90]

The gala *beija-mão* honoring Izabel Maria's ennoblement defined the high point in Pedro's public establishment of a polygamous family. However, his triumph proved ephemeral, even his undoing. Empress Leopoldina did not recover from the public humiliation and the private slights she received from her husband's privileging of Izabel Maria and Domitila. By late December, Pedro was a widower and, given how Empress Leopoldina died, an unpopular monarch. The healthy and athletic empress, whose pregnancies had never been complicated, succumbed to childbed fever after going into premature labor. The miscarriage she suffered had been induced by her deteriorating emotional health, for she was confined to bed due to a depression that produced hallucinations and loss of sanity. Some cast blame for Leopoldina's death on Domitila de Castro, but fundamentally an immensely devoted public laid responsibility at the emperor's door. In 1827, when Pedro and Domitila hosted another gala *beija-mão*, on the occasion of Izabel Maria's third birthday, the absence of the Austrian and French ambassadors was portentous for the emperor's rapidly deteriorating reputation abroad.[91]

The Last of the "Imperial Series": Two Maria Izabels

The last two children born to Pedro and Domitila did not enjoy the rank or splendor conceded the duchess of Goyaz, but not because of their father's predilection. Although Domitila's expulsion from court, effected by Pedro between October 1827 and June 1828, meant the monarch was now doubly bereft of a consort, Pedro demonstrated that his paternal sentiments did not depend on his attachment to the marquise of Santos. On August 13, 1827, a fourth child was born to Pedro and Domitila. Baptized seven days later in her mother's home in the city center, the new daughter united the widower emperor's dual families despite his growing estrangement from Domitila. Pedro named the child "Maria Izabel," after his other older sister, the wife of Ferdinand VII who in 1818 had died cruelly in childbirth at the hands of the surgeon. The heir to the Brazilian throne, future Emperor D. Pedro II, served as godfather, but his tender age of twenty months meant that the marquis of Palma stood as proxy. The godmother was the duchess of Goyaz, age three and a half. When Pedro first visited his new daughter, he arrived with a sealed parchment for her mother, to be opened on the baptism day. The document, executed in Pedro's own hand, bestowed the title of duchess of Ceará on the infant.[92] Ever determined, D. Pedro refused to permit the stigma of bastardy to remain on his household.

In October, the emperor ordered both little duchesses removed from their mother's house and installed in his São Cristovão Palace. Intent on forcing Domitila to leave Rio de Janeiro, he ended their liaison. Pedro, however, would not part with his daughters and Domitila returned to São Paulo without them. The emperor intended to induct Maria Izabel formally into the imperial nobility the following year, when his annual list of those elevated to the peerage would be published on October 12. He reasoned that the departure of the marquise of Santos, who definitively abandoned the Corte only in June 1828, would be sufficient to remove any objections. As a widower, the emperor drew advantageously on the legal point that Maria Izabel was only matrilineally adulterine. She had been born, even conceived, when he was a widower, making her his natural child. But the marquis of Mareschal, Austrian minister to the court and Pedro's informal adviser, expressed concern over the emperor's prospects as a bridegroom in a European marriage market. When he argued that formally raising Maria Izabel to duchess of Ceará would scandalize public opinion abroad and deprive Pedro of a suitable second wife, then the emperor deferred to his counsel.[93]

The argument proved irrelevant, for the infant succumbed to meningitis at fourteen months, on October 25, 1828—a mere two weeks after the annual list of titles was announced without mentioning her name. Although the marquis of Mareschal stated that the child's funeral was accomplished in secrecy, before only a palace staff, Mello Moraes the Elder stated it took place with "uncommon pomp" befitting an emperor's daughter. According to him, her body was carried to the old church in Engenho Velho in a coach of state, followed by others carrying the friends and higher nobles in Pedro's circle. Maria Izabel was laid to rest beside the infant Pedro, her adulterine brother.[94]

The determination that D. Pedro must remarry—and his advisors' apprehension that he might recall Domitila from banishment for an eventual marriage—spelled the demise of Pedro's polygamous family. Yet the star-crossed couple, briefly reunited by Domitila's 1829 "comeback," brought one last child into the world. The triumphant return to court that the marquise of Santos staged in April 1829 proved a pyrrhic victory. On May 30, a royal marriage was arranged in Canterbury with representatives of the only candidate on Pedro's short list of six possible brides who would accept him as a husband. She was Amélie Auguste Eugénie Napoleona von Leuchtenberg, the daughter of the deceased Eugene Beauharnais of Leuchtenberg, a duke and Napoleon's stepson. The marriage contract amounted to an interdict for Pedro's polygamous family. It contained a clause prescribing Domitila's definitive exit from court as a precondition for the marriage to be consummated. On August 2, 1829, three weeks after performance of the proxy marriage in Munich, Amelia of Leuchtenberg embarked for Rio de Janeiro. She did so under the contractual understanding that she would not relive Empress Leopoldina's experience. She was to be stepmother only to Pedro's legitimate children.

On October 3, the young bride's arrival being imminent, the duchess of Goyaz, now five years old, was removed from the São Cristovão Palace and ferried across the Bay of Guanabara to temporary quarters in Niteroi. On November 24, she sailed for Brest, never again to see Brazil. She would remain in a Paris boarding school for the next ten years. Nor would she ever see her mother again. Three years hence, she would meet her father in Paris, in his new incarnation as the duke of Bragança, claimant to the Portuguese throne usurped by his brother, Miguel. Goyaz would afford Pedro opportunity to listen to his "very pretty and precocious" daughter playing the piano. Ironically, Amelia, ex-empress of Brazil, did acquire a role as stepmother to Goyaz, once Pedro died. "My wife the duchess esteems her as if she were one of her own children," Pedro wrote after being reunited with Izabel Maria.[95] She alone was the child Pedro singled out in his 1832 will as "my beloved daughter." Her father, who had given Izabel Maria the jewels that should have gone to Amelia after Leopoldina died, left testamentary instructions to Amelia of Leuchenberg, asking her to take charge of Goyaz "as soon as her education in Paris is concluded." The legacy he left this very special daughter, one-half of his *terça*, was a bequest his widow faithfully executed.[96] Once again, family unanimity overrode the rules of heirship, for, technically, succession law excluded Izabel Maria from a bequest from her father's *terça*, given his five legitimate children.

The "last in the imperial series" of offspring born to Pedro and Domitila was conceived in June 1829, at the end of a brief interlude when her mother returned to court. At the time of her birth, on February 28, 1830, the marquise of Santos was living in irreversible banishment in São Paulo. Named "Maria Izabel," after her deceased sister, the duchess of Ceará, the child was baptized "of unknown parents." Because Pedro and Amelia were not married by proxy until the first week in July 1829, technically this Maria Izabel should have been the emperor's natural daughter. Yet the close timing of her conception, within weeks before his proxy marriage, and her birth some eight months afterward meant that Maria Izabel would bear the stain of paternally adulterine birth. The fact that she was indisputably maternally adulterine, coupled with Domitila's inglorious expulsion from court due to Amelia's imminent arrival, meant that Maria Izabel would always bear the stigma of being spurious, above all, as Pedro's bastard.

The harsh treatment Maria Izabel would later suffer resulted from Pedro's new role as a royal husband. Not only would her father be unable to grant her a title but he also could not recognize her as his natural daughter, given his marriage contract. Consequently, Pedro's last will and testament touchingly attempted to rectify her situation, for he used it to confer recognition on the last of his love children with Domitila. Posthumous testamentary recognition also explained why in adulthood Pedro's daughter signed her name variously, as "Maria Izabel de Bourbon" or "Maria Izabel de Bragança." Eventually, she did acquire a title. Her marriage to Pedro Caldeira Brant, count of Iguassu and the son of D. Pedro's trusted friend and adviser, the marquis of Barbacena, entitled her to be treated as a noblewoman and addressed as countess of Iguassu. D. Pedro generously dispatched an expensive layette to São Paulo for his newborn daughter, the only gesture left to a monarch whose role had been rehabilitated as monogamous bridegroom. Pedro's days in Brazil were numbered. Although he would never lay eyes on the last daughter he fathered with Domitila, Pedro reasserted paternal concern only four months after he returned to Europe as an exile. He made representations to Domitila in August 1831, through the count of Rezende, asking her to send their infant child to him in Paris. Domitila tactfully consented, but did not relinquish Maria Izabel. She was the only one of their love children whom Domitila raised to adulthood. Goyaz, who ceased to speak Portuguese, already was lost to her.

Pedro's paternal devotion to his illegitimate family found final expression in his 1832 last will and testament. He died two years later, ravaged by tuberculosis. The terms of the instructions he left for his widow to execute, and the fact that Amelia sought to carry them out, demonstrated the genuine paternal concern Pedro held for the adulterine and natural children he posthumously recognized. His behavior did not differ from what thousands of Brazilian fathers customarily arranged as similar testamentary acts. Only the fact that Pedro was ex-emperor of Brazil made his final testament singular. He entrusted to Amelia the raising of Maria Izabel, describing his daughter with uncustomary delicacy, as "that little girl I told her [Amelia] about and who was born on February 28, 1830, in the city of São Paulo in the Empire of Brazil." The imperial father did not abandon his prerogative of personally choosing his children's names, even from beyond the grave. Maria Izabel was to take a new name appropriate to residence on a new continent: "I wish this girl to be named 'Europa' in order that she receive an upbringing equal to that which my above-mentioned daughter, the duchess of Goyaz, is receiving; once her education is completed." Although Pedro stipulated that Amelia would "call her" to Europe and take charge of Maria Izabel, he left no patrimony for her. She remained permanently in the Empire of Brazil.[97] Maria Izabel's exclusion was striking, given that Pedro did leave one-sixth of his *terça* to the adulterine son he fathered in 1823 with Domitila's sister—Rodrigo Delfim Pereira. He similarly remembered Pedro Brasileiro Alcantara, the paternally natural son he fathered in 1828 with a French seamstress, who was born in Paris in 1829. Another sixth of his *terça* he left to Amelia. Ever doting on the duchess of Goyaz, Pedro favored her over all the others, leaving her one-half his *terça*.[98]

Of course, legally, neither the adulterine nor the natural child of a noble father could inherit a bequest from the paternal *terça*, whenever legitimate children existed. Never one to be deterred by the letter of the law, Pedro may have deceived himself in believing that his testamentary recognition—simple legitimization—was sufficient to equip his spurious and natural children to receive bequests from his *terça*. Yet he probably placed his faith in social practice for overriding the letter of the law. Amelia of Leuchtenberg carried out her husband's testamentary instructions, in spite of how his bequests diminished the inheritance portion of their one legitimate child, not to mention Leopoldina's five surviving children, on whose behalf D. Pedro had also instructed Amelia to act. As Pedro's *meeira*, Amelia saw her own patrimony proportionately reduced by Pedro's assignment of his *terça* to three of his illegitimate children.[99] She sent British bankers to Brazil in 1839 and 1840, seeking to persuade Domitila to send "Europa" to the Continent for an education appropriate to her station.[100] The marquise of Santos diplomatically demurred, keeping Pedro's daughter in her company. Maria Izabel was brought up in the new family that Domitila established in 1832, when she began living in *mancebia* with Brig. Raphael Tobias de Aguiar, a liberal imperial deputy who was also provincial governor of São Paulo.

LIBERTINE EMPEROR AS LIBERAL DISSENTER

A consistent thread running through Pedro's behavior toward his illegitimate children was his refusal to defer to the cardinal convention that adulterine paternity should be legally denied and socially left tacit, even concealed. The punitive spirit of canon and positive law he found wholly repugnant. Emotional and passionate, D. Pedro was described by many who closely observed him as a genuinely interested and devoted father. On one occasion, for instance, he wrote Domitila to confirm that he had vaccinated the first Maria Izabel against smallpox.[101] The Rev. Robert Walsh characterized the emperor as "strict and severe" with his children, adding immediately, "he is an affectionate father."[102] One conclusion to be drawn from Pedro's unconventional behavior is that his own upbringing prompted him to act with devotion toward the children he fathered with Domitila. Dissimulation over the paternity of several of his younger siblings meant that he grew up with uncertainty over paternity as a subtext in his family of origin. As an adolescent, he had to have been deeply affected by the doubt cast on D. João's fatherhood of several of his sisters, in light of the gossip about Carlota Joaquina's multiple liaisons. The cruel rhymes that circulated among the populace about his younger brother, Miguel, with whom he shared little physical resemblance, doubtlessly made a lasting impression on Pedro.[103]

It was Pedro himself, not his Brazilian paramour, who determined their children would be honestly recognized in terms of his paternity.[104] He expressed his intention to recognize the first Maria Izabel and elevate her to duchess of Ceará during the low point in his relationship with Domitila, a circumstance confirming that he acted out of a paternal responsibility unprompted by the child's mother. Earlier, Pedro's failed attempt to legitimize Izabel Maria before the Desembargo do Paço responded to the repugnance he felt in falsifying the parish registry concerning her parentage. Maintaining silence over his paternity ran against his basic disposition, which tended to be forthright, even reckless. Furthermore, the fraud of a baptismal record tacitly assumed the convention that he should distance himself from an adulterine daughter, when his inclination was to lavish every attention on her. That he should treat Izabel Maria ostensibly as a foundling, to be raised by foster parents in a separate household, amounted to a hypocrisy that Pedro regarded as personal affront.

As emperor, of course, D. Pedro possessed prerogatives denied other adulterous fathers. And he was not one to forget for an instant that he was the sovereign. He used the privileges and powers at his command to lessen or remove the stigma visited on his spurious children as punishment for his own behavior. Boldly, he publicly recognized Izabel Maria and her sister, the first Maria Izabel, on the assumption that even simple legitimization canceled the stain of bastard birth. Moreover, law agreed with that assumption, although it withheld rights in patrimony. By ennobling the older daughter, he placed her on a par with his legitimate daughters.

The fact that Pedro's dynastic destiny, and that of another beloved daughter who was legitimate—Maria da Gloria—ultimately lay not in Brazil, but in Europe, best explains why Pedro could be persuaded by his ministers first to set Domitila aside and then to relinquish his illegitimate daughters. In the end, Brazil's monarch sacrificed his polygamous family to a European dynastic marriage with the granddaughter of Josephine Beauharnais. Pedro's reasons for banishing his illegitimate children, however, were to be found less in his desire to remarry than in imperial ambition. He wanted his eldest legitimate daughter to fulfill a monarchical destiny in Europe. The exile of the adored duchess of Goyaz, consequently, followed from Pedro's dynastic position in 1829. Maria da Gloria, heir to the throne of Portugal, after her father definitively renounced his claim in her favor, still needed Pedro's backing to remove her uncle, the "usurper" Miguel. In banishing Goyaz to Paris, Brazil's emperor bowed to the political destiny of his legitimate, eldest daughter and reasons of state that extended beyond his marriage to Amelia of Leuchtenberg.

Despite overwhelmingly negative reaction, at court and among national legislators, Pedro's paternal recognition and ennoblement of Izabel Maria in 1826—as well as his thwarted efforts to do the same for Maria Izabel, as duchess of Ceará in 1828—by no means were public acts devoid of positive consequences. True, he was strongly condemned for exceeding the limits of court decorum. Some even blamed him for causing the death of the empress, but many more concluded that he had simply been at fault for expressing terribly bad taste and poor judgment. His deliberate decision to make his paternal recognition of an adulterine daughter no less than "notorious and scandalous knowledge" broke a cardinal taboo. Although Pedro acted more from what he deemed a royal prerogative than any liberal values, the fact remained that the emperor defied both the "damnable and punishable" spirit of canon law and the letter of national positive law. In offering a royal gloss on behavior that was "notorious and scandalous," he suggested that the formula of silence applying to adulterine paternity, incorporated into Pombaline positive law, no longer served a useful purpose.

In retrospect, the impetuous emperor offered a boldly unconventional example of an adulterous father who in one royal stroke cut the Gordian knot of "damnable and punishable" birth. Pedro did not so much lead the way to reforming the civil status of adulterine children as he demonstrated on a grand scale that both ecclesiastical and national positive law deserved to be disregarded. Through paternal action he eroded the authority of both, paving the way for radical legislators to propose bills that explicitly ran against the grain of the sacred canons and Pombaline law.

The deeper side of the emperor's rebellious attitude was one that many men in the political elite had no difficulty intuiting, even when they might be shocked over the emperor's effrontery in elevating an adulterine daughter to a duchess. Pedro chose to divulge his declaration of paternity of Izabel Maria by the most public means available to him—the daily newspaper. His use of this new medium enhanced the impact of his flaunting of convention and official morality. For instance, the occasion when he formally presented Izabel Maria to Empress Leopoldina, on June 6, 1826, horrified many. However, he dictated that on the same day *Diario Fluminense* would devote its "Unofficial Items" column to listing examples of individuals who historically drew advantage from their "bastardy."[105] His outrageous behavior struck a powerful blow against the conventional notion that fathering a spurious child was a "crime." His action threw into question prevailing wisdom that the stain of "damnable and punishable birth" was justly deserved as payment for parental conduct.

Pedro's insistence on recognizing his spurious offspring demonstrated an instance in which his self-proclaimed, often confused, "liberalism" rang true. Personal antipathy to the dogmatic morality of canon law meant that he tacitly concurred on the need for a modern redefinition of the dictum that the sins of the father should be visited on his children. Although his personal actions as an adulterous father were rendered infinitely more complex by his constitutional role as protector of the church, the immediate political context did not support rigid orthodoxy to the sacred canons. By 1829, Brazil's lawmakers had extinguished the Tribunal of the Mesa do Desembargo do Paço. Consequently, liberals in both houses perceived the end of the Paço as an unprecedented opportunity for rewriting the rules of paternal recognition and heirship. In so doing, they were obliged to take into account the social consequences of *mancebia,* or "*amasia,*" as consensual unions increasingly were called.

At the very moment the emperor was bidding good-bye to the five-year-old Goyaz and establishing a second legitimate family, liberal reformers in both houses of Parliament were drawing up radical bills designed to recast succession rules and paternal recognition on behalf of natural and spurious offspring—or their parents. For the first time, they prepared to address polygamous family organization at the elite level. In 1830, it would be the turn of legislators to propose that some adulterous fathers be legally permitted to "acknowledge" their spurious offspring—and that clerics also recognize their children in order to make them natural rather than sacrilegious. Without intending such an impact, the emperor behaved so as to provide legislators with a "dress rehearsal" for redefining attitudes toward illegitimate paternity at the highest level of Brazilian society. He placed at center stage the notion of paternal devotion, within the context of polygamous family organization. In the final months of Pedro's brief reign, consequently, national legislators were preparing to deliberate revised procedures for paternal recognition and inheritance rights applicable to a plurality of non-legitimate offspring, and based on the reality of *mancebia*, whether lay or clerical. Their willingness to do so reflected a bold apprehension of the need to bring national law into line with historically Brazilian patterns of family organization and cultural values.

PART III

Reforming Illegitimacy and Heirship
in the Regency

CHAPTER 6

Undoing "Damnable" Birth

First Reforms

———◆◆———

I called for the register and found that in the last thirteen years
nearly 12,000 children had been received, but scarcely 1000 were
forthcoming, the Misericordia not knowing in fact what had become of them.
D. Pedro I, Report on the Foundling Hospital, 1823[1]

1830 marked the beginning of an effort to reform Brazilian succession law on
behalf of illegitimate offspring that would stretch over two decades. The bills
introduced in Parliament would respond to dramatic changes in the national
government as it moved from a constitutional monarchy to a de facto republic and finally returned to a reinvigorated imperial monarchy. Legislators
turned their attention to reforming the position of illegitimate offspring in
1830, because recasting succession rights followed logically from their preceding efforts to sanction clerical *mancebia*, introduce civil marriage, and
abolish entail. The latter effort, which failed by a single vote in the Senate in
1829, refocused efforts to reform the inheritance system.

By 1830, three broad circumstances shaped the context in which two important proposals addressing the position of non-legitimate individuals in
succession law were introduced in the Chamber of Deputies. First, the subject
of succession—dynastic succession—defined a significant theme in legislative
debate throughout the 1820s and 1830s. Second, 1830 witnessed the arrival of a
political opening permitting liberals to engage in radical reform. And third,
the forces of social change were being felt in the Corte as well as the provinces.
Urbanization, population growth, and increased importation of slaves from
Africa introduced important factors that rapidly transformed social life.

THE CONTEXT OF CHANGE

Dynastic Succession: Leitmotif of the Twenties

Throughout the 1820s, succession defined a theme in legislative debate,
not necessarily in terms of inheritance law but, quite literally, in terms of the

fate of the Brazilian monarchy. At the national level, from the moment Brazilians declared their independence in September 1822, questions of dynastic succession pertaining to the Brazilian throne turned on the heirship of D. Pedro I, who remained his father's successor to the throne of Portugal. Title I, Article 4, of the Constitution of 1824 provided that Brazil's "imperial dynasty is that of D. Pedro I, current emperor and perpetual defender of Brazil," eliminating even the remote possibility that Pedro's brother Miguel might succeed him. However, the Portuguese government did not recognize Brazil as an independent nation until August 1825, meaning the question of who would succeed D. João VI to the throne of Portugal clouded relations between the two countries for the first three years of Pedro's reign. In the treaty of independence signed with Portugal, D. João VI formally recognized Pedro as emperor of Brazil and heir to the Portuguese throne, further complicating Brazil's position.

When news of D. João's death arrived in Rio de Janeiro, on April 25, 1826, D. Pedro resolved the dilemma of his heirship to the Portuguese throne by proclaiming himself king of Portugal for five days—from April 29 through May 3. The interim was long enough for him to promulgate a new constitution for the former metropole, drawing on the charter authored by the Liberal Cortes of Lisbon. He then renounced all claim to the Portuguese throne, abdicating in favor of his eldest daughter, Maria da Gloria, on May 3.[2] Subsequently, by the decree of July 3, 1827, Pedro invested Miguel with all of the powers of the monarchy for the Kingdom of Portugal and the Algarve—the powers he had abdicated—by virtue of the legal minority of Maria da Gloria. On February 26, 1828, Miguel took an oath to observe the Liberal Constitution, in the presence of the bicameral Cortes.

The fact that the emperor had already betrothed Maria da Gloria in infancy to Miguel, and that she preceded her uncle on the ladder of succession in the royal line, supposedly resolved any claim to the Portuguese throne that Miguel might later make. By virtue of Pedro's 1827 investiture of power in his brother, and the latter's seventeen years of seniority over his child-fiancée, Miguel could anticipate becoming de facto king, as well as regent. In 1827, Miguel celebrated his twenty-fifth birthday, attaining the legal age of majority for succession to the throne of Portugal. However, Maria da Gloria's formal betrothal to Miguel, followed by a civil marriage celebrated by proxy in Vienna in February 1828, proved a dynastic "backfire." Miguel immediately betrayed Pedro, given that Pedro reaffirmed his abdication of all rights to the throne of Portugal, on March 3, 1828. Support for Miguel in Lisbon therefore mushroomed. In late April, the Lisbon Municipal Council acclaimed Pedro's brother king. Repudiating the Portuguese liberals, Miguel convened the ancient Cortes, breaking a 131-year hiatus, so that Portugal's historical Estates General could declare him the nation's legal king—on June 23, 1828. Five days later, he issued an ordinance confirming that decision and formally assumed the title of king, repudiating any claim by Pedro or his immediate line. Thus Miguel ambitiously both ruptured a carefully crafted design of state and severed a relationship between brothers who in boyhood had been inseparable.

For Brazilians, initially, Pedro's abdication of all claim to the throne of Portugal came as a relief. Despite his initial abdication, in 1826, the emperor continued to act as if he were king of Portugal. Given the birth of a male heir in December 1825, Brazilians breathed more easily. The conclusion followed that the thrones of Portugal and Brazil would not be reunited. The departure of the nine-year-old Maria da Gloria for Vienna, in July 1828, and the expectation that Francis of Austria would uphold his granddaughter's claim to the Portuguese throne against Miguel, further confirmed Pedro's intention to insure that the Portuguese throne passed to his daughter. However, doubt over Pedro's involvement in Portugal's dynastic politics was not altogether stilled. Should the three-year-old male heir to the Brazilian throne die, then Maria da Gloria would again be heir to the throne of Brazil as well as Portugal. Thus a dynastic question mark kept succession uppermost as a theme of state even after a male heir to the Brazilian throne arrived. Pedro's determination to defend the right of his eldest daughter to succeed him to the throne of Portugal, in defiance of his brother, merely increased political uncertainty in Brazil about his European aspirations.

Although dynastic succession regularly punctuated legislative debate, it did not touch directly on illegitimacy. Legislators' deliberations nevertheless raised a number of concerns that kept the inheritance system routinely within the purview of public power, such as the series of matrimonial and dowral contracts that had to be approved for the royal princesses, the emperor's sisters. Then, in 1827–1828, legislators began deliberations on a second round of matrimonial contracts, for Maria da Gloria and her sisters. The diplomatic and financial details of dynastic succession regularly punctuated parliamentary debate as if to make the rules of *ab intestato* succession writ large for the nation, with patrimony consisting of the crowns of Portugal and Brazil. The marriages of the royal princesses implied constitutional obligations for the legislature, involving careful budgetary scrutiny in setting the terms and payment of their dowries. The emperor's liaison with Domitila de Castro continued against this backdrop of routine preoccupation with matters of dynastic succession during the two and one-half years when Pedro was a widower. Lack of an empress added to anxiety over any domestic political repercussions that might derive from the emperor's illegitimate family, especially if Domitila bore him a son. The introduction of a few bills seeking to rework legal marriage or the rights of illegitimate offspring, within the more modest context of the elite corporate family, accompanied almost naturally the domestic political concerns generated by the patrimonial destinies of the imperial family.

Political Change

The arrival of a political opening for liberals to engage in more radical reform offered the second circumstance encouraging the introduction of bills addressing the succession rights of illegitimate offspring. 1830 demonstrated serious weaknesses in D. Pedro's monarchy and exposed new fissures in the edifice of state. Partisan strife escalated to the point where popular mobs became important participants in daily politics. A climate of conflict and impending change afforded liberals in the national legislature renewed opportunity to extend their agenda attacking the colonial society of estates to new issues. May 1830 witnessed the opening of the Second Legislature, meaning that a newly elected chamber of Deputies would hold office for another four years. The political climate, however, had begun to change in late 1828, when elections for the 1830 session were held. During the intervening eighteen months, opposition to the emperor and his Portuguese coterie sharpened considerably. The mutiny of German mercenaries in the imperial army, loss of the war over the Banda Oriental, D. Miguel's usurpation of the throne rightfully belonging to Maria da Gloria, and the appalling situation of the national treasury undercut D. Pedro's political support. Nor could he now rely on the army to secure the throne. As if to test the constitutional ban on criticism of the emperor's person, the national legislature's mood had shifted by 1829 to one of harsh condemnation.

In the Chamber of Deputies, Bernardo Pereira de Vasconcellos emerged as the indisputable liberal leader, after shepherding the Judiciary Act and the Ministerial Responsibility Act to adoption in 1828. A Coimbra graduate and a great orator, the Mineiro deputy who headed the largest delegation in the Chamber of Deputies proved a moderate. Not only for defending vigorously the interests of the slavocratic planters who dominated the lower house but also for his authorship of harsh sections of the 1830 Criminal Code, Vasconcellos defined a centrist liberal position that would be outstripped by more radical deputies in the opening year of the Second Legislature.

Even in the Senate, greater dissent was openly expressed toward the emperor's leadership, but the most important change turned on how politics had moved into the streets. Legislation adopted to protect freedom of speech and insure habeas corpus meant that the number of newspapers in Brazil doubled between 1828 and 1830. Rapid emergence of a political press served as the catalyst for the emperor's downfall. Although newspapers of every political stripe emerged, those controlled by the radicals known as Exaltados fanned the flames of opposition to the emperor and his Portuguese-dominated coterie. Evaristo da Veiga, an intellectually gifted bookstore owner and founder of the *Aurora Fluminense*, one of the most popular of these newspapers, joined Minas Gerais' parliamentary delegation as a liberal deputy in 1830. His editorials, together with those of more irresponsible editors, steadily attacked the emperor's decisions—and attracted mass opposition to Pedro and his choice of cabinets. High levels of public strife characterized political activity and threw into question the nature of the monarchy and even the fate of constitutional government. By the end of the 1830 session, as pro- and anti-imperial ranks polarized and journalists appealed to the populace to come into the streets, factional conflict threatened the foundations of national government. The 1830 legislative session, having gained a solid position and broader political ground in which to enact legislation, concluded by being faced with a situation where it found itself bowing, not to the emperor, but to pressure from the crowd.

Social Change and the Reform Impetus

Although legislators paid attention to the succession rights of both natural and spurious offspring from motives that were fundamentally political, social change had also altered perceptions of illegitimacy at all levels of society by 1830. Greater urbanization in the 1820s, accompanied by unprecedented population growth, constituted the two most important elements of change in the Corte. By 1828–1829, Rio de Janeiro had a population of 150,000, exclusive of another 16,000 resident foreigners. Between thirty-three and thirty-eight percent of the city's inhabitants were slaves, a decline of over ten percent from the last years of D. João's reign. As many as 56,000 slaves may have lived in Rio de Janeiro in 1828–1829. The Rev. Robert Walsh was impressed with what historians later viewed as the progressive Africanization of the city, a process accelerated by the approaching 1830 deadline for abolishing the African slave trade, one dictated by the 1826 treaty between Great Britain and Brazil. He calculated forty-five thousand Africans were imported into Rio de Janeiro during 1828 alone. Noting that "a great many of these are sent up the country," Walsh stressed that "a great proportion remains in the town, to supply the demands of the expanding white population, so that their increase has been beyond all ordinary calculation."[3] One liberal deputy, Pernambuco's Almeida e Albuquerque, alluded to the impact that an abundance of slaves exerted on family formation. He condemned the practice of "many *fazendeiros* in the Province of Minas Gerais . . . [who] abandon their youngest slave children, because it is easier for them to find slaves at the Valongo"—Rio de Janeiro's embarcadero slave market.[4]

Walsh proved overly optimistic in concluding that the 1826 treaty would end the traffic in slaves. After 1830, Rio de Janeiro continued to be the principal slave market for the expanding coffee sector in the adjacent Paraíba Valley. Production there peaked in the 1830s, offering sufficient reason for the Brazilian government to ignore any treaty obligation to close the Atlantic trade. After a sharp decline in slave imports in 1830–31, the trade quickly returned to its 1829 high over the next five years. New peaks in importations occurred in the 1840s, ending only when the trade was effectively abolished in 1850.[5]

Urbanization and demographic change brought about an increase in the absolute number of individuals who were illegitimate as well as a proportionate rise in their number. The establishment of municipally sponsored foundling wheels throughout Brazil, largely a phenomenon of the first four decades of the nineteenth century, testified to the higher proportion of children born outside legal wedlock. By the end of the 1830s, a dozen more foundling wheels had been added to the three created during the colonial period. Although foundling wheels in Salvador and Rio de Janeiro dated to 1726 and 1738, respectively, the city of São Paulo acquired one only in the late 1820s. Until the first years of the nineteenth century, "the natural absorption of *expostos* in rural areas" explained the fact that they were not mentioned as a social problem in the towns of the province or in the [Capital]. In Recife, where the Casa de Expostos dated to 1788, a foundling wheel was established early in the nineteenth century, and in Olinda a school associated with an orphanage, also administered by the Misericórdia, opened in 1831.[6] Municipal councils, which had been contributing to the support of foundling homes established by the Santa Misericordia since the eighteenth century, were not the only sponsors of those institutions. Beginning in 1828, the national legislature authorized a budgetary appropriation for "the most urgent" charitable ends in legally constituted cities and towns, "where there are no Casas de Misericordia," and "principally for providing the upbringing of *expostos*, their education, and that of other poor orphans and the helpless."[7] Although establishment of foundling wheels testified to rising rates of illegitimacy after 1808, they represented only the tip of an iceberg, given that foundlings and orphans amounted to a miniscule proportion of the country's population of natural and spurious offspring.

Despite public rhetoric pointing to rising illegitimacy, the motives of legislators for changing legal rules of heirship did not fundamentally respond to the impoverished majority of the country's population. Nor did the focus of reform necessarily fall on the illegitimate offspring themselves. Rather, legislators attempted to modify the position of illegitimate individuals in succession law largely on behalf of patrimonial interests that directly touched the propertied elite, a rural stratum of large landowners reinforced by incipient middle classes whose incomes derived largely from commerce, civil service, the military, and the professions. Furthermore, legislators responded primarily to the legal situation of fathers—or, tangentially, to that of mothers—rather than addressing the perspective of children born out-of-wedlock. After all, the stigma of "damnable" birth, though visited on the offspring, testified to the parent's "crime."

On the other hand, legislators personally confronted the evidence of rising numbers of individuals whose illegitimacy condemned them to poverty and baseborn occupations every day. The houses of Parliament were located a stone's throw from the Misericordia's foundling wheel. The magnitude and ubiquitousness of the population marginalized by poverty and illegitimacy served as a reminder that the legal condition of spurious and natural offspring deserved attention. By and large, however, legislators sought changes that offered the means by which, on an individual basis, fathers could rectify the legal situations of their natural or spurious offspring. Secondarily, they sought to protect the interest of the legitimate family vis-à-vis illegitimate counterparts, a motive that did not exclude genuine feelings of attachment and responsibility for non-legitimate children. Finally, offspring legally identified "of unknown father" hypothetically posed a threat to the patrimony of "good" families. Motives for reforming law, consequently, admitted exclusionary as well as inclusionary intentions. Placing the power to decide whether an illegitimate child deserved to be called to succession directly in his or her father's hands offered an individual solution for a general problem.

Given the centrality of property to succession law, it would be wrong to conclude that the intended beneficiaries of legal reform were illegitimate persons of color, even though out-of-wedlock births registered a preponderance of children of color. White anxiety over being a minority in a population predominantly of color derived not only from the high proportion of slaves but also from the rapidly expanding free population of color. Although it is tempting to argue that conferring rights in succession on a small proportion of illegitimate offspring of color was intended to contribute to the resilience and stability of slavery, which it did, such a conclusion ignores the fundamental motives of legislators. Reform of the patrimonial position of natural or spurious offspring did not proceed as a kind of implicit policy of race relations due to the fact that illegitimacy inscribed a cross-racial population, including many individuals who were white.

White individuals from "good" families did not always take care to be properly married. For instance, those who were legally separated by an ecclesiastical court were almost always white. Although they could not remarry until the death of their spouse, "divorced" individuals formed de facto marriages by living in *mancebia*. Otherwise, *mancebia* relationships were common between individuals who were white, due to the canonical prohibitions on marriage. Finally, the failure of wealthy individuals, the majority of whom were also white, to marry at all sometimes was directly traceable to the rules of heirship. Throughout the 1830s, for instance, Domitila de Castro Canto e Mello and Raphael Tobias de Aguiar offered the most well known example of a couple of substantial wealth and landed property who lived openly in *mancebia*. D. Pedro's former concubine and São Paulo's provincial governor established a joint household in early 1833, but they did not marry until 1842. All of their five natural children were recorded "of unknown mother" in the baptismal register, despite Domitila's becoming a widow in 1834. However, Tobias de Aguiar recognized all of their offspring, who were paternally as well as maternally natural. A patrimonial strategy on behalf of Domitila's last child with D. Pedro I, the maternally adulterine Maria Izabel, accounted for her decision not to recognize these natural children. Eventually, they were legitimized by their parents' subsequent marriage, an occasion for which Tobias de Aguiar executed a prenuptial contract bestowing dower on Domitila that was intended as Maria Izabel's dowry.[8] The pervasiveness of illegitimacy in a society where authentic divorce and remarriage were impossible encouraged ad hoc strategies in heirship that sometimes led parents of considerable wealth to postpone or decline legal marriage on behalf of patrimonial benefits for children, especially when a parent had offspring who were both natural and spurious.

In embarking on reform of the inheritance system, Brazil's legislators could be confident that the changes they sponsored would introduce no revolutionary element in terms of race and class. Their bills were predicated on the assumption that reform would reach only a small minority of the population, largely propertyowners. By attempting to give fathers greater discretionary power, they anticipated greater opportunity to create individual exceptions to the rules of heirship, not any massive change throughout society. They thought in terms of paternal recognition as the key for patrimonially endowing a limited number of illegitimate offspring. As upwardly mobile entrants to elite ranks, a small proportion of illegitimate children would be equipped to succeed, largely due to a father's voluntary recognition.

Biographical Dimensions

In 1830, Dep. Jozé Lino Coutinho launched what became a two-decade campaign to reform succession rights pertaining to illegitimate offspring. Far in advance of his time, the Coimbra-trained physician was "in religion a deist and in principle, a republican." He believed in the dissolubility of marriage—in legal divorce—an idea deemed much more dangerous in orthodox Catholic circles than civil marriage.[9] It is impossible to know how Lino Coutinho reacted to D. Pedro's public declaration of his adulterous paternity of the duchess of Goyaz; however, he did enjoy a personal relationship with the emperor, as his medical adviser. More to the point, Lino Coutinho was himself the father of a natural daughter whose mother's identity had been deliberately withheld, due to her respectable reputation. In assuming responsibility for his daughter Cora's upbringing, he had entrusted her education to a talented governess, none other than the child's biological mother. Cora Coutinho, however, remained a legal *exposta*, a circumstance that facilitated her marriage around 1834, and, eventually, her elevation to the peerage as baroness of Alagoinhas, by virtue of her husband's title. Cora's legal identity as a foundling similarly enabled her concealed biological mother to contract an exceptionally late first marriage in 1836.[10]

Given that Lino Coutinho represented his native province of Bahia, it is just as likely that his bill addressing natural and spurious offspring responded to the circumstances of his birthplace and hometown, Salvador. Indeed, the competing proposal that vanquished his own bill was introduced by another Baiano, his fellow deputy Antonio Pereira Rebouças. In the former viceregal capital of Salvador, both de facto marriage and concubinage were ubiquitous and openly acknowledged. Lino Coutinho, moreover, attained a social position among elite networks that inscribed prominent Bahians who themselves, either informally or tacitly, acknowledged adulterine or sacrilegious children. In 1833, he married into such a family network, Salvador's very prestigious and intermarried Sodrés and Moniz de Aragãos. That he remained a bachelor until he was nearly fifty years of age may have been on account of his modest social origins, assuming his "inequality" was an obstacle. The English physician Robert Dundas met Lino Coutinho around the time Cora was born, in 1819, and remained his friend for life. Dundas, who also attended Lino Coutinho when he died, said that the celebrated liberal politician had "sprung from the humblest origins" and died "poor and unpensioned." In 1819, Lino Coutinho held a medical degree for six years, but he remained "a simple physician apparently absorbed in the duties of his profession."[11] Probably the modest income of a clinician, coupled with the relatively low status medical doctors enjoyed, excluded him from a good marriage, despite a Coimbra degree. On the other hand, he may also have declined to marry Cora's mother because ambition drove him to take a wife from a higher social level.

Lino Coutinho has recently been construed as a mulatto, although the evidence to show he was a "*branco da Bahia*"—putatively white—does not support that conclusion.[12] Certainly, he was not counted among a select group of imperial legislators who included the future baron of Cotegipe (João Mauricio Wanderley), the viscounts of Jequitinhonha (Francisco Gê Acayaba de Montezuma) and Inhomirim (Francisco de Salles Tôrres Homem), in addition to Jozé de Assis Mascarenhas, son of the marquis of São João da Palma. They were men whose African ancestry and physical features were left publicly unremarked by colleagues in Parliament, but revealed to be mulattoes in the memoirs and political caricatures left by their contemporaries.[13] Although Lino Coutinho's family of origin was nondescript, both his parents have been identified as "Portuguese residents in Brazil."[14] Given Dundas' comment about his "humblest origins," it is not known how Lino Coutinho financed his medical training at Coimbra University.

Professional success and a spectacular political career came to Lino Coutinho as a result of his election to the Lisbon Cortes in 1821, and, subsequently, membership in Bahia's revolutionary junta in 1822. When he did marry, in 1833, he was at the height of his political career—a distinguished legislator recently reelected to the Chamber of Deputies, an imperial councilor, and a former minister of empire, not to mention a member of Lisbon's Royal Academy of Sciences and the director of Bahia's newly created Faculty of Medicine. Consequently, it was as an accomplished and powerful politician that Lino Coutinho married the legitimate daughter of Francisco Maria Sodré Pereira, the administrator of a sizable entail known as the Morgado of Sodré. Within three years, his death ended the matrimonial union he formed with Maria Adelaide Sodré Pereira, one exemplifying an intergenerational interweaving of legitimate and illegitimate family branches commonplace in Salvador.[15] Cora Coutinho, who married shortly after her father, became the wife of the natural son of Francisco Maria Sodré Pereira—her father's father-in-law. Her husband, also Francisco Maria Sodré Pereira, could not be heir to the family entail because he lacked the *qualidade* of legitimate birth. However, in 1879, he became baron of Alagoinhas, as if to demonstrate that for a paternally recognized natural offspring quality of birth posed no barrier to ennoblement during the mature reign of D. Pedro II.[16]

The legitimate and illegitimate lines of Lino Coutinho and his wife, Maria Adelaide Sodré Pereira, eventually united in marriage, when one of Cora Coutinho's eleven children, Maria Leopoldina (1845–1915), married Dr. Egas Carlos Moniz Sodré de Aragão, the son of Maria Adelaide and her second husband, Antônio Ferrão Moniz de Aragão (1813–1887). On the other hand, Maria da Purificação, the daughter of Lino Coutinho's only legitimate child, Maria Jozé Coutinho da França, married a well-known magistrate of the Second Empire who was a *sacrílego*. Tranquilino Leovigildo Torres was one of several spurious children born of the stable consensual union that Pe. Belarmino Silvestre Torres (1829–1896), the Bahian Conservative Party politician and priest, established with the widow Umbelina Emilia dos Santos (1824–1887).[17] After his death, Maria da Purificação and her cousin, Gonçalo Moniz de Aragão—son of the above Maria Leopoldina and Cora's grandson—cohabited in *amasia* and had three natural children between 1898 and 1903. Eventually, these respective descendants of Lino Coutinho's natural and legitimate daughters legitimized their natural children by subsequent marriage.

The bill proposed by Lino Coutinho in 1830 touched on his personal circumstance as the minimally noble father of a natural daughter, for he enjoyed civil nobility by virtue of his medical diploma. Furthermore, D. Pedro I had admitted Lino Coutinho to the Order of Christ in the mid-1820s, although, as Dundas lamented, he died "untitled."[18] Theoretically, Lino Coutinho could have equipped Cora as his *ab intestato* successor prior to his legitimate daughter's birth in 1834. However, it would have entailed legitimizing her before either the Desembargo do Paço or, after 1828, a parish judge, due to his civil nobility. Once Lino Coutinho fathered a legitimate child, in 1834, then it was unlikely that he could equip Cora as his legitimized his successor. Due to his possession of civil nobility, technically, she was ineligible for even a bequest from her father's *terça*, given that he had a legitimate daughter. On the other hand, Cora probably remained an *exposta* because Lino Coutinho did not want to cause "notorious scandal" for her mother, whose marriage in 1836, when she was well into her thirties, confirms such a motive. Thus his 1830 bill, addressing the situation of many men of property, who, like himself, were the minimally noble fathers of natural children, or alternatively, those who had fathered spurious children, confronted the "thicket of endogamy and illegitimacy" in Bahia. All of his social relations "conveyed how important, or perhaps how ordinary, the question of illegitimacy was in Bahia, even in families of the elite."[19] The same could be said, of course, for the parliamentary circles in which he circulated in the Corte.

A Radical Proposal: Lino Coutinho's Omnibus Bill

The bill introduced by Dep. Jozé de Lino Coutinho on May 18, 1830, defined the genesis of a reform effort that his colleagues pursued until 1847. His omnibus proposal was not only modern in a nineteenth-century context but also far in advance of proposals that would be adopted throughout most of the twentieth century. Initially, no debate followed the reading of the bill into the record, but Lino Coutinho offered a brief supporting argument that appealed to natural law, which "equalizes all men." Although he did not explicitly attack the society of estates, the Bahian legislator implied what everyone knew—that differences in succession rights derived from "distinctions" pertaining to the legal vestiges of a society of estates. Having in mind Article 1 of the bill, he bluntly referred to how Brazilians were still divided into noble and non-noble estates—"There are these differences of names, although there would be marquises, counts, and councilors." His goal was to remove the distinction of estate that barred the natural offspring of a noble parent from succeeding *ab intestato* on a par with that parent's legitimate offspring. "The equality of law is for all Brazilian citizens, whether they use titles or not," he insisted.[20]

The fact that the bill was returned for discussion only at the end of the legislative year, on September 30, suggested that it lacked sufficient backing to pass; however, it could not be dismissed outright or indefinitely tabled because a core of liberal deputies favored it as a valuable means for pushing "equality before the law" in a new direction. Lino Coutinho's bill consisted of five substantive articles. A sixth and final article merely revoked existing legislation to the contrary. Only the first article addressed the situation of natural offspring in succession law, for the other four treated paternal recognition of spurious individuals. Article 1 proposed revision of the *Ordenações Filipinas*, Book 4, Title 92. Referring to its famous dictum that recognized natural offspring enjoyed rights in *ab intestato* succession "as if they had been born in a legitimate marriage," this article placed that equality of rights in a new context by referring to natural offspring "born to a Brazilian citizen of whatever class [*classe*] or condition [*condição*]." Thus it presumed to equalize all natural offspring regardless of the father's—or the mother's— legal estate, disregarding the parent's legal condition as either a titled noble, merely gentle-born (*fidalgo*), or "ennobled by the law" with civil nobility. It proposed that any natural offspring, of whatever class or condition, provided he or she was recognized by the parent, would possess "the right to succeed their parents, as if born of legitimate marriage, and together with those children born subsequent to marriage."[21]

Hence liberal action singled out natural offspring unlucky enough to be fathered by men of any noble rank—or, less often, born to a noble mother. As the preceding volume explained, the *Ordenações Filipinas* excluded them from *ab intestato* succession. Lino Coutinho, ever the liberal, posed the question in constitutional terms: "We know that the legislation regarding the parental act of recognition [*perfilhação*] for natural offspring makes a big distinction between those who are the natural offspring of commoners and those who are the natural offspring of nobles, *escudeiros*, or *cavalheiros*. Will this continue among us?" Article 1 supplied his answer: "It cannot, because every citizen of any condition will be able to recognize his offspring according to the same form, without distinction among commoners, nor between nobles and *fidalgos*—and this is exactly what this law proposes." Although he argued the bill would bring law into line with the 1824 Constitution, ending discrimination between natural offspring fathered by nobles and commoners, he did not raise the crucial issue of minimal nobility per se. The latter explained why Article 1 survived through seventeen years of legislative debate and revision, to be adopted in 1847.

Article 1 also implied revised procedural changes for parental recognition. Henceforth, recognition of paternity would have to be declared either by the father's affidavit, whether executed privately or with a notary, or by a testamentary declaration conferring posthumous recognition, or by means of a "judicial determination" rendered by a judge of the first instance. The latter option followed from the 1828 Judiciary Act, placing the power to grant the solemn legitimization formerly conferred by the crown in the hands of judges. Unless a father documented his declaration of paternity in an affidavit or his will, or he had obtained judicial legitimization of his natural offspring, then his paternal recognition would be null, conveying no legal effects. In other words, Article 1 also sought to end much of the subjectivity—and legal arbitrariness—inherent in the kind of evidence accepted for paternal recognition, by obliging fathers for the first time to commit their acts of recognition to writing. Where historically natural offspring enjoyed the right to have a judge establish paternal filiation, this article left such a recourse intact. The procedural importance of the provision lay in the fact that, where law had also left paternal recognition customarily informal, either tacit within families or openly acknowledged in the community, no longer would those expressions be sufficient to convey legal effects.

The thread connecting the patrimonial interests of natural offspring and their noble parents lay first in the changing nature of nobility in Brazil. By the end of the 1820s, minimal nobility was accessible to many men, due to being conferred most commonly "by the law" as civil nobility. Alternatively, attainment of a title or merely the "honors" of admission to a noble order had privileged a much smaller group between 1808 and 1830. Otherwise, where children inherited *fidalguia* by descent, from parents and grandparents, they discovered that it opened fewer doors after 1822 than in the eighteenth century. Diplomas awarded for higher education, especially in law and medicine, now defined the common credentials for entry-level careers. Yet they continued to confer civil nobility. Finally, life-tenure titles of nobility carried less advantage for the holder's children; they were no longer heritable. The nature of noble status had changed. Although *fidalguia* still mattered socially more than civil nobility, it no longer translated into the career credentials that had made it coveted in the eighteenth century. Nor did either nobility by descent or that conferred by the law signify great advantage for the corporate family group. Yet noble parents, especially fathers, were barred, however minimal their noble rank, from making their recognized natural offspring their *ab intestato* heirs. Nor could they expect to confer testamentary succession rights whenever they also had legitimate children. *Fidalguia* and civil nobility, even the distinction of a noble title, stood as mixed blessings wherever a parent wanted a natural child to be a forced heir.

Article 2 represented the bill's most iconoclastic proposal, because it addressed the consequences of clerical concubinage. Although Lino Coutinho anticipated a break with canon law, his ingenious strategy left that circumstance tacit, given that Article 2 deftly prescribed, "The children of ecclesiastical or religious individuals are understood to fall under the disposition of the preceding article." That is, Article 1 also applied to *sacrílegos*, transforming them into natural offspring. Any religious, whether secular or regular, including nuns, would be free to recognize his or her offspring in the same manner as the unmarried parents of the natural offspring described in Article 1. In the eyes of the church, of course, Article 2 was "heretical" for contravening canonical prohibitions contained in the Articles of Trent. Although Lino Coutinho drew inspiration from the views of his priestly colleague and political ally in the Chamber of Deputies, Diogo Antônio Feijó, he crafted Article 2 as a compromise between Feijó's extremist position that priests be permitted to marry and the church's orthodox rigidity on clerical celibacy. Article 2 tactfully gave the nod to clerical concubinage, upholding the arrangements of priests who lived in *mancebia*, but it stressed the offspring's entitlement to equal rights in heirship, redressing the legal situation of the children of clerics analogously to those of noble parents. Thus *sacrílegos*, like the natural offspring of a noble parent, deserved to be equated with the children of lay persons—commoners—wherever rules of *ab intestato* succession mattered.

In defending Article 2, Lino Coutinho stood on the firm ground of recent practice, arguing that in the past "the Desembargo do Paço had issued documents to clerics enabling them to establish legal kinship with their off-spring." Therefore, from his bill, "It follows that there are no sacrilegious off-spring, only natural offspring." Implying the practical change introduced by the 1828 Judiciary Act, he asked, "If before the Desembargo do Paço had possessed this right, why did not the legislature now have it?" He referred to the sovereign's former identity as the legislator, recently delegated by the General Legislative Assembly to the judiciary. The 1828 Judiciary Act had not specifically instructed judges on how to proceed in terms of awarding either *ab intestato* or testamentary succession rights concurrent with solemn legitimization, but it did stipulate that the procedural rules of the Desembargo do Paço would remain in force. Because it was an act of the legislature that abolished the Desembargo do Paço, Lino Coutinho argued in blunt affirmation of Article 2 that the General Legislative Assembly—Parliament as a whole—still possessed authority to bestow legitimization, by means of adopting his bill.

Lino Coutinho avoided pointing out that the 1828 Judiciary Act had left priests in legal limbo, knowing his colleagues apprehended that fact. Unlike parents belonging to the laity, priests could not routinely resort to a judge of the first instance for obtaining a child's certificate of legitimization. Since 1828, such action entailed a very public confession of paternity, one discouraging priests from petitioning for solemn legitimization. If they were living in *mancebia*, then petitioning a judge placed them in jeopardy, confession of "notorious and scandalous" behavior that often was also "ongoing," *prima facie* evidence for episcopal disciplining and in some instances prosecution for a crime. Priests thus might be vulnerable to reprisals from political enemies that led to criminal charges. Formerly, clergy who possessed substantial financial means had petitioned the Tribunal of the Mesa do Desembargo do Paço in largely closed proceedings. Normally their petitions had been posthumously habilitated. The 1828 Judiciary Act, consequently, discouraged clerics from seeking solemn legitimization for their children. More and more, priests were living in open *mancebia*. Lino Coutinho, however, wanted to do more than facilitate solemn legitimization for *sacrílegos*. He intended no less than outright removal of the stigma of sacrilegious birth. He viewed children born to priests as analogous to those with a parent possessing a degree of nobility, deserving "equality before the law."

Article 3 addressed a social taboo as much as a point in canon law, albeit one that positive law echoed less loudly. Namely, fathers of adulterine children, even more than priests, were expected to remain silent about their paternity, leaving their blood tie to the child tacit in social contexts. Although Article 3 also pertained to canonically incestuous offspring, they did not suffer the opprobrium reserved for adulterine children. In upholding the taboo—"adulterine and incestuous children cannot be recognized"—Article 3 proposed that paternal clandestinity take second place to paternal responsibility. "Once their fathers so declare" paternity by providing for the child, Article 3 stipulated, or "if the spurious child's filiation to the father had been judicially established for child support, then the latter should become the sole responsibility of the declaring father."

In fact, this was not new law, but an attempt to make a specific statute articulating a broad principle on child support that originated in the *Ordenações Filipinas*. Book 1, Title 88, Section 11, obligated all fathers, of either natural or spurious children, to assume responsibility for supporting and raising their offspring, after the mother's primary responsibility ceased at age three. In Pombal's era, the *assento* of April 9, 1772, Section 3, had expressly reaffirmed such paternal responsibility. As Borges Carneiro noted, this *ordenação* amounted to "the voice of nature," compelling even the rapist to support and raise his offspring. Drawing additional juridical authority from Heiniccius and Stryk, he pointed to the "barbarous disposition of Roman law" that had denied any category of illegitimate offspring the right of paternal support. Article 3 nonetheless reaffirmed the duty of only those fathers who had come forward at some point in the past, and made their identity known in order to provide support to their non-legitimate children. It implied that those who chose to remain consistently silent and conceal their identity would continue to enjoy such a privilege of evasion, unless the child's relatives went to court to establish paternity for the exclusive purpose of child support. Consequently, Article 3 was confirmatory, given that both Book 1, Title 88, Section 11, and Book 4, Title 99, Section 1, were already interpreted that way.[22]

Article 3 nevertheless represented a bold attempt to address the stigma of spurious birth, by underscoring that a father's provision of child support for his spurious offspring, by means of a tacit declaration of his blood tie to the child, would not be taken as an admission of a criminal act. By upholding the existing legal prohibition on paternal recognition of adulterine children, the article avoided antagonizing the defenders of law in force. From the hindsight of over a century, Article 3 represented a modest first step in moving toward paternal recognition for adulterine children, a legal development that did not gain momentum in Brazil until the 1940s. Finally, Article 3 proved to be of practical assistance in a society where the numbers of adulterine and canonically incestuous children were growing. Should the father die, his informal declaration of adulterous paternity, tied to child support, would benefit the child. The mother or other relatives could go to court to claim some right of support from the father's estate, one in the hands of his legitimate heirs.

However modest these changes might appear, they were largely canceled out, due to the fact that Article 4 reaffirmed the conventional silence demanded from the fathers of adulterine children, especially when their wives were living. It flatly stated, "The declaration of adulterine offspring has no place in the constancy and harmony of matrimony." This provision curbed the freedom of such fathers to "acknowledge" their paternity publicly, even for the sole purpose of child support, a circumstance that Pombaline law had ignored. The caveat of Article 4, largely a contradiction of Article 3, offered a clue to the growing importance of legal marriage in post-independence Brazil. Silence on adulterous paternity now mattered more for the honor of the conjugal family. Canonical incest, although bracketed with adulterine liaisons in Articles 3 and 4, never acquired the character of a social taboo that adultery projected, given social norms regarding consanguineous marriage. Otherwise, Lino Coutinho knew that few legislators were willing to ignore the full force of custom on the cardinal point on adultery and family honor. When a married man brought an adulterine child to be raised under his own legitimate family's roof, he did not acknowledge—declare—his paternity in a way that publicly compromised his wife or himself. He left it unspoken, tacitly understood, usually by concealing the child's relationship.

Article 5 posited a radical redefinition of incest, in effect underscoring that adulterine birth remained a category set apart. "Incest" amounted, of course, to canonical incest; therefore it did not enjoy the same broad condemnation that adulterine paternity produced. Hence, Article 5 effectively sought to abolish canonical incest as it had been received in Luso-Brazilian positive law, by redefining the legal incest taboo so shallowly that any necessity to obtain an ecclesiastical dispensation to marry was obviated. Article 5 was as terse as it was thoroughly radical: "Incestuous offspring are those who come from sexual unions between relatives in lineal degree; in a collateral degree, only between siblings."

Article 5 thus prohibited marriage only between consanguine relatives who were ascendants and descendants or between siblings. Yet it promised even greater social impact in terms of how it kept silent on matrimonial impediments that were either affinal—based on kinship by marriage—or spiritual—based on kinship by godparenthood. Both of the latter went to the heart of marriage arrangements in Brazil, accounting for a larger absolute number of dispensations than those granted for prohibited degrees of consanguinity. By all but eliminating prohibitive degrees of kinship, Lino Coutinho's bill sought no less than to "nationalize" the rules of marriage and to bring impediments into line with Brazilian social realities. Consequently, Article 5 rendered most matrimonial dispensations hypothetical, by placing Brazilians in the "free state" to contract marriage, but it also anticipated a break with ecclesiastical procedures that provided important income to parish priests and bishops alike.

Yet the Roman Catholic rite of marriage remained the sole form of legal marriage in Brazil. Most priests would not perform marriages in disregard of canon law's prohibitions—or condone the elimination of indispensable clerical fees. Article 5 deserved to be read as a deliberate provocation to the ecclesiastical hierarchy and to Rome. It also implied adoption of a civil registry for marriages. Article 5 would have been resisted by many parish priests, who would have refused to marry couples in disregard of Tridentine rules— not to speak of surrendering to a precipitous loss of income from clerical fees. Furthermore, parish priests would have been reduced merely to performing the marriage ceremony, that is, converted into agents of the state by virtue of impediments that were civil. The "sweetener" was Article 2, offering to make the children of priests natural, removing the stigma of "*sacrílego*."

A reading into the record of Lino Coutinho's bill "on the recognition of natural offspring of Brazilian citizens" took place on June 5, but without any discussion having been recorded. The bill was not returned for an indicated second discussion until October 14, when little more than a week remained in the 1830 legislative year. Although the minutes described the bill as carried to a second discussion, the redactor reported no exchange of views or oratorical support for the measure. By placing the bill so late on the Camara's calendar, the president of the lower house intended to postpone consideration until 1831, or perhaps indefinitely. As a precedent-shattering set of proposals addressing the most controversial facets of illegitimate family life, Lino Coutinho's bill was fated to draw the ire of Archbishop D. Romualdo de Seixas, throwing into high relief the rapidly deteriorating relationship between the Brazilian government and the Holy See.[23]

Meanwhile, a very different bill treating the recognition of illegitimate offspring, introduced a week after Lino Coutinho's initial presentation on May 18, better accounted for the postponement of his bill. A more modest proposal, it, too, aimed to bring law into line with social behavior. By substantially undercutting the appeal of Lino Coutinho's radical proposal, it obviated demands for a third discussion of the latter.

RECASTING LEGITIMIZATION PER

RESCRIPTUM PRINCIPIS

A Modest Proposal

On June 26, 1830, Aureliano de Souza e Oliveira Coutinho, an imperial deputy for the Province of Minas Gerais, introduced a resolution in the Chamber of Deputies that addressed the position of "children of damnable sexual union" in inheritance law.[24] Because his resolution overlapped considerably with Articles 2 through 4 of Lino Coutinho's bill, it further testified to liberals' concentrated effort to reform the succession rights of illegitimate individuals as they dismantled the juridical framework of a society of estates.

Aureliano, the envoy who had been entrusted with negotiating the marriage contract of D. Pedro I and Amelia of Leuchtenberg, was a Coimbra civil law graduate and only thirty years old. He had already made a brilliant political career for himself, having arrived in the Chamber of Deputies from Rio de Janeiro's high court, the Relação. A gentleman of the imperial household and a member of Pedro's Council of State—on whom the emperor had bestowed the Orders of Christ and the Rose—Aureliano was the consummate self-made man. His family background in the province of Rio de Janeiro is somewhat obscure, but his father was a military officer. He possessed indigenous and probably African ancestry, although he was of predominantly European descent.[25] Politically, Aureliano de Souza Oliveira was a moderate liberal who would soon join the Regency executive and then hold various cabinet posts, alongside Diogo Antonio Feijó, Jozé Lino Coutinho, and Nicolao Vergueiro.

Aureliano's resolution proposed that the parents of "offspring of damnable unions"—spurious children—be permitted to use their wills to institute their offspring as testamentary heirs in succession, wherever they lacked necessary, or legitimate, heirs. In contrast to Lino Coutinho, Aureliano introduced a conservative measure that offered a limited, but very important, remedy for the Philippine Code's legal exclusion of spurious offspring from paternal or maternal succession rights. It obviated solemn legitimization in a key context. Rather than using the extinction of the Tribunal da Mesa do Desembargo do Paço as a means for radically extending law in a new direction, the tactic adopted by Lino Coutinho, Aureliano reaped advantage from the procedural opportunity presented by the Paço's disappearance. Equally important, he envisioned bringing law into conformity with existing social practice, namely that many parents of spurious offspring, contrary to law, had not bothered to legitimize them before the Desembargo do Paço—or to indicate in their wills they intended the offspring subsequently be legitimized by the crown.

The text of Aureliano's resolution presumed to state law in force, but it amounted to a half-truth: "Neither the *ordenação* of Book 4, Title 93, nor any national law prohibits that the offspring of damnable unions may be instituted by their parents as heirs by virtue of a will, in the absence of necessary heirs."[26] The bill's lone article was correct in concluding that the *ordenação* of Book 4, Title 93, "did not prohibit this practice." For that matter, better authority could be found in Book 2, Title 35, Section 12, wherein the *Ordenações Filipinas* expressly stated that in cases where a parent lacked necessary heirs, spurious children could be made testamentary successors. But the bill's text was wrong where it referred to the absence of any national law prohibiting a parent from using a will to institute the spurious child as a testamentary heir. As we have seen in the preceding volume, and contemporary legal commentaries continued to emphasize after 1800, law strictly circumscribed a parent's use of a will for instituting a spurious child as an heir in succession. Authorization from the Tribunal of the Desembargo do Paço was required, implying the parent had to petition for crown legitimization with concurrent rights in succession. The laws of September 9, 1769, and January 31, 1775, were still interpreted to apply to wills written for the purpose of nominating universal heirs in testamentary succession.[27] Finally, the 1828 Judiciary Act, by adopting the *Regimento* of the Desembargo do Paço, gave force to that manual of rules and procedures, which upheld the need for solemn legitimization as a prerequisite for testamentary succession.

By means of clever paraphrasing, and neglecting to interpret law accurately, Aureliano's bill conferred directly on parents the independent authority to institute their spurious offspring, that is, those of damnable and punishable birth, as testamentary successors, provided the parents lacked legitimate descendants or ascendants. That is, the resolution eliminated the required step of solemn legitimization, currently awarded by a judge of the first instance, as a prerequisite for conferring testamentary succession on this class of heirs. Aureliano's measure proposed, for the first time, that simple legitimization would be sufficient to enable a parent to institute a spurious offspring as testamentary successor, that is, parental recognition conveyed in a notarial affidavit or a clause in a will. However, Aureliano's resolution applied only to situations where neither legitimate children, parents, or grandparents existed, that is, where the parent potentially enjoyed the privilege of naming universal heirs, consistent with the application of testamentary succession rights.[28]

Argumentation over the resolution offers historians a context in which to situate post-1828 change in the courtroom, in the wake of the Judiciary Act. Aureliano thus provided a glimpse of the confusion reigning in the new judicial system, one that implied a lack of qualified judges of the first instance who ruled on legitimization or inheritance disputes. Calling for "urgency" due to the impact of the 1828 Judiciary Act, he pointed to cases arising daily in the courts, where collateral heirs sought to overturn testamentary dispositions on behalf of illegitimate children. Often, the reason was the testator's use of a will to institute an offspring "of damnable union" as a testamentary successor—when, presumably, the child had not been solemnly legitimized. Alternatively, the bill's sponsor continued, legal challenges occurred in court because the parent had omitted recognition of the spurious offspring in his or her will, leaving the door open to collateral relatives who challenged those dispositions as null. Testators also named such offspring beneficiaries of bequests from the *terça*, in situations where the *Ordenações* prohibited leaving spurious offspring a bequest, or when a natural offspring's parent possessed some degree of noble rank.[29]

Aureliano did not always offer sufficient details to make those actions fully comprehensible, because he deliberately avoided any explicit reference to solemn legitimization. Nevertheless, he offered sufficient details to make courtroom behavior comprehensible. The most important revelation about courtroom practices concerned spurious offspring who themselves went to court to bring actions for judicial legitimization, or *perfilhação solemne*. As we have seen from the chapter devoted to the latter, in Volume 1, unless a father left evidence of his intent to legitimize a spurious offspring, then law barred the latter from petitioning for a judicial determination of paternity. Aureliano's extended remarks on the confusion occurring in courtroom proceedings suggested that public perceptions about the rights of spurious offspring were changing, and not necessarily in accordance with law in force. They also suggested that the impact of the 1828 Judiciary Act may not have been what legislators intended—to make it easier for spurious offspring of commoner parents, as well as both the natural and spurious offspring of a noble parent, to obtain legitimization certificates from a local judge, awarded concurrently with succession rights.

By 1830, the aggressiveness of collateral heirs had became proverbial, due to their unwillingness to step aside in favor of both legally equipped spurious and natural offspring, including those whose solemn legitimization was pending. José de Alencar demonstrated how the hostile insistence of collateral relatives would soon penetrate national fiction. In *Senhora*, Lourenço Camargo, the elderly grandfather of the protagonist, Aurelia, is driven to fury by the patrimonial ambitions of his nephews and nieces. They refuse to be restrained even by Lourenço Camargo's last will and testament, a document recognizing Aurelia as the old man's natural granddaughter and sole heir. Eventually, he suffers a stroke and dies from the onslaught of "a mob of idlers who claimed to be his nephews, and with them their wives ... and kinfolk." Lourenço Camargo is beset by his collateral relatives because "they had been informed by a reliable source that the old man had made his will at the courthouse and surmised that he had bequeathed his entire estate to a girl, the daughter of some fallen woman, a former mistress of Pedro Camargo," Lourenço's dead, legitimate son. The conflict is telling, for, indeed, Lourenço Camargo's collateral relatives enjoyed no patrimonial rights whatsoever. The will he wrote guaranteed that his sole granddaughter would be his *ab intestato* successor, by underscoring he recognized her as the daughter of his legitimate son. In the scene precipitating the elderly man's death, his nephews descend on him with a notary in tow in order to cajole him into drawing up a new will. Camargo is told—wrongly—that his will is invalid and that his granddaughter cannot succeed him.[30]

As the novel suggests, confusion over the meaning of law was one thing. However, the greed of collateral heirs excluded from the ladder of *ab intestato* succession was a problem beyond the reach of legislators to correct. As Aureliano de Souza Oliveira acknowledged to his fellow deputies, wills were disputed in court regardless of whether a parent had "either recognized them [the spurious offspring] or omitted recognition."[31] Yet more than merely the impact of the Judiciary Act had fostered an increasingly litigious ambience in the courts.

Muriel Nazzari's examination of the legitimization proceedings of the Desembargo do Paço in Rio de Janeiro, between 1808 and 1828, sheds additional light on why courts of the first instance became the battleground for conflicting claims by collateral heirs and spurious offspring. Normally, she confirmed, the Tribunal of the Desembargo do Paço awarded legitimization with succession rights only when the decedent lacked necessary heirs—legitimate descendants and ascendants—and the collateral heirs waived their rights and agreed to admit their legitimized relative to *ab intestato* succession. Otherwise, when collateral heirs withheld their consent, then the Tribunal of the Desembargo do Paço preferred to grant solemn legitimization without any succession rights mentioned in the legitimization certificate. That is, the Desembargo do Paço upheld the Provisão of January 18, 1799, and declined petitions for concurrent succession rights wherever collaterals—and sometimes ascendants—defended their prior *ab intestato* rights. However, post-1808 judicial practice in Brazil confronted both natural and spurious children who, in posthumous contexts, presented less than the ideal documentation as evidence for a parent's earlier intent to legitimize them. In addition, natural off-spring went to court for the same reason that Lobão had pronounced there was no "half-noble" state: They sought to convince a judge that their parents did not enjoy minimal nobility and, therefore, that they could succeed *ab intestato* as a recognized child.

Ambiguity increasingly complicated rulings. Instead of passing judgment on the recommendation of the *ouvidor*, the judge of the first instance, whose task it was to conduct a preliminary consultation with competing heirs, the high crown judges of the Paço inclined toward making that lower judge the final arbiter among competing claimants. In effect, they abandoned their mandate to bestow succession rights concurrently with legitimization and, according to Nazzari, remanded contested cases to the lower courts. When illegitimate offspring were legal minors, then the Desembargo do Paço instructed the surviving parent to take a claim for succession rights to the orphans judge. The Paço, in other words, pronounced an important shift had taken place in the position collaterals historically occupied on the ladder of *ab intestato* succession. Their prior rights in heirship no longer were defended absolutely by the crown's high court of privilege. Those rights had become subject to *ad hoc* litigation in the lower courts.[32] After 1808, the emergence of a judicial policy that no longer regarded the rights of collaterals as sacrosanct suggested that the Desembargo do Paço had nodded in a direction giving greater opportunity to non-legitimate offspring. Beginning in 1828, when succession rights concurrent with solemn legitimization, now referred to as legitimization *"por escrito,"* were decided by either the justice of the peace (parish judge) or the orphans judge, the new judiciary was ill-equipped to render consistent rulings. The cause was either the judges' fundamental ignorance of law or their vulnerability to subornation, and the national legislature's failure to provide consistent doctrinal principles. The lower courts now required guidance, and the acrimony and confusion arising from collateral challengers who aggressively pushed their patrimonial claims, Aureliano and others believed, would be resolved by removing altogether this contentious area of litigation from the courtroom.

Aureliano resorted directly to Pombaline legal doctrine for repudiating the claims of collateral heirs. He charged that considerable court time was being wasted, due to situations where collateral heirs used Roman law to contest the inheritance claims of spurious offspring. Correctly, he invoked the 1769 Law of Right Reason (Lei da Boa Razão) to point out that collaterals could not use Roman law to argue that spurious offspring were prohibited from inheriting. Instead, he had in mind the *Ordenações*, Book 2, Title 35, Section 12, which offered parents without legitimate children opportunity to make anyone a testamentary heir. Therefore, it did not follow that parents' testamentary dispositions on behalf of spurious offspring were null. Of course, he neglected to mention the Pombaline emphasis on solemn legitimization before a judge. Appealing directly to the intellectual authority of "Jurisconsult Pascoal José de Mello [Freire]," Aureliano referred to the new vernacular title by which that Pombaline jurist's commentary was by then known—the *Instituições de direito patrio*."[33] He cited Section 13 of Title 8, Book 3, to show how national law departed from Roman law. In Roman law, he explained, "only natural offspring are legitimized, and not spurious offspring, nor those born of damnable unions, in the absence of legitimate offspring . . . ." He correctly noted, contrary to Luso-Brazilian legal tradition, that legitimization of a natural offspring in Roman law took place "only at the father's request." Emperor Justinian "introduced this method of legitimization" and did not permit the offspring themselves to petition for it.[34] Basing his reasoning on legal nationalism—*direito pátrio*—Aureliano dismissed Roman law for being contradictory. The legislative body therefore was competent to perform a "corrective" function wherever Roman law was at issue, given the mandate of the celebrated Law of Right Reason.

More than ignorance of *direito pátrio* was at work in the judiciary, he charged. Chicanery, too, played a role:

Hundreds of [court] cases are pending on this theory [of the relevance of Roman law], the judges varying at each step in either good or bad faith and this . . . opens the door to prevarication. Many have committed even the abuse of basing their opinions on the text of Roman law, founded indubitably (but shallowly) on the charter of the Law of 18 August 1769, which, very much to the contrary, in §10, expressly prohibits restricting national laws wherever they are corrective of Roman law (as occurs concerning the just cited *ordenação*).[35]

Roman law was being interpreted in Brazil's courtrooms, sometimes successfully, to set aside national law. That fact disclosed serious intellectual deficiencies in the country's fledgling judiciary. Judges did not always know how to apply the 1769 Law of Right Reason—to the point where they were reading it in reverse. By the same token, controversy over the rights of collateral heirs exposed the liabilities of the new judicial system, where the parish judge was chosen by popular election. He often lacked legal training. In 1827, Dep. Feijó had warned, to no avail, that the newly created justice of the peace required oversight from the imperial judge, a law school graduate, in order to make his rulings "more prudent" and avoid arbitrary decisions.[36] Otherwise, the fact that only six Brazilians had graduated from the Coimbra Law Faculty since 1826, while the newly created law faculties in Recife and São

Paulo had yet to produce their first crop of graduates, contributed to the dearth of qualified personnel at the critical level of imperial judge, the magistrate occupying the rung immediately above the parish judge.

Aureliano confined himself to the practical situation of parents writing wills on behalf of spurious offspring, neglecting to comment that many parents did not bother to obtain solemn legitimization for their children or, alternatively, to include the requisite conditional clause of future intent in their wills: "if legitimization is obtained" (*se obtiver legitimação*). Legitimization could only follow from the parent's express wish, meaning a judge could never bestow it over parental opposition or enigmatic silence. Aureliano did not want an argument over his goal of replacing solemn legitimization with the simple, usually testamentary form, because on that point Mello Freire had been adamantly explicit. The latter had construed testamentary nomination of a spurious offspring in heirship as not "true legitimization." Yet Aureliano's resolution proposed precisely that. "Explicit approval of royal authority" beforehand, according to Mello Freire, was indispensable for rights in heirship: "If the Prince has not approved the nomination [in heirship], in his own hand and made him [the offspring] legitimate," then "the nominated does not acquire the rights of the legitimate offspring."[37] The prince's dispensation of law, now wielded in Brazil by a judge of the first instance known as the parish judge, accounted for the peculiar redaction of Aureliano's bill. The text spoke of "nominating" or "instituting" the illegitimate offspring as an heir, as opposed to "legitimizing" the individual, and it remained silent on "succession," referring to the result only as a testamentary heir.

Consequently, Aureliano never directly confronted the fact that formerly the Tribunal of the Mesa do Desembargo do Paço had to be petitioned for what were exceptions to Book 4, Title 93, of the *Ordenações*—succession rights for spurious offspring. Instead, he argued ipso facto, following his bill's redaction, that the *Ordenações* did "not prohibit, as it is to be understood, that similar illegitimate offspring [i.e., those of damnable birth] might be instituted as heirs by their parents in a will, wherever the latter lacked necessary heirs."[38] Technically speaking, he was correct, but only if he ignored Lobão's famous caveat that the parents did not enjoy "a plenary right" to nominate an offspring in testamentary succession—independently of the crown.

Most historians of Brazil have labored under the same misconception, for they have encountered wills appearing to confirm that parents enjoyed the independent right prior to 1831 to use a will to institute their spurious children as their heirs in succession. Nor have they discerned that the law instituted them testamentary heirs rather than *ab intestato* ones. What needs clarification is that wills had to carry the proviso that the testator had already obtained solemn legitimization. Or, if conferring simple legitimization, mere recognition, then the testator had to note "if [solemn] legitimization is obtained" in the future. Until 1831, simple testamentary legitimization merely repaired bastardy. It removed the stain of spurious birth and equipped the offspring to use the parent's names or honors, but it could not convey rights in patrimony.[39]

When Aureliano pointed to hundreds of pending cases disputing the succession rights of spurious offspring, it should not be assumed that only the collateral challengers were at fault. Leaving aside bad juridical reasoning founded on Roman law, many collateral claimants presumably attacked testamentary dispositions that really were invalid. From this perspective, it can be concluded that the social practice of writing invalid wills was gaining the upper hand against the letter of the law. By 1830, the courtroom had become the arena where these two forces clashed. The 1828 Judiciary Act, for the first time, offered a local venue for competing collateral relatives to challenge spurious offspring who asserted rights in heirship. This new window of judicial opportunity, rather than the strict enforcement of inheritance law in drawing up *partilhas*—a development coming later in the century—turned the issue of succession rights for illegitimate offspring into a Pandora's box.

Aureliano denounced the judiciary, condemning Brazil's new parish judges not only for "divergences" from accepted jurisprudence, but also for incompetence. It was they who "opened the door to prevarication and impunity, bringing vacillation and uncertainty to the property and fortune of so many heirs and legatees, due to the theoretical interpretation in question."[40] The patrimonial fate of a growing population of spurious offspring, in his view, now clearly lay in the hands of judges who were as venal as they were confused or ignorant over the meaning of the Law of Right Reason. Referring derisively to those judges of the first instance as "*julgadores*"—"those doing the judging," he pointed to what many of his colleagues viewed as "the chaos" of legal decisions following on the heels of the 1828 Judiciary Act. Therefore, the solution Aureliano proposed was simply to remove the patrimonial destiny of spurious offspring, when they lacked legitimate half-siblings, from the courts altogether. By letting parents alone decide whether to "nominate" them a testamentary successor, the competing claims of spurious offspring and collateral heirs could be largely eliminated from the courts. Hence Aureliano de Souza's resolution looked to a "quick fix" that legislatively redefined the ladder of *ab intestato* succession in a way prejudicial to the rights of collateral heirs.

Amending a Modest Proposal

The urgency enjoined by Aureliano de Souza Oliveira meant that his resolution was returned to the floor of the lower house for debate near the close of the 1830 session, on September 30. Now formally designated "Resolution No. 99," the measure definitely was regarded as a clarification of existing law, rather than a bill introducing new law. In fact, new legislation, what a bill implied, was being proposed. Its purpose was to displace collateral heirs from their historic position on the ladder of *ab intestato* succession, to favor spurious offspring normally excluded from succession rights. Without saying in so many words what he was doing, Aureliano shrewdly clung to the idea that he was merely clarifying law on the books. The second time the resolution came up for a discussion, on October 1, Jozé Paulino de Albuquerque, the sole deputy sitting for the Province of Rio Grande do Norte, confronted Aureliano over the point that a bill, not a resolution, was pending: "The *ordenação* was not clear . . . thus the resolution is not clear." He called for a bill amounting to new law, given that "a legal interpretation of law" was at issue, having in mind the need for a committee report to be produced prior to any vote taken.[41] Nuances of legal interpretation, procedures, and doctrinal consistency would be resolved by the committee report, including a legal opinion on how the bill fit into existing law, known as a *parecer*, as well as a revised redaction, which would be presented to the full house. Consequently, Paulino de Albuquerque sought to discard the resolution in favor of a bill making new law. Instead, Aureliano obfuscated, anticipating a speedy conclusion that would thereby avoid tying up his proposal in committee.

Aureliano's resolution was saved thanks to the oratory and legal argumentation of Antonio Rebouças, who overrode Paulino de Albuquerque's objections, seconded by Jozé da Silva Maia and other deputies who argued vainly the resolution represented new law. Rebouças offered an amendment insuring that adoption of the resolution would also let prior judicial rulings stand undisturbed. Newly elected, Rebouças belonged to Bahia's parliamentary delegation. Although he took exception to Aureliano's redaction, condemning the wording as equivocal, he strongly disagreed with both Maia and Paulino de Albuquerque. Worse, he argued, the text was "ill-conceived" for incorporating the phrase "offspring of damnable unions," a phrase that derived from canon, not civil, law. Rebouças basically sought to prepare the ground for his own version of the resolution, by amending Aureliano's text. The fiction of a "resolution" was nevertheless retained, even though Rebouças' amended version amounted to a new law encompassing all types of illegitimate offspring: "Neither the *ordenação* of Book 4, Title 93, nor any other law prohibits that spurious and adulterine offspring, or those from any other illicit and damnable union, might be instituted as heirs by their parents, where the latter lack other legitimate heirs, descendants or ascendants."[42]

Redundancy regarding "spurious and adulterine offspring" presumably derived from concern over how adulterine offspring were set apart in public opinion, as well as law, from those who were either incestuous or *sacrílegos*. However, in redundantly defining "legitimate heirs" as encompassing descendants and ascendants, Rebouças addressed popular confusion over the definitional scope of the term. He would have been better off using "necessary heirs." The wording, in fact, warned collateral relatives they could not claim to be legitimate heirs, something that in the eighteenth century would not have been the case. Rebouças offered no explanation about why his text ambiguously joined those born of an illicit union to those deemed "damnable," but the change presumably reflected behind-the-scenes negotiations with backers of Lino Coutinho's bill. By adding offspring born in merely "illicit" unions, the amendment significantly widened the scope of the original resolution and attracted substantially greater support for adoption.

Amended, the resolution now inscribed natural offspring, overlapping substantially Article 1 of Lino Countinho's bill. Therefore, it explicitly addressed the natural offspring of noble parents. Furthermore, although testamentary succession rights were less advantageous to such offspring than rights that were *ab intestato*, the same conclusion did not necessarily follow from a parent's perspective. The resolution implied only testamentary succession, meaning a parent was free to rescind the child's status as a testamentary heir simply by altering the will. Hence, this feature appealed to legislators because it kept control in a father's hands. Finally, Rebouças' text for the first time mingled two categories of illegitimacy, natural and spurious, confounding legal doctrine on each. As a result, a precedent existed for blurring distinctions between natural and spurious offspring that would recur in later proposals. The initial step had been taken in altering the definition of bastardy in Luso-Brazilian legal tradition.

A Genealogical Parenthesis: "Damage Control" for Men of Property

Rebouças wanted many more fathers to be able to favor their non-legitimate offspring with patrimony. No particular defender of nobility, he proposed his amendment having in mind the complicated family situations that many men and some women faced as a result of how law differentiated between offspring of natural and spurious birth within the same family. A parent's noble rank imposed yet another dimension of rules especially resented by fathers. Rebouças' amendment to Aureliano's resolution, consequently, offered the means for many men to avoid court proceedings in seeking legitimization of their children. The experience of testifying in court obliged individuals to reveal humiliating details of personal and family life. In 1830, the most sensational instance of high exposure vis-à-vis judicial legitimization focused on the nuclear family of Col. Antonio da Silva Prado, São Paulo's first entrepreneurial genius and big-time financier. By his death in 1875, Antonio Prado enjoyed a reputation as the Second Empire's wealthiest citizen. Ennobled as baron of Iguape in 1848, eighteen years earlier he had gone to unprecedented lengths to legitimize his only son, all to no avail. In the words of one of his descendants, Antonio Prado went to the extreme of "taking his family's scandalous births to the national legislature," where even his considerable influence proved insufficient to the task.[43]

Precisely at the moment Aureliano's resolution was being deliberated in the Chamber of Deputies, Antonio Prado awaited the outcome of an appeal he had directed to the Chamber's Committee on Civil Justice. He had petitioned it to "dispense the law prohibiting the succession of adulterine offspring," on behalf of "one of his children born to a married woman who was legally divorced." Presumably under the assumption that the Chamber now possessed the sovereign's former authority to dispense law, but more likely out of personal political influence as a man with friends in high places, Col. Antonio Prado had pleaded for the Chamber "to conclude legitimization proceedings" he then had pending "before São Paulo's judge." In fact, he appealed out of misgivings that the unnamed judge of the first instance would grant his petition to legitimize his older, maternally adulterine child, Verissimo da Silva Prado. Very likely, the judge had already refused him. The Committee on Civil Justice replied in a formal opinion, denying his petition. It explained that since the extinction of the Tribunal of the Desembargo do Paço, in 1828, judges of the first instance now authorized solemn legitimization, not the national legislature. In counseling Antonio Prado to apply to São Paulo's local judge for Verissimo's legitimization, the committee alluded to the family complication that stood as the nub of his problem, when it offered this warning: Legitimization "always should be contemplated when it is without prejudice to a third party." Therefore, the report concluded, "the petitioner's formal request should be dismissed as ineffectual."[44]

Antonio Prado's situation had been compounded by the birth of a daughter in February 1825. Veridianna Valerianna da Silva Prado, Verissimo's younger, full sister, had been born a year and a half after their mother's husband died. Therefore, she was a natural offspring. In contrast, Verissimo had been conceived before their mother's husband died, in June 1823, making him adulterine. Therefore, Veridianna, as a natural offspring, was her mother's *ab intestato* heir, while Verissimo was excluded from the maternal *legítima* due to his quality of spurious birth. Nor was he equipped to succeed in the paternal line, notwithstanding that he was Antonio Prado's natural son. Antonio Prado enjoyed minimal nobility by descent, a circumstance excluding both Verissimo and Veridianna from his *legítima*. This circumstance can be deduced from the officer's patent he held in the colonial militia.

On the face of it, Rebouças' amended version of Aureliano's resolution was tailored to resolve situations that were analogous to Verissimo's position in paternal succession, assuming that Antonio Prado had no legitimate children. In reality, however, the situation proved much more complex and even irresolvable, for not only did Verissimo remain perpetually unequipped to succeed in the maternal line, but his sister was legitimized. His rights in paternal succession were denied after his father's death in 1875, confirmation that his father never obtained solemn legitimization for him. Published genealogies omit mention of the fact that Antonio da Silva Prado and Maria Cândida de Moura [Leite] Vaz were living in *mancebia* as early as 1822 or 1823, when Verissimo was born, and that neither of their children was of legitimate birth. They also neglect to identify Maria Cândida as "divorced"— legally separated by an ecclesiastical tribunal—unique information supplied in 1830 by Antonio Prado himself in the petition directed to the Chamber of Deputies. Nor do genealogies offer a date for the couple's marriage, a truly remarkable omission for a literary genre obsessively devoted to recording when the "legitimate marriages" in illustrious families like the Silva Prados of São Paulo took place.[45]

The reason the Committee on Civil Justice warned Antonio Prado that legitimization was contingent on not prejudicing the rights of third parties was the same reason that had impelled him to take the extraordinary step of petitioning the national legislature for Verissimo's legitimization. Presumably, São Paulo's judge of the first instance would not maternally legitimize Verissimo for inheritance purposes, because Maria Cândida already had two legitimate daughters born during her long marriage to Capt. Antonio Jozé Vaz. They would have had to consent to Verissimo's judicial legitimization with concurrent succession rights. Presumably, either they, their father's relatives, or the judge himself declined to waive their prior rights on Verissimo's behalf. As his mother's heir in succession, Verissimo would have reduced his two legitimate half-sisters' patrimony by one-third. To complicate matters more, Verissimo could not succeed to his father's *legítima* on a different ground: He was his father's natural offspring, but Antonio Prado enjoyed nobility by descent. Thus Antonio Prado sought solemn legitimization for Verissimo not only to remedy his situation as maternally adulterine but also to equip him to succeed as his own natural offspring.

Yet a final twist further differentiated Antonio Prado's two natural children, accounting for Verissimo's tragic position in succession law. It turned on the as yet unestablished date when Veridianna became legitimized by the subsequent marriage of her parents, an option that did not apply to Verissimo as a spurious child. If, as one Prado family tradition has it, Antonio Prado did not marry Maria Cândida until 1838, on the very eve of Veridianna's wedding, then earlier he could have profited from Rebouças' revised amendment of Aureliano's resolution. That is, Antonio Prado could have made both of his illegitimate children his testamentary heirs, as long as he lacked legitimate children, obviating altogether solemn legitimization by a judge.[46] That he did not do so is confirmed by the family oral tradition positing a marriage in 1838. On the other hand, it can be also inferred from Antonio Prado's 1830 petition to the national legislature that he had already married Maria Cândida by that date, probably following Veridianna's birth in 1825. The family recollections that she was legitimized by subsequent marriage also posited a date much earlier than 1838. In other words, it can be deduced that what prompted Antonio Prado's petition of legitimization to the legislature was the circumstance that in 1830 he had only one illegitimate offspring, the spurious Verissimo. His petition did not speak of Veridianna, because she had already been legitimized by her parents' subsequent marriage and therefore was automatically equipped to be the *ab intestato* successor of both her father and her mother. Otherwise, their minimal nobility still would have been a barrier preventing her as a natural child from succeeding *ab intestato*. Instead, her parents' nobility posed an additional barrier only for Verissimo, one distinct from his maternal exclusion from succession as adulterine. Antonio Prado's minimal nobility meant that his paternally natural son Verissimo could not be his *ab intestato* successor. In fact, once Antonio Prado married Verissimo's mother, the law prohibited him from leaving Verissimo even a bequest from his *terça*, due to Veridianna's automatic legitimization. She, consequently, became equipped as her father's sole *ab intestato* heir, as well as her mother's. Precisely the fact of his marriage to the children's mother explained the urgency with which Antonio Prado mounted his effort to obtain solemn legitimization for Verissimo in 1830. His children illustrated the dire effect of inheritance law on full siblings who nevertheless possessed different qualities of illegitimate birth, once their parents married.

If Antonio Prado had not already been married to Maria Cândida in 1830, then he would have petitioned both judge and legislature to legitimize both his children. But Antonio Prado's petition ignored Veridianna and focused exclusively on Verissimo as maternally adulterine. In 1868, Verissimo was not called to succession when his mother died, an exclusion further compounded by the fact that, after forty years, Maria Cândida's half of the community property inscribed an enormous proportion of Antonio Prado's assets. Had his parents delayed marriage until after 1831, they could have made him a testamentary heir, together with Veridianna, by resorting to the measure proposed by Antonio Pereira Rebouças. Instead, Veridianna became the sole heir of her mother's *meia*, Maria Cândida's half of the matrimonial community property she shared with Antonio Prado. The estrangement that developed between brother and sister after Antonio Prado's death in 1875 probably emerged in 1868, for it derived from the vastly different positions each occupied in heirship vis-à-vis their father's immense patrimony. Verissimo's legal *qualidade* in 1868 remains unclear, but he may well have enjoyed a paper identity as a legal *exposto*, or at least "of unknown mother," due to the convention of concealing the mother's name in documents wherever an individual enjoyed an adulterine quality of birth. Subsequently, Veridianna alone became her father's heir, at his death in 1875, a circumstance that kept lawyers contesting Iguape's fortune into the twentieth century.[47]

Rebouças Takes Up a Liberal Cause

Antonio Pereira Rebouças proved a unique backer of the resolution he would sagaciously expand to cover different sub-categories of illegitimate offspring in the same family. He came from a lower middle-class stratum in the free population of color, one that exemplified a talented, upwardly mobile, and usually urban group, whom the era of independence favored with political opportunity. A *pardo* whose African ancestry and dark color can easily be detected from a sole surviving portrait, he was singular as the only legislator in the 1830s to whom, publicly, "both a name and a mixed racial identity" could be attached.[48] Rebouças contrasted starkly with several other legislators who shared African ancestry, but sought to be taken as white. Nor did he, like they, remain silent on issues affecting the free population of color, although his views tended to be conservative. For instance, he defended the right of *libertos* to enlist in the National Guard.[49] In 1837, he introduced a bill to prohibit the importation of Africans, as well as the commerce of slaves, within Brazilian territory. Atypically, he married a woman "of African features more pronounced than his own, without worrying about 'improving the race.'"[50] A moderate liberal like Aureliano de Souza Oliveira, Rebouças opposed what was known in Bahia as the "aristocratic party," the clique of sugar planters who occupied the cupola of provincial power.[51]

Neither his biographers nor those of his more famous son, the abolitionist André Rebouças, have dug deeply into Antonio Pereira Rebouças' family origins in Maragogipe, Bahia. His family was respectable, but poor. His grandfather has been presumed to be a Portuguese immigrant, while his father was a small businessman of limited success whose three very gifted sons individually distinguished themselves in music, art, and the law. His mother may have been a freed slave, a point on which printed sources are silent. Nor do they offer any information on his parents' marriage, leading to speculation about whether Rebouças himself was of illicit birth.[52] Lacking the resources to acquire higher education, Rebouças had worked from boyhood, initially as an apprentice typesetter and then as a clerk in a public notary's office. These experiences made him determined to study law independently and to qualify professionally as a lawyer, without benefit of a law degree. He would be assisted in his goal by Brazil's famous imperial jurist, Teixeira de Freitas, a native of Cachoeira, where Rebouças lived until the mid-1830s. In 1847, Rebouças was admitted to the bar by a special act of Parliament, in testimony to the achievement that he was superbly self-taught.[53] In 1830, however, he was a genuine "*rábula*"—a lawyer without academic credentials— whose grasp of jurisprudence belied the ridicule that in the Senate was reserved for self-schooled lawyers who lacked law degrees. Turning politician in the 1828 elections, Antonio Rebouças won a seat in the Chamber of Deputies.

Rebouças demonstrated a sophisticated understanding of legal doctrine during his first opportunity to debate. When Dep. Jozé Antonio da Silva Maia pointed out that although Book 4, Title 93, of the *Ordenações Filipinas* did not specify the sub-categories of offspring born of damnable unions, the Bahian concluded they could be deduced, "as Mello Freire says." Maia argued that Mello Freire made it clear that spurious offspring could not be called to *ab intestato* succession, given that Book 4, Title 92, showed a preference for only the natural offspring of commoner parents. He concluded that spurious offspring, as well as those born of "trivial sexual unions," were excluded from *ab intestato* succession.[54] Erroneously, Maia further presumed that natural offspring had to be the result of concubinage relationships, for he took Book 4, Title 92, of the *Ordenações* quite literally. As we have already seen, by 1800, legal commentaries leaned toward the interpretation that natural offspring could be the result of either stable concubinage or casual sex—Maia's "trivial unions."[55] The solution that Maia proposed was to avoid mingling the rights of what he implied were bona fide natural offspring with all sub-categories of spurious offspring, and to treat the latter in a separate law. In other words, he supported Lino Coutinho's six-article bill precisely because it carefully discriminated natural from spurious offspring.

Rebouças cleverly responded to Maia that a different *ordenação*, that of Book 2, Title 85, permitted parents of an adulterine child to adopt "any off-spring of damnable union," meaning even their own spurious children. It thus enabled the latter "to be admitted to succession as testamentary heirs, whether by *adrogação* [adoption of a legal adult] or ordinary adoption." Correctly, he claimed that such a loophole altered, while clarifying, the *ordena-ção* of Book 4, Title 93, which barred calling spurious offspring to *ab intestato* succession.[56] Yet, like Aureliano, Rebouças declined to add that, until 1828, either adoption with succession rights or writing the will in universal heir-ship to confer those rights on spurious children required solemn legitimiza-tion by the Tribunal of the Desembargo do Paço. It still mattered, in other words, that the rules and regulations of the Paço's *Regimento* applied, as a stipulation of the 1828 Judiciary Act. If adoption was a device explicitly sanc-tioned by the Philippine Code for repairing spurious birth, according to Re-bouças' argument, then his resolution departed from law in force, because it proposed dispensing with authorization by a judge of the first instance.[57]

Passage and Defeat

When the resolution came up for a third and final discussion, on October 1, Lino Coutinho tried unsuccessfully to amend it to exclude all adulterine children, as well as those who were incestuous in lineal degrees or collater-ally, as siblings. That is, he tried to tailor Aureliano's resolution to address Articles 3, 4, and 5 of his own bill, and to limit the beneficiaries who could be instituted heirs in a parent's will. Clearly, he was not inclined to revise exist-ing law on behalf of adulterine individuals, even when no legitimate half-siblings existed, although he favored liberalizing the legal position of the children of priests and almost everyone else who was canonically incestuous. Aureliano's resolution came very close to approximating Article 2 of Lino Coutinho's bill, given that only rarely did priests have legitimate children. Furthermore, it encompassed the situation of many parents described in the same bill's Article 4, meaning parents who were not in the free state to marry in the church. When Aureliano objected, however, Lino Coutinho withdrew his amendment. Yet Rebouças' amended version of the resolution, by offer-ing opportunity to the noble parent's natural offspring, suffered quick defeat. Presumably, the backers of Lino Coutinho's bill, one more favorable to *sacrílegos* and the canonically incestuous, withheld their votes from Rebouças' resolution. Thanks to Aureliano's opposition, Rebouças' amended text failed to carry the vote, leaving the Chamber to adopt Aureliano's original resolution. Forwarded to the Committee on Redaction, it did not mention children of illicit birth, but only the "offspring of damnable unions."[58] It would move to the Senate in 1831.

Two weeks later, on October 14, Lino Coutinho's six-article bill returned to the floor for a second discussion. No more than the bill's full text was read into the official record, suggesting that debate was brief and inconclusive.[59] Lino Coutinho's complex and radical proposal had parted company from Aureliano's well-tempered and modest resolution. Of course, Aureliano's resolution no longer possessed the attraction of partially accomplishing what Lino Coutinho's bill proposed to do for natural offspring, given that, once again, its language referred to only those of spurious, or "damnable" birth. On the other hand, the last had not been heard of Rebouças' attempt to expand the scope of Aureliano's proposal to encompass natural offspring. When the General Legislative Assembly convened in April 1831, completely different circumstances would prevail. D. Pedro I would no longer occupy the throne and a Regency representing the liberal majority in the Chamber of Deputies would govern Brazil. Under its aegis, succession rights for those of illicit as well as "damnable and punishable" birth would move forward, even in the Senate.

DIREITO PÁTRIO ACQUIRES
A BRAZILIAN GLOSS

Despite the introduction of a number of radical proposals for reforming both the laws of marriage and illegitimate succession, Brazilian legislators made only limited progress in 1830. A small group of liberals in each chamber of the legislature had introduced bills on civil marriage, the right of priests to live in *mancebia* free from state punishment, and the abolition of entail, without any success. They had looked to both legal nationalism— *direito pátrio*—and the standard of natural law it implied for proposing a revision of rules of heirship laid down by the Philippine Code. For the first time, a Brazilian legislator had proposed rewriting those rules in order to bring them into conformity with social practice. Thus Aureliano de Souza Oliveira boldly advocated setting aside the prior rights of collateral heirs in *ab intestato* succession, wherever a parent who lacked necessary heirs (ascendants and descendants) so disposed, making spurious children take precedence as testamentary successors. By the same token, Rebouças had proposed placing in the hands of those parents the same right to endow natural offspring, in addition to spurious offspring, addressing the barrier of a parent's noble rank that barred natural offspring from succeeding. Thus both proposals responded to a social context that was Brazilian, at the expense of positive law received from Portugal.

The notion that priests be allowed to declare paternity of their children, and that law treat the latter no differently from natural offspring, while too radical to gain adoption by the Chamber, echoed a similar refrain. National law should reflect the customary arrangements defining family in Brazil. Lino Coutinho, in being the first to propose a law explicitly permitting fathers to "acknowledge" adulterine or incestuous paternity, albeit very circumscribed, sought to transfer a responsibility vaguely articulated in the Philippine Code to a precise, national statute that was Brazilian. Willingness to offer child support, to assume paternal responsibility, might then be weighed against an otherwise "criminal" declaration of adulterine paternity. Finally, in a society where non-legitimate children were becoming increasingly common at high social levels, the boundaries of family were to be drawn more narrowly, against collateral heirs. The nuclear family was to be privileged over the wider kindred, even when it implied children who were adulterine, sacrilegious, or canonically incestuous. Of course, greater emphasis was placed on their rights in law only in the absence of legitimate children as well as parents or grandparents. Yet the ancient claim of the kindred to patrimony, historically epitomized in legal rights assigned to the brother of the deceased, it was now proposed, should pass without restriction to a class of lineals whom law historically regarded as "damnable and punishable." In addition, Aureliano's reform, by seeking to obviate a great deal of judicial legitimization proceedings, made the notary or local record clerk, acting on behalf of a parent, the decisive actor in family scenarios on patrimony. It displaced the recently invented judge of the first instance, the locally elected parish judge, on behalf of a recordkeeper for whom family patrimony would include the very documents he was paid to validate and file.

Although only modest progress had been accomplished in the reform of either family or inheritance law by 1830, the triumph of the 1828 Judiciary Act lay in transferring legitimization proceedings from the Tribunal of the Mesa do Desembargo do Paço to a local, elective judiciary. The process proved problematic, quickly forcing legislators to consider rewriting certain rules of heirship. If the solution called for directly empowering parents to institute their spurious offspring as testamentary successors, whenever they lacked necessary heirs, then it was one bound to be popular. Men and women of property could avoid the public exposure of courtroom proceedings for legitimization simply by having a notary draw a will on behalf of their spurious children—as long as they had no legitimate children and their parents were dead. They could circumvent a judge who might be unfavorable to legitimization, especially in situations where the collateral heirs, like a brother or a nephew, refused to waive their rights. Legislators could endorse Aureliano's resolution enthusiastically because it did not step substantially beyond the theoretical restrictions of the *Ordenações Filipinas*. It merely repealed Pombaline oversight. The fact that it undercut the key parts of Lino Coutinho's bill only contributed to the success and speed with which it was approved by the lower house.

Finally, the 1830 legislative initiatives addressing the rules on succession for non-legitimate individuals did not stand in isolation. They deserve appreciation as part of a larger movement that encompassed Vergueiro's 1829 bill on civil marriage and Feijó's 1827 proposal to sanction clerical *mancebia*, as well as future efforts to lower the age of legal majority, abolish entail, and introduce civil impediments to marriage. All these bills and resolutions took issue with the society of estates, the common denominator for how colonial law treated marriage, illegitimacy, and succession rights. They brought into focus the legal implications of individual quality of birth. The institutional obstacles to change, however, lay in the monarchy, with its privileged, nobilary elite, or in the established church. Constitutional establishment of a religion presumed that canon law would continue to be embedded in family and succession law. The nature of the constitutional monarchy itself, therefore, would have to be altered before radical reform of inheritance rights could be adopted. Precisely this opening for change arrived in 1831, when Brazil's first emperor was forced to abdicate in favor of his five-year-old son.

CHAPTER 7

The Regency and Liberal Reform of
Succession Law

━━━━◆◆◆━━━━

> What is certain is that before any popes existed . . . the same impediments to marriage were established by Roman law that afterward the church adopted from the same Civil Law. . . . It seems an error therefore for the law doctors to say that impediments to marriage and their dispensation always were the primary jurisdiction of the church and never of the temporal power.
>
> Manoel de Almeida e Souza de Lobão, "Analysis of the
> *Ordenação* for Book 2, Title 35, Paragraph 12"[1]

On April 6, 1831, angry citizens of Rio de Janeiro assembled on the Campo de Santana, the largest public gathering place in the city, demanding that D. Pedro I restore the ministry he had dissolved the day before. He refused. Despite the urgings of certain magistrates, the emperor stood firmly behind his "ministry of the marquises," appointed on the preceding evening. Several divisions of the army and militia, as well as the emperor's imperial guard, joined the irate populace. Abdication came as the final answer of the people to their emperor. Within hours, Pedro renounced his claim to the throne in favor of his small son and prepared to forsake his adopted country.

Open opposition to Pedro publicly emerged in September 1830. The arrival of the news of the July Revolution in France acted as a catalyst on the political fortunes of Brazil's impetuous monarch. As an emperor who had always taken personal pride in characterizing himself as a liberal, he was infuriated at being compared with Charles X. In October, Pedro closed the annual session of the General Legislative Assembly uttering only a terse and chilling conclusion to assembled senators and deputies: "August and Dignified Representatives of the Nation, the session is closed."[2] Having wished to abdicate on that occasion, it was said that he requested a secretary to draw up a declaration renouncing the throne. Judging from the speed with which the paper was handed to him, he calculated that his abdication was wanted from behind-the-scenes and tore up the paper.[3]

Early in the morning of April 7, "*vivas*" from the crowd acclaiming the five-year-old heir to the throne echoed through the streets of Rio de Janeiro, even as Brazil's first emperor prepared to depart for Europe. In the pre-dawn hours, Pedro had written a succinct declaration of abdication. Taking consolation from the fact that he could now directly embrace the dynastic cause of his twelve-year-old daughter, Maria da Glória, the newly styled duke of Bragança eagerly anticipated a confrontation over the Portuguese throne with his usurping brother. The same morning, ex-ministers of state and legislators assembled in the Senate building to appoint a provisional Regency, the "*vivas*" from the streets punctuating their discussion. Following the Constitution, an interim executive would be comprised of three senators: Nicolao Pereira de Campos Vergueiro, Francisco de Lima e Silva, and Jozé Joaquim Carneiro de Campos, marquis of Caravellas.

April 9 was designated the first court day of Brazil's future emperor, even while his father remained aboard ship in the harbor. The boy Pedro arrived in triumph from São Cristovão Palace, his destination the ceremony of acclamation in the Senate building. A Te Deum in the imperial chapel and a review of the troops followed. An "immense concourse of people, wearing the leaves of the 'nacional tree' as a badge of loyalty, filled the downtown streets."[4] The crowd detached the horses and drew the carriage of the "infant sovereign" to the City Palace, reverting to a tradition historically reserved for Portuguese monarchs, one the boy's father had declined to perpetuate.[5] "On reaching the Palace, the boy's jubilant subjects watched as he was placed in a window so that the multitude, followed by the diplomatic corps, could pass before him."[6] Now the "orphan of the nation," the heir to the throne had become the cipher for an experiment in de facto republicanism under the auspices of a liberal-dominated Regency.

MONARCHICAL INTERLUDE

Abdication

The forced abdication of D. Pedro I opened the most turbulent decade in Brazil's history. Known as the Regency, the era inscribed from April 7, 1831, to July 23, 1840, would be recalled as a time when Brazil's imperial government resembled a monarchy in name only. During the outpouring of popular enthusiasm for the "boy emperor," national politicians congratulated themselves over the exodus of his father, who on April 9 left on a British naval vessel. In the final hours of D. Pedro's reign, Sen. Vergueiro had deliberately failed to present himself at the palace after the emperor summoned him—too late—for advice on saving his throne.[7] The national political elite, whether ultra-monarchist or radical republican, concurred that Pedro had exhausted his mandate to rule. Legislators immediately began to shape a new national government based on the constitutional provision for a three-man Regency to govern in the boy emperor's name until he reached his eighteenth birthday, the age of majority. On June 17, the jointly constituted General Assembly elected a permanent Regency, a triumvirate of legislators consisting of Francisco de Lima e Silva, Jozé da Costa Carvalho, and João Braulio Muniz. With subsequent substitutions that included Diogo Antonio Feijó and Aureliano de Souza e Oliveira Coutinho, the new executive would govern Brazil over the next four years, giving way in October 1835 to a government organized under a sole regent.

In political terms, D. Pedro I became an unpopular monarch with both the people and legislators for two broad and interconnected reasons. First, he identified the interests of the nation too closely with his daughter's dynastic situation in his native country. By persistently tying Brazil's political destiny to the dynastic fortunes of the former metropole, Pedro surrounded himself with a pro-Portuguese faction that his Brazilian-born subjects regarded as suspect. When his coterie's most influential advisers were banished to Europe, in 1829, on the insistence of the cabinet, then they continued to operate from the Continent as the emperor's "secret cabinet." They reinforced Pedro's determination to defend Maria da Gloria's cause on his native soil and increased apprehension among Brazilians that their monarch would return to Portugal.[8]

The emperor's identification with a Portuguese faction at court found further validation in the many noble titles he bestowed on Portuguese who had rendered service either to him or his father. By virtue of their arrival in Brazil with the court of D. João VI, the senior members of this nobilary clique of favored intimates encountered disapproval and hostility from native-born Brazilian politicians who associated them with absolutism and colonialism. For many of the latter, Brazil's 1824 Constitution stood in sharp contrast to the new Portuguese Constitution imposed by Pedro's "autocratic" brother, after Miguel's forces routed liberals from government in Lisbon. Patriotic Brazilians regarded their emperor's inner circle of Portuguese advisors and intimates with suspicion, because they also feared their own constitution might suffer a fate similar to the one Pedro had promulgated for Portugal.

Pedro's growing preoccupation with Portugal's dynastic and political affairs encouraged the other propensity explaining his subjects' growing animosity, namely, his predilection for authoritarian rule. That he took pride in claiming authorship of the 1824 Constitution, as a liberal document he had bestowed on his subjects, did not imply that he would necessarily honor that charter's limited role for monarchy. His "liberal" convictions had not stopped him from closing Parliament in 1824. Nor had he fulfilled his commitment to summon another Constituent Assembly to rewrite the Constitution. Hence, the events of 1830–1831 suggested that perhaps the emperor would replay the crisis of 1823–1824 and again close the national legislature. This time, however, the possibility that an autocratic coup could intersect with Pedro's dynastic ambitions in Europe produced a volatile mix that raised the specter of Brazilian involvement in a Portuguese civil war. After extricating himself from the seven-year liaison with Domitila de Castro Canto e Mello and contracting a European dynastic marriage that proved extremely popular with both sovereign and people, Pedro still managed to lose his throne over his European ambitions and associations. The monarch who so adored his adopted land found himself sentenced to irreversible banishment from its shores, simply because he failed to be the Brazilian sovereign his subjects had demanded.

The New Polity: Federalism

An interim between two eras of empire, the Regency proceeded under liberal auspices as an experiment in decentralizing political power as well as a continuation of efforts to impose "equality" at the expense of legal "distinctions." Between 1831 and 1835, the political space of the national capital was contested by hostile factions, each claiming to be "liberal," with the most extreme wing embracing a contradictory republicanism. Initially, the pro-Portuguese faction loyal to D. Pedro, popularly dubbed "Caramarus" after the sixteenth-century's most famous Portuguese castaway, defined the common target. The polarization of self-proclaimed liberals into Exaltados and Moderados, following Pedro's unceremonious exit, frequently handed over the streets of the national capital to angry mobs. Encouraged by a new, incendiary journalism, popular mobilization became a principal concern for the new government. Street manifestations were not divorced from elite politics but integral to a demagogical style that flourished from 1829 onward. Effective suspension of the monarchy encouraged factional rivalry for power among competing politicians in the national legislature and afforded additional advantage for factional hostilities in the provinces to spawn civil discord and war. The maintenance of "law and order," keeping the body politic intact, became the central problem of all Regency governments.

Diogo Antonio Feijó, first in his capacity as a member of the tripartite interim Regency and then as minister of justice from July 5, 1831, to August 3, 1832, gradually emerged as the singular figure in the new government. Nominated a senator for São Paulo in 1834, the cleric who styled himself a "rustic" and was a native of the city of São Paulo would go down as a Moderado in the history books. Notwithstanding radical positions on civil marriage, clerical celibacy, and inheritance rights for the children of priests, Feijó repudiated the tactics of violence and disruption characteristic of the Exaltados' political style. Six years of political experimentation in a decentralized system of national government lay ahead. By means of the Additional Act of 1834, Brazilian legislators modified significantly the centrist government defined by the 1824 Constitution. D. Pedro's authoritarian tendencies had drawn on two features of the Constitution's distribution of power, both of which proved significant casualties to reform in 1834: the Moderating Power and the Council of State. The Moderating Power exercised by the emperor was deliberately withheld from the sole regent, leaving the national executive weakly empowered. The Council of State, which under Pedro acquired the aura of a clandestine advisory body unaccountable to either public opinion or the national legislature, similarly was suppressed.

On the other hand, the Additional Act innovated in two important respects that responded to conflicting currents of federalism and centralism. First, the creation of provincial assemblies (replacing general councils) in 1835, with assemblymen elected for two years, imposed an electoral system on the nation that within five years would produce an embryonic party system. This feature of the Additional Act was never rescinded after liberal tinkering with the Constitution was reversed in 1841–1842. In the eyes of the 1834 reformers, legislative power at the provincial level would counterbalance the concentration of national power synonymous with the Corte. Constitutional reformers reasoned that tipping the scales in a federative direction would dilute the influence of the primate city in the nation, redressing geographical imbalance as much as it would militate against an authoritarian direction. Second, the tripartite Regency was abolished in favor of a sole regent, to be elected every five years until the emperor reached his majority in December 1843. Stripped of an advisory council and denied the Moderating Power, the sole regent would be unable to dominate the national legislature.

When legislators elected Diogo Antonio Feijó regent in October 1835, their choice of "the man of iron" admitted a certain irony. An unbending figure of great personal conviction, Feijó would nevertheless find it difficult to impose his will on the legislature. The sole regent's constitutionally circumscribed authority proved an effective barrier to centralization; yet he was expected to quash regional rebellion and impose peace on situations that were tantamount to civil war. As early as 1836, significant countertendencies emerged favoring acclamation of the boy Pedro as emperor and auguring the expeditious abolition of the Regency. They testified to the neutralization of national executive authority by the ascendancy of the legislature, especially in the provinces.

A new political generation came of age after 1831. Of the men who held ministries under the Regency, almost none had served in the same capacity under D. Pedro I.[9] Abdication also carried profound consequences for both the legal privileges and personal prerogatives of the titled nobility. The Regency awarded no noble titles for the remainder of the decade, due to an express law.[10] The political influence of a titled nobilary elite waned—especially where the latter had been of Portuguese birth. In the Chamber of Deputies, titles fell out of favor as partisans of "equality" militated against further ennoblement. The key to the survival of Brazil's titled nobility over the long run, however, still lay in second estate's constitutional position as quasi-corporate. The guarantor of its permanence was the Senate, given the high proportion of noble titles its members commanded and the life tenure in office they enjoyed. An attempt to amend the Constitution in 1832, in order to set finite terms of office for senators, failed by one vote, although only one senator, Jozé Ignacio Borges, cast a vote in favor of the amendment.[11]

By the mid-1830s, death began to claim many senior politicians "on whom the emperor first bestowed titles."[12] The Empire's first cohort of political leaders, men like Caravellas and Cayru, had been raised to political influence under the Regency of D. João VI, although their adolescence stretched to the reign of Maria I. In some instances, their careers dated to the pre-Napoleonic era or D. João's first years as de facto monarch. The Regency represented much more than a generational transition in national politics, for it amounted to nothing less than Joaquim Nabuco's oft-quoted summation—"a de facto republic, a provisional republic."[13] Yet the decisive factor in shaping political outcomes throughout the remainder of the decade would be the centrifugal pull exerted by the provinces against the national government. In the end, the priority of maintaining the polity intact foreclosed a promising opening for the reform of family and inheritance law initiated in 1830.

UNFINISHED BUSINESS

Resolution No. 99 of 1830

On July 20, 1831, the resolution originally introduced by Dep. Aureliano de Souza Oliveira in the Chamber of Deputies, in June 1830, reached the Senate floor. As a proposal directed exclusively at the parents of spurious offspring, it had again been altered, by the Chamber's Committee on Redaction, prior to sending it to the Senate. The text no longer pertained exclusively to offspring of "damnable" birth, as it had when the Chamber voted adoption.[14] Now it amounted to "a resolution on illegitimate" offspring with a definitive wording: "Neither the *ordenação* of Book 4, Title 93, nor any other legislation in force prohibits that illegitimate offspring of any type whatsoever be instituted heirs by their parents in a will, the latter having no necessary heirs."[15] In other words, Rebouças' earlier substitution of "illicit and spurious offspring" had carried the day, albeit with the language of canon law transformed into the language of the civil law in readying it for the Senate.

The more inclusionary wording may have been reinforced by contemporary juridical currents from Portugal. Borges Carneiro's *Direito civil de Portugal*, published in 1826–1828, argued that now legitimate heirs were implied in the term necessary heirs—following a line of argumentation that reduced the rights of collateral heirs. Discussing legitimization certificates, he asserted that the clause stipulating succession rights had to be "without prejudice to the legitimate heirs," and then interpreted the latter to mean only children, not collaterals. In the absence of legitimate children, the natural offspring of a noble parent did have succession rights: "Because these [collaterals] do not have a right so sacred to their inheritances as do children, and they can be excluded by the father."[16]

Clearly, a consensus had crystallized around the resolution, favoring maximum inclusion of both the natural offspring of noble parents and all spurious offspring. By proposing that all "illegitimate offspring be instituted heirs by their parents in a will, in the absence of necessary heirs," Resolution No. 99 of 1830 thus encompassed the natural children of noble parents. The resolution passed first and second discussions in rapid succession on July 20, leaving both a final discussion and the Senate's adoption of the resolution for July 26. The speed with which it passed the Senate and received the Regency's sanction doubtlessly reflected Diogo Antonio Feijó's appointment as minister of justice. July 26 proved a marathon day of senatorial deliberation, accounting for why the final discussion of Resolution No. 99 was concluded only at the close of the day's order of business. The press of urgent business explained why the Senate's redactor failed to supply any debate, notwithstanding the resolution became law under Feijó's signature two weeks later, on August 11, 1831.

The new right of a parent to institute any spurious or natural offspring a testamentary heir remained as arbitrary as it was plenary, turning solely on parental volition. Testamentary succession meant that the parent remained free to withdraw the nomination in heirship, simply by rewriting the will or destroying it, leaving the estate to pass in *ab intestato* succession to collateral heirs. Furthermore, a minimally noble father might institute a natural off-spring his testamentary heir, but decline to equip his spurious children with the same right. Hence, what became known as "the Law of August 11, 1831" catered to parental, and especially to paternal, preferences. Testamentary succession, as opposed to *ab intestato* succession, gave fathers or mothers the choice of deciding whether all or merely certain illegitimate children would be instituted their heirs.

It will be recalled that the *Provisão* of January 18, 1799, was cited regularly to uphold the requirement of Pombaline law that collaterals had to con-sent—be consulted—to being displaced on the ladder of *ab intestato* succes-sion, wherever illegitimate offspring were candidates for legitimization with concurrent succession rights. Although the Resolution of August 11, 1831, al-lowed parents lacking legitimate children or living parents to override the rights of collateral heirs on behalf of their illegitimate children, the *Provisão* of 1799 continued to apply in a more restricted sense. Whenever collaterals challenged illegitimate offspring who did not have a sound basis in a will for arguing their parents had intended they be instituted heirs, then the *Provisão* was invoked. As we have seen, the Resolution of August 11, 1831, also under-cut pressure to broaden further the rights of spurious offspring, above all, where the parent had legitimate children. Its adoption explained why Lino Coutinho's radical omnibus bill on illegitimate offspring, introduced in June 1830, never returned to the floor. Until 1847, the "Law of August 11" served as the principal loophole for noble parents who lacked legitimate offspring to institute their illegitimate offspring their testamentary successors.

Mitigating "Damnable and Punishable" Birth

Legislators of the early Regency removed some of the stigma law assigned to spurious birth when they adopted the 1832 Code of Criminal Procedure. Its language evinced a slight departure from the morally punitive language of the *Ordenações Filipinas* that drew on canon law. Spurious children ceased to be legally described as "the fruit of damnable and punishable sexual unions" and became regarded as simply of "damnable" birth. The change reflected no less than the famous Pombaline distinction imposed by the 1769 Law of Right Reason: National law no longer punished "sin," merely "crime." Nev-ertheless, deletion of "punishable" amounted to a cosmetic change, given that "damnable" birth continued to be punished by excluding all spurious offspring from *ab intestato* succession.

In 1832, legislators also lowered the age of legal majority from twenty-five to twenty-one years of age. This change affected only the patriarchal prerog-atives exercised over legitimate children, for the law denied a father *pátrio poder* over a recognized natural offspring. Sponsored by the viscount of Al-cantara (João Ignacio da Cunha), the bill was enacted as law on October 31, 1831, but it also became incorporated in the section of the 1832 Code of Criminal Procedure treating juries. The reason given for lowering the age of majority was that it had been done "all over Europe." Education was credited as another reason, for "today it is recognized that as a general rule a man reaches his maximum development before age twenty-five."[17] The impact of this change, while not redounding specifically to illegitimate individuals, largely benefited sons, especially those who previously could not be emanci-pated from *pátrio poder* by virtue of holding a higher degree or an officer's patent in the military. However, the consent of the parent possessing *pátrio poder* over the child was still required for legal emancipation. If "unfairly de-nied" by the parent, then the orphans judge could judicially emancipate the individual.[18] Over time, the change worked to give sons a greater voice in choosing a wife under a system of parentally imposed marriages.

Legislators still looked to reforming marriage as a means for lifting the stain of bastardy. During the Regency, they revisited the section on impedi-ments in Lino Coutinho's omnibus bill of 1830 as well as Vergueiro's 1829 unsuccessful proposal to introduce civil marriage. The suspension of the vow of clerical celibacy proposed by Feijó in 1827–1828 also reappeared on the Re-gency's legislative docket. Although all those bills failed, they articulated lib-eral social positions that were radical for the first half of the 1830s. Further-more, they provided an impetus for what became the cornerstone of an al-tered Luso-Brazilian legal tradition concerning succession rights for natural offspring—the law of September 2, 1847. In the same regard, both bills on civil marriage introduced in the 1830s are noteworthy as precursors of the Civil Marriage Act of 1890. For that matter, they foreshadowed legislation that during the 1860s permitted Protestants to marry.[19]

Civil Marriage: Redefining Impediments

The Regency's first bill on civil marriage bore the stamp of Diogo Antonio Feijó and the authorship of the Ecclesiastical Committee of the Chamber of Deputies. By means of what were defined as "impediments in the civil law," the bill of June 11, 1831, asserted the right of the state to define impediments that would supplant the canonical impediments received in national positive law. On May 25, 1832, the Chamber of Deputies began debate on the meas-ure, what the official agenda described as "a bill on the formulas and essen-tial conditions for the contract of marriage to have validity."[20] Feijó, in his capacity as minister of justice, took the floor to introduce the proposal, for he retained his seat in the Chamber. Despite the awkward paraphrase, this was a very shrewd proposal that offered civil marriage on behalf of Brazilians of all religious creeds, but without explicitly referring to "civil marriage." Its primary substance encompassed three areas of matrimony theretofore exclusively reserved to the church.[21]

First, the bill proposed civil impediments to marriage that set aside almost all of those sanctioned by the Council of Trent. Second, the bill explicitly proposed for the first time that civil registries be established for marriages, which, in true liberal fashion, would be maintained under the exclusive supervision of the municipal councils and their presidents. Finally, also for the first time, the bill defined grounds for granting a legal separation (*divórcio*) in the civil law and it enumerated multiple reasons justifying the latter, providing for an "amicable division" of the married couple's community property. Thus the members of the Ecclesiastical Committee intended no less than to preempt on behalf of the imperial courts the legal determinations on matrimony theretofore exclusively reserved to ecclesiastical tribunals.

Feijó's introduction of the bill drew on arguments he had set forth in his famous 1827 and 1828 speeches advocating the suspension of clerical celibacy. He rejected the notion that impediments were divinely ordained, consequently, and maintained they were disciplinary and man-made—subject to error. He and other adherents of the bill also criticized episcopal authority throughout Brazil for failing to dispense matrimonial impediments in a uniform manner. Argument thus returned to the theme legislators had exhausted in 1827, when they promulgated *De Reformatione Matrimonii*. In 1832, however, they went a step further. Because bishops had failed to apply a uniform standard in granting dispensations to marry, liberal legislators charged, the national legislature now should assume the "indispensable" role of establishing those impediments.[22]

In addition to Francisco de Paula Araujo e Almeida, Lino Coutinho's friend in the Bahia delegation, and Manoel Odorico Mendes, supporters of the bill included newcomers to the lower house: Antonio Pedro da Costa Ferreira and Antonio de Castro Alves. However, it was a priest, Antonio Maria de Moura, another newcomer, who proved the most vocal spokesman for the bill. His endorsement echoed the Chamber's 1827 discourse criticizing the expense of matrimonial dispensations. In blunt language, Moura situated marriage within class privilege: "No one who is rich fails to marry, because only a head nodding in the direction of money will bring to an end all of the impediments. But the poor, no matter how much they work to follow the standard procedures, do not achieve the same."[23]

Legislators' objections centered not only on the arbitrary way that dispensations were awarded but also on the circumstance that they could be withdrawn. Feijó's charge that dispensations served only "to further the business of bishops" extended to the view that even marrying in the free state could be precarious, due to post-matrimonial reversibility of episcopal dispensations. According to complaining deputies, the legislature's involvement in such "formulas and essential conditions" for marriage therefore became justified, given that clerical arbitrariness approached caprice. The constitutional consideration that the Chamber of Deputies legislated on behalf not only of Brazilian Catholics, but of all Brazilians, proved a fruitful argument to pursue. As in 1829, legislators concerned themselves with how marriage defined a contract in civil law. Feijó protested that the Chamber of Deputies "was not a council to take up the sacrament of marriage, but to treat it only as a contract." Echoing Vergueiro's position on civil marriage in 1829, he argued that "it is not necessary [for marriage] to be a sacrament in order for the contract to be present." In concluding that the moment had arrived to adopt what he and others assiduously declined to construe as "civil marriage," Feijó pointed to "all the other countries of the world" that had taken such a step.[24]

On June 18, when legislators addressed the bill's plethora of articles, thirteen in all, opponents readily made one objection very clear: Almost all canonical impediments were missing from its text. Extensive attention cannot be paid to this innovative bill, but, some idea of how radically it redefined canonical impediments deserves mention.[25] Paragraph 3 prohibited marriage only between either first-degree consanguines—ascendants and descendants—or first-degree collaterals—siblings. Curiously, the bill used canonical, rather than civil, degrees of kinship. Thus it broke completely with the canons on marriage, which prohibited as a dire impediment matrimony between collateral relatives within the fourth canonical degree—those having a common great-great grandparent.[26] Paragraph 4 added a prohibition on the first affinal degree of kinship, that is, pertaining to in-laws, a provision absent in Lino Coutinho's 1830 bill. By remaining silent on the dire impediment of a vow of celibacy, the bill implied that priests and nuns were free to marry in civil law.[27] Jozé Ribeiro Soares da Rocha, the only priest in Bahia's delegation, correctly leveled the charge that the bill was a "cover" for clerical marriage, asserting the Chamber of Deputies had no authority in spiritual matters. Antonio Maria de Moura shot back that "the bill's effect was limited, for it still left canonical impediments intact."[28]

Moura stressed the bill's value in permitting the mixed marriages of Catholics and Protestants. He referred to the recently deceased bishop of Rio de Janeiro, D. Jozé Caetano da Silva Coutinho, who had presided over the Senate through 1831. Moura claimed to have seen "some instructions from the prelate of Rio de Janeiro on the marriages of men of different religious faiths," implying that D. Jozé Caetano had not concurred in mixed marriages where a Brazilian priest officiated. In cases where religiously mixed couples wished to marry, Moura explained, D. Jozé Caetano had required the Protestant partner to renounce his religion. However, the bishop's written instructions also disclosed that he had not known how to proceed in situations where one partner refused to give up his or her creed and declined to embrace the Catholic faith. Civil marriage, Moura expounded, offered a way that couples whose unions the church refused to sanctify could gain the civil effects following from a matrimonial contract.[29]

Although the minutes of the Chamber of Deputies make no more mention of the bill after June 19, 1832, when it was debated for a second time, it definitely passed the lower house. Presumably, it did so in the same year, when the minutes for after September 3 were lost. The bill was definitely forwarded to the Senate, implying passage in the Chamber. On May 6, 1834, a directive from the Provincial Council of São Paulo to the Senate specifically requested that "the bill of June 11, 1831, on the facilitation of marriages," be placed on the Senate's agenda for discussion.[30] On the other hand, the bill died in the upper house, no doubt because the more urgent issue of clerical celibacy consumed attention throughout June and July 1834.

Fundamentally, the 1831 bill defining civil impediments to marriage was laid to rest because its fate was inextricably linked to the issue of suspending the vow of clerical celibacy, given that both proposals contravened canonical impediments. They were publicly debated as connected issues in an atmosphere highly charged in the national press, thanks to the campaign waged against them by Brazil's metropolitan, the archbishop of Bahia, D. Romualdo Antonio de Seixas. Marquis of Santa Cruz since 1825, D. Romualdo regained his seat in the Chamber of Deputies in 1834. Now the opponents of "forced celibacy" arrayed against him included not only Feijó, who had used his position as minister of justice in 1831 to advance the bill on civil impediments in the Chamber of Deputies, but also a discrete constituency of priests in the diocese of São Paulo. In 1834, they petitioned their bishop to suspend the vow of celibacy. They were abetted by fellow priests within the Chamber of Deputies who held radical views on both the vow of celibacy and civil marriage. Their principal spokesman was Antonio Maria de Moura, vice-president of the Chamber of Deputies in 1834, but better known since 1833 as the bishop-elect of Rio de Janeiro—the candidate whom Pope Gregory XVI would not confirm. Liberal ascendancy in the legislature since 1830 merely persuaded D. Romualdo to oppose relentlessly the bill on civil impediments, from his vantage point outside the Chamber between 1831 and 1833. In a thirty-page treatise addressed directly to the national legislature, he laid out his arguments condemning the bill on civil impediments.[31]

In the final analysis, the issue of "forced celibacy" was resolved in favor of canonical orthodoxy, explaining why the bill of June 11, 1831, on civil impediments would be buried in the Senate, consigned to historiographical oblivion. In that regard, the warfare that much later erupted between church and state, due to the promulgation of the Civil Marriage Act of 1890, deserves reassessment. The republican controversy over civil marriage, resolved only in the 1930s, has to be appreciated in terms of the efforts of liberals a century earlier, in light of D. Romualdo's original and long standing opposition to a very similar list of civil impediments.

Recasting "Marriage According to the Ordenações"

The other bill on civil marriage introduced during the Regency adopted a different tack than that of civil impediments. Sponsored by Sen. Patricio Jozé de Almeida e Silva, it looked backward, to the *Ordenações Filipinas*, rather than to liberal contract theory. Almeida e Silva's bill was introduced in the Senate on August 18, 1835, in the aftermath of Feijó's 1834 defeat on the issue of the rule of celibacy. The bill did not reach the floor for what became a sole discussion until May 14, 1836.[32] Each of its two articles addressed the situation of couples who could not be legally married in Brazil, albeit for drastically different reasons. Legislative impetus followed from a practical necessity dictating the bill's raison d'être, one lying in considerations of matrimonial property. The nature of property held by couples living in consensual unions accounted for the bill, due either to the fact that the partners were of mixed religious faiths or that, as Catholics, they faced canonical impediments prohibiting marriage in the church. No community property regulation applied in either of these situations.

The bill's first article sought to remedy the situation of mixed marriages between Catholics and Protestants, null of civil effects due to the withholding of the sacrament in the Catholic rite of matrimony. By giving "the same civil effects to marriage contracts celebrated between individuals of different beliefs, as if they were Roman Catholics," the bill proposed bestowing civil effects on such unions.[33] Thus Roman Catholics living in mixed marriages that had been celebrated in the rites of another faith were assured of the same civil effects that followed from marriage in the church. Article 1 addressed illegitimacy, for it implied that children born in such mixed marriages would enjoy all the rights of those of legitimate birth.

The second article, however, attempted to revitalize *mancebia* as de facto, or assumed, marriage. It alone explained why the bill would fail, for the article stood as a sign that some legislators still favored upholding "marriage according to the *Ordenações*." Article 2 extended "the same disposition" of civil effects equal to those that followed from Roman Catholic marriage—"to persons mentioned in the first article who [instead of being married in a different creed] fall within the provision of the *Ordenações*, Book 4, Title 46, Section 2." In other words, Article 2 addressed Brazilian Catholics who lived in *mancebia*, but as de facto husband and wife, having in mind couples who lacked dispensations for matrimonial impediments of consanguinity and affinity. The situation of Protestant couples was also subsumed under Article 2, for it implied they, too, would enjoy the civil effects of legal marriage, by virtue of living in the public reputation of man and wife.

Title 46 of the *Ordenações Filipinas* governed the matrimonial community, mandating that in the absence of a contract to the contrary, couples would live under community property regulation as *meeiros*. Section 2 of Title 46, previously abrogated by promulgation of *De Reformatione Matrimonii*, had applied to couples living in the public reputation of husband and wife, but who had not exchanged marriage vows before a priest. Hence Almeida e Silva's bill sought to retrieve for Brazilian Roman Catholics an ancient customary form of marriage that in an age of liberal contract theory was assumed to have died a legal death. There was no going back. Having repromulgated Tridentine marriage a decade earlier, and pronounced *mancebia* as pertaining exclusively to concubinage, legislators were not willing to revive de facto marriage. When Sen. Nicolao Vergueiro responded to Almeida e Silva's bill on the floor in 1836, he proposed that it be sent to the Senate's Committee on Legislation as well as to the Ecclesiastical Committee. The reason he offered was to give the bill's text "the necessary development," meaning a redaction designed to make it less objectionable.[34] Although it was remanded to those committees, following a positive vote that passed the bill on the first discussion, the measure never returned to the floor, dying in committee, probably due to Vergueiro's influence.

Almeida e Silva's bill faced opposition from both conservatives and liberals. Conservative Catholics upheld the church's objection to mixed marriages, to clandestine marriage between Catholics, and, of course, to concubinage arrangements between Catholics. As the 1829 debate on civil marriage had revealed, conservative legislators and the church hierarchy preferred to leave *mancebia* intact as legal concubinage, rather than to use it as a "back door" to civil marriage, by giving juridical effect to a customary form of marriage. Nor, they argued, should mixed-creed couples receive effects in civil law denied to Roman Catholics who lacked dispensations for marrying in the church. Conservatives believed that those couples should be obliged to live in *mancebia* as a status appropriate for individuals who would not marry in the true church. Progressive liberals had not given up on a bill to enact civil marriage, but based on contract theory rather than the force of custom. They did not ordinarily support *mancebia* as de facto marriage, regarding the latter as occupying the higher plane of concubinage. Vergueiro, no admirer of *mancebia*, would again sponsor a bill to introduce civil marriage, but only eleven years later.[35] Hence Almeida e Silva's bill died because both conservative religious values and liberal ideology militated against it. The fate of civil marriage was sealed until the 1860s, when its effect was confined exclusively to Protestants.[36]

Abolishing "Forced Celibacy": A New Context

Despite the extended public debate over clerical celibacy from 1827 onward, and an impressive number of legislators in both houses who favored the right of Catholic priests to marry, 1834 marked the last time Brazilian lawmakers seriously entertained abolition of "forced celibacy." The controversy was definitively resolved due to a unique context. In 1834, the bishop of São Paulo, D. Manoel Gonçalves de Andrade, brought "the necessity of having the vow of celibacy suspended" before the General Council of the Province of São Paulo. The Council, a deliberative body lacking the power to make law, was constitutionally charged with proposing measures to the provincial president that addressed specifically local matters, especially if they were urgent. It responded to the bishop by requesting him to dispense with the vow of celibacy in his diocese, given that a majority of the Council's twenty-one delegates believed such authority resided within a bishop's discretionary authority. Aureliano de Souza Oliveira, as minister of justice, sought to enlist the Regency government's support on behalf of Bishop D. Manoel Gonçalves de Andrade, given that the initiative to act now rested with the latter, who was personally sympathetic to the Council's position. After listening to arguments from both sides and concurring that "a state of immorality existed" among the clergy of his diocese, São Paulo's bishop went on record to state he rejected the use of force for restoring clerical discipline. He declined, in other words, to punish priests who had not kept their vows of celibacy. In June 1834, Aureliano forwarded to the Ecclesiastical Committee of the Chamber of Deputies a request from D. Manoel, accompanied by documentation that simultaneously was being presented to São Paulo's Provincial General Council.[37]

Stating he was reluctant to take sole responsibility for suspending the vow of celibacy in his diocese, the bishop asked the imperial government for its "advice," thereby obliging the Regency government to take a position on the vow of celibacy. The Chamber's Ecclesiastical Committee, through its authority over the placet, technically possessed such power. On June 30, Jozé Bento Leite Ferreira de Mello, a priest who belonged to that Committee, seconded the determination of São Paulo's General Council and deemed suspension of the rule of celibacy of "urgent magnitude." He proposed that the committee address the bishop's request in an official opinion.[38] On July 26, 1834, João de Santa Barbara, another priest on the Ecclesiastical Committee, introduced the latter's report, a formal response to the bishop's formal solicitation for advice. He noted that São Paulo's General Council had reported that clerical celibacy in São Paulo, "with a few honorable exceptions," was "a dead letter." In that diocese, "many parishes were abandoned of a priest," the Council's report noted, and "the faithful, lacking any religious recourse, ask the bishop to dispense the law" of celibacy. The bishop of São Paulo, who had seconded the difficulty of recruiting candidates for the priesthood in his diocese, attributed the lack of new blood to the unpopularity of the vow of celibacy in the province.[39]

Strictly speaking, suspension of clerical celibacy defined an issue far afield of the inheritance rights of illegitimate offspring. Yet, on closer examination, it camouflaged the proposition that priests be allowed to marry, meaning their children could be legitimate. The controversy over the vow of "forced celibacy" mattered, consequently, because it impeded the recent efforts of legislators to modify law on behalf of illegitimate offspring. Opposition to "forced celibacy" threw canon law into question and, in the eyes of the official church, challenged official dogma. As a result, the furor over clerical celibacy made it more difficult, if not impossible, to deliberate any alteration of the legal norms that defined either spurious or illicit birth, given that they, too, were embedded in canon law. Feijó's 1831 bill defining civil impediments to marriage reignited the controversy engendered in 1827 by drawing the renewed ire of Archbishop D. Romualdo de Seixas. Brazil's paramount prelate perceived the bill of June 11, 1831, as part of a broader assault on the sacred canons.

Even in absentia, D. Romualdo played a crucial role in the deliberations of São Paulo's Provincial General Council, because his position on the vow of celibacy was solicited by the Council. The documentation that Aureliano conveyed to the Ecclesiastical Committee, on behalf of the bishop of São Paulo, expressed the opinions of "different persons," in addition to "those of the metropolitan." Among the clerics the General Council consulted, pro and con, D. Romualdo stood out as the foremost exponent of clerical celibacy. By means of a formal "Reply," submitted to Minister of Justice Aureliano de Souza Oliveira, D. Romualdo condemned any suspension of the vow of celibacy. Consequently, the report issued by the Chamber of Deputies' Ecclesiastical Committee amounted to a rebuttal of D. Romualdo's "Reply" to Aureliano of June 14, 1834. The controversy, once more inflamed in the national press, thus invaded the Chamber of Deputies.[40]

In "soliciting the opinion of the government," Bishop Gonçalves de Andrade perceived the difficulty of his personal position. Were he to concede what the Provincial General Council wanted—and "almost all those he had consulted in São Paulo" agreed on the advisability of dispensing the rule of celibacy—then his action would eventually provoke a break with the Vatican. Thus the specter of schism underlay why "D. Manoel did not want the responsibility to fall exclusively on himself" for any determination that the vow of celibacy should be suspended. In addressing the Regency government for advice, he undoubtedly intended either to obtain its support for suspending the vow or, alternatively, in the absence of its support, to abandon any intention of upholding the General Council's request.[41]

The response of the Ecclesiastical Committee was positive, up to a point. It reaffirmed widespread opinion by "recogniz[ing] that today clerical celibacy is not a necessary quality, as in early times . . . . Neither the current needs of the church nor the circumstances of its clergy nor sentiment in Brazil would now recommend this practice diametrically opposed to nature, to the interests of morality, or to the advantages of society." Although the Committee's report drew directly on the argument in Feijó's 1828 treatise, that clerical celibacy was a matter of discipline, rather than dogma, it left the final determination to suspend the vow of celibacy squarely in the hands of São Paulo's bishop. In the end, the Ecclesiastical Committee evasively countered that the Provincial General Council had not requested "anything from the temporal power," but directed to the diocesan bishop a request for the "suspension of a condition the canons judge necessary in a priest for the exercise of his ministry." A decision on suspension of the vow, the report concluded, was "completely ecclesiastical, appropriate for him [the bishop] to decide, in view of reasons that ought to be best known to him and according to principles of ecclesiastical jurisprudence." On the other hand, the Ecclesiastical Committee recommended offering the support of the Chamber of Deputies, "whatever the bishop's deliberation might produce in effecting the General Council's representation." Finally, it issued a warning, presumably intended for Brazil's metropolitan, D. Romualdo: The "government would never consent to the slightest persecution" that might ensue over the means the bishop adopted to carry out the General Council's decision."[42]

Although São Paulo's D. Manoel Gonçalves de Andrade was the bishop in question, D. Romualdo took aim at every Brazilian bishop who might be tempted into believing his episcopal authority entitled him to dispense the rule of celibacy in his diocese. Warning that any suspension of the rule of celibacy would be "imprudent and dangerous," Romualdo emphasized that the rule of celibacy "belongs to the integrity of national religion, the Apostolic Roman Catholic Religion." According to his reasoning, suspension of the vow of celibacy would destroy Brazil's identity as a Roman Catholic nation. The consequence—the "moral results" of suspending the vow—Romualdo admonished, would "place the nation, or a given diocese, outside the communion of the Apostolic Roman Catholic Church." Abolition of celibacy, he insisted, would create "a new church" and "a special creed" that "sacrifices the mass, confession, and all sacraments." A determination permitting priests to marry would therefore constitute a body that was "schismatic, apostate, and excommunicated."[43] In short, D. Romualdo threatened the Chamber of Deputies, in addition to São Paulo's liberal bishop, with the label of schismatic.

On July 30, the Chamber also passed two related instructions, introduced by Dep. Antonio João de Lessa, another priest holding Jansenist views. They were addressed to the Regency's executive branch, and required information on constitutional points for the guidance of the legislature. Each addressed the international dimension of church-state relations and was specifically designed to antagonize the Holy See.[44] The first instruction employed the engendered metaphor of the "forgotten state of concubinage" into which Brazil's bishops had fallen vis-à-vis Rome. It requested information on the steps the Regency government had taken in pursuing unspecified "just complaints" of Brazil's bishops, in conformity with the Constitution and national legislation. In effect, the directive lamented the state of episcopal authority explicitly in terms of impediments to matrimony and ordination, and the relevant papal dispensations. It amounted to an admonition to Rome that rejected the excessive authority of the Roman Curia on questions of dispensing the Tridentine canons: "The bishops of this empire, of little strengthened dignity with respect to what constitutes their bishoprics, have to beg the Court of Rome for the favors and powers to dispense in their aforesaid jurisdictions."

The second instruction took aim at the papal nuncio in Brazil, no doubt because he had denounced the Brazilian clergy's laxity with respect to the rule of celibacy—and named names. The nuncio had also advised against papal confirmation for Antonio Maria de Moura as bishop of Rio de Janeiro. De Lessa's second instruction therefore requested the Regency executive to instruct the lower house on "the precise type of jurisdiction that papal nuncios exercised, or intended to exercise, in Brazil," and the nature of their "subordinate relationship to bishops."[45] It amounted to a plea for the intervention of the executive power to restrict the nuncio's authority.

Despite widespread anti-clerical sentiment, few deputies wanted to carry conflict with Rome to the point of risking schism and sponsoring a national church, the road logically following from a suspension of the vow of clerical celibacy. In the end, cooler heads prevailed. The bishop of São Paulo did not accede to the determination of the General Council of the Province of São Paulo. Together with the rest of the Brazilian hierarchy, he upheld the rule of celibacy, at least by paying it official lip service. On the other hand, the bishop, like most of his counterparts elsewhere in the country, declined to use coercion to impose that rule. As a result, clerical *mancebia* flourished throughout both Regency and Second Empire, meaning the unabated censure of papal nuncios carried no weight. Furthermore, the "Law of August 11" regularized the legal position of the offspring of priests in succession law. Although they would continue to be *sacrílegos* in positive law until 1890, their posthumous testamentary recognition by their fathers conferred simple legitimization, repairing their social position. The will itself became available as the legal instrument for instituting them the testamentary heirs in succession of their clerical parents.

A FINAL ASSAULT ON NOBLE PRIVILEGE:
EXTINGUISHING ENTAIL

Abolishing the Morgado

The adoption in 1835 of a law gradually abolishing entail demonstrated both the high point of the attack on legal distinctions and the limits of reform during the Regency. Notwithstanding public rhetoric on the matter of noble titles, many legislators balked at removing what amounted to the fundamental privilege historically associated with nobility, the establishment of a private or family entail known as a *morgado*. Under the Regency, liberals renewed their effort to extinguish entail, one that had come close to succeeding in 1829. Yet it took six years for the bill to win adoption, largely due to Senate opposition. Resistance to abolishing entail underscored the fundamentally conservative outlook of national legislators. In 1829, the Senate debate acknowledged that relatively few *morgados* had been created in Brazil. Nevertheless, senior senators like Cayru put forward the classic argument that *morgados* were necessary "to sustain the monarchy against the anarchy of the people."[46] Although few senators were the heirs of family *morgados*, debate not only associated the defense of entail with the defense of nobility, but sometimes conflated the latter with the Senate itself. Not every senator believed that Brazil's upper house should stand as a deliberative body analogous to the House of Lords, but commitment to the principle of senatorial life tenure was similarly justified on the ground that it secured the throne. As long as the Senate remained an appointive body of life tenure members, unanswerable to the public in elections, opportunity to reform the noble privilege of establishing an entail proved difficult.

The establishment of an entail, an exclusive prerogative of those who possessed natural nobility, was defended in historical terms. The cliché perpetuated by the *Ordenações Filipinas*, that entail was essential for the "splendor of a noble house," suggested the attraction the *morgado* exercised. Given the diffusion of noble rank from the 1760s onward, those who instituted entails tended to be bereft of ancestry traceable to a noble house. Civil nobility, as much as *fidalguia* by descent, entitled individuals to entail their property as a *morgado*, provided they met the Pombaline rules for minimum income and assets. By the 1830s, consequently, the *morgado* conferred prestige on institutors who were successful in commerce, the liberal arts, or the high judiciary and crown bureaucracy, as much as it did on either noble titleholders or the descendants of Portugal's great houses.

The fact that assets, once entailed, became indivisible and inalienable protected a *morgado*'s administrator and subsequent heirs from foreclosure. Those features meant that entail often preserved large properties intact and served as a mechanism for concentrating land. For example, one of the last entails to be established, the Morgado of Cabo, whose administrator was the marquis of Recife (Francisco Paes Barreto), inscribed "immense properties" and nearly a dozen sugar mill complexes.[47] The advantageous circumstance that legally an entail was a trusteeship also explained why individuals succeeded *ab intestato* only to the administration of the entail, but not its ownership. The *morgado* passed only in legitimate succession, excluding solemnly legitimized heirs, and according to rules contractually defined by the person who instituted the entail; therefore the administrator also had to possess minimal nobility. To those who argued that indivisibility and inalienability of real property favored the stability of the nobility, and therefore the throne, opponents responded that the *morgado* was the refuge of inept administrators as well as the hallmark of a society of estates. They demanded that real property freely circulate in the national economy.

Like *morgados*, the ecclesiastical entails known as *capelas* similarly tied up assets in perpetual trusteeship. Even where legitimately dedicated to charitable ends, the "splendor" of a family often was memorialized by a *capela*. In dismissing the *morgado* as of little consequence in Brazil, historians have assumed that entail did not play a significant role in the economic arrangements of wealthier families. In that regard, the *capela* deserves more attention, as do the *"vínculos," ad hoc* entailments devised by individual families for conveying assets across generations. During the 1829 Senate debate on entail, the longest, sustained legislative discourse on Brazil's inheritance system prior to 1907, legislators affirmed the identity of both *capelas* and *"vínculos"* as family entails. Furthermore, their debate eventually conceded that those two forms of entail, more than the *morgado*, served to "privilege" the second estate. In social practice, legislators explained, *capelas* offered a mechanism, loosely construed, for certain individuals and their families to contravene law, subverting for narrower family purposes what ostensibly was a charitable institution pertaining to the church.

The liberal attack on entail, although rhetorically justified in terms of "equality before the law," followed essentially Pombaline lines. The *morgado* constituted "privilege" par excellence, for defining the exception to *ab intestato* succession. Constituted from the *legítima*, it violated the principle of "equal shares for all," by favoring one heir at the expense of all others. As an aberration in natural law, only the sanction of "the Legislator" had formerly authorized it. Furthermore, the *morgado* offended liberal principles by compounding privilege, due to being reserved only for those possessing a degree of nobility as well as legitimate birth.

Following the 1829 defeat of the Senate's resolution to abolish entail, by only one vote, the measure was returned to the lower house.[48] Dep. Manoel Odorico Mendes, the unflagging sponsor in 1827 and 1829 of the Chamber's bill, reintroduced it in 1830. The wording of his bill's five articles did not change. Article 1 encapsulated the key provision: "The establishment of *morgados, capelas* and any other entailments of whatever nature or denomination is prohibited."[49] After reading his bill into the record, nothing more transpired until it was brought up a year later, on June 7, 1831. A first discussion was waived, and, on August 12, now designated Bill No. 96 of 1831, the measure came up for a second discussion. Although no record of that debate, covering Articles 1–3, was entered in the minutes, presumably it was minimal. A third discussion, required for an adoptive vote, was postponed. Then the bill was tabled for four years.[50] In 1831, a much bigger issue, the adoption of a law abolishing noble titles and orders, took precedence. The debate it generated, despite the fact that the law establishing the Regency had already placed a moratorium on titles, consigned consideration of entail to limbo.[51] The 1832 vote defeating the constitutional amendment to revoke life tenure in the Senate also put a damper on plans in the Chamber to adopt Odorico's bill on entail and again send it to the upper house.

During the first half of the 1830s, entail continued to exercise a symbolic significance within the Senate, probably because titles of nobility no longer defined a prestigious reward. Very likely, the Chamber of Deputies strategically delayed further action on abolishing entail until the Senate decided to move on the issue. That development occurred only in 1835, when, almost immediately, the Senate opened debate on its own resolution to extinguish entail. A changed political context, following from the radical impetus to pass the Additional Act of 1834, again made the issue of entail a priority. Undoubtedly, advocates of abolishing entail in the Chamber of Deputies put pressure on the Senate. Unlike the ambience surrounding Senate debate over entail in 1829, monarchy now enjoyed a suspended state, newly created provincial legislatures were getting organized for the first time, and the ruling Regency triumvirate was about to be exchanged for a sole regent whose powers were drastically limited. Thus the abolition of entail reemerged at a moment when legislators enjoyed a brief and heady sensation of dominance vis-à-vis the executive. In a highly charged political atmosphere, where demagoguery pitted "privilege" against "equality" in a new era of "liberty," entail and primogeniture could hardly be sustained as institutional pillars of a throne that was vacant.

Senate debate engendered significant discussion in 1835, although substantially less than in 1829. Compared to the Chamber's Bill No. 96 of 1831, whose text was fundamentally fixed, the Senate resolution proved structurally complex and eminently amendable. Although Senate debate faintly reprised the pro's and con's argued in that body in 1829, there were new overtones. The Senate basically adopted the Chamber's old bill, but with the proviso that extinction of entail would be immediate. It rejected the gradualist approach favored by the Chamber, one permitting entails to run for the life of their incumbent administrators.

The major protagonists in Senate debate remained nearly identical to those in 1829, for life tenure produced a nearly static line-up. Again, except for the maverick Caravellas, the key proponents of abolition lacked noble titles, while the principal defenders of entail had been ennobled by D. Pedro I in 1825 and elevated in the peerage in 1826.[52] Vergueiro, the marquis of Caravellas, and J. I. Borges took the floor as the main sponsors of immediate abolition of all arrangements of entail—both *morgados* and ecclesiastical *capelas*. They received assistance from a capable and outspoken newcomer to the Senate, who had arrived from the Chamber of Deputies in July 1833: Francisco de Paula Souza e Mello. Paula Souza, standing for São Paulo, played a key role in adoption of the resolution. As a seasoned debater, he had long advocated the abolition of entail in the lower house.

Arrayed against the liberal opponents of aristocratic privilege were the veteran defenders of *morgado* and *capela* from 1829, especially João Evangelista, who earlier had argued that abolition of entail violated the rights of private property. The viscount of Cayru had led the defense of entail in 1829. Now in his eightieth year and failing, he played a more modest role in opposing the resolution, dying two months after the bill became law. The paralytic marquis of Queluz (João Severiano Maciel da Costa), another 1929 defender of entail, was carried into the chamber on a stretcher to cast his vote against the resolution. Similarly, the marquis of Inhambupe, who had championed ecclesiastical entail in 1829, defended the *morgado* in 1835, again with support from the viscount of Congonhas do Campo. However, Jozé Saturnino da Costa Pereira proved the most vocal defender of entail in the final debates, assisted by the viscount of Caethé (Jozé Teixeira da Fonseca e Vasconcellos).

Although the line-up was largely familiar, this time the defense of entail proved largely symbolic, due to fundamental political change that brought 1835 starkly into contrast with 1829. Brazil no longer had an emperor. Consequently, defenders of entail and primogeniture proved reluctant to depend on what formerly had been the keystone of their argument: the *morgado*'s necessity for the stability of the throne. Only João Evangelista ventured a brief remark in that respect, when he paraphrased Montesquieu to sound a threatening note: "As the monarchy goes, so goes aristocracy; as aristocracy goes, so goes nobility."[53] But precisely nobility was at issue in 1835, given the question mark hanging over the monarchy. As Francisco Carneiro de Campos, brother of Caravellas, summed up the new political context, "The necessity to perpetuate nobility" could be dismissed, because service to the Imperial House was an idea no longer "in vogue." He could not resist a pun on entail's indispensability for the "splendor" of a noble house. Any law based on such a premise, he concluded, would be unsuitable for "a country in which liberty is [now] in its splendor."[54] If the *morgado* was no longer necessary for the splendor of a noble house, then it was much less necessary for a monarchy now relegated to a symbolic role.

Not surprisingly, the proponents of abolishing entail made its "privileging" feature the centerpiece of attack. Carneiro de Campos condemned the *morgado* outright with a subtle, Pombaline inflection, denouncing it as owing to "the law of odious exceptions." That is, entail did not obey the force of natural law, which imposed "equal shares for all" and found validation in natural succession—alternately known as legitimate succession. Beyond indicting entail with the cliché that it was a "feudal" institution, he deprecated it for being "Spanish." Nativist sentiment now being ascendant, Carneiro de Campos also dismissed entail and primogeniture for having originated among the Goths and the Franks. In delivering the coup de grace, Paula Souza located the *morgado*'s origin in northern Europe. Recklessly rhetorical, he followed up by arguing that Brazil's Lusitanian legal heritage drew on the Roman Empire's "Mohammedan-occupied southern lands," where entail had been unknown.[55] Noticeably absent from the attack in 1835 was J. I. Borges' finely articulated 1829 argument that nobility should be based on merit and virtue, implying it no longer required the privileging of a *morgado*. The accent on merit and virtue had vanished, because, as Carneiro de Campos derided, nobility was no longer in style.

Debate in 1835 took a more practical turn than in 1829, concentrating on how opponents of entail could—or should—implement the institution's extinction. Abolition was a foregone conclusion, but whether entail would be gradually eliminated—and whether all forms of *capela* should be abolished— occupied central attention. Consequently, most of the debate explored various amendments to what eventually became the Senate's five-article resolution, but deserves to be regarded as a bill. When the Senate adopted the measure, on May 25, 1835, the text differed in one major respect from the Chamber's identical bill of 1827, 1829, and 1831. In 1829, the Senate had nearly adopted Odorico Mendes' bill prohibiting only "the establishment of *morgados, capelas,* and any other entails of whatever nature or name that might be" (Article 1). That is, the bill contemplated only establishment of new entails, but it left in place existing ones and prescribed that they would revert to forced heirship at the incumbent administrator's death. The Senate's 1835 bill proved more drastic, for it offered no grace period for existing entails. The marquis of Caravellas amended the Chamber's bill to call for "all *morgados, capelas* and any other entails of whatever other nature or name that might be to end as of now." The previously timid Senate proved more daring than the lower house in 1835, calling for "abolition now."[56]

Law No. 57 of 1835

After the Senate approved the amended resolution and returned it to the Chamber of Deputies, on May 25, 1835, the lower house restored the provision of life tenure for incumbent *morgados* in the final version that became law. Those who administered family entails when the bill was signed into law would continue to administer their *morgados* until death. On October 2, the Chamber of Deputies adopted the revised bill and sent it to the Regency. It was quickly signed into law, on October 6, as Law No. 57 of 1835. Article 1 provided the crucial social change: "The establishment of *morgados, capelas* or any other entails, of whatever nature or name that might be, is hereby prohibited; those in existence will become extinct with the death of their current, legitimate administrators."[57] Thus a cautionary approach determined that the institution of entail would run the course of the Empire rather than suffer abrupt extinction.

Technically speaking, entail outlived the monarchy's collapse in 1889, a circumstance causing Clovis Bevilaqua to observe in the early republic that "abolition of the feudal privilege of masculinity and primogeniture had succeeded in remaining in force in national legislation." However, he had in mind only the preservation of "a vestige of it . . . one whose erasure our legislators demand. I refer to the exceptional rule permitting succession in emphyteusis, or lifetime lessorship." The special case of emphyteusis, commonly assumed a concession only to the heirs of the Bragança royal line, for collecting taxes on urban properties and lands whose administration was inherited from D. Pedro II, actually was more widely enjoyed.[58] Thus a variant of entail eluded extinction under Law No. 57 of 1835, notwithstanding the provision of the Constitution of 1891 that definitively ended noble titles and, presumably, privileges of birth.[59]

Article 2 of Law No. 57 of 1835 paid careful attention to what had been Article 3 of the original Senate bill. It spelled out the fate of entails after their incumbent administrators died. The rules of legitimate, or *ab intestato*, succession would apply, meaning that all family or private entails would be consigned to the pulverizing impact of forced heirship once the incumbent administrator died. Article 2 also took specific notice of legal devices for evading the rules of legitimate succession, by addressing what Article 1 vaguely described as "any other entails of whatever other nature or name that might be." Rather than being vague, the latter phrasing was a catch-all intended to apply to a plethora of entailed arrangements—the elusive "*vínculos*" that families employed to remove real property from *ab intestato* succession. These "entails of whatever other nature" were often hybrid forms—what João Evangelista had candidly described as "quasi-*morgados*" in 1829, because they diverted assets into *capelas* rather than *morgados*, but served private, family ends just the same.[60]

Consequently, Article 2 incorporated a tough prohibition barring the terminal administrator from "being able to dispose of [entails] by means of a will or some other formal document."[61] In fact, the Senate version of the bill had left a loophole in this respect that the Chamber of Deputies firmly closed.[62] In anticipating that the final administrator might use contracts or a will to evade the rules of *ab intestato* succession, this article made absolutely clear that all forms of private entail would revert to the administrator's forced heirs at his or her death. No one dared propose in 1835 what Cayru advocated in 1829, that after the current administrator of an entail died, then his brothers should succeed to it in birth order. Such a postponement of reversion to *ab intestato* succession now was unthinkable. Consensus in the national legislature affirmed that no exceptions to "the General Law" regulating natural succession would be tolerated.

In further cognizance of the complex ways that wealthy families either illegally or extralegally employed entail to evade the rules of legitimate succession, Law No. 57 of 1835 carefully distinguished between entail created on behalf of families—conventionally termed the *morgado*—and "all other kinds." In fact, this dichotomy confirmed that legislators understood that in social practice family entails were often a mélange of arrangements. In reality, the latter defied the standard legal textbook explanations that abstracted entails into either "family" (*morgado*) or "ecclesiastical" (*capela*) forms. What really mattered, debates revealed, was simply "*os vínculos*"—entailment in a generic sense. Nevertheless, in their zeal to curtail the *morgado*—"family entail"—legislators left the door open to perpetuating the *capela*. The latter, rather than simply defining an ecclesiastical entail, was better described as a corporately administered entail—in contradistinction to a privately, or family, administered entail.

Article 3 of the 1835 law, in referring to Article 2's provision for disposing of a family entail after the final administrator's death, left the fate of *capelas* that fell under ecclesiastical, or corporate, administration moot. That is, Article 3 bracketed *capelas* as exempt from the law's reach: "The above dispositions pertain only to entails belonging to families, administered by their individual members." Furthermore, in prescribing gradual extinction for both *morgados* and *capelas*, Article 1 failed to address the special nature of *capelas*, that their administrators were not living individuals with finite lifespans, but corporations that conceivably could survive for centuries. By the same token, Article 4, addressing entails that enjoyed irregular situations, that is, those lacking legitimate administrators or that had fallen into forfeiture, sidestepped the corporately administered *capelas*. That article, too, pertained largely to *morgados*. Only when a religious brotherhood abandoned an ecclesiastical entail, or where terms of the contract establishing the entail were not fulfilled—for instance, if a religious order ceased to say prayers for the soul of the *capela*'s institutor—did Article 4 imply a *capela*'s extinction via forfeiture.[63]

An Unresolved Issue: Capelas

The 1835 gradual abolition of entail left the fate of existing *capelas* moot. Only when they were administered by individuals, such as a *cóngrua*, or clerical stipend, provided by a family for a member who was a priest, did Article 1 prescribe their extinction. Ordinarily, *capelas* were administered by cathedrals, chantries, religious orders, and lay brotherhoods. As legal corporations, they did not fall under the "lifetime of the administrator" provision of Article 1 of Law No. 57 of 1835. Although no more new contracts for ecclesiastical entail could be established, those already being administered by ecclesiastical corporations could continue to exist in perpetuity as long as they remained solvent. The Senate debates in both 1829 and 1835 explained why corporately administered entails slipped through the 1835 curtailment of entail. Sentiment was divided over whether or not to eliminate ecclesiastical entails outright, given that they defined a nearly exclusive source for financing almost all charitable undertakings in Brazil. Abolishing corporately administered *capelas*, consequently, meant eliminating most of the arrangements that addressed genuine social welfare needs. Many senators were inclined to accept a role for patrimony dedicated to ecclesiastical charities, despite their anti-clerical views. However, on liberal grounds, they objected to the contractual establishment of funds as a trusteeship irrevocably and indivisibly pledged to narrow ends. Equally, important, they subscribed to a Pombaline ideology that had imposed legal limits on how much of an estate individuals could entail as a *capela*. Additionally, Pombaline law had excluded altogether real property—land and buildings—from passing into *capelas*, construing such arrangements as "mortmain."

Jozé Teixeira da Matta Bacellar unsuccessfully proposed a sixth article for the Senate resolution that defined an important exception to Article 1's prohibition on the future establishment of *capelas*: "Entailed assets whose income is applied to public necessity and assistance, administered by corporations of mortmain, are not contemplated in the disposition of the present law." Borges and Vergueiro forced him to amend it, by striking out "entailed assets" [*bens vinculados*] and substituting "donated assets" [*bens doados*]. In other words, gifts would be permitted to finance charities, but entailment of assets for specifically defined corporate funds would not be permitted. Clearly, the intention was to permit legitimate charities to continue, where ecclesiastical bodies were understood to discharge that responsibility positively.

Sen. Matta Bacellar's sixth article nonetheless had to be withdrawn, in favor of what Vergueiro successfully amended as a compromise to the final

Senate version of the resolution. *Morgados* were differentiated from *capelas*, by qualifying Article 2 to "pertain only to entails belonging to families, administered by their individual members"—what later became Article 3 of the law. Thanks to his amendment, Article 3 of Law No. 57 of 1835 would explicitly exclude any action pertaining to the fate of *capelas* already in church hands. The omission of any provision applying to the future extinction of corporately administered *capelas* represented a compromise between the defenders of ecclesiastical charities and the draconian heirs of Pombal. The latter wanted to strip the church of assets that they believed unnecessarily withdrew wealth from free circulation and to liberate those assets for investment in productive enterprises. As even the wills of liberal legislators demonstrated, they did not necessarily believe in leaving the church any more payment than what was required to say a modest number of masses for their immortal souls.

Omission of a provision abolishing currently existing *capelas* also represented a tactical delay, one designed to effect passage of Law No. 35 in 1835. In 1837, however, legislators revisited the question of entail. Not much of their debate has survived, but clearly some legislators, like Sen. Borges, still wanted to stop the perpetuation of existing *capelas*. They partly resolved the latter issue, albeit indirectly, by taking social practice more into account than the letter of the law. At the same time, they focused on both *capelas* and *morgados* in what was a new law designed to clean up "loose ends" remaining after passage of Law No. 57 of 1835. Decree No. 2 of May 29, 1837, a brief paragraph, rendered null—by declaring them "as unwritten"—any testamentary disposition or gifts "of *vínculos* and *morgados* that cannot be verified." Verification referred to proving an entail had been legally established. Those that were unverifiable would be regarded as "unwritten"—therefore null—and "the assets composing those entails would belong to the heirs of their institutors."[64]

The law's raison d'être turned on legislators' sage appreciation that most entails, whatever their nature, were not legally constituted. It will be recalled from the preceding volume's discussion of entail that, in Pombaline times, the contractual establishment of *morgados* and *capelas* that had required approval by the Tribunal of the Desembargo do Paço came under stricter crown enforcement. However, with the abolition of the Paço, in 1828, central oversight lapsed. Consequently, the 1837 law struck hard at what had to be the majority of existing entails. That is, it offered confirmation that legislators knew very well that many entails, perhaps most, did not meet the test of being legally instituted. Pombaline law, still in force, had confined *capelas* to assets disposed from the *terça*, restricted them to cash funds, and imposed minimum incomes for their institutors. These provisions were designed to discourage future establishment of *capelas* as well as to eliminate those of inconsequential size.[65] Eighteenth-century law had similarly restricted the creation of *morgados*.

After 1837, law still permitted individuals to write testamentary bequests from the *terça* on behalf of the church and to make gifts to ecclesiastical entities. Such provisions did not establish *capelas*, because they were not contractual arrangements establishing a fund into which the institutor's heirs then usually paid installments. Nor could funds be corporately constituted. Nevertheless, donations might increase the capital accumulated by charities for their own investment and expenditure. On the other hand, entailed assets already in church hands, including real property that historically originated in *capelas*, remained untouched wherever they could be verified as lawfully instituted.

Applying the Law: A Postscript from Bahia

Arrangements of family entail would continue to appear in inheritance documents after 1835. Given that the law of October 6 required *morgados* to revert to *ab intestato* succession with the incumbent administrator's death, entails would be enumerated as assets distributed in *partilhas* after 1835. Sometimes, however, families conspired to divert a *morgado* from the law's impact. The entail known as the Morgado of Sodré, mentioned earlier as administered by Lino Coutinho's father-in-law, the elder Francisco Maria Sodré, illustrated such a development. His eldest legitimate son, Jeronymo Sodré, succeeded to the administration of the Morgado of Sodré when Francisco died, on October 24, 1835. That he did so several weeks after Law No. 57 of 1835 went into effect, on October 6, gives pause to reflect on social practice.[66] Perhaps the situation of this Bahian entail prompted Antonio Pereira Rebouças, deputy for that province, to introduce a resolution in June 1837 clarifying Article 1 of Law No. 57 of 1835. Its purpose was to make even more unambiguous Article 1's clear pronouncement that "*morgados* in existence will become extinct with the death of their current, legitimate administrators." Rebouças' resolution, which failed, ludicrously expounded on the foregoing interpretation as "comprehending everyone who would have died after the said law [was passed, i.e., October 6, 1836]."[67] Just how orderly the gradual extinction of entails proceeded after October 6, 1835, remains for historians to discover. Scattered evidence suggests that government intervention was still needed to bring families into compliance.[68]

Jeronymo Sodré personified another problem in applying Law No. 57 of

1835, one turning on legitimate birth. The last administrator of the Morgado of Sodré, he never married. However, Jeronymo left several natural children fathered with his slaves, whom he recognized properly in a notarial affidavit and indicated as his heirs in his will. Freed, they became his natural successors and sole heirs, for, when he died in 1881, law no longer distinguished between the natural offspring of nobles and commoners. On his death, Jeronymo's surviving siblings or their children claimed the Morgado of Sodré in *ab intestato* succession, according to Law No. 57 of 1835. However, his natural children contended that they, not Jeronymo's collateral heirs, were the lawful *ab intestato* successors of the entail's passage into forced heirship. Several of them took over their father's sugar mill by force.[69] Jeronymo Sodré's collateral heirs resorted to the courts for upholding their claim. They argued, successfully, that the personal property of their uncle belonged to his "recognized bastards"—his necessary heirs. However, the real property constituting the Morgado of Sodré, they insisted, should pass to them under the rules governing *ab intestato* succession.

Jeronymo Sodré's siblings and nephews recovered the entail because Article 2 of the 1835 law stipulated that when the entail terminated, it "would pass according to the laws regulating legitimate succession to the heirs of the last administrator." Those regulating laws included the famous royal *Provisão* of January 18, 1799, one that, it may be recalled, stipulated *morgados* passed only in the legitimate line. In the end, nobility by descent, implying legitimate birth, settled the conflict. Jeronymo's illicit progeny, however lawfully he had recognized them, could not be the heirs to the Morgado of Sodré. Thus in the 1880s, nearly a half-century after the abolition of entail, the late medieval rules determining how a *morgado* passed in succession still applied. The privilege of legitimate birth was upheld. Jeronymo Sodré's children lost the entail on yet a second ground. Their father had violated Article 2 of Law No. 57 of 1835, which prohibited the final, incumbent administrator from using "a will or any other document" to dispose of the assets constituting the *morgado*.

Reversion of the Morgado of Sodré to *ab intestato* succession, on behalf of Sodré's legitimate siblings, or their children *per stirpes*, demonstrated a rare example of collateral kin displacing recognized natural offspring on the ladder of *ab intestato* succession—and the continuing, if restricted, applicability of the *Provisão* of January 18, 1799. At least in this special situation, the rights of collateral heirs would be upheld over those of recognized natural offspring, notwithstanding the Law of August 11, 1831.

LIBERAL DENOUEMENT

Although the Regency was an era of political experimentation for Brazilian liberals, the reforms they enacted in inheritance and family law fell far short of introducing radical change. The Law of August 11, 1831, modified the *Ordenações Filipinas* in light of changing social realities. Illegitimacy often characterized family organization and parents who lacked legitimate children deserved to be able to institute illicit or spurious offspring as their successors. In clearly favoring children over collateral heirs, and empowering parents to determine the patrimonial destinies of such children, legislators did not break with the logic of their legal tradition. Instead, they accommodated the latter to a new political context where the oversight of an absolutist state, embodied in the Desembargo do Paço, no longer mattered and a new imperial judiciary was considerably relieved of responsibility for dispensing solemn legitimization.

In the political ambience of 1835, where "liberty was in vogue," the national legislature was loath to reconfirm the *morgado* as the special privilege of the second estate. Similarly, it was reluctant to endorse *capelas*, not so much from anti-clerical sentiment as on the same ground of noble privilege. By foreclosing the future establishment of all entails, legislators completed a reform program originating with the marquis of Pombal during the 1760s. They redefined the new national inheritance system by making it rest exclusively on partitive succession, but they left the door open to individual testamentary bequests on behalf of ecclesiastical entities. Because the vast majority of Brazilians were landless, freeing property from entailment mattered as a change only for those at the very top of society.

Radical reform of inheritance and family law depended on redefining the relationship between church and state. It is interesting that those legislators most committed to such a goal included a high proportion of clerics. They were priests who favored some form of civil marriage and the end of "forced celibacy," if not the freedom to marry. They held those beliefs largely because they had been inculcated in a Portuguese political tradition diffused within Brazil's heterodox seminaries in the final decades of colonial rule. That tradition located religious authority in the sanctions of church councils, or individual bishops, but not in the Vatican. However, in the end, expectations of secularizing marriage, divorce, and "damnable" birth gave way to the policies of more practical politicians who, rather than disestablish the church, negotiated rapprochement with Rome. The radical agenda in private law that was shelved after 1835 would have to await the arrival of a republic.

The ideological tide that produced the Additional Act of 1834 conceivably could have led to a broader agenda of reform. Theoretically, more measures removing "distinctions" embedded in family and inheritance law might have become the order of the day, once Diogo Antonio Feijó became Brazil's sole regent, on October 12, 1835. Instead, the Additional Act proved to be a high water mark from which most liberals beat a hasty retreat. They rethought their political positions as Feijó devoted the two years of his Regency to quelling rebellion or confronting partisan resistance that realigned Parliament. Issues of family and inheritance law had to be relegated to the periphery. On September 19, 1837, Feijó abruptly wrote out his resignation and headed homeward, to São Paulo. The statement he left offered vague reasons for resigning, but his temperament had been no match for the tumultuous events and parliamentary fragmentation that plagued his tenure in office.[70] He created a situation where he could not count on support from his own Moderado faction, above all, from the key figure in the lower house, Bernardo de Vasconcellos. The murder of Evaristo Ferreira da Veiga, at the opening of the 1837 legislature, not only removed an important reform-minded Moderado from the Chamber but it also signaled the disintegration of that faction, initiating the political crisis that compelled Feijó to resign.

The momentum for reforming family and inheritance law that might have been positively exploited instead continued to wane after Feijó's departure from the executive. Furthermore, the ranks of liberal legislators inclined to sponsor such reform suffered drastic attrition by 1838. Death took its toll, leaving Sen. Nicolao Vergueiro isolated as the principal reformer of private law. First, Lino Coutinho failed to return to the Chamber of Deputies after reelection in 1834, due to a fatal illness. Soon after his death, in July 1836, his fellow Bahian in the Senate and Vergueiro's old ally, the marquis of Caravellas, also died.[71] Jozé Ignacio Borges followed in 1838. Finally, Feijó became very ill in early 1838, when he suffered a second episode of paralysis, a condition that limited his participation when he returned to the Senate for a final year in 1839.[72] Vergueiro, who, together with Caravellas, had stood in the Senate as the most important liberal leader on reform of family and inheritance law, quickly found his views anachronistic. No longer enchanted by the spirit of liberty, liberals were disavowing their earlier positions. As the Regency government began to disintegrate, they reconsidered the attractions of an authoritarian and centralizing national government.

In the highly politicized transition from Regency to restored monarchy that spanned 1837 to 1842, Sen. Vergueiro chose to put forward one, last novel proposal, Bill BU of 1836. It addressed the procedures of legal recognition, legitimization, and inheritance rights for individuals born outside wedlock. Not debated until 1838, this comprehensive bill paid attention to many of the same issues that the bills of Lino Coutinho and Feijó had identified in 1830–1831. Yet Vergueiro's bill differed from their radical solutions, for being proposed when liberal ideals were being consciously abandoned and reaccommodation to the monarchy was the order of the day. His vocal sponsorship of Bill BU of 1836, at the opening of the 1839 legislative year, can be taken as the final opportunity to remove the stigma of illegitimacy by rewriting positive law. Vergueiro's own political views, on the other hand, were also adjusting to the rapidly shifting national configuration of power. He would leave his mark on a final piece of legislation addressing the inheritance rights of illegitimate offspring within a new political context that was less experimental, one where the watchword of "equality before the law" would be overshadowed by the rising claims of a bourgeois family grounded on legal marriage and patriarchal control of legitimate patrimony.

CHAPTER 8

Scandal in the Courtroom

—•✦•—

I vote for the article, because it is going to avoid those scandalous
filiations of kinship that were just mentioned . . . . And if the article removes the embarrassment of so many awkward revelations
from the courtroom, I fail to comprehend why passage of the law
is opposed . . . .

Sen. Francisco Carneiro de Campos, 7 May 1839[1]

Marriage should be promoted as much as possible and the offspring thereof regarded with greater honor and esteem than the
offspring of customary unions. Therein lies the reason for this bill
not to give illegitimate children the same rights as legitimate children.

Sen. Nicolao Pereira Vergueiro, 8 May 1839[2]

The Second Empire opened when the fourteen-year-old heir to the throne
was declared "already of age" on July 23, 1840. On the same day, he took the
oath of office as D. Pedro II.[3] Although proclamation of Pedro's majority officially brought the Regency to a close, historians have defined his investiture
as part of a transition that began in 1837 and continued until 1842. The progressive repudiation of federalism and Regency that culminated in the accelerated proclamation of the boy emperor's majority led to new political
alignments. Despite Brazil's return to monarchy, Conservatives and Liberals,
aligned as rudimentary national parties by late 1840, continued to dispute the
features of a reorganized national political system. The fact that the Additional Act of 1834 had created provincial legislatures explained why periodic
elections, coupled with factional politicking, produced the Empire's two enduring political parties. Throughout Feijó's Regency, conviction grew that a
return to monarchy would resolve the fragmentation of civil war and regional revolt, as well as institutionalize a stable national political system.
Moderate liberals, disavowing many of their ideals, entered the ranks of the
"Regresso"—the "return" to monarchical rule that implied their "reactionary" turn—one that Bernardo de Vasconcellos informally sponsored as early
as 1836.

An uneasy coalition of recommitted monarchists, an influential palace clique, and, above all, chastened moderate liberals, the Regresso eventually divided liberal ranks. Formally inaugurated by Vasconcellos in an 1838 speech, the Regresso accelerated in momentum, defining the context for legislative debate between 1838 and 1840.[4] If Feijó had been distant and unceremonious with Brazil's boy emperor, then those in the Regresso's conservative ranks reversed his approach, cultivating the prince's affection and allegiance in order to manipulate him. Aureliano de Souza e Oliveira Coutinho, moderate liberal of the early 1830s, played a key role in proclaiming the emperor's majority, both as his tutor and a leader of the influential palace clique. The latter still opposed many of Aureliano's former colleagues from the early 1830s who, in the aftermath of Pedro's acclamation, fused as the Liberal Party.

The genesis of a Conservative Party—"the Party of Order"—coincided with the special elections called in 1838 to install a regent to replace Feijó: Pedro de Araujo Lima, future marquis of Olinda. His term of office was to conclude in 1843, coinciding with the attainment of Pedro's majority at age eighteen. Restoration of the monarchy, however, was tied to jettisoning the Additional Act of 1834, ending the nation's short-lived federal organization and reinstating most of the 1824 Constitution. The accomplishment of that task, during 1839–1840, still left the monarch and his cabinet subject to parliamentary divisions, attenuating executive power by virtue of a judiciary that remained locally defined. Consequently, Conservatives viewed proclamation of Pedro II's majority as preliminary to a political restructuring that would impose a strong and independent national executive. Nothing less than restoration of the Moderating Power and the Council of State would satisfy them.

Momentous shifts in national political organization between 1837 and 1842 provided the initial context for historical liberals in the Senate to deliberate Nicolao Vergueiro's Bill BU of 1836. Before it became law in 1847, the tortured evolution of the bill that redefined the inheritance rights of natural and spurious individuals mirrored the changing ideological fulcrum of the Liberal Party. In retreat from a commitment to removing distinctions of birth, legislators reevaluated the impact of the 1828 Judiciary Act that had facilitated judicial determinations of paternal recognition and legitimization proceedings. Debate over procedures of legal recognition and inheritance rights for non-legitimate individuals fundamentally disputed two, contested views of family. One was founded on legitimate marriage and the other, rooted in custom, was defended as "natural" marriage. Similarly, changing attitudes toward property—construed as family patrimony—accounted for the bill's revision and eventual adoption in 1847. Consequently, juridical notions pertaining to the family's legal constitution, historically traceable to the eras of Pombal and Philip II, came under critical scrutiny and were discarded.

The protracted legislative debates conducted on Sen. Vergueiro's bill, first in 1838–1839 and again from 1845 to 1847, deserve special attention beyond their illumination of two, contested views of the family. Nowhere else can historians of Brazil find primary sources as forthcoming about the official attitudes those in the Empire's political elite expressed toward concubinage, bride abduction-elopement, paternal recognition, legitimate or "natural" marriage, and, above all, the quality of illicit birth or genuine bastardy. All were subjected to intense examination in a public debate that spanned a decade. Thus legislative deliberation on the bill that evolved into Law No. 463 of 1847 generated a unique discourse on the meaning of family within the forum of the national legislature and established how public power would reinforce legitimate birth at the expense of bastardy for the remainder of the Empire.

Although legislative debate registered rhetorical statements ranging from absurd idealization to outright mendacity, the fact that lawmakers argued passionately over the provisions in Bill BU of 1836, from the venue of what can be regarded as the Empire's most exclusive male club, obliged them to reveal personal opinions otherwise rarely committed to their era's primary sources. Similarly, their antagonistic exchange provides valuable information about how the imperial court system functioned, how inheritance fraud was perpetrated, or what constituted appropriate evidence in trials. For a historiography woefully bereft of private letters and diaries, the public discourse of imperial legislators on the subject of illegitimacy and patrimony yields a wealth of insights and interpretive glosses on the personal attitudes held by this group of powerful middle- and upper-class men. Reflective of their intimate views, sometimes their own private lives, the comments they expressed were uniquely illuminating for the meaning of the family within the context of public power, during a transitional decade that led to the Second Empire.

THE GENESIS OF INHERITANCE REFORM

A Daring Proposal

On July 20, 1838, the Senate began consideration of Bill BU of 1836.[5] Spelled out initially in ten detailed articles, the measure introduced changes pertaining to procedures for legally recognizing illegitimate offspring and their rights in succession law. No explanation was offered as to why the bill, authored by Sen. Nicolao Vergueiro, took two years to reach the floor for debate. A notation in the *Anais do Senado* for May 8, 1837, enigmatically indicated that, on the very day it was introduced, the bill passed the first of three, standard debates on the floor. Nothing was recorded about what was a puzzling, rapid endorsement of a complex and controversial bill. On May 11 and 12, 1837, the bill came up for a second discussion, but debate was abruptly curtailed shortly after Article 1 was introduced. Sen. Manoel Caetano de Almeida e Albuquerque objected so strongly to the bill's wording that it went to the Committee on Legislation "in order to make those changes that are judged suitable."[6]

Bill BU of 1836 deserves interpretation as the lineal successor to Dep. Lino Coutinho's 1830 omnibus bill on illegitimate offspring. It will be recalled that he had proposed a redefinition of the rules by which fathers might either recognize natural offspring and *sacrílegos*, making the latter of illicit birth, or "acknowledge" adulterine and canonically incestuous children. Lino Coutinho's bill could not be easily revived, however, due to adoption of the Resolution of August 11, 1831. Consequently, Vergueiro's 1836 bill drew from Lino Coutinho's proposal in a negative respect as well, by declining to concede paternal recognition or succession rights to adulterine offspring. Equally significant, the bill deserves to be understood in terms of the senator's frustrated efforts to secure adoption of a bill introducing civil marriage. Most notably, Vergueiro's bill studiously avoided mention of either natural or spurious offspring. Eschewing the language of canon law, it spoke generically of only "illegitimate" offspring, following the cue introduced by Antonio Pereira Rebouças in 1830. That tactic imparted more than merely faithfulness to the language of civil law, for, by semantically blurring individuals born outside wedlock as "illegitimate," Vergueiro's measure implied that even *sacrílegos* could enjoy the same rights as natural offspring.

Finally, the bill's wording could be said to be careless, injecting genuine confusion into debate. Ambiguity, omission, and imprecision of redaction hampered the ability of legislators to grapple effectively with the bill's proposals. Vergueiro's remarks suggested nonetheless that he relied deliberately on ambiguity of language as a device for persuading his colleagues of the bill's utility. His intentions emerged gradually over the course of debate, for he took little active part in 1838, deferring instead to the bill's principal supporters: Jozé Ignacio Borges, Luiz Jozé de Oliveira, and Francisco Carneiro de Campos. Presumably, Feijó also could be counted among them, when he returned to the Senate in 1839. However, his role as president of the Senate barred him from debate.[7]

By 1839, Vergueiro's motives clearly emerged. They were threefold. First, he wanted to make paternal recognition the cornerstone of inheritance rights for all illegitimate children. Maternal recognition would similarly require legal validation. Consequently, the bill's first goal was to redefine the procedures by which the courts would accept proof of parental recognition. Second, the bill's restrictive approach toward parental recognition of illegitimate children called for suppressing altogether judicial investigation of paternity. This goal sought to end any opportunity for illegitimate children, or their relatives, to petition the court for judicially determined paternal recognition, wherever succession rights were the motive. The third purpose of Vergueiro's bill was to modify the ladder of *ab intestato* succession, where it applied to appropriately recognized illegitimate offspring. Thus the bill privileged legitimate heirs over illegitimate offspring—placing the latter's grandparents, in addition to legitimate half-siblings, on an equal or higher footing. Above all, it modified the size of the inheritance portion devolving to recognized illegitimate offspring, given the existence of legitimate heirs. No longer would recognized illegitimate children automatically enjoy parity with legitimate offspring.

Collectively, the bill's articles implied that positive law would cease to make distinctions between types of recognized illegitimate offspring, except for *adulterinos*. Henceforth, the division between "natural" and "spurious" no longer would apply. What would matter instead would be the legal line drawn between illegitimate offspring who enjoyed parental recognition and those who did not. Respecting inheritance rights, no mention was made in any of the original bill's ten articles about a parent's legal condition as a commoner or a noble.

Senator Vergueiro's bill revised the position of non-legitimate individuals in inheritance law by setting aside a substantial amount of legal doctrine derived from the *Ordenações Filipinas* that had been reformulated or clarified as national law in the second half of the eighteenth century. His complex bill bears independent scrutiny, prior to turning to the substance of debates, not only for clarifying the changes it proposed but also for eliciting the key points of controversy the bill generated. In 1839, the Senate adopted all of the bill's articles, although with several important amendments, leaving most of the objections raised in the Senate to be addressed by the Chamber of Deputies. Even where amendments initially failed, or objectionable provisions were not eliminated in the Senate, debate revealed an important divergence over the relevance of precepts and procedures intrinsic to a Luso-Brazilian inheritance system. The proposed changes eventually divided legislators into two camps, the proponents of "modern" juridical precepts and the defenders of what essentially remained a Pombaline legal tradition.

Reapplying Legitimization by Subsequent Marriage

Article 1 of Bill BU of 1836 significantly broadened the legitimizing effect of subsequent marriage. In 1838, the latter applied exclusively to natural off-spring, regardless of whether parents were of noble rank or commoners. The original text of Article 1 was not recorded, but debate suggested it closely conformed to the version adopted by the Senate in 1839: "Subsequent mar-riage legitimizes offspring who are not adulterine, born to the spouses prior to marriage, and confers on them all family rights as if they had been born during marriage, even the name of the legitimate offspring."[8] Canonically in-cestuous offspring were the main beneficiaries of this article, but *sacrílegos* might, at a future date, be subsumed within its provision, if priests were permitted to marry in civil law. By applying the notion of legitimization by subsequent marriage to all illegitimate children "other than adulterine," Ar-ticle 1 found in positive law a remedy for removing the stain of spurious birth for those whom the church continued to define as "*incestuosos*," even when their parents married with an ecclesiastical dispensation subsequent to their birth.

Article 1 rested implicitly on the interpretation of Pombaline jurist Pas-choal José de Mello Freire, specifically on *De jure personarum*, Book 2 of his *Institutiones juris civilis lusitani*, published in 1791. However, he had applied legitimization by subsequent marriage more radically than Sen. Vergueiro, following Boehmer's arguments: "I am of the opinion that the children born before marriage, even if spurious [sacrilegious], adulterine, or incestuous, are legitimized by virtue and by force of law, causing the preceding impedi-ment to cease, when followed by true and legitimate matrimony."[9]

Like Mello Freire, Vergueiro's bill defied canon law by extending legitimi-zation via subsequent marriage beyond the boundary established by the Council of Trent: natural offspring. What mattered most throughout the legislative discourse over Article 1, especially in the lower house, was the legal tradition earlier adumbrated by Mello Freire. It explained legislators' often sincere, but mistaken, assumption that canon law permitted legitimization by subsequent marriage for incestuous and even adulterine children. Article 1 therefore opened the door for the state to give the civil effects of legitimiza-tion by subsequent marriage to children whom the church defined as spuri-ous even after it permitted their parents to marry. Article 1 suggested that positive law could remedy their quality of birth and address a rising rate of out-of-wedlock births.

A Bill to Alter Legal Tradition: Paternal Recognition

Article 2, in tandem with Article 4, envisioned changes that would tempt legislators to produce a new definition of paternal recognition. Both articles reacted to the 1828 Judiciary Act that designated courts of the first instance as the appropriate bodies for issuing certificates of solemn legitimization, on behalf of any category of spurious offspring or, alternatively, the natural child of a noble parent. Article 2 reiterated that an illegitimate individual's rights in inheritance rested on legal recognition: "The illegitimate offspring does not have the right to the father's inheritance, nor that of the mother, who does not legally recognize him."[10] What it changed was the inclusion of spurious offspring, implied in "illegitimate offspring." That is, Article 2 extended the same rights to spurious offspring, excepting adulterine offspring, that natural offspring historically enjoyed. Article 4 spelled out the procedures for recognizing them.

The first half of the original Article 4 (revised as Article 2 in 1839) generated controversy that even Vergueiro did not anticipate: "Legal recognition can only be made, as much on the father's part as on the mother's, [whether] declaring or not [declaring] the person with whom the child was conceived, by one of the following means . . . ."[11] An awkward syntax raised the possibility that the recognizing parent might, or could, mention—by "declaring or not declaring"—the name of the child's other parent. By no means innocuous, this provision provoked a great deal of acrimonious exchange. Opponents of the article, correctly, charged that a "voluntary" declaration sanctioned revelation of the mother's name—whereas custom, as well as Pombaline law, demanded silence. Despite the neutrality of gender suggested by reliance on "other person," debate made absolutely clear that the perspective of the text presumed paternal recognition, implying the father's revelation of the identity of his child's mother. The inverse of the gender-neutral language was left aside. For many proponents of the article, "voluntary" declarations did not go far enough. They argued that paternal recognition be given legal effect only when both parents' names were declared by the father.

Controversy over whether the "other" parent should be named by the one seeking to recognize the illegitimate child spoke to how the bill directly challenged precepts clearly articulated in a Luso-Brazilian legal tradition. Pombaline law reinforced an etiquette of silence over the mother's identity in situations where she was of "good" family and even enjoined against disclosure of her name. Royal jurisconsult Lobão expounded on this point when he parsed the second article of the law of January 7, 1750. Written around 1805, his interpretation highlighted the shift proposed by Vergueiro's bill. Following Mello Freire, Lobão interpreted the 1750 law as permitting crown legitimization for any canonically incestuous, adulterine, or sacrilegious offspring, before the Tribunal of the Desembargo do Paço, while "suppressing the name of the mother." The petitioner merely had "to state that declaration of the [mother's name] was omitted for the sake of decency, and not to defame a woman of honest reputation." By the same token, Lobão explained, "It is enough to say that the mother was unmarried, without having to point out that she was a virgin, widow, or noblewoman, etc., because everything [i.e., every sub-category of spuriousness] is encompassed within vices that are dispensable . . . ."[12] Muriel Nazzari's research has confirmed this usage was followed without exception in legitimization proceedings before the Desembargo do Paço of Rio de Janeiro. When fathers brought legitimization petitions on behalf of children who were legal foundlings, for example, then the mother's name was always omitted "for decency's sake"—or, as one father noted, "so as not to broadcast her fault."[13]

After substantial and heated debate, Article 4 (revised as Article 2 in 1839) was rewritten to require that both parents' names be declared for recognizing the illegitimate child. Furthermore, where the declaring parent was the mother who had concealed maternity, then she would have to provide the father's name:

Recognition of illegitimate offspring, by the father as well as by the mother who would conceal childbirth, can only be legally executed by one of the [five] prescribed means in this article; and, unless declaration is made of the [name of the] person with whom the child was conceived, the declaration will not produce any [legal] effect . . . .

Mandatory declaration of the other parent's name defined a new criterion for recognition. Customarily, parents who employed wills, notarial affidavits, or private affidavits for declaring recognition (perfilhação) also used discretion in naming the other parent. When the mother was of "respectable" social station, she might be named if deceased. In making any of five procedural means for declaring paternity directly dependent on the father's naming the "person who presumably was begotten of the child," the revised bill sought nothing less than to inhibit paternal recognition, on the assumption the etiquette of silence pertaining to the mother's identity would be respected.

Article 4 diverged dramatically from Luso-Brazilian legal tradition by redefining paternal recognition of an illegitimate child according to one of five procedures, stipulated in four succinct paragraphs. The first four procedures required recognition to be executed in writing. Where the parent was illiterate, a proxy signature carried effect. To wit, recognition would have legal effect according to one of the five options: 1) "the Public Registry of Baptisms or Births, signed by the declarant and two witnesses"; or 2) a notarized public affidavit (*escritura pública*); or 3) a will or codicil—"even when lacking legal formalities that [otherwise would] invalidate, provided that it contains ordinary proof of recognition"; or 4) a private affidavit (unnotarized). The fourth option required the signatures of five witnesses indicated by the parent—the same number required for a deathbed will. The fifth option, an oral declaration dictated *in extremis*, was the classic "deathbed confession" of paternity, analogous to a nuncupative will. In perpetuating that ancient practice, the final procedure engendered opposition, on the ground that oral declarations were highly susceptible to fraud. After significant debate, it was struck from the bill in 1839.[14]

Paragraph 5 of the original Article 4 provoked more controversy than any other provision, although it merely reiterated law in force, by exempting mothers who did not conceal their maternity from executing one of the preceding five written procedures: "A mother recognizes her illegitimate child by not concealing its birth."[15] Paragraph 5 shifted debate to the thorny issue of whether maternal recognition should continue to be "obvious" in judicial determinations, by calling attention to the circumstance that, historically, documentation had not been required for maternal recognition.

In summary, Article 2, in tandem with Article 4, determined that legal recognition would henceforth depend on the father's (parent's) execution of a written document. No longer would the conjectural evidence enumerated by Borges Carneiro, in *Direito civil do Portugal* (1826–1828), be admissible in court. Gone therefore was the reliance on hearsay evidence—testimony confirming a notable physical resemblance between father and child, on a father's publicly demonstrated acts of child support or affection for the child, or, above all, on an observable relationship of concubinage he maintained with the child's mother.[16] The first four procedures enumerated by Article 2 therefore imposed mandatory documentation that would replace what in practice often amounted to guesswork substituting for evidence.

Collectively, procedures for recognition implied yet another divergence from Luso-Brazilian legal tradition. Now only the parent, meaning ordinarily the father, would possess the legal power to confer recognition on the child. The fourfold set of procedural options for recognition declined to mention the right of the child to seek a judicial determination of paternity, a cardinal right the *Ordenações* extended to all natural offspring fathered by commoners for safeguarding their position in *ab intestato* succession. The bill signified no less than a historic shift in rights—at the child's expense in favor of the father. Consolidated in 1839 as Article 2 of the revised bill adopted by the Senate, the original Articles 2 and 4 mattered as the bill's key provision.[17]

Originally, Article 3 did no more than bar adulterine offspring from succession, echoing law in force: "The illegitimate offspring, even legally recognized, has no right to the inheritance of the father, nor of the mother, who has recognized the child, [where], at the time of conception, the former had been married." Dissonantly, it suggested a father could legally recognize an adulterine child, a right he did not have. By the same token, it explicitly referred to a married woman who made her maternity of an adulterine child obvious, a rare occurrence, tantamount to maternal recognition. Law in force did not permit such recognition. Because it was redundant and contradictory of several other articles, not to mention awkwardly worded, Article 3 was eliminated altogether when the Senate adopted the bill in 1839.

In compensation, senators substituted a different provision, one no longer narrowly focused on adulterous maternity. They derived it from the debate addressing whether the doctrine that maternity was obvious should continue to enjoy the force of law. Consequently, a recrafted Article 3 reiterated the conventional presumption: "When the mother does not conceal childbirth, the illegitimate child will be taken to be legally recognized by her, independent of any other declaration." Yet a man's concealed paternity of an illegitimate child was legally protected, wherever he chose not to reveal it by absenting himself from the baptismal font. Furthermore, a woman's maternity, taken as self-evident, also operated to shield the child's father from public scrutiny. Law in force already restricted judicial investigation of maternity, denying offspring the right to initiate such proceedings, even when their mother was not married. When she was married, then that right belonged exclusively to her husband, not to the child. Sole exception was made for testimony given in closed chambers to a judge in order to divulge information on a mother's concealed maternity for the exclusive purpose of preventing an incestuous marriage. Otherwise, legal doctrine, in presuming maternity to be self-evident, conferred maternal succession rights unilineally, normally on the assumption the child was a natural offspring.

Not surprisingly, a redefined Article 3, in tandem with the four procedures for recognition enumerated in Article 4, required mothers who had concealed the birth of their illegitimate child to execute formal recognition. That is, the same procedures imposed on the fathers of illegitimate children applied to them. Article 3 was hardly an innovation. In practice, mothers who wished to declare maternity after concealing the birth of a child often availed themselves of a notary for executing an affidavit of recognition, either in preparation for solemn legitimization before a judge of the first instance—

for legitimization *por rescrito*—or for changing a baptismal registry to permit entry of an *exposto*'s name. Alternatively, they used wills to reveal posthumously "confessed" maternity.

Suppression of judicial investigation of paternity led senators to redraft Articles 2 and 4 in a final respect. The bill maintained silence on a key point that in practice gave rise to petitions for a judicial determination of paternity, one that in an exclusively male legislature amounted to a most problematic area of social behavior: *rapto*. Definitionally elusive, due to the divergent family situations it encompassed, the crime of *rapto* admitted interpretation as kidnapping—bride abduction—but it also amounted to no more than elopement, implying female agency and consent. The Senate, consequently, sought to clarify family situations of immense complexity, because elopement posed a rebellious reaction to parentally imposed marriage—and *rapto* was on the rise. Therefore, a revised Article 4 addressed the bill's key lacuna by defining paternity *a priori* in situations of *rapto*: "When the illegitimate child's conception coincides with the abduction of the mother, the child will be taken to be fathered by the abductor, as if he had been legally recognized by the father."

In summary, the first four articles of Sen. Vergueiro's bill thoroughly redefined the legal position of illegitimate individuals of all types. First, legitimization by subsequent marriage acquired a new inclusiveness, removing the stain of bastardy for canonically incestuous offspring and potentially offering the same for *sacrílegos* at a future date. In failing to distinguish natural from spurious offspring, the bill obliterated an ancient and carefully constructed juridical distinction, that full *ab intestato* succession rights to the parent's *legítima* belonged to recognized natural offspring, while ordinarily spurious offspring, unless solemnly legitimized with testamentary succession rights, were excluded from succession.

Second, the fivefold means for declaring recognition of illegitimate children, underscoring the new precept that recognition of illegitimate offspring would now depend exclusively on paternal volition, deprived natural offspring of their historic right to petition a judge for an investigation of paternity to determine who had illicitly fathered them. Finally, discourse over the bill left implicit a new notion, that simple parental recognition of spurious offspring would be tantamount to solemn legitimization, obviating a judicial determination of paternity by the parent to produce the same effect. On the other hand, the bill's treatment of illegitimate offspring was far from reactionary wherever a father chose to recognize his child, because it proposed that recognition, tantamount to simple legitimization, be extended to those of canonically incestuous birth. The fact that Article 4 mentioned not only "public registries of baptism" but also those of "of birth," anticipated establishment of a civil registry—and civil marriage—in the future. Senators who favored legitimization of sacrilegious children looked not only to Article 1 but also to Article 2 for facilitating reversal of the *sacrílego*'s legal status as a bastard. The "trade-off" for placing the power to recognize exclusively in the father's hands, meaning suppression of judicial investigation of paternity, lay in the bill's ostensible blurring of distinctions between types of illegitimate offspring—in how it would lessen the stain of bastardy across society. Now paternal recognition implied that any illegitimate child, except *adulterinos*, might be legally equipped for heirship via paternal recognition. Thus the bill extended and complemented the Law of August 11, 1831, by ignoring whether legitimate children were living.

A Bill to Reduce Rights in Heirship

The last six articles of Vergueiro's bill tied the appropriate procedures for conferring legal recognition directly to *ab intestato* inheritance rights in several innovative respects. Article 5 explicitly spelled out the new legal precept, deducible from Articles 2–4, that made rights in patrimony directly dependent on paternal (or maternal) volition. Revised, it read: "The illegitimate offspring has only the right to the inheritance of the father who recognizes him according to the means prescribed in Articles 2 and 4, and of the mother who recognizes him according to one of the means prescribed in Articles 2 and 3. . . ." Without mentioning judicial investigation of paternity, the article effectively suppressed it.[18] The same article specifically excluded from succession rights those children recognized by a parent "who had been married at the time of the child's conception."

The original Article 5 redefined the succession rights of recognized illegitimate offspring in three paragraphs that, revised in 1839, became Article 6.[19] Collectively, new rules of heirship modified the position of recognized offspring on the ladder of intestate succession vis-à-vis necessary heirs. Furthermore, the size of their inheritance portions under the new rules was now contingent on the existence or the absence of necessary heirs, especially grandparents:

1. In the absence of either descendants or ascendants, paternally or maternally, the [recognized] illegitimate child will succeed to the totality of the estate.

2. In the absence of legitimate descendants, and accompanied by surviving ascendants, the illegitimate child will inherit one-half the estate, the other half remaining with the ascendants.

3. Accompanied by the legitimate descendants, the right of each illegitimate child to inherit will be equal to one-half the inheritance right of each legitimate child.

Paragraph 1 of Article 6 (originally Article 5) confined the right of a recognized illegitimate offspring to be the sole successor to the entirety of the *legítima* to one situation: the absence of both legitimate descendants and ascendants. By extending the axis of necessary heirs upward, to ascendants, it qualified the patrimonial rights of recognized illegitimate offspring. This paragraph therefore conformed to the Resolution of August 11, 1831, which provided that ascendants, as necessary heirs, would exclude spurious offspring from succession, as well as the natural offspring of a noble parent. However, Paragraph 2 of Vergueiro's bill explicitly privileged the deceased parent's ascendants—the recognized child's grandparents. Law in force gave grandparents sole *ab intestato* succession rights in the absence of legitimate, legitimized, *and* recognized natural grandchildren of a commoner parent. Spurious grandchildren, in other words, had to be solemnly legitimized under current law and receive their grandparents' consent in order to gain succession rights at the latter's expense. In the absence of legitimate half-siblings, the Law of August 11, 1831, permitted spurious children to succeed only if the grandparents were deceased. Yet Paragraph 2 of Vergueiro's bill stipulated that recognized illegitimate offspring would share their parent's *legítima* equally with their surviving grandparents, making both categories co-heirs. Thus spurious offspring gained rights, while the natural offspring of a commoner parent had them reduced.

Paragraph 3 of Article 6, the heart of succession reform, redefined the position of recognized offspring vis-à-vis their legitimate half-siblings, making them unequal co-heirs with the latter, for they were entitled to receive a share of the parent's *legítima* that amounted to only one-half the size of the share the legitimate half-siblings received. Consequently, the bill redrew the line between legitimate and non-legitimate birth, pushing those of illicit birth—natural offspring—much closer to bastardy, by merging them with spurious offspring. Recognized natural offspring therefore lost their privileged position of parity with legitimate offspring. They ceased to be tantamount to legitimate, thanks to the imputation of bastardy. On the other hand, the canonically incestuous, and, by implication, *sacrílegos*, acquired the right to succeed *ab intestato*, albeit it on an unequal basis with legitimate half-siblings.

Articles 6, 7, and 8 of the original Bill BU of 1836 regulated the succession rights of a recognized offspring vis-à-vis the parent's close relatives or, conversely, in terms of the former's descendants.[20] Revised as Articles 7, 8, and 9, they extended succession rights *per stirpes* to the descendants of all recognized illegitimate offspring, or restricted the *ab intestato* succession rights of recognized offspring to a parent's collateral relatives. Although they prohibited inheritance from the latter, they stipulated a reciprocity of rights where a recognized illegitimate offspring died without descendants. A new Article 10 was added to favor analogously the recognized offspring's *ab intestato* heirs. Finally, Articles 9 and 10 of the bill's original text reiterated law in force, respectively, by barring adulterine offspring from succeeding *ab intestato* to the parent's relatives and confirming the legal right of adulterine children to petition for child support from their fathers.[21]

The inheritance provisions of Bill BU of 1836 ended the ancient legal presumption of "equal shares" in *ab intestato* succession between recognized natural and legitimate offspring, assigning priority to the necessary heirs by displacing all recognized illegitimate offspring to a secondary plane, except when no necessary heirs existed. The revised ladder of *ab intestato* rights favored the legitimate family's lineal axis, including grandparents, but it imposed a new inferiority of rights on all recognized natural offspring. On the other hand, it simultaneously extended succession rights to recognized spurious offspring beyond what the Resolution of August 11, 1831, had conferred—albeit in terms of inheritance portions that were reduced by halves. Unequal in rights, and no longer clearly discriminated from spurious offspring, natural offspring would move closer to bastardy.

THE SENATE DISPOSES, 1838–1839

Main Currents

Bill BU of 1836 was debated in the Senate ten times between July 20 and September 15, 1838, when deliberation ceased.[22] By August 22, Article 1 was adopted and Articles 2–4 passed the second discussion with amendments. Deliberation resumed in 1839, during the first two weeks of May, testifying to the priority the Senate placed on the bill's passage. Three extensive debates revealed considerable division on each of the bill's provisions and a great more detail about how the inheritance system functioned in practice. On May 10, 1839, the Senate passed the bill. After amendments and several revisions were adopted by the Committee on Redaction, the bill left the Senate for the lower house on May 31.[23]

Senators reacted to Bill BU of 1836 in diverse ways. Illegitimacy, as the pivot of debate, exposed painful contradictions in values and revealed that the fundamental issue was not to draw a line between illegitimate individuals who were recognized by a parent and those who were not. Law, as well as society, had long drawn such a line. Rather, the issue was how to redraw that line—and whether to move recognized natural offspring closer to bastardy. The bill's underlying logic implied that the legitimate family's boundaries had to be made less ambiguous vis-à-vis illegitimate offspring, less capable of idiosyncratic inclusion. Those whose quality of birth was illicit henceforth were to be more sharply differentiated in rights from legitimate offspring, even if they were legally recognized and enjoyed intimate membership within the same family core. New rules of heirship were intended to etch a clear division between legitimate and natural offspring in social practice, implying that all illegitimacy would be less susceptible to nuanced recognition within respectable society.

Article 1, calling for legitimization by subsequent marriage to apply to all but adulterine offspring, generated significant controversy, largely because several senators voiced the opinion that adulterine offspring also deserved to be legitimized by means of subsequent marriage. When Oliveira persuasively moved to amend, by striking out "not adulterine" and substituting "not sacrilegious," then Patricio Jozé de Almeida e Silva surpassed him. He amended the bill to read "legitimize all the offspring," meaning adulterine and sacrilegious, as well as canonically incestuous individuals. Passing on a first and a second vote, his pithy and plenary entitlement failed on a final vote, probably because of greater respect for the prevailing social taboo against recognizing adulterine children than for any deference to canon law.[24]

Attitudes toward the "punishment" positive law demonstrated toward adulterine children were at best ambivalent. They responded as much to a rapidly solidifying bourgeois ethic as they did to either the tenets of liberalism or the dogma of canon law. On the other hand, willingness to use positive law to override canonical prohibitions on marriage followed not only from Luso-Brazilian regalism but also from the Regency's badly deteriorated relations with the Vatican. Many legislators continued to be defiant toward Rome, especially after papal confirmation for Antonio Maria de Moura, as bishop of Rio de Janeiro, was not forthcoming and he withdrew his candidacy in 1838. Harmonious relations were reestablished with the Holy See by May 1839, when the diplomatic impasse was ended, thanks to legislators' nomination of a new candidate suitable to the Vatican. The Speech from the Throne, delivered by Regent Araujo Lima in May 1839, pronounced the misunderstanding with the Vatican concluded; however, the Senate remained defiant. In fact, the committee appointed to reply to the Regent's verbally delivered annual report rejected it.[25]

Paternal recognition procedures acted as a red flag to what in the Senate was an assemblage of lawyers, judges, and law degree holders. On one side could be found the partisans of a new and draconian procedural compliance that eventually constituted the essence of legal reform. Appealing to the French Civil Code, which had inspired Vergueiro, advocates of written declarations of paternity denounced the chicanery and fraud associated with verbal declarations and private affidavits. They were also the promoters of the dubious innovation that a parent (the father) who recognized an illegitimate child would have to declare the name of the child's other parent (the mother). Arraigned against them, partisans of more modest reform backed procedures that minimally tied both filiation and inheritance rights to a parental declaration preserving the ancient convention of protecting the identity of the mother—"the other parent." The *parecer*, or formal opinion, presented in the report of the Committee on Legislation largely defended the latter position. When Chairman Cassiano Espiridião de Mello e Mattos read the Committee's full report to the Senate, on July 20, 1838, it proved downright hostile to the bill, accounting for the one-year delay in releasing the report.[26]

Committee critics intended not to defeat the bill, but to pare down its provisions to focus exclusively on recognition procedures. The report made no mention of inheritance rights, addressing only Articles 1 through 4 of the bill, because two of the three members opposed the bill's alteration of succession rights. Besides the signature of Mello e Mattos, the *parecer* bore that of Patricio José de Almeida e Silva, the senator who in 1835 had introduced a bill extending the legal effects of marriage to couples living in *mancebia*. The third author of the report, Francisco Carneiro de Campos, dissented from the report and submitted a separate opinion. He endorsed the bill almost as Vergueiro had drafted it, although he defended written paternal recognition as the exclusive means for equipping what he consistently and dissonantly identified as "natural" offspring. He declined to use the bill's language and to speak of "illegitimate" offspring throughout debate, whether from disagreement with the bill's scope or on the assumption that its provisions would not apply in practice to spurious offspring was unclear. Carneiro de Campos also proposed confining the execution of paternal recognition to the father's lifetime. Unlike his colleagues on the Legislative Committee, he strongly endorsed Article 6, reducing inheritance portions for recognized offspring to one-half of what their legitimate half-siblings received.[27]

Clearly, Mello e Mattos and Almeida e Silva, as the bill's harshest critics, sought to bracket the procedures for recognizing illegitimate offspring as the bill's exclusive objective. Consequently, they declined to debate either legitimization by subsequent marriage or *ab intestato* inheritance rights. Their report presented a substitute bill confined to five succinct articles outlining recognition procedures that required the same documentation for parental recognition as the bill—baptismal registry, notarial affidavit, and will or codicil. However, they excluded the fourth and fifth means for parental recognition proposed by Vergueiro: private affidavits and verbal declarations.[28] In that respect, their opinion stood as more modern than the bill. Above all, the report opposed the bill's requirement that a parent who declared filiation—recognition—to an illegitimate child be required to divulge the name of the other parent. The report saw through the "voluntary" disclosure of the mother's name and treated it as the mandatory revelation it was. Mello e Mattos set the tone for the opposition, insisting that Article 2, by "forcing a person to declare [the woman] with whom he lives," was simply "immoral." Instead, saying merely once, "So-and-So is my child" should satisfy the law. Likewise, a declaration by the mother to the same effect, he concluded, "offends the principles of public morality."[29] Proposing the time-honored means of the baptismal registry, he and Almeida e Silva argued such information must be offered optionally, at each parent's inclination.[30]

Clear consensus emerged in debate over the need to tighten procedures for declaring paternity, by moving away from reliance on evidence condemned as conjectural, for being conducive to fraud, a position endorsed by the Committee on Legislation.[31] Thus "those who do not have rights"— bogus heirs—became uppermost in Sen. Caetano Maria Lopez Gama's attack on the procedural means for declaring paternity. He pressed the point that chicanery routinely ensued where verbal declarations equipped individuals with paternal recognition. Once someone was dead, it was easy for a fraudulent heir to gather five "witnesses" who would then swear the deceased earlier had declared paternity in their presence. Consequently, he argued to suppress verbal declarations: "The man who wants to recognize his illegitimate child should go to a notary and have him draw up a notarized affidavit."[32]

Oral declarations were largely defended on account of the country's low literacy—and flagging liberal determination to uphold equality. When a father did not know how to write, "the child falls into a condition worse than other children. It is not fair to favor some and punish others for the wrongs that are not their fault, but those of their parents."[33] Vergueiro defended verbal declaration of paternity, having in mind "those living in remote places without recourse to notaries." The bill specifically waived the crucial issue of a will's validity in order for testamentary declarations of filiation to have overriding legal effect. As for improperly executed declarations in wills, what had in 1830 so troubled Aureliano de Souza Oliveira, Vergueiro countered, "In France it is not necessary for a will to reflect all the legal formalities [in order to be valid]."[34] Such arguments were in vain. A majority of senators voted to strike verbal declarations and to uphold their own legal tradition: Where a will lacked legally stipulated procedures, then valid effects could not follow.

The Shibboleth of French Law

On a number of occasions, Vergueiro referred authoritatively to the French Civil Code of the restored monarchy, promulgated on July 17, 1816, as the inspiration for provisions in the bill he authored in 1836.[35] In fact, he took almost no provisions outright from the French model. Except for the explicit suppression of judicial investigation of paternity, and a considerably modified notion of reduced inheritance portions, he preferred to tailor his bill to Brazil's special circumstances.[36] Nevertheless, he drew rhetorical advantage from invoking France's *Code civil*, given legislators' lack of sound preparation in the law of post-revolutionary France. Older senators, including Coimbra graduates, had not been formally schooled in the French Civil Code.

It was the much younger Antonio Pereira Rebouças, the autodidact of color and genuine "*rábula*" of 1830, who would quote Savigny with greatest authority in the Chamber of Deputies. Younger legislators with law degrees suffered from the deficiencies of a fledgling legal curriculum established for Brazil's new law faculties after 1827. As Joaquim Nabuco later observed about his father's student years at the Olinda Law Faculty during the early 1830s: "They did not yet have courses on the French expositors of the French Civil Code . . . or Roman law, as our teachers had in the 1850s and afterward . . . ." In fact, he aptly summed up the impact of eighteenth-century legal nationalism on Brazil's juridical formation. The work of Savigny, "which revealed the new school of Italian law, was not yet translated" into Portuguese. "Law was treated as a series of practical questions, not abstract ones," he explained. The peers of the elder Nabuco, "like our old jurisconsults," reminisced his son, "were schooled in the law by practicing as judges, lawyers, and sometimes as legislators."[37]

Vergueiro crafted a bill addressing his personal views on illegitimacy in imperial Brazil, albeit ones shared by many of his colleagues. In seeking to restrict paternal recognition, as well as to liberalize legitimization by subsequent marriage, he offered those proposals as French-inspired when he knew they embodied his ad hoc adaptations. Although the French Civil Code appealed to him on the subject of paternal recognition, he had no intention of adhering strictly to French precedent. For instance, in French law, paternal recognition depended only on a formal procedure—"an official instrument" (*un acte authentique*)—something that mattered a great deal to Sen. Vergueiro. He saw formal procedure as the device for cutting through the plethora of customary and conjectural proofs admissible in judicial determinations of paternity in the courts. Yet he considerably modified the notion of "an official instrument" to fit both legal culture and social practice in a Brazilian context, by falling back on time-honored written means of documenting paternal recognition: baptismal registry, public or private affidavits (*escrituras*), and wills. Moreover, he argued to retain verbal declarations before five witnesses, in deference to Brazil's low literacy rate—perhaps ten percent in 1838—and the dispersion of over ninety percent of the population in the countryside.

In contrast, French law from the 1790s until 1843 made recognition of a natural offspring a considerably less private act than the options Vergueiro's bill endorsed. A notarized act of recognition was to be appended to the margin of the civil birth registry, in conformity with what had to be recorded by an officer of the civil state.[38] Not until 1843 would French parents be permitted to rely exclusively on what, throughout Regency and Empire, Brazilians routinely availed themselves of—separately notarized and witnessed affidavits of recognition that never amended a "public" baptismal registry unless a parent deliberately so petitioned.[39]

Vergueiro, like many liberals, looked forward to the adoption of a civil registry after the French model. Yet he tried to construe a Brazilian context along French lines when he knew it did not fit. The text of the original Article 4, for instance, specifically mentioned the "public registry of baptisms or births" as one of five means by which a parent conferred legal recognition.[40] Parish registers maintained exclusively by the clergy, however much deemed "public" registries in Brazilian positive law, far from satisfied the modern notion of a civil registry that France introduced to the western world. Priests, if they could be construed "public" record clerks, followed only record-keeping prescriptions dictated by the *Constituições primeiras do Arcebispado da Bahia* of 1707.

The major arguments against Vergueiro's bill contested all of his assertions about the *Code civil* of France, foreshadowing a more vehement reaction offered by the Chamber of Deputies in 1846–1847. Reducible to three overlapping points of controversy, those arguments also exposed senators' personal attitudes about the position individuals of illicit or bastard birth should occupy in society, in addition to the value they placed on legal marriage, consensual unions, and the changing importance of property as family patrimony. The controversial points encompassed gender, investigation of paternity, and the size of inheritance portions. They illuminated sometimes astonishing opinions and assumptions legislators held about a wife's fidelity, a "concubine's" propensity to manipulate for personal gain, or a baby's susceptibility to being switched in the cradle—that is, a husband's confidence in his paternity of legitimate children.

ENDURING CONTROVERSIES

Reconsidering Gender: Maternity

The first major area of disagreement concerned the recognizing parent's "voluntary" declaration of the name of the "other parent with whom the child had been conceived." Although Vergueiro strongly endorsed the principle of paternal recognition as "the only irrefutable proof of filiation and legitimization," he also insisted on the necessity of identifying the illegitimate child's mother. He sided with proponents of a mandatory declaration of the mother's name, although initially he used sophistry to stress what Article 4 ostensibly left optional: "Declaring or *not declaring* the parent with whom the child was conceived." He dismissed the significance of what he proposed, given that ". . . most of the time the other person is declared because someone judges it necessary."[41] He neglected to note that the French Civil Code did not demand mandatory identification of the mother's name.[42]

Vergueiro's interlocutors grasped his logic, one he never acknowledged: To discourage fathers—and mothers—from declaring recognition by means of a procedure insuring that embarrassment and scandal ensued from the obligatory revelation of the other parent's name. Costa Ferreira bluntly told him the only reason to oblige the father to name the mother was "to defame the mother—without any benefit to her offspring." Thus Article 4 amounted to a device drastically curtailing paternal recognition. Knowing the child would be harmed by revealing her maternity, no father would defame the mother. Lopez Gama chose to point to succession law, correctly observing that rights were unilineal, flowing from recognition discrete to each parent: "If the father is the one to make declaration of the child's mother, [then] it does not benefit the child at all in terms of maternal inheritance." His mention of the mother's name was not only "useless" for maternal inheritance rights, but it also "could be harmful to the mother," serving to "discredit an honest lady."[43]

In arguing he was merely following current juridical practice, Vergueiro opened a window to the courtroom, one instructive for connecting the bill's procedural reforms to how judicial investigation of paternity had evolved since 1828. He pointed to what he claimed was a shift in how judges conducted those investigations. "Today," he insisted, "in the courts, proof of paternal filiation is not admitted without declaring maternity, because, respecting paternity, there is no proof; there is only conjecture and therefore maternal declaration becomes necessary." In arguing that fathers who recognized illegitimate offspring knew that silence over the mother's identity "left the matter of their paternity in doubt," he referred primarily to contexts that were posthumous, including those where testamentary declarations of paternity did not exist or competing heirs had challenged the latter.[44] Initially, Vergueiro argued that the "principal objective of the present legislation is to avoid having issues of fact that offend morality and family reputation raised in court." He acknowledged that "this situation already can be safeguarded, for the father is able to say, 'So-and-So is my child,' without however declaring who is the mother. And the mother can say the same thing, without saying who is the father."[45]

Yet he did not want to safeguard such declarations, but rather to remove confessions or accusations of paternity and maternity from the venue of a public courtroom. By deeming "families" one and the same with respectable society, he was demanding they enjoy greater shielding from harmful gossip and scandal. His argument thus amounted to an attempt to suppress investigation of paternity by inhibiting it. It strikingly echoed the argument of French legislators prior to adoption of the French Civil Code of 1804. Bigot-Préameneu had invoked what he deemed "a general cry" in the old regime against such investigation, asserting that "these law suits exposed the courts to the most scandalous debates, to the most arbitrary judgments, to the most variable jurisprudence."[46] Yet, when pressed by opponents, Vergueiro dismissed the notion that grave injury could be avoided simply by maintaining silence over the mother's identity. Paternal declarants would, in any event, he claimed, divulge the woman's name. "What does it matter," he asked, "that a father, in recognizing the child, states with whom it was conceived? What right follows from that? None." Returning to his mantra, he concluded, "What is well known is that such a declaration is worthless unless it refers to with whom the child was conceived."[47]

Mello e Mattos introduced the unreliability of the conventional instruments for paternal recognition, suggesting, they too, did damage to women of good family. He played on widespread anxieties over bogus heirs and the uncertainty a husband felt over his paternity of his wife's child. He also injected the detestable figure of the father whose testamentary declaration of paternity lied—by naming as the mother of his child a "woman unembarrassed [by scandal], who possessed great wealth, even though she is not the true mother." In order to end the "lacerating questions that violate decorum," he called for "all or nothing," coming down in favor of each parent executing a mandatory declaration of recognition. Otherwise, the bill would "fall apart if left unamended."[48]

Costa Ferreira's protest, that "a declaration which serves only to defame a woman deserves to be replaced," was not shared by the majority, for Vergueiro's position carried the Senate.[49] Revised as Article 2, the original Article 4 was amended to require mandatory declaration of the other parent's name by the parent recognizing the illegitimate child. Consequently, the Senate adopted a procedure relying directly on fear of scandal—even slander—to discourage fathers, and an infinitesimal proportion of mothers, from recognizing their illegitimate offspring.

Controversy shifted to focus on the closely related issue of whether mothers should be routinely required to declare maternity of an illegitimate child, in a notarized affidavit, after the manner required of fathers. Senators favoring notarized maternal declarations objected that Article 3's reiteration of the old legal dictum that maternity was "obvious" did not go far enough: "A mother recognizes her illegitimate offspring whenever she does not conceal the birth." Yet biology manifest no longer satisfied those eager to move in a modern direction. A vocal minority, they favored mandatory written declarations of maternity. No one mentioned that most unwed mothers already executed written maternal declarations—dictated to priests before at least two witnesses who were godparents for a baptismal registry.

Carneiro de Campos argued for parity, on the ground a legal wife enjoyed opportunity to betray her husband's honor. A bill requiring fathers to declare paternity in writing should also do so for mothers. Otherwise a husband might be forced to accept another man's child as his own. Why should "this very open door"—that mothers did not have to execute written declarations—"be left open"? He appealed to the deep-seated anxiety over baby switching. "Great harm [could] be permitted, given that many times there would be substitutions of one child for another." When he erroneously claimed the French Civil Code "had been notable for investigation of maternity," Vergueiro corrected him. "Regarding maternity," the French Civil Code "said nothing."[50]

Vergueiro attempted to quell fears voiced about the mother who falsely represented as her own child one born to another woman—the crime of baby switching. With dramatic flourish, he referred to "no less than a European monarch" who currently personified such a development, cautioning his colleagues that even children who were legitimate could be exchanged in the cradle.[51] In order to evade Mello e Mattos' charge that imposing a foreign legal tradition destroyed the coherence of legal doctrine fundamental to Brazilian national law, Vergueiro dismissed the French Civil Code as irrelevant for declaring maternity and interpreted his bill as uniquely tailored to Brazilian circumstances. Article 341 of the *Code civil* also presumed maternity to be obvious, where unconcealed. Brazilian legislators would have found it nonetheless repugnant that in most situations the French code denied husbands the right to investigate the maternity of their wives.[52]

"Hard line" insistence by certain senators on written declarations of maternity derived from yet a different reason, the same one that made wills indispensable in an Anglo-American legal tradition: protection of minor children from relatives intent on denying them their inheritance rights. Mello e Mattos pushed his fellow legislators to go beyond the "obvious" nature of maternity and adopt legislation requiring mothers of illegitimate offspring to declare maternity in wills or unnotarized affidavits, but protecting their privacy. The "embarrassments that will take place," he noted with subtle disparagement, pertained to inheritances that otherwise would be contested by relatives: "The bill does not take into account situations where the mother dies, leaving a child [biologically] recognized by her, but, for lack of a declaration in a will, there is no effect to her recognition." As a result, he warned, "the *ab intestato* heirs will arrive to dispute the child's inheritance," and the child's parentage would be cast in doubt.[53]

Finally, discussion logically examined the indelicate situation of maternity occasioned by "bride abduction" and elopement. This deliberate omission added a new article to the bill that covered the umbrella term of "*rapto*." Article 4, revised, stipulated that offspring fathered during a mother's abduction would automatically enjoy the abductor's paternal recognition. Yet it did not satisfy many senators who were aware of *rapto*'s ambiguous character, as well as the multiplicity of situations explaining a daughter's flight from her parental home, an event further complicated by her age. Subsequent debate in the lower house better illuminated the problematic nature of *rapto* for both paternity and patrimony. *Rapto* raised legal concerns challenging the father's *pátrio poder*, his legal authority over a minor child, because usually the woman was abducted from her parents' home. Normally, when she lived under the paternal roof, even after turning twenty-one, she was not legally emancipated. Everyone understood that, beyond contravening the father's *pátrio poder*, *rapto* often involved criminal charges of what amounted to either forcible or statutory rape, the latter legally defined as "seduction."[54]

Denial of paternity in situations of *rapto* deprived the child born of an abduction of paternal succession rights, but concern in a Brazilian context also focused on the abductor's patrimonial advantage. Article 228 of Brazil's 1830 Criminal Code provided that, where a woman married her abductor, punishment thereby was rendered null.[55] In the Chamber of Deputies, the charge that *rapto* could be a strategy enabling the abductor to gain the patrimony of his "victim's" parents followed from that provision. If the mother died, opportunity was enhanced and her family could suffer patrimonial loss due to claims the abductor-father made on behalf of the orphaned child. Further compounding such situations, according to a majority of senators, an abducted woman might not be pregnant by her abductor, but by another man. What, then, would become of her family's patrimony if a man who was not the father of her child acquired it?

For these reasons, the viscount of Congonhas do Campo left no doubt as to the unwisdom of categorically suppressing investigation of paternity. His amendment to Vergueiro's bill duplicated the one exception in French law. Article 4, revised again, passed: "All investigation of paternity is prohibited, except in cases of *rapto*."[56] The French code, however, allowed only the child conceived during abduction to bring a legal action for investigation of paternity. Significantly, Congonhas do Campo and his colleagues thought in terms of the mother, especially her family of origin. In France, by the late 1840s, on the other hand, the glaring contradiction in the civil code between suppression of paternity investigation and the right to sue for personal injury began to be taken into account. Judges gradually permitted an unwed mother to sue the father of her child for injury suffered due to pregnancy.[57] In Brazil, however, the higher priority placed on patriarchalism and family honor, rather than personal injury that was individual and female, better suggested why Congonhas do Campo's single exception to investigation of paternity passed the Senate. Neither injury to the abducted woman nor her impaired ability to support a child fathered by the abductor was raised in debate.

Efforts to amend the bill to permit investigation of paternity in situations of *rapto*—or to extend abduction (kidnapping) explicitly to rape (forcible or statutory)—were almost as strongly resisted. As Antonio Jozé Veiga, a career judge, would later insist in the Chamber of Deputies, Portugal's law of October 6, 1784, had clarified the notion of seduction, so confused by the *Ordenações Filipinas* (Book 5, Title 18): "When an abducted woman is over seventeen and the *rapto* is by seduction, it denies her the criminal action conceded by Book 5, Title 23."[58] Carneiro de Campos, who wanted the bill to conform to the Penal Code of 1830, did not succeed in confining *rapto* to what amounted to forcible rape, meaning to victims seventeen years and older.[59] No qualification to that effect was written into the bill because Sen. Vergueiro strenuously opposed such an amendment on the ground it was an arbitrary distinction. He doubted that only women age seventeen and older were susceptible to violent abduction.[60] On the other hand, he probably wanted to avoid introducing the concept of "seduction" into the bill, thereby compounding the notion of injury which was raising problems in French courts.

Suppressing Judicial Investigation of Paternity

The second major area of disagreement in the bill pertained to the elimination of judicial investigation of paternity. Mello e Mattos and Almeida e Silva did not want to suppress such investigation altogether, as their hostile committee report indicated. Basically, they defended the status quo permitting wide latitude for natural offspring to seek a judicial determination of paternity, one the bill extended to spurious offspring. However, they agreed on an important restriction—limiting judicial investigation of paternity to the father's lifetime. Thus they favored ending posthumous proceedings, probably the majority of judicial determinations of paternity. The latter came under heavy criticism from legislators, due to their susceptibility to fraudulent testamentary declarations of paternity and perjured witness testimony. Mello e Mattos and Almeida e Silva also recommended ending the practice of letting fathers appeal judicial determinations that recognized an illegitimate child.[61] Finally, Mello e Mattos found it contradictory to accepted legal doctrine to base judicial recognition on a will that was invalid, a point Vergueiro's bill endorsed. He rejected it: "A will that in civil law has no validity is able to give validity to those rights in heirship." His argument led to that provision being struck from the bill.[62]

Vergueiro attempted to deflect attention from the fundamental issue that paternal recognition implied in the context of the bill: succession rights for all natural and canonically incestuous offspring. Incredibly, he argued that fathers placed recognition clauses in wills "not as free dispositions in inheritance, but dictated by moral obligations." Mello e Mattos returned debate to the basics by affirming what was common knowledge: "A judicial determination of filiation that has not been moved by a petition asking for either honors or property is very rare." Vergueiro persisted in hammering at the benefits derived from suppressing investigation of paternity. Eventually, he came around to the argument flatly asserting the father should be required to name the mother of his illegitimate child. He insisted the bill's principal objective was "to avoid having issues of fact that offend family morality and modesty raised in court," and returned to the subject of how court proceedings had been evolving since the 1828 Judiciary Act. He ascribed the fact that judges were demanding revelation of the mother's identity in legitimization proceedings and judicial determinations of paternity to the failure of conventionally accepted evidentiary norms for establishing paternity unequivocally.[63] The testimony of witnesses in posthumous proceedings where paternal declarations were private—unnotarized—Vergueiro dismissed as "conjecture." Customarily, such evidence testified either to a father's habitual visits to the child and mother, or it ascribed a physical resemblance between father and child. Often, it amounted only to hearsay or a subjective impression.

Conjectural evidence, always susceptible to fraud, was part of a larger problem signifying the courtroom had become an important venue for projecting "scandalous and notorious" behavior in the community. Rather than fraud, rising litigiousness seems a better explanation for why judges were soliciting witnesses to disclose the mother's name in court. The 1828 Judiciary Act simply facilitated wider access to courts of the first instance, but demographic growth and a rising incidence of illegitimacy overloaded judicial dockets. Disclosure of the mother's name to the court offered a practical means of resolving cases, because judges frequently heard opposing sets of witnesses contradict each other on paternal identity. Relying on either the mother's corroborating testimony of the father's identity, or on witnesses who knew the identity of the dead father's *manceba*, offered a practical means for cutting the Gordian knot of contested paternal identity. No senator contradicted Vergueiro when he stated that judges resorted to either the testimony of the mother—or the introduction of her name—for corroborative evidence.

What mattered most for Vergueiro was the development that, in the late 1830s, a woman's maternity of an illegitimate child was likely to be introduced as evidence in open court. He and Carneiro de Campos focused on an emergent sensibility that asserted the privacy of the bourgeois family and argued it deserved greater protection. Not merely the woman but also her family group would be exposed to censure and ridicule by courtroom revelations. Inspired by the French *Code civil*, Vergueiro turned to the precept that voluntary paternal "recognition is the only proof of filiation and legitimization," and the direct means for shielding families from open scandal.[64] That refrain underscored throughout debate that only the father's voluntary act would bestow legal recognition on an illegitimate child. However, the inverse, expressed in Napoleon's famous dismissal, now had greater relevance: "Society has no interest in recognizing bastards."[65]

Mello e Mattos, of course, disagreed. He impugned the bill on the ground it "contained clearly identifiable provisions that are going to attack existing law." New juridical precepts would contravene the logic of accepted legal tradition. He derided the procedure that identified the child's mother, but gave as the main reason for voting against the bill its suppression of judicial investigation of paternity. He heaped scorn on Vergueiro's motive of social propriety, by trivializing it as "the irritating demands about filiation that arise in the courtroom." Family embarrassment, in Mello e Mattos' calculation, amounted to the justifiable price to be paid for a legal tradition that endowed illegitimate individuals with impressive rights in patrimony.[66]

When Carneiro de Campos rose to Vergueiro's defense, he equated the honor of the family with the right to privacy: "I vote in favor [of the article], because it is going to avoid these scandalous filiations that are being put forth [in court]. . . ." By specifying limited procedures for declaring filiation, he explained, "the article removes the embarrassment of so many awkward revelations from the courtroom." Rodrigues de Carvalho, another liberal who agreed with Carneiro de Campos and Vergueiro, argued in favor of procedures to restrict paternal recognition. To repudiate this bill "would be to return all legislation respecting filiation to the chaos where we found it."[67] The reference to "chaos" was not accidental. French legislators had applied the same word to legislation on illegitimacy adopted prior to the Directory. They viewed the law of 12 *brumaire* as embodying "order," just as they viewed a civil code as bringing "order" by tracing "between two kinds of descendants a perfect line of separation."[68] Vergueiro's lengthy disquisition on behalf of ending investigation of paternity persuaded his peers the new priority of protecting family privacy should be uppermost. The suppression of investigation of paternity, except in situations of *rapto*, was adopted by the Senate over vocal objection. In dictating revised rules of heirship for illegitimate offspring, Vergueiro would similarly anchor them in the same moral foundation advanced to suppress judicial investigation of paternity.

Redefining the Rules of Heirship

The final area of intense disputation arose from how the bill redefined inheritance rights. Articles 6 through 10 reordered the position of recognized offspring—or their close kin—on the ladder of *ab intestato* succession, but Article 6 explicitly modified the size of their inheritance portions. Many senators expressed reluctance to tamper with what was a highly inclusionary legal tradition of succession rights, vis-à-vis recognized natural offspring. Given that the Resolution of August 11, 1831, had liberalized the position of offspring who were spurious, as well as the natural offspring of a noble parent, proponents of Bill BU of 1836 built on that precedent. In fashioning new rules of heirship, Vergueiro had borrowed from how the Law of August 11 generically mixed natural and spurious offspring, as "illegitimate offspring." However, he misrepresented French law by implying it, too, blurred distinctions between natural and spurious offspring.

Bill BU of 1836 broke with Luso-Brazilian legal tradition by retaining a position of parity in heirship for recognized illegitimate offspring only when they lacked legitimate half-siblings and ascendants. Favoring grandparents to succeed equally with recognized non-legitimate grandchildren, whenever the parent had no legitimate children, followed French law only to an extent, because the latter also favored the dead parent's siblings and collateral heirs. When legitimate half-siblings existed, Vergueiro's bill provided the recognized offspring would succeed to only one-half the portion the legitimate children inherited. French law, on the other hand, accorded natural offspring one-third of that portion.[69] The bill thus stripped recognized natural offspring of their ancient right to be called to succession in a division of patrimony imposing equal shares for them and descendants who were legitimate. Only in the absence of all necessary heirs, legitimate descendants or ascendants, would a recognized illegitimate offspring succeed to the entirety of the parent's *legítima*. On the other hand, the bill considerably liberalized rights for spurious offspring who were canonically incestuous and recognized. They were called to succeed *ab intestato* merely by virtue of the parent's simple recognition.

Vergueiro proposed these new patrimonial rules in terms of the same rationale that French lawmakers had used to justify an inequality in inheritance shares for recognized offspring during the 1790s, albeit with differently proportioned shares.[70] For Vergueiro, legitimate marriage deserved to be valued by society; therefore, inheritance rights must be altered to reflect the higher priority it demanded:

It is my understanding that marriage ought to be promoted as much as possible and the offspring thereof regarded with greater honor and esteem than the offspring of customary unions. Therein lies the reason for this bill not to give illegitimate children the same rights as legitimate children. Competing with the ascendants, they inherit only one-half the estate, the other half belonging to the ascendants. If they were legitimate, they would have inherited the entirety of the estate.[71]

Given that Vergueiro's bill did not distinguish between natural and spurious offspring, except to exclude those who were adulterine, he was obliged to assure colleagues that the "offspring of a crime"—canonically incestuous individuals—would not be called to succession as the sole heirs, but only when no forced heirs existed. Normally, then, incestuous offspring would divide patrimony equally only when called to succession in the company of ascendants, according to the bill. Otherwise, he explained, they would similarly receive half the portion that legitimate children received.[72] The rule inscribing ascendants as co-heirs with recognized offspring copied French law, but, contrary to Brazilian law, French law tenaciously preserved patrimonial rights on behalf of collateral heirs to a degree that was striking. The latter enjoyed rights in forced heirship to the twelfth degree. Recognized natural offspring, therefore, could not be sole heirs in France unless no collaterals existed. Otherwise, even in the absence of necessary heirs, they received only three-quarters of the parent's estate. The final quarter devolved to collaterals.[73]

Moreover, Vergueiro declined to tell his colleagues that in France only recognized natural offspring were called to succession. Sen. Costa Ferreira was obliged to point out, correctly, that Vergueiro's use of "illegitimate offspring" diverged from French law, when some senators assumed that term also subsumed adulterine children. Mello e Mattos further pointed out that French law drew a careful line between all spurious offspring and those who were natural. Correctly, he explained that the French Civil Code carefully specified only "natural offspring" were equipped for forced heirship, because incestuous as well as adulterine children were excluded from succession. Of course, the Articles of the Clergy had extinguished *sacrílegos* as legal persons in French civil law, rendering them natural offspring.[74]

Consistent with the progressive marginalization of collateral heirs in Luso-Brazilian inheritance law, they were not mentioned in Vergueiro's bill. Instead, the bill innovatively privileged ascendants in terms of a new family axis reinforced around lineal kin connected by legitimate birth. An unsuccessful amendment to strike the succession rights that Article 6 assigned to grandparents, as co-heirs with recognized offspring, failed to carry, but it revealed deep division over that innovation.[75] Rewriting the rules of heirship to withdraw rights from natural offspring, Mello e Mattos insisted, threatened what was a historic model of family porosity in Brazil. "It is understood," he complained, "that new principles of hereditary division, as stated in the bill, cannot be received among us for establishing law ... They are, doubtlessly, to alter our system of law regulating succession."[76] He brought up the bill's generic treatment of illegitimate offspring, one that ignored logical connections to what had always been two, parallel systems of *ab intestato* and testamentary succession, respective to natural and spurious offspring. The underlying logic of succession would therefore be lost, he correctly predicted, and the integrity of legal reasoning undermined.

Taking Vergueiro to task for interpreting all illegitimate individuals as "the offspring of a crime," Mello e Mattos vehemently objected that natural offspring were "not bastards." Protesting they "should not be so defined," he insisted it was unjust to harm the inheritances of "those who have rights to them."[77] Mello e Mattos' accusation, that the principles of hereditary division proposed by Vergueiro's bill would "alter our system of law regulating succession," echoed again in the lower house during the 1840s.

When Bill BU of 1836 left the Senate for the Chamber of Deputies, on May 31, 1839, it no longer contained ten articles, but thirteen. The Committee on Legislation renumbered several of the original articles and incorporated two substantial amendments. In addition to striking oral declarations of paternal recognition, the revised bill now required a recognizing parent, normally the father, to name the illegitimate child's other parent, normally the mother. A new article pertaining to judicial determination of paternity, in cases of *rapto*, defined the latter as the sole exception to suppressing investigation of paternity. A separate Article 11 guaranteed succession rights for parents and the descendants of a recognized illegitimate offspring, in the event the child predeceased the parent; it reiterated the *terça* was to remain of free disposition. Article 12 reconfirmed existing law on the right of adulterine children to receive child support from their fathers, following the original bill's final article.[78] A final article, strictly pro forma, revoked all contrary legislation.

A HISTORIC BILL GOES AWRY

In May 1839, simultaneously with Senate passage of Vergueiro's bill, the bill for the Act of Interpretation that would repeal the 1834 Additional Act was nearing completion in the Chamber of Deputies. Adopted in the Senate in May 1840, it meant that Brazil's political structure would revert to the constitutional foundation defined in 1824. D. Pedro's accelerated investiture as emperor, in July 1840, brought the Regency to a close, but transition to a recentralized monarchy was still incomplete. The task of restructuring the central state awaited revision of the liberal-inspired 1832 Code of Criminal Procedure. Parliamentary elections were called, following the legislature's adjournment in September 1840. The institutional modifications needed to secure a reinvigorated throne for D. Pedro II, however, depended on the full implementation of the Regresso's agenda. That anomalous factional coalition needed to retain a parliamentary majority after elections, from May through October 1841, the final year of the Fourth Legislative General Assembly (1838–1841).

The Chamber of Deputies declined to match the Senate's enthusiasm, even urgency, in adopting Bill BU of 1836, although the Senate immediately dispatched the measure to the Chamber on June 1, 1839, one day after final amendments were inserted. Action was deferred indefinitely, for the Law of Interpretation, rescinding or revising the Additional Act of 1834, had just gone into effect. Pending resolution of the crisis over the nation's political reconstitution, the Chamber of Deputies was not inclined to regard the rights of illegitimate offspring with urgency. Renewed Liberal sponsorship of Sen. Vergueiro's bill therefore emerged in the lower house only in 1845, but it took firm hold only in 1846. Nevertheless, the Senate had passed a historic bill, however lengthy and complex. The revisions in the rules of heirship it proposed would be subjected to careful scrutiny in the lower house: altered rights of natural and spurious offspring vis-à-vis the ladder of *ab intestato* succession; reaffirmation of child support for spurious children, implying a narrowly circumscribed paternal recognition for that purpose; suppression of judicial determination of paternity and curtailment of a father's prerogative to recognize his natural offspring, using the inhibiting device of naming the mother; and extending legitimization by subsequent marriage to canonically incestuous children or, at a future date, the children of priests.

For the first time, legislators introduced the notion that Brazil should borrow legal innovations in the private law of the family and inheritance system from an alien legal tradition, one embodied in the French Civil Code. Modernity arose in debate as legislators proved even more willing to base the procedures of paternal recognition exclusively on written documentation, abandoning the reliance their legal tradition placed on oral testimony before witnesses. The raison d'être for diverging from notions of heirship enshrined in the *Ordenações do Reino*, redefined by Pombaline positive law, lay in the new emphasis placed on the value of privacy and a heightened fear of "scandal in the courtroom," not to mention the growing significance of family patrimony. For an emergent middle class, the sharp departure from an accepted legal tradition signified a new idealization of the conjugal family based on legitimate marriage, one demanding greater patriarchal control of economic resources and the exercise of paternal discretion in either incorporating or declining to recognize non-legitimate members of the family.

PART IV

Redefining Bastardy in Imperial Brazil

CHAPTER 9

Placing Conscience in Conflict with Interest

Who, hoping to make a marriage happy and fortunate, will then
have in mind the embarrassment of natural offspring, if they do
not have to exist except at a time when the father chooses? . . . No
one turns toward concubinage from duty . . .

Dep. Jozé Vieira Rodrigues de Carvalho e Silva, 3 July 1846[1]

We ought very much to flee from legislating in opposition to
deeply rooted customs, as if we were creating a new religion. It will
be difficult to impose a foreign language—these difficult new customs—on the people by force and impossible to destroy the existing ones by means of laws.

Dep. Angelo Moniz Ferraz, 15 May 1846[2]

The crisis of a recentralized monarchy crystallized in 1840, around the government that would hold power under the elections called for the Chamber
of Deputies. In 1839, factional realignment had transformed the Regresso
cabinet, but not before it obliged Araujo Lima's Regency government to face
eclipse. Starting with Bernardo de Vasconcellos, moderate liberal cabinet
ministers were driven into opposition, fragmenting the Regresso and leaving
the government in the hands of those backing the premature proclamation
of D. Pedro's majority. Identified as the "elections of the cudgel," the 1840
elections relied on violence and fraud in order to impose a majority favorable to a nascent Liberal Party. In the aftermath of the October–November
elections, whose winners would not take their seats until 1842, the Regresso
opposition emerged as the chrysalis of the Liberal Party. However, the fall of
the cabinet, in March 1841, upset majoritarian expectations for 1842. The
Conservative cabinet appointed by D. Pedro II as its successor proved decisive for counteracting the electoral outcome and denying Liberals the control of both cabinet and legislature.

Opening in May 1841, Parliament adopted the centralizing program of
Bernardo de Vasconcellos, who, as the Regresso's erstwhile leader, together
with Jozé Clemente Pereira and Aureliano de Souza Oliveira, shed partisan
scruples and joined the Conservative cabinet. A strong government insured,

the cabinet organized voting majorities for adoption of the key legislation needed to guarantee a recentralized government. The law of November 23, 1841, reinstated the principal organ of monarchical rule, the Council of State. Ten days later, the notorious "Law of December 3" ended the historical liberals' experiment with a decentralized judiciary and police power. As an amendment to the 1832 Code of Criminal Procedure, the Law of December 3 further divided the ranks of what was still an emergent Liberal Party, one that throughout the decade would be distinguished by deep factional divisions and contradictory currents.

The Law of December 3, 1841, imposed the key shift in Brazil's local political organization by redefining the judicial-police branch of government. Placing judicial and police power throughout the nation under the control of provincial presidents, who became imperial appointees, the new law centralized authority and power in the ministries of the imperial government. The political party that named the minister of justice now exercised infinite advantage in manipulating elections, because he controlled the imperial bureaucracy devoted to police and judiciary. The judiciary ceased to be elected at the lowest levels. Now local police officials "were delegated the authority to investigate, arrest, judge, and sentence petty offenders right in the police station, without the intervention of lawyers, prosecutors, or higher judicial authority."[3] The magistrate who would embody the monarchy throughout the Second Empire was also an imperial appointee: the *juíz de direito*, or "district judge." A law school graduate, he became the agent overseeing the imperial government's interests in local jurisdictions. The Law of December 3 projected the police and judicial power of the imperial government downward, onto the *municípios*, or local units of government, undermining patronage relationships and the electoral support of many Liberals who still opposed the rejuvenated monarchy. The law also strengthened the imperial government's power to tax and to enforce regulation of commerce and agriculture in the provinces, measures that further eroded Liberal Party voting strength.[4]

In the short run, the Law of December 3 enabled the lame-duck Conservative cabinet of 1841 to organize a political revanche that displaced Liberals elected in 1840, keeping Conservatives in power from 1842 to 1844. The cabinet, above all, Aureliano de Souza Oliveira, persuaded D. Pedro to dissolve Parliament on the ground that new elections had to be called, given the abuses committed by Liberals in winning the 1840 election of the cudgels. By consenting, the emperor permitted the Conservatives to carry the election of 1842 and prevent the Liberals from gaining a majority. The Conservatives relied on appointive powers they exercised under the amended Criminal Procedural Code, which facilitated fixing elections.[5] In May 1842, however, the so-called Liberals of the South (São Paulo and Minas Gerais) revolted against the central government. They reacted to the emperor's dissolution of the Chamber of Deputies in order to call new elections, but the Law of December 3 represented the root cause of their hostility. The leaders of this Liberal Party "rump" opposition were from São Paulo: Dep. Raphael Tobias de Aguiar, the former provincial governor, and Sen. Nicolao Vergueiro. Tobias de Aguiar enlisted the symbolic support of his friend, Sen. Diogo Antonio Feijó. As the leaders of "the Liberal Revolt," they intended to force the resignation of the imperial cabinet, curtail new elections, and demand repeal of the detested Law of December 3. Arrested and charged with treason, all three were confined to exile distant from Rio de Janeiro while they awaited the Senate's determination of their fate.

A forgiving Senate amnestied Vergueiro and Tobias de Aguiar in 1843, permitting them to return to national politics in 1844. The vote went against amnesty for the terminally ill Feijó, who died in October 1843, unforgiven by his colleagues and nearly unnoticed by the press. In an act of political rehabilitation and reconciliation, Nicolao Vergueiro, who steadfastly had refused offers of ennoblement, maintained his aversion to titles but permitted himself to be inducted into the Imperial Order of the Cruzeiro, receiving the medal directly from the hands of D. Pedro II. Initially urged by Aureliano de Souza Oliveira, Pedro sought to solidify support for his monarchy by issuing a generous number of noble titles as soon as his majority was proclaimed. Similarly inspired, Araujo Lima had reinstituted the court ceremony of the *beija mão* and become the first to kneel before the young emperor and kiss the royal hand.[6]

During the festivities for Pedro's formal investiture, in July 1841, Diogo Antonio Feijó had also received from Brazil's new emperor the medallion bearing the great cross of the Imperial Order of the Cruzeiro. The former regent, who was almost unable to walk and losing the power of speech, made an exhausting journey to the imperial capital to receive that honorary distinction—indispensable for a complementary, more coveted pension to sustain him for the few remaining years of his life. The liberal delegate to the Lisbon Cortes, who twenty years before had declined in the presence of the entire court to kiss the royal hand of Pedro's father, knelt and accepted the hand extended by his adolescent son. Feijó's bestowal of the obligatory *beija mão*, in a gesture of gratitude that his liberal convictions had withheld from Brazil's first emperor, must have struck observers as sublime as it was absurd.[7] A titled nobility would again flourish under the second Pedro. Liberals, as much as Conservatives, would find themselves flattered to be the bearers of nobiliary distinctions that ordinarily proclaimed them barons and viscounts.

A BILL AWAITS A LIBERAL MAJORITY

The quashing of "the Liberal Revolt of 1842" marked the effective reestablishment of the Second Empire. Thanks to a magnanimous emperor, the Liberal Party met pragmatic reversal and regained a majority in the Chamber of Deputies in 1845, having carried the 1844 elections. Although the party would be largely relegated to the role of an opposition until the 1860s, Liberals held their first majority until 1848. Their cabinet, however, fell in September 1847, barely in time for them to adopt Sen. Vergueiro's heavily rewritten Bill BU of 1836. Initially, despite the Senate's enthusiasm, the Chamber of Deputies failed to act in concert on the bill. Vergueiro's 1836 bill, redesignated General Assembly Bill No. 14 of 1839, was swiftly dispatched to the printer after being immediately placed on the agenda of the lower house on June 4. Then it was completely ignored for over two years. Again placed on the agenda toward the end of 1841, the bill "regulating the succession rights of illegitimate offspring" then received terse attention from a sole and influential member. When Honorio Hermeto Carneiro Leão, future marquis of Paraná and a Conservative Party founder, deemed its provisions "very obscure," the Chamber followed his recommendation to send it to the Committee on Civil Justice for rewording and a formal opinion.[8] Despite a binding proviso to return the bill to the floor within eight days, postponement stretched into four years, notwithstanding that the required committee report was produced within three weeks.

The amendments contained in the *parecer* prepared by the Chamber's Committee on Civil Justice offer no clues about why deliberation in the lower house was effectively postponed for the period stretching from 1839 to 1845. They merely embodied perfunctory touches polishing or rendering precise the redaction of the bill received from the Senate on June 1, 1839.[9] The causes for tabling the bill must instead be sought in the great changes transpiring in Brazil's national politics between 1839 and 1845. Political events pivoting on the restoration of a strong monarchy, especially the appointments of two centralizing cabinets in 1841 and 1843, account for why Liberal supporters of the bill directed attention to more urgent matters. The house arrest and exile of the bill's prime mover better explains the delay. The trial of Sen. Nicolao Vergueiro for sedition took place in 1843. Only after he was amnestied and reintegrated in national politics, in 1844, did Bill No. 14 of 1839 begin to move through the Chamber of Deputies. More to the point, revived interest in passage of the bill responded to the election of a Liberal Party majority in the lower house in 1844. Taking office in May 1845, Liberals again dominated the Chamber of Deputies. Although initial debate on Bill

No. 14 of 1839 began in mid-August 1845, parliamentary deliberation was diverted in the final month of that legislative year—to renewal of the commercial treaty with Britain, in anticipation of a crisis over the continuation of the Atlantic slave trade.

Despite the Senate's expeditious approval, the lower house demonstrated strong objection to most of the bill's provisions, once debate resumed in earnest in 1846. The Chamber proved more factionally divided than the Senate, and imperial deputies expressed a wider spectrum of views on the bill, defying partisan cohesion. Without leadership similar to what Vergueiro had exercised in the Senate during the late 1830s, the bill's progression in the Chamber ran afoul of acrimonious criticism, making debate protracted and inconclusive, to the point where key deputies rewrote its provisions before giving it final consideration in 1847. The provocative changes proposed by Bill No. 14 of 1839 elicited a complex and fractious discourse, one reflective at mid-century of important changes in social attitudes toward the legitimate family, "natural" marriage, and the quality of illegitimate birth. The issues connected to these changing attitudes were framed against the backdrop of competing claims in heirship that conferred new, public importance on family patrimony. Otherwise, concern over a plethora of fraudulent practices in the courtroom, that many legislators claimed to have witnessed personally, fueled the heated debate over how to recast the rules of heirship for those born outside legitimate marriage.

REFORM MOVES FORWARD

An Incompatibility of Legal Traditions (1845)

As soon as Bill No. 14 of 1839 came to the floor of the Chamber of Deputies, on August 14, 1845, objection was raised over the lack of any committee assessment in the requisite report offering a *parecer* relevant to existing law. That report had not been printed and distributed beforehand, suggesting proponents anticipated sidestepping further delay. Nicolao Rodrigues de França Leite asked that the bill be returned to committee prior to deliberation. Correctly apprehending that what the bill proposed "is going to alter not only our positive law but also the uniformity of practice in the courts," he leaned toward careful reconsideration, if not indefinite postponement. Deeming the bill to be "of great transcendence," he objected that it "contains many dispositions taken from the Civil Code of France" and expressed misgivings. Could its dispositions "be entirely applied to our country today, in light of our customs, our legislation, practice in the courts, our laws, and our peculiar jurisprudence?"[10] João Jozé de Moura Magalhães seconded França

Leite, noting that "new legislation"—law departing from established legal doctrine—was before the house. He cited what seemed to him "an enigma" in the bill, and termed the bill a "dangerous innovation": "The rights of legitimized offspring are not equal to those of legitimate offspring."[11] Neither deputy was placated; after a pause of four days, debate resumed on August 18 without the guidance of a *parecer*. Then, as more pressing matters occupied deputies in the final month of the 1845 legislative year, the bill was tabled.

The central role played by one deputy, Manoel Jozé de Souza França, in the sessions of August 14 and 18, 1845, together with the disinclination of the president of the Chamber to send the bill to a committee for a legal opinion, suggested that proponents of the bill assumed they could impose it more successfully if they prevented a careful committee study of the bill's impact on prevailing legal doctrine. Hence Gabriel José Rodrigues dos Santos argued that the bill was too important to go to a committee. Pointing out that "jurisconsults were in great number in the house," he carried the day. Previously, Souza França had used the advantage of surprise to inject a different interpretive accent for the bill, one inspired by an amendment originally proposed by Sen. Francisco de Souza Paraiso in 1838. Reacting to the reality that noble titles were no longer being issued, that they were held only in life tenure, and, probably, to the personal circumstance that his own eldest son was a natural offspring, Paraiso had proposed amending the original Senate bill's Article 5 to read: "Natural offspring called to succession with the legitimate offspring inherit equally from the father who has recognized them, even when they are noble, and according to the same terms." In 1845, a wave of new titleholders finally made Paraiso's amendment to extinguish differences of estate in succession law now very timely.[12]

On the first occasion when Souza França gained the floor, August 14, he diverted attention from the fundamental issue of legal doctrine to the old theme of distinctions of estate. The bill's treatment of succession, he maintained, ambiguously raised the issue of rights differentiated according to estate: "This bill establishes a new right of succession that revokes existing right, which excludes from succession the natural offspring of the so-called gentlemen [*cavalheiros*], but not of the so-called plebeians [*peões*], from succession." Claiming the bill also raised potential conflict with the existing succession rights enjoyed by the noble parent's relatives, he endorsed Article 1, believing that only legitimization by subsequent marriage should equip natural offspring for succession, never paternal recognition.[13]

When debate resumed on August 18, Article 1 was enigmatically "approved" in an initial discussion, without comment by the Chamber's redactor. Nevertheless, the rapid adoption the Senate had accorded the bill was

not to be repeated in the Chamber, where the proposal to extend legitimization by subsequent marriage to spurious offspring encountered strong resistance. Article 2, it will be recalled, had been amended before leaving the Senate, to read that recognition of an illegitimate offspring would convey inheritance rights only when the parent made "declaration of [the name of] the
person with whom the child was conceived."[14] Legislators in the Chamber
initially addressed the four procedures conferring legal recognition adopted
by the Senate: 1) baptismal registry, requiring two witnesses; 2) notarized affidavit; 3) will or codicil, even if lacking the solemn procedures invalidating
them; or 4) informal (private) affidavit in the presence of five witnesses.

Several deputies enthusiastically denounced evidence for paternal filiation
accepted in current law, especially wills—"for being written in life's last
moments."[15] Notable anxiety emerged over the oral testimony of witnesses
procedurally required for private affidavits. Dep. João Jozé de Oliveira Junqueira, for example, claimed that reliance on the latter "has resulted in decisions where children are taken as offspring of men who are not their fathers."
Evoking the menacing specter of the imposter, he asserted that "introducing
children as family members who are strangers" only "disturbed the order of
succession for the legitimate heirs."[16] Therefore, the oral testimony of all witnesses ought to be excluded as evidence for any paternity posthumously determined in court.

On the other hand, in the Chamber's blanket condemnation of hearsay
evidence, a parallel tendency to condemn illegitimacy outright could be
clearly detected. Mendes da Cunha summed up an attitude of moral condemnation typically shared by many: "Those who live in illegitimate unions
are susceptible to many intrigues, and all kinds of discord could lead the
mother to the idea of revenge that would deny the child's [true] paternity."[17]
He opposed legitimization for spurious offspring in current law not only because it often depended on courtroom testimony that was hearsay but also
because it revealed the parents' involvement in "incest." Turning to how the
bill privileged canonically incestuous children and implied the same for
sacrílegos, he demanded to know, "Why are incestuous and sacrilegious offspring any different from those who are adulterine?" The good reputation
and honor of spurious individuals would not benefit, he argued, because
"reason dictates, religion approves, and morality prescribes" that legitimization of incestuous and sacrilegious children should not be permitted. My-
sogenistically, Mendes da Cunha refocused the bill's attention from the father of a spurious offspring to the mother: "Those who are born outside
conjugal union belong only to their mothers. Why do we forbid [recognition
for spurious offspring]? To save the mother from the shame of revealing her

lack of [morality]."[18] Following Souza França's lead, Mendes da Cunha captured the central importance of legitimate marriage in the longer debate that ensued in 1846. His accent directly opposed liberalizing rights for illegitimate children, a theme that found its strongest expositor in Souza França.

Souza França initially condemned succession rights even for natural offspring, on the ground they were "contrary to the morality of good custom and the constitutive principle of society." His line of argument quickly carried the institution of matrimony beyond questions of morality, privileging it in terms of the new importance he ascribed to civil, as opposed to natural, law. Although he acknowledged that "man has a natural propensity for [legal] marriage, he often denies society's responsibilities by substituting natural marriage, thus contravening society's laws." The offspring of such consensual unions, he reasoned, "cannot have the same protection of the same laws [of civil society], in order to succeed together with legitimate offspring to a father's property." Moreover, the right to *ab intestato* succession derived from civil law, "not from natural law." Therefore, the only way natural offspring should succeed would be by the subsequent marriage of their parents—the means prescribed by the same civil law, which "validates what initially was invalid."[19]

By resting his position on the logic that only civil law created rights in succession, Souza França denied prevailing legal nationalism, dating to the Pombaline reforms of 1754 and 1769, which equated legitimate succession with natural, or *ab intestato*, succession. Ever since, Luso-Brazilian legal tradition derived the succession rights of both legitimate and natural offspring from natural law, but reserved for legitimized spurious offspring the artifact of civil law known as testamentary succession. Yet Souza França's iconoclastic line of argumentation was hardly novel, for French legislators had used it in the late 1790s, in order to repudiate the law of 12 *brumaire* (November 2, 1793). The latter briefly repaired the legal position of illegitimate individuals by signifying "there are no more bastards in France."[20] Souza França echoed Siméon, who had construed the civil law as a higher achievement than natural law: "The law of inheritance pertains to the realm of the civil law . . . it is not part of natural law, and if it were, the cause of children born out of wedlock would be no less unfortunate."[21] By denying an equality of rights depending on natural law, he sought to privilege legal marriage in order to condemn "the clamor of debauchery."[22]

Moving to contract theory, he reasoned that the natural offspring "is outside the law" because, as the product of natural marriage, such an individual originated from a union lacking a legitimate contract. Therefore, he insisted, "no natural offspring [should] able to succeed his father by the mere fact of recognition by the same father." Instead, either "legitimization by the subsequent marriage of the parents" or "a legitimization certificate issued by the competent [judicial] authority" should be the sole means of legitimizing a natural offspring. However, he declined to support the bill's procedures for paternal recognition, unless they applied exclusively to a judicial legitimization that did *not* produce *ab intestato* succession rights. Paternal inheritance rights by virtue of paternal recognition he deemed "prejudicial to the rights of the [legitimate] family to which [the father] belongs." It followed that law in force "protected immorality and the transgression of public order."[23]

Rising to defend the status quo, Rodrigues dos Santos responded in terms of eighteenth-century legal doctrine: "Under natural law all children born in marriage, what [Souza França] calls 'natural' [marriage], are equal under the law." He called on his colleagues "not to lose sight of the principles of natural law." Reaffirming Pombaline legal tradition, he implied the great distance that separated recognized natural offspring from bastardy in law: "It is incontestable that under natural law whether [or not] a child is born of marriage conforming to written [positive] law is not going to be investigated." His line of reasoning, therefore, made "natural marriage" as much the contested issue as the rights of natural offspring.[24] Significantly, no legislator spoke of "*mancebia*," although several proponents of the bill chose to speak of "concubinage" rather than "natural marriage." Yet, clearly, sentiment supportive of natural marriage demonstrated that the concept of "marriage according to the *Ordenações*" was far from dead.

Souza França introduced argumentation resting on contract theory that was well suited to the restored monarchy, precisely at the moment when it was being reestablished on an oligarchical foundation articulated within preexisting webs of family alliances.[25] His assertion that civil society was composed of "small societies" which were "families organized in conformity with the [civil] law" repeated familiar political theory, but it also synthesized a socio-political core of family power appropriate to the newly constituted Second Empire. A nation, he continued, "is no more than an aggregation of many families. These families, or small societies, have their constitutive rights . . . [coming] from public authority." In maintaining that "no one can constitute family outside the law," Souza França flatly denied natural marriage could constitute a valid family. In short, "no contract, even of marriage, can be protected by public authority when it is reputed as illicit." Therefore, "illegitimate offspring, as the effect of an illicit contract, have no right to succeed the father, because the father did not respect, but contravened, the law." This reasoning, he added, further explained why the recognized natural offspring of nobles were still barred from *ab intestato* succession.[26]

Souza França propounded a second, related point that would become central to the bill in 1846. Law governing illegitimacy should make no distinction between nobles and commoners, because to do so was to contravene the 1824 Constitution. In support of that position, Junqueira alluded directly to the courts, where some lawyers were arguing—and he indicated some judges agreed—that recognized natural offspring should succeed to a noble father's *legítima* even when legitimate offspring existed. Not to do so "discriminated" generically against natural offspring. Having carefully worded a logically persuasive argument dedicated to withholding succession rights from natural offspring, Souza França was obliged to wait until 1846 before addressing Junqueira's position.[27]

"New Legislation on Old Law": Resolution No. 53 of 1846

Getting down to business, on May 14, 1846, the Chamber of Deputies resumed debate on General Assembly Bill No. 14 of 1839. Beginning with Article 2, a second and third discussion saw the latter quickly adopted; therefore, temporarily, deliberation closed on the procedural means by which paternal recognition could legally be conferred.[28] As in the Senate, verbal declarations of recognition failed to gain support, leaving deputies concurring on the four, alternative written declarations: baptismal registries, notarial affidavits, privately executed affidavits, and wills or codicils. Dissenting from the Senate's endorsement, however, the Chamber rewrote the requirement of Article 2—the stipulation that a father's declaration of paternity must include the name of the mother of his illegitimate child. The Chamber made disclosure of the other parent's name genuinely voluntary, by severing it as a precondition for any legal rights. Articles 3, 4, and 5 were approved with similar alacrity on the same day, apparently with little debate. Behind-the-scenes negotiating explained the rapidity of business on May 14, freeing legislators to focus argumentation on how the bill treated inheritance rights in *ab intestato* succession. Those provisions required a third and final discussion for adoption, meaning that the dissenting opinions voiced over the first five articles continued to matter for final approval. That is, the specific procedures for declaring paternity, and the pro's and con's of legitimization by subsequent marriage, would arise anew when debate addressed the articles defining inheritance rights.

Angelo Ferraz, future baron of Uruguayanna, took the lead in defending the status quo. His query, "What need allows . . . our customs should be destroyed?" provoked Antonio Pereira Rebouças to a lengthy oratorical contest.[29] Only too pleased to respond, Rebouças invoked Cambacére's legal opinions on the relevant sections of the French *Code civil* as the means for discrediting Luso-Brazilian legal tradition's generosity toward natural off-spring. Cambacére was a principal author of the French *Code*'s Articles 331–342, treating natural children, as well as Articles 756–766, stipulating their inheritance rights. The French Empire's future arch chancellor had brought his full authority to bear in suppressing investigation of paternity and reducing the inheritance portions of recognized natural offspring in *ab intestato* succession to one-third the size of those disposed for legitimate offspring.[30]

Not to be intimidated, Ferraz retorted that he had in mind "the reason" for Cambacére's *volte face* over the law of 12 *brumaire*, legislation that in 1793 the French jurist had enthusiastically endorsed. His point was that the law of 12 *brumaire*, as part of the so-called transitory legislation of the radical Revolution, had "contradicted all the received customs in French territory over a long period." The *Code civil* originally adopted in 1803 therefore returned the legal position of illegitimate individuals to more or less what it had been during the *ancien régime*. Because French legal tradition reflected "customs" that almost totally excluded illegitimate offspring from *ab intestato* succession, Ferraz gloated, the law of 12 *brumaire* was destroyed—with Cambacére's blessing. Consequently, he concluded, "there is militancy among us against receiving the system of the French Civil Code as law."[31]

The fact that Ferraz had earlier digressed on legitimization by subsequent marriage, arguing it should apply to *sacrílegos* as well as to adulterine offspring, gave Rebouças opportunity to take the high ground. The Bahian bluntly corrected Ferraz on his mistaken assumption that the *Ordenações Filipinas* permitted legitimization by subsequent marriage on behalf of adulterine children. Rebouças delivered the dramatic lesson to the lower house that, despite adoption of Article 1 in 1845, the latter directly conflicted with how the church applied canon law. He more than fulfilled Nabuco's estimation of him, as "a living tradition in the Chamber, where his conversation, attitude, and language attracted the attention of the newly arrived." Rebouças cogently and correctly dissected how Ferraz had confused legitimization by subsequent marriage with "legitimization *por graça e rescrito*," that is, "by the sovereign's grace" and, beginning in 1828, the judiciary's writ that formerly emanated from the Tribunal of the Desembargo do Paço "*per Rescriptum Principis*."[32] Rebouças' persuasiveness proved decisive for Article 1, causing the Chamber to reopen debate over its acceptability.

That many deputies genuinely believed legitimization by subsequent marriage applied to spurious offspring, in contradiction of how the Vatican orthodoxly upheld canon law, testified to the pervasiveness of Mello Freire's radical interpretation—and even more so to Lobão's post-1824 popularization of Book 2 of the *Institutiones juris civilis lusitani*. The controversy dissected by Ferraz and Rebouças seemingly confirmed Joaquim Nabuco's characterization of legal education in Brazil prior to 1850 as "the co-reign of Mello Freire and Merlin."[33]

Angelo Ferraz, the most outspoken proponent of applying legitimization by subsequent marriage to spurious offspring, invoked "in first place, the opinion of Mello Freire." He appealed to "the great weight of his authority" by quoting from his "excellent work" in Latin. He also enlisted Lobão's *Notas à Mello* to stress the "uncertainty" of the Philippine Code on the same point, but argued, correctly, that the Code of 1603 had been obliged to favor ecclesiastical law. In that respect, he correctly pointed to how "the legislation of all Christian nations had received canon law," using that circumstance to argue that in national positive law the doctrine on legitimization by subsequent marriage basically derived from the latter. Thus, he reasoned, "the dispositions adopted by the Council of Trent and the commandments of our Holy Mother Church" sanctioned such legitimization for spurious offspring. Inevitably, he invoked Mello Freire's favorite authority, "the great Dr. Boehmer," to underscore a view widely held by European jurisconsults. Ferraz played down the distinction between natural and spurious offspring by attributing it, correctly, to Roman law, in order to underscore that the introduction of legitimization by subsequent marriage was first permitted by Justinian—whence it was appropriated by the church.[34] In other words, he fell back on Lobão's argument that the secular arm fundamentally possessed the power to define matrimonial impediments.

What this argument failed to note was that the church—pope and Curia—legitimized certain spurious offspring, but always on an ad hoc basis, even when their parents received an ecclesiastical dispensation to marry. The process was analogous to determinations rendered formerly by the Tribunal of the Desembargo do Paço, acting *per Rescriptum Principis* to suspend law in force. As the Brazilian jurist Lafayette Rodrigues Pereira noted in 1869, "Boehmer's ingenious opinion had against it the practical intelligence of canon law, the opinion of the most gifted canonists, and the interpretation of Benedict XIV."[35] Yet in a Luso-Brazilian juridical context, proponents like Ferraz started from the assumption that canon law in the 1840s was not necessarily what the pope and Curia pronounced it to be. As a confirmed regalist, Ferraz assumed that canon law was subject to interpretation within a national context, given the privileges (*regalias*) of the imperial government over the church. In his view, the sacred canons were subject to conciliar consensus and the pope's pronouncements on them far from infallible. Moreover, as the preceding volume noted, throughout the nineteenth century, Brazilian as well as Portuguese jurists disagreed over whether legitimization by subsequent marriage should apply to spurious offspring. It was one thing for a judge to rule in favor of an individual petition, but quite another for the national government to adopt such a law. In the end, the issue came down to the constitutional role of the established church and D. Romualdo's position that canon law prohibited marriage between partners possessing forbidden degrees of incest or engaging in adultery, much less where one had taken a vow of clerical celibacy. Their only remedy, therefore, lay in an episcopal dispensation, given that the church determined the free state to marry. The same authority applied to children born in such unions. If the bishop did not dispense their defect of birth when dispensing their parents' prohibition to marry, then the state could not do so.

On the other hand, Sen. Vergueiro, as the bill's sponsor, had calculated that an ideology of legal nationalism would override the orthodoxy of canon law, gaining adoption for Article 1's endorsement of legitimization by subsequent marriage for canonically incestuous individuals and *sacrílegos*. He gauged his bet correctly until Antonio Pereira Rebouças took the floor in 1846. It was the task of Bahia's deputy to bring his colleagues to an accurate awareness of where Article 1 would lead, if adopted as national law. After persuading them that the church did not apply canon law in the manner Ferraz claimed, Rebouças did not have to articulate the obvious, that Article 1's adoption would inevitably lead to a direct confrontation with the Vatican. His clarification of canon law having penetrated the Chamber's collective consciousness, its members grasped the diplomatic implications. In fact, neither chamber of the legislature was eager to produce a rupture with the Holy See, given that the Brazilian government had mended its relations with Rome only in 1839. Consequently, Rebouças rendered Article 1's interpretation of legitimization by subsequent marriage a dead letter, justifying Nabuco's praise that he was the legislator whose "opinions made him compete with Teixeira de Freitas."[36] In the revised bill the lower house adopted in 1846, Article 1 simply disappeared.

On May 15, the debate between Ferraz and Rebouças moved to inheritance rights, although Ferraz stubbornly tied the latter to the issue of legitimization by subsequent marriage, persuasively appealing to history, custom, and fairness. If *ab intestato* succession rights of illegitimate offspring were left in place, he argued contra Articles 2–4, then legitimization by subsequent marriage would resolve the injustice of excluding spurious offspring from succession. Although he exhibited a genuinely liberal commitment to mitigating the position of "damnable" offspring, Ferraz also insightfully touched on the strategy for adopting the bill, when he alluded to the powerful role that Sen. Vergueiro was playing behind the scenes. By pointing out that a bill of major importance was being deliberated without benefit of a formal legal opinion from the Chamber's Committee on Civil Law, he suggested the bill's proponents, prompted by Vergueiro, wanted no less than to "ramrod" their reforms through the lower house.[37]

Starting on May 15, Ferraz took up the cause of the natural offspring's right to a judicial investigation of paternity, a right resting on Brazil's "ancient custom." Rebouças countered by stressing the need to "rectify ancient custom." His position was interesting, due to the support the bill offered for ascendants as *ab intestato* heirs, meaning those whom law in force had displaced in favor of recognized natural offspring. Article 6, he argued, redressed that situation, for it prevented a natural offspring from "despoiling" his paternal grandparents of their dead son's patrimony, due to proposing those two categories of heirs divide equally the *legítima*. With an eye for courtroom conflicts between grandparents and their non-legitimate grandchildren, Rebouças explained: "This law foresees . . . that the father's recognition in favor of the natural offspring should never have the incompatible power of disinheriting absolutely the legitimate grandparents."[38] In fact, the *Ordenações Filipinas* had followed the preceding Manueline Code (1521) when they privileged recognized natural children over a dead parent's parents, meaning that the practice reached to medieval times. Article 6 addressed a very recent situation, one occasioned by the Resolution of August 11, 1831, that had facilitated the equipping of spurious offspring as testamentary heirs and, secondarily, the natural offspring of noble parents, but only in the absence of grandparents. If parents survived a son who had fathered natural offspring, they could find themselves in court, forced to surrender their son's *legítima* to natural grandchildren who availed themselves of the 1828 Judiciary Act. The latter obtained judicial recognition of paternity, or even legitimization, and asserted preemptive claims over grandparents.

Rebouças' assertions thus took as their starting point the impoverishment of grandparents, as a result of recent legislation—what he construed as "the scandal of the [natural] grandson's enriching himself" as an upstart *ab intestato* heir. Striking a misogynistic note, he impugned the mothers of natural offspring as women manipulated by the greed of their relatives. He was by no means alone in his assertion:

So great is the repugnance of the grandparents to the filiation of the grandchildren [of their deceased son], that the mothers [of the natural child] give in to discord and are surrounded by protectors who, with pharisaical zeal employ every means of opposition [to the grandparents], such that, when the inheritance is not paltry, all she ends up doing is satisfying her protectors . . . there remaining from this repugnant battle of blood and all the family relatives a perpetual enmity between the [natural] children and their parent's parents, between nephews and their uncles and aunts or cousins, and between the uncles and aunts and their nephews and nieces.[39]

Rebouças declined to assert the argument used by Ferraz, that inheritance rights should be equal between recognized natural and legitimate offspring, because both were equal in natural law. Yet he echoed Mello Freire almost word-for-word on the subject of child support: "A natural offspring in succession law should not be equal in everything to a legitimate offspring, not because of our customs, but because the upbringing of the natural offspring is almost never equal to that of the legitimate offspring."[40] That position also relied on Lobão, for both jurisconsults defined paternal responsibilities more modestly vis-à-vis children who were not legitimate. Yet elsewhere both affirmed the paternal succession rights of recognized natural offspring were equal to those of legitimate children. In other words, a new notion of family was implicit in Rebouças' privileging of the rights of legitimate offspring vis-à-vis those who were natural. Souza França articulated that notion more brutally when he pronounced that recognized natural offspring "cannot have rights, except to equity, to favor, and to charity." In defense of inheritance portions one-half the size of those for legitimate offspring, Souza França returned to his 1845 contract argument that acknowledged "the natural offspring is as good as the legitimate, but he has no right to succeed his father." Because his father had "married naturally, not legitimately, as the law of the Empire wants," he insisted, the natural offspring was "born of an illegitimate contract."[41]

França Leite dramatically rebutted those who asserted an inequality between illicit and legitimate birth, on the ground the latter had "different conditions to fulfill in society." Invoking the pedigree of Brazil's young sovereign, he exclaimed, "How wrong they are! Look at the throne and see that it came from natural succession. Our *ordenação* concedes equal rights to both [natural and legitimate offspring]."[42] Presumably, his reference was to the founder of the Bragança line, D. João I, not to D. João VI's paternity of D. Pedro I. Nevertheless, in condemning the bill, França Leite became the most eloquent defender of the values enshrined in legal tradition, drawing on Book 4, Title 92—and implicitly on "marriage according to the *Ordenações*"—what legislators rechristened "natural" marriage in liberal parlance. He grounded the legal status quo on historical practice, but appealed to the social reality that defined many Brazilians at mid-century. Furthermore, he declined to speak of offspring who were incestuous, sacrilegious, or adulterine "because they are not natural offspring":

Among us, our legislation understands that natural marriages cannot be excluded from society; we do not authorize them, but we tolerate them. And while we do not concede to spouses in these marriages full plenitude of rights that those in legitimate marriage enjoy, succession for offspring born in them is still established with plenitude of rights . . . . We do not want to dress up marriage with so many conditions and say outside this there are no rights. There are many considerations in society that often lead a man not to enter legitimate marriage and oblige him to [enter] one that is natural. It is not the legislator who can destroy these considerations; it is custom, it is civilization.[43]

França Leite larded his lengthy defense of "natural" marriage with numerous references to modern contexts, including "Gretna Green" situations where Scottish village blacksmiths posted signs advertising they could marry couples on the spot. In Rome, "in the company of a member of the Curia, D. Dominico Brutti," he had encountered a maternity residence for unwed mothers that "was defended on the ground not of punishing a crime, but of saving their innocence." Brazil's legislation, similarly, should "protect the man who is found in our society"—the natural offspring. He "ought to have the rights that we have."[44]

Theory Yields to Reality: Sociological Considerations

Rebouças largely sidestepped his critics' most powerful argument, that the bill would alter "the large part of succession legislation," meaning a logically coherent legal tradition of complementary precepts in positive law. Manoel de Souza Martins (viscount of Parnaíba) seconded Ferraz on current legislation "staying in place" and pointed to the confusion that an alteration of rights would have on jurisprudential doctrine and the application of law: "What we will do with this law is impose new legislation on old legislation, changing [only] a part of legislation and leaving in force some to which new law will be attached."[45] When backers of the bill failed to address his reservation, he adopted a different tack. On May 18, still debating Article 6, deputies moved to the key issue: the rule halving portions for recognized illegitimate offspring in comparison to what legitimate half-siblings received. Souza Martins pointed to the bill's destructive social impact, insisting that recognized illegitimate offspring be equipped to succeed on a par with legitimate children. To do otherwise, he argued, would invite social disintegration and, he predicted, a scenario of doom that spoke directly to the high proportion of natural offspring in the total population. Denying that the bill "would oblige fathers to contract marriage," he reasoned the contrary. Assuming "the action of succession law to be very slow, constant, and perpetual," he asked what the cumulative effect would be if legitimate offspring monopolized inheritance portions over generations.

Souza Martins' answer directly rebutted the motive the bill's advocates defended, that it favored the stability of the legitimate family: "The monopoly of inheritances will remain among certain families and the larger part of society will be reduced to what today are the proletariats of England," Souza Martins predicted. In an aside, he explained he was referring to "the evil of pauperism that today afflicts the British nation." Then he offered the "research" he had conducted in his province of Minas Gerais for driving home the point: "According to the statistical data I have collected on births in Brazil, one third are natural offspring, while among European nations the proportion of natural offspring to legitimate offspring is in the range of 1 to 8, to 10, to 15, to 17, etc." His percentage of one-third derived "from a report on deaths, births, and marriages in the province—what was officially collated." In what is the earliest documented appeal to the archetype of the "Mineira family," a stand-in for the "Brazilian family," he pronounced Minas far from deviant, being persuaded that "this province is not one of those in Brazil that can be reputed to have more dissolute customs, or where there are fewer marriages [than elsewhere]."[46]

Souza Martins reasoned according to a simple algebraic progression, one spelling social ruin for future generations, given how the proposed law would progressively deprive natural offspring of inheritance rights and leave wealth more concentrated within legitimate families over successive generations. His argument was striking for being a frank acknowledgment that one-third of Brazil's population consisted of natural offspring. Yet what stands out even more starkly among his assertions is the singularly candid connection he drew between illegitimacy and slavery. Souza Martins was responding within the context of the recent parliamentary hesitation over renewal of the commercial treaty with Great Britain, in 1845, when many of his colleagues stubbornly refused to uphold an interdict on the international traffic in slaves. Souza Martins left no doubt that he believed slavery constituted a social malady as well as an injustice, causing him to tie it to the country's high proportion of out-of-wedlock births:

Well, if a third part of our population comes in each generation to be defrauded of one-half of the paternal inheritance shares, what then will be the slow action of this law over a succession of centuries? Above all, because among us natural offspring are much more numerous than in Europe, an inevitable consequence of slavery's establishment among us. [What is] an inevitable result of the two races, when one is the owner of the other—as a thing and not a person—[gets] turned into the easy instrument of satiating the other's passions.[47]

Like Ferraz, Souza Martins recommended the bill not be adopted, "because it does not conform to our legislation." In saying that it "fit badly" within established legal tradition, he provided a prescient warning. Once adopted, the law would necessitate more regulatory laws and become "an interminable source of [legal] disorder, huge doubts, and contradictory rulings on the part of judges of the first instance." Seizing the moment, he proposed that changes such as the half-shares contemplated by Article 6 would be more appropriate for legislators to ponder "when we want to adopt our civil code." Wisely, he observed that the multiplicity of novelties the bill proposed would be better contemplated "when we want to form a new set of laws whose parts harmonize with each other, establishing new rules of succession as much for ascendants as descendants, as much for legitimate as for natural, adulterine, incestuous, and sacrilegious offspring."[48]

Precisely at the moment when Souza Martins articulated his fundamental objection to the bill, Souza França rejoined the debate. Ignoring the overarching issue of abandoning legal tradition, he deftly introduced a pivotal shift in the evolution of discourse. Turning to the old theme of equality, he charged that the *Ordenações Filipinas*, Book 4, Title 92, presented a conflict with the 1824 Constitution, because the *Ordenações* "created two different rights, that is, the succession rights of illegitimate offspring of the nobles and the succession rights of the illegitimate children of the plebes, here called *peões*." Waxing rhetorical, he indicted the outmoded "injustice" of the *Ordenações Filipinas*: "Can we today, after having a liberal Constitution, maintain this law from other times, in which is consecrated the principle of inequality of rights? Ought the natural child of a plebe to have other family rights that are not the same as the illegitimate offspring of the nobles? Surely not!"[49]

Souza França's focus on the inequality of rights carried great appeal. Not only had a titled nobility already made a spectacular "comeback," but the point was also subsequently made that a majority of Brazil's active citizenry, including legislators, was subsumed within a minimal degree of nobility. Either they were gentlemen by birth or they had acquired civil nobility by virtue of Pombaline and Joanine laws. That circumstance created support for Souza França's appeal: "Our legislation ... prescribes that the illegitimate child of a noble or a gentleman [*cavalheiro*] is unable to inherit from his father," he lamented. "But regarding the natural offspring of a plebeian, it orders they inherit from their fathers, even being called to succession with legitimate children." The only thing to do, he urged, "is to adopt a new law in this respect that will end this legislation belonging to other times and customs."[50] Yet the issue was not quite what he proposed.

Turning directly to property, Souza França denied that natural offspring succeeded as coheirs with a father's legitimate children by virtue of natural right: "Succession is completely derived from civil law. A father has an obligation, yes, under natural law, of feeding [his child] always until his physical or intellectual faculties fail him. But he has no obligation to leave him his property." This flat repudiation of positive law and legal tradition derived from the new value that he and others now placed on private property as patrimony: "Property belongs to the family and the family is constituted legitimately; its members have among themselves reciprocal rights of succession that derive from legitimate marriages." Therefore, he concluded, "It is necessary to have a new law that in this respect will put an end to the legislation and customs of past time."[51]

Rebouças seconded Souza França's call for discarding "the ancient legislation and custom" enshrined in the *Ordenações Filipinas*, arguing the latter were "incompatible with the enlightenment of the century." He appealed to national pride for repudiating the inequality of rights enshrined in Book 4, Title 92: "We have been presented with all the crudeness of a new society and we have acquired all the vices of the old countries in decadence."[52] Like other supporters of the bill, Rebouças preferred to emphasize the motive of ending fraud, one he asserted was practiced by presumptive natural offspring who were ersatz. It alone justified withdrawal of rights from natural offspring. By hammering on how decent families were defrauded by bogus heirs, he and other legislators avoided addressing the rights of natural offspring who genuinely were a father's recognized natural children. No one was more cynically aware than Rebouças of the fundamental role that patrimony played in court proceedings:

Since the year 1814, when I studied courtroom law, I have yet to see a court action moved [only] in order for an offspring to have his father determined, or the father [merely] to take his offspring as his own. All of these legal actions are petitions for inheritance, and almost always the children are intending to have as their fathers those who are patrimonially the best endowed, purely in terms of their material fortune.[53]

When the bill passed a second discussion, on May 20, it was referred to the Committee on Civil Justice. On June 17, the final discussion resumed. Dep. Jeronymo Vilella Tavares charged the bill had been altered and objected it had not been printed and distributed in revised form. When Ferraz denied it had been altered, noting only that the committee had "suppressed" part of it, "prejudicing" the articles treating inheritance (Nos. 5 through 11), then he alluded to the fact that a rewriting had begun in earnest.[54] No further debate occurred in 1846, for drastic revision was already under way.

A RESOLUTION BECOMES A LAW (1847)

From Punishing the Libertine to Rewarding Nobreza

Once the Chamber of Deputies convened in 1847, deliberation began immediately on what had become a very different bill. Relabeled Resolution No. 53 of 1846, Vergueiro's bill had metamorphosized. Legislators no longer contemplated a bill proposing new law, but merely a resolution clarifying existing law. Furthermore, the focus had shifted to a narrowly inscribed population: natural offspring. Liberalization of rights still mattered, but Resolution No. 53 focused only on one aspect: the unfair treatment that inheritance law meted out to the natural offspring of a noble parent. It explicitly proposed "extinguishing Book 4 of the *Ordenações*, Title 92, in the part that establishes distinctions between the natural offspring of nobles and commoners in relation to inheritance law."[55] Souza França took the initiative in redefining the bill as a resolution. In maintaining the measure represented a mere clarification of the *Ordenações*, Book 4, Title 92, he called for "equalizing" the succession rights of a natural offspring whose parent was noble with the succession rights of the offspring of commoners. Thus a distinction of estate and a sole class of illegitimate individual, natural offspring, initially absorbed legislators' attention.

On May 8, Rodrigues dos Santos opened a debate that would span six days of heady deliberation, before adoption of an amended resolution on May 17.[56] In a long speech, he supported the resolution, noting the *Ordenações Filipinas* stood in contradiction to Brazil's Constitution, which abolished privileges between citizens unless they followed from public officeholding. However, the country's higher courts had upheld the distinction founded on estate in Book 4, Title 92, in resolving appeals from the lower courts. In short, the resolution was needed to overturn the country's highest courts, because "various judicial decisions that had been forthcoming to the contrary," had led to doubts that had also created numerous scandals." "As a rule," Rodrigues dos Santos objected, "this issue is decided [in the courts] according to the importance of the litigants," that is, by personal influence. "This state of affairs cannot go on," he explained, because natural law did not distinguish the children of the same father according to whether they were born in legitimate marriage or an illicit union. Persuaded to compromise since 1845, he acknowledged, "We have to recognize that we can modify prescriptions in natural law when there are strong reasons for so doing, grounded in social interest."[57] Expounding the social interests that justified the resolution, he dismissed the argument that families headed by a noble parent would be troubled by admitting natural offspring to legitimate succession.

Moving to "a stronger argument" that testified to the political reality of the Second Empire, he noted, "In Brazil a large number of citizens can be considered as noble." His amounted to a majoritarian argument, an appeal to the new consciousness of Brazil's emergent middle classes. Rodrigues dos Santos took as a given that contemporary social divisions reflected a "mass vs. class" dichotomy. Construing the former to be "proletarians" and the latter, "nobles," he made a cardinal observation revealing how legislators defined the country's emerging middle classes, and the basis on which they dichotomized imperial society, at least for the free population:

If almost all the officers in the National Guard, all the diploma holders in the humanities, all the officers in the militias and *ordenanças*, etc., in a word, all the middle class of Brazilian society—or, more to the point, all who are not proletarians—are able to be considered noble, the injustice of this legislation [Book 4, Title 92] can be verified on a much greater scale. . . . I am certain that a large part of the population has an inheritance to leave their children, but finds itself embarrassed by the disposition of legislation in force because, almost everyone being noble, or reputed to be such, their [natural] children cannot succeed *ab intestato* whenever they have legitimate children.[58]

Rodrigues dos Santos pursued a line of reasoning whose logic confirmed that "Brazilians" existed only in the upper social echelons of imperial society, as minimally noble individuals. Receiving applause when he invoked the Constitution's dictum that all citizens enjoyed equal rights before the law, he criticized how law in force made an exception of one class of Brazilians—those whose fathers enjoyed any noble rank. His rhetoric also equated "citizen" closely with the Constitution's "active citizenry"—voters and electors. He quickly got to the point of the resolution: "Of course, we know that in our country the class [*classe*] of natural offspring can be counted in a very high number." Inspired by Souza Martins' statistical data on Minas Gerais, Rodrigues dos Santos doubled the proportion: "Nearly two-thirds of all individuals born can be taken to be natural offspring." Thus the resolution "would extend to the interests of at least one-half of the Brazilians."[59]

The resolution's mastermind, Souza França, pursued the line of reasoning that relied on civil nobility for arguing that succession rights should be extended to vast numbers of Brazilians, the offspring of that "class." When discussion resumed on May 10, he avoided his previous theoretical formulations about natural and civil law, in favor of propounding a working definition of nobility for the Second Empire. It was a definition that today deserves

historians' attention. Far from confining "nobility" to titleholders, Souza
França demonstrated that a Pombaline notion of nobility still penetrated
Brazilian society to the core. If historians deign to speak of the legal
"immunities" attached to *bacharelismo*, or the "prerogatives" accorded to the
imperial officer corps, then they have not fully grasped the nature nor the
extent of minimal nobility in the Second Empire. Souza França left no doubt
that legislators regarded minimal nobility itself to be the operative social
construct, at least where society was congruent with the free population. Improving on Rodrigues de Santos' majoritarian inversion of nobility, Souza
França touched directly on the pervasive nature of nobility's lowest rung,
confirming that Brazil's emerging middle classes were circumscribed within
the protective cocoon of what usually was the minimal civil "nobility of the
law."

When the Philippine Code had been drafted, he explained, "plebeians
constituted the large majority of the Portuguese nation . . . the class of nobles
then was not very numerous at all. Today in our country we see the opposite.
How numerous among us indeed is the class of citizens who have the right to
aspire to the prerogatives of nobility?" In referring to the social reality of
minimal nobility, he could have been paraphrasing Lobão's juridical definition forty years earlier. Now, however, minimal nobility was a concept that
corresponded to Second Empire's active citizenship:

Many are those who have the patents of officers in the National Guard, of officers of
the first line in the army, of the former corps of militias and *ordenanças*; many others
are decorated with some of the ranks of different honorific orders, many have been
awarded academic diplomas, and, finally, many are those who, not exercising a
manual occupation, can bear arms and maintain a horse—which is all the *ordenação*
requires for a man to qualify as a gentleman and, consequently, be noble. Thus perhaps over two-thirds of the active citizenry of our country comes to be considered
noble. Given that all of them are invested with the privilege of excluding their natural offspring from hereditary succession, it is certain that the established exclusion
has been converted into a rule of civil law, as the exception to the *ordenação*.[60]

Opponents of Resolution No. 53 of 1846 defended the *ordenação* of Book
4, Title 92, from several perspectives. Some, like the viscount of Goyanna
(Bernardo Jozé da Gama), countered that the resolution had in its favor only
the "celebrated mania of destroying everything old for the sake of its being
old, and approving everything that is modern for being garish." Although he
drew laughter and approval, Goyanna earlier had argued on behalf of the *ordenação*, in the name of "solid principles of impartiality and morality," adding that the *ordenação* "does not spare nobles the punishment judged appropriate . . . The purpose is to protect marriages and punish vice-ridden celi-

bates [bachelors] with the loss of their [biological] production." A firm conservative who believed in social hierarchy as a positive good, he explained: "The ordinary common person looks up to his superiors in order to imitate them." Not believing "vice-ridden bachelors" merited emulation by "plebeians," but rather "correction" and "punishment," Goyanna complained that they offered "examples of corruption for the people to imitate," when, indeed, marriage should define the universal standard. In his view, fathers of natural offspring, far from being celibate, were libertines refusing to conform to the married state. He dismissed an inequality of rights between legitimate and natural offspring, given their differences: "Inequality here is the greatest justice I know in the disposition of the [*ordenação*]."[61]

More measured objection came from Antonio Jozé da Veiga, a practicing judge since 1824. He seized on the issue of "interests" that proponents of the resolution tied to the "privilege" the *ordenação* bestowed on noble parents—that is, the barring of their natural offspring from succeeding to their *legítima*—in order to favor "the concentration of property."[62] In support of the legal status quo, Veiga found no conflict with the Constitution in what he insisted was a "privilege" favoring the noble class. His view was echoed by João da Silva Carrão, who also opposed the resolution, because he endorsed how the relevant *ordenação* favored "the social superiority of the nobility," by protecting the rights of families with a concentration of property. Believing the *ordenação* deserved to be preserved, he did not construe it as "punishment" or a feature of discrimination (inequality). Rather, it privileged families of noble birth by shielding them from the rules of *ab intestato* succession that applied to society at large, thereby preserving their property for legitimate members.[63]

Moura Magalhães expressed different reservations, in further demonstration of the wide range of opinion in the Chamber. As to the presumption that the *ordenação* exercised the moral function of "impeding concubinage among the nobles," he asked why it had not also done so among plebeians. Granting that "everyone concurs marriage ought very much to be favored, and that a legitimate offspring ought to be paid major consideration over one who is natural," he called on his colleagues to "make legislation uniform for everyone."[64] Diverging from the elitist perspectives of Rodrigues dos Santos and Souza França, Moura Magalhães objected that the *ordenação* of Book 4, Title 92, "established a dividing line between the classes of society." It "conceded extraordinary favor to the legitimate children of the so-called *cavalheiros*," by excluding their "natural brothers" from succession, but did not do so for those whose fathers belonged to "the so-called *peões*." "We ought not to treat of legislating only on behalf of one class of individuals; we

ought to look also to the great mass of citizens, to that part that truly constitutes the people." In order to be fair, he argued, legislators should also exclude the natural offspring of plebeians from succession rights, thereby protecting patrimony for everyone who was legitimate and discouraging concubinage. More to the point, he spoke of the need to revise the *ordenação*
"precisely because of the difficulty among us of having to prove [in court]
what a true gentleman is . . . who has this or that nobility." Echoing Lobão's
earlier complaint about Portugal's courts, and the recent remarks of the viscount of Goyanna, Moura Magalhães alluded to contradictory rulings by
judges whenever they had to determine "where the noble condition exists."
Therefore, he proposed the converse. Law ought to exclude the natural offspring of commoners from *ab intestato* succession, just as it excluded those
of nobles. In fact, Moura Magalhães voted in favor of the resolution, because
he believed that the impressive diffusion of minimal noble rank meant that
nearly all natural offspring were excluded from succession. "Either all should
succeed or none."[65]

A Historic Compromise

On the final day of debate, May 17, 1847, Souza França proclaimed a majority consensus—one obviously achieved off the floor. The Chamber had
"resolved that the offspring of nobles will inherit from their fathers jointly
with the offspring of commoners."[66] He then introduced a well-calculated
amendment that further integrated Vergueiro's key proposal and made legal
recognition follow solely from a father's voluntary act. In calling for a vote
on the amendment, Souza França returned to the theme of fraudulent claims
perpetrated in court by natural offspring. The impact of the amendment
would be far-reaching:

In order for the natural offspring to divide his father's inheritance with that of the legitimate issue, it will be necessary to obtain recognition from him, by means of a
notarized affidavit executed at a time prior to marriage.[67]

The amendment reflected a speech Souza França had made on the second
day of debate, expounding on the marriage contract, when he claimed the
latter presumed rules of *ab intestato* succession in the event that a married
couple died without issue. Husband and wife, by virtue of their contract, understood that a ladder of legitimate succession implicitly defined their respective forced heirs "up to the tenth degree." "Then how can it be admitted
in law," he queried, "that afterward a stranger may come to say, 'I belong to
this family? I want you therefore to give me a share from this inheritance'?"
Plainly, disclosure of the existence of a surprise heir was a development for-

eign to the marriage contract, but such an eventuality altered the legal basis of that contract. For this reason, he argued, a natural offspring could only be assumed to share succession rights with legitimate children when the marriage contract was drawn up in full knowledge of that offspring's existence: "It is necessary for the natural offspring to be recognized by the father at least at a time prior to the marriage contract," in order for him or her "to inherit from the parents." In principle, however, Souza França confessed that he did not believe natural offspring should inherit, except in the absence of necessary heirs. Finding current law "contrary to good custom," he favored altering the resolution, not in favor of the offspring of a noble parent, but to "protect" parents who were plebeian. Their natural offspring, like those of a noble parent, should similarly be barred from sharing a parent's *legítima* with legitimate children.[68]

Souza França proposed a "hard-line" policy confining paternal recognition to a sole procedure, a notarized affidavit. His dismissal of wills as the most commonly employed instrument received careful justification. To that end, he resorted to the specter of the surprise heir who, as a "stranger," was also a bogus heir. Having in mind declarations of paternity that were oral, even if committed to wills, he argued it was necessary to prevent fraud from being perpetrated by "two false witnesses"—individuals who swore on behalf of a will recognizing natural offspring who tried "to inherit from a family to which he does not belong." Souza França's evocation of the ghostly stranger who spelled the ruin of family patrimony occurred at the very close of debate. Given that his amendment further limited execution of a notarial affidavit for paternal recognition, to a time prior to a father's marriage, opportunity to bestow paternal recognition was further restricted. Nor would widowers with legitimate children be able to recognize the natural children they fathered after the death of a wife. Appealing to widespread anxiety over fraud, Souza França assailed "well-known courtroom practice [and] the swindles of ambition that have introduced many strangers into the inheritance arrangements of families." To the figure of the menacing stranger who appeared suddenly as the surprise heir, he added "the arbitrariness of judges regarding the testimony of witnesses"—that is, courtroom practices—and pronounced the reliance current law placed on wills for proving paternal recognition "an evil."[69]

Souza França's amendment proposed one exception to the use of a notarized affidavit for declarations of paternity. Where a father lacked legitimate offspring, a will would be accepted as proof of paternal recognition. This provision was consistent with the Resolution of August 11, 1831, permitting fathers or mothers to use wills to institute any type of illegitimate offspring a successor whenever they lacked legitimate children. In effect, the 1831 law contemplated the natural offspring of a noble parent. However, Souza França proposed a novel twist, that inheritance rights in succession for natural offspring be treated "in all respects like a bequest." He wanted to revise dramatically the Law of August 11, 1831, and to treat such patrimony as a voluntary disposition from the *terça*—to sever it from the *legítima* and *ab intestato* heirship in order to permit collateral heirs again to benefit from *ab intestato* succession. The father could thereby reduce the amount of patrimony disposed in favor of an illegitimate child or impose special conditions on his recognized natural offspring as heir, neither option being permitted under *ab intestato* succession.[70] This final blow struck against established legal tradition failed to attract consensus, but it revealed how far certain legislators were willing to curtail the succession rights of recognized natural offspring.

With Souza França's amendment accepted, the Chamber of Deputies quickly concluded its work, by adopting Resolution No. 53 of 1846 on May 17, 1847. Approved, the measure was sent to the Committee on Redaction, in preparation for forwarding to the Senate. First, however, the Committee profoundly altered the resolution, without further deliberation from the floor, and imposed the final form that became law:[71]

1. The same inheritance rights that the *Ordenações*, Book 4, Title 92, confer on the natural offspring of commoners are extended to the natural offspring of nobles.[72]
2. The father's recognition, made by public notarial affidavit before his marriage, is indispensable in order for any natural offspring to partake of the paternal inheritance, [when], succeeding together with the legitimate offspring of the same father.[73]
3. In other situations [i.e., where no legitimate children exist], the evidence for filiation can only be made by one of the following means: notarized public affidavit or a will.[74]
4. Any dispositions to the contrary are revoked.[75]

Consisting of four succinct articles, three of which were substantive, the resolution demonstrated that Vergueiro's original bill had been stripped bare, except for its keystone of suppressing judicial investigation of paternity.

Upholding Gender "Inequality": The Senate Responds (1847)

Seven weeks later, on August 6, the president of the Senate reported the resolution of the Chamber of Deputies "on the inheritance rights of natural offspring" to the floor.[76] First and second discussions of the resolution defined most of the day's business, each ending with an affirmative vote. Judging from the rapidity with which the resolution was "approved without debate and passed to the second discussion," during the single day of August 6, considerable consultation between both houses must have already occurred.

The *Anais do Senado* do not tell the full story, offering few clues about what had been "backroom" negotiation. Earlier, on May 22, the formation of a new Liberal cabinet, under Manoel Alves Branco, had placed Sen. Nicolao Pereira de Campos Vergueiro in the pivotal position of minister of justice.[77] The text of the Chamber's resolution was not altered in the Senate. This is not to say that senatorial unanimity reigned, but that Vergueiro's influence contributed to a confident majority prior to bringing the bill to the floor.

Article 1, deriving from Souza França's 1846 amendment, offered a new sense of "equality" that became the bill's raison d'être, granting to the children of nobles the same succession rights enjoyed by the children of commoners. Paternal recognition, detailed in Article 2, testified to Vergueiro's original determination that the father's voluntary declaration of paternity, prior to marriage, should be the sole criterion for conferring succession rights on natural offspring, whenever legitimate children existed. Even as widowers, they would be denied opportunity to recognize their natural children as heirs in succession, wherever legitimate children existed. However, Article 2 narrowed what originally had been four procedural options for declaring paternal recognition to a single procedure: notarial affidavit. It incorporated the heart of Souza França's amendment. Fathers would be deprived of the opportunity to institute their natural children as *ab intestato* heirs once they married and had legitimate children. They could use a will for recognizing natural children for succession rights only when they lacked legitimate offspring. The resolution rendered the majority of this enormous population of natural offspring permanently incapable of succeeding— "*filhos insucíveis*" by virtue of procedural rules.

The *Anais do Senado* indicate that Article 1 was "approved without debate" during a second discussion on August 6, signifying a high consensus over removal of the legal barrier denying the natural offspring of a noble parent succession rights. Article 2, however, was a different story. It raised the familiar issue of gender differences in inheritance law that generated most of the day's controversy. Some legislators demanded a change in redaction, insisting that Article 2 apply "equally" to mothers, by requiring them to execute declarations of maternity before a notary. Their objections centered on one word: "*pai*." The marquis of Olinda (Pedro de Araujo Lima), now in the Conservative opposition, complained that redaction was ambiguous, because "*pai*" could mean either "father" or "parent." In fact, as his colleagues reminded him, legal usage supported by the most authoritative jurists had long determined that the word "*pai*" exclusively implied "father." That is, Book 4, Title 92, was understood to regulate only paternal filiation and succession.[78] In insisting the resolution focused exclusively on paternity,

Mello e Mattos intoned the well-known formula that law took maternity to be "obvious" and stuck to his 1839 position: Mothers should not be required to make written declarations of maternity.

The gender issue raised by Olinda was more than a mere quibble over semantics, for it grappled with maternal succession rights, a subject that occupied almost all debate on the final day. Olinda inferred a sexual double standard, in favor of the natural offspring's maternal succession rights. He insisted on clarifying "*pai*," arguing it should mean "parent"—fathers *and* mothers—because, otherwise, law would continue to favor natural offspring with maternal patrimony, while restricting access to paternal patrimony. In claiming, correctly, that natural offspring would, as a matter of course, be called to maternal succession with their legitimate half-siblings, Olinda responded to the circumstance that very few women concealed maternity. Conceding that maternity was obvious, he protested precisely on the same ground: Natural offspring enjoyed automatic succession rights in the maternal line, whereas in the paternal line they depended on a father's voluntary recognition. A natural child born prior to marriage—when fathered by a man with an unmarried woman—retained maternal succession rights by virtue of the mother's public acknowledgment of her pregnancy and personal tie to the child.[79] He objected that Resolution No. 53 did not address this engendered situation, given that it denied paternal succession rights to most natural children.

Olinda and several others decried the gender "disparity" produced by the resolution, insisting that mothers of natural offspring be obliged to execute declarations of maternity before a notary. Their objective, to deny the overwhelming majority of natural offspring *all* succession rights, would only be served by also curtailing matrilineal rights. Olinda even questioned whether legitimization by subsequent marriage should take effect when the natural child's mother had not executed a notarized declaration of maternity prior to marriage. Although he was bluntly informed that husbands did not have to execute such an affidavit in such situations, he stubbornly persisted.[80] Sen. Antonio Luiz Dantas de Barros Leite demurred, alluding to the uncertainty men habitually faced in not knowing if they had fathered their wife's child. As husbands, however, they would not want to be embarrassed by a wife's notarized declaration of maternity whenever, prior to marriage, another man had fathered her natural child. To require a mother to execute a notarized declaration of maternity, consequently, would be "an immorality":

Our legislation treats only paternal filiation, and not maternal. And what reason would there be for it to do so? Our jurisconsults say that motherhood is always certain, that it is sufficient she baptize the child and raise it as her own. These are the precepts for proving maternal filiation. This cannot be so with respect to a father, and the present law disposes on behalf of his [case].[81]

Other senators rebuffed Olinda's demand for notarized declarations of maternity, by invoking the need to protect a woman's honor. Manoel dos Santos Martins Vellasques reminded the assemblage of the unwritten etiquette of decorum applying to women from "good" families: "A gentlewoman who has a natural child, and prior to marriage, goes to execute recognition by means of a notarized affidavit, exposes herself to public censure, and the man who would have desired to marry her should, naturally, refuse the marriage for the same reason." Of course, he and the majority of senators wanted just as much to shield the honor of not only her suitor or husband but also her father and brothers. They could not have it both ways: Either everyone of "good family" would be insulated from scandal or women would declare maternity openly before a public notary. The latter outcome insured that embarrassment and censure would become the price "respectable families" paid for legal gender equality. In Mello e Mattos' words, "What kind of man would think of marrying a woman who had declared, prior to [his marrying her], that she had an illegitimate child?"[82]

Brazil's outstanding jurisprudential authority, Perdigão Malheiro, later concurred with Olinda that the resolution was flawed, for leaving natural offspring equal to their legitimate half-siblings vis-à-vis the maternal *legítima*. Legislators indeed faced a conundrum inherent in legal precepts that were engendered. They chose the higher value of gender inequality rather than violate the social etiquette of family honor, fueling later objections that natural children should not be called to maternal succession "when those of her husband cannot," merely to "avoid scandal" or "protect marriage."[83]

Finally, Bernardo de Vasconcellos became disgusted with the petty bickering over whether women should make written declaration of maternity and chided his colleagues, protesting he was afraid to join in the discussion "when I remember in what century we are living." Now an ally of the Conservative Party, he had not disavowed all tenets of liberalism. With greatly exaggerated effect, Vasconcellos reminded his colleagues of the law adopted in 1831, prohibiting the granting of titles of nobility. He argued it rendered Article 1 of the bill unnecessary—irrelevant—because, "It had already been declared there are no more nobles in the Empire." Then he took deadly aim at Article 2 for not admitting natural children to succession unless a father executed a notarial declaration of paternity prior to marriage. Referring to what was the unacceptable solution of eliminating Article 2 altogether, he said that otherwise he would vote "no."[84]

CALLING THE VOTE

"Placing Conscience in Conflict with Interest"

A lifelong bachelor, Vasconcellos refocused the issue on the injustice of denying inheritance rights to natural offspring whose fathers failed to execute recognition within the strict confines of Article 2. He succinctly captured the overarching moral dilemma that would follow from adoption of the resolution:

A father who has natural children and who will be interested in getting married can sacrifice his affections, his natural obligations; he can compromise with his own conscience by not recognizing those children in order not to lose out in marriage. It is an article that places conscience in conflict with interest, and it seems to me that the law ought not to promote such conflicts. To treat in a law, to modify law, when it is connected to so many other ends, without looking to place in harmony the alterations that have to be made in all the other dispositions with which that law has affinity, is dangerous. . . . I deem it preferable to eliminate the article.[85]

Article 3, following from Souza França's 1846 amendment, permitted wills to be used for declaring paternity in order to confer succession rights, but only where legitimate offspring did not exist. Earlier, legislators criticized the bill for focusing exclusively on inheritance rights, to the neglect of "honors" and child support. As adopted, however, Article 3 failed to permit either. Criticism leveled by Sen. Vellasques against Article 3 struck at the drastically restricted means for bestowing paternal recognition. Having in mind the ease with which a father could repudiate a natural child, even when he had publicly recognized the offspring by raising the child in his own household, Vellasques lamented, "This has happened many times." He pleaded to revive debate on judicial investigation of paternity on behalf of natural children whose fathers denied child support. Why should not the child have ways of obligating the father to recognize him for child support, while he was alive, if the father would not do so voluntarily?[86] Mello e Mattos' terse and callous reply to Vellasques captured perfectly the cynical mood of the Senate's prevailing majority: "What this law purports is that no one would be obligated to be a father. Against this spirit of the law you want to impose procedures for obligating [fathers to recognize natural offspring]? You want to enact the opposite logic? It cannot be."[87]

Mello e Mattos' pronouncement was the last word recorded in the *Anais do Senado* on the merits of Res. No. 53 of 1846. With this apt closing, Article 3 was put to a vote on August 16. The Senate approved the resolution in a third discussion without debate, and the verbatim text of the resolution, as it had come from the Chamber of Deputies, stood. On August 19, the Senate remanded the resolution to the emperor for his signature.[88] On September 2, the imperial sanction rendered it Law No. 463 of 1847. Fittingly, Sen. Nicolao Vergueiro co-signed the law, in his capacity as minister of justice.[89] A sole change struck out "resolution" and substituted "law," in anticipation of what Perdigão Malheiro authoritatively confirmed: The legislation "was not simply clarifying the *Ordenações*, Book 4, Title 92." Article 1 introduced new doctrine and Articles 2 and 3 derived from modifications of the French Civil Code (Articles 334 and 337). *Ipso facto*, it had been a bill that introduced new law.[90]

New Law for a New Family

As Law No. 463 of September 2, 1847, the final version of Sen. Vergueiro's bill stood almost unaltered for seventy years. Yet what amounted to a drastic revision of the *Ordenações*, Book 4, Title 92, would not go unremarked or uncontested. The law remained highly controversial—a circumstance confirmed a decade later when Perdigão Malheiro published his useful "Commentary on Law No. 463 of 1847, Regarding Succession of Natural Offspring and Their Filiation (1857)." First published as newspaper articles in the early 1850s, the treatise was written in the didactic but accessible format of a series of questions expressing the myriad of legal quandaries that Souza Martins had predicted the law would engender. When clear answers were impossible, Perdigão provided inferences. He ended with a list of the law's "defects," appending final suggestions for correctives that future legislation should address.

Although no roll call vote had been recorded, the attention the *Anais do Senado* paid to dissenting opinions in the final debate suggested that the bill was adopted by a narrow margin, rather than by an overwhelming majority. Liberals, whose political party demonstrated what one historian has construed as "an ideological schizophrenia," divided over the bill. In Roderick Barman's apt view, one partisan current interpreted "liberty, security, property, and resistance to oppression as committing it to the defense of vested rights and established interests." The opposing current embraced "radical social and political changes such as land reform, abolition of slavery, and the elimination of privilege," seeking to impose France or Great Britain as the relevant model.[91] Bernardo de Vasconcellos, the most outspoken opponent of the bill in the upper house, had raised no objection until 1847. Now a Conservative, he repudiated the reconstituted bill in August 1847, preferring the status quo. "Liberty," in his view, could not be reconciled with Article 2, which rewarded concealment of paternity and barred its judicial investigation. A minority of Liberals shared his reservation. Vergueiro took no formal part in the final Senate debate due to his identity as minister of justice. In the end, the comprehensive bill he authored and the appeal to the French Civil Code he advocated were reduced to the single article suppressing judicial investigation of paternity by virtue of voluntary paternal recognition.

Mello e Mattos' triumphant pronouncement, "What this law has in mind is that no one would be obligated to be a father," resounded in the ears of legislators, jurists, lawyers, and law professors into the twentieth century. His words, however, echoed more as reproach than triumphant boast. Over time, the impunity with which fathers could evade responsibility for their natural offspring received significant condemnation. Yet until the arrival of a republic in 1889, legislators stood firm, declining to reopen the Pandora's box of judicial investigation of paternity. On the other hand, no sooner was Law No. 463 adopted than problems arose about its interpretation and application. Vasconcellos' point on the matter of *"pai,"* that passage of the bill would make the issue of maternal recognition moot, did not go away. Within months, a ministerial interpretation, the *Provisão* of February 23, 1848, offered the first, logical response to the new law. It reiterated what Olinda had feared: Natural offspring would continue to share a maternal *legítima* with their mother's legitimate offspring, independently of any notarial affidavit executed by her. In the words of the minister of the treasury, "The baptismal certification ought to produce the equipping [for maternal succession and] . . . exemption from the *décima*," the tax levied on heirs who were not *ab intestato*.[92]

Confusion persisted. Five years later, the minister of justice issued an interpretive advisement on a point of existing law, known as an *aviso*, that reiterated the ancient assumption that neither evidence of recognition nor documentary declarations would be required to guarantee matrilineal *ab intestato* rights for natural offspring, wherever maternity was common knowledge.[93] The reputations of respectable women would continue to be shielded by law, relieving mothers of making public notarial declarations of maternity for the remainder of the Second Empire.

Suppression of judicial investigation of paternity, including whenever *rapto* led to criminal prosecution of the male abductor, accomplished legislators' tacit goal of imposing total silence in the courtroom. Neither the father's nor the more vexing identity of the mother, as respectable wife, sister, or daughter, would be raised in court. The heir who was either fraudulent or a genuine natural offspring similarly was silenced by suppressing judicial determinations of paternity. Solemn legitimization continued on the books, largely a dead letter. Layfayette Rodrigues Pereira noted that prior to 1847 such judicial legitimization almost always had been dedicated to obtaining patrimony. "Today, *perfilhação solemne* is perfectly useless," he pronounced. "For the offspring to acquire all the effects that it can produce (except honors), the father's simple recognition is enough." The benefits derived from judicial legitimization for natural offspring were reduced to only what Law No. 463 of 1847 withheld: "the right to enjoy the honors and privileges of legitimate offspring" that derived from the parent's noble rank. A very select group of parents, usually noble by descent, availed themselves of solemn legitimization after 1847, in order to permit their natural children to share their honors. As we have seen, judicial legitimization had formerly equipped the natural offspring of noble parents to be candidates for the Military Academy at Realengo, given that the 1757 Law of the Cadets remained in force. After 1847, a military career continued to offer the most salient reason for a minimally noble father to legitimize his natural son before a judge of the first instance, given that the Law of Cadets remained in force into the 1890s. Natural offspring legitimized "*por rescrito*" prior to 1847 had also received *ab intestato* succession rights and been equipped to divide a noble father's *legítima* equally with their legitimate half-siblings.[94] After 1847, solemn legitimization conferred only honors on them.

Law No. 463 of 1847 was complementary to the Resolution of August 11, 1831, because Article 2, imposing mandatory notarial affidavits as the means for recognizing natural offspring for inheritance purposes, applied only when legitimate children existed. Otherwise, Article 3 stipulated that wills could be used as an alternative to notarized affidavits for conveying recognition on natural offspring, or for equipping them with succession rights "in other situations," meaning when there were no legitimate children. In this regard, Article 3 reiterated the Law of August 11, 1831; the latter also continued in force, applicable to spurious offspring whenever legitimate children did not exist. The latter option continued to render solemn legitimization an artifact, however. On the other hand, natural offspring recognized prior to marriage in notarial affidavits remained tantamount to necessary heirs. So recognized, they preempted the succession rights of spurious offspring who otherwise a parent was still free to institute as a testamentary successor under the Law of August 11.[95]

THE NEW PATRIMONY

The law of September 2, 1847, stood as the most important revision of Brazil's inheritance system between 1822 and 1907, when the ladder of intestate succession was fundamentally altered. Long after the Liberal Party's majority of the 1840s was forgotten, Law No. 463 of 1847 continued to matter and to generate important controversy. Legislators imposed a law inspired by a provision of the French Civil Code, one alien to Luso-Brazilian legal tradition, arguing from the moral high ground that privileged the legitimate family and, conversely, condemned natural marriage as concubinage. They reacted to the embarrassment inflicted on legally constituted families by public revelation of a husband's concubine or paramour in court, or the even greater scandal produced when a respectable woman, sometimes a wife, had to testify in court about children she had borne outside legal wedlock. Yet the brunt of the protracted debate that produced Law No. 463 of 1847 fell implicitly on patrimonial issues rather than on "scandal in the courtroom," given that rising litigation explicitly treated inheritance rights. In Perdigão Malheiro's estimation, the law was adopted "not to privilege legitimate birth or marriage but to avoid surprises" among the respectable families synonymous with the Empire's active citizenry.[96]

If the courtroom of the Regency Era had been transformed into a menacing public space, then legislators viewed the latter as a stage for fraudulent behavior and the rules of evidence as extremely susceptible to common chicanery. Reading between the lines of parliamentary debate leads to the inescapable conclusion that the nature of evidence, and its manipulation, acquired important new significance after 1828. Notwithstanding assertions of legislators like Rodrigues dos Santos, personal reputation and influence no longer operated as strongly to persuade judges in making legal determinations. As accessibility to the courtroom became "democratized" by liberal reform, judges no longer faced a largely elite population of litigants drawn from the *homens bons*—the good men of property. Instead of individuals who were their peers, and those they often knew face-to-face, plaintiff and defendant might be strangers drawn from social groups that before 1828 had appeared infrequently in court. Even the amount of their property might be insufficient to stamp them as individuals deserving social deference as the "better sort." Alternatively, where the parties possessed worthy reputations and were known to the judge, then their litigation posed dilemmas that judges of the first instance were obliged to resolve locally and publicly.

Legitimization proceedings conferring rights in testamentary or *ab intestato* succession, not to mention petitions for determining paternity, placed local judges in difficult positions. They might have to find publicly against one party when neither was personally known to them. If, on the other hand, both parties enjoyed equal status of membership in a "good family," and belonged to the judge's social network, then he was bound to antagonize one of them. By emphasizing evidence, including the identify of a natural child's mother, judges found a means for resolving their own very public predicament in court proceedings. Evidence, as opposed to personal reputation, acquired greater importance in court. Testimony on the identity of an illegitimate child's mother, if not her immediate presence in the courtroom, consequently relegated the etiquette of silence to the colonial past. The chorus of complaints legislators expressed over the misuse or admission of evidence in court must also be appreciated in light of legal proceedings that now had become local and very public. Legislators' denunciations of every sort of deception admissible in court, consequently, deserve to be read as part of a general dissatisfaction over judges' greater reliance on direct evidence.

On the other hand, the disdain legislators voiced toward charlatans bent on posing as genuine heirs, in order to steal a family's patrimony, must be set against their own acknowledgments that the "stranger" was indeed a father's biological child. Resentment expressed over grandparents forced to cede rights to natural grandchildren also implied that many such strangers were genuine, not bogus, heirs. The challenge to the legitimate family did not fundamentally rest on the false identity of the surprise heir but on the genuineness of the claim he or she exerted.

Where natural children were not openly recognized, their existence was often tacitly registered in the consciousness of the father's legitimate family. The "surprises" noted by Perdigão Malheiro then pertained not to real discoveries, but to the reaction of legitimate offspring when they learned their natural half-siblings expected to be called as co-heirs to succession. Rugendas, in the 1820s, had best captured customary understandings that no longer could be taken for granted, when he described the arrangements made for the consensual "wives" of propertied young white men in Recife, whose parents later arranged their sons' legitimate marriages. The women of color who were set aside and given a dowry were expected to know their place.[97] Their natural children, it was tacitly agreed, were not to be called to succession, although a bequest from the father's *terça* might be the price of silence. By 1847, however, natural offspring enjoyed unprecedented juridical opportunity to demand paternal patrimony in court. Furthermore, they posed a challenge to the legitimate family at a point when the nature of property was changing.

The anecdotes about switching babies in the cradle, of the wife who brought her natural child to live under her husband's roof, threatening the patrimony of their legitimate children—or the grandparents turned out in old age by a natural offspring—registered genuine alarm. More typically, however, those anecdotes indicated that the surprise heir who stepped forward to claim patrimony was a genuine co-heir. The "surprise" arising from such "strangers" turned as much on their assertion of a legal demand for rights in patrimony as on a sudden disclosure of consanguine identity. That is, legitimate offspring frequently knew of the existence of their father's natural offspring. Even in the absence of solid information, they often possessed disturbing intimations. Now propertied groups confronted a surprise heir who increasingly obliged them to divide family patrimony among more heirs. Demographic and judicial change, rather than the scenario of fraud and deception recounted on the floor of Parliament, provided the major impetus for a momentous redefinition of Brazil's inheritance system.

By 1846, legislators refocused the original Bill BU of 1836, reducing it from a comprehensive effort to address illegitimacy to a narrow, collective expression of anxiety centered on threats to the legitimate family's patrimony. The figure of the fraudulent heir therefore bore the brunt of a collective threat to patrimony by virtue of an unacknowledged awareness that neither law in force nor lawyers nor judges could adequately contain the rising courtroom challenge to family assets. Moreover, marriage now appeared as a phase of the life cycle that threatened patrimony as much as death. Parents did not know if a prospective son-in-law would introduce concealed natural children into their daughter's household, once the marriage occurred, and deprive their legitimate grandchildren of maternal patrimony. The "new marriage bargain," highlighted in Muriel Nazzari's study of the dowry, was a fact of urban life by the 1840s. It presumed the novel arrangement that expected a husband to be the "good provider" for his wife, as well as to assume primary or sole financial responsibility for the couple's children.[98] In a context of "disappearing dowries," the assumption of the *Ordenações Filipinas*, that both parents' property would sustain the couple's family, had become an anachronism. Wives no longer were expected to provide property to support their children, and dowries became commensurably smaller. Natural heirs thus posed a greater threat to a husband's patrimony than formerly. The legitimate family came to depend more on the father's liquid income and less fundamentally on family wealth in land—what historically had defined the basis of both dowry and dower. A steady flow of income provided by the household head now mattered urgently to the legitimate family. Wives and widows, together with legitimate children and maternal grandparents, more readily perceived natural offspring as interlopers threatening to despoil them of collective patrimony.

The focus of Law No. 463 of 1847 amounted to a leveling of estates that removed the ancient legal privilege protecting the patrimony of families either noble by descent or by the law from the claims of a father's illegitimate offspring. However, the same law placed complete discretion as to whether natural offspring should be recognized for succession rights solely in the father's hands. Reform of succession law in 1847, consequently, deserves interpretation as self-serving of legislators' social interests, starting with their immediate families. As members of the Empire's politico-social elite, they raised an important point. Why should their natural offspring not be their heirs, when nobility offered ephemeral reward? For those with titles, nobility was further debased by no longer being heritable.

On the other hand, Law No. 463 of 1847 did not open the floodgate to larger numbers of natural offspring equipped for *ab intestato* succession. A father's voluntary recognition confined those equipped to succeed to a small proportion, reserving substantially greater family patrimony for the legitimate heirs. When Sen. Vergueiro argued that "marriage should be promoted as much as possible and its results [legitimate offspring] regarded with greater honor and esteem than the results of customary unions," he and Souza França had in mind conservation of family patrimony on behalf of a smaller number of heirs: legitimate children. Even in 1836, by tying reform of succession law vis-à-vis illegitimate individuals to a more inclusive interpretation of legitimization by subsequent marriage, Vergueiro anticipated that henceforth an infinitesimal minority of spurious offspring would benefit.

Adoption of Law No. 463 of September 2, 1847, occurred when the nature of family wealth was shifting from a landed base to the more liquid income of urban pursuits in commerce, the professions, and the imperial bureaucracy. Souza Martins explicitly noted this circumstance when he contradicted Vergueiro's contention that a wife's dowral wealth exceeded her husband's inherited and accumulated wealth. "As a rule, he contended, wives receiving a dowry are not as well equipped to augment [their wealth] as are men. The latter have employment in the lucrative professions; they earn their fortunes with greater facility than wives."[99] Ergo, husbands, rather than wives, could better afford to make their natural children their *ab intestato* successors. By rewriting the succession rights of natural offspring to depend exclusively on the principle of paternal recognition, sworn before a notary prior to marriage, the bill's backers made it impossible for almost all natural offspring who had legitimate half-siblings to be equipped as heirs in paternal succession. New law thus rendered the *quaesito*—the surprise heir's juridical alter ego—an irrevocably disinherited figure. Now permanently incapable of succeeding—legally, a *"filho natural insucessível"*—the *quaesito* was transformed into the irreversibly tragic figure of the Second Empire's novels.

In reforming the inheritance system along more exclusive lines in 1847, Brazil's national politicians employed law in order to circumscribe the legitimate family, setting it apart juridically from the polygamous society in

which it was constituted. They vested fathers with a greater patriarchal prerogative over illegitimate offspring, one denying the latter juridical personal-
ity by refusing recognition. There was irony in this change, for the revolt of
legitimate sons and daughters against patriarchy was well under way.[100] Legislators' political response turned on reaction, for the suppression of judicial
investigation of paternity occurred precisely at the moment when *pátrio poder* had begun to erode. Protracted argumentation over the finer points of
what one imperial deputy mocked as "the trivial matter [*negociozinho*] of
rapto" extended to collective laughter when the Chamber of Deputies turned
to the subject of "*fujonas*"—daughters fleeing the paternal home with "ab-
ductors" who were, in fact, preferred mates. The jokes amounted to a nerv-
ous admission that children were defecting from patriarchal control in increasing numbers.[101]

Profound modification of the rules of heirship for Brazil's enormous
population born outside legal wedlock followed directly from the changing
nature of property and marriage in 1847. The emergence of a bourgeois family ethic in the Second Empire demanded greater recognition of the indispensability of legitimate matrimony. Law No. 463 of 1847 effectively sealed
legislative debate on the subject of paternal recognition for the rest of the
century. The discourse that had opposed its adoption, however, was not silenced. Dual concerns over the changing nature of heritable property and the
ethical definition of paternal responsibility survived into the twentieth century. They troubled individual conscience and called into question the wisdom of importing alien law that broke with Luso-Brazilian legal tradition's
reliance on custom. Rekindled in the early twentieth century, the dissonance
over judicial investigation of paternity, the French formula of smaller inheritance portions for recognized offspring, and the "damnable" birth of
adulterine individuals would be all revisited in the debates addressing Brazil's
long-postponed project of adopting a civil code.

Conclusion

A Brazilian Legal Tradition

———•◆•———

> If you have natural offspring and wish to escape paternal obliga-
> tion, then marry a woman to whom you do not confess that error.
> That is what the law says.
>
> Bernardo de Vasconcellos on the Law of September 2, 1847,
paraphrased in Direito (1889)[1]

Reform of succession law accompanied Brazil's transition from colony to independent nation and implied more than merely cutting political ties to
Portugal. During the first three decades of independence, Brazil's political
elite recast the rules of heirship in important respects where they applied to
individuals born outside wedlock. In directly changing the mechanisms by
which property could be transferred intergenerationally within a system of
forced heirship, legislators relied largely on altering the procedures by which
recognition of paternity could be legally declared. Changes adopted between
1828 and 1847 deserve appraisal in terms of both the repudiation of the colonial society of estates and the eighteenth century's absolutist state. They testified to the liberal values of Brazilian reformers who sought to revise positive law received from Portugal, in order to bring it into conformity with the
1824 Constitution's commitment to equality before the law for "all" citizens.
By the middle of the nineteenth century, the emergence of a new pattern of
family organization, modeled on the conjugal couple of the bourgeois family, persuaded a Liberal-dominated legislature to draw a firm line between
what they privileged as the legitimate family and what opponents defended as
a parallel, "natural" family based on customary *mancebia*, or "*amasia*."

In the same year that Brazilians expelled their first emperor and his "Portuguese faction"—1831—legislators took several important steps to break with
the Portuguese legal heritage so fundamental to the operation of rules of heirship in colonial Brazil. For this reason, the commonplace that Portugal's early
modern law code, the *Ordenações Filipinas* of 1603, remained in force
throughout the nineteenth century—despite the 1824 Constitution's call to

adopt a national civil code—can be taken as accurate only to a point. What is less recognized and deserves greater appreciation by political and social historians alike is the piecemeal fashion by which Brazil's lawmakers immediately began to modify the Philippine Code, rendering some of its most fundamental provisions null within a decade of independence. Inheritance law is an instructive case in point. Succession rules fell under legislative scrutiny in the First Empire and the Regency, because liberal values clashed with those of the society of estates. The task of bringing the *Ordenações Filipinas* into line with the political and economic realities of the eighteenth century had been undertaken by Pombaline jurists. Brazilian liberals, however, fulfilled the latter's incompletely attained reforms by adapting the inheritance system to their own modern era. They accepted axiomatically that a Luso-Brazilian system of inheritance rested fundamentally on *ab intestato* succession rules ordaining a partitive inheritance distribution of "equal shares for all," regardless of gender, birth order, or affiliation of estate. Those rules, they understood, pertained to arrangements in civil law. However, the partitive division on which they rested derived basically from "the General Law"—the law of nature.

Those who defended the right of paternally recognized natural offspring to be called to succession on an equal basis with a father's legitimate offspring argued on behalf of the natural equality existing between children of illicit and legitimate birth. Civil law, they insisted, merely validated what natural law had established. Although succession law was firmly anchored in natural law under Pombal, thanks in large part to the reinterpretation by royal jurisconsult Paschoal José de Mello Freire, Brazilian liberals also thought in terms of written constitutions. Their own, by incorporating the principle of "equality before the law," contradicted an eighteenth-century legal heritage of privilege, monopoly, and exemption, resting on legal distinctions of estate—and birth. Therefore, reformers demanded that rules of heirship in the new nation uniformly insure "equal shares for all." In consonance with a partitive system of heirship, they opposed entailed wealth. After an eight-year struggle, they abolished family entails in 1835 and then, in 1837, narrowly circumscribed ecclesiastical entails to serve largely charitable ends. In confronting how individual quality of birth determined rights in inheritance, radical liberals also attempted to abolish or diminish the exclusionary rules that rested on damnable and punishable birth.

Taking note of legal bastardy's derivation from canon law, liberal reformers sought to bring the rules of heirship into conformity with enlightenment values that opposed punishing offspring for the "crimes" of their parents. Rescinding the "punishable" quality of spurious birth in positive law was just a first step for more emboldened reformers, some of whom also questioned whether, or to what extent, national positive law should construe spurious birth as "damnable," given that it derived from canon law. Reformers made solemn legitimization more readily available through the lower courts by means of the 1828 Judiciary Act, and then they adopted the Resolution of August 11, 1831, placing the opportunity to institute spurious offspring as testamentary successors in the hands of their parents—at least when there were no legitimate offspring. The "Law of August 11" also privileged the noble parent of a natural offspring in the same situation. An even more determined core of radical liberals attempted to remove the stain of bastardy altogether, in direct contravention of how canon law was received in positive national law. They embraced the controversial argument articulated by Mello Freire during the 1780s and 1790s, one popularly disseminated by a dissenting Manoel de Almeida e Souza de Lobão in the 1820s, that legitimization by subsequent marriage applied to spurious children as well as to those of illicit birth.

In 1830, Dep. Jozé Lino Coutinho's now forgotten, iconoclastic bill was debated in the Chamber of Deputies, testifying to the substantial support for extending paternal recognition to spurious children who were not adulterine. The following year, a bill authored by the Ecclesiastical Committee of the Chamber of Deputies mitigated the stain of bastardy by redefining the canonical impediments to matrimony as minimally civil impediments. Adopted by the Chamber, the bill ran afoul of the national controversy over suspending the vow of clerical celibacy and died in the Senate. Far from being a "crackpot" idea, the proposal that priests should be free to marry—or at least to live in *mancebia* without reprisals from the spiritual or the temporal arm—received substantial support within both ecclesiastical and political hierarchies, and, above all, enjoyed a popular consensus. Yet polarization over the issue of "forced celibacy," once a bill was introduced to suspend it, in 1827, undercut support for civil marriage as well as diluted support for civil matrimonial impediments that would have redefined the position of spuriously illegitimate individuals in inheritance law. The established church proved an indomitable foe of liberal reform of family and inheritance law due to how the latter defied canon law.

Under Sen. Vergueiro's sponsorship in 1836, a final, very different bill would have obliterated the pivotal distinction between natural and spurious offspring that determined differential rights in positive law. By treating most individuals born out-of-wedlock as simply "illegitimate," and permitting paternal recognition to apply generically to all except adulterine individuals, this bill anticipated procedural reforms making bastardy eminently more reversible in positive law. While embracing the interpretations of Mello Freire, derived from the Protestant jurist G. L. Boehmer, Vergueiro's Bill BU of 1836 proved Janus-headed. It offered the possibility for conservative reaction on the position of natural offspring in succession law, even as it proposed changes that contraverted the canon law adopted at the Council of Trent.

Natural offspring who enjoyed paternal recognition had long been free of the imputation of bastardy in Luso-Brazilian legal tradition. They enjoyed opportunity for social acceptance on a par with legitimate offspring, because law differentiated and privileged them from those stigmatized by the defect of spurious birth, individuals who were canonically incestuous and adulterine or deemed *sacrílegos*. On the other hand, even natural offspring who were paternally unrecognized, as *quaesitos*, still benefited from how positive law left them maternally natural offspring—equipped to succeed in the maternal line. By altering the procedural rules in 1847, legislators profoundly changed ancient rules of heirship in favor of a new norm of family organization. Bastardy, historically a mutable quality of birth, became much less susceptible to reversal.

Simultaneous with reforming the inheritance system, liberal legislators of the 1820s and 1830s attacked "aristocratic privilege" as a common target, given the perception that distinctions of estate belonged to the Portuguese colonial regime. Yet the colonial past offered precedents that reached to Pombal's era, demonstrating how noble privilege could be curbed and diluted, if not eliminated altogether. Although Brazil's national charter mandated equality before the law for all who were citizens, it also conceded arbitrary power to the sovereign to bestow noble titles and honors. Liberals succeeded in tempering the enthusiasm of Emperor D. Pedro I for a hereditary nobility, by pressuring him to bestow noble titles only for the holder's lifetime. Having weakened the force of aristocratic privilege in the newly independent polity, they then prohibited any granting of noble titles between 1831 and 1840.

Although noble titles ceased to be heritable, natural nobility—nobility by descent—as well as the civil nobility so widely diffused during the reigns of D. José I, D. Maria I, and D. João VI, was so extensively enjoyed as to be congruent with Brazil's active citizenry. Yet inheritance rules still excluded the natural child of a noble parent from rights in heirship while calling the natural child of a commoner parent to *ab intestato* succession. Minimal nobility therefore inscribed virtually all national legislators, accounting for why so many of them objected to the exclusion of natural offspring from paternal or maternal inheritance rights. Thus a steady diffusion of civil nobility before and after 1822 produced a reaction to what were colonial rules of heirship. Alternatively, those whose nobility rested directly on titleholding or honorific orders appreciated that historically the value of nobility had been degraded. Their titles could not be transmitted from parent to legitimate off-spring. The contradiction between the diminished value of such titles and the rigidity of rules of heirship that inscribed their bearers presented the latter, as well as their minimally noble counterparts, with a serious patrimonial dilemma.

That a society of estates continued to prescribe legal privilege in Brazil prefigured the liberal reform impetus that challenged the position natural offspring occupied in Luso-Brazilian legal tradition. On the other hand, deeply rooted values appropriate to multiple forms of family organization, and deriving from widely shared historical experience, underlay the peculiar situation those natural offspring enjoyed. In 1847, a critical majority of reformers, led by the Liberal Party, decided to set aside the historical and customary underpinnings that explained rules of heirship derived from the *Ordenações Filipinas*. In their zeal to eliminate distinctions of estate, to correct evidentiary abuses in juridical determinations of paternity, and, above all, to insulate and protect the bourgeois family's interest in property, many legislators who formerly favored liberalizing rights turned to a foreign legal tradition as the means to restrict those rights. Thus the frontal attack liberals mounted on the society of estates in the 1820s eventually became transformed into a reaction that rigidly fixed inequality of inheritance rights in law, redefining bastardy as a more inclusive legal condition. Erstwhile reformers set aside what their opponents upheld as the wisdom of "our customs," as well as the legal nationalism that had served as the foundation for validating the latter in national positive law. What amounted to a widely diffused social consensus on multiple patterns of family organization, openly tolerant of all categories of illegitimate birth, irrevocably broke down. Political power exercised by the national legislature rendered legally irrelevant patterns of social organization that historically had admitted the co-existence of legitimate and natural families, or even the inclusion of individuals whose spurious birth was redeemed by solemn legitimization, in an intermingling of patrimonial rights, family names, and intra-familial matrimonial pacts.

It is important to appreciate the legal watershed defined by Law No. 463 of 1847. Not only was it the nineteenth century's most important piece of legislation pertaining to the inheritance rights of illegitimate individuals—and, indeed, for Brazil's system of *ab intestato* succession—but it also stood as a reaction to earlier efforts to liberalize the legal position of illegitimate individuals. Judicial determination of paternity had defined the bedrock of Luso-Brazilian legal tradition that privileged the position of natural offspring in succession, starkly differentiating it from Roman law. Law generously accorded natural offspring the right to petition a judge to determine the identity of a father who would not, or could not, recognize them. Legal rules of evidence for establishing paternity in court further favored natural offspring. Total suppression of judicial investigation of paternity in 1847, even for child support, signified that the 1828 Judiciary Act, by permitting larger numbers of illegitimate individuals to use the courts to acquire their patrimonial rights, had succeeded all too well.

Liberalized opportunity to acquire rights in heirship after 1828, in other words, carried consequences that few liberals anticipated. A new accessibility to the courts, both for the natural offspring of a noble parent and for any spurious individual seeking judicial legitimization, opened a floodgate of litigation. Demographic trends merely swelled the ranks of petitioners and counterclaimants. The protests of grandparents against patrimonial claimants who were a son's or a daughter's non-legitimate offspring further transformed courtrooms into stages for family conflict, for what one legislator termed "family revenge." Reform impelled collateral relatives seeking to defend *ab intestato* inheritance rights vis-à-vis both natural and spurious offspring to go to court. Their grievances were compounded by the Resolution of August 11, 1831, vesting in parents who lacked legitimate children the right to use wills to institute any type of illegitimate offspring as their testamentary heirs. Moderate legal reform obviated the need for solemn legitimization, "*por escrito.*" Although the "Law of August 11" facilitated transmission of a parent's *legítima* to non-legitimate children, it caused the disgruntled collateral heirs whom it displaced to petition judges to overturn wills or contest declarations of paternity, burdening the dockets of lower courts. The courtroom became the stage for an endless chain of rival claimants to reenact sordid family dramas bringing scandal and embarrassment to respectable families.

Dep. Souza Martin's assertion that one-third of all Brazilians were natural offspring was not unreasonable. His estimate made the phenomenon of the surprise heir understandable. Suddenly appearing after a father's death to demand a share of the paternal *legítima*, this familiar figure became more menacing to propertied families in the 1830s. Legitimate heirs, as collateral relatives, and even necessary heirs, resorted to court for defending their succession rights against natural offspring, the only means for setting aside a father's customary recognition. Confronted by such claims—and counterclaims relying on hearsay testimony—judges demanded that the identity of the mothers of such non-legitimate offspring be revealed for corroborating a father's alleged paternity. Fear of the post-funeral catastrophe epitomized by the appearance of the surprise heir also derived from the abuse of procedural rules. Abuse of procedures implied fraud was being validated in the court-

room, for Luso-Brazilian legal tradition sanctioned a wide spectrum of conjectural evidence for determining filiation that facilitated perjury and was
practiced with impunity.

Far from being a figment of legislators' overstimulated imagination, the
surprise heir introduced anxiety within the legitimate family because his or
her appearance disturbed patrimonial arrangements that earlier had been
anticipated, often already settled informally. Fraud of a different nature represented a concern when propertied families arranged a good marriage for
their daughters. Eligible bachelors could conceal from future in-laws the
natural offspring they had fathered prior to marriage, passing themselves off
as childless in successful matrimonial negotiations. Between 1838 and 1847,
legislators in both houses regularly returned to the theme of a wife's dowry—
the devolving wealth of her family of origin—to voice concern over natural
offspring who gained recognition as a husband's *ab intestato* successor only
to render the wife's matrimonial property forfeit. The convention of a community property regulation left open the possibility, especially when a wife
predeceased her husband, that he, as her executor and the father of her minor children, might allow uxorial patrimony to pass to his natural children.
Undoubtedly, legislators exaggerated the draining of a wife's dowral wealth
in favor of her husband's recognized natural heir. And certainly they never
once paid attention to the most frequent despoiler of a married woman's
dowry—the profligate husband. But the changing nature of wealth, especially
among the growing middle classes who resided in Brazil's larger cities,
proved pivotal for grasping what was a new anxiety over maternal patrimony
susceptible to appropriation by an heir who was a "stranger."

The "new marriage bargain" that implied "disappearing dowries" defined
the surprise heir as a greater threat to a husband's and a father's patrimony
than formerly had been the case. The legitimate family now depended less
inclusively on wealth derived from both maternal and paternal lines, and
more exclusively on a father's earned income.[2] Less and less did land, real
property, constitute its wealth. Legitimate offspring also required a father's
patrimony, perceived as a reliable income flow, with greater urgency. Maternal grandparents and widows, together with legitimate children, were more
readily inclined to view the claims of the natural offspring of a dead son or
husband as interlopers. The words of Sen. Vergueiro merely belied the fundamental dilemma: "Marriage should be promoted as much as possible and
its results [legitimate offspring] regarded with greater honor and esteem than
the results of customary unions." By arguing that it was appropriate, even
socially beneficial, to change law in order to reward legal marriage and
thereby discourage *mancebia*, Brazilian lawmakers effectively shored up the

patrimonial interests of what was rapidly becoming a conjugally defined legitimate family. They thereby preserved its property for a limited population of heirs whose sine qua non would be legitimate birth.

The property at issue for the bourgeois family increasingly consisted of reliable income flows from salaries and pensions that derived from the imperial civil service, including the judiciary and the military, or from income from commerce and stocks and bonds, not to mention the many perquisites of government employment that rendered expenditure of liquid income unnecessary. The legitimate family found it harder to give up portions of regular income to natural offspring, because it was increasingly committed to paying for the higher education and the professional training of legitimate sons, as well as underwriting urban expenditure devoted to conspicuous consumption, especially the domestic labor of expensive household slaves.

In 1847, Brazil still lacked a commercial code. Wherever a family head was a businessman in a legal partnership, the common form of joint ventures, then his death brought home the devastating consequences of inheritance law. The latter did not distinguish between business assets and family patrimony. Legal partnerships had to be dissolved in order to auction the dead partner's assets and convert them to cash for division among his necessary heirs. Such an occurrence pushed many nuclear families into dire straights and militated against a modern capitalism. Consequently, the division of a father's business assets among one or more of his natural heirs, in company with his legitimate heirs, threatened the latter, especially when one or more of them wanted to reconstitute the dissolved partnership. By restricting the forced heirs to legitimate children, the likelihood of buying back paternal assets—of the legitimate children selling their inheritance shares to each other—became greater. Moreover, the claims of natural heirs were harder to resolve in an urban economy. No longer was it simply a question of the legitimate heirs dividing a substantial landed property into seven pieces instead of six. Nor was the situation as susceptible to manipulating the substance of individual portions, as in rural economy, in order to favor certain heirs over others—and make natural children look equal on paper.

In the monetized economy of the city, calling natural offspring to succession directly depleted the ready cash and stocks needed by legitimate children. Changing the rules of heirship in 1847 therefore promised financial redress for the legitimate family. The surprise heir could be eliminated by obliging future sons-in-law either to declare their natural offspring prior to marriage, or, otherwise, to forsake making them co-heirs in succession with any future legitimate offspring. Parents no longer would have to be concerned that a daughter's dowry could be diverted to support children who were not her own—but those of her husband who did not disclose them at their engagement. Their grandchildren's paternal *legítima* would remain an exclusive inheritance channeled within the legitimate family.

The official raison d'être of Law No. 463 of 1847, a leveling of estates that removed the last vestige of aristocratic privilege and equalized rights between the children of nobles and commoners, developed very late in the evolution of Sen. Vergueiro's bill.[3] Only in 1847 did the issue capture a consensus. By the mid-1840s Brazil's legislators were cognizant of an expanding population of noble rank that consisted largely of gentlemen and gentlewomen who personified the exponential impact of civil nobility. Law and medical degrees, like officers' patents in either the imperial army and navy or the rural National Guard, conferred minimal nobility and testified to the new mania of credentialing an imperial bureaucracy. Growth in the number of noble title-holders also followed the proclamation of D. Pedro II's majority in 1840, adding impetus to the goal of imposing a legal equality between the natural children of nobles and commoners in succession law. Yet, despite the advantageous legal leveling of estates imposed by Law No. 463 of 1847, the insulation of legitimate patrimony against "strangers" mattered a great deal more. By rewriting the succession rights of natural offspring to depend exclusively on the principle of voluntary paternal recognition, executed before a notary prior to marriage, Brazil's legislators made it impossible for most natural offspring to acquire a legal status in heirship. In reforming the inheritance system along more exclusive lines, the national political elite employed law to redefine individual rights in property as patrimony. They circumscribed the legitimate family tightly, setting it apart in a society still strongly disposed to accept natural marriage, de facto serial marriage, and polygamous unions. In doing so, they vested in fathers a greater patriarchal prerogative over natural offspring than they had ever previously exercised.

In turning away from a liberal agenda of reform that had initially sought to mitigate the "defect" of bastardy during the Regency, the Chamber of Deputies responded to political change at the national level. In a new climate of centralizing power around the throne, and the frank repudiation of federalism, the Liberal Party also responded to economic and social change at the elite level. Rather than acknowledge illegitimacy matter-of-factly as an inherent feature in national family organization, and address it in terms of the constitutional precept of equality before the law, a majority of legislators opted to rewrite Sen. Vergueiro's 1836 reform bill along more reactionary lines. Metamorphosed as Res. No. 53 of 1846, it deleted any reference to either spurious offspring or legitimization. Instead, it imposed the ostensibly liberal goal of abolishing a distinction of estate that prohibited many in the active citizenry—including legislators themselves—from making their natural offspring their *ab intestato* successors.

It is equally important to appreciate the limits that legislators imposed on reform in 1847. Law No. 463 represented a compromise with the existing rules laid down by Luso-Brazilian legal tradition. A redefinition of family membership in law still preserved important space, albeit greatly diminished, for natural offspring, contingent on voluntary paternal recognition prior to marriage. Although a more limited access to full family membership on the part of natural offspring spoke to enhanced patriarchal power by virtue of voluntary recognition, after 1847, properly recognized natural offspring continued to be called to succession on a par with their legitimate half-siblings. Equal shares remained the rule. Law No. 463 of 1847 represented a compromise, because the defenders of Luso-Brazilian legal tradition effectively blocked the outright adoption of "alien" rules of heirship that would have reduced the inheritance portions of natural offspring vis-à-vis legitimate children. They prevented full nullification of the custom that Book 4, Title 92, of the *Ordenações Filipinas* had perpetuated for more than two and a half centuries. Those who expected national law to be in harmony with "our customs" successfully upheld the important precept that recognized natural offspring should inherit on a par with legitimate offspring. They also upheld the legal nationalism articulated by Pombaline jurists even as the modern precepts of the French *Code civil* were finding greater acceptance in Portugal's 1867 Civil Code. In Brazil, at least, "new law" had proved impossible to impose in totality.

If notorious scandal had been silenced in the courtroom, then the propensity for constituting families outside the boundaries of legal matrimony had not. Recognized natural offspring, as well as socially acknowledged adulterine offspring, in company with *sacrílegos* raised by clerical fathers, continued to populate the social landscape of early republican Brazil. Patrimonially endowed as *ab intestato* successors, recognized natural offspring claimed a place beside those of legitimate birth by virtue of what was now taken to be a *Brazilian* legal tradition, one that still generously regarded them as paternally equipped for heirship, acceptable in respectable society, and, most important of all, free of the stain of bastardy.

Reconsidering Bastardy in
Republican Brazil

The 1916 Civil Code

———— ·✦· ————

> In Brazil, the average conscience does not recognize a difference
> between the obligations of the natural father and the legitimate
> father. All the litigation brought in this arena we owe to the law of
> September 2, 1847, whose rigor jurisprudence has sought to at-
> tenuate, although applying precepts that clearly contrast with the
> express letter of the law. . . . The goal of the Code Project's dispo-
> sition therefore is no less than revocation of the said law, one re-
> cently hammered by criticism.
>
> Clovis Bevilaqua, commenting on Article 1605,
the Civil Code Project (1902)[1]

Once the Law of September 2, 1847, was adopted, it remained controversial
for two generations. Republican lawmakers charged with adopting a civil
code continued to wrangle over the changes the law had imposed, even as
they debated the Civil Code Project between 1900 and 1916. Consequently,
what Law No. 463 of 1847 suppressed—judicial investigation of paternity—
generated considerable disagreement. Judges and law professors vented their
objections in articles and rulings published in legal journals. The adoption of
a republic in 1889 produced separation of church and state. Promulgation of
the Civil Marriage Act, Law No. 181 of January 24, 1890, offered the first opportunity to make slight revision pertinent to judicial investigation of paternity. However, the law was most significant for defining civil impediments to
marriage that challenged canon law. For the first time since the sixteenth
century, the canonical impediments promulgated at the Council of Trent
ceased to be received *in toto* in Brazilian positive law. As a result, the sub-
category of spurious birth defining *sacrílegos* was eliminated. The sub-category pertaining to canonically incestuous offspring was redefined in minimally civil terms. Most couples who formerly could not marry in the church
now could marry "in the civil."[2]

Where illegitimate offspring mattered in family and inheritance law, the Civil Code Project produced by Professor Clovis Bevilaqua in 1899, and approved by the Ministry of Justice in 1900, offered legislators impressive opportunity to turn back the clock to before 1847 and reconnect with Luso-Brazilian legal tradition.[3] Indeed, the author, a distinguished young professor from the Olinda Law Faculty, was himself a *sacrílego*. Not surprisingly, Bevilaqua condemned Law No. 463 of 1847 because it suppressed investigation of paternity and restricted paternal recognition to prior to the father's marriage. His Civil Code Project proposed that both provisions be revoked. Once again, the Senate proved willing to ease restrictions on paternal recognition and acknowledge a limited right to judicial investigation of paternity, while the Chamber of Deputies remained firmly opposed to any liberalization of rights, especially for spurious offspring. In contrast to the Senate, the Chamber committed itself to further reducing rights, along the lines of the French Civil Code. Nevertheless, legislators rescinded the most controversial feature of Law No. 463 of 1847 in several important respects. Brazil's new civil code reinstated judicial investigation of paternity on a limited basis and revised procedures for recognizing natural offspring, but it dealt even more harshly with adulterine and incestuous offspring than had nineteenth-century law.

The 1916 Civil Code completed the transformation of the legal position of natural offspring initiated in 1847, notwithstanding the concessions it made to judicial investigation of paternity. As a result, what had historically been a unique position for recognized natural offspring within a Luso-Brazilian inheritance system disappeared during Brazil's first republican era (1889–1930). A very different generation of self-styled liberal legislators, most of whom had entered politics in the final two decades of the Second Empire, again chose to alter law by privileging the legitimate family. They proved even more firmly committed to using legal change as the instrument for upholding legitimate matrimony than had the Chamber of Deputies in 1847. The revisions imposed on Bevilaqua's original Civil Code Project by the Special Committee of the Chamber of Deputies countermanded the generosity of rights that his draft accorded to individuals born out-of-wedlock.[4] Although Bevilaqua's Code Project proposed undoing most of Law No. 463 of 1847, subsequent revisions, first in 1902 and then under Sen. Rui Barbosa's direction, redefined the position of recognized natural offspring in succession law, causing them to lose their historical position of parity with legitimate children.

Adoption of the 1916 Civil Code meant that legislators succeeded in accomplishing a redefinition of how twentieth-century Brazilians would think about illegitimacy. For instance, wherever it referred to "illegitimate" off-spring, the Code usually had in mind only adulterine children, notwithstanding that it could apply that generic term idiosyncratically to encompass either incestuous or natural offspring. The new connotation of "illegitimate equals adulterine" originated in the Civil Marriage Act of 1890, whose provisions were faithfully incorporated in the 1916 Civil Code. The 1890 law markedly reduced the barriers to marriage, striking down most of the canonical impediments that had accounted for why so many in colonial and imperial Brazil never attained the free state to marry. First cousins and uncles and nieces, or aunts and nephews, as well as double (carnal) cousins, became free to contract marriage "in the civil." As a result, civil impediments of incest minimally inscribed only lineal relatives or siblings, a change that explained why adulterine children suddenly became the largest group of spurious offspring. The civil impediments maintained silence on marriage with a priest or nun, declining to refer to vows of clerical celibacy. Consequently, *sacrílegos* simply ceased to exist in civil law. Legal redefinition, therefore, meant that, practically speaking, adulterine individuals became synonymous with bastardy after 1916.

The Civil Code of 1916 also implied that natural children would be subsumed within the new equation of "illegitimate equals adulterine," due to how the generic of "illegitimate" applied to them, and the avoidance of any reference to illicit birth. The canonical category of spurious birth also failed to be mentioned. Although natural offspring had to be identified as a discrete group in certain contexts, the Code preferred to merge them with all others who were "illegitimate." As a result, the Code blurred the crucial distinction that natural offspring were not the "fruit of a crime," producing a conflation of natural with adulterine. This shift in redaction held important significance in law, but even greater importance for colloquial speech and popular attitudes. Although a generation or more would pass before people ceased to distinguish "natural" from "spurious" in ordinary speech, linguistic reliance on the generic application of "illegitimate" grew. After several generations, language obliterated the special position that natural offspring historically possessed in popular consciousness. Eventually, "illegitimate" conflated natural offspring with "bastard," although the Code still drew a thin but fundamental line between them. Today, younger Brazilians often apply "bastard" indiscriminately to everyone born outside legal wedlock, in contradiction to their legal tradition prior to 1916. The process of reevaluation, of course, has occurred over nearly a century, for mere legal redefinition did not rapidly produce new social attitudes.

The fact that the Civil Code of 1916 redefined the succession rights of recognized natural represented the last step in dislodging them from quasi-legitimacy and pushing them toward bastardy in a popular mentality. Sen. Vergueiro's insistence on borrowing new rules of heirship from the French Civil Code finally found acceptance in Brazil's 1916 Civil Code. Article 1605 rather misleadingly provided that recognized natural offspring—together with both those who were legitimized by their parents' subsequent marriage or legally adopted—were to be equipped for succession in the same manner as legitimate offspring. However, this meant only that they would be called to succession as *ab intestato* heirs together with their parent's legitimate offspring. Setting aside Clovis Bevilaqua's recommendation, the national legislature revised the Civil Code Project to impose an inequality of inheritance portions for those who were recognized natural offspring, legitimized by the subsequent marriage of their parents, or adopted. All of the latter would inherit portions one-half the size of their legitimate half-siblings' portions. This formula stood unchallenged until the late 1980s.[5]

The notion of half-shares for natural offspring, a Brazilian modification of the French *Code civil*'s prescription of thirds, it will be recalled, was first proposed by Sen. Vergueiro in Bill BU of 1836. Since 1916, consequently, wherever legitimate half-siblings exist, then recognized natural offspring receive inheritance shares equal to only one-half the size of the shares devolving to legitimate children. The drastic nature of this change is most readily perceived by noting that even natural offspring legitimized by the subsequent marriage of their parents suffered the identical diminution in their inheritance portions vis-à-vis their full, legitimate siblings. Historically, jurists had always defined those legitmized by subsequent marriage as equal to legitimate children. After 1916, only when natural offspring were the sole successors of the deceased parent—that is, in the absence of legitimate children—would they succeed on the same basis as the latter. The French formula, modified to half-shares as a token of Brazilian generosity, prevailed throughout the twentieth century.[6]

In a related change, the 1916 Civil Code administered the coup de grace to judicial legitimization. Nearly a dead letter, given that the Law of September 2, 1847, had whittled away most of its raison d'être, solemn legitimization remained useful only for conferring a noble parent's honors on a spurious child. The Constitution of 1891, however, abolished all distinctions of nobility and honors. In a related revision, investigation of paternity for establishing a spurious offspring's right to child support continued to be suppressed by Article 353 of the 1916 Civil Code. Nor could a parent recognize an adulterine or incestuous child. The same article stipulated that henceforth the sole basis of legitimization would be that "resulting from the marriage of the parents," meaning only natural offspring could be legitimized after 1916, through the civil marriage of their parents. As a result, the quality of spurious birth, now confined to either incestuous or adulterine children, ceased to be reversible in law after 1916. Therefore, bastardy became a permanent legal condition for the first time. All but properly recognized natural offspring were excluded from *ab intestato* succession and law afforded no loophole of legitimization.

On the other hand, the size of the *legítima* was decreased as early as 1907, due to adoption of a new law redefining the ladder of *ab intestato* succession. The *legítima*, rather than being defined as two-thirds of the parent's estate, was reduced to a minimal one-half, giving testators freedom to dispose of one-half of their patrimony, not one-third. This revision, incorporated in the 1916 Civil Code, expanded testamentary freedom and facilitated the transfer of greater amounts of property as bequests. Of course, all types of illegitimate individuals, including those who were spurious, could receive bequests disposed from one-half of the *legítima*.

The most maligned feature of reform in 1847, total suppression of judicial investigation of paternity, received significant attention from the authors of the 1916 Civil Code. Despite substantial backing in the Senate, Bevilaqua's novel proposal to grant the right to a judicial determination of paternity to both natural and spurious offspring was struck down by the Chamber of Deputies. However, wherever his draft code restored the right to investigation of paternity on behalf of only natural offspring, it gained limited endorsement in the lower house. Article 363 adopted three of his four proposals, thanks to the fact that Bevilaqua discretely circumscribed investigation of paternity to situations: 1) where the mother was living in concubinage with the presumed father at the time of the child's conception; 2) where the conception of the natural child had coincided with either the mother's *rapto* by the presumed father or his sexual relations with her; 3) and where the father had already executed a written affidavit attributing his own paternity, that is, had expressly recognized the offspring, but not by a notarial declaration.[7]

In the first instance, Brazil's legislators returned to a very old definition of natural offspring enshrined in the *Ordenações Filipinas* that jurists in Pombal's era had rendered outmoded. Since the second half of the eighteenth century, as we have seen, natural offspring had been paternally recognized without requiring the mother to be the father's concubine. They could be the result of even a casual encounter. In the second instance, legislators revived a provision of Sen. Vergueiro's original 1836 bill that his colleagues insisted should address the important circumstance of *rapto*. It, too, looked to older notions that redressed family honor when *rapto* resulted in a child being fathered by the abductor. In the final instance, they reopened what had been debated constantly between 1838 and 1847, namely, the kind of evidence admissible for proving paternal recognition. In permitting a wider degree of written evidence, the 1916 Civil Code partly turned back the clock to a pre-1847 situation. However, although legislators permitted testamentary recognition and private affidavits, properly witnessed, they again deliberately excluded oral testimony.

Although judicial investigation of paternity became a reality for several select groups of natural offspring in 1916, it applied only to those who fell within the above three situations. Article 363 also permitted a natural offspring to demand a judicial determination of paternity vis-à-vis a deceased father's heirs, meaning that a father's paternity of his legitimate children might be impugned in a judicial investigation of paternity. However, legislators rejected a fourth and very compelling situation proposed by Bevilaqua, one that went straight to the heart of customary arrangements in Brazilian society: Natural children who already "enjoyed the continuous state of being a natural offspring" of the person "presumed to be the father" were to be permitted judicial determination of paternity. In other words, those taken by the community—by a popular voice—to have always been paternally natural were to be deemed recognized by their fathers. By striking down what amounted to tacit recognition, the Chamber of Deputies left a father free to repudiate a natural offspring he had formerly recognized by the constancy of his actions—including cohabitation with the child and/or the mother over a long time. The Chamber of Deputies left those natural children without any legal recourse for recognition.[8]

On the other hand, what mattered most about a partly restored right to judicial determination of paternity was that it promised the possibility of conferring *ab intestato* succession rights under Article 1605 of the Civil Code. Of course, the pre-1847 rules were not fully restored, meaning many natural offspring did not fall under the provisions of Article 363. Where a father's written declaration did not exist, children of casual unions, like those whose parents' relationship had been concealed, could not expect to gain judicial recognition of paternity and, therefore, succession rights. Most objectionable was the situation where the father cohabited with the child and the mother, but had lived apart from her at the time of conception. Then the child could not demand judicial investigation of a paternal filiation.

Republican legislators were willing to reverse considerably the suppression of judicial investigation of paternity, because it had been widely condemned since 1847. The new precept of 1847, that paternal recognition, when declared for the purpose of bestowing succession rights, had to be made in a publicly executed affidavit prior to marriage, had proved highly unpopular on the ground of fairness. Reestablishment of a circumscribed right to judicial determination of paternity in 1916 also followed from an 1890 relaxation of the standard of evidence admitted in court. Yet none of the means reintroduced in 1890 for declaring recognition conferred succession rights. Law No. 463 of 1847 had limited the evidence to notarized affidavits and wills, with only the former conferring succession rights when legitimate children existed. Promulgation of the 1890 Civil Marriage Act expanded opportunity for fathers to declare recognition of natural offspring beyond the standard notarial declaration or will. Article 7, Section 1, defined the civil birth registry, introduced in 1881, as well as "other authentic documentation offered by the father," as acceptable evidentiary means for recognition. It even reintroduced "spontaneous confession"—what amounted to the "verbal declaration" that legislators eliminated in 1847. However, the father himself had to make the spontaneous declaration; hearsay testimony as to its having taken place, even if corroborated by five witnesses, remained prohibited.[9] None of these evidentiary means, it must be emphasized, conferred paternal succession rights.

Adoption of the 1916 Civil Code conveyed legal effect for succession rights in terms of two new procedural means for declaring paternity: the civil birth registry and wills (Art. 357). Contrary to Law No. 463 of 1847, the 1916 Civil Code allowed natural offspring to be equipped for succession when the parent executed recognition either before or after marriage. The counterbalancing feature for rescinding a great deal of Law No. 463 of 1847 could be found in Article 358. It flatly stated that "incestuous and adulterine children cannot be recognized." The Senate, in a vote reminiscent of 1839, suppressed Article 358 of the Civil Code Project, precisely because it denied paternal recognition to incestuous and adulterine individuals. A majority of senators favored liberalizing their rights. Echoing 1846, the Chamber of Deputies refused to follow suit. The prohibition against recognizing adulterine and incestuous children therefore stood without exception until 1942.

For the first time, Law No. 4737 of 1942 conferred on parents the right to recognize adulterine children, but only when the courts had already granted a *desquite* to the adulterine parent. A legal separation, implying separation of the matrimonial society—dividing the community property and establishing separate residences for husband and wife—thus permitted mostly husbands to recognize their adulterine children. Thus a first step was taken to rectify the position of adulterine children born to parents who were legally separated, but who had established second families—much in the manner of couples a century earlier who were viewed in their communities as living in customary or "natural" marriages. In 1949, a new law broadened the same right, including for adulterous parents not legally separated, by stipulating a sealed and irrevocable will could be used for recognition, either before or after the child's birth.[10]

In reaffirming the ancient condemnation law visited on spurious birth, the Chamber's Special Committee on the Civil Code Project revived what liberals in the 1830s had condemned: punishing children for the crimes of their parents. The task force in the Chamber of Deputies subsequently drew up its own version of the Civil Code Project, one that used language much more devastating than their nineteenth-century predecessors. The Chamber's moralizing pronounced that the legitimate family needed to be protected from "spurious offspring [understood] to be a category originating from a crime that is punished, besides being an affront to morality and the traditional good customs of our society."[11]

Whereas liberals in the 1830s had found it impossible to redress the punitive impact of law on adulterine birth, largely due to the established church, liberal republicans labored under no such limitation in the early twentieth century. No longer were they obliged to respect the rules of canon law. The Civil Code they promulgated in 1916 might have embodied some of the liberalizing features advocated by their predecessors in the 1830s. Instead, by reintroducing the pre-1830 accent on "punishable" birth, republican liberals maintained legal non-recognition for both adulterine and incestuous offspring. In the First Republic, it was therefore impossible for such children to gain child support from a father who refused it. By banning investigations of paternity, legislators further distanced themselves from an eighteenth-century Luso-Brazilian legal tradition that had acknowledged such a right in a limited sense. The *Assento* of April 9, 1772, §3, had permitted spurious offspring to petition for child support from the father, necessitating a judicial investigation of paternity confined to that end.[12] Canon law similarly had prescribed a father's obligation to support his spurious offspring, even when the father was a priest. In contrast, the 1916 Civil Code projected unprecedented harshness toward adulterine and incestuous children by offering them nothing.

In 1916, Brazil was a society where divorce still did not exist, but it was also one where religious marriage alone now implied no legal effect. Unlike liberal legislators during the Regency, who proposed ingenious bills designed to extend the effects of legal marriage, the republican liberals who presided over the 1916 Civil Code restricted legal matrimony to mandatory "marriage in the civil." They also declined outright to support any form of divorce. Legal separation, now styled a "*desquite*" to distinguish it from modern divorce (*divórcio*), was incorporated in the new code. It remained faithful to the ca-nonical precept that the bond of matrimony, when properly contracted, was indissoluble except by death. The *desquite* signified merely dissolution of the matrimonial society.[13] *Desquites* would become fashionable among the mid-dle class of the 1920s, offering another reason for why illegitimacy rates would remain high after 1916. By continuing to exclude adulterine children from any paternal recognition, the Chamber of Deputies perpetuated the stigma attaching to adulterine children for most of the twentieth century. More to the point, the line between bastardy and legitimacy was drawn starkly in 1916 in order to underscore how all illegitimate children would be distinguished as generic bastards.

Finally, in 1916 legal matrimony was not gaining popular acceptance in the linear fashion legislators had anticipated at the dawn of the republic. Mandatory civil marriage came under direct siege in many parts of Brazil as soon as the Civil Marriage Act of 1890 was promulgated. Thanks to the oppo-sition of the church, thousands of couples declined to marry "in the civil."[14] Mutually antagonistic, republican legislators would not make peace with the church over the issue of civil marriage until the era of the Estado Novo ar-rived in 1937. Widespread non-compliance with civil marriage continued for two more decades after adoption of the 1916 Civil Code. Republican legisla-tors stubbornly refused to give religious marriage civil effect. This contre-temps perpetuated relatively low rates of civil marriage before 1940. Children of couples married only in the church remained natural offspring— illegitimate—in the eyes of the law. Consequently, the Civil Code boded ill for the patrimonial fate of all children born outside civil marriage.

The harsher treatment meted to adulterine offspring by the 1916 Civil Code, like the diminished size of the inheritance portion disposed on behalf of recognized natural offspring, deserves interpretation against a twentieth-century imperative of middle-class respectability. The bourgeois family that Sen. Vergueiro had sought to privilege indeed became a legal reality only in 1916. Brazil's first national code of law conferred on legitimate marriage the shibboleth of social stability, precisely in a historical context where enor-mous social and economic change were transforming family and polity. The privileging of the legitimate family, at the expense of all children born out-side legal wedlock, followed from the widespread social change that coin-cided with Brazil's passage from monarchy to republic. Abolition of slavery, only in 1888, produced demographic as well as economic change. National politicians viewed the migration of many former slaves to Brazil's larger cit-ies as a threat to the private sphere as well as to public order. To the wide-spread fact of urbanization, European mass immigration added a different

dimension, beginning in the late 1880s, changing the nation's ethnic and racial composition in fundamental respects, but similarly calling into question
the political elite's social control.

Like Vergueiro, his liberal counterparts in the First Republic demonstrated little tendency to recognize the pliability that family in Brazil had
demonstrated historically. Twentieth-century legislators were drawn even
more from the ranks of the urban professional and commercial classes than
in the 1840s. They no longer inscribed the planter-patriarchs who cohabited
amongst a throng of blood relations, family dependents, and slaves, in testimony to the ambiguous ties of blood and concubinage that defined such
extended families. The propensity of a native-born clergy for clerical *mancebia* had also begun to change, albeit much more slowly. By the 1880s, such
cohabitation came under increasing censure from the higher clergy, pressured by Rome. Twentieth-century bishops demanded conformity to a public image that did not proclaim a priest's private family life, although the
rank-and-file was slow to change.

If the recasting of class, race, and ethnicity did not provide sufficient impetus for persuading republican legislators to buttress the legitimate family
juridically, then the assault on patriarchy mounted after 1900 by suffragists
and emancipationists—women whom jurists insisted on labeling "*spin-
sters*"—convinced them that it deserved to be defended. A growing number
of middle-class women demanded the right to pursue law and medical degrees, to enter the higher civil service, and to vote. They persuaded lawmakers that the values of the nineteenth-century patriarchal family had eroded to
the point where only a new family could supplant it. Now conjugally based,
but oriented around a male head, the new, legitimate family deserved every
protection the law could define. Its defense, they reasoned, depended on the
new capacity of the national state to intervene directly in family life.[15]

In reality, a reorganization of patriarchy under the 1916 Civil Code, not its
demise, subordinated wives to their husbands within a more conjugally focused family. Married women therefore did not acquire legal control of their
own property, either as *ab intestato* heirs in 1907 or as co-owners of the matrimonial community in 1916.[16] They did, however, make small gains reflecting the new importance of wives and mothers in the rearing of the legitimate
family's children. For the first time, "due to the necessity of maintaining
harmony in the conjugal home," wives received the right to refuse to raise a
husband's illegitimate child.[17] In consigning all children who were not legitimate, sanctified by "marriage in the civil," to a secondary position vis-à-
vis patrimony, or depriving them of inheritance rights altogether, the 1916
Civil Code drew a firmer line, circumscribing the conjugal couple and their

children. The insulation of the legitimate family's members required distancing them from others who were ambiguously defined as members—for being born outside legal marriage. Law, as Vergueiro had proposed in 1839, could be used to draw a line between the offspring of "natural marriage" and legitimate matrimony, with rights turning on differential access to patrimony.

Where long-term change mattered, the 1916 Civil Code proved definitive for eroding the inheritance rights of collateral relatives. This development illuminated the importance that legislators had, since the 1830s, consistently accorded a conjugally defined family. In 1907, they altered the ladder of *ab intestato* succession in ways that were comparable to how Pombaline reform had redefined the system of *ab intestato* succession, beginning in 1754. Law No. 1839 of 1907 provided that surviving spouses would be privileged over all collaterals on the ladder of intestacy. For the first time, instead of calling collaterals to the tenth degree to succession, in the absence of necessary heirs, succession law called surviving spouses as the next group of *ab intestato* heirs on the ladder of intestacy. As for the enormous population of collateral relatives who might be called to legitimate succession, in the absence of necessary heirs or surviving spouses, they were reduced. The range of collateral heirs was redefined from ten to six degrees in an effort to insure that very distant collaterals would never be called to succession. Both changes were incorporated in the 1916 Civil Code (Articles 1611 and 1612).

Although collaterals still inherited as intestate successors, in the absence of necessary heirs and surviving spouses, testamentary freedom after 1907 implied they would be less important. In reducing the *legítima* from two-thirds of the decedent's estate to one-half, legislators acted on the assumption that greater testamentary freedom would redound to the benefit of either a surviving spouse or minor children, including the physically and emotionally impaired. They thus fundamentally revised the system of inheritance as one that would be mixed, demonstrating equal commitment to forced heirship and testamentary freedom.[18] Rules of heirship continued to favor forced heirs—children, ascendants, and surviving spouses—within a conjugally defined legitimate family. Alternatively, where neither surviving spouses nor legitimate children existed, they privileged testamentary freedom as the means for selectively disposing of patrimony in favor of individuals closer to the conjugal family core—whether they were favorite collaterals or friends construed as "strangers" within a perspective oriented toward kinship.

Significantly, the 1916 Civil Code perpetuated the device of universal heirship, restored in the late eighteenth century after Pombal failed to redirect it from the church toward collateral kin. The term itself was not used in the Civil Code, but Article 1725 detailed the rules of heirship appropriate to nominating a universal heir. The testator who lacked necessary heirs, consequently, enjoyed freedom to dispose of the entire *legítima*—as well as the testamentary half of his or her goods—by means of a will. A testator nominating a universal heir could even exclude the surviving spouse, simply by using a will (Article 1721).[19] However, surviving spouses still had one-half of the community property reserved for them. Given the advantageous situation of testamentary freedom over the entire estate, the rights of collaterals mattered less and less to testators. Instead, they disposed on behalf of closer collaterals, like siblings, nieces, or nephews—or an illegitimate child. They excluded cousins and other distant collaterals altogether from *ab intestato* succession. As a final proof signifying the shift in a redefined family fulcrum in inheritance rights, brothers lost their ancient right to impugn a will that nominated a universal heir. No longer could they do so by charging the latter was "vile and of bad habits."[20]

Until the 1940s, Brazil's legislators assumed that the legal changes they introduced in family and inheritance law, by means of the new Civil Code, would alter social behavior and mold patterns favoring the legitimate family. Yet the promotion of legal marriage turned out to be a goal that they themselves impeded. By refusing to give civil effect to religious marriage until the late 1930s, and by withholding the remedy of divorce until 1976, they created a situation where millions of individuals were legally defined as either natural or adulterine offspring. Yet the difficulty in promoting legal marriage occurred not only because legislators and the church remained at war over civil marriage from 1890 to 1938. Law simply proved an ineffective remedy for encouraging legitimate marriage, given that illegitimate children remained integral to family formation. Opponents of Law No. 463 of 1847 had based their objections on the underlying premise that good law must be consistent with the historical experience and customs of a people. In protesting that they should uphold legal doctrine consistently, legislators who defended the status quo in 1847 often spoke as lawyers or judges, yet they raised abstract objections on the ground that existing doctrine appropriately addressed customary values and behavior. What constituted family could be located in customary behavior, because they took into account a multiplicity of family arrangements that historically had tended to make the legitimate family's boundaries highly permeable—testifying to the long significance of illegitimacy. The words of Dep. Angelo Moniz Silva Ferraz still rang true in 1916: "We ought to flee from legislating in opposition to deeply rooted customs, as if we were creating a new religion. It will be as difficult as a foreign language to impose these difficult new customs on the people by force and impossible to destroy the existing ones by means of laws."[21]

Twenty-five years after 1916, the pendulum began to swing from programmatic legal reform toward recognizing the role of "our customs." In taking small steps during the 1940s to permit parents to recognize adulterine children, once the marriage bond attenuated, a new generation of lawmakers eventually reinstated the right of any illegitimate individual (incestuous, adulterine, or natural) to bring a judicial action for the purpose of obtaining child support—at least in secret.[22] In 1946, a better case in point pertained to the drastic withdrawal of succession rights from collateral heirs. Law limited them to the fourth civil degree: first cousins. Legislators scaled down the blood kindred to encompass only close, collateral members. In drawing a new line that circumscribed the legal kindred at first cousins, legislators did not so much innovate as bring to conclusion a long-term trend. The Brazilian tendency to favor the conjugal family reached a logical end point.

In this respect, the social organization of Brazilian families may well have differed significantly from that of Portugal throughout the nineteenth century. Thomaz Lino D'Assumpção, a Portuguese traveler in Brazil during the late 1870s, believed so. "Happily," he did not see in Brazil "the interminable *parentela* [horde of relatives] that accompanies an individual everywhere" in Portugal, which he deplored as "one of our defects."[23] For him, "family" in Brazil was fundamentally construed lineally, meaning more narrowly over generations.[24] Perhaps due to the circumstance that Brazil was always a nation of continuous immigration, from both Europe and Africa, ties between parents and children or between discrete siblings sets, defined the family's historical pivots. Migration within Brazil also weakened the collateral ties binding an extended family. For these reasons, children born out-of-wedlock probably always mattered more to Brazilians than to their Portuguese counterparts, notwithstanding that historically high rates of non-legitimate births prevailed in Portugal. D'Assumpção described family in Brazil as "much more reduced, consisting of only what lives in the conjugal nest: father, mother, and children." Other relatives were confined "to more intimate visits," with the exception of grandparents, who were "always welcome in every house . . . ."[25]

The notion that in Brazil family has been, at least for several centuries, defined around a conjugal core of parents, children, and grandparents is not the same as saying that legitimate marriage has necessarily coincided with that core. This observation is an appropriate one on which to bring this study of illegitimacy and inheritance to a close, given that today the legitimate family represents only one of several norms in family organization in Brazil.

Nor should this exploration of the changing inheritance rights of illegitimate offspring in imperial Brazil end on a note that emphasizes the exclusionary features of the 1916 Civil Code. No longer do Brazilian legislators view law as the instrument for repudiating customary patterns of family organization upheld for so long by a popular voice. Today one can say that they have either become much more accepting of social realities that admit non-legitimate children as integral to family organization or that they simply are more willing to grant what was argued less successfully throughout the nineteenth century: Under natural law, all children are indistinguishable and deserve the parent's recognition, support, and affection.

Did not the 1988 Constitution adopt the principle that "discrimination with respect to filiation is prohibited"? And did it not stipulate that "regardless of whether born in or out of wedlock, or adopted, children shall have the same rights"?[26] This is indeed heady doctrine for Brazilian succession law as the twenty-first century opens. On the other hand, if history is consulted, and the customary social arrangements of the nineteenth and twentieth century are considered, then one must conclude that, finally, positive national law is catching up with custom and the standards of "a popular voice" are again being heard. If so, the arguments first articulated over one hundred and fifty years ago, by the likes of Jozé Lino Coutinho, Diogo Antonio Feijó, the marquis of Caravellas, Antonio Maria de Moura, and Angelo Moniz Ferraz, not to mention their juridical muse, Paschoal José de Mello Freire, will again be heard on the floor of the Brazilian Congress, as the nation deliberates the family sections of a new civil code for a new century.

Reference Matter

Abbreviations

———◆·◆·◆———

PARLIAMENTARY DEBATES, COLLECTIONS OF LAWS,
AND THE OFFICIAL GOVERNMENT NEWSPAPER

ACD   *Anais da Camara dos Deputados do Imperio Brasileiro, 1826–1847*
AS   *Anais do Senado do Imperio Brasileiro, 1826–1847*
CDGIB   *Collecção das decisões do Governo do Imperio Brasileiro, 1808–1889*
CLIB   *Collecção das leis do Imperio do Brasil 1808–1889*
CLP   *Collecção da legislaçao portuguesa 1750–1820*, Antonio Delgado da Silva, compiler
JC   *Jornal do Commercio*, Rio de Janeiro, 1846–1847

STANDARD DESIGNATIONS FOR LAWS, EXECUTIVE ORDERS, JUDICIAL
CLARIFICATIONS, OR RULINGS CARRYING THE FORCE OF LAW

Al.   *Alvará* (plural: *Als.*)*
Ass.   *Assento*
Av.   *Aviso*
Dec.   *Decreto*
Of.   *Ofício*
Prov.   *Provisão*
Reg.   *Regimento*
Regul.   *Regulamento*
Res.   *Resolução*

COMPONENT PARTS OF LEGAL COMMENTARIES OR THE 'ORDENAÇÕES
DO REINO' (i.e., the *Ord. Filipinas*, *Ord. Manuelinas*, and *Ord. Afonsinas*)

L.   *Livro* (Book)
Pte.   *Parte* (Part [synonymous with "*Livro*"])
v.   *Volume* or *Tomo* (Volume or Tome)
Cap.   *Capítulo* (Chapter)
T.   *Título* (Title)
§   *Seção* (Section)

*"Alvará" was used interchangeably with "law" (*lei*) until independence (1822). After independence, "law" (*lei*) and "decree-law" (*decreto-lei*) were used interchangeably.

§§   *Seções* (Sections)
Art. *Artigo* (Article)
Par. *Parágrafo* (Paragraph)
N.   *Número* or *Item* (Number or Item)
n   Nota (Note)

Notes

PREFACE

1. Francisco de Souza Martins, 18 May, *ACD 1846*, 1:104.
2. The *Anais do Parlamento Brasileiro* were written by redactors whose skills varied considerably, but did not always capture every participant's comments. The *Anais* for the Senate in 1835, 1836, and 1838, for example, were exceptionally sparse. Generally speaking, a half dozen speakers dominated any debate. Customarily, a vote on a given law was not recorded, except to note whether it passed or failed. Therefore, it was not possible to discern patterns of bloc voting that derived from roll call votes for the bills discussed herein. I have usually relied on the original series of the *Anais*, published in the second half of the nineteenth century through the 1910s, as well as on their detailed membership lists for the Chamber of Deputies. In some cases, however, I relied on reprint editions published in Brasília after 1970, another factor explaining why the title of the series varies.
3. All references to the *Ordenações Filipinas* herein refer to Candido Mendes' monumental 14th edition: *Codigo Philippino ou Ordenações do Reino de Portugal* . . . . The following abbreviations, used in notes throughout this book, apply to its divisions: Ord. (*Ordenações*), L. (*Livro*), T. (*Título*), § (*Seção*), Art. (*Artigo*), and Par. (*Parágrafo*). References to "Candido Mendes, *Ord.*," followed only by page and/or footnote numbers, refer to his annotative notes interpreting the *Ordenações*. Otherwise, the *Ordenações Filipinas* is abbreviated "*Ord. Filipinas.*" A single *ordenação* is abbreviated "*ord.*" NOTE: Unless otherwise indicated by a generic context, references herein to the "*Ordenações do Reino*," or "the *Ordenações*," refer to the *Ordenações Filipinas*.

LANGUAGE, ORTHOGRAPHY, AND NAMES

1. *Family Marriage Europe*, p. 7.
2. *Subsídios direito pátrio*, 4:37. Direct reference herein to laws applying in Brazil's colonial period draw on Delgado da Silva's comprehensive, nine-volume compilation spanning 1750–1820: *Collecção da legislação portugueza desde a ultima compilação das Ordenações*, abbreviated herein "*CLP.*" Laws cited for imperial Brazil have been drawn from the government's overlapping *Collecção das leis do Imperio do Brasil de [year]*, whose title varies, abbreviated herein as *CLB*. In addition, the verbatim texts of both colonial and imperial laws can be found in Candido Mendes' appendices to each book of the *Ordenações Filipinas*, or in legal commentaries.

CHAPTER 1

1. Mello Moraes [Pai], *Chronica Geral*, 2:243, 273.

2. Ibid., 2:223. Barman, *Forging Brazil*, pp. 65ff., 272n1.

3. Ribeiro, "'Brasileiros, vamos a eles!'"; Reis, "O jogo duro"; Peter Wood, "'The Dream Deferred'"; and M. J. M. Carvalho, "Hegemony and Rebellion in Pernambuco."

4. Murilo de Carvalho, *Teatro de sombras*, p. 50.

5. Ibid., p. 51. By treaty, the Atlantic slave trade was abolished on 13 Mar. 1830; in domestic law, by the Law of 7 Nov. 1831 (*CLIB 1831*, Pt. 1:182).

6. Marinho de Azevedo explores the doomed abolitionist position in the 1820s: *Onda negra, medo branco.*

7. On dissolving the Constituent Assembly (12 Nov. 1823), Pedro promised to convoke another to produce a constitution "*more liberal* than the one the extinct Assembly had ended up making." Fleiuss, "Organização," p. 300. Italics added.

8. Barman, *Forging Brazil*, p. 101.

9. Seed, *Ceremonies*, p. 134 (citing Marcelo Caetano, *Lições da historia*, p. 225). Macaulay, *Dom Pedro*, pp. 130–31.

10. Macaulay, *Dom Pedro*, p. 131.

11. Ibid.

12. Ibid., p. 135 (citing Sousa, *Vida Pedro I*, 2:76–78; and Rodrigues, *Independência*, 1:270–71). Italics added.

13. On the Constitution's affinities with Constant's theory, see Gomes B. Câmara, *Subsídios direito pátrio*, 3:29–38. On "charter," see Viotti da Costa, *Brazilian Empire*, p. 60. Around half the country's municipal councils approved the 1824 Constitution, frustrating Pedro's convocation of a second Constituent Assembly. Fleiuss, "Organização," p. 312; Macaulay, *Dom Pedro*, p. 161. All references to the *Con. 1824* herein are taken from the text published in IHGB, *Diccionario*, 1:304–13.

14. Fleiuss, "Organização," p. 301. Pedro's 1823 Address From the Throne called for "a constitution with only three branches." Ibid., p. 300.

15. *Teatro de sombras*, p. 162.

16. Moreira Alves, "Panorama," pp. 87, 90 (citing Law of 20 Oct. 1823); Gomes B. Câmara, *Subsídios direito pátrio*, 3:54–55

17. Hale, "Revival," p. 159.

18. The first secret Masonic lodge in Brazil, the "Areópago Itambé," was founded around 1808 in Itambé, Pernambuco, by Manuel Arruda da Câmara (1752–1810). Vasconcellos Pedrosa, "Estudantes brasileiros," pp. 55, 62. The Patriotic Masonic Lodge, founded in Recife in 1817, defined a regional turning point in the influence of "liberal" revolutionary thought. Sousa Montenegro, *Liberalismo radical*, pp. 73–77, 81–82.

19. Paim, *História idéias*, p. 71.

20. Pamphlet cited by Nizza da Silva, *Império luso-brasileiro*, p. 408; Viotti da Costa, *Brazilian Empire*, p. 16.

21. Boehrer, "Flight Brazilian Deputies," p. 499 (citing *O Diario do Governo*, 15 Apr. 1822).

22. Ibid., p. 498 and 498n4; Mello Moraes [Pai], *Chronica geral*, 2:223. Egas, *Feijó*, 1:16; Bethell, "Independence of Brazil," pp. 28–30.

23. Sousa Montenegro, *Liberalismo radical*, pp. 64–69, 77–93.

24. This section draws importantly on Hale's "Revival," pp. 161–66, and his classic *Mexican Liberalism*, esp. pp. 55–63. On the "absolutist face" of the 1824 Constitution, see Murilo de Carvalho, *Teatro de sombras*, pp. 162–63.

25. Hale singles out Constant's essay "Principes de politique applicables á tous les gouvernements représentatifs et particuliérement á la constitution actuelle de la France" (1815) as the early inspiration for Spanish liberals, noting that Antonio López published a "free selection" of Constant's abridged writings relevant to Spain, rendering his ideas in a post-1814 context: *Curso de politica constitucional*, 1823. *Mexican Liberalism*, pp. 56n36, 69–71.

26. Hale, "Revival," p. 164.

27. Ibid., p. 165.

28. Ibid., pp. 161–66; and Hale, *Mexican Liberalism*, pp. 55–63. In France after Robespierre's fall, Constant opposed Napoleon once the latter eliminated him from the government in 1804.

29. *Mexican Liberalism*, pp. 44, 67–68.

30. "Revival," p. 167.

31. Hale, *Mexican Liberalism*, p. 58. In Mexico, the "safeguards" envisioned by Constant for militating against an excess of democracy were located in organs of local government—the *ayuntamientos* of the 1820s. Brazilians aspired to analogous safeguards on central authority when they created provincial legislatures in 1834.

32. Coelho da Rocha, *Ensaio*, p. 179.

33. Mello Moraes [Pai], *A independencia*, p. 305.

34. Livermore, *New History*, p. 264.

35. Sousa Montenegro, *Liberalismo radical*, p. 34.

36. Ibid., p. 122 (citing Frei Caneca's 1824 written statement presented to the Recife Municipal Council). Machado Portella, "Supplicio da Caneca," pp. 137–39.

37. Haitian slaves rose in mass insurrection in August 1791, inspired by the free population of color's revolt. The result was full citizenship for those of free color (4 Apr. 1792) and abolition of slavery in the French colonies (4 Feb. 1794). The 1794 decree, widely diffused throughout the Caribbean, brought to Salvador news of slave revolts as distant as Louisiana (1795). Hall, *Africans in Louisana*, pp. 346–47.

38. Nizza da Silva, *Império luso-brasileiro*, p. 362 (citing 1798 testimony by J. J. de Veiga, in *Inconfidência da Baía*, 1:8). Andrada, *Representação escravatura*. See also Dep. Jozé Eloy Pessoa da Silva's 1826 proposal to end the slave trade: *Memória escravatura*; and Azevedo, *Onda negra*, pp. 41–42ff.

39. The Spanish Constitution created "passive" and "active" citizens by introducing a three-tiered system of indirect elections and property requirements. Hale, *Mexican Liberalism*, pp. 96–97. The abolition of tribute levied according to racial or ethnic criteria (Indians and mulattoes) defined a rare instance where Mexicans applauded the Spanish liberal attack on the society of estates. Lynch, *Spanish-American Revolutions*, pp. 300–302.

40. Flory, "Race and Social Control," p. 207. M. J. M. de Carvalho, "Slave Resistance," p. 14. This view, aired in Recife's anti-liberal *Amigo do Povo*, was denounced by the liberal *Diario de Pernambuco* [Recife], on 11 Nov. 1829; quoted ibid., p. 14. At most, conceded *Amigo do Povo*, "those of color should be 'passive' citizens," voting in two-stage elections as voters, not electors.

41. Macaulay, *Dom Pedro*, pp. 161, 163. In revising the draft constitution, D. Pedro I examined the Constitutions of Portugal (1822), France (1814), and Norway (1814).

42. The 1812 Spanish Constitution curtailed the corporate privileges of nobility (including the military) and church (including the Inquisition), as well as the corporate nature of the mint, the guilds, and Spanish America's indigenous communities. Hale, *Mexican Liberalism*, p. 114.

43. Melchor Gaspar Jovellanos attacked the *mayorazgo* in his famous 1795 *"informe de ley agraria."* In 1796, the Bourbon government called in the church's loans and amortized ecclesiastical property; in 1804, Charles IV turned to disentailment. Hale, *Mexican Liberalism*, pp. 119–20, 135–37. Ladd, *Mexican Nobility*, pp. 153–55. Regarding the *fuero militar* in Mexico, see Linda Arnold's revision, "Privileged Justice?"

44. Livermore, *New History*, p. 264. Art. 246 of Brazil's Constitution provided, "The princes of the royal house are senators by right, on reaching age 25."

45. "Slavery gives the lie to liberal ideas . . . ." Schwarz, "Misplaced Ideas," p. 22.

46. Ibid., p. 29.

47. Ibid., pp. 23, 28–29.

48. Hale, "Revival," p. 166.

49. Schwarz, "Misplaced Ideas," p. 20.

50. *Brazilian Empire*, p. 59. See also Carvalho Franco, "Idéias no lugar," pp. 61–64.

51. *Brazilian Empire*, pp. 53–59.

52. On D. João's post-1793 reorganization of censorship, see Neves, "Do império ao império," pp. 78–79.

53. Schwarz, "Misplaced Ideas," p. 20.

54. Maxwell, *Pombal*, p. 91.

55. Pires, "Teologia jansenista," pp. 327–28. Gérson, *Regalismo brasileiro*, pp. 24n6–26, 27–29. Entitled *Catechismo da doutrina cristã conforme o Codigo da Igreja Nacional* (s.d.), Silva Lisboa's catechism conformed to the *Con. primeiras* (1707). Ibid.

56. Walsh, *Notices*, 2:181–82. On the religious devotion of a singular liberal anticlerical, Dep. Clemente Pereira, see ibid., 1:202, 211.

57. Gérson, *Regalismo brasileiro*, p. 13.

58. Beal, "Regalismo Brasil," pp. 25, 50. Gottfried van Swieten, Maria Teresa's Dutch surgeon and "the soul of Jansenist propaganda at the Court of Austria," exerted the primary influence on Pombal. Ibid.

59. Ibid., p. 27.

60. Pombal turned to the ex-Oratorian, Pereira de Figueiredo, for writing his defense. Using arguments analogous to those of Febronius, both his *Tentativa teológica* and *Demonstração teologica* claimed rights on behalf of Portugal's bishops that until then had been reserved to the Holy See. Ibid., p. 50.

61. On Charles III and Spanish Bourbon reliance on Jansenist principles, see Brading, *Origins Mexican Nationalism*, pp. 32–34.

62. Beal, "Regalismo Brasil," pp. 56–57 (citing Archivio Segreto Vaticano, Nunziatura Portogallo, 119A, fols. 48–49).

63. Gérson, *Regalismo brasileiro*, p. 38 (citing *al.* of 20 May 1814). Beal, "Regalismo Brasil," p. 146n49 (citing Candido Mendes, *Dir. civ. eccles.*, 1:247–49); and p. 132 (citing *Dec.* 3 Aug. 1813).

64. Beal, "Regalismo Brasil," pp. 104–5 (citing Archivio Segreto Vaticano [ASV], Vatican City; Nunziatura Portogallo, Ano 1829, Rubrica 250).

65. Ibid., Appendixes C, D, E, and F (pp. 247–51). There were 23 clerics seated as delegates in the 1823 Constituent Assembly. Ibid.

66. Ibid., p. 112 and App. A (pp. 243–46).

67. The 1810 Commercial Treaty provided the precedent of an unmarked church not deemed a public edifice. Walsh, *Notices*, 2:181.

68. Hale has argued similarly that "equality," even "democracy," implied merely juridical equality in the face of corporate privilege. *Mexican Liberalism*, p. 123.

69. Walsh, *Notices* 1:258.

CHAPTER 2

1. *ACD 1827*, 3:259.

2. Ibid., 3:260.

3. *Forging Brazil*, pp. 102 and 273n17. Pope Leo XII's bull, *Proclara Portugaliae Algarbiorum que regum*, confirmed Pedro as Grand Master. 10 Oct., *ACD 1827*, 5:121. See also Schwarcz, *Barbas imperador*, Chap. 8.

4. Barman, *Forging Brazil*, p. 102.

5. Coelho da Rocha, *Ensaio*, p. 186.

6. Ibid., pp. 186–87, 187n1, citing *als*. 10 Mar. 1764, 18 Jan. 1765, 4 July 1768, 12 May 1769, and 9 Sept. 1769 (§12).

7. Dauphinee, "Church and Parliament," p. 102n1.

8. Ibid., p. 91n2.

9. 12 July, *ACD 1827*, 3:129, upholding Mello Freire on Pope Leo X's brief to D. Manoel I, "confirming the ancient rights of the *Padroado*"; and 8 July, *ACD 1826*, 3:95. Quoted in Dauphinee, "Church and Parliament," p. 16.

10. Vainfas, *Trópico dos pecados*, pp. 291–92. The Portuguese Inquisition tried cases of bigamy in Brazil, especially among slaves, in 1753, 1799, and 1804. Ibid., p. 292. Borges Carneiro, *Dir. civ. Port.*, L.1, v.1, T.11, §104, N.13a (p. 24), citing the Law of 26 May 1689, defining bigamy as a crime *mixtifori*, tried by the Inquisition.

11. Art. 1 of Vergueiro's bill (citing *Con. 1824*, Art.179, Par.17), quoted in Dauphinee, "Church and Parliament," p. 92 (citing 19 June, *ACD 1826*, 2:200).

12. Art. 2 of Vergueiro's bill, ibid.

13. Ibid., pp. 98–105 (citing 29 July, *ACD 1826*, 2:352). The bill passed the lower house on 29 July. Ibid., 2:357. Dauphinee, "Church and Parliament," pp. 15–17.

14. Coelho da Rocha, *Ensaio*, p. 185.

15. Ibid., quoting Ribeiro Sanches, p. 73.

16. Ramos de Carvalho, *Reformas pombalinas*, p. 73. As late as the five-year period ending in 1769, enrollment in Coimbra's faculties (totaling 20,453 students) reflected canon law's preeminence: theology, 566; medicine, 966; civil law, 2,493; and canon law, 16,398. Ibid., p. 142.

17. *Notices*, 1:200–201.

18. Ibid., 1:203.

19. 16 July, *ACD 1828*, 3:128.

20. Ramos de Carvalho, *Reformas pombalinas*, p. 140.

21. Following ecclesiastical law, formerly crown law prohibited marriage with or between slaves, conceding them only *contubernio*, a consensual cohabitation destitute of civil effects. Borges Carneiro, *Dir. civ. Port.*, L.1, v.1, T.11, §101, N.5 (p. 18a).

Nizza da Silva noted that the *Con. primeiras* of 1707 endorsed marriage for slaves, forbidding owners to impede such unions or to separate conjugal partners. *Sistema casamento*, p. 139.

22. *Travels*, pp. 391, 398n.

23. *Notices*, 1:204.

24. Ibid., 1:203–4.

25. "Slave Resistance," p. 14; "Bispos de Olinda," n.p.

26. Guerra Ferreira and Silva Formiga, *Catálogo dos processos*. This catalog summarizes responses from 1852 to 1987 to the *processos de Genere, Vita et Moribus* and *do Patrimônio* that screened candidates for ordination, in terms of biological background and income sources in what became the archdiocese of Paraíba in 1894. I have deliberately suppressed herein candidates' names and relevant page numbers.

27. Ibid. The dispensation noted "his mother and grandmother were ex-slaves." The only other *pardo* candidate to be ordained supplied both his parents' full names, presumably indicating he was of legitimate birth. Two others (1886 and 1897) had "defects" of birth that were physical handicaps. Ibid.

28. 17 Sept., *ACD 1827*, 5:45, that is, "*sangue limpo e puro.*"

29. Fernandes Pinheiro, "Padres do Patrocínio," pp. 138–39 [*sic*].

30. Ibid.

31. Nizza da Silva, *Império luso-brasileiro*, p. 313. The same policy prohibited kings and queens being elected by the membership, in *irmandades* reserved to slaves [*negros*]. Ibid.

32. Boschi, *Leigos e poder*, p. 162.

33. Higgins, "*Licentious Liberty*," pp. 104–5.

34. Schwarcz, *Barbas imperador*, p. 173.

35. Ibid., p. 523.

36. *Notices*, 1:289.

37. Mota, *Nordeste - 1817*, p. 142.

38. Von Leithold and von Rango, *Dois prussianos*, p. 63, quoted in Nizza da Silva, *Império luso-brasileiro*, p. 524.

39. Jansen, "Nobiliario," p. 167.

40. Kraay, "Black Militias," p. 44 (citing Cunha Mattos, *Repertório legislação militar*, 2:112, 322).

41. Vieira da Cunha, *Nobreza brasileira*, p. 13 (citing *al.* of 24 June 1806, responding to a councilor of state who lacked nobility by descent). Nascimento e Silva, *Synopse legislação militar*, 2:139.

42. Paula Cidade, *Cadetes alunos militares*, p. 26. The texts of the *prov.* of 26 Oct. 1820, elaborating the Law of 4 Feb. 1820 (anticipated by the *res.* of 6 Sept. 1819), are reproduced ibid., pp. 260–28. Cunha Mattos, *Repertorio legislação militar*, 2:62. Vieira da Cunha, *Nobreza brasileira*, p. 13.

43. Separate criteria for recruiting first and second cadets were spelled out by the Supreme Military Council in the *prov.* of 22 Oct. 1824, still in force in 1889. Vieira da Cunha, *Nobreza brasileira*, p. 35.

44. Cunha Mattos, *Repertorio legislação militar*, 2:191 (citing *reguls.* of 1763 and 1764, Cap.13, §7).

45. Nascimento e Silva, *Synopse legislação militar* 1:132 (citing circular of 27 July and *prov.* of 12 Aug. 1848).

46. Bills annulling Art. 1 of the Law of 16 Mar. 1757—the Law of the Cadets—were introduced in 1829 and 1830. Vieira da Cunha, *Nobreza brasileira*, pp. 23–29n55-A&B, citing *ACD 1850*, 2:569.

47. *Repertorio legislação militar*, 2:327.

48. Vieira da Cunha, *Nobreza brasileira*, p. 44 (citing Law of 18 Aug. 1831, Arts. 69–70, creating the National Guard).

49. Ibid., pp. 42–45 (citing Law No. 602 of 19 Sept. 1850). *Ofício* N.66 of *prov.* Gov. of Maranhão, 5 Mar. 1854; *res.* of 16 Nov. 1853.

50. Ibid., p. 44 (citing the Law of 18 Aug. 1831, Arts. 69–70, creating the National Guard); and pp. 52–53 (citing *ACD 1848* 11:103–4). Law of 2 Sept. 1847, Art.1.

51. Law of 16 Mar. 1757, Art.1. Nascimento e Silva, *Synopse legislação militar*, 1:136 (citing *res.* of 18 Oct. 1862). See also the case of Sgt. Manuel Pedro Alves, natural son of National Guard Lieut. Samuel Hartman, denied admission as a second cadet on appeal to the Council of State (*res.* 17 Nov. 1883). Vieira da Cunha, *Nobreza brasileira*, p. 54.

52. Paula Cidade, *Cadetes alunos militares*, p. 29. Thus Mar. Floriano Peixoto failed to attain the status of a second cadet or private soldier, but Mar. Deodoro da Fonseca and the duke of Caxias became cadets, thanks to the natural nobility they possessed. Ibid.

53. *Als.* of 31 May 1777, 21 Oct. 1763 (§6); *res.* 30 Aug. 1823 and *prov.* & *av.* of 19 Aug. 1837; on house arrest and "consideration": orders of the army of 10 Aug. 1809 and 3 Jan. 1817; circular of 17 July 1855. Cited in Nascimento e Silva, *Synopse legislação militar*, 2:247–53.

54. Candido Mendes, *Aux. juridico*, p. 524 (citing *Ord.*, L.1, T.86, §42).

55. *Cód. processo penal 1941*, Art. 295, §§1–11. The following laws complement the 1941 Criminal Procedural Code: Nos. 1799 (1949), 2860 (1956), 3313 (1957), 3988 (1961), 4878 (1965), 5256&5350 (1967), 5606 (1970), 35 (1979), 7102&7172 (1983), 8069 (1990), 75& 80 (1993&1994, respectively). I am grateful to Osvaldo Agripino for providing these refererences.

56. 17 July, *ACD 1827*, 3:195.

57. The Law of 9 Sept. 1769, §§12,14; *Notices*, 1:201, 256.

58. Beal, "Regalismo Brasil" (citing Law of 11 Aug. 1827), p. 216.

59. 3 June, *ACD 1828*, 2:16.

60. Ibid.

61. 9 June, ibid., 2:65.

62. Ibid., 2:66.

63. Ibid., 2:66–72.

64. Ibid., 3:30–32, 65, 88.

65. *AS 1828*, 2:121; 9 July, *AS 1829*, 2:72ff.

66. Holloway, *Policing Rio de Janeiro*, pp. 28–33, 44–45. Like Portugal's 1821 Constituinte, Brazil's 1823 Constituent Assembly favored the "individual guarantee" of trial by jury; however, it was deleted from D. Pedro's revised 1824 Constitution, leaving jury trials contingent on the legislature's adoption of legal codes. Flory, *Judge and Jury*, pp. 116–17.

67. Candido Mendes, *Aux. juridico*, p. 775–76. The Regidor das Justiças, who presided over the Casa da Suplicação, almost always possessed royal blood. Schwartz, *Sovereignty and Society*, p. 9.

68. Nizza da Silva, *Império luso-brasileiro*, pp. 316, 318–19. In 1812, creation of a separate *Relação* for Maranhão removed appeals to Lisbon.

69. Candido Mendes, *Aux. juridico*, p. 777n3; Rheingantz, *Titulares*, p. 67.

70. See Dauphinee, "Church and Parliament," pp. 33–34, 33n34. Neves has recently clarified the role of the Mesa da Consciência e Ordens in the 1820s: *E receberá mercê*. Beal, "Regalismo brasileiro," p. 156n76; Nizza da Silva, *Império luso-brasileiro*, pp. 307–8n3.

71. Neves, *Receberá mercê*, p. 121. On the papal dimension of Pedro's role as Grand Master—bargaining over the *Padroado Régio*—see pp. 126–28.

72. Ibid., p. 121 (citing the Law of 22 Sept. 1828, Art.1).

73. Candido Mendes, *Aux. juridico*, p. 775.

74. 3 July, *AS 1828*, 2:90. On legislators' disdain for the high crown courts, their Coimbra-trained *desembargadores*, and the venality of judges, see Flory, *Judge and Jury*, pp. 31–38.

75. 3 July, *AS 1828*, 2:90.

76. Ibid. Italics added.

77. Law of 22 Sept. 1828, Arts.3–5, *CLIB 1828*, Pt.1, pp. 47–50.

78. Candido Mendes, *Aux. juridico*, p. 777n3. Palma moved from presiding judge (*regidor*) of the Casa da Suplicação (1824–1825) to President of the Desembargo do Paço in 1825, serving in that capacity after 1828. Ibid.

79. Law of 22 Sept. 1828, Art.2, §§1,6, and 9. The justice of the peace, or parish judge, was created by the Law of 15 Oct. 1827. He amounted to a magistrate "at first set adrift in the uncomplementary and hostile structure of the largely unchanged colonial judiciary." Flory, *Judge and Jury*, p. 50. See also Holloway, "Justice of the Peace," pp. 65–72.

80. Law of 22 Sept. 1828, Art.2, §6.

81. Flory, *Judge and Jury*, pp. 113–15.

82. The bill that became the 1828 Judiciary Act was amended (Art.2, §1) in the Senate, changing "orphans judge" to "judge of the first instance," thereby making it possible for the justice of the peace *or* the municipal judge to substitute for the orphans judge, whenever the latter office was vacant. 28 June, *AS 1828*, 1:76.

83. Lafayette, *Dir. familia*, Cap.3, T.3, §§117,119 (pp. 241–47). The Law of 31 Oct. 1831 lowered the age of majority to twenty-one, but the *filho-famílias* still lacked legal capacity for civil acts, due to his father's exercise of *pátrio poder*.

84. Flory, *Judge and Jury*, pp. 51, 59, 62, 64.

85. Law No. 143, 15 Mar. 1842, Art.2, §5.

86. Nazzari, "Urgent Need To Conceal," p. 120; Nizza da Silva, "Desembargo do Paço," p. 74 (both citing AN, *Legitimações*, cxa. 127, *pac.* 2, *doc.* 21).

87. Flory, *Judge and Jury*, p. 34.

88. Ibid., pp. 50–51, 59, 69.

89. 28 June, *AS 1828*, 1:77–78.

90. *Ord.*, p. 944n1 (quoting Teixeira de Freitas, *Consol.*, Art. 217n1).

CHAPTER 3

1. *ACD 1827*, 2:163.

2. *Travels*, pp. 141–42.

3. "Such connexion unsanctioned by marriage is the usual domestic arrangement of all Brazilians of this class, particularly in the interior." Walsh, *Notices* 2:53. Thomas Ewbank, who deemed "the priesthood of this country superlatively corrupt," quoted an old resident of Rio de Janeiro to the effect that "with country priests concubinage is universal." *Life in Brazil*, pp. 141–42. Dain Borges estimated that "about half of the priests in Salvador had children in the late nineteenth century"; in rural parishes "most priests openly kept mistresses and families." *Family Bahia*, p. 167. In eighteenth-century Minas Gerais, "concubinage was very common among the clergy, owing in large part to the secular character of priests." Mello e Souza, *Desclassificados*, p. 176.

4. Dunshee de Abranches, *O captiveiro*, pp. 50–51, excerpted as "Racial Conflict Maranhão," ed. and trans. Conrad, p. 229.

5. Gardner, *Travels*, p. 142.

6. Ibid. Gardner identified the senator-priest as "the son of the vicar of Crato [Miguel Carlos da Silva Saldanha]." In fact, he was his godson. Beal, "Regalismo Brasil," p. 178n37.

7. Londoño, *Concubinato y iglesia*, p. 38. The relative independence of parish priests often derived from privately established *capelas*, making them answerable to local families who established those ecclesiastical entails as income funds more remunerative than clerical stipends. Ibid.

8. Higgins, "*Licentious Liberty*," p. 109.

9. Ramos, "Gossip, Scandal, Popular Culture," pp. 889–90.

10. L.5, T.22, §979.

11. Ramos identifies responses to Monteiro da Vide's 1720 *Regimento do auditorio ecclesiastico* as the key repository of injunctions derived from a popular voice. A manual for conducting ecclesiastical visitations, 24 of the *Regimento's* 40 questions qualified sinful behavior as producing scandal that was either "common knowledge" or "public and well known." "Gossip, Scandal, Popular Culture," pp. 890–91.

12. Lewcowicz, "Fragilidade celibato," p. 64. Nazzari, "Concubinage," pp. 112, 122n36. Denunciation of *mancebia* amounted to over 80% of the sins reported in episcopal visits in eighteenth-century Minas Gerais and Mato Grosso. Ibid. In the Archbishopric of Bahia, an 1813 episcopal investigation found *mancebia* amounted to 35.7% of sins denounced (213 accusations), the largest category. Among 291 individuals prosecuted for *mancebia*, 28% were married to other partners (64 men and 17 women) and 17% cohabited as unmarried individuals. Mott, *Pecados*, pp. 13–14. In a 1734 episcopal visit to Sabará, Minas Gerais, 93.2% (221) of the 237 individuals were charged with *mancebia*, but only 6 (4.2%) of 142 men were accused of adultery. Higgins, "*Licentious Liberty*," pp. 111–12.

13. Gama Lima, "Padre e moça," pp. 25–36.

14. Law of 5 Apr. 1821, cited in Coelho da Rocha, *Ensaio*, p. 234.

15. On the "panic" and "complicity" produced by the Inquisition in denunciations of sin, see Vainfas, *Trópico dos pecados*, pp. 224–32. Parish priests used mandatory Lenten confession and threat of excommunication for revealing concubinage. Nazzari, "Concubinage," p. 112.

16. For an 1800 case of "stonewalling" the episcopal investigator, in the diocese of Mariana, see Lewcowicz, "Fragilidade celibato," pp. 66–67.

17. See Seed, *Love, Honor, Obey*, esp. Part II; and Nancy Farriss, *Crown, Clergy, Mexico*.

18. L.5, T.24, §§1000, 1001 (cited in Vainfas, *Trópico dos pecados*, p. 74). Priests were punished with admonition and a fine of 10 *cruzados* for a first offense. Subsequent offenses brought deprivation of clerical fees, stipend, and pension; those refusing to abandon *mancebia* could suffer excommunication. Vide, *Con. primeiras*, L.5, T.24, §§994–96.

19. 1750s cases from four provinces are discussed in Gama Lima, "Padre e moça," pp. 28–32; see Vainfas, "Condenação adultérios," pp. 40–41. Priests guilty of "qualified concubinage" (canonically "prohibited" sexual intercourse) were punished by ecclesiastical authority, but their paramours were punished by the civil authorities. Nizza da Silva, *Sistema casamento*, p. 44.

20. *Con. primeiras*, L.5, T.24, §1000.

21. Londoño, *Concubinato y iglesia*, p. 38. On the failure of episcopal reform in the eighteenth century, see Venâncio, *Ilegitimidade e concubinato*, pp. 8–9.

22. Londoño compares how adulterous concubinage was treated respectively by the *Ord. Filipinas*, the Council of Trent, and the *Con. primeiras*. *Concubinato y iglesia*, pp. 35–52.

23. *Con. primeiras*, L.5, T.22, §980. Nazzari, "Concubinage," p. 112, 121n35 (for clerics, citing *Con. primeiras*, T.19, §968).

24. *Con. primeiras*, L.5, T.22, §988. See the 1785 case of Leonardo Soares de Souza, in Londoño, "Crime do amor," pp. 17–18. For exceptions, see the cases of Manoel Pires Dias, in Nazzari, "Concubinage," p. 112 (citing *Con. primeiras*, L.5, §789); and Jacinto Pacheco Pereira, in Higgins, "*Licentious Liberty*," pp. 110–11.

25. *Dir. civ. Port.*, L.1, T.17, §159, N.3a (p. 197).

26. Ibid., N.9 (p. 197, citing *Ord.*, L.5, T.25, §3; and *al.* of 26 Sept. 1769). On illegal prosecution, see the examples of a São Paulo provincial governor (1780) and the crown *ouvidor* (1805), in Nizza da Silva, *Sistema casamento*, pp. 44–45.

27. *Con. primeiras*, Appendix to L.5, showing "how the *Constituições* are altered or revoked by the laws of the Empire and finally modified by usage and customs" (pp. 149–71). On adultery, see T.19, §§966–68 (p. 165).

28. On the survival of honor and morality in the 1830 Criminal Code, vis-à-vis gender, see Caulfield, *Defense of Honor*, pp. 23–24ff. On the Code's assumption that a wife's adultery exerted pernicious effect on her family, in contrast to the innocuousness of her husband's "meanderings," see Malerba, *Brancos da lei*, pp. 47–48.

29. Malerba, *Brancos da lei*, pp. 27, 36; 46–47. As proof "the figure of the father was religiously preserved in the code," Malerba quoted Dep. Manuel Mendes da Cunha Azevedo, who deplored that the Code failed to exact a greater penalty for parricide than for homicide. Ibid., p. 46.

30. Ramos, "Gossip, Scandal, Popular Culture," p. 892.

31. Malerba, *Brancos da lei*, p. 48 (citing Paula Pessoa, *Cod. Criminal Imperio*, 2nd ed. [1885], p. 423).

32. *Cod. Penal Império [1830]*, pp. 165–265.

33. Cunha Mattos, claiming the privileges of the state over the Brazilian church were equal to or greater than those of the state over the Portuguese church. 21 June, *ACD 1827*, 2:128.

34. Dauphinee, "Church and Parliament," p. 142n1. Until the law of 27 Aug. 1830 abolished it, by converting it into a tribunal of the second and final instance, Brazil's metropolitan appellate marriage court known as *De legacia* remanded con-

flicts over the validity of a marriage, often with important civil consequences, to Rome. See the case of Maria and Lucio, analyzed ibid., p. 173. Candido Mendes, *Ord.*, p. 1231.

35. *ACD 1827*, 2:156–61.

36. *De Reformatione Matrimonii* instructed the parish priest to join the couple in matrimony "*na face da igreja*"—before the altar—with two or three witnesses present, once the banns revealed no impediment. On pain of a null marriage, couples were to be married only by their parish priest, unless permission came from the parish's ordinary, who was authorized to dispense the banns. "Decreta da Reforma do Matrimonio" [trans. of *De Reformatione Matrimonii*], Cap.1, 2:633.

37. "[T]here being no impediment . . . our permission or that of the Provisor is not necessary . . ." *Con. primeiras*, L.1, Tit.68, §291. 18 June, *ACD 1827*, 2:89.

38. 18 June, *ACD 1827*, 2:89. The bishop-elect of Maranhão resisted standardization, believing that, within their own dioceses, Brazilian bishops enjoyed "the right to make statutes and take other disciplinary means for good organization of the dioceses, and to regulate the grounds and evidence pertaining to those [free] to marry, as long as they did not run counter to canonical rules and the civil law of the Empire." 26 June, *ACD 1827*, 2:157.

39. 18 June, *ACD 1827*, 2:89.

40. On the absence of this arrangement in northern dioceses, see 27 June, ibid., 2:163. For accusations against specific dioceses, see statements by the bishop-elect of Maranhão and Deps. Cunha Mattos, Clemente Pereira, and Teixeira de Gouvêa, for 26 June, ibid. 2:157–58, 162.

41. Mesquita Samara, *Mulheres, poder, família*, p. 91. Nizza da Silva, *Sistema casamento*, p. 132–33.

42. Vergueiro, 26–27 June, *ACD 1827*, 2:157–59, 163. Saint-Hilaire rrecorded the 1796 appeal of the town council of Caeté, Minas Gerais, to Maria I, protesting episcopal directives to pay diocesan priests and the "ridiculous proceedings" for enabling couples to marry. *Segunda viagem*, p. 84.

43. 26 June, *ACD 1827*, 2:158.

44. 27 June, ibid., 2:163–64. Vainfas pointed to bigamy as "meriting the greatest vigilance and punishment of moral crimes by inquisitorial authority," in late eighteenth- and early nineteenth-century Minas Gerais, including among slaves. *Trópico dos pecados*, pp. 253, 289–90, 292. On Minas Gerais, where "bigamy was frequent," see also Mello e Souza, *Desclassificados*, p. 156.

45. To the first bishoprics in Brazil, those of Bahia (an archbishopric and, under Pombal, seat of the metropolitan), Maranhão, and Rio de Janeiro, were added four more in the late colonial era: Pernambuco, Mato Grosso, São Paulo, and Mariana (Minas Gerais). In 1827, the aforementioned dioceses of Cuiabá (Goiás) and Mato Grosso were proposed by the pope, but could not be confirmed by him until 1839.

46. 26 June, *ACD 1827*, 2:157.

47. 27 June, ibid., 2:162.

48. 26 June, ibid., 2:160–61; 12 July, ibid., 3:141. Bishops in older dioceses (Rio de Janeiro, Salvador, and Maranhão) received one *conto*. The stipend in the newer diocese of Mariana had risen to 1:600$, generating Dep. Custodio Dias' amendment to equalize all stipends, including those for the future bishoprics of Goiás and Mato Grosso. It failed. 9–10 Aug., *ACD 1827*, 4:89–91.

49. See Chap. 17, "Arancel Disputes," of Taylor's pathbreaking analysis for the late colonial era: *Magistrates of the Sacred*.

50. Venâncio, *Ilegitimidade e concubinato*, pp. 8–9. For a dissenting view, that cost was not an obstacle to contracting marriage, see Vainfas, *Trópico dos pecados*, pp. 85–87. 27 June, *ACD 1827*, 2:162.

51. 26 June, ibid., 2:158.

52. *Segunda viagem*, p. 84. "In 1796 the town council of the *vila* of Caeté sent a delegation to Queen Maria I to protest the directives of the bishops of Mariana, making them pay the priests of their dioceses, as well as to object to the ridiculous proceedings that two persons, who were in admirable understanding with each other, were forced to undertake in order to contract marriage. The government initially ordered some information taken down, but the delegation did not produce results." Ibid.

53. Ibid. The "generous bishop" was D. Jozé Caetano da Silva Coutinho.

54. 30 June, *ACD 1827*, 2:195; 2 July, ibid. 3:20. 3 July, *AS 1827*, 1:345; 1–2 Oct., ibid., 3:92–95; Aug. 18, ibid., 2:204–6. 6 and 11 Oct., *ACD 1827*, 5:107–8, 123. *Dec.* of 13 Nov. 1827, *CLIB 1827*, p. 1128. Congonhas do Campo, former provincial president of São Paulo, singled out his own diocese of Mariana (Minas Gerais), in addition to those of Rio de Janeiro and São Paulo, as notorious examples of deviating from the dicta of the *Con. primeiras* on matrimony. *AS 1827*, 2:205–6. Amendment citing *Con. primeiras*, L.1, T.64, §269: 1 Oct., *AS 1827*, 3:93.

55. 26–27 June, *ACD 1827*, 2:158, 163; Sacramento Blake, *Diccionario*, 5:7. Lino Coutinho, *Cartas sobre educação Cora*.

56. Couples who lived "in reputation of husband and wife, sharing bed and board, signing contracts, etc.," were not punished with death for transgressing a dire impediment—the fate of the adulterer (*Con. primeiras*, L.5, T.26, §1). But the married man who maintained a concubine (*barregã*) was subject to exile to Africa or imprisonment (T.28).

57. An 1813 episcopal investigation in the diocese of Bahia revealed that, of the total 213 denunciations for concubinage, 46 (21%) cases referred to couples who maintained stable relationships. In 17% of the cases, couples lived "*de portas a dentro*"—cohabiting—and otherwise men confessed they lived with concubines "as if they were married" (*teúdas e manteúdas*).

58. Nizza da Silva identified clandestine marriage as a strategy of the poor (motivated by impediments of affinity) or the propertied (motivated by impediments of consanguinity). *Sistema casamento*, p. 113 (citing Alexandre Herculano's reference to "*mariage à la Gaulmine*," in *Estudos sobre o casamento civil*).

59. Candido Mendes, "Axiomas e brocardos," p. 566 (citing Art. 248 of *Cod. Penal Imperio [1830]* and *al.* of 13 Nov. 1651). The Council of Trent condemned clandestine marriage performed without a priest, wherein the parties married themselves. It recognized the form of clandestine marriage known in English as "secret marriage" ("*casamento oculto*" or "*em segredo*"), i.e., performed in private by a priest who dispensed the banns and used the words of "present promise." Lobão, *Notas*, L.2, T.8, §4, N.3 (p. 241). In the 1820s, Borges Carneiro referred to clandestine marriage as "marriage of conscience" [*matrimônio de consciência*], normally prohibited, but celebrated with a bishop's dispensation. *Dir. civ. Port.*, L.1, v.2, T.11, §111, N.17 (p. 50).

60. 17 July, *AS 1829*, 2:128.

61. *Dir. civ. Port.*, L.1, v.2, T.11, §112, Par. 1 (p. 52). Borges Carneiro also referred to a variant of concubinage that formerly in common law "was considered unequal marriage and less solemn." He pronounced it "completely repudiated and without civil effects." Ibid., T.17, §159, N.1 (p. 197).

62. *Notas*, L.2, T.8, §4, N.2 (p. 240).

63. Ibid., N.1 (p. 240).

64. Vainfas, *Trópico dos pecados*, p. 71 (citing Teofilo Braga, *Povo português, costumes*, 1:182).

65. Lobão, *Notas*, L.2, T.6, §2, Ns.2–3 (pp. 181–82); T.8, §4, N.2 (pp. 240–41).

66. Ibid., p. 74. As Vainfas notes, Moraes e Silva's 1813 *Diccionário lingua portuguêsa* defined "*concubina*" as both "*manceba*" and "*amásia*," in addition to "*amiga de um só*"—a female friend exclusive to one man! Ibid., p. 72.

67. Ibid., citing *Ord.*, L.5, T.28: "Para prova do casamento do que se diz ser barregueiro casado, bem assim bastará provar-se que elle está em voz e fama de casado . . . ."

68. *Notas*, L.2, T.8, §4, Ns.1–2 (pp. 240–41).

69. Ibid., N.2 (p. 141); T.6, §2 (p. 181).

70. Pereira Freire, *Instituiçoens*, L.2, T.9, §27 (pp. 55–56), trans. of Paschoal José de Mello Freire, *Institutiones juris civilis luzitani*, Book 2. References herein to Book 2 of Mello Freire's *Institutiones* [also *Institutionum*] henceforth cite Pereira Freire's vernacular translation as follows: Mello Freire, *Instituiçoens* (1834). NOTE: Brazilian legislators referred to the original Latin edition with a Portuguese title, as "the *Instituições de direito civil* of José [Mello] Freire."

71. Nizza da Silva, *Sistema casamento*, p. 44 (quoting *Classes de crimes*). Pereira e Souza reiterated that the law of 26 Sept. 1769 prohibited criminal proceedings for simple (illicit) concubinage. However, Pereira e Souza's *Classes de crimes* was identified by Candido Mendes as "an appendix" to his *Primeiras linhas* (1785), meaning the latter's refutation of marriage according to the *Ordenações* presumably predated Mello Freire's 1788 defense of customary marriage. "Epitome," p. 788.

72. 26 June, *ACD 1827*, 2:159.

CHAPTER 4

1. "Demonstrasão," 2:119.

2. "Reflexoens," 2:387, 403.

3. The Spanish crown council received only eight petitions to legitimize *sacrílegos* between 1716 and 1775, all of which were granted. Between 1776 and 1793, the only two petitions filed were denied. Twinam, *Public Lives*, pp. 248, 252–54, 260, 264–65 (Tables 12–14).

4. Nizza da Silva, "Filhos ilegítimos," p. 123.

5. Ibid., p. 124. Priests' close relatives usually waived their *ab intestato* rights in favor of equipping legitimized *sacrílegos* as successors. Ibid.

6. *Notices*, 1:208–9.

7. Sousa, *Feijó*, p. 81.

8. On Abbot Manuel Joaquim de Miranda, whose parish of Sant'Ana was in Rio de Janeiro, and Mon. Antonio Marinho, an imperial deputy for Minas Gerais, both of whom lived in concubinage and fathered children, see Beal, "Regalismo Brasil," p. 179n41. On the 1846 wedding of the daughter of a priest to the son of the Vicar of São

José Parish (Rio de Janeiro), who publicly acknowledged his large family, see Ewbank, *Life in Brazil*, p. 142.

9. Kidder, *Sketches of Residence*, 1:64.

10. Moura was nominated bishop on 22 Mar. 1833. He withdrew his nomination five years later, after the Vatican refused to consecrate him, on the ground of his improper dispensations for defects of illegitimacy and "paralysis" (epilepsy), meaning outside the appropriate diocese of Mariana. Beal, "Regalismo Brasil," pp. 188n62–90n66. Sacramento Blake, *Diccionario*, 1:258.

11. Barman, *Citizen Emperor*, pp. 221, 399 (citing Magalhães Jr., *Três panfletários*, pp. 3–43; and Taunay, *Reminiscências*, pp. 33–80). Sacramento Blake, *Diccionario*, 3:114–15.

12. Walsh, *Notices*, 1:208.

13. Ibid., 1:209.

14. 10 Oct., *ACD 1827*, 5:115.

15. 3 Sept., ibid., 5:11.

16. 10 Oct., ibid., 5:115. Feijó's verbally delivered report appears ibid., 5:115–19, and debate in 5:119–21.

17. Feijó's rhetoric teacher was Estanislau João de Oliveira, a former Coimbra University professor who fled persecution under Maria I. Beal, "Regalismo Brasil," p. 180.

18. Fernandes Pinheiro, "Padres do Patrocínio," p. 140 *passim*.

19. Egas, *Feijó*, 1:3–18. Letter of Dr. Richard Gumbleton Daunt to baron Homem de Mello, 17 July 1856, reprinted in Ellis Júnior, *Feijó*, pp. 472–75. See also Ricci, *Padre-Regente*.

20. Barman describes Feijó as the father of five. *Forging Brazil*, p. 171. Beal denies Sousa's allegation that Feijó was the "unknown" father of his unmarried cousin's (Maria Luisa Camargo) six children. "Regalismo Brasil," p. 176n33 (citing Sousa's *Feijó*, pp. 107–9; and *A Matraca dos Farroupilhos* [Rio de Janeiro], Nos. 6&9 [17 Jan. and 7 Feb. 1832]).

21. 10 Oct., *ACD 1827*, 5:120–21. Romualdo quoted Erasmus, who viewed Martin Luther "with an air of comedy, because everything [in the Reformation] came down to marriage." Ibid.

22. "Demonstrasão," 2:98–156. Beal identified the professor as Jozé Manoel da Veiga, author of *Memoria contra o celibato clerical* (Coimbra, 1822). "Regalismo Brazil," p. 173n22.

23. "Demonstrasão," 2:108–30.

24. Ibid., p. 100.

25. 10 Oct., *ACD 1827*, 5:119 ("Demonstrasão," Arts. 1&2).

26. Ibid. ("Demonstrasão," Art. 3).

27. Ibid.

28. Feijó's 1827 response was "Resposta ás parvoices," in Egas, *Feijó*, 2:157–73.

29. Seixas, "Resposta [14 June 1834]" to the *av.* of 4 Mar. 1834 of Min. of Justice Aureliano de Souza Oliveira, 2:369.

30. Ibid., 2:357–58.

31. *Life in Brazil*, p. 143.

32. "Demonstrasão," 2:115–23. Feijó emphasized a standard argument, that at

Trent the Christian princes had been nearly unanimous in calling for abolition of clerical celibacy.

33. "Resposta," 2:355. Romualdo fell back on the 10 March 1791 encyclical of Pius VI, directed to the Bishops' Assembly in revolutionary France, "showing clearly that points of discipline connected to dogma are equal to dogma." Ibid.

34. In 1827, Vergueiro had opposed the government's sponsorship of Swiss German immigration as incompatible with the interests of São Paulo planters. His efforts to bring European colonists to São Paulo dated to 1842–1845. Viotti da Costa, *Brazilian Empire*, pp. 94–95, 100–101.

35. Forjaz, *Sen. Vergueiro*, p. 341.

36. The redactor omitted the bill's text from the *AS 1829* for July 4 and 17: 2:25–26, 128–32.

37. In 1832, D. Romualdo publicly argued that "heterodox" marriages between Catholics and "heretics" taking place with a dispensation from a prelate would enjoy standing "only in custom" (*á face de costume*), i.e., with the sacrament withheld. Consequently, his "toleration" amounted only to not making the demand of conversion from the non-Catholic partner—a precondition meaning the ceremony would establish legal marriage. "Representação," 2:297.

38. 4 July, *AS 1829*, 2:25–26.

39. D. Romualdo even acknowledged that marriage was a contract in both natural and divine law that prefigured the sacrament of matrimony. However, "so great was the weight of doctrine derived from the Council of Trent, that no distinction was made between the contract and the sacrament." "Representação," 2:279, 281.

40. 4 July, *AS 1829*, 2:25–26.

41. Vergueiro, 17 July, ibid., 2:131.

42. "Necrologia Caravellas," pp. VII-VIII.

43. "Não tem os paes [*pátrio poder*] nos filhos naturaes e espurios." Candido Mendes, "Axiomas e brochardos," p. 575 (citing Lobão, *Acções summarias*, §368).

44. See Nazzari, "Widows as Obstacles to Business," p. 795. Conflicts of foreign and Brazilian inheritance law, vis-à-vis surviving non-Brazilian spouses of legally married couples, largely had to be resolved by treaties guaranteeing extra-territoriality of inheritance rights. Ibid., pp. 784–85.

45. Carneiro de Campos, 17 July, *AS 1829*, 2:128.

46. Ibid.

47. 4 July, ibid., 2:25.

48. Ibid., 2:26.

49. 17 July, ibid., 2:129, 132.

50. Ibid., 2:129–31.

51. Ibid., 2:132.

52. Ibid., 2:130.

53. Seixas, "Representação [20 July 1832]," 2:297, 302–3.

54. Beal, "Regalismo Brasil," pp. 231–32. Ewbank reported that Bedini delivered a sermon in Petrópolis, declaring "all married Catholics among [the Protestants] are living in concubinage; their marriages are void, and their children illegitimate." *Life in Brazil*, p. 393.

55. Lavrin, *Women Argentina, Chile, Uruguay*, p. 228.

56. Ibid., p. 227. Civil marriage in these contexts was "performed by a servant of the state," and mandatory for any civil effects.

57. Joaquim Nabuco construed his father's bill as "the first on civil marriage elaborated by the Government," that is, by the Cabinet, not the legislature. *Estadista imperio*, 1:217.

58. Seixas, *Representação à sua magestade* (1859); and Seixas, *Representação às camaras* (1859).

59. *Narrativas*, pp. 77–78.

CHAPTER 5

1. "Declaration of Recognition of Izabel Maria de Alcântara Brasileira by D. Pedro I," 24 May 1826; reprinted in Rangel, *Pedro e Santos*, p. 383.

2. Walsh, *Notices*, 1:196; Mello Moraes [Pai], *Chronica geral*, 2:116. Rheingantz, *Titulares*, pp. 16 and 46.

3. Graham, *Journal*, p. 126.

4. Mello Moraes [Pai], *Chronica geral*, 2:282. A free woman of color, the daughter's existence was recalled in the 1820s because "Joanna Parda" [Mosquera] bore a son to Emperor D. Pedro I.

5. Rugendas, *Viagem pintoresca*, p. 130.

6. *Journal*, p. 112.

7. On the appropriation of malicious gossip, see Freyre, *Ordem e progresso*, 1:clix; and Levi, *The Prados*, p. 234n83.

8. Ibid., pp. 120–21n82 (citing *In memorium, Martinho Prado Júnior*).

9. Macaulay, *Dom Pedro*, pp. 102, 236 (citing Sousa, *José Bonifácio, 1763–1838*, pp. 19–94).

10. *Journal*, p. 169; p. 166–67.

11. Holloway, *Policing Rio de Janeiro*, pp. 47, 314n38.

12. Ibid., pp. 186, 326n35 (citing Police Chief Antonio Simões da Silva's 1849 report on a crackdown and deportation of 15 foreigners, mostly Portuguese, some of whom ran bordellos where "orgies were constant").

13. Ibid., pp. 46–47.

14. Macaulay, *Dom Pedro*, pp. 50 (citing Arago, *Narrative*), 79.

15. Rangel, *Pedro e Santos*, p. 65 (citing José Delavat y Rincón).

16. *Journal*, p. 225.

17. Rangel, *Pedro e Santos*, p. 65.

18. Saint-Hilaire, *Segunda viagem*, p. 85.

19. Walsh, *Notices*, 1:261.

20. Rangel, *Pedro e Santos*, p. 65.

21. Macaulay, *Dom Pedro*, p. 50 (citing Arago, *Narrative*, pp. 79–80).

22. On Mangue's history, see Caulfield, "Birth of Mangue." On Mangue's recent demolition, see Muello, "Rio de Janeiro's Oldest Red Light." I am grateful to Elizabeth Lewin for bringing this article to my attention.

23. Engel, *Meretrizes e doutores*, pp. 39 and 56n6.

24. Rangel, *Pedro e Santos*, p. 65.

25. Karasch, *Slave Life*, p. 207 (citing Schlichthorst, *O Rio de Janeiro como é*, p.

208n71; and Toussaint (Samson), *Parisian in Brazil*). See also Lauderdale Graham, "Slavery's Impasse."

26. Karasch, *Slave Life*, p. 295.

27. Quoted in Mesgravis, *Santa Casa Misericordia*, p. 175 (citing *Viagem a São Paulo* [*sic*] [São Paulo, s/d, s/p]).

28. Ibid.

29. Rangel, *Pedro e Santos*, p. 65.

30. Karasch, *Slave Life*, p. 23 (citing Harro-Harring, *Tropical Sketches*).

31. Ibid., p. 207n70 (citing *Diario 2*, 29 Sept. 1821:188).

32. Ibid., p. 363n84 (citing *O Diario do Rio de Janeiro*, 6 July and 26 Oct. 1821, pp. 37, 182).

33. Alencar, *Senhora* [1875], p. 89.

34. *O captiveiro*, p. 228.

35. Dean, *Rio Claro*, Table 3.10, pp. 60, 62, 74–75.

36. Ibid., pp. 68, 75, and notes.

37. Pang, *Pursuit of Honor*, pp. 191, 261 (citing Leoni Iorio, *Valença de ôntem*, p. 191).

38. Ibid., pp. 258–59. NOTE: Presumably, the will was written under universal heirship and the father had freed his children.

39. Karasch, *Slave Life*, p. 208.

40. Ibid.

41. Graham, *Journal*, p. 197.

42. Ibid., pp. 125–26.

43. Sousa, *Vida Pedro I*, 1:3.

44. Ibid., pp. 10–11; Macaulay, *Dom Pedro*, pp. 9n9 (citing William Beckford, *Travel Diaries*, 5:370–71), 9n11, and 307.

45. Mello Moraes [Pai], *A independencia*, pp. 239–40.

46. Rangel, *Pedro e Santos*, pp. 66, 87.

47. Ibid., p. 75.

48. Ibid., p. 73.

49. Macaulay, *Dom Pedro*, p. 53.

50. Ibid., p. 122n63. On Pedro's abusive treatment of a woman of good family, see Seidler, *Dez annos Brasil*, pp. 82–83.

51. *Al.* of 9 Jan. 1817; Mello Moraes [Pai], *Chronica geral*, 2:24.

52. Sousa, *Vida Pedro I*, p. 79.

53. Ibid., pp. 77–79; Rangel, *Pedro e Santos*, p. 70. An account of the affair can be found in Graham, *Journal*, pp. 113, 186–87ff; and Mello Moraes [Pai], *Chronica geral*, 2:73–74.

54. D. João arranged for Moemi to be married. Rangel, *Pedro e Santos*, p. 70; Sousa, *Vida Pedro I*, pp. 80–81; Mello Moraes [Pai], *Chronica geral*, 2:259–61; Rheingantz, *Titulares*, p. 41.

55. The corpse, discovered in Pedro's apartments by Regency officials, was buried in 1831 by order of Min. of Justice Feijó. Sousa, *Vida Pedro I*, pp. 79–81; Rangel, *Pedro e Santos*, p. 70.

56. On the 12 July 1873 petition of naval officer Theotonio Meirelles (b. 1822) to Emperor D. Pedro II, misrepresenting himself as a "natural offspring" of Pedro I, when he was really adulterine, see Rangel, *Pedro e Santos*, p. 74n1.

57. Seidler, *Dez anos*, p. 82.

58. Rangel, *Pedro e Santos*, p. 131. Domitila and Felicio Pinto Coelho de Men-donça signed their final separation agreement seven months later, on 10 Jan. 1825.

59. Baptismal entry for "Izabel, *exposta*," 31 May 1824, Livro de Batismos, Arquivo da Igreja de S. Francisco Xavier do Engenho Velho, Rio de Janeiro; reprinted ibid., p. 440. Empress Leopoldina gave birth to her sixth child, Francisca Carolina, on 2 Aug. 1824.

60. Walsh, *Notices* 1:153. The first-born son of Pedro I and Leopoldina, João Carlos (b. 1821), died in 1822.

61. Rangel, *Pedro e Santos*, p. 137.

62. Baptismal entry for "Pedro," 27 Dec. 1825, Livro de Batismos, Arquivo da Igreja de S. Francisco Xavier do Engenho Velho, Rio de Janeiro; reprinted ibid., p. 441. NOTE: The Corte's first registry for secret marriages was established around 1800 at the Engenho Velho church. Nizza da Silva, *Sistema casamento*, p. 114; Alencar, *Senhora*, p. 64.

63. Rangel, *Pedro e Santos*, pp. 144–45.

64. Ibid., p. 146. Paranaguá was minister of the navy; Palma, Pedro's close friend, was mayordomo of the Palace.

65. Walsh, *Notices*, 1:272; Toussaint (Samson), *Parisian in Brazil*, pp. 130–31.

66. Rangel, *Pedro e Santos*, pp. 146–47.

67. Ibid., p. 153, referring to "um solemne processo de reconhecimento de filia-ção."

68. MacDonald, "Alfonso's Reform," p. 161.

69. Oliveira Marques, *From Lusitania to Empire*, pp. 126–27.

70. *Notas*, L.2, T.5, §§5–6 (p. 187); Liz Teixeira, *Curso dir. civil port.*, Pt.1, T.6, §5 (p. 126), glossing *Ord.*, L.5, T.92, §7.

71. Schneider, *Marquês Pombal*, pp. 8, 20.

72. Information on Bernardo and Francisco de Lorena is from Rangel, *Pedro e Santos*, pp. 93–94; and Maxwell, *Pombal*, p. 79.

73. Rangel, *Pedro e Santos*, pp. 93–94.

74. Gérson, *Regalismo brasileiro*, pp. 25, 27; Graham, *Journal*, p. 321.

75. Walsh, *Notices*, 1:205.

76. *Av.* of 28 Apr. 1821, cited in Gérson, *Regalismo brasileiro*, p. 52.

77. Walsh, *Notices* 1:206.

78. Rangel, *Pedro e Santos*, pp. 166, 169.

79. Ibid., p. 153; Mello Moraes [Pai], *Chronica geral*, 2:257.

80. Rangel, *Pedro e Santos*, p. 383.

81. "Declaration of Recognition of Izabel Maria de Alcântara Brasileira by D. Pedro I, 24 May 1826"; ibid., p. 383.

82. The priest's acknowledgment of the correction for "Izabel Innocente," of 28 May 1826, is reprinted in Rangel, *Pedro e Santos*, pp. 440–41.

83. The full text of the decree, dated 17 Oct. 1826, is reprinted ibid., p. 439. NOTE: Orthography for Domitila's name, including her own signature, varies considerably.

84. Ibid., pp. 436–37, reprinting marriage registry entry for Boaventura Delphim Pereira and Maria Benedicta de Castro, 8 July 1812, Livro de Casamentos, Arquivo da Sé, São Paulo.

85. "Will of Pedro Alcântara Bragança e Bourbon," reprinted in Rangel, *Pedro e Santos*, pp. 446–47.

86. Pedro's letter of 19 June 1822 to D. João, cited by Walsh, *Notices*, 1:176, 176n. Sousa, *Vida Pedro I*, p. 81. By custom, the king's eldest daughter married a close relative. Ibid., p. 174.

87. *Journal*, p. 263.

88. On Pedro's slapping Paula for being reluctant to kiss Goyaz, see Mello Moraes [Pai], *Chronica geral*, 2:254.

89. Rangel, *Pedro e Santos*, p. 154.

90. Ibid. and p. 60; Seidler, *Dez anos*, p. 82.

91. Rangel, *Pedro e Santos*, p. 154; Mello Moraes [Pai], *Chronica geral*, 2:253–54.

92. On Leopoldina's death, see Walsh, *Notices*, 1:148–54; Mello Moraes [Pai], *Chronica geral*, 2:257–59; Rangel, *Pedro e Santos*, pp. 193, 244; and Seidler, *Dez anos*, pp. 79–83.

93. Ibid., pp. 208–9.

94. Ibid., pp. 244, 276.

95. Mello Moraes [Pai], *Chronica geral*, 2:287.

96. Rangel, *Pedro e Santos*, p. 60.

97. "Will of Pedro Alcântara Bragança e Bourbon [21 Jan. 1832]," reprinted in Rangel, *Pedro e Santos*, pp. 446–47. The duchess of Goyaz married baron von Holzen, count of Treuberg, on the twelfth anniversary of her father's abdication—Apr. 7, 1843—and retained her Brazilian title. Ibid., p. 285.

98. Rangel, *Pedro e Santos*, pp. 446–47. Pedro wrote another will on 17 Sept. 1834, shortly before he died. It stated the 1832 will executed in Paris would stand as a codicil, leaving the dispositions for his illegitimate children unchanged. It is reprinted in São Clemente, *Estatisticas e biographias*, vol.2, pt. 1, pp. 226–29.

99. Rangel, *Pedro e Santos*, pp. 446–47. Pedro's affair with Mdme. Saisset ended when he packed her and her husband off to Paris, on 30 Dec. 1828. Ibid., p. 73.

100. Mello Moraes [Pai], *Chronica geral*, 2:293.

101. Ibid., 2:286.

102. Pedro to Domitila de Castro (Rio de Janeiro), letter of 24 Dec. 1827; quoted in Rangel, *Pedro e Santos*, p. 59.

103. Walsh, *Notices*, 1:251.

104. A popular rhyme offered one variant on Miguel's father, identifying him as "Neither Marialva nor João/But the caretaker at Romalhão"—Carlota Joaquina's country retreat. Quoted in Macaulay, *Dom Pedro*, p. 307n11.

105. Rangel, *Pedro e Santos*, p. 155.

106. Ibid., p. 154.

CHAPTER 6

1. Speech of 3 May 1823, Eng. trans. by Graham, *Journal*, p. 240.

2. Mello Moraes [Pai], *Chronica geral*, 2:259–60.

3. Karasch, *Slave Life*, Tables 3.1 and 3.3 (pp. 61–63); *Notices*, 2:199–200.

4. 29 May, *ACD 1828*, 1:184.

5. Eltis, "Transatlantic Migrations," p. 262 (Graph 1).

6. Marcílio, *Criança abandonada*, pp. 148, 150, 161; Mesgravis, *Santa Casa Misericôrdia*, p. 171; João Alfredo dos Anjos, "A roda dos enjeitados," pp. 37, 59, 191.

7. Law of 1 Oct. 1828, in *CLIB 1828*, Pt.1, pp. 85–86. See also Marcílio, *Criança abandonada*, pp. 135, 143.

8. Rangel, *Pedro e Santos*, pp. 283–89; Domitila's will and marriage registry entry are reproduced on pp. 443–45, 437. Her estate was valued at over one million *contos* in 1867. Pang, *Pursuit of Honor*, p. 254.

9. Dundas, *Sketches of Brazil*, p. 392; Berbert de Castro, *Cartas Cora*, pp. 6–8, 68.

10. Cora's mother was Ildefonsa Laura Pereira, Brazil's first published poetess (*Ensaios poeticos*, 1844). Berbert de Castro, *Cartas Cora*, pp. 17–19. Sacramento Blake, *Diccionario*, 3:280.

11. *Sketches of Brazil*, p. 392.

12. Peard, *Race, Place, Medicine*, p. 93n70 (citing photographs and captions in Torres, *Esboço histórico*). The photographed portrait (facing p. 16), a painting, conveys no hint of African ancestry, but reveals stereotypically Portuguese features.

13. Pang, *Pursuit of Honor*, p. 44, 173; Flory, "Race and Social Control," p. 213; Freyre, *Ordem e progresso*, 1:281, 285–87, and 2:301, 346; Barman, *Citizen Emperor*, p. 221. One of two legitimized mulatto sons of the marquis of São João da Palma, Mascarenhas was taken to be of color, due to maternal African descent. Ibid., 122n55.

14. Berbert de Castro, *Cartas Cora*, p. 11 (citing *AGB* [SP], 2 (1940):84). Lino Coutinho's mother was identified as "*dona*," a marker for white parentage.

15. Unless otherwise noted, material on Lino Coutinho's extended family is from Borges, *Family Bahia*, pp. 259–61.

16. Ibid., pp. 259, 377/n66; Rheinghantz, *Titulares*, pp. 9, 85. NOTE: Sodré acquired his title after the Law of 2 Sept. 1847.

17. Borges, *Family Bahia*, p. 377n69.

18. Sacramento Blake, *Diccionario*, 5:7; Dundas, *Sketches*, p. 393.

19. Borges, *Family Bahia*, p. 261.

20. 18 May 1830, *ACD 1830*, 1:172.

21. Ibid. Arts. 2–5, discussed below, including Lino Coutinho's May 18 commentary, are found in 1:172. Ibid.

22. Borges Carneiro, *Dir. civ. Port.*, L.1, v.1, T.19, §168 (p. 218), also citing *Ord. Filipinas*, L.4, T.99, §1; Lobão, *Notas*, L.2, T.6, §17, citing *Ord.*, L.4, T.99, §1 (p. 197); Mello Freire, *Instituiçoens* (1834), L.2, T.6, §17 (p. 90). All cited canon law, esp. Pope Benedict's Diocesan Synod 13.

23. Lino Coutinho, 5 June, *ACD 1830*, 1:329, and 14 Oct., ibid., 2:601.

24. *ACD 1830*, 1:495.

25. Sacramento Blake avoids the convention that Aureliano was a "legitimate son," noting only he was the "son of Col. Aureliano de Souza e Oliveira," omitting reference to his mother. *Diccionario*, 1:373. On his mixed ancestry, see Barman, *Citizen Emperor*, p. 77.

26. 26 June, *ACD 1830*, 1:498.

27. Candido Mendes, *Ord.*, p. 945n (citing *prov.* of 18 Jan. 1799 and *res.* of the Desembargo do Paço of 17 Jan. 1770; Teixeira de Freitas, *Consol.*, Art.218n).

28. Candido Mendes, *Ord.*, p. 944n1, quoting Teixeira de Freitas on suspending *Ord.*, L.4, T.92, §1; T.93; and L.2, T.35, §12 (*Consol.*, Art.217n1).

29. 26 June, *ACD 1830*, 1:498.

30. *Senhora* [1875], p. 90.

31. 26 June, *ACD 1830*, 1:498.

32. Personal communication from Muriel Nazzari, 1 Oct. 1995.

33. 26 June, *ACD 1830*, 1:498.

34. Mello Freire, *Instituiçoens* (1834), L.2, T.5, §17 (p. 64).

35. 26 June, *ACD 1830*, 1:498.

36. Holloway, *Policing Rio de Janeiro*, p. 50.

37. Mello Freire, *Instituiçoens* (1834), L.2, T.5, §17 (p. 67, citing *Ord.*, L.1, T.3, §1; T.35, §12).

38. 26 June, *ACD 1830*, 1:498.

39. *Ord.*, L.2, T.35, §12; Candido Mendes, *Ord.*, p. 945; Lobão, *Notas*, L.2, T.5, §§17–19 (pp. 157–58).

40. 26 June, *ACD 1830*, 1:498.

41. 30 Sept., *ACD 1830*, 2:570–71.

42. Ibid.

43. Silva Prado family oral history came from Jorge Pacheco Chaves Filho, great-grandson of Veridianna Prado, interviewed at the IHGB, Rio de Janeiro, on 22 and 27 June, 4 July 1990, and used with his permission.

44. Verbatim "Parecer da Commissão da Justiça Civil, 20 Oct. 1830," 30 Oct., *ACD 1830*, 2:626.

45. Published information on the Silva Prados is from Broteiro, *Família Jordão*, pp. 57–65, 89, 98; and Azevedo Marques, *Apontamentos São Paulo*, pp. 120–21. NOTE: Maria Cândida's husband died on 12 June 1823, but Verissimo's baptism, on 8 Oct. 1823, may have been postponed, given that genealogies omit his birth date, contrary to convention.

46. Information from Pacheco Chaves Filho, 22 June and 4 July 1990. A search of parish registers suggested by Pacheco Chaves Júnior, on or around 24 June 1838, revealed neither marriage. Arquivo da Arquidiocese do Rio de Janeiro, 17 July 1990.

47. Brotero, *Família Jordão*, p. 61. Jorge Pacheco Chaves Filho attributed the estrangement between Verissimo and Veridianna to Verissimo's exclusion from his father's *legítima*, in favor of Veridianna, Antonio Prado's sole *ab intestato* heir. Interviews of 22 June, 4 July 1990, IHGB.

48. Flory, "Race and Social Control," p. 213.

49. Ibid., p. 205n18.

50. Santos, *André Rebouças*, p. 523 (citing Pinho Osborne, "André Rebouças," *Rev. CTC*, No. 29 (Sept. 1946): 140.

51. Ibid., p. 13. On the baron of Cotegipe's (João Mauricio Wanderley) racial insult of Rebouças in the Chamber of Deputies, see Flory, "Race and Social Control," p. 213 (citing *ACD 1846*, 2:571).

52. Santos, *André Rebouças*, pp. 9–10, 523–24 (citing Pinho Osborne, "André Rebouças," p. 523); and Sacramento Blake, *Diccionario*, 5:125. Rebouças was the youngest of the three sons of Gaspar Pereira Rebouças and Rita Basília dos Santos.

53. Santos, *André Rebouças*, p. 10 (citing Dec. No. 647 of 4 Sept. 1847).

54. 30 Sept., *ACD 1830*, 2:571.

55. Mello Freire, *Instituiçoens* (1834), L.2, T.6, §4 (p. 79). Borges Carneiro, *Dir. civ. Port.*, v.1, T.20, §179 (pp. 250–53); Candido Mendes, *Ord.*, pp. 947–48n7.

56. Rebouças, 30 Sept., *ACD 1830*, 2:571; citing also *Ord.*, L.4, T.83. NOTE: I have

translated Rebouças' "*subrogação*" as "*adrogação*," assuming either a redactor's error or a slip of the tongue.

57. Ibid.

58. 1 Oct., *ACD 1830*, 2:573.

59. 14 Oct., ibid., 2:601.

CHAPTER 7

1. Lobão, "Analyse da ordenação," pp. 9, 20.

2. Rangel, *Pedro e Santos*, p. 41.

3. Ibid., p. 214.

4. Fletcher and Kidder, *Brazil and Brazilians*, p. 214.

5. Macaulay, *Dom Pedro*, p. 214.

6. Fletcher and Kidder, *Brazil and Brazilians*, p. 214.

7. Mello Moraes [Pai], *Chronica geral*, 2:408.

8. Viotti da Costa, *Brazilian Empire*, pp. 63–67; Barman, *Forging Brazil*, 150–59; Holloway, *Policing Rio de Janeiro*, pp. 64–67.

9. Of the 22 ministers holding law degrees in the Regency, 18 graduated from Coimbra after 1816. Barman, "Law Graduates," p. 435.

10. Barman, "New World Nobility," p. 47. Between late 1829 and Apr. 7, 1831, only 8 noble titles were awarded. Ibid.

11. *AS 1832*, 1:vi, ix.

12. Petrônio Portella, "Apresentação," in *AS 1835*, p. 3. The following senators died in 1835: A. Gonçalves Gomide; Jozé da Silva Lisboa, viscount of Cayru. In 1836: Affonso de Albuquerque Maranhão; Manoel Ferreira da Camara Bittencourt; Francisco Maria Gordilho Vellozo de Barbuda, marquis of Jacarepaguá; Jozé Caetano Ferreira de Aguiar; Jozé Joaquim Carneiro da Campos, marquis of Caravellas; Antonio Vieira da Soledade; Francisco Santos Pinto. In 1837: Antonio Luiz Pereira da Cunha, marquis of Inhambupe. *AS 1835–1837*.

13. *Estadista imperio*, 2:32.

14. 20 July, *AS 1831*, 2:169; 1 Oct., *ACD 1830*, 2:174.

15. 26 July, *AS 1831*, 2:175. "Nem a Ordenação do L. 4, T. 93, nem outra alguma Legislação em vigor, prohibe que os filhos illegitimos de qualquer especie, sejam instituidos herdeiros por seus pais em testamento, não tendo estes herdeiros necessarios." *CLIB 1831*, Pt. 1, pp. 42–43.

16. L.1, v.2, T.22, §208 (p. 331).

17. João Ignacio da Cunha, 22 June, *AS 1831*, 2:3–4; 1 Aug., ibid., 2:184.

18. Trigo de Loureiro, *Inst. dir. civ. bras.*, L.1, T.4, §69 (p. 40, citing 1828 Judiciary Act, Art.2, §4). Lafayette, *Dir. familia*, Sec.2, Cap.3, §112 (p. 225).

19. Law No. 1.144 of 11 Sept. 1861 bestowed the civil effects of marriage on non-Catholics. *CLIB 1861*, Pt.1, p. 21.

20. *ACD 1832*, 1:41. The bill of June 11, 1831 is not mentioned until 1832. See also Seixas, "Resposta," 2:277–303.

21. Debate on Art. 1 (9 pars.) ran from May 25 to June 18. *ACD 1832*, 1:41–42, 113. Arts. 2–4, pertaining to impediments, received no attention in the minutes, but were approved on June 18. Ibid., 1:113. On June 19, Arts. 5–13 (below) were debated. Ibid., 1:114.

22. Speeches of Feijó, Carneiro da Cunha, Maria de Moura, and Paula Araujo, 25 May. *ACD 1832*, 1:41–42.

23. Ibid., 1:41.

24. Ibid., 1:41–42

25. Six of Article 1's nine paragraphs reiterated canonical impediments unrelated to kinship. 19 June, ibid., 1:114.

26. Lafayette, *Dir. familia*, Sec.1, Cap.2, T.1, §15 (pp. 23–25).

27. Ibid., §13 (p. 21), citing Sess. 24, Council of Trent.

28. 25 May, *ACD 1832*, 1:42.

29. Ibid.

30. 19 June, *ACD 1832*, 1:115. The third debate ended in the bill's adoption, but presumably proved a casualty to the lost minutes for 4 Sept. to 20 Oct. 1832, omitted from ibid., vol. 2. The redactor reported they "were not found." Ibid., 2:264. Confirmation of the Chamber's adoption of the bill appears in 6 May, *AS 1834*, 1:15.

31. "Representação," 2:277–305.

32. Bill of 18 Aug., *AS 1835*, p. 309; 14May, *AS 1836*, p. 46.

33. Ibid.

34. Ibid.

35. Bill No. 92 of 7 Aug. 1847. I am very grateful to Librarian Eliane Pereira, Biblioteca Nacional, for supplying a copy of the bill.

36. 14 May, *AS 1836*, p. 46.

37. 17 June and 30 June, *ACD 1834*, 1:144, 201. On the Conselhos Gerais de Provincia, see *Con. 1824*, Arts. 71–89, esp. Art. 81.

38. Ibid., 1:201.

39. The report and its legal opinion justifying no action by the Chamber appear in 27 June, ibid., 1:144–47. The other committee member, Lourenço Marcondes de Sá, was also a priest.

40. Seixas, "Resposta." Santa Barbara obtained permission to publish the Ecclesiastical Committee's report in the press. 30 June, *ACD 1834*, 1:201.

41. "Ecclesiastical Committee Report," 17 June, *ACD 1834*, 1:144.

42. 26 July, ibid., 2:144, 147.

43. "Resposta," 2:359, 362.

44. 30 July, *ACD 1834*, 2:167.

45. Ibid.

46. 11 June, *AS 1829*, 1:88.

47. Ferraz, *Liberais*, pp. 189, 191.

48. Pedro Araujo Lima, "Officios," 16 July, *ACD 1829*, 4:121.

49. Odorico Mendes, 26 June 1830, *ACD 1830*, 1:184.

50. 7 June, 8 and 13 Aug., *ACD 1831*, 1:129–30 and 2:41.

51. See 20 June, *ACD 1831*, 1:159–67.

52. Rheingantz, *Titulares*, pp. 13, 50, 64, 88 (Caethé, Cayru, Congonhas do Campo, and Inhambupe).

53. 15 May, *AS 1835*, p. 42.

54. Ibid., pp. 39–40.

55. Ibid., pp. 41–42. The Laws of Toro (1502) invigorated the *mayorazgo*.

56. 14 May, *AS 1835*, p. 43.

57. 2 Oct., *AS 1835*, p. 452; *CLIB 1835*, Pt.1, pp. 64–65.

58. *Dir. successões*, pp. 98–99. Emphyteusis, the "last vestige" of entail, was an exception to Law No. 57 of 1835, because Art. 115 of the *1824 Con.* stipulated that D. Pedro I's property in land and houses was "to belong always to him and his successors." Emphyteusis surfaced at the 1988 Constitutional Convention, when Dep. José Ulisses de Oliveira again proposed its extinction. Besides the Bragança descendants, he referred to others "who avail themselves of this privilege: the traditional families of the country, private entities, the Catholic Church, and the federal government." "Ataque à realeza," p. 76.

59. *Con. 1891*, Art. 72, §2: "All are equal before the law. The Republic does not admit privileges of birth, recognize patents of nobility, create titles of *fidalguia* or honorary distinctions [*condecorações*]."

60. 11 July, *AS 1829*, 2:87.

61. Article 2: "In view of the preceding article, assets ceasing to be entailed will pass according to the laws regulating legitimate succession, to the heirs of the last administrators, the latter not being able to dispose of them by a will or some other formal document. Law No. 57 of 6 Oct. 1835, *CLIB 1835*, 2:64.

62. 16 May, *AS 1835*, p. 45.

63. Art. 4: "Existing laws will remain in effect regarding the extinction of entails that do not have legitimate administrators or have been forfeited." *CLIB 1835*, Pt.1, p. 64. Art. 5 revoked all contradictory laws.

64. Although notaries explicitly cited *Dec.* No. 2 of 29 May 1837 as extinguishing the *capela*, that law actually targeted entails generically, as "*vínculos.*" Cf. Pereira de Vasconcellos, *Nov. man. tabelliães*, p. 116.

65. Laws of 9 Sept. 1769 and 3 Aug. 1770; *CLP* 3:424–25 & 3:478.

66. Data on the Morgado of Sodré is from Borges, *Family Bahia*, p. 259–61n66.

67. 10 June, *ACD 1837*, 1:225; and 11, 13–14 July, ibid., 2:83, 90, 98, 100, 104. Rebouças returned to the Chamber in 1837.

68. See the case of the "*vínculo de Jaguará,*" brought to the Chamber's attention when Minas Gerais' provincial assembly proposed its extinction. 2 Sept. 1837, *ACD 1837*, 2:450.

69. Borges, *Family Bahia*, p. 259, 261n66, citing Antônio Ferrão Moniz' journal.

70. Feijó to Min. Pedro de Araujo Lima, letter of 19 Sept. 1837, 19 Sept., *ACD 1837*, 2:547; reprinted in Mello Moraes [Pai], *Necrologia Feijó*, p. 37. 19 Sept., *AS 1837*, p. 425.

71. "Necrologia Caravellas," *AS 1837*, 1:vii; Sacramento Blake, *Diccionario*, 4:471.

72. *ACD 1834*, 1:ii; *AS 1837*, i-xvi; Mello Moraes [Pai], *Chronica geral*, 2:339.

CHAPTER 8

1. *AS 1839*, 1:10. NOTE: The redactor incorrectly identified Sen. Carneiro de Campos as "Sr. C. da Cunha" on May 7–8, an error corrected below.

2. Ibid., 1:18.

3. Fletcher and Kidder, *Brazil and Brazilians*, pp. 222–23.

4. Homem de Mello, "*Apresentação*," *AS 1838*, p. ii. NOTE: On 3 Oct. 1838 Vasconcellos moved from the Chamber to the Senate. Ibid.

5. 20 July, ibid., p. 147. The full text of Bill BU of 1836 has not survived, but, where quoted verbatim in this chapter, discrete articles appeared in the *AS 1838* and *AS 1839*.

The bill's revised, complete text, adopted on 31 May 1839, also omitted from the *AS 1839*, was published unaltered in *JC*, 143 (15 May 1846):3. I am grateful to Eliane Pereira, of the Biblioteca Nacional, and to José Gabriel da Costa Pinto of the Arquivo Nacional, Rio de Janeiro, for providing me with a microfilm copy of the latter.

6. Almeida e Albuquerque, 12 May, *AS 1837*, p. 61. Bill BU of 1836, "establishing the inheritance rights of illegitimate offspring," is mentioned for the first time on 6 May, ibid., p. 45. NOTE: A single volume format for *AS 1836* through *AS 1838*, uncharacteristically sparse, paraphrased little debate.

7. Vergueiro's comments were recorded only once in 1838: 7 Aug., *AS 1838*, p. 181. Baron Homem de Mello, "*Apresentação*," *AS 1839*, 5:ii.

8. *JC*, 143 (15 May 1846):3.

9. *Instituiçoens* (1834), L.2, T.5, §§14–16 (pp. 60–64), glossing the *ordenação* of L.2, T.35, §§12,16.

10. 7 May, *AS 1839*, 1:10. Articles 2–4 of Bill BU of 1836 were renumbered and revised by the Senate's Committee on Redaction in 1839. Initially, this chapter refers to original article numbers. For consistency between Chaps. 8 and 9, however, the renumbering when the bill was adopted, on 31 May 1839, is also noted. The latter, published in *JC*, 143 (15 May 1846):3, is referred to below as "revised articles."

11. 7 May, *AS 1839*, 1:11.

12. Lobão, *Notas*, L.2, T.5, §3, N.10n (p. 160).

13. "Questionable foundlings," p. 21.

14. 7 May, *AS 1839*, 1:11–12.

15. Ibid., 1:11.

16. *Dir. civ. Port.*, L.1, v.2, T.20, §180, Nos.5&10; §181 (pp. 253–55).

17. Ibid.

18. Ibid. Revised Art. 5 pertained only to the first part of the original Art. 5. 7 May, *AS 1839*, 1:17.

19. The original Article 5, 3 paragraphs long, was revised as Art. 6, for clarity and corrected syntax. Ibid., 1:20.

20. The original texts for Arts. 6, 7, and 8, were not recorded in the *AS 1838–1839*, but debates established the revised texts were little altered. 8 May, *AS 1839*, 1:21–23.

21. Ibid.

22. The bill was debated on 20–21, 26–27 July; 3–4, 7, 14, 16–18, 20–22 Aug.; and 12, 15 Sept. *AS 1838*, pp. 147–49, 158–61, 173–75, 177–78, 181–82, 193–97, 200, 203, 205, 209–11, 253, 260. NOTE: The *AS 1838* offered a meager record of debate, accounting for this chapter's principal reliance on the more substantial *AS 1839*'s third discussion.

23. 10 and 27 May, *AS 1839*, 1:27, 207; 4 June, *ACD 1839*, 1:268.

24. 27 July and 3–4 Aug., *AS 1838*, pp. 160, 175, 177–78.

25. Homem de Mello, "Apresentação," *AS 1839* 5:i.

26. 20 July, ibid., pp. 147–49.

27. Ibid., p. 149.

28. The Committee on Legislation offered a set of amendments (18 July 1838) to the articles on recognition, labeled "K." Ibid., pp. 148–49; *JC*, 26 (19 July 1838):1. They failed to pass. 7 Aug., *AS 1838*, p. 193.

29. 7 May, *AS 1839*, 1:11.

30. Art.2, §1, of the committee's report stipulated recognition be made by "declaration in the public registry of baptism, *specifying or not, the person with whom the*

child was conceived, signed by the declarant and two witnesses present." 20 July, *AS 1838*, p. 148. Italics added.

31. Almeida e Silva, 20 July, *AS 1838*, p. 147.

32. 7 May, *AS 1839*, 1:15.

33. Costa Ferreira, ibid., 1:12.

34. Ibid., 1:13.

35. This was the third promulgation of what had originally been the French Civil Code (1804) and then the *Code Napoléon* (1807), although the latter title was not reestablished until 1852. Mourlon, *Répétitions écrits*, 1:26. Citations herein pertain to the commentary on the reestablished *Code Napoléon* (27 Mar. 1852): Gilbert, ed., *Les Codes annotés de Sirey*, v. 1: *Code Napoléon*. English quotations or paraphrasing from the latter are from Cachard, ed., *French Civil Code*, with attention paid to what was in force between 1838 and 1843. I am greatly indebted to Louise Avila, who undertook research on French law for this chapter.

36. Gilbert, *Code Napoléon*, Art. 340 (pp. 178–79): "La recherche de la paternité est interdite."

37. *Estadista imperio*, 1:12.

38. Vienne, *Étude sur légitimation*, p. 253.

39. Notaries were authorized to receive such declarations, in the presence of a second notary or two witnesses, by Art. 2, "Loi sur la formes des Actes notariés," No. 10,713 of 21 June 1843, p. 519.

40. 7 May, *AS 1839*, 1:11.

41. Ibid., 1:14.

42. Cachard, *French Civil Code*, Ch.3, "Of Natural Children," Art.336 (p. 87). Cf. Arts.333&765 (pp. 86 & 182).

43. 7 May, *AS 1839*, 1:11, 14–16.

44. Ibid., 1:12, 14, 16.

45. Ibid., 1:12.

46. Brinton, *Revolutionary Legislation*, p. 56 (citing P.A. Fenet, *Recueil complet des traveaux préparatoires du Code civil* (Paris: 1827), X, 154). Brinton rejected the claim. Ibid., p. 58.

47. 7 May, *AS 1839*, 1:16–17.

48. Ibid., 1:16. NOTE: The redactor identified Mello e Mattos (1:15) as "Sen. Cassiano."

49. Ibid.

50. Ibid., 1:11, 13. It was a crime for a woman to simulate pregnancy; to pass off another woman's childbirth as her own; to substitute another child as her own; to steal or conceal or exchange her child for another. *Cod. Criminal 1830*, Art. 254, §4.

51. 7 May, *AS 1839*, 1:13.

52. Gilbert, *Code Napoléon*, L.1, T.7, Cap.1, Arts.313–16. Traer, *Marriage and Family*, pp. 93, 103, 155.

53. 8 May, *AS 1839*, 1:20.

54. *Rapto* was "taking any woman from her house or the place where she was for libidinous ends, by violence." *Cód. Criminal Império [1830]*, Art.226. Art. 227 extended *rapto* to a woman under seventeen "in the house of her father, guardian, or anyone having authority or guardianship over her."

55. According to Gaby Oré-Aguilar, staff attorney with the Center for Repro-

ductive Rights, today the laws of fifteen Latin American countries, including Brazil, prohibit prosecution of a rapist (and co-defendants in gang rape) whose offer of marriage is accepted by his victim. Calvin Simms, "Justice in Peru," pp. 1, 8.

56. 7 May, *AS 1839*, 1:10.

57. Art. 340 conflicted with Art. 1320 of the Civil Code: "Any act of man which causes injury to another obliges him by the fault which he has committed to make reparations." Demars-Sion, *Femmes séduites*, p. 445. Brinton, *Revolutionary Legislation*, p. 51.

58. 3 July, *ACD 1846*, 2:37. Veiga cited the 1830 Criminal Code to explain that *rapto* by violence, against a victim over age sixteen, carried a penalty of ten years in prison and provision of a dowry. Where seduction was used with a victim under seventeen, the penalty was a three-year prison sentence. Ibid.

59. 12 Sept., *AS 1838*, p. 253. *Rapto*, when applied to a woman under 17 years who was (or taken to be) a virgin, could also be accomplished by seduction ("por meio de afago e promessas"). *Cod. Penal Império [1830]*, Art.227.

60. 7 May, *AS 1839*, 1:10.

61. Report, Committee on Legislation, Art. 3, 20 July, *AS 1838*, pp. 148–49.

62. 7 May, *AS 1839*, 1:11.

63. Ibid., 1:17, 16, 12. NOTE: Mello e Mattos is identified here (1:16) as "Cassiano."

64. 7 Aug., ibid., p. 181; 7 May, ibid., 1:12.

65. Garaud, *Révolution Française*, p. 180: "La societé ná pas intérêt à ce que les bâtards soient reconnus." Brinton, *Revolutionary Legislation*, p. 70.

66. 7 May, *AS 1839*, 1:10–11.

67. Ibid.

68. Brinton, *Revolutionary Legislation*, pp. 55–56 (quoting Boulay de la Meurthe from Fenet, *Recueil complet*, X, p. 132).

69. Cachard, *French Civil Code*, Art.756.

70. Garaud, *Révolution Française*, p. 177.

71. 7 May, *AS 1839*, 1:18.

72. Ibid.

73. Cachard, *French Civil Code*, Arts.755–58.

74. 7 May, *AS 1839*, 1:12; 8 May, ibid., 1:22–23. Cachard, *French Civil Code*, Arts. 756,762,335, and 342. Garaud, *Révolution Française*, pp. 116, 124, 213.

75. 21 Aug., *AS 1838*, p. 210.

76. 20 July, ibid., p. 148.

77. 7 May, *AS 1839*, 1:10.

78. 8 May, ibid., 1:22–23.

CHAPTER 9

1. *ACD 1846*, 2:41, 44.

2. Ibid., 1:79.

3. Holloway, *Policing Rio de Janeiro*, p. 165.

4. Faoro, *Donos poder*, 1:333–34; Barman, *Forging Brazil*, p. 213.

5. Flory, *Judge and Jury*, pp. 171, 174.

6. Barman, *Citizen Emperor*, p. 64.

7. Ibid, p. 40; Sousa, *Feijó*, p. 290 (citing *Dec.* of 23 Dec. 1840).

8. 20 Aug., *ACD 1841*, 2:710.

9. The text of General Assembly Bill No. 14 of 1839, published in *JC*, N.143 (15 May 1846), p. 3, included amendments extracted from the *parecer* (of 13 Sept. 1841) of the Chamber's Committee on Civil Justice.

10. *ACD 1845*, 2:557.

11. Ibid., 2:558.

12. 20 Aug., *AS 1838*, p. 205. The amendment also recognized rights in succession from a noble mother. In 1843, Paraiso's natural son succeeded to his *legítima* in company with his legitimate children. Borges, *Family Bahia*, p. 258, 376n63.

13. 14 Aug., *ACD 1845*, 2:558.

14. "O reconhecimento dos filhos illegitimos, tanto pelo pai como pela mãi, que tiver occultado o parto, só se pode ser legalmente feito por um dos quatro meios prescriptos neste artigo; sem se exigir declaração da pessoa com que forão havidos, nem poder tal declaração produzir effeito algum . . . ." 18 Aug., *ACD 1845*, 2:586.

15. Mendes da Cunha, ibid., 2:589.

16. 14 Aug., ibid., 2:557.

17. 10 May, ibid., 1:32; 18 Aug., ibid., 2:590.

18. 18 Aug., ibid, 2:589.

19. Ibid., 2:586–87.

20. Brinton, *Revolutionary Legislation*, pp. 26, 29.

21. Ibid., p. 53 (citing Simeón, *Rapport sur la successibilité des enfans naturels*, 18 messidor, an V; Conseil des Cinq-Cents [Paris: 1797], p. 7).

22. Ibid., p. 54 (citing Pollart, *Motion d'ordre sur les enfans nés hors du mariage*; Conseil des Cinq-Cints [Paris: 1798], p. 3). Souza França, 18 Aug., *ACD 1845*, 2:587.

23. 18 Aug., *ACD 1845*, 2:587.

24. Ibid., 2:588.

25. Graham, *Politics and Patronage*, pp. 155–56, 234–35; Flory, *Judge and Jury*, pp. 134, 193; Needell, "Provincial Origins State," pp. 133–36.

26. 18 Aug., *ACD 1845*, 2:588.

27. 14 and 18 Aug., ibid., 2:557, 588.

28. 14 May, *ACD 1846*, 1:70. The full text of the revised bill appears in *Jornal do Commercio*, No. 167 (18 June 1846), p. 3.

29. 15 May, *ACD 1846*, 1:79.

30. Brinton, *Revolutionary Legislation*, pp. 34, 51.

31. 15 May, *ACD 1846*, 1:81; Brinton, *Revolutionary Legislation*, pp. 24–25, 30–31, 51.

32. 15 May, *ACD 1846*, 1:80–81. NOTE: Ferraz' reference to *Ord.*, L.2, T.35, §12, erroneously identified it as L.4, T.35, §12. *Estadista imperio*, 1:38.

33. *Estadista imperio*, 1:12.

34. 7 July, *ACD 1846*, 2:86 (2:85–87 for full speech), citing Mello Freire, *Instituiçoens* L.2, T.5, §16. Ferraz also cited Borges Carneiro for Portugal, Merlin and Potier on French law, Dieck's dissertation on the legitimization of adulterine offspring in German lands and his treatise on legitimization published in Halle in 1832, and esp. M. L. J. Kenigswarter's "Legislação comparativa dos filhos naturais," published in France in 1842. Ibid.

35. *Dir. familia*, "Nota XI (§169)," p. 400. Refuting Protestants Boehmer and Rieger, Lobão endorsed Pope Benedict XIV (letter to the archbishop of Hispañola—*Reddite novis*) and the canonist Berardo: "It is understood in court that the *Ord.*, L.4,

Ts.92&93, legitimize only natural offspring by subsequent marriage ... not those incestuous and spurious." *Notas*, L.2, T.5, §§14–16 (pp. 149–53).

36. Speech from the Throne, 3 May 1839, announcing "the removal of misunderstandings between the imperial cabinet and the Vatican," in *Discussão Senado 1839*, p. iii. Nabuco, *Estadista imperio*, 1:38.

37. "Was this bill elaborated by a committee of the Senate? No again. It was presented by *one* of their members." Ferraz, 15 May, *ACD 1846*, 1:79. Italics added.

38. Ibid., 1:81.

39. Ibid.

40. Ibid. Mello Freire, *Instituiçoens* (1834), L.2, T.6, §§23–24 (pp. 95–96); Lobão, *Notas*, L.2, T.6, §12, Nos.6–8; §17, Nos. 1–2 (pp. 188–93, 197–98).

41. 15 May, *ACD 1846*, 1:82.

42. Ibid., 1:83.

43. Ibid.

44. Ibid.

45. 18 May, ibid., 1:102. NOTE: Following the redactor, Parnaíba is identified herein by his family names.

46. Ibid., 1:104.

47. Ibid.

48. Ibid.

49. Ibid.

50. Ibid.

51. Ibid.

52. 9 July, ibid., 2:9.

53. 1 July, ibid., 2:8.

54. 17 June, 1:374.

55. "Res. N.53 de 1846, derogando a ordenação, L. 4, T. 32 [*sic*], na parte em que estabelece distincção entre os filhos naturaes de nobres e peões em relação ao direito hereditario." 8 May, *ACD 1847*, 1:27.

56. 8, 10–12, 14, 17 May, ibid., 1:27–29, 30–34, 43–48, 57–60, 67–70, 87–94.

57. 8 May, ibid., 1:27–29. He implied the perquisites and immunities conferred by officeholding.

58. Ibid., 1:28.

59. Ibid., 1:28–29.

60. 10 May, ibid., 1:33–34. To this comprehensive list defining noble condition, Moura Magalhães later added "accredited businessmen and wealthy farmers." 17 May, ibid., 1:90.

61. 11 May, ibid, 1:43–44.

62. Ibid., 1:45.

63. 14 May, ibid., 1:69.

64. 17 May, ibid., 1:89.

65. Ibid., 1:89–90; Goyanna, 5 May, ibid., 1:43–44.

66. Ibid., 1:94.

67. "Para que o filho natural possa partilhar a herança de seu pai conjunctamente com os legitimos, será necessario que obtenha delle o reconhecimento por escriptura publica outorgada em época anterior ao seu casamento." Ibid.

68. 10 May, ibid., 1:32.

69. 17 May, ibid., 1:94.

70. Ibid.

71. Ibid. NOTE: The final text of Res. N.53, adopted on 17 May 1847, was not recorded in *ACD 1847*. The Committee's revised text, cited below in terms of 4 articles, appeared on 6 Aug., *AS 1847*, 3:72; also in *JC*, N.167 (18 June 1846), p. 2.

72. Art. 1: "Aos filhos naturais dos nobres ficam extensivos os mesmos direitos hereditarios que pela *ordenação*, livro 4, título 92, competem aos filhos naturais dos plebeus." Ibid.

73. Art. 2: "O reconhecimento do pai, feito por escritura publica antes de seu casamento, é indispensável para que qualquer filho natural possa ter parte na herança paterna, concorrendo elle com filhos legitimos do mesmo pai." Ibid.

74. Art. 3: "A prova de filiação natural, nos outros casos, só se poderá fazer por um dos seguintes meios, escritura publica ou testamento." Ibid.

75. Art. 4: "Ficam revogadas quaisquer disposições em contrário." Ibid.

76. *AS 1847*, 3:72.

77. Nabuco, *Estadista imperio*, p. 58; Secretaria da Camara dos Deputados, *Organizações ministeriais*, p. 99. Vergueiro briefly substituted for Manoel Alves Branco, as minister of empire, between 20 October and 18 November 1847. Ibid.

78. *AS 1847*, 6 Aug., 3:72. Mello e Mattos and Vasconcellos, ibid., 3:75 and 81, respectively.

79. Ibid., 3:74–83.

80. Ibid., 3:73.

81. Ibid., 3:82.

82. Ibid., 3:75–76.

83. Perdigão Malheiro, *Com. Lei N. 463*, pp. 131–32.

84. 6 Aug., *AS 1847*, 3:79–80. The Law of 12 June 1831 had withheld the executive attributes of the monarchy from the Regency, including the granting of titles and honors. Barman, *Forging Brazil*, p. 163.

85. 6 Aug., *AS 1847*, 3:79–80.

86. Ibid., 3:83.

87. Ibid.

88. Ibid.; 19 Aug., *ACD 1847*, 2:542. Perdigão Malheiro, *Com. Lei N. 463*, pp. 6–8, citing *JC*, No. 229 (19 Aug. 1847).

89. *Dec.* No. 463 of 2 Sept. 1847, *CLIB (1847)*, Pt.1, §28 (p. 48). Vergueiro served as minister of justice from 22 May 1847 to 2 Jan. 1848.

90. *Com. Lei N. 463*, pp. 10–11, 11n20, and 13.

91. Barman, *Forging Brazil*, p. 229.

92. *CDGIB (1848)*, pp. 30–31. NOTE: Children of unmarried mothers were matrilineally natural for succession rights, whenever the father was married.

93. *Av.* N.279 of 17 Dec., *CLIB 1853*, p. 250.

94. Lafayette, *Dir. familia*, Sec.3, Cap.1, T.3, §130 (p. 271n1&2). Perdigão Malheiro, *Com. Lei N. 463* (citing *Ord.*, L.1, T.3, §10; L.2, T.35, §12; *Regimento novo do Des. do Paço*, §118; Mello Freire, *Dir. civil*, L.2, T.5, §21), p. 68, 68n135.

95. Perdigão Malheiro, *Com. Lei N. 463*, pp. 44, 59, 63, 66, 68, 68n135, 69, and 69n137; Lafayette, *Dir. familia*, Sec.3, Cap.1, T.3, §130 (p. 271n2); Trigo de Loureiro, *Inst. dir. civ. bras.*, L.1, T.5, §83 (p. 47).

96. *Com. Lei N. 463*, p. 56.
97. *Viagem pintoresca*, p. 148.
98. Nazzari, *Dowry*, pp. 136–40 and 147–48.
99. 18 May, *ACD 1846*, 1:103. He rejected Vergueiro's point that natural offspring defrauded legitimate children of maternal dowries.
100. Lewin, "Repensando patriarcado," pp. 121–33; Borges, *Family Bahia*, p. 49.
101. Dep. Mendes da Cunha argued the unrevised bill was "good for *fujonas*," but "an evil for seducers." 15 May, *ACD 1846*, 1:81. On the rising incidence of *rapto*, see Lewin, *Politics and Parentela*, pp. 183–91.

CONCLUSION

1. "Os filhos legitimados gozam dos mesmos direitos que os legitimos?" p. 321.
2. Nazzari, *Dowry*, pp. 164–67.
3. The official abstract of Law No. 463 of Sept. 2, 1847, read: "Declaring that the same inheritance rights that the *Ordenações*, Book 4, Title 92, bestow on the natural offspring of plebeians will become extended to the natural offspring of nobles." *CLIB 1847*, Pt.2, §28, p. 48.

EPILOGUE

1. *Proj. Cod. Civil CD*, 1:45. Quoted in Alves, *Cod. Civil 1916*, pp. 1130–31.
2. Dec.-Law No. 181 of 24 Jan. 1890, Art.7, §1, in Souza and Montenegro, eds., *Leis usuaes Republica*, pp. 236–37.
3. Bevilaqua, *Proj. Cod. Civil*, Arts. 417–31, 1775 (pp. 48–49, 171).
4. Alves' first-edition commentary to *Cod. Civil 1916*, reprints in parallel columns Bevilaqua's *Proj. Cod. Civil* and the *Proj. Cod. Civil CD*, to indicate the modifications made to the former by the latter, article-by-article, or to leave standing Bevilaqua's recommended adoptions.
5. Alves, *Cod. Civil 1916*, Art.1605 (p. 1130). Bevilaqua proposed assigning half shares only to natural offspring recognized during marriage. Ibid.
6. Until 1916, adopted children enjoyed ambiguous succession rights. Alves, *Cód. Civil comentado*, Art.1605, §2 (p. 1130).
7. Ibid., Art.363 (pp. 283–85). Cf. commentary of A. Bevilaqua, *Cód Civil comentado Clovis Bevilaqua*, 2:262–66.
8. Achilles Bevilaqua blamed Sen. Andrade Figueira for eliminating the consuetudinary context ("in possession of the state of being a natural offspring") from the revised Civil Code Project. Ibid., 2:262–63.
9. A limited right to secret judicial determination of paternity existed when the father refused, and disclosure of an impediment to matrimony was at issue. Another ascendant could disclose the paternity. Dec.-Law No. 181 of 24 Jan. 1890, Art.8 (p. 237).
10. Law No. 4.737 of 24 Sept. 1942 was superseded by Law No. 883 of 21 Oct. 1949, §1, Par.1, permitting voluntary or judicially coerced recognition once the conjugal society was dissolved for any reason (i.e., death, *desquite*, or annulment). A. Bevilaqua, *Cód. Civil comentado Bevilaqua*, 6:51 and 51n.
11. Consistent with the Chamber's Special Committee, Alves construed spurious offspring "a species originating from a punishable crime, beyond being a blow struck

against morality and the traditional good customs of our society." *Cod. Civil 1916*, p. 281 (re Art. 358).

12. See Lewin, "Repensando patriarcado," pp. 121–33; Alves, *Cod. Civil 1916*, pp. 281–82, 307–8 (re Arts.358&405).

13. The term *"desquite"* was invented in 1902, by Dep. Andrade Figueira. Sen. Rui Barbosa then applied it to Art. 315, to mean a legal separation. *Proj. Cod. Civil CD*, Art.315, 6:573. Bevilaqua's *Proj. Cod. Civil*, however, retained *"divórcio."* Gusmão, *Dicionário direito família*, p. 380. Bevilaqua, *Proj. Cód. Civil*, 2:208–10. See Azevedo, *Moda desquite*.

14. See Lewin, "Republic and 'Unholy' Matrimony."

15. See Besse, "On Shoring Up Marriage" and "Updating Child Rearing," Chaps. 2&3, of *Restructuring Patriarchy*, esp. pp. 80–88.

16. Lewin, "Repensando patriarcado," pp. 129–31.

17. Alves, *Cod. Civil 1916*, Art.359 (p. 281).

18. Law No. 1839 of 1907; see 1 Oct., *AS 1907*, 6:8–25; and 11 Dec., *ACD 1907*, 8:573–75, 616–26.

19. Alves, *Cod. Civil 1916*, re Arts.1721&1725 (pp. 1213–14, 1216). Alves deemed Art. 1725 "lacunose," for failing to protect surviving spouses.

20. Ibid. (p. 1216).

21. 15 May 1846, *ACD 1846*, 1:79.

22. Law No. 883 of 21 Oct. 1949, Art.4, cited in A. Bevilaqua, *Cód. Civil comentado Bevilaqua*, 6:51n.

23. *Narrativas*, pp. 48–49; reprinted in Leite, *Condição feminina*, p. 46.

24. On nineteenth-century family fragmentation and first cousins, see Lewin, *Politics and Parentela*, pp. 139–47.

25. *Narrativas*, p. 46.

26. "1988 Constitution of the Federative Republic of Brazil," Art.227, §6 (p. 495).

Legal Primary Sources Cited

————— ✦ ◆ ✦ —————

I. JURIDICAL COMMENTARIES, TREATISES,
DISSERTATIONS, OPINIONS, AND NOTARIAL MANUALS

Azevedo, Noé. *A moda do desquite: o velho instituto do casamento defendido pelo advogado* . . . . São Paulo: *Revista dos Tribunais,* 1927.

Bevilaqua, Clovis. *Direito das Successões.* Bahia [Salvador]: Liv. Magalhães, 1899.

Borges Carneiro, Manoel. *Direito civil de Portugal contendo três livros: I. Das pessoas; II. Das cousas; III. Das obrigações e acções.* 3 vols. Lisbon: Typ. de Antonio José da Rocha, 1826–1828, 1844.

Cunha Mattos, Raymundo Jozé da. *Repertorio da legislação militar, actualmente em vigor no exercito e armada do Imperio do Brazil,* 3 vols. Rio de Janeiro: Typ. Imperial e Constitucional de Seignot & Plancer, 1834–1842.

"Os filhos legitimados gozam dos mesmos direitos que os legitimos?" *Direito* 50 (1889): 321–25.

Liz Teixeira, Antonio Ribeiro. *Curso de direito civil portuguez, ou commentario às Instituições do Sr. Paschoal José de Mello Freire, sobre o mesmo direito, por* . . . . 3rd ed. Coimbra: J. Augusto Orcel, 1856.

Lobão, Manoel de Almeida e Souza de. "Analyse da Ordenação, L. 2, T. 35, Art. 12; Porém se tal filho, etc." In *Collecção de dissertações juridicas, e praticas por* . . . *Lobão,* 3–35. Lisbon: Imp. Regia, 1826.

———. *Notas de uso pratico, e criticas, addicções, e remissões (á imitação das de Müller á Struvio), sobre todos os titulos dos livros 1, 2 e 3 das Instituições de Direito Civil Lusitano do Dr. Paschoal José de Mello Freire.* Lisbon: Imp. Regia, 1818–1824.

Mellii Freireii, Paschalis Josephi. *Institutionum juris civilis lusitani, cum publici, tum privati.* 4 vols. Lisbon: Ex Typis Regalis Academiae Scientiarum Olisponensis, 1789–1793.

Mendes de Almeida, Candido. *Auxiliar juridico servindo de appendice a decima-quarta edição do Codigo Philippino ou as Ordenações do Reino do Portugal recopiladas por mandado de El-Rey D. Philippe I, a primeira publicada no Brasil a que se dedicão ao estudo do direito e da jurisprudência patria por* . . . . Rio de Janeiro: Typ. de Instituto Philomathico, 1869.

———. "Axiomas e brocardos de direito, extrahidos da legislação brazileira, antiga e moderna." In Candido Mendes de Almeida, *Auxiliar jurdico de appendice a decima-quarta edição do Codigo Philippino* . . . . , 517–602. Rio de Janeiro: Typ. do Instituto Philomathico, 1869.

————. "Bibliographia." In *Ordenações Filipinas* . . . , pp. X–LXII. Rio de Janeiro: Typ. de Instituto Philomathico, 1870.

————. "Epitome dos trabalhos juridico-litterarios dos jurisconsultos." *In Auxiliar juridico* . . . , pp. 781–88. Rio de Janeiro: Typ. de Instituto Philomathico, 1869.

Mourlon, M. Fr. *Répetitions écrits sur le premier examen du Code Napoléon contenant l'exposé des principes généraux, leurs motifs et la solution des questions theoriques.* 6th ed. Paris: A. Masesqu et E. Dujardin, 1858.

Nascimento e Silva, Manoel Joaquim do. *Synopse da legislação militar brazileira até 1874 cujo conhecimento mais interessa aos empregados do Ministerio da Guerra.* 2 vols. Rio de Janeiro: Typ. do *Diario do Rio de Janeiro*, 1874.

Paula Cidade, F. de. *Cadetes e alunos militares através dos tempos (1878–1932).* Rio de Janeiro: Biblioteca do Exército, 1961.

Perdigão Malheiro [Augustinho Marques]. *Commentario à lei N. 463 de 2 de setembro de 1847 sobre successão dos filhos naturaes, e sua filiação.* Rio de Janeiro: Eduardo e Henrique Laemmert, n.d. [1857].

Pereira de Vasconcellos, F. M. P. *Novissimo manual dos tabelliães, ou collecção dos actos, attribuições e deveres d'estes funccionarios, contendo a collecção de minutas de contractos e instrumentos mais usuaes . . . ordenada sobre o Manual de José Homem Corrêa Telles por* . . . . Rio de Janeiro: Liv. dos Editores Antonio Gonçalves Guimarães & C.ª, 1864.

Pereira e Souza, Joaquim José Caetano. *Classes de crimes, por ordem systematica: com as penas correspondentes, segundo a legislação actual.* 2nd ed., emendada e accrescentada. Lisbon: J. F. M. de Campos, 1816.

————. *Primeiras linhas sobre o processo criminal.* 2nd ed. Lisbon: Typ. Lacerdina, 1810.

Pereira Freire, Francisco. *Instituiçoens de direito civil luzitano tanto publico como particular por Paschoal José de Mello Freire traducidas do latim por* . . . *livro segundo do direito das pessoas.* Pernambuco [Recife]: Typ. de Pinheiro & Faria, 1834.

Rodrigues Pereira, Lafayette. *Direitos de familia por* . . . . Rio de Janeiro: B. L. Garnier, 1869.

Vienne, R. Mathieu de. *Étude sur la légitimation des enfants naturels en droit roman et en droit français.* Paris: Imprimerie Arnous de Riviére, 1876.

II. CONSTITUTIONS, CODES, STATUTES, AND COLLECTIONS OF LAWS

Alves, João Luiz. *Codigo civil da Republica dos Estados Unidos do Brasil, promulgado pela lei de Nº 3.071, de 1 de janeiro de 1916, annotado pelo Doutor* . . . . Rio de Janeiro: F. Briguiet e Cⁱᵃ, 1917.

Bevilaqua, Achilles. *Código civil dos Estados Unidos do Brasil, comentado por Clovis Bevilaqua, por* . . . . 11th ed., updated. 6 vols. Rio de Janeiro: Liv. Francisco Alves, 1956.

Bevilaqua, Clovis. *Projecto de Codigo Civil Brazileiro, organizado pelo* . . . *Lente Cathedratico de Legislação Comparada da Faculdade de Direito do Recife, por ordem do Exmo. Dr. Epitacio Pessôa, Ministro da Justiça e Negocios Interiores.* Rio de Janeiro: Imp. Nacional, 1900.

Brazil. *Collecção das decisões do Governo do Imperio do Brazil* [Title varies]. Vol. 11 (1848). Rio de Janeiro: Typ. Nacional, 1849.

―――. *Collecção das leis do imperio brazileiro.* [Title varies.] Rio de Janeiro: Typ. Nacional, 1808–1889.

―――. Ministerio do Interior. *Projecto do Codigo Civil Brazileiro: Trabalhos da Commissão Especial da Camara dos Deputados (mandados imprimir pelo ministro do interior, Dr. Sabino Barros Junior).* 8 vols. Rio de Janeiro: Imp. Nacional, 1902.

―――. Ministerio da Justiça. *Commissão revisora do projecto de Codigo Civil: Actas dos trabalhos . . . elaborados pelo Dr. Clovis Bevilaqua.* Rio de Janeiro: Imp. Nacional, 1901.

Cachard, Henry, ed. *The French Civil Code With the Various Amendments Thereto, As in Force on March 15, 1895.* New York & Albany: Banks and Brothers, 1895.

Código Criminal do Império do Brasil [1830]. In *Códigos penais do Brasil: Evolução histórica,* edited by José Henrique Pierangelli, pp. 167–265. Bauru, São Paulo: Ed. Jalovi Ltda., 1980.

Código de Processo Penal, Dec.-Lei No. 3689 de 3 Oct. de 1941, com todas as alterações em vigor. São Paulo: Saraiva, 1971.

Constituição Politica do Imperio do Brasil [1824]. In *Diccionario historico, geographico e ethnographico do Brasil (commemorativo do Primeiro Centenario da Independencia),* 2 vols., edited by the Instituto Historico e Geographico Brasileiro, 1:304–13. Rio de Janeiro: Imp. Nacional, 1922.

Constituição da República dos Estados Unidos do Brasil, de 24 de fevereiro de 1891. In *Tôdas as Constituições do Brasil: Compilação das textos, notas, revisão e índices,* edited by Adriano Campanhole and Hildon Lôbo Campanhole, 457–86. São Paulo: Editôra Atlas, 1971.

Decree-Law No. 181 of 24 January 1890 [1890 Civil Marriage Act]. In *Leis usuaes da Republica dos Estados Unidos do Brazil,* edited by Tarquinio de Souza and Caetano Montenegro, 235–52. Rio de Janeiro: Imp. Nacional, 1903.

"Decreta da Reforma do Matrimonio" [trans. of *De Reformatione Matrimonii*]. In *Direito civil ecclesiastico brazileiro, antigo e moderno, em suas relaçoes com o direito canonico ou collecção completa chronologicamente disposta desde a primeira dynastia portugueza até o presente comprehendendo . . . por . . . . ,* 2 vols., edited by Candido Mendes de Almeida, 2:663–67. Rio de Janeiro: B. L. Garnier, 1873.

Delgado da Silva, Antonio. *Collecção da legislação portugueza desde a ultima compilação das Ordenações, redigida pelo . . . .* 9 vols. Lisbon: Typ. Maigrense, 1825–1847.

Gilbert, P., ed. *Les Codes annotés de Sirey, contenant toute la jurisprudence des arrêts et la doctrine des auteures; édition entiérement refondue par . . . .* 3rd ed. Vol. 1: *Code Napoléon.* Paris: Librairie Générale de Jurisprudence Cosse, 1855.

"*Loi sur la formes des Actes notariés,* No. 10,713 of June 21, 1843." In *Bulletin des Lois du Royaume de France* [Paris], IXe série, 26 (1843): 519–35.

Mendes de Almeida, Candido. *Codigo Philippino ou Ordenações e Leis do Reino de Portugal recopiladas por mandado d'El-Rey D. Philippe I, decima-quarta edição, segundo a primeira de 1603, e a nona de Coimbra de 1824.* Rio de Janeiro: Typ. do Instituto Philomathico, 1870.

―――. *Direito civil ecclesiastico brazileiro, antigo e moderno, em suas relações com o direito canonico ou collecção completa chronologicamente disposta desde a primeira dynastia portugueza até o presente comprehendendo . . . por . . . .* 2 vols. Rio de Janeiro: B. L. Garnier, 1873.

1988 Constitution of the Federative Republic of Brazil. Keith S. Rosenn, trans. and annotator. In *A Panorama of Brazilian Law,* edited by Jacob Dolinger and Keith S. Rosenn, pp. 383–518. Miami: University of Miami Press, 1992.

"Novo Regimento da Mesa do Desembargo do Paço (Lei de 27 de julho de 1582)." Reprinted in Candido Mendes de Almeida, *Ordenações Philippinas . . . ,* 241–53. Rio de Janeiro: Instituto Philomathico, 1870.

Pierangelli, José Henrique, ed. *Códigos Penais do Brasil: Evolução histórica.* São Paulo: Edição Jalovi, 1980.

Souza, Tarquinio de, and Montenegro, Caetano, eds. *Leis usuaes da Republica dos Estados Unidos do Brazil.* Rio de Janeiro: Imp. Nacional, 1903.

Teixeira de Freitas, Augusto. *Consolidação das leis civis.* Rio de Janeiro: Typ. Universal de Laemmert, 1857.

Vide, Sebastião Monteiro da. *Constituições primeiras do Arcebispado da Bahia feitas, e ordenadas pelo illustrissimo, e reverendissimo senhor D. Sebastião Monteiro da Vide, 5° Arcebispo do dito Arcebispado, e do Conselho de Sua Magestade: propostas, e aceitas em o synodo diocesano, que o dito senhor celebrou em 12 de junho do anno de 1707.* São Paulo: Typ. 2 de Dezembro, 1853.

———. *Regimento do auditorio ecclesiastico do Arcebispado da Bahia, Metropoli do Brasil, e da sua relacam, e officiaes da justiça ecclesiastica, e mais cousas que tocão ao Bom Governo do dito arcebispado ordenando . . . .* Coimbra: Off. do Real Collegio da Companhia de Jesus, 1720.

Other Sources Cited

INTERVIEW

Jorge Pacheco Chaves Filho. Instituto Histórico e Geográfico Brasileiro, Rio de Janeiro. June 22, 27, and July 4, 1990.

BOOKS, ARTICLES, AND CATALOGUES

Alencar, José [Martiniano] de. *Senhora: Profile of a Woman*. Translated by Catarina Feldman Edinger. Austin: University of Texas Press, 1994.

Andrada, Jozé Bonifacio de. *Representaço á Assembléa Geral Constituinte e Legislativa do Imperio do Brasil sobre a Escravatura*. Rio de Janeiro: Cabral, 1840.

Anjos, João Alfredo dos. "A roda dos enjeitados: Enjeitados e órfãos em Pernambuco no século XIX." Master's thesis, Universidade Federal de Pernambuco, 1997.

Arago, Jacques. *Narrative of a Voyage Around the World in the Uranie and Physicienne Corvettes, commanded by Capt. Freycinet, in 1817, 1818, 1819, and 1820*. London: Treuttal & Wurtz, Treuttal, Jun, & Richter, 1823.

Arnold, Linda. "Privileged Justice? The *Fuero Militar* in Early National Mexico." In *Judicial Institutions in Nineteenth-Century Latin America*, edited by Eduardo Zimmerman, 48–64. London: University of London Institute for Latin American Studies, 1999.

"Ataque à realeza: Constituinte contra os lucros imobiliários da família dos Orleans e Bragança." *IstoÉ*. 3 June 1987, pp. 76–77.

Azevedo, Célia Maria Marinho de. *Onda negra, medo branco: O negro no imaginário das elites—século XIX*. Rio de Janeiro: Paz e Terra, 1987.

Azevedo Marques, José Manoel Eufrazio de. *Apontamentos historicos, geographicos e biographicos da Provincia de São Paulo*. Rio de Janeiro: n. p., 1879.

Balderston, Daniel, and Donna J. Guy, eds. *Sex and Sexuality in Latin America*. New York: New York University Press, 1997.

Barman, Roderick J. *Brazil: The Forging of a Nation, 1798–1852*. Stanford: Stanford University Press, 1988.

———. *Citizen Emperor: Pedro II and the Making of Brazil, 1825–91*. Stanford: Stanford University Press, 1999.

———. "A New-World Nobility: The Role of Titles in Imperial Brazil." In *University of British Columbia Hispanic Studies*, edited by Harold Livermore, 39–50. London: Tamesis Books Limited, 1974.

Barman, Roderick J., and Jean Barman. "The Role of the Law School Graduates in the Political Elite of Brazil." *Journal of International Studies and World Affairs* 18 (1976): 423–50.

Beal, Tarcisio. "Os Jesuítas, a Universidade de Coimbra e a Igreja Brasileira, subsídios para a história do regalismo em Portugal e no Brasil, 1750–1850." Ph.D. diss., The Catholic University of America, 1969.

Beckford, William. *The Travel Diaries of William Beckford of Fonthill.* Cambridge: On the University Press for Constable & Co., 1928.

Berbert de Castro, Dinorah d'Araújo. *Cartas sobre a educação de Cora do Dr. José Lino Coutinho.* Cidade do Salvador: Universidade Católica do Salvador, 1977.

Besse, Susan K. *Restructuring Patriarchy: The Modernization of Gender Inequality in Brazil, 1914–1940.* Chapel Hill: University of North Carolina Press, 1996.

Bethell, Leslie. "The Independence of Brazil." In *Brazil: Empire and Republic, 1822–1930,* edited by Leslie Bethell, 45–113. Cambridge: The Cambridge University Press, 1989.

"Os bispos de Olinda, diocese criada pelo Papa Inocêncio XI em 16 de novembro de 1676." Library of the Cúria Metropolitana do Recife e Olinda, s. p., s. d. Mimeographed.

Boehrer, George C. A. "The Flight of the Brazilian Deputies from the Cortes Gerais of Lisbon, 1822." *Hispanic American Historical Review* 40 (Nov. 1960): 497–512.

Borges, Dain. *The Family in Bahia, Brazil, 1870–1940.* Stanford: Stanford University Press, 1992.

Boschi, Caio César. *Os leigos e o poder (Irmandades leigas e política colonizadora em Minas Gerais).* Editora Ática, 1986.

Brading, D. A. *The First America: The Spanish Monarchy, Creole Patriots, and the Spanish State, 1492–1867.* Cambridge: Cambridge University Press, 1991.

———. *The Origins of Mexican Nationalism.* Cambridge: Centre of Latin American Studies, 1985.

Brazil. Parlamento. *Discussão no Senado e na Camara dos Deputados sobre a falla do trono em 1839 na parte relativa aos negocios com a Santa Sé Apostolica.* Rio de Janeiro: Imp. Americana de L. P. da Costa, 1839.

———. ———. Camara dos Deputados. *Annaes do Parlamento Brazileiro; Camara dos Srs. Deputados [1826–1847].* Rio de Janeiro: Typ. de Hyppolito José Pinto & Cia., 1874–1880.

———. ———. Secretaria. *Organizações e programmas ministeriaes desde 1822 a 1889: Notas explicativas . . . com alguns dos mais importantes decretos e leis, resumo historico . . . .* Rio de Janeiro: Imprensa Nacional, 1889.

———. ———. Senado. *Annaes do Senado do Imperio do Brazil . . . [1826–1834, 1837, 1839–1846].* Rio de Janeiro: n. p., 1911–1923.

———. Senado. *Anais do Senado do Império do Brasil [1835, 1836, 1838, 1847].* Brasília: Senado Federal, Subsecretaria de Anais, 1978–1979.

Brinton, Crane. *French Revolutionary Legislation on Illegitimacy, 1789–1804.* Cambridge: Harvard University Press, 1936.

Broteiro, Frederico de Barros. *A família Jordão e seus afins.* São Paulo: Instituto Genealógico Brasileiro, 1948.

Burns, Robert I., ed. *The Worlds of Alfonso the Learned and James the Conqueror: Intellect and Force in the Middle Ages.* Princeton: Princeton University Press, 1985.

Carvalho, Marcus Joaquim Maciel de. "Hegemony and Rebellion in Pernambuco (Brazil), 1821–1835." Ph.D. diss., University of Illinois, Urbana-Champagne, 1989.

———. "Slave Resistance in Pernambuco in the Age of the Liberal Rebellions, 1817–1848." Paper presented at the Pacific Coast Conference of Latin American Studies, California State University at San Diego, 1995.

Carvalho Franco, Maria Sylvia de. "As idéias estão no lugar." *Cadernos de Debate* 1 (1976 [2nd ed.]): 61–64.

Caulfield, Sueann. "The Birth of Mangue: Race, Nation, and the Politics of Prostitution in Rio de Janeiro, 1850–1942." In *Sex and Sexuality in Latin America*, edited by Daniel Balderston and Donna J. Guy, 86–100. New York: New York University Press, 1997.

———. *In Defense of Honor: Sexual Morality, Modernity, and Nation in Early Twentieth-Century Brazil*. Durham: Duke University Press, 2000.

Coelho da Rocha, M[anoel] A[ugusto]. *Ensaio sobre a historia do governo e da legislação de Portugal para servir de introducção ao Estudo do direito patrio por . . . .* 2nd ed. Coimbra: Imp. da Universidade, 1843.

Conrad, Robert Edgar. *Children of God's Fire: A Documentary History of Black Slavery in Brazil.* Princeton University Press, 1983.

Dauphinee, Bede A[nthony]. "Church and Parliament in Brazil During the First Empire, 1823–1831." Ph.D. diss., Georgetown University, 1965.

Dean, Warren. *Rio Claro: A Brazilian Plantation System, 1820–1920.* Stanford: Stanford University Press, 1976.

Demars-Sion, Veronique. *Femmes séduites et abandonées au 18ᵉ siècle, l'exemple du Cambrésis.* Hellemmes: ESTER, 1991.

D'Incao, Maria Angela, ed. *Amor e família no Brasil.* São Paulo: Contexto, 1989.

———. "O amor romántico e a família burguesa." In *Amor e família no Brasil*, edited by Maria Angela D'Incao, 57–71. São Paulo: Contexto, 1989.

Dolinger, Jacob, and Keith S. Rosenn, eds. *A Panorama of Brazilian Law.* Miami: University of Miami Press, 1992.

Dundas, Robert. *Sketches of Brazil, Including New Views on Tropical and European Fever.* London: John Churchill, 1852.

Dunshee de Abranches [João]. *O captiveiro (memórias).* Rio de Janeiro: *Jornal do Commercio*, 1941. Excerpt reprinted as "Racial Conflict in Nineteenth-Century Maranhão," in *Children of God's Fire: A Documentary History of Black Slavery in Brazil*, edited and translated by Robert Edgar Conrad, 225–29. Princeton: Princeton University Press, 1983.

Egas, Eugenio. *Documentos*, vol. 2 of *Diogo Antonio Feijó*, 2 vols. S. Paulo: Typ. Levi, 1912.

Ellis Júnior, Alfredo. *Feijó e sua época. Boletins da Faculdade de Filosofia, Ciências e Letras*, XVI. Rio de Janeiro, 1940.

Eltis, David. "Free and Coerced Transatlantic Migrations: Some Comparisons." *American Historical Review* 88 (Apr. 1983): 251–80.

Engel, Magali. *Meretrizes e doutores: Saber médico e prostituição no Rio de Janeiro (1840–1890).* São Paulo: Brasiliense, 1989.

Ewbank, Thomas. *Life in Brazil; Or a Journal of a Visit to the Land of the Cocoa and the Palm.* New York: Harper & Brothers, Publishers, 1856.

Faoro, Raimundo. *Os donos do poder: Formação do patronato político brasileiro.* 2nd ed., rev. and exp. 2 vols. São Paulo: Editora Globo/Editora da USP, 1975.

Farriss, Nancy. *Crown and Clergy in Colonial Mexico, 1759–1821: The Crisis of Ecclesiastical Privilege.* London: Athlone Press, 1968.

Feijó, Diogo Antonio. *Demonstrasão da necessidade da abolição do celibato clerical pela Assemblêa Geral do Brasil: e da sua verdadeira e legitima competência nesta materia.* Rio de Janeiro: Imprensa Nacional, 1828. Reprinted in Eugênio Egas, *Diogo Antonio Feijó,* 2:98–156. São Paulo: Typ. Levi, 1912.

————. "Resposta as parvoices, absurdos, impiedades, e contradisões do Sr. Pe. Luiz Gonsalves dos Santos na sua intitulada defeza do celibato clerical . . . ." In Eugenio Egas, *Diogo Antônio Feijó,* 2:157–72. São Paulo: Typ. Levi, 1912.

Fernandes Pinheiro, J. C. "Os padres do Patrocínio ou o Porto Real de Itú." *Revista do Instituto Histórico e Geográfico Brasileiro,* 33, Pt. 2 (1870): 137–48.

Ferraz, Soccorro. *Liberais e liberais: Guerras civis em Pernabuco no século XIX.* Recife: Editora Universitária UFPE, 1996.

Fleiuss, Max. "Organização política." In *Diccionario historico, geographico e ethnographico do Brasil, commemorativo do Primeiro Centenario da Independencia,* 2 vols., edited by the Instituto Histórico e Geográfico Brasileiro, 1:299–304. Rio de Janeiro: Imprensa Nacional, 1922.

Fletcher, James C., and D. P. Kidder. *Brazil and the Brazilians Portrayed in Historical and Descriptive Sketches.* 9th ed. Boston: Little, Brown, and Company, 1879.

Flory, Thomas. *Judge and Jury in Imperial Brazil: Social Control and Political Stability in the New State.* Austin: University of Texas Press, 1981.

————. "Race and Social Control in Independent Brazil." *Journal of Latin American Studies* 9, no.2 (1979): 199–224.

Forjaz, Djalma. *O Senador Vergueiro: sua vida e sua epoca, 1778–1859.* São Paulo: Cia. Melhoramentos de São Paulo, 1922.

Freyre, Gilberto. *Ordem e progresso (Processo de disintegração das sociedades patriarcal e semi-patriarcal no Brasil sob o regime do trabalho livre: Aspectos de um quase meio século de transição do trabalho escravo para o trabalho livre; e da monarquia para a República).* 3rd ed. 2 vols. Rio de Janeiro: José Olympio Editora/Instituto Nacional do Livro, 1974.

Gama Lima, Lana Lage da, ed. *Mulheres, adultérios e padres.* Rio de Janeiro: Raymundo Paula de Arruda, 1987.

————. "O padre e a moça: o crime de solicitação no Brasil no século XVIII." *Ler História* [Lisboa], No. 18 (1990): 25–36.

Garaud, Marcel. *La Révolution française et la famille.* Paris: Presses Universitaires de France, 1978.

Gardner, George. *Travels in the Interior of Brazil, Principally Through the Northern Provinces, and the Gold and Diamond Districts during the Years 1836–1841.* 2nd ed. London: Reeve, Benham, and Reeve, 1849.

Gérson, Brasil. *O regalismo brasileiro.* Rio de Janeiro: Liv. Editora Cátedra, 1978.

Gomes B. Câmara, José. *Subsídios para a história do direito pátrio.* 4 vols. Rio de Janeiro: Liv. Brasiliana Editôra, 1966.

Goody, Jack [John Rancine]. *The Development of the Family and Marriage in Europe.* Cambridge: Cambridge University Press, 1983.

Graham, Maria [Dundas] [Lady Calcott]. *Journal of a Voyage to Brazil and Residence*

There During Part of the Years 1821, 1822, and 1823. London: Longman, Hurst, Rees, Orme, Brown, and Green, 1824.

Graham, Richard. *Patronage and Politics in Nineteenth-Century Brazil*. Stanford: Stanford University Press, 1990.

Guerra Ferreira, Lúcia de Fátima, and Zeluiza da Silva Formiga, eds. *Catálogo dos processos de ordenação*. João Pessoa: Arquivo do Arcebispado da Paraíba, n.d. [1993].

Gusmão, Paulo Dourado de. *Dicionário de direito de família*. 2nd ed. Rio de Janeiro: Forense, 1987.

Hale, Charles A. *Mexican Liberalism in the Age of Mora, 1821–1853*. Yale University Press, 1968.

———. "The Revival of Political History and the French Revolution in Mexico." In *The Global Ramifications of the French Revolution*, edited by Joseph Klaits and Michael H. Haltzel, 158–76. Cambridge: Cambridge University Press, 1994.

Hall, Gwendolyn Midlo. *Africans in Colonial Louisana: The Development of Afro-Creole Culture in the Eighteenth Century*. Baton Rouge: Lousiana State University Press, 1992.

Harro-Harring, Paul. *Tropical Sketches From Brazil, 1840*. Rio de Janeiro: Instituto Histórico e Geográfico Brasileiro, 1965.

Higgins, Kathleen. *"Licentious Liberty" in a Brazilian Gold-Mining Region: Slavery, Gender, and Social Control in Eighteenth-Century Sabará, Minas Gerais*. University Park: The Pennsylvania State University Press, 1999.

Holloway, Thomas H. "From Justice of the Peace to Social War in Rio de Janeiro." In *Judicial Institutions in Nineteenth-Century Latin America*, edited by Eduardo Zimmerman, 65–85. London: University of London Institute of Latin American Studies, 1999.

———. *Policing Rio de Janeiro: Repression and Resistance in a 19th-Century City*. Stanford: Stanford University Press, 1993.

Instituto Histórico e Geográfico Brasileiro, ed. *Diccionario historico, geographico e ethnographico do Brasil, commemorativo do Primeiro Centenario da Independencia*. 2 vols. Rio de Janeiro: Imprensa Nacional, 1922.

Iorio, Leoni. *Valença de ôntem e de hoje (subsídios á história do Município de Marquês de Valença, 1789–1952)*. Valença, Rio de Janeiro: Jornal de Valença, 1952.

Jansen, José. "Introdução ao nobiliario maranhense." *Anais do Museu Histórico Nacional* 21 (1969): 165–69.

Johnson, Lyman L., and Sonya Lipsett-Rivera, eds. *The Faces of Honor: Sex, Shame, and Violence in Colonial Latin America*. University of New Mexico Press, 1998.

Jornal do Commercio (Rio de Janeiro). No. 143 (15 May 1846), p. 3; and No. 167 (18 June 1846), p. 2.

Karasch, Mary. *Slave Life in Rio de Janeiro, 1800–1850*. Princeton: Princeton University Press, 1987.

Kidder, Daniel P. *Sketches of Residence and Travels in Brazil*. 2 vols. Philadelphia: Sorin & Hall/London: Wiley & Putnam, 1845.

Klaits, Joseph, and Michael H. Haltzel, eds. *The Global Ramifications of the French Revolution*. Cambridge: Cambridge University Press, 1994.

Koster, Henry. *Travels in Brazil*. London: Longman, Hurst, Rees, Orme, and Brown, 1816.

Kraay, Hendrik, ed. *Afro-Brazilian Culture and Politics: Bahia, 1790s–1990s*. Armonk, New York: M. E. Sharpe, 1998.

———. "The Politics of Independence-Era Bahia: The Black Militia Officers of Salvador, 1790–1840." In *Afro-Brazilian Culture and Politics: Bahia, 1790s–1990s*, edited by Hendrik Kraay, 30–56. Armonk, NY: M. E. Sharpe, 1998.

Ladd, Doris. *The Mexican Nobility at Independence, 1780–1826*. Austin: University of Texas Press, 1976.

Lauderdale Graham, Sandra. "Slavery's Impasse: Slave Prostitutes, Small-Time Mistresses, and the Brazilian Law of 1871." *Comparative Studies in Society and History* 33–34 (1991): 669–94.

Lavrin, Asunción, ed. *Sexuality and Marriage in Colonial Latin America*. Lincoln University of Nebraska Press, 1989.

———. *Women, Feminism, and Social Change in Argentina, Chile, and Uruguay, 1890–1940*. Lincoln: University of Nebraska Press, 1995.

Leal, Aureliano. "Historia judiciaria do Brasil." In *Diccionario historico, geographico e ethnographico do Brasil (Commemorativo do Primeiro Centario da Independencia)*, edited by the Instituto Histórico e Geográfico Brasileiro, 1: 1107–1187. Rio de Janeiro: Imp. Nacional, 1922.

Leite, Míriam Moreira. *A condição feminina no Rio de Janeiro, século XIX*. São Paulo & Brasília: HUCITEC/PRÓ-MEMÓRIA & Instituto Nacional do Livro, 1984.

Leithold, T. von, and L. von Rango. *O Rio de Janeiro visto por dois prussianos em 1819*. São Paulo: Cia. Editora Nacional, 1966.

Levi, Darrell E. *The Prados of São Paulo, Brazil: An Elite Family and Social Change, 1840–1930*. Athens & London: The University of Georgia Press, 1987.

Lewcowicz, Ida. "A fragilidade do celibato." In *Mulheres, adultérios e padres*, edited by Lana Lage da Gama Lima, 53–68. Rio de Janeiro: Raymundo Paula de Arruda, 1987.

Lewin, Linda. "Natural and Spurious Offspring in Brazilian Inheritance Law from Colony to Empire: A Methodological Essay." *The Americas* 48 (1992): 351–96.

———. "Patrimony, Paternity, and Republicanism in Brazil: The 1916 Civil Code." Paper presented at the Annual Meeting of the American Society for Legal History, 1995.

———. *Politics and Parentela in Paraíba: A Case Study of Family-Based Oligarchy in Brazil*. Princeton: Princeton University Press, 1987.

———. "Repensando o patriarcado em declínio: De 'de pai incógnito' a filho ilegítimo no direito sucessório brasileiro do século XIX." *Ler História* [Lisbon], No. 29 (1995): 121–33.

———. "The Republic and 'Unholy' Matrimony: The Adoption of Civil Marriage in Brazil." Paper presented at the Annual Meeting of the Western Association of Women Historians, San Marino, California, 1994.

Lino Coutinho, José [dos Santos]. *Cartas sobre a educação de Cora, seguidas de um Cathecismo moral, politico e religioso pelo finado Conselheiro Dr. José Lino Coutinho, publicado por João Gualberto de Passos*. Bahia: Typ. de Carlos Pongetti, 1849.

Lino D'Assumpção, Thomaz. *Narrativas do Brasil (1876–1881)*. Rio de Janeiro: Liv. Contemporanea de Faro & Lino, 1881.

Livermore, H. V. *A New History of Portugal*. Cambridge: Cambridge University Press, 1969.

Livermore, Harold, ed. *University of British Columbia Hispanic Studies*. London: Tamesis Books Limited, 1974.

Londoño, Fernando Torres. *El concubinato y la iglesia en el Brasil colonial*. ESTUDOS CEDHAL, No 2. São Paulo: CEDHAL/USP, n.d. [1988?].

———. "O crime do amor." In *Amor e família no Brasil*, edited by Maria Angela D'Incao, 17–30. São Paulo: Editora Contexto, 1989.

Lynch, John. *The Spanish-American Revolutions*. New York: Norton, 1973.

Macaulay, Neill. *Dom Pedro: The Struggle for Liberty in Brazil and Portugal, 1798–1834*. Durham: Duke University Press, 1986.

MacDonald, Robert A. "Law and Politics: Alfonso's Program of Political Reform." In *The Worlds of Alfonso the Learned and James the Conqueror*, edited by Robert I. Burns, 150–202. Princeton: Princeton University Press, 1985.

Machado Portella, Joaquim Pires. "Supplicio da Caneca: Recordaço de factos acontecidos á mais de meio seculo por uma testemunha ocular." *RIHGB* 51, *Supplemento* (1888): 119–39.

Malerba, Jurandir. *Brancos da lei: Liberalismo, escravidão e mentalidade patriarchal no Império do Brasil*. Maringá, Paraná: Editora da Universidade Estadual Maringá, 1994.

Marcílio, Maria Luiza. *História social da criança abandonada*. São Paulo: HUCITEC, 1998.

Maxwell, Kenneth. *Pombal: Paradox of the Enlightenment*. Cambridge: Cambridge University Press, 1995.

Mello e Souza, Laura de. *Desclassificados de ouro: A pobreza mineira no século XIX*. Rio de Janeiro: Graal, 1982.

Mello Moraes [Pai], A[lexandre] J[osé] de. *Chronica geral do Brazil por dr. . . . systematisada e com uma introdução por Mello Moraes Filho*, 2 vols. Vol. 2, *1700–1900*. Rio de Janeiro: B. L. Garnier, 1886.

———. *A independencia e o imperio do Brazil*. Rio de Janeiro: Typ. do Globo, 1877.

———. *Necrologia do Senador Diogo Antonio Feijó*. Rio de Janeiro: Typ. Brasileira (J. J. do Patrocinio), 1861.

Mesgravis, Laima. *A Santa Casa da Misericórdia de São Paulo (1599?–1884): Contribuição ao estudo da assistência social no Brasil*. São Paulo: Conselho Estadual de Cultura, 1977.

Mesquita Samara, Eni de. *As mulheres, o poder e a família: São Paulo, século XIX*. São Paulo: Editora Marco Zero & Sec. do Estado da Cultura de São Paulo, 1989.

Moraes e Silva, Antonio de. *Diccionário da lingua portuguêsa, recopilado dos vocabularios impressos até agora . . . novamente emendado, e muito accrescentado, por . . . .* 2nd ed. Lisbon: Lacerdina, 1813.

Moreira Alves, José Carlos. "A Panorama of Brazilian Civil Law from Its Origins to the Present." In *A Panorama of Brazilian Law*, edited by Jacob Dolinger and Keith S. Rosenn, 87–120. Miami: University of Miami Press, 1992.

Mota, Carlos Guilherme. *Nordeste—1817: Estrutura e argumentos*. São Paulo: Editora da USP/Editora Perspectiva, 1972.

Mott, Luiz R. B. *Os pecados de família na Bahia de Todos os Santos (1813)*. Salvador: Centro de Estudos Baianos/Universidade Federal da Bahia, 1982.

Muello, Peter. "Urban Renewal Turns Off Rio de Janeiro's Oldest Red Light." *Seattle Times*, 5 Jan. 1996, sec. A, p. 1.

Murilo de Carvalho, José. *Teatro de sombras: a política imperial.* Rio de Janeiro: Edições Vértice e IUPERJ, 1988.

Nabuco, Joaquim. *Um estadista do imperio, Nabuco de Araujo: sua vida, suas opiniões e sua epoca por seu filho.* 2nd ed. São Paulo & Rio de Janeiro: Cia. Editora Nacional/Civilização Brasileira, 1936.

Nazzari, Muriel. "Concubinage in Colonial Brazil: The Inequalities of Race, Class, and Gender." *Journal of Family History* 21 (Apr. 1996): 107–24.

———. *The Disappearance of the Dowry: Women, the Family, and Property in São Paulo (1600–1900).* Stanford: Stanford University Press, 1991.

———. "Questionable Foundlings: The Fake Abandonment of Infants in Colonial Brazil." Paper presented at the Annual Meeting of the American Historical Association Annual Meeting, 1995.

———. "An Urgent Need To Conceal: The System of Honor and Shame in Colonial Brazil." In *The Faces of Honor: Sex, Shame, and Violence in Colonial Latin America,* edited by Lyman L. Johnson and Sonya Lipsett-Rivera, 103–26. Albuquerque: University of New Mexico Press, 1998.

———. "Widows as Obstacles to Business: British Objections to Brazilian Marriage and Inheritance Laws." *Comparative Studies in Society and History* 37 (1995): 781–802.

"Necrologia, 8 de setembro de 1836: Marquez de Caravellas." *Jornal do Commercio,* 15 Sept. 1836. Reprinted in *Annaes do Senado de 1837,* VII-XVI.

Needell, Jeffrey D. "Provincial Origins of the Brazilian State: Rio de Janeiro, the Monarchy, and National Political Organization, 1808–1853." *Latin American Research Review* 36, no. 3 (2001): 132–53.

Neves, Guilherme Pereira das. "Do império luso-brasileiro ao império do Brasil (1789–1822)." *Ler História,* Nos. 27–28 (1995): 78–79.

———. *E receberá mercê: A Mesa da Consciênca e Ordens e o clero secular no Brasil - 1808–1828.* Rio de Janeiro: Arquivo Nacional, 1997.

Nizza da Silva, Maria Beatriz. *Cultura e sociedade no Rio de Janeiro (1808–1821).* São Paulo: Cia. Editora Nacional, 1977.

———. "A documentação do Desembargo do Paço e a história da família." *Ler História* (Lisbon), No. 20 (1990): 61–77.

———. "Os filhos ilegítimos no Brasil colonial." In *Anais da Sociedade Brasileira de Pesquisa Histórica, XV ª Reunião* (1995): 121–24.

———. *O império luso-brasileiro, 1750–1822.* Vol. 8 of *Nova história da expansão portuguêsa,* edited by Joel Serrão and A. H. Oliveira Marques. Lisbon: Editora Estampa, 1986.

———. *Sistema de casamento no Brasil colonial.* São Paulo: Editora da USP, 1978.

Okihiro, Gary Y., ed. *Resistance Studies in African, Caribbean, and Afro-American History.* Amherst: University of Massachusetts Press, 1986.

Oliveira Marques, A. H. de. *From Lusitania to Empire,* vol. 1 of the *History of Portugal.* 2 vols. New York & London: Columbia University Press. 1972.

Paim, Antonio. *História das idéias filosóficas no Brasil.* São Paulo: Editôra Grijalbo, 1967.

Pang, Eul-Soo. In *Pursuit of Honor and Power: Noblemen of the Southern Cross in Nineteenth-Century Brazil.* Auburn: University of Alabama Press, 1988.

Peard, Julyan. *Race, Place, and Medicine: The Idea of the Tropics in Nineteenth-Century Brazilian Medicine*. Durham: Duke University Press, 1999.

Pessoa da Silva, Jozé Eloy. *Memoria sobre a escravatura e projecto de colonização dos europeus e pretos da Africa no Imperio do Brazil*. Rio de Janeiro: Plancher, 1826.

Pires, Heliodoro. "Uma teologia jansenista no Brasil." *Revista Eclesiástica Brasileira* 8 (June 1943): 331–34.

Portella, Petrônio. "Apresentação." In *Anais do Senado do Império do Brasil [março a outubro de 1835]*, pp. 3–4. Brasília: Senado Federal, Subsecretaria de Anais, 1978.

Ramos, Donald. "Gossip, Scandal, and Popular Culture in Golden Age Brazil." *Journal of Social History* 33 (Summer 2000): 887–912.

Ramos de Carvalho, Laerte. *As reformas pombalinas da instrução pública*. Boletim No. 160 (1952), Universidade de São Paulo, Faculdade de Filosofia, Ciências e Letras.

Rangel, Alberto. *D. Pedro Primeiro e a Marquêsa de Santos: A vistas de cartas íntimas e de outros documentos públicos e particulares*. 2nd ed., exp. and rev. Tours, France: Typ. de Arrault e Cia., 1928.

Reis, João José. "O jogo duro do Dois de Julho: O Partido Negro na independência da Bahia." In *Negociação e conflito: A resistência negra no Brasil escravista*, edited by João José Reis and Eduardo Santos, 79–98. São Paulo: Cia. das Letras, 1989.

Reis, João José, and Eduardo Santos, eds. *Negociação e conflito: A resistência negra no Brasil escravista*. São Paulo: Cia. das Letras, 1989.

Rheingantz, Carlos G. *Titulares do império*. Rio de Janeiro: Min. da Justiça e Negócios Interiores/Arquivo Nacional, 1960.

Ribeiro, Gladys Sabina. "'Brasileiros, vamos a eles!': Identidade nacional e controle social no Primeiro Reinado." *Ler História*, Nos. 27–28 (1995): 103–24.

Ricci, Magda [Maria de Oliveira]. *Assombrações de um padre-regente: Diogo Antonio Feijó (1784–1843)*. Campinas, São Paulo: Editora da Universidade de Campinas, 2002.

Rodrigues, José Honório. *Independência, revolução e contrarevolução*. 5 vols. Rio de Janeiro: Liv. F. Alves Editora, 1975–1976.

Rugendas, Johann Moritz. *Viagem pintoresca através do Brasil por João Maurício Rugendas*. 8th ed. Translated by Sergio Milliet. Belo Horizonte: Editora Itatiaia, 1979.

Sacramento Blake, Augusto Victorino Alves. *Diccionario bibliographico brazileiro, pelo doutor . . . .* 7 vols. Rio de Janeiro: Typ. Nacional, 1883–1903. Reprint: Guanabara: Conselho Federal da Cultura, 1970.

Saint-Hilaire, Auguste de. *Segunda viagem do Rio de Janeiro a Minas Gerais e a São Paulo (1822)*. Translated by Vivaldi Moreira. Belo Horizonte & São Paulo: Editora Itatiaia/ Editora da USP, 1975.

Santos, Eugenio dos. "A legislação pombalina e os novos marginalizados do Brasil: Uma abordagem." *Revista de Ciências Históricas* [Universidade Portocalense] 11 (1996): 151–61.

Santos, Sydney M. G. dos. *André Rebouças e seu tempo*. Petrópolis: Editora Vozes, 1985.

São Clemente, baron of (José dos Santos). *Estatisticas e biographias parlamentares portuguezas pelo . . . .* 3 vols. Porto: Typ. do Commercio do Porto, 1887–1892.

Schlichthorst, C. O. *Rio de Janeiro como é, 1824–1826 (huma vez e nunca mais): Contribuições dum diario para a historia atual, os costumes e especialmente a situação da tropa estrangeira na Capital do Brazil*. Translated by Emmy Dodt and Gustavo Barroso. Rio de Janeiro: Editora Getúlio Costa, 1943.

Schneider Susan. *O marquês de Pombal e o vinho do Porto; dependência e subdesenvolvimento em Portugal no sêculo XVIII*. Lisbon: A Regra do Jogo, 1980.

Schwarcz, Lilia Moritz, and Angela Marques da Costa. "Como Ser Nobre no Brasil." Chapter 8 of *As barbas do imperador: D. Pedro II, um monarca nos trópicos*, by Lilia Moritz Schwarcz. São Paulo: Cia. das Letras, 1998.

Schwartz, Stuart B. *Sovereignty and Society in Colonial Brazil: The High Court of Bahia and Its Judges, 1609–1751*. Berkeley and Los Angeles: University of California Press, 1973.

Schwarz, Roberto. "Misplaced Ideas: Literature and Society in Late-Nineteenth-Century Brazil." In *Misplaced Ideas*, edited by Roberto Schwarz, with an introduction by John Gledson, 19–31. London & New York: VERSO, 1992.

Seed, Patricia. *Ceremonies of Possession in Europe's Conquest of the World*. Cambridge: Cambridge University Press, 1995.

———. *To Love, Honor, and Obey in Colonial Mexico: Conflicts over Marriage Choice, 1574–1821*. Stanford: Stanford University Press, 1988.

Seidler, Carl. *Dez annos no Brasil*. São Paulo: Liv. Martins, [1942].

Seixas, Romualdo Antonio de. *Collecção das Obras completas do . . . .* 3 vols. Pernambuco: Typ. de Santos & Cia, 1839.

———. "Reflexoens offerecidas à Camara dos Deputados, sobre o Parecer da respeitiva Commissão Ecclesiastica, acerca do Celibato Clerical [1834]." In *Collecção das obras completas do D. Romualdo Antonio de Seixas*, 3 vols., 2:373–405. Pernambuco [Recife]: Typ. Santos & Cia., 1839.

———. "Representação dirigida à Assembléa Geral Legislativa, sobre hum Projecto de Lei, relativo aos Impedimentos, e Causas Matrimoniais [20 July 1832]." In *Collecção das obras completas do D. Romualdo Antonio de Seixas*, 3 vols., 2:277–303.

———. *Representação dirigida às camaras sobre o casamento civil*. Bahia [Salvador]: 1859.

———. *Representação dirigida à sua magestade o Imperador sobre a proposta do governo acerca do casamento civil*. Bahia [Salvador]: 1859.

———. "Resposta a hum aviso do Exmo. Min. da Justiça, exigindo o seu parecer sobre a questão do Celibato, suscitada em S. Paulo [14 June 1834]." In *Collecção das obras completas do D. Romualdo Antonio de Seixas*, 3 vols., 2:349–71. Pernambuco: Typ. de Santos & Cia, 1839.

Simms, Calvin. "Justice in Peru: Rape Victim Is Pressed to Marry Attacker." *New York Times*, 12 Mar. 1997, A:1, 8.

Sousa, Octávio Tarquínio de. *A vida de D. Pedro I*. 3 vols. Rio de Janeiro: Biblioteca do Exército e Liv. José Olympio Editores, 1972.

Sousa Montenegro, João Alfredo de. *O liberalismo radical de Frei Caneca*. Rio de Janeiro: Tempo Brasileiro, 1978.

Taylor, William B. *Magistrates of the Sacred: Priests and Parishioners in Eighteenth-Century Mexico*. Stanford: Stanford University Press, 1996.

Torres, Octavio. *Esboço histórico dos acontecimentos mais importantes da vida da Faculdade de Medicina da Bahia, 1808–1946*. Salvador: Tip. Vitória, 1952.

Toussaint (Samson), Mme. [Adéle]. *A Parisian in Brazil*. Translated from the French of Mme. Toussaint-Samson by Emma Toussaint. Boston: J. H. Earle, 1891.

Traer, James F. *Marriage and the Family in Eighteenth-Century France*. Ithaca: Cornell University Press, 1980.

Twinam, Ann. *Public Lives, Private Secrets: Gender, Honor, Sexuality, and Illegitimacy in Colonial Spanish America*. Stanford: Stanford University Press, 1999.

Vainfas, Ronaldo. "A condenação dos adultérios e padres." In *Mulheres, adultérios e padres*, edited by Lana Lage da Gama Lima, 35–52. Rio de Janeiro: Raymundo Paula de Arruda, 1987.

———. *Trópico dos pecados: moral, sexualidade e inquisição no Brasil colonial*. Rio de Janeiro: Editora Campus, 1989.

Vasconcellos Pedrosa, Manoel Xavier de. "Estudantes brasileiros na Faculdade de Medicina de Montpellier no fim do século XVIII." *Revista do Instituto Histórico e Geográfico Brasileiro* 243 (1959): 35–71.

Vega, Manoel da. *Memoria contra o celibato clerical*. Coimbra: 1822.

Venâncio, Renato Pinto. *Ilegítimidade e concubinato no Brasil colonial: Rio de Janeiro e São Paulo*. ESTUDOS CEDHAL, No. 1. São Paulo: CEDHAL/USP, 1988.

Vieira da Cunha, Rui. *Estudo da nobreza brasileira: I—Cadetes*. Rio de Janeiro: Min. da Justiça e Negócios Interiores/Arquivo Nacional, 1966.

Viotti da Costa, Emília. *The Brazilian Empire: Myths and Realities*. Chicago: University of Chicago Press, 1985.

Walsh, *Notices of Brazil in 1828 and 1829*. 2 vols. Boston: Richardson, Lord & Holbrook, William Hyde, Crocker & Brewster, *et. al.*, 1831.

Wood, Peter. "'The Dream Deferred': Black Freedom Struggles on the Eve of White Independence." In *Resistance Studies in African, Caribbean, and Afro-American History*, edited by Gary Y. Okihiro, 166–87. Amherst: University of Massachusetts Press, 1986.

Zimmerman, Eduardo. *Judicial Institutions in Nineteenth-Century Latin America*. London: University of London Institute of Latin American Relations, 1999.

Index

In this index an "f" after a number indicates a separate reference on the next page, and an "ff" indicates separate references on the next two pages. A continuous discussion over two or more pages is indicated by a span of page numbers, e.g., "57–59." *Passim* is used for a cluster of references in close but not consecutive sequence.

Crato (Ceará), 81–82, 341n6
Criminal Code of 1830, 44, 64, 71, 88ff,
 100f, 105, 255f, 262, 342n27,n28,n29
Cruz Ferreira, Jozé da Cruz, 46, 61–62
Cunha, João Ignacio da, viscount of
 Alcantara, 208
Cunha Mattos, Raymundo Jozé da, 46f,
 55–56, 58–59, 81, 108, 111f, 342n33,
 343n40
"curfew of Aragão," 130f
Curia, Roman 32, 91–95 *passim*, 108, 112f,
 217, 247, 279, 361n36

"damnable birth," *see* Adulterine offspring; Incestuous (canonical) offspring; *Sacrílegos*
damnable offspring, Res. No. 99 of 1830
 (26 June) on, 181–99 *passim*, 205–7.
 See also Resolution of August 11, 1831
Dantas de Barros Leite, Antonio Luiz,
 294
D'Assumpção, Thomaz Lino, 327
Dean, Warren, 134f
décima, 298
Declaration of the Rights of Man and
 Citizen, 17
"defect of birth," 36, 48f, 114, 125, 338n27
"defect of color," *see* Race
defectu natalium, 50. *See also* "Defect of
 birth"
De jure personarum (Mello Freire), 104,
 238
Delavat y Rincón, José, 130, 348n15
De legacia, 342n34
*Demonstration of the Necessity to Abolish
 Clerical Celibacy* (Feijó), 111
de pai incógnito, 138. *See also Quaesito*
de portas a dentro (cohabitation), 344n57.
 See also Mancebia
De Reformatione Matrimonii, debate on,
 92–106 *passim*, 125, 213, 343n36,n37. *See
 also* Marriage, sacramental
desembargador (high crown judge), *see*
 Desembargo do Paço
Desembargo do Paço: Mesa do, xix, xxx,
 66–70, 159, 340n78; Tribunal of, 12,
 36–40 *passim*; abolition of, 68–70, 127,

177, 181f, 191, 227, 340n74; and legitimization certificates, 71–75 *passim*,
 107–8, 147, 182–87 *passim*, 240, 277. *See
 also* Legitimization, solemn
desquite, *see* Legal separation
Deus e Silva, Candido de, 96
Diario Fluminense (Niterói), 150, 159
Dias, Jozé Custodio, 112, 343n48
Dinis I (1279–1325), 145
Direito civil de Portugal (Borges
 Carneiro), 206
direito pátrio, *see* Legal nationalism
district judge, imperial (*juíz de direito*),
 71, 82, 268
divorce, 115, 230, 322. *See also* Legal separation (*divórcio*)
dom, xxviii–xxix, 57, 147
doutor, 59
dower, 302
dowry, 302–3, 312–13, 363n99
Dundas, Robert, 171, 173
Dunshee de Abranches, João, 134

Ecclesiastical Committee, Chamber of
 Deputies, 43–46, 92, 93–94, 108
ecclesiastical privilege, *see Mixti fori*, bill
 on
Ecuador, Confederation of, *see* Pernambuco revolts
elections, 166, 267
elopement, *see Rapto*
emphyteusis, 224, 356n58
Engenho Velho, church of São Francisco
 Xavier do, 143f, 350n59,n62
English in Brazil, 130
entail, xxii, 16, 22, 39ff, 336n43, 356n58;
 abolition of *morgado*, 60–64, 218–25,
 230, 356n61,n63,n64; and *capela*, 226–
 28, 230. *See also Capela; Mayorazgo;
 Morgado; Vínculos*
"equality before the law," xix, 22–23, 42f,
 77, 120, 177, 205, 220, 284, 287
Escragnolle Doria, 138
Estates General of Portugal, 13
estilos, xxx
Evangelista, João, *see* Faria Lobato, João
 Evangelista de